Macworld® Illustrator 6 Bible

Macworld® Illustrator 6 Bible

by Ted Alspach

Foreword by Pierre Bézier

IDG Books Worldwide, Inc.
An International Data Group Company

Foster City, CA ♦ Chicago, IL ♦ Indianapolis, IN ♦ Braintree, MA ♦ Dallas, TX

Macworld Illustrator 6 Bible

Published by
IDG Books Worldwide, Inc.
An International Data Group Company
919 E. Hillsdale Blvd.
Suite 400
Foster City, CA 94404

Library of Congress Catalog Card No.: 95-81812

ISBN: 1-56884-494-8

Printed in the United States of America

10 9 8 7 6 5 4 3 2 1

2B/QU/QR/ZW

Distributed in the United States by IDG Books Worldwide, Inc.

Distributed by Macmillan Canada for Canada; by Computer and Technical Books for the Caribbean Basin; by Contemporanea de Ediciones for Venezuela; by Distribuidora Cuspide for Argentina; by CITEC for Brazil; by Ediciones ZETA S.C.R. Ltda. for Peru; by Editorial Limusa SA for Mexico; by Transworld Publishers Limited in the United Kingdom and Europe; by Al-Maiman Publishers & Distributors for Saudi Arabia; by Simron Pty. Ltd. for South Africa; by IDG Communications (HK) Ltd. for Hong Kong; by Toppan Company Ltd. for Japan; by Addison Wesley Publishing Company for Korea; by Longman Singapore Publishers Ltd. for Singapore, Malaysia, Thailand, and Indonesia; by Unalis Corporation for Taiwan; by WS Computer Publishing Company, Inc. for the Philippines; by WoodsLane Pty. Ltd. for Australia; by WoodsLane Enterprises Ltd. for New Zealand.

For general information on IDG Books Worldwide's books in the U.S., please call our Consumer Customer Service department at 800-762-2974. For reseller information, including discounts and premium sales, please call our Reseller Customer Service department at 800-434-3422.

For information on where to purchase IDG Books Worldwide's books outside the U.S., contact IDG Books Worldwide at 415-655-3021 or fax 415-655-3295.

For information on translations, contact Marc Jeffrey Mikulich, Director, Foreign & Subsidiary Rights, at IDG Books Worldwide, 415-655-3018 or fax 415-655-3295.

For sales inquiries and special prices for bulk quantities, write to the address above or call IDG Books Worldwide at 415-655-3200.

For information on using IDG Books Worldwide's books in the classroom, or ordering examination copies, contact Jim Kelly, Director of Corporate, Education and Government sales, at IDG Books Worldwide, 800-434-2086.

For authorization to photocopy items for corporate, personal, or educational use, please contact Copyright Clearance Center, 222 Rosewood Drive, Danvers, MA 01923, or fax 508-750-4470.

About the Author

Ted Alspach is the author of several books, including the best-selling *Illustrator Filter Finesse, Macworld Illustrator 5.0/5.5 Bible, The Complete Idiot's Guide to Photoshop,* and *The Complete Idiot's Guide to QuarkXPress.* Considered one of the leading experts on computer graphics and Adobe Illustrator, Ted has given hundreds of seminars in the areas of graphic design and illustration. In addition, Ted is a forum consultant on America Online, running the Adobe Illustrator special interest group.

Joined by his five unruly and quite furry sidekicks, Ted fights the evil menace of pixel-based images from his secret hideout somewhere in the untamed desert of Arizona.

ABOUT IDG BOOKS WORLDWIDE

Welcome to the world of IDG Books Worldwide.

IDG Books Worldwide, Inc., is a subsidiary of International Data Group, the world's largest publisher of computer-related information and the leading global provider of information services on information technology. IDG was founded more than 25 years ago and now employs more than 7,700 people worldwide. IDG publishes more than 250 computer publications in 67 countries (see listing below). More than 70 million people read one or more IDG publications each month.

Launched in 1990, IDG Books Worldwide is today the #1 publisher of best-selling computer books in the United States. We are proud to have received 8 awards from the Computer Press Association in recognition of editorial excellence and three from Computer Currents' First Annual Readers' Choice Awards, and our best-selling ...*For Dummies*® series has more than 19 million copies in print with translations in 28 languages. IDG Books Worldwide, through a joint venture with IDG's Hi-Tech Beijing, became the first U.S. publisher to publish a computer book in the People's Republic of China. In record time, IDG Books Worldwide has become the first choice for millions of readers around the world who want to learn how to better manage their businesses.

WINNER
Eighth Annual Computer Press Awards 1992

Our mission is simple: Every one of our books is designed to bring extra value and skill-building instructions to the reader. Our books are written by experts who understand and care about our readers. The knowledge base of our editorial staff comes from years of experience in publishing, education, and journalism — experience which we use to produce books for the '90s. In short, we care about books, so we attract the best people. We devote special attention to details such as audience, interior design, use of icons, and illustrations. And because we use an efficient process of authoring, editing, and desktop publishing our books electronically, we can spend more time ensuring superior content and spend less time on the technicalities of making books.

You can count on our commitment to deliver high-quality books at competitive prices on topics you want to read about. At IDG Books Worldwide, we continue in the IDG tradition of delivering quality for more than 25 years. You'll find no better book on a subject than one from IDG Books Worldwide.

John Kilcullen
President and CEO
IDG Books Worldwide, Inc.

WINNER
Ninth Annual Computer Press Awards 1993

IDG Books Worldwide, Inc., is a subsidiary of International Data Group, the world's largest publisher of computer-related information and the leading global provider of information services on information technology. International Data Group publishes over 250 computer publications in 67 countries. Seventy million people read one or more International Data Group publications each month. International Data Group's publications include: **ARGENTINA:** Computerworld Argentina, GamePro, Infoworld, PC World Argentina; **AUSTRALIA:** Australian Macworld, Client/Server Journal, Computer Living, Computerworld, Digital News, Network World, PC World, Publishing Essentials, Reseller; **AUSTRIA:** Computerwelt, PC TEST; **BELARUS:** PC World Belarus; **BELGIUM:** Data News; **BRAZIL:** Annuário de Informática, Computerworld Brazil, Connections, Super Game Power, Macworld, PC World Brazil, Publish Brazil, SUPERGAME; **BULGARIA:** Computerworld Bulgaria, Networkworld/Bulgaria, PC & MacWorld Bulgaria; **CANADA:** CIO Canada, ComputerWorld Canada, InfoCanada, Network World Canada, Reseller World; **CHILE:** Computerworld Chile, GamePro, PC World Chile; **COLUMBIA:** Computerworld Colombia, GamePro, PC World Colombia; **COSTA RICA:** PC World Costa Rica/Nicaragua; **THE CZECH AND SLOVAK REPUBLICS:** Computerworld Czechoslovakia, Elektronika Czechoslovakia, PC World Czechoslovakia; **DENMARK:** Communications World, Computerworld Danmark, Macworld Danmark, PC World Danmark, PC World Danmark Supplements, TECH World; **DOMINICAN REPUBLIC:** PC World Republica Dominicana; **ECUADOR:** PC World Ecuador, GamePro; **EGYPT:** Computerworld Middle East, PC World Middle East; **EL SALVADOR:** PC World Centro America; **FINLAND:** MikroPC, Tietoverkko, Tietoviikko; **FRANCE:** Distributique, Golden, Info PC, Le Guide du Monde Informatique, Le Monde Informatique, Reseaux & Telecoms; **GERMANY:** Computer Business, Computerwoche, Computerwoche Extra, Computerwoche Focus, Electronic Entertainment, GamePro, I/M Information Management, Macwelt, PC Welt; **GREECE:** GamePro, Macworld & Publish; **GUATEMALA:** PC World Centro America; **HONDURAS:** PC World Centro America; **HONG KONG:** Computerworld Hong Kong, PCWorld Hong Kong, Publish in Asia; **HUNGARY:** ABCD CD-ROM, Computerworld Szamitastechnika, PC & Mac World Hungary, PC-X Magazine; **INDIA:** Computerworld India, PC World India, Publish in Asia; **INDONESIA:** InfoKomputer PC World, Komputek Computerworld, Publish in Asia; **IRELAND:** ComputerScope, PC Live!; **ISRAEL:** PC World 32 BIT, People & Computers; **ITALY:** Computerworld Italia, Computerworld Italia Special Editions, Lotus Italia, Macworld Italia, Networking Italia, PC Shopping, PC World Italia, PC World/Walt Disney; **JAPAN:** Macworld Japan, Nikkei Personal Computing, SunWorld Japan, Windows World Japan; **KENYA:** East African Computer News; **KOREA:** Hi-Tech Information/Computerworld, Macworld Korea, PC World Korea; **MACEDONIA:** PC World Macedonia; **MALAYSIA:** Computerworld Malaysia, PC World Malaysia, Publish in Asia; **MEXICO:** Computerworld Mexico, GamePro, Macworld, PC World Mexico; **MYANMAR:** PC World Myanmar; **NETHERLANDS:** Computable, Computer! Totaal, LAN Magazine, Macworld, Net Magazine; **NEW ZEALAND:** Computer Buyer, Computerworld New Zealand, MTB, Network World, PC World New Zealand; **NICARAGUA:** PC World Costa Rica/Nicaragua; **NIGERIA:** PC World Africa; **NORWAY:** Computerworld Norge, Computerworld Privat, CW Rapport Klient/Tjener, CW Rapport Nettverk & Telecom, CW Rapport Offentlig Sektor, IDG's KURSGUIDE, Macworld Norge, Multimedia World, PC World Ekspress, PC World Nettverk, PC World Norge, PC World's Produktguide, Windows Spesial; **PAKISTAN:** Computerworld Pakistan, PC World Pakistan; **PANAMA:** GamePro, PC World Panama; **PARAGUAY:** PC World Paraguay; **P. R. OF CHINA:** China Computerworld, China Infoworld, Computer & Communication, Electronic Product World, Electronics Today, Game Camp, PC World China, Popular Computer Week, Software World, Telecom Product World; **PERU:** Computerworld Peru, GamePro, PC World Profesional Peru, PC World Peru; **POLAND:** Computerworld Poland, Computerworld Special Report, Macworld, Networld, PC World Komputer; **PHILIPPINES:** Computerworld Philippines, PC Digest, Publish in Asia; **PORTUGAL:** Cerebro/PC World, Correio Informático/Computerworld, Mac•In/PC•In Portugal; **PUERTO RICO:** PC World Puerto Rico; **ROMANIA:** Computerworld Romania, PC World Romania, Telecom Romania; **RUSSIA:** Computerworld Rossiya, Network World Russia, PC World Russia; **SINGAPORE:** Computerworld Singapore, PC World Singapore, Publish in Asia; **SLOVENIA:** MONITOR; **SOUTH AFRICA:** Computing S.A., Network World S.A., Software World; **SPAIN:** Computerworld España, COMUNICACIONES WORLD, Dealer World, Macworld España, PC World España; **SWEDEN:** CAP&Design, Computer Sweden, Corporate Computing, MacWorld, Maxi Data, MikroDatorn, Nätverk & Kommunikation, PC/Aktiv, PC World, Windows World; **SWITZERLAND:** Computerworld Schweiz, Macworld Schweiz, PCtip; **TAIWAN:** Computerworld Taiwan, Macworld Taiwan, PC World Taiwan, Publish Taiwan, Windows World; **THAILAND:** Thai Computerworld, Publish in Asia; **TURKEY:** Computerworld Monitör, MACWORLD Turkiye, PC WORLD Turkiye; **UKRAINE:** Computerworld Kiev, Computers & Software Magazine, PC World Ukraine; **UNITED KINGDOM:** Acorn User, Amiga Action, Amiga Computing, Amiga, Appletalk, CD Powerplay, CD-ROM Now, Computing, Connexion, GamePro, Lotus Magazine, Macaction, Macworld, Open Computing, Parents and Computers, PC Home, PC Works, The WEB; **UNITED STATES:** Cable in the Classroom, CD Review, CIO Magazine, Computerworld, Computerworld Client/Server Journal, Digital Video Magazine, DOS World, Electronic, InfoWorld, I-Way, Macworld, Maximize, MULTIMEDIA WORLD, Network World, PC World, PUBLISH, SWATPro Magazine, Video Event, WebMaster; **URUGUAY:** PC World Uruguay; **VENEZUELA:** Computerworld Venezuela, GamePro, PC World Venezuela; and **VIETNAM:** PC World Vietnam 10/17/95

Acknowledgments

Rewriting a book this size was a task I'm quite glad I didn't have to face alone. Because I got it in my head at some point that I wanted a total revamp of the book, from the order of the chapters to the chapter content itself (not to mention updating each sentence to reflect Version 6 of Illustrator), I was faced with a monumental pile of work. And the work would've ruined me, beating me senseless if it wasn't for the help of the following people, all of whom I thank tremendously:

First and foremost, Jennifer deserves all the thanks in the world for her contributions to this book. Most of the artwork is based on her work for the first edition of the book, and she was kind enough to update several figures, as well as organize artwork. And then there are the other things, only some of which are directly relevant to this book, but instead, are responsible for keeping me alive in various ways.

Erik at Cytopia Software: I've said it before, but it bears repeating. Erik knows more about Illustrator than anyone I know. I conned him into tech-editing this book, and as expected, he did a marvelous job telling me, "What the hell were you thinking, Ted?" without actually saying just that. In addition to just fixing mistakes and booboos that I created, Erik provided several ideas that have been incorporated into various chapters.

Ken at IDG Books has been a delight to work with, through several delays and a last-minute marathon rush to get this book out and into your hands. His well-thought-out comments and suggestions helped to refine this book into the information-packed volume it is.

Actually, everyone at IDG whom I worked with on the *Illustrator 6 Bible* this time 'round did an amazing job of turning this book around so quickly, including Nancy, Kathy, Earl, Valery, and Shelley.

I thought I'd finally write a book where I didn't have to thank Rob at Teeple Graphics for something, anything, but alas, that's not to be. His graciousness in loaning equipment allowed the book to be finished on time. And of course, he was the person who got me started in Illustrator, for which I can't thank him enough.

Sean, Ellen, and Patricia, three of my favorite people in Mountain View, were instrumental in answering questions for me and providing me with help that goes way beyond the call of their jobs. And they're just really nice people, too. Sean even returned one of my calls, a fact that many say should appear in the weekend edition of *Ripley's Believe It or Not.*

Sandee, of *FreeHand: A Visual QuickStart Guide* fame, provided valuable input into all areas of this book. In addition, she provided me with stacks of information for Appendix F.

This book would be missing several tens of pages if it weren't for Intrepid Systems' Sree and Marci, who together brought KPT Vector Effects into being. They've helped to put the "fun" back into Illustrator, so now it's spelled "Illfunustrator."

A special thanks to all the wonderful people who participate in the America Online Illustrator SIG, including Sharon, Mordy, Gary, Mary, and many more, although I think all of them have an "r" somewhere in their first names... Their comments and ideas have been incorporated throughout this book.

I'd mention more people, but who knows, one of them might leave town unexpectedly, owing everyone money, return a year later, and then attempt to sue for slander because he doesn't have any marketable skills...

In closing, I would like to thank Pierre Bézier, whose "Foreword" graces the front of this book.

(The Publisher would like to give special thanks to Patrick J. McGovern, without whom this book would not have been possible.)

Credits

Senior Vice President and Group Publisher
Brenda McLaughlin

Aquisitions Editor
Nancy E. Dunn

Brand Manager
Pradeepa Siva

Editorial Assistant
Suki Gear

Production Director
Beth Jenkins

Production Assistant
Jacalyn L. Pennywell

Supervisor of Project Coordination
Cindy L. Phipps

Supervisor of Page Layout
Kathie S. Schnorr

Production Systems Specialist
Steve Peake

Pre-Press Coordination
Tony Augsburger
Patricia R. Reynolds
Theresa Sánchez-Baker

Media/Archive Coordinators
Leslie Popplewell
Michael Wilkey

Developmental Editor
Kenyon Brown

Copy Editors
Kathryn Duggan
Earl Jackson, Jr.

Technical Reviewer
Erik-Paul Gibson

Project Coordinator
Valery Bourke

Graphics Coordination
Shelley Lea
Gina Scott
Carla C. Radzikinas

Production Page Layout
Shawn Aylsworth
Dominique DeFelice
Angela F. Hunckler
Todd Klemme
Laura Puranen

Cover Design
Kavish + Kavish

Cover Illustration
Steven Lyons

Book Design
Beth Jenkins
Shelley Lea

Proofreaders
Jenny Kaufeld
Christine Meloy Beck
Gwenette Gaddis
Dwight Ramsey
Carl Saff
Robert Springer

Indexer
Sharon Hilgenberg

Contents at a Glance

Table of Contents

Foreword by Pierre E. Bézier

Around 1960, engineers and technicians in the European car industry were divided into two groups: those who worked on mechanical parts and those who worked on car body parts.

For the mechanical group, the surfaces that could be manufactured were clearly defined with dimensions and limits — there was no place for haggling or bargaining at inspection time, and the verdict was simple: GOOD or SCRAP.

For the body-design group, things were far from being simple. From the stylist's small scale mock-up to the full-scale drawing of the "skin," to the clay model, to the final drawing, to the master model, to the stamping tools — each rendering was supposed to be in accordance with the preceding one. Designers used French curves, sweeps, and lathes (plastic splines), but small discrepancies could not be avoided at each step. These minor errors added up, to the detriment of the final product.

Although these problems had gone on for decades, people were not satisfied and still looked for a solution. They believed, as Plato said, that "Number is the expression of everything," and, as Lord William Kelvin said, that "No one can claim to have mastered a phenomenon as long as he has not been able to express it with figures."

By 1960, a small number of people believed that the computer could provide an acceptable solution to the problem of discrepancies in measurements. The aircraft industry was probably the first industry in the U.S. to use computers, but the automotive industry rapidly followed suit.

At this time, two solutions were considered. The first solution was to keep the general process of manufacturing and, with the help of computers (CRT or numerically controlled machine tools), improve one or two steps. The second solution was to forget the existing scheme and start from scratch to take full advantage of the computer's capabilities. This step entailed greater risks but also had greater advantages.

For those who chose the latter solution, the first task was to build a list of requirements that included the following:

- Creating or adopting a mathematical system that could be easily understood and operated by draftsmen, designers, and methods people. The system needed to describe space curves — not only conics and surfaces — and to provide an accurate, complete, and distortion-free definition of the curves. It needed to be easily transmitted between offices, shops, and subcontractors.

- Providing the body- and tool-drawing offices with full-scale drawing machines, controlled completely by computers that work in interactive mode, such as those capable of tracing curves at a speed of one foot per second.
- Equipping the drawing offices, not the tool shops, with rapid milling machines that could carve large portions of a car — the top, the hood, and so on — in a soft material, such as Styrofoam, urethane foam, or plaster.
- Devising the relevant software.
- Equipping the tool shops with heavy NC milling machines for manufacturing stamping units.

In 1960, the mathematical theory was based on the use of conics — nonrational polynomials with vector coefficients. Mathematical theory now includes B-splines and NURBS, but mathematicians still search for other solutions.

By the end of the '60s, some simple systems were operative, but a complete system was not fully operative until the end of the '70s. Since that time, many basic improvements in car design have been developed, including color, reflection lines, perspective viewing, animation, finite elements, crash simulation, aerodynamics, stress and strain, vibration and noise, and so on.

No doubt, the advent of CAD/CAM has been one of the most important changes that took place in the industry during the present century. Of course, it is not necessary for the lay user to master the complete theory — one can play basketball without referring to Galileo, Newton, Keppler, or Einstein — but students and engineers who take part in the development or improvement of a system will find plenty of food for thought in this book.

Pierre E. Bézier

Pierre Bézier is the creator of Bézier Curves, a unique mathematical system used for defining curves. Bézier Curves were adopted by Adobe when they created the PostScript page description language. Illustrator is very much a "front end" for PostScript, and the software would undoubtedly be quite different today if not for Bézier's (unknown at the time) contribution. Pierre Bézier lives in Paris, France.

Introduction

Wait! Before you do anything else, be sure to lift this book with your legs, not your back. Or pick up the handy *Macworld Illustrator Bible Tote* (sold separately), so you can pull it behind you on your way home from the bookstore.

With the 2nd edition of this book, I've managed to cram in almost twice as much information as before, effectively doubling the physical weight of the book. But even with all those extra facts leaking out of the pages, the reading continues to be light and conversational.

When I first wrote the *Macworld Illustrator 5.0/5.5 Bible,* I was aiming to create the first book to show current and potential Illustrator users all the "good stuff" there is in Illustrator, while sneaking in the basics of drawing in a high-end illustration program. To that end, I succeeded, but for this edition, I have a higher goal. I want everyone who uses Illustrator to get the most out of that software that they possibly can.

What's New in the 2nd Edition

After finishing the first edition, I looked back and saw some things I didn't like. I wished this chapter was there, I wish I had never put that chapter in the book, and I wish I had written another section on this thing or that thing. Not that there was anything wrong with the *5.0/5.5 Bible,* but it could be better, faster, stronger...you know the drill.

More than 95% of the art in this edition is new or changed from the previous edition. There are more examples and steps than before. There's less emphasis on Macintosh operations (I never said I was David Pogue, now, did I?) and more on Illustrator. There's a new chapter just on third-party filters, with emphasis on KPT Vector Effects, the darling software of Illustrator users. The filter section has been expanded even as the number of filters in Illustrator declined from 5.5 to 6.0. Adobe Dimensions has pages and pages devoted to creating special illustrations with its capabilities. A new chapter on troubleshooting has been added. And, of course, the new features in Illustrator 6 are covered extensively.

Icons

I've never been a big fan of icons, so in this edition they're used more sparingly, only when really appropriate, and I've whittled them down to just three varieties, so you aren't bombarded by little symbols on every page. Speaking of whittling, I've disposed of the hideous little woodcut style of icons, replacing them with a more modern, mid-nineties look.

This icon tells you that there's some sort of super "I can be a power-user, too" kind of tip.

This icon is one of those oh-by-the-way sort of things. Like having Cliff Claven sitting next to you while you read. (Speaking of Cliff, I bet he'd look dandy on a book cover...)

Concerned, cautious, and overly careful? Read these icons ahead of time to help prevent screwups.

Ask Toulouse

I've also added a new kind of sidebar called "Ask Toulouse." Toulouse is my screen name on America Online, where I moderate the Illustrator special interest group, constantly responding to Illustrator users with Illustrator questions. I provide Illustrator answers when possible; other times I quote passages from *Internet E-Mail Quick Tour* and hope no one notices.

The Ask Toulouse sidebars show common questions and concerns and how they would be answered were I typing you a response online. It's like being there, except you can't specify the question, and you don't need to be using your computer to get the answer.

Complete Third-Party Filter Coverage

I've weeded out the trash and provided a complete rundown of the best third-party filters there are for Illustrator. Not only are the filters explained in detail, but there are tips and techniques to make using them more effective than ever.

Personally, I wanted the filters section of the *Macworld Illustrator 6 Bible* to be even bigger, but my editor nixed the idea of a 1600 page book, saying that people would mistake it for a giant cube. I eventually backed down, but with lots of filter information and nowhere to go, I wrote a book just on Illustrator filters: *Illustrator Filter Finesse*. So if you need more information on filters than I could give you here, you know where to look.

Is This the Illustrator Book for You?

Hey, I don't live in a cave (though I've been known to draw on the walls...), so I know there are other Illustrator books out there. That's one of the reasons that the *Macworld Illustrator 6 Bible* was written in the first place, because I didn't think any of the other books out there did a good enough job in explaining Illustrator. But why should you buy this book, when the one on the shelf next to it has a shinier cover?

I'm glad you asked. The following is a partial list of things that differentiate this book from all the others:

- **The most complete coverage of Illustrator.** This book isn't big because I wanted a big book spine, but because I've included every possible thing you'd want to know about Illustrator. From learning to draw to special effects to obscure keyboard commands, it's all here.
- **Fun, original, *different* artwork to illustrate the techniques and capabilities of Illustrator.** By different, I don't mean when you look at bizarre modern art, and all you can say is, "That's really...uh...different," but instead that the artwork on page 334 is different from the art on page 335. If you saw a simplistic drawing of Groucho on every page of this book, you might learn Illustrator...but you'd never want to watch another Marx brothers movie again. No, variety is what you'll find, making turning each page a new experience.
- **Clean artwork without those annoying jaggies.** I didn't cut corners when it came to illustrating a point. Or a path. Instead of taking screen shots and slapping them in the book as a figure, I've redrawn paths, points, and Control Handles so that the artwork looks sharp, not jagged and boxy.
- **Top-notch technical prowess.** This book was reviewed by the former lead technical engineer for Adobe Illustrator for technical accuracy. There are things in here the engineers don't even know about. In fact, the *Macworld Illustrator Bible* is the book Adobe uses to train their technical support staff. Peter Chase of Adobe Systems used this book as his sole reference material while writing the manuals for Illustrator 6.
- **The most in-depth coverage of filters.** Filters and Plug-Ins are integral parts of Illustrator, this book contains more pages, tips, and information about third-party filters than any other general Illustrator book.
- **Real world examples and advice.** When relevant, topics include information pertinent to getting files printed quickly and accurately, controlling fonts, trapping issues, avoiding banding in gradients and blends, and other issues that affect Illustrator in the real world.

- **A CD-ROM with filters, QuickTime tutorials, and more.** The CD-ROM is stuffed full of files that will make you more productive with Illustrator than ever before, including tutorials that show you right on your computer how to do a variety of things, from the basics to tricky effects.
- **The only "Illustrator for FreeHand users" guide.** Appendix F is a complete reference to Illustrator for the FreeHand user, listing comparable features and how they work differently in Illustrator, things Illustrator doesn't have that FreeHand does have, and Illustrator features that FreeHand users have never experienced.

I've written the *Macworld Illustrator 6 Bible* to be as readable as possible without losing sight of my goal of a thorough and complete education of the readers of the book.

You don't need to be an artist, a computer geek, or anything else to learn Illustrator with this book. No matter what your level of Illustrator experience — from the person who calls tech support when the shrink wrap won't come off the box to the tech person who takes the call — you'll undoubtedly find new things to try, and learn more about Illustrator along the way.

Stuff You Should Know Before Reading

There're a few things that you might want to be aware of before you dive too deeply into the mysteries of vector-based graphics, Adobe style:

- **Versions.** When you see the word "Illustrator," I'm referring to all versions of Illustrator. When I stick a number after the word Illustrator, it's relevant to that version only. Versions change rapidly in the world of software; version 6.0 may change into 6.0.1 or 7.0 before you know it. When I say Illustrator 6, I'm referring to Illustrator 6.0.1, 6.1, or whatever numbers Adobe decides to put after the number 6.
- **Menu and keyboard commands.** To indicate that you need to choose a command from a menu, I'll write *MenuName⇨Command.* For instance, File⇨Save. If there's a keyboard command, I'll stick it right after the menu command. For instance, File⇨Save (⌘-S).
- **Avoid Eyestrain.** This book wasn't meant to be read in one sitting. It's best read in digestible, chapter-at-a-time chunks.

Inside, You'll Find...

...great stuff on every page. Here's a brief overview:

Part I: Introducing Illustrator does just that. I'll point out points and help you get a Handle on your paths. You'll learn how to color things, how to uncolor things, and how to delete the things you don't like the color of. I'll even show you how to customize Illustrator so that it works better for you.

Part II: Putting Illustrator to Work will actually put you to work learning about type and fine tuning paths, and about the hard stuff like compound paths and masks. I'll also show you how to use Blends, Gradients, Patterns, Graphs, and Layers.

Part III: Filters is all about the different filters in Illustrator and how to use them. There's a chapter on third-party filters, and another on using Photoshop filters right in Illustrator.

Part IV: Mastering Illustrator is where the gloves come off (one at Bundy, the other at Rockingham) and you give Illustrator a real workout. Techniques for getting the most out of Illustrator are everywhere.

Part V: Appendixes contains information on all the shortcuts in Illustrator, taking Illustrator filters from Macs to PCs and back, and even includes a special appendix that explores some of the differences between FreeHand and Illustrator.

Yo, Ted!

Sometimes you'll be reading something, and it doesn't quite make sense to you. After pounding yourself repeatedly alongside your head, send me a note telling me what you're having difficulty with, and maybe I'll be able to help you out. If you don't get a response right away, I've pounded myself silly and will be out of touch for a few weeks.

Send me comments, critiques, or suggestions for future editions via e-mail at **toulouse@aol.com**. Or even better, stop by the AOL Mac Graphics Forum conference room (Keyword MGR) on Tuesday nights around 9 pm ET/6 pm PT and bug me while I'm helping to host the Illustrator SIG chat.

Oh, and if I don't respond for some reason, I'm either (1) being held captive by FreeHand purists who have no reason to live after discovering all the zippy new features in Illustrator 6; (2) on my yacht, somewhere in the South Pacific, and my cel-modem is out; or (3) too darn lazy to write back. I do try and answer readers' e-mail whenever possible.

PART I

Introducing Illustrator

The first time you run Adobe Illustrator, you might be overwhelmed by the number of tools and menu items that you have to choose from. As if that weren't bad enough, you also have a blank white page staring you in the face, daring you to create something — anything.

Part I will take the apprehension and fear away from learning Illustrator. The section includes such basic concepts as drawing, painting, and how Illustrator works with files. Throughout this part, I've included samples and interactive lessons, so that you can try out the concepts that are introduced.

Illustrator Basics

CHAPTER 1

In This Chapter

- The length of time it takes to learn a PostScript drawing program
- How to learn faster
- Outline theory
- Pierre Bézier and his curves
- Basic editing functions: Cut, Copy, Paste, and Clear
- Undoing and redoing
- Working in Preview mode
- Using palettes and windows

Not too long ago, artists and illustrators worked by hand, not on computers. It may seem hard to believe, but artists spent hours and hours with T squares, rulers, French curves, and type galleys from their local typesetters.

Now, of course, artists and artist wanna-bes spend hours and hours with their Macintosh, a mouse, a monitor, and on-screen type that they've set themselves. Some traditional artists are still out there . . . although they seem to be a dying breed. Eventually, most serious computer artists come face to face with Illustrator, the king of PostScript drawing programs. And they're frightened by what they see.

The Learning Curve

Quite a few years ago, I was setting type with PageMaker at the service bureau where I worked. I noticed that the specs called for type to be set at a 15° angle. In those days, type at any angle on the computer was a big deal because none of the desktop publishing programs at the time had that capability. PageMaker Version 3 had more options and menus than almost any other software currently on the market, and I spent considerable time searching for "rotate" or something similar. No such luck. I got so desperate that when I spied the manual out of the corner of my eye, I began to reach for it.

"What troubles you, young Skywalker?" asked my boss.

Out of instinct, I punched ⌘-S on my keyboard. (The boss, a former soldier, had this thing about saving often; his method of enforcement was a lightning fast flick of my Mac's power switch.) "I can't find where you rotate type in PageMaker," I replied sheepishly.

He nodded. And then he spoke two simple, forceful words: "Adobe Illustrator."

Thus began my journey into the land of Illustrator, and my subsequent PageMaker productivity slide.

Figuring out how to rotate type wasn't too difficult, but then I started playing with some of the other tools and features of the software. Confusion ensued. Hours of staring at an Illustrator document and wondering "Why?" took up most of my time those days. I didn't understand Fills and Strokes, I didn't understand how to make things certain colors, and I didn't understand why what I drew was so different from what I printed (see Figure 1-1).

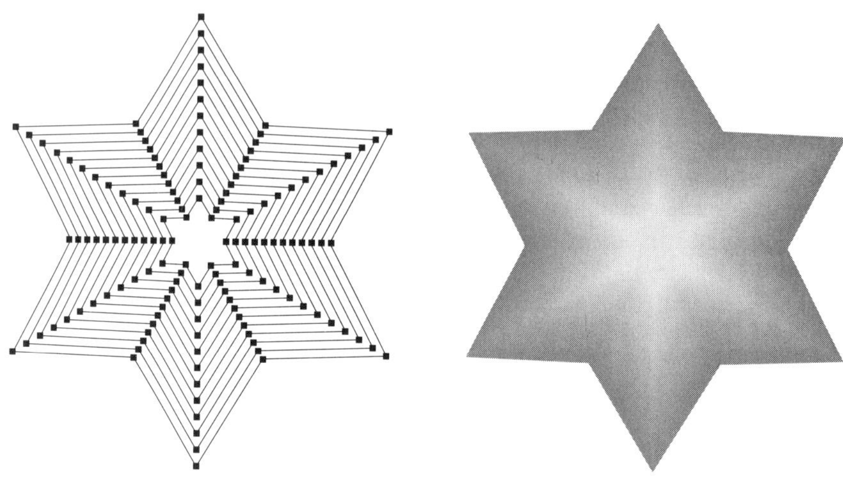

Figure 1-1: Artwork as it appears in Artwork mode (left) and the printed result (right)

Even my boss couldn't help me much with Illustrator; questions to him resulted in a knowing nod and the now-customary tilt and swivel of his head toward the Illustrator manual. I went through the tutorial three times, but when I tried to mask anything but those darn fish, it wouldn't work. I was convinced that the Pen tool was Satan's pitchfork in disguise. Patterns made about as much sense as differential equations (those I'll *never* understand, much to my math-teaching mother's chagrin). Then there were things like flatness (huh?), miter limits (yeah, right), and splitting paths (wouldn't know a clue if I was sitting on one...) — all subjects that might as well have been written in third-century Chinese dialect.

I had never used or seen software as *different* as Illustrator.

That Was Then, This Is Not Then

The version of Illustrator I was introduced to was Illustrator 88, an incredible improvement over Illustrator 1.1, but still not a user-friendly piece of software. Version 3, introduced in 1990, was a little better, but most of its improvements were in functionality, not user interface. In the summer of 1993, Illustrator 5 was introduced, with a full load of not just new features but better ways for people to access those features.

Finally, in 1996, Illustrator 6.0 arrived in all its glory. But there's still a problem with Illustrator — although the program is now easier for beginners to understand, most of the intermediate and advanced areas of Illustrator are still beyond the scope of the majority of users.

Techniques for Learning More

There are a number of ways you can "pick up" Illustrator faster than the average Joe D. Designer:

- **"Playing" the right way:** I used to hate the term "playing," which has been typically used to describe trying out new features and areas of the software you aren't familiar with. Normally, "playing" is said in a negative way, although if done correctly, it can be the most important and valuable time spent while learning software. When playing with Illustrator, follow these rules for the most effective "playtime":
    - Create something that you want to keep, like a business card, a new logo (especially if your company currently has a hokey one designed in the 70s by the owner), a letterhead, or a graphic masterpiece.

- Even if you don't like what you're doing, *don't* delete it. It may look awful, but it could be a starting point for another illustration in the future. Save it.

- Print everything. After an hour of playing, you will (1) feel better about the time your coworkers and boss think you spent playing with new software and (2) have a file of stuff you did that you can review in the future. I love going back to artwork I did three months before and remembering a feature I used for that art that I've just plain forgotten about since then. (Imagine if you had year's worth of this stuff — you'd have a treasure chest full of Illustrator experiments at your fingertips that could save you lots of time and effort in the future.) Or, if you'd like to take the hi-tech route, save the paper and add the Illustrator files to your favorite Fetch catalog (Illustrator 6 automatically saves Fetch previews).

- Don't do real-life projects during playtime. Real-life projects consist of two possible things: artwork you are doing for someone else, which has to be perfect, and artwork you are doing for yourself, which — surprise! — also has to be perfect. Either way, you will invariably delete quite often, and hardly ever print anything but the final product. Try to separate real life from playtime. (I'm currently just trying to distinguish what exactly *is* real life, so you're already a step ahead of me.)

- Don't do too much in one sitting. The more you do at one time, the more you'll forget. More than a couple hours of play at one time starts becoming detrimental.

- **Dissect existing illustrations:** "How'd they do that?" You can figure out all but the most complex artwork by opening it up in Illustrator and selecting different pieces. You can discover techniques that you probably would never have come across on your own.

The *Macworld Illustrator 6 Bible CD-ROM* contains every piece of artwork that you see here in the book. Just open up the folder called MIB6 Artwork, and find the chapter and figure number you're looking at. You can see how Jennifer and I created the artwork that graces these pages by dissecting and examining it.

- **Talk to other Illustrator users:** By talking to other users, you can discover ways they approach similar illustrations or learn of their pitfalls before they become yours. One of the best places to do this is at the frequent Illustrator Conferences sponsored by Thunder Lizard Productions (1-800-221-3806), where hundreds of top-notch Illustrator users gather for several days of talks and seminars about every aspect of Illustrator. Another great place to "talk Illustrator" is at the weekly Illustrator Special Interest Group chat on America Online, each Tuesday night at 9PM ET in the Mac Graphics conference room (keyword "MGR").

- **Attempt the impossible:** If you can successfully use Illustrator to create a replica of the ceiling of the Sistine Chapel, including the proper shading and discoloration associated with aging, you will undoubtedly master the software. Realistically, if you try something that you believe is beyond either your skills or the capabilities of the software, you may be surprised at what you know and what Illustrator can do with you in the driver's seat. And, in the process, you'll probably also come up with new techniques and procedures for creating similar, simpler artwork.
- **Read the entire *Macworld Illustrator 6 Bible*:** Just because you never understood masking before, and never thought you would need it in the future, doesn't mean that nothing else in the chapter on masking is going to be of interest to you. Throughout this book, I've tried to show new and exciting ways of doing everything, from the basics of drawing a line and creating a simple closed shape to reversing gradients and accessing the Convert Direction Point tool while using a pressure-sensitive brush.
- **Watch the CD-ROM tutorials:** If you think a tutorial on basic pattern creating is too elementary, you just might miss out on that new way of creating a cloverleaf in a few simple steps. Most of the tutorials on the CD I've included with this book show more tricks on side topics than they do on their main subject.

The *Macworld Illustrator 6 Bible CD-ROM* tutorials are arranged in the same order as this book, with each section corresponding to a book chapter.

Mousing Around

Illustrator requires the use of a mouse for selecting items, pulling down menus, moving objects, and clicking buttons. Learning to use the mouse efficiently requires a great deal of patience, practice, and persistence (the three-p's, which is where American Indians might have lived but for that H&R Block). In most programs, you can master using the mouse quickly, but using the mouse with Illustrator's Pen tool takes those p's to a new extreme. If you're unfamiliar with using a mouse, a fun way to get used to working with it is by playing a Macintosh mouse-driven game, such as *Eric's Ultimate Solitaire* from Delta Tao. After several hours of play (providing you don't get fired by your employer or kicked out of the house by your irritated spouse), you'll become Master of Your Mousepad, King of Your Klicker, ...

You use the mouse to perform three basic functions in Illustrator:

- **Clicking,** which is pressing and releasing the mouse button in one step. Clicking is used to select points, paths, and objects, and to make windows active.
- **Dragging,** which is pressing the mouse button and keeping it pressed while you move the mouse. You drag the cursor to pull down menus, select contiguous characters of text, move objects, and create marquees.
- **Double-clicking,** which is quickly pressing and releasing the mouse button twice in the same location. Double-clicking is used to select a word of text, select a text field with a value in it, access a dialog box for a tool, and run Illustrator (by double-clicking on its icon in the Finder).

Cursors

When I refer to a cursor, I don't mean someone whose favorite phrase is "@#&*%!!" — although this is a popular phrase for people who are using Illustrator for the first time.

The cursor is the little animated picture (usually an arrow) that moves in the same direction as the mouse. (If the cursor seems to be moving in the opposite direction from the mouse, check to make sure that the mouse isn't upside down, or, heaven forbid, that you aren't upside down.)

In Illustrator, the cursor often takes the form of a tool that you are using. When the computer is busy — doing whatever it is a computer does when it is busy (computing, probably) — an ugly little watch takes its place. Figure 1-2 shows most of the standard cursors that appear in Adobe Illustrator.

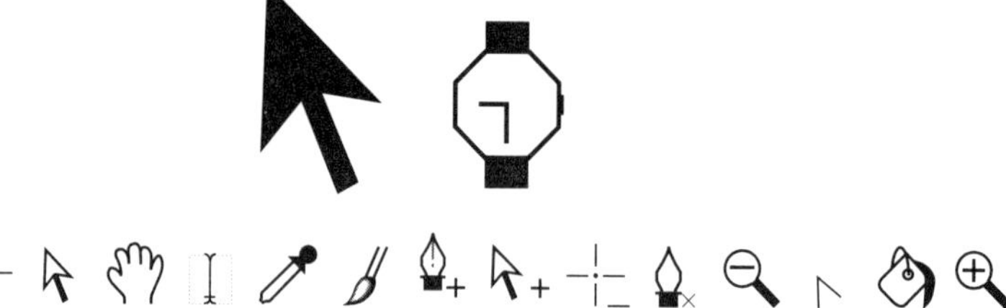

Figure 1-2: An assortment of cursors from Illustrator

Keyboard Commands

Keyboard commands are shortcuts for common activities that you perform in Illustrator. Ninety percent of the shortcuts use the Command key (the one with the cloverleaf symbol ⌘ and the) in combination with other keys.

Many of Illustrator's menu items have keyboard shortcuts listed next to their names. Pressing the key combination does the same thing as choosing that menu item from the menu. Some menu items do not have keyboard commands; usually, you have to choose those items from the menu.

Common keys that are used with the Command key are the Option key (located handily next to the Command key) and the Shift key. The Control key has also been used much more recently than it was in the past (long ago — circa 1986 — Macintosh keyboards did not have a Control key). You hold down these keys while you press another key or click the mouse. Figure 1-3 shows these four modifier keys.

Figure 1-3: The four keyboard modifier keys

Keyboard commands are as important to an Illustrator artist as the mouse is, and with a little practice, you can learn them quickly. Besides, many keyboard commands are the same from program to program, which will make you an instant expert in software that you haven't even used yet!

Commanding Attention

Mrs. C: Do you know the "Illustrator Alphabet" commands?

Toulouse: Sure. A is for Select All, B is for Paste Behind, C is for Copy, D is for Repeat Transform....

Mrs. C: Wait, D is for Repeat Transform? What happened to R?

Toulouse: R is for Show/ Hide Rulers.

Mrs. C: What about T then?

Toulouse: T is for the Character palette.

Mrs. C: Oh.

Toulouse: O is for Open.

Mrs. C: I See.

Toulouse: I is for the Paint Style palette, C, as I said before, is for Copy.

Mrs. C: You and ....

Toulouse: Ungroup. New Document.

Mrs. C: Why ....

Toulouse: Preview.

Mrs. C: Heyyyyyyy!

Toulouse: What, are you Fonzie? You know, I know the Command-Shift alphabet as well.

Mrs. C: Sometimes I really wish *Brooklyn Bridge* would've stayed on the air.

Illustrator Terminology

The language of Illustrator users sounds kinda funny to normal people and FreeHand users.

Sometimes Illustrator users, in their enthusiasm, start spouting off all manner of ungodly terms, such as *RAM, Pantone colors, megabytes, PostScript Level 2, dpi,* and *Option-clicking.* Then there are the power users, who are into *megahertz, gigabytes, Bézier curves, line screens,* and *Command-Option-Shift-clicking.* In this book, such terms are discussed as they come up.

A word of advice: don't use Illustrator language in front of people who have never used (or never plan to use) Illustrator. You might get put away in one of those places where the walls are soft and so is the food, as should anyone who spouts off "Thank God for TIFF support in 6.0!" at the drop of a bitmapped hat.

Fonts

Fonts are a big deal to Illustrator users.

For the seasoned graphic artist, the thousands of typefaces that are available for the Mac provide a typesetting heaven on earth. For a newcomer to Illustrator and typesetting, fonts can be overwhelming. Illustrator ships with about 300 Adobe PostScript Type 1 fonts; others are available for purchase at costs that range from about $2 per face to hundreds of dollars for a family.

Fonts for the Macintosh come in various formats, each format having advantages and disadvantages over other formats. Fonts fall into the following categories:

- Bitmap fonts, also known as screen fonts
- PostScript fonts, also called Type 1 or Type 3
- TrueType fonts

Bitmap Fonts

A bitmap font is a font that is made up of a series of dots inside a grid pattern. Bitmap fonts were the original fonts for the Macintosh, and they worked well on both the screen and the dot-matrix printers that were prevalent at the time they were introduced.

Each character in a bitmap font has a certain number of square black dots that define its shape. Some bitmap fonts include different point sizes, with the smaller point sizes having fewer dots than the larger point sizes. The larger the point size of the bitmap fonts, the more detail is available, and the better the letter looks.

A problem arises when a point size is specified for which no corresponding bitmap font is available. Then dots from the point size that is closest to the specified size are scaled to the new size. The result is usually large, blocky-looking letters. The larger the size specified, the larger the "blocks" as shown in Figure 1-4.

Figure 1-4: Different point sizes of bitmapped type

Because bitmap fonts were originally designed for a Macintosh screen, the dots in a bitmap font are set at 72 dpi (dots per inch), as are most Macintosh screens. When you print a bitmap font on a laser printer, which has a resolution of at least 300 dpi, the letters look blocky, even when their sizes are supported by the typeface. A typical viewer of such a font might be heard to say, "bitmapped…too jaggie...must find outline font."

PostScript Fonts

PostScript fonts are the most popular font format (see Figure 1-5), but they also are the most confusing and frustrating fonts to use because they have two parts: the screen fonts (which are really bitmap fonts) and the printer fonts.

Garamond Eras **Poplar**

Figure 1-5: Three PostScript typefaces

In order for the computer to recognize a PostScript font in the different programs you use, its corresponding screen font must be installed. If the printer font is installed but the screen font is not installed, you can't use the font at all. Screen fonts for PostScript fonts are usually in little suitcases. Double-clicking on the suitcases reveals the bitmap fonts inside the suitcase, and each point size has its own file. Double-clicking on a bitmap font (in System 7) displays a screen with that font in that point size and a sentence that contains all the letters in the alphabet. This makes for sentences that are pretty bizarre. Nothing like reading "How razorback-jumping frogs can level six piqued gymnasts!"

Printer fonts are needed, as their name implies, for printing. Printer fonts consist of outlined shapes that get filled with as many dots as the printer can stuff in that particular shape. Because these printer fonts are outlines, and not a certain number of dots, they make characters look good at any point size. In fact, PostScript printer fonts are *device independent,* meaning that the quality of the type depends on the dpi of the printer (which is device dependent). The higher the dpi, the smoother the curves and diagonal lines look. If printer fonts are missing, the printer either uses the corresponding bitmap font or substitutes another font whose printer font is available (usually Courier...ick).

PostScript fonts were developed by Adobe, who, just by coincidence, created the PostScript page description language, which is also, just by coincidence, based on outlines instead of dots. Adobe also created typefaces in PostScript format, called Type 1 format. They released a set of specifications for third-party manufacturers to use in creating other fonts, called Type 3 fonts. Type 3 fonts have one advantage over Type 1 fonts in that the outlines of these fonts can be Stroked, not just filled, and they can be filled with various shades of gray instead of just black. However, Type 1 fonts are easier to program and to test, and they also have hinting (which increases their viewability at small point sizes at low resolutions). Then Adobe released the specifications for Type 1 fonts, and third-party manufacturers having been creating fonts in the Type 1 format ever since.

Things wouldn't be so bad if printer fonts were needed only for printing, but they are also needed for drawing good fonts on the screen at any point size. If a control panel called Adobe Type Manager (ATM) is installed, the screen font information is supplemented by the printer font outline.

Since the rise of desktop publishing, the standard in fonts has been PostScript. In 1990, Apple teamed with Microsoft and developed a new font format, called TrueType.

TrueType Fonts

The greatest advantage of TrueType fonts is that they have only one part. There's no separate screen font and printer font, just the TrueType font. Actually many TrueType fonts do include screen fonts because hand-tuned screen fonts at small sizes tend to look better than Filled outlines at screen resolution. The difference is that both the TrueType font and the bitmap are contained in the same suitcase. Believe me, when you are used to finding two of everything, this idea of one font, one file, and so on, is a godsend. The quality of TrueType fonts is comparable, if not better, to that of PostScript typefaces. Apple includes TrueType fonts with every new computer it sells. True, there are some potential quality advantages to TrueType fonts, such as the Quadratic curves used to draw TrueType outlines and the supposedly superior hint ability.

Why, you ask, haven't the high quality type vendors (like Lino, ITC, and so forth) jumped on the TrueType bandwagon? My sources tell me that TrueType fonts are harder to engineer and draw. The comparison is this, TrueType font creation environment feels more like an engineering environment, the Type 1 environment feels more like a design environment. Obviously, we are talking about the high end here. A program like Fontographer uses the same interface to create both TrueType & Type 1 fonts. But the high-end folks go in and hand-tune everything to the nth degree, and the difference shows.

Battles between the two formats are still raging, but PostScript appears to be winning the war. In this case, competition isn't really better for the consumer, just confusing.

Fonts and Adobe Illustrator

Adobe makes PostScript. Adobe makes Illustrator. What type of fonts should you use? Although PostScript is the obvious answer, Illustrator also supports the use of TrueType fonts. One thing that Illustrator does *not* support, however, is having two fonts with the same name, one in PostScript and one in TrueType. If this event should occur, you may end up with some strange results, such as invisible type.

Make sure that you have only one type of font format per typeface.

Adobe Type Manager

Adobe Type Manager (ATM) is to computer screens what PostScript is to printers. ATM is a sort of link between the screen fonts and the printer fonts. If the point size that you choose is unavailable for a certain typeface, the screen font references the printer font for its outline and fills the outline with dots. The result is a smooth character, whatever the point size on-screen.

Because of screen-resolution limitations (72 dpi), type below 8 points can be hard to read, even with ATM. When type gets below this size, many software applications use *greeking*, which changes small type into gray bars, saving the application a great deal of processing time. (They figure that if you can't read it anyway, no reason exists to put all those dots in the right places.) And remember that in the smaller point sizes, it is better to have the hand-tuned bitmap font installed.

If you start up a Macintosh with extensions off (by pressing Shift until the "Welcome To Macintosh" screen appears), ATM will be disabled, and you can see bitmap fonts in all their glory (this isn't recommended for those with weak stomachs). Oddly enough, the fonts will still print correctly to a PostScript printer, which doesn't use ATM to generate font outlines.

TrueType automatically renders type at various point sizes without the use of ATM.

Multiple Master Fonts

Multiple Master Fonts, again from Adobe, provide an impressive, if not somewhat complex, way to vary typestyles. Normally, a typeface may come in several weights, such as bold, regular, light, and black. But what if you want a weight that is between bold and black? Usually, you're out of luck.

The theory behind Multiple Master Fonts is that a font has two extremes — black and light, for example. Multiple Master technology creates any number of in-betweens that range from one extreme to the other. Multiple Masters don't stop with weights, though. They also work to step between regular and oblique, wide and condensed, and serif or sans serif.

Multiple Master Font capabilities are built into many high-end graphics applications, such as Illustrator and QuarkXPress.

PostScript and Printing

Up until the mid-'80s, computer graphics were, well, crusty. Blocky. Jagged. Rough. If a mid-'90s person saw graphics that were done on computers in 1981 and printed to a black-and-white printer, we'd laugh so hard we couldn't breathe, stopping the laughter only when we realized...that we couldn't breathe. Of course, in 1981, the world was gaga over the capabilities of computers and computer graphics. Those same pictures were admired, and the average person was generally amazed (the average designer, on the other hand, shuddered and prayed that this whole computer thing wouldn't catch on).

Desktop publishing was pushed to a level of professionalism in 1985 by a cute little software package called PageMaker. With PageMaker, you could do typesetting *and* layout on the computer screen, seeing everything on a screen just as it would eventually be printed. Well, almost. Aldus was the company that created PageMaker. In 1994, Adobe swallowed Aldus, and now PageMaker is "made" by Adobe as well.

The worst acronym this planet has ever seen was coined at this time: *WYSIWYG,* pronounced about the way it reads (wizzy-wig), and standing for "*w*hat *y*ou *s*ee *i*s *w*hat *y*ou *g*et." Oddly, a more accurate term would have been *WYSISSTWYGIYGIAL,* (pronounced wizzys-twiggy-guyal), meaning "*w*hat *y*ou *s*ee *i*s *s*omewhat *s*imilar *t*o *w*hat *y*ou *g*et *i*f *y*ou *g*et *i*t *a*t *a*l*l*." The screen representation was poor, and the likelihood that anything remotely complex would actually print was even poorer. Figure 1-6 shows a common response to these silly acronyms.

Figure 1-6: What you see here is just another unnecessary acronym.

Problems aside, PageMaker would not have been a success if the laser printer hadn't handily arrived on the scene. Even so, there were problems inherent with laser printers too: at 300 dpi (*d*ots *p*er *i*nch), there were 90,000 dots in every square inch. An $8^1/_2$ x 11-inch paper had 8.5 *million* dots to put down. Computers were finally powerful enough to handle this huge amount of dots, but the time it took to print made computers pretty much useless for any real work.

Capital *S*?

Al's Diner: So, what's up with that capital *S* in the middle of the word PostScript?

Toulouse: I believe it was a creative way to establish a trademark, considering the word "Postscript" is quite common. Adobe's pretty conservative about that sort of thing normally. They didn't do "IllusTrator" or "PhotoShop" or "StreamLine" or "DimeNsions" or "PreMeire."

Al's Diner: That's the best you could come up with?

Toulouse: Oh, and the name of your restaurant was thought up by a team of marketing whizzes?

Al's Diner: What about PageMaker?

Toulouse: Aldus did that. It's too late to change it, really.

Several systems were developed to improve the printing process, and the one standout was PostScript from Adobe Systems. Apple licensed PostScript from Adobe for use on its first LaserWriter, and a star was born. Installed on every laser printer were two things from Adobe: the PostScript page description language and the Adobe Base fonts, including Times, Helvetica, Courier, and Symbol.

PostScript became fundamental to Apple Macintosh computers and laser printers, and it was an unchallenged standard. In order to use PostScript, Apple had to pay licensing fees to Adobe for every laser printer it sold. Fonts were PostScript, and if there ever was a standard in graphics, the closest thing to it was PostScript (commonly called EPS, for *E*ncapsulated *P*ost*S*cript).

Today, the majority of fonts for both Macintosh and Windows systems are PostScript, and almost all graphics and desktop publishing software can read PostScript in some form. However, technically speaking (I'm supposed to speak technically aren't I?) there is actually greater number of TrueType fonts available.

What PostScript Does

A typical graphic object in "painting" software is based on a certain number of pixels that are a certain color. If you make that graphic larger, the pixels get larger, giving a rough, jagged effect to the art (see Figure 1-7). To prevent the *jaggies,* two things can be done: Make sure that there are enough dots per inch in the image so that when enlarged, the dots are too small to appear jagged, or define graphics by mathematical equations instead of dots.

Figure 1-7: A bitmap image at normal size (left) and enlarged by 300%

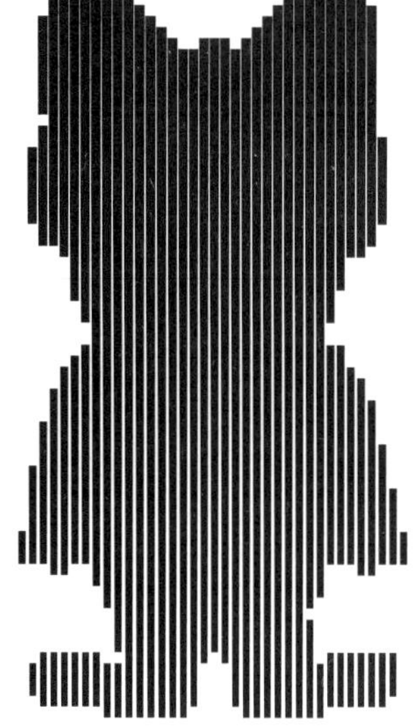

PostScript is a mathematical solution to high-resolution imaging. Areas, or *shapes,* are defined, and then these shapes are either Filled or Stroked with a percentage of color. The shapes are made up of paths, and the paths are defined by a number of points along the path (*Anchor Points*) and additional points off the path (*Control Handles*, sometimes called *curve handles* or *direction points*) that control the shape of the curve. Figure 1-8 shows a PostScript outline around a bitmapped image and the enlarged outline Filled with Black.

Figure 1-8: A PostScript outline surrounds the original bitmapped image.

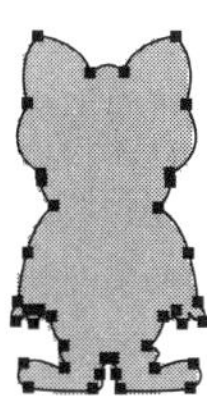

Because the Anchor Points and Control Handles have real locations on a page, mathematical processes can be used to create the shapes based on these points. The mathematical equation for Bézier curves is quite detailed (at least for someone who fears math, like me).

PostScript is not just math, though. It is actually a programming language, and more specifically, a *page description language*. Like BASIC, Pascal, or C, PostScript is made of lines of code that are used to describe artwork.

Fortunately, the average user never has to use PostScript code but instead uses a simplified *interface,* like Illustrator. Software that has the capability to save files in PostScript or to print to a PostScript printer writes this PostScript code for you. Printers that are equipped with PostScript then take that PostScript code and convert it to dots on a printed page.

Why PostScript Is So Cool

Obviously, the fact that most applications can handle EPS files and that most printers can print PostScript is a great benefit to users, but the strength of PostScript is not really in its widespread use.

If you create a 1-inch circle in Photoshop or any other pixel-based drawing software and then enlarge that same circle in any application, the circle will begin to lose resolution. A 300-dpi circle at twice its original size becomes 150 dpi. This makes those jagged edges more apparent than ever.

If you create a 1-inch circle in Illustrator, you can enlarge it to *any size possible* without losing one iota of resolution. The Illustrator circle stays perfectly smooth, even enlarged to 200%. In fact, the resolution of that circle depends on the laser printer or imagesetter that prints it. That means that a perfect 1-inch circle has the potential to be a perfect 2-foot circle (providing you can find a printer or imagesetter that can print a 2-foot x 2-foot circle).

But scaling objects is only the beginning. You can distort, stretch, rotate, skew, and flip objects created in Illustrator to your heart's content, and still the object will print to the resolution of the output device (see Figure 1-9).

Here's an example: A company wants its tiny logo on a 3-inch wide poster. Using conventional methods, the edges will become fuzzy and gross looking, pretty much unacceptable to your client. Your other conventional option is to redraw the logo at a larger size or to trace the blown-up version — a time-consuming proposition either way.

Figure 1-9: The original PostScript mouse (we'll call him "Theme") is in the upper-left corner. The other mice are, appropriately, "Variations on a Theme."

The Illustrator solution? Scan the logo, trace it either in Adobe Streamline or with the Auto Trace tool, touch it up, and build your design around it. Afterwards, output the illustration on a printer that can handle that size of a poster. There is no loss of quality; instead, the enlarged version from Illustrator will often look better than the scanned original.

Paths

The most basic element in Illustrator is a *path*. A path in Illustrator must have at least one Anchor Point. Most paths will have a minimum of two Anchor Points, in which case there will be a line segment between those two Anchor Points (see Figure 1-10). Conceptually, there is no limit to how many Anchor Points or segments can be in any one path. Depending on the type of Anchor Points that are on either end of a line segment, the segment may be straight or curved. Actually, a path really must have two Anchor Points because without two Anchor Points, there is no place to draw a path segment (the line between the points). A single Anchor Point will never print anything.

There are three major types of paths:

- **Open paths** are paths that have two distinct End Points, with any number of Anchor Points in between.
- **Closed paths** are paths that are circular. There are no End Points and no start or end to a closed path — it just continues around and around.
- **Compound paths** are paths that are made up of two or more open or closed paths. It may be difficult to determine whether a path is a compound path or not. (For a detailed look at compound paths, see Chapter 11.)

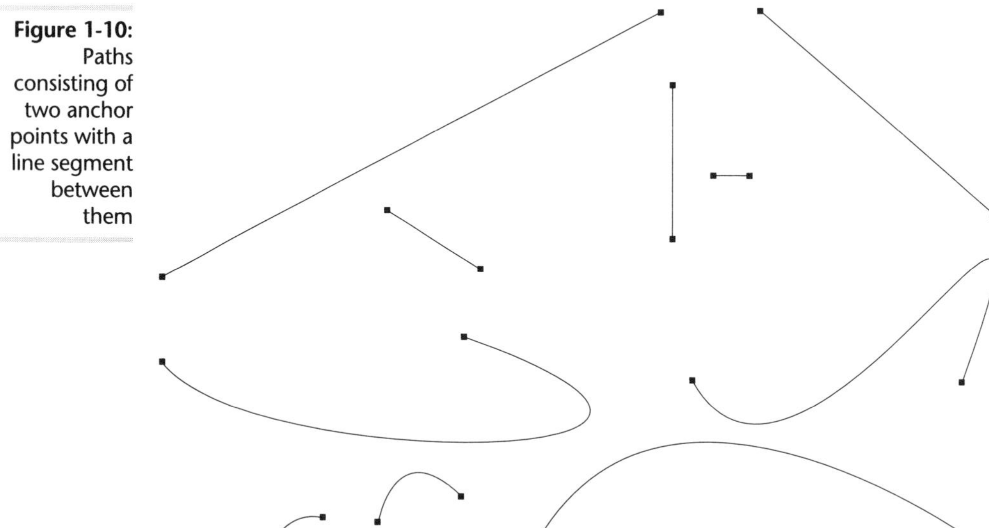

Figure 1-10: Paths consisting of two anchor points with a line segment between them

When you are working in Illustrator in Artwork mode (View⇨Artwork), only paths are visible. In Preview mode (View⇨Preview), Fills and Strokes applied to paths are visible. Unless a path is selected in Preview mode, that path (Anchor Points and line segments) isn't visible.

Paths in Illustrator can be Filled with a tint of color, a pattern, or a gradient. Closed paths always use the color to Fill the inside of the shape they form (see Figure 1-11).

Open paths also can be Filled; the Fill goes straight across the two End Points of the path to enclose the object. Figure 1-12 displays how different types of open paths are Filled. Filling an open path is usually not desirable, although in some circumstances it may be necessary.

Filled one-dimensional line mistake: In PostScript, when a Fill is specified but there is only one dimension to an object (a straight line), it prints (rasterizes) at one "device pixel." At 100% on screen, the Filled line looks exactly like a 1-point Stroked line (72 dpi = 1 device pixel = 1/72 of an inch, 1 point = 1/72 of an inch.) When you zoom in to 200% the Stroked line scales by 200%, but the Filled line stays the same (1 device pixel or 1/72 of an inch). When you print this line to a laser printer, one device pixel is as tiny as 1/300" or 1/600 of an inch. By the time you print to a typical Imagesetter, one device pixel will be 1/2570 of an inch, making it too small to see in most situations.

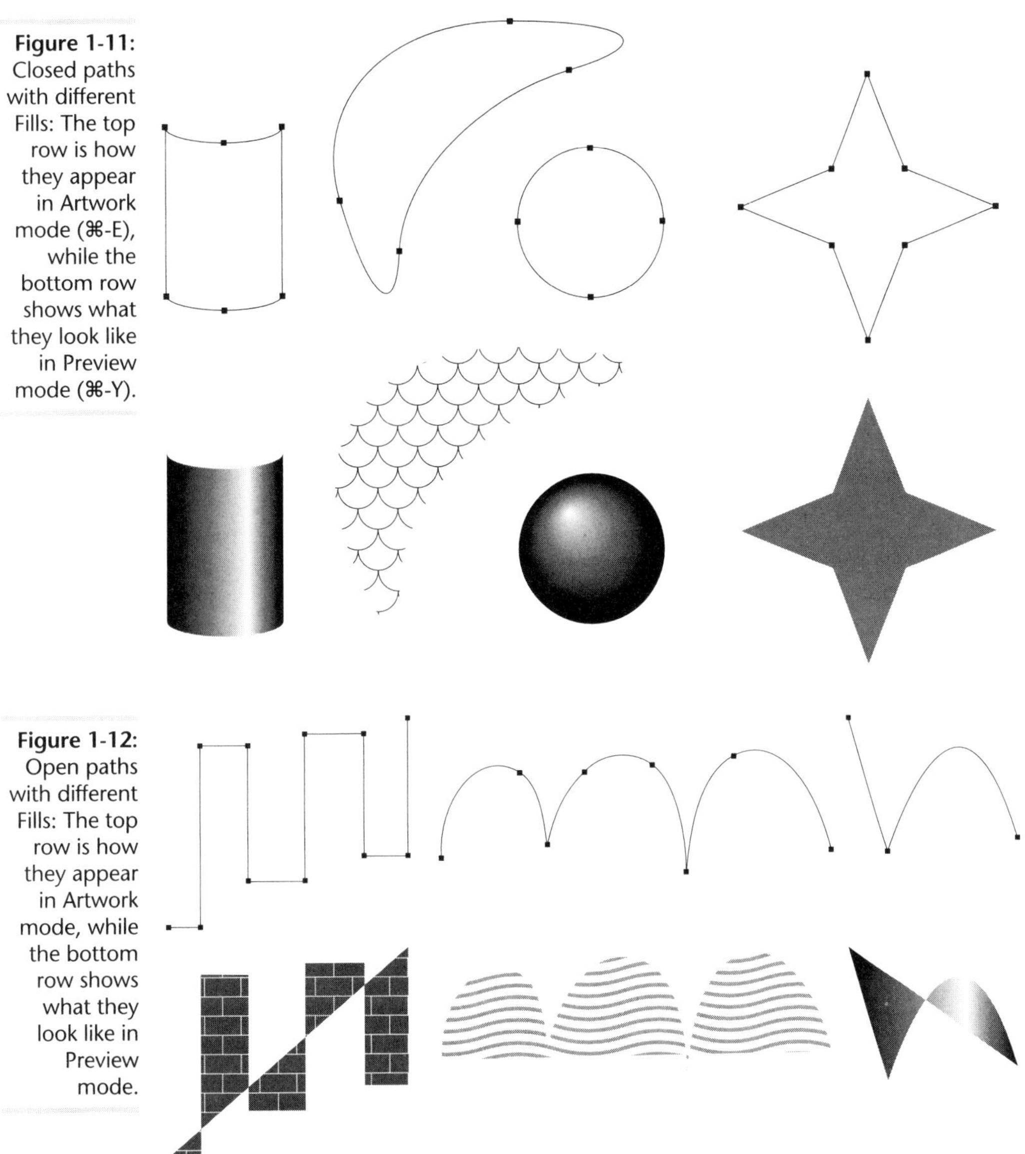

Figure 1-11: Closed paths with different Fills: The top row is how they appear in Artwork mode (⌘-E), while the bottom row shows what they look like in Preview mode (⌘-Y).

Figure 1-12: Open paths with different Fills: The top row is how they appear in Artwork mode, while the bottom row shows what they look like in Preview mode.

Besides Filling paths, you can also Stroke paths with any tint of any color or a pattern. These Strokes can be any weight (thickness), and the width of the Stroke is equally distributed over each side of the path. Open paths have ends on the Strokes; these ends can be either cropped, rounded, or extended past the end of the Stroke by half the width of the Stroke. Several different paths with Strokes are shown in Figure 1-13.

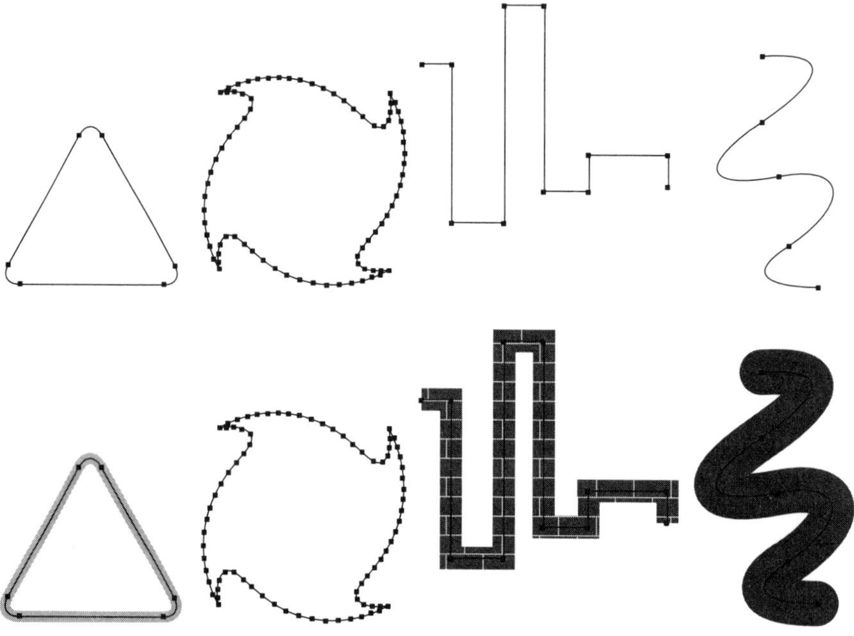

Figure 1-13: Various paths with different Strokes applied to them (sans Gary Coleman)

A single point is also considered a path, but in Illustrator, single points can have no printable qualities. This isn't readily noticeable because you can assign a Fill or Stroke color to a single point, although it can't be seen in Preview mode or when printed. When the document is color separated, it will cause a separation of the color to print even if nothing else on that page is using that same color, and the separation will be blank. If you think you may have individual Anchor Points floating around your illustration, you can select all of them at once by choosing Filter⇨Select⇨Select Stray Points and then deleting them.

Fills and strokes in Illustrator can be tints of colors or an opaque white, which knocks out any color underneath. Fills and Strokes may also be *transparent,* in which case the Stroke or Fill will not be opaque. Transparency in Illustrator is commonly referred to as a Fill or Stroke of None.

Anchor Points

Paths are made up of a series of points and the line segments between two points. These points are commonly called *Anchor Points* because they anchor the path; paths *always* pass through or end at Anchor Points. There are two classes of Anchor Points:

- **Smooth Points** are Anchor Points that have a curved path flowing smoothly through them; most of the time you don't know where a Smooth Point is unless the path is selected. Smooth Points keep the path from changing direction abruptly. There are two *linked Control Handles* on every smooth point.
- **Corner Points** are a class of Anchor Points in which the path changes direction noticeably at those specific points. There are three different corner points:
  - *Straight Corner Points* are Anchor Points where two straight line segments meet at a distinct angle. There are no Control Handles on this type of Anchor Point.
  - *Curved Corner Points* are points where two curved line segments meet and abruptly change direction. There are two *independent Control Handles* on each Curved Corner Point.
  - *Combination Corner Points* are the meeting place for straight and curved line segments. There is one independent Control Handle on a Combination Corner Point.

Figure 1-14 shows the different types of Anchor Points in Illustrator.

Anchor Points, Control Handles, and Control Handle Lines do not appear on the printed output of your artwork. In fact, they only appear in Illustrator, never on artwork imported into other applications.

Bézier Curves

Not knowing all that much about geometry (or maybe not remembering that much…it was eighth grade, after all), the very concept of creating curves using math frightens me. Most of the curve creation in Illustrator takes place behind the scenes in the PostScript language code we almost never see.

PostScript curves are based on Bézier curves (pronounced Bez-ee-ay), which were created by Pierre Bézier (see Figure 1-15) in the early '70s as a way of controlling

Figure 1-14: The different types of Anchor Points in Illustrator

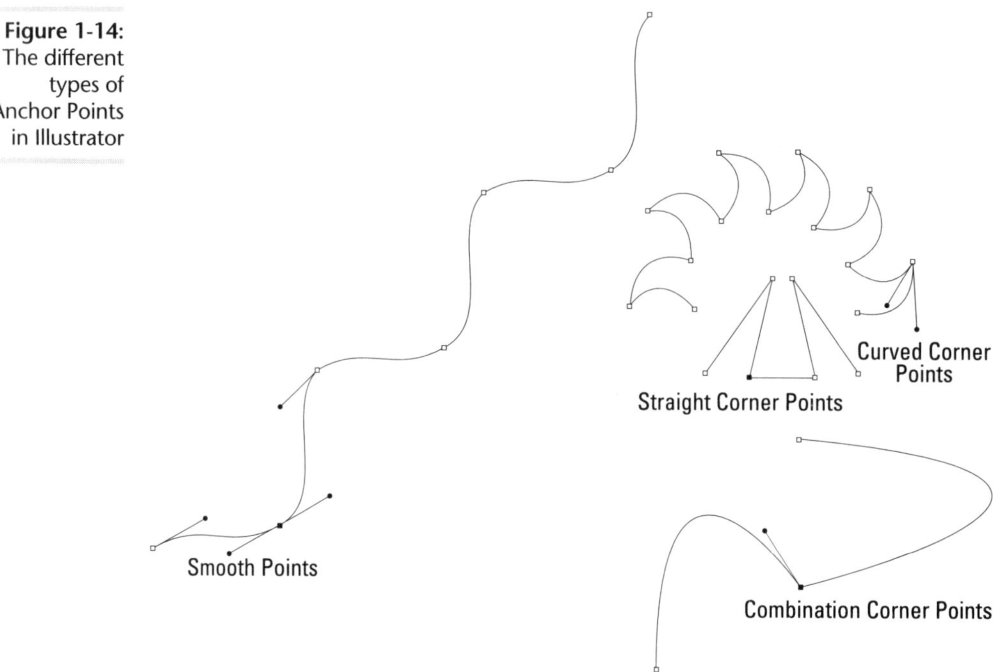

mechanical cutting devices, commonly known as Numerical Control. Bézier (see the Foreword) worked for Renault (the car manufacturer) in France, and his mission was to streamline the process by which machines were controlled.

A mathematician and engineer, Bézier developed a method for creating curves using four points for every curved segment. Two of these points lay at either end of the segment (we call them Anchor Points in Illustrator), and two points just floated around the curve segment, controlling the shape of the curve (Control Handles). Using these four points, a person could conceivably create any curve; using multiple sets of these curves, one could create any possible shape. The two PostScriptateers, John Warnock and Chuck Geshke of Adobe, decided that Bézier curves were the best method for creating curves for a page-description language, and suddenly those curves became a fundamental part of high-end graphic design.

Bézier curves are anything but intuitive. I believe that Bézier curves represent the most significant stumbling block in learning to use Illustrator well. After you've mastered the concept and use of these curves, everything about Illustrator suddenly becomes easier and friendlier. Don't try to ignore them because they won't go away. You'll find it easier in the long run to try to understand how they work.

You already know half of what a Bézier curve is: two Anchor Points. Here comes the hard part (brace yourself).

Figure 1-15: Pierre Bézier, who laid the groundwork for PostScript and, thus, Illustrator

Control Handles and Control Handle Lines

If an Anchor Point has a Control Handle coming out of it, the next segment will be curved. No Control Handle, no curve. Couldn't be simpler.

Control Handles are connected to Anchor Points with *Control Handle Lines*. Figure 1-16 shows what happens when an Anchor Point with no Control Handle and an Anchor Point with a Control Handle are connected to another Anchor Point.

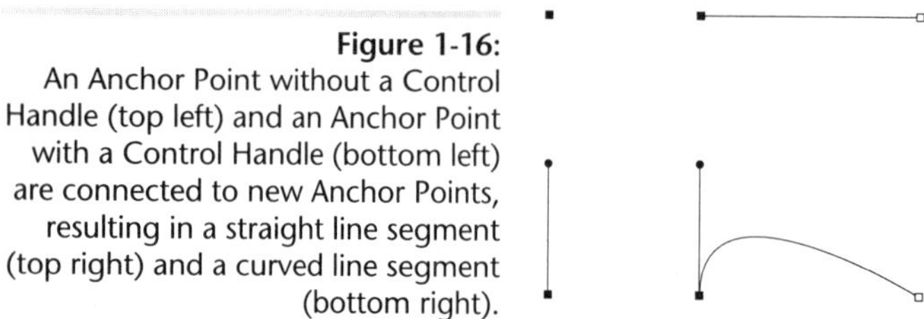

Figure 1-16: An Anchor Point without a Control Handle (top left) and an Anchor Point with a Control Handle (bottom left) are connected to new Anchor Points, resulting in a straight line segment (top right) and a curved line segment (bottom right).

The Control Handle Lines themselves really have no function other than to show you which Anchor points the Control Handles are attached to. You cannot select a Control Handle Line. The only way to move a Control Handle Line or change the length of a Control Handle Line is by moving its corresponding Control Handle. Figure 1-17 displays how Control Handles and Lines work with curves and Anchor Points.

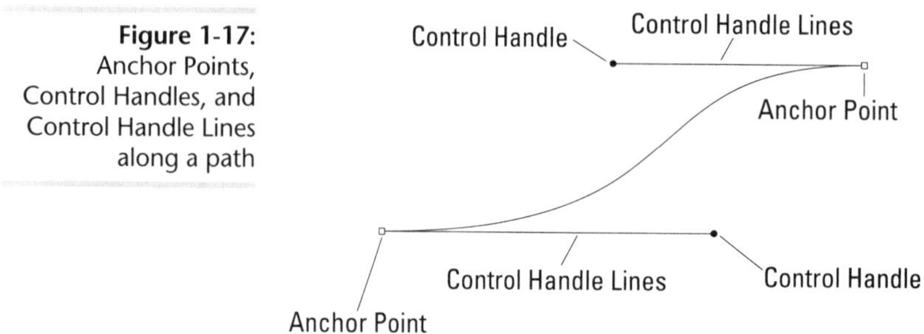

Figure 1-17: Anchor Points, Control Handles, and Control Handle Lines along a path

The basic concept concerning Control Handles is that Control Handles act as magnets, pulling the curve towards them (see Figure 1-18). This presents an interesting problem because there are usually two Control Handles per curved line segment. Just as you might suspect, the Control Handle exerts the greatest amount of force on the half of the curved segment nearest to it. If there is only one Control Handle, then the segment is curved more on the side of the segment with the Control Handle than the side with no Control Handle.

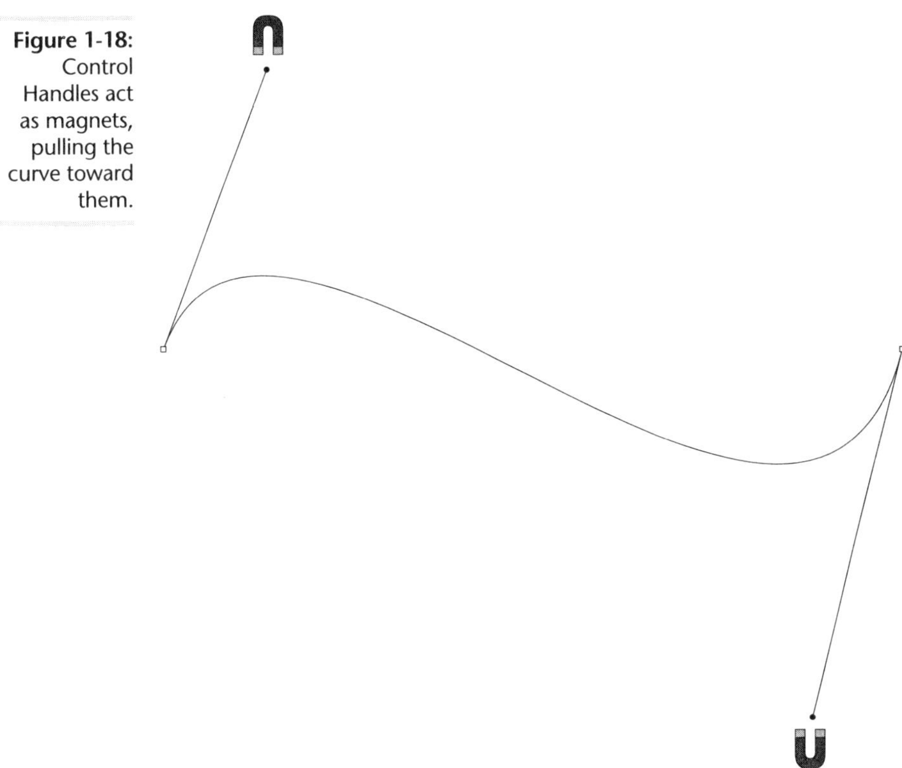

Figure 1-18: Control Handles act as magnets, pulling the curve toward them.

The greater the distance between a Control Handle and its corresponding Anchor Point, the farther the curve (on that end of the curve segment) will pull away from an imaginary straight segment between the two points (see Figure 1-19). If the Control Handles on either end of the segment are on different sides of the curved segment, the curved segment will be somewhat *S* shaped, as the bottom path in Figure 1-19 shows. If the Control Handles on the ends of the curved segment are on the same side, the curve will be somewhat *U* shaped, as shown in the top path of Figure 1-19.

Control Handle Lines coming out of an Anchor Point are always *tangent* to the curved segment where it touches the Anchor Point, regardless of whether the Anchor Point is a Smooth point, a Curved Corner Point, or a Combination Corner Point. By tangent, I'm referring to the angle of both the Control Handle Line and the angle of the curved segment as it crosses the Anchor Point (see Figure 1-20).

In Chapter 3, you'll learn how to use the Pen tool for drawing with Anchor Points, Control Handles, and Control Handle Lines. Rules are also given to help you determine the placement, length, and angle of the various points and Control Handle Lines that are encountered using this tool.

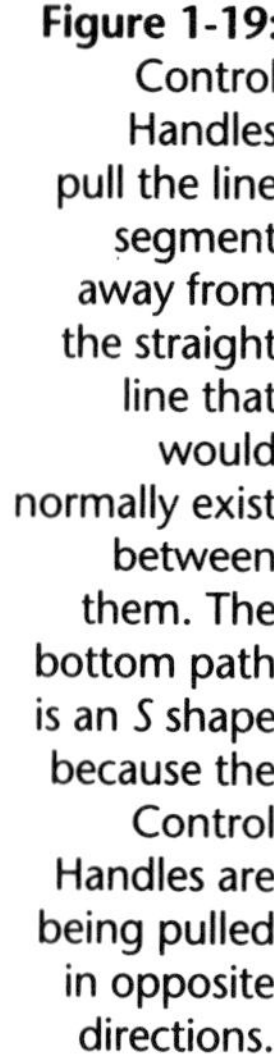

Figure 1-19: Control Handles pull the line segment away from the straight line that would normally exist between them. The bottom path is an *S* shape because the Control Handles are being pulled in opposite directions.

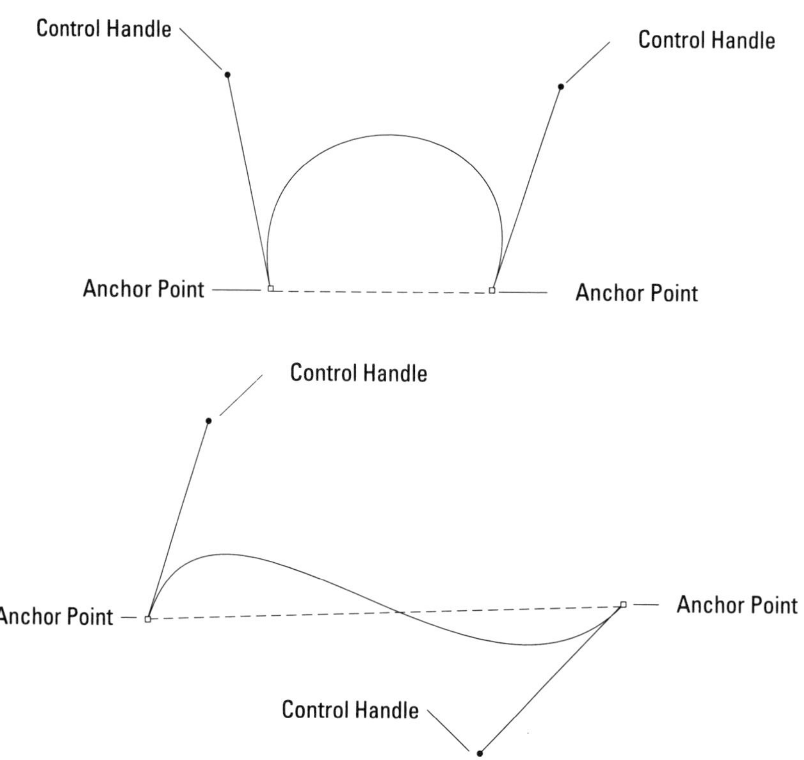

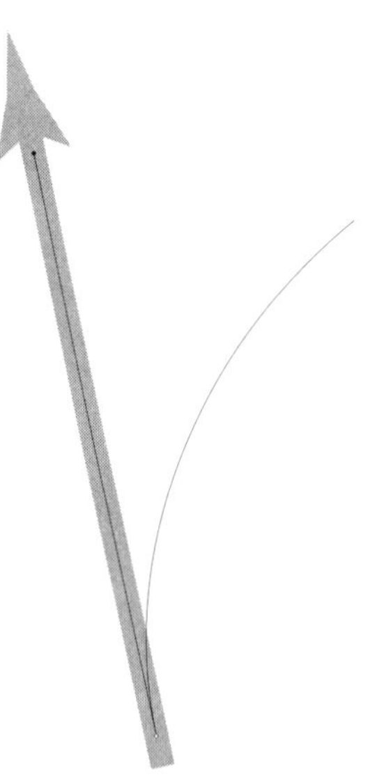

Figure 1-20: Control Handle Lines run tangent to the path where the path meets the Anchor Point.

Clear, Cut, Copy, and Paste

In most Macintosh software, including Illustrator, many of the most basic functions of the Edit menu work the same way. If you have used the Edit menu in QuarkXPress or Microsoft Word, for example, you should have no trouble using the same functions in Illustrator because the menu options are located in the same place in each program.

Clear

The most simplistic of these commands is Clear, which in Illustrator works almost exactly like the Delete key on the keyboard. When something is selected, choosing Clear will delete, or get rid of, what is selected.

You're probably asking yourself: "If the Delete key does the same thing, why do we need Clear?" or "Why didn't they just call the Clear command *Delete*?" Ah, the makers of Illustrator are a step ahead of you in this respect. Note that I said "almost" the same way; there actually is a subtle yet important difference in what the Clear command does and what the Delete key does, due to Illustrator's abundant usage of palettes in Version 6.0.

If you are working on a palette and (1) have just typed a value in an editable text field; (2) tabbed down or up to an editable text field, highlighting text; or (3) dragged across text in an editable text field, highlighting text; the Delete key will (1) delete the last character typed; or (2) and (3) delete the highlighted characters. In all these situations, the Clear command will delete anything that is selected in the document.

Curves Are Tough

Potsie: I'm having trouble with curves.

Toulouse: What kind of trouble?

Potsie: Moving the Control Handles around is really difficult.

Toulouse: You know, there's an easier way...but it's not quite as accurate.

Potsie: Tell me! At this rate I'll never finish my drawing of Jennie Piccolo.

Toulouse: Wow. Lots of curves there. Looks like you might need to add a few extra Anchor Points....

Potsie: (blush)

Toulouse: To adjust the curves without moving the Control Handles, just click on the curve and drag it.

Potsie: Wow!

Toulouse: Keep in mind that you're changing both Control Handles at once with that, and it's very imprecise. Sort of like your occasional musical outbursts.

Potsie: Was I really that bad?

Toulouse: Ever notice the lack of work after the series ended?

Cut, Copy, and Paste

The Cut, Copy, and Paste commands in Illustrator are very handy. Copying and Cutting selected objects places them onto something called the Clipboard. The Clipboard is a temporary holding place for objects that have been cut or copied. After an object is in the Clipboard, it may be pasted into (1) the center of the same document, (2) the same location as the cut or copied object, or (3) another document in Illustrator, Photoshop, Dimensions, or Streamline.

Choosing Cut (⌘-X) from the Edit menu deletes the selected objects and copies them to the Clipboard, where they are stored until another object is cut or copied or the Macintosh is shut down or restarted. Quitting Illustrator *does not* remove objects from the Clipboard. Cut is not available when no object is selected.

Choosing Copy (⌘-C) from the Edit menu works like Cut, but it doesn't delete the selected objects. Instead, it just copies them to the Clipboard, at which time you can choose Paste and slap another copy onto your document.

Choosing Paste (⌘-V) from the Edit menu places any objects on the Clipboard into the center of the document window. If type is selected with the Type tool or highlighted in another application on the Pasteboard, either a Rectangle type, Area type, Path type, or Point type area must be selected with the Type tool. Paste is not available if nothing is in the Clipboard or if the contents of the Clipboard were copied there from another application.

Now, the really cool part: Just because you've pasted the object somewhere doesn't mean it isn't in the Clipboard anymore; it is! You can paste again and again, and keep on pasting until you just get plain bored, or until your page is an indecipherable mess, whichever comes first. However, the most important rule to remember about Cut, Copy, and Paste is that whatever is currently on the Clipboard will be replaced by anything that gets cut or copied subsequently to the Clipboard. Cutting or copying an object or objects twice will put the second copy on the Clipboard, and the first will be gone.

Cut, Copy, and Paste also work with text that you type in a document. Using the Type tools, you can select type, cut or copy it, and then paste it. When you're pasting type, it will go wherever your blinking text cursor is located. If you have type selected (highlighted) and you choose Paste, the type that was selected is replaced by whatever you had on the Clipboard.

You can cut or copy as much or as little of an illustration as you choose; you are only limited by your hard disk space. A good rule of thumb is that if you ever get a message saying you can't cut or copy because you are out of hard disk space, it is time to start throwing out stuff on your hard drive that you don't need or simply get a bigger hard drive.

Thanks to Adobe's PostScript on the Clipboard, Illustrator can copy paths to other Adobe software, including Dimensions, Streamline, and Photoshop. Paths created in those packages can be pasted into Illustrator. With Photoshop 3.0 and later, you have the option of pasting your clipboard contents as an actual Photoshop image instead of as paths.

With Illustrator 6 and Photoshop 3.0.4 and later, you have the ability to drag Illustrator artwork from an Illustrator document right into a Photoshop document. In addition, because Adobe "goes both ways," you can drag a Photoshop selection from any Photoshop document right into an Illustrator document.

The Clipboard

You can view the contents of the Clipboard by going under the Edit menu to Show Clipboard. Unfortunately, the only thing you'll usually see in Illustrator is (1) the PostScript logo with the number of objects you have selected and the layers those objects are on or (2) copied text. In order to see text in the Clipboard, it must be copied using the Type tools. Type that is cut or copied using the selection tools will not appear as type, but instead as an "object." When you view type, it will usually not look like the type you selected; the words are there, but the font and style information isn't. Instead, the type is displayed in Geneva, at either 12 points or 9 points, depending on what you have copied prior to copying your text.

The Clipboard is actually a file in the main (root) level of your System Folder called (oddly enough) "Clipboard."

Selecting Show Clipboard from the Edit menu opens a window that shows the current contents of the Clipboard. You can keep this window open and put it anywhere on the screen, but it will always be behind all palettes and the active document once you click within any of the palettes or the document. When a portion of the Clipboard is visible behind the palettes or document window, clicking on the visible part of it will bring it back to the front (of course, you can also just select Show Clipboard from the Edit menu again).

You can't do anything to the Clipboard by displaying the Clipboard window. You may only resize the window and move it around on your screen for the sole purpose of displaying what you have copied last. The Clipboard can be resized with the box in the lower-right corner, toggled between the current size and the full screen with the box in the upper-right corner, and closed with the box in the upper-right corner. The only way the contents of the Clipboard window can be altered is when something is cut or copied. Figure 1-21 shows two examples of how the Clipboard can look when different things are copied.

Figure 1-21: The Clipboard when several objects on different layers have been copied or cut (left), and the Clipboard when text selected in a type tool has been copied or cut (right)

Selecting Hide Clipboard from the Edit menu hides the Clipboard. This option is available only if the Clipboard window is *active* — that is, in front of all open documents.

Undo and Redo

In most Macintosh applications, you can undo the last thing done by choosing Undo from the Edit menu. That works in Illustrator, but Adobe has taken the undo concept just a little further: You can keep undoing in Illustrator up to 200 times, providing your system has enough memory and you have enough patience. After you have undone, you can redo by choosing Redo, right below Undo in the Edit menu. And, guess what — you can redo up to 200 times as well.

Choosing Undo (⌘-Z) from the Edit Menu undoes the last activity that was performed on the document. Successive undos undo more and more activities, until (1) the document is at the point where it was opened or created or (2) you have reached the undo limit, set in the General Preferences dialog box (File⇨Preferences⇨General or ⌘-K).

The default number of undos in Illustrator is 10. To change the number of undos, go to the General Preferences dialog box (File⇨Preferences⇨General, or ⌘-K) and type in the number of undos that you want. You *can* set the undo levels to 0, but I wouldn't recommend it; this will disallow any undo or redo operations. If you *do* set the number of undos too low and later realize you want to undo more actions, the cold, hard truth of the Undo levels box will raise its ugly head: You can't increase the number of undos after you have run out of them.

Undos are the chief source of Illustrator's occasional memory woes. All those undos are being kept track of in Illustrator's RAM partition; when it fills up, you'll be presented with a dialog box to get rid of the oldest undos. Never do this. Instead, click the cancel button and manually change the number of undos to a smaller amount and try again. This way you can control the number of undos Illustrator has available at all times.

Choosing Redo (⌘-Shift-Z) from the Edit Menu redoes the last undo. You can continue to redo undos until (1) you are back to the point where you started undoing or (2) you perform another activity, at which time you can no longer redo any previous undos.

If you undo a couple of times and then *do* something, you won't be able to redo. You have to undo the last thing you did and then actually do everything again. In other words, all the steps that you undid are gone.

It is fine to use the Undo feature to go back and check out what you did, but after you have used multiple undos, don't do anything if you want to redo back to where you started undoing from. Got that???

The Undoables

Not Opie: I think my Undo command is broken.

Toulouse: Uh-oh. Are you sure it's not set to zero in your preferences?

Not Opie: Yeah, it's set to 10. Most of the time it undoes fine, but every once in a while....

Toulouse: What types of things can't you undo?

Not Opie: Well, my receding hairline, for one thing. Why do you think I'm *behind* the camera now? I can't undo my saves, either.

Toulouse: Ah-ha! Saving has no impact on Undo or Redo. Saving is not considered to be an option that can be undone, or done again, so its very existence is ignored by Undo and Redo. After you save, you'll undo the last thing you did before you saved.

Not Opie: Oh. Well, I can't undo my zooms or scrolls either.

Toulouse: Two more things that Illustrator ignores when it comes to undoing and redoing. Sorry.

(continued)

(continued)

Not Opie: Anything else I should look out for?

Toulouse: Undo and Redo only work on actions that actually change your document. Zooming and scrolling don't affect your document. Neither does changing tools or selecting or deselecting things.

Not Opie: I guess my hairline doesn't affect my documents either.... (sigh)

Artwork and Preview Modes

Ah...Gone are the days of working blind, having to wait to see what you were illustrating until you chose Preview and then not being able to work again until you chose Artwork. I'm being sarcastic, of course. Aldus FreeHand has allowed artists to work in Preview for many-a-year (since 1989, to be exact), and Adobe finally included this capability for Macintosh owners in 1993 with the release of Illustrator 5.

Artwork Mode

Many artists who have used Illustrator in the older versions (1.1, 88, and 3.2) actually *like* working in Artwork mode because it's faster, you can see every path in the document (and select those same paths), and the Anchor Points and Control Handles stand out more. Artwork mode is much closer to what the printer sees: paths that define the edges of the objects you are working with.

"Artwork" mode seems to be a misnomer. "Wireframe" mode would be more descriptive — or maybe "Paths" mode. The only thing visible in Artwork mode is the paths that make up the objects, and all paths are always visible.

Since Illustrator 5, Artwork mode has worked slower than in previous versions. The reason? Layers could be colored via the Layers Palette, and selected points and paths reflected those colors. To give that little extra boost of speed back to Artwork mode, install the Artwork View Speedup Plug-In from the Extra Plug-Ins folder in your Illustrator folder by placing it in the Plug-Ins folder. When installed, all points and paths will be black, not their layer colors. This speed difference is determined by the difference in redraw times between 1-bit (black and white) and 8-bit (256 colors) color.

Preview Mode

In Preview mode, you see on-screen what your illustration really looks like when it prints (with the exception of displayed paths, which don't print). Figure 1-22 shows Illustrator art in both Artwork and Preview modes.

Figure 1-22: Art from Illustrator shown in Artwork mode (left) and Preview mode (right)

Illustrator can't show overprinting when previewing. To see overprinting, open, paste, or drag the artwork to Photoshop.

Instead of selecting a path by clicking it, you can select entire paths by clicking the inside of those paths in a Filled area. It becomes a little more difficult to select certain points on paths because the Strokes on those paths are also visible. Sometimes, there is so much stuff on your screen in Preview that you don't know what to click. The option that allows this is called "Area Select," a checkbox (turned on by default) in the General Preferences dialog box (⌘-K).

The inside of a compound path is considered a Fill for Area Select functionality. It may look trasparent, but you can't directly select an object appearing behind the transparent portion of a compound path. When Area Select is on, clicking the transparent portion of a compound path results in the compound path being selected.

The major drawback to Preview mode is not the inability to select paths or parts of paths, but the amount of time it takes for certain types of Fills and blends to redraw accurately on your screen. The first time a slow redraw takes place in your document, you hardly notice it; you are too busy looking at how that object appears now that it has, say, a pattern Fill. After that, though, you may not be working with that object but others, and you still have to wait for that pattern-filled object to completely redraw every time you change views, move that object, or move something in front of that object.

Fortunately, Illustrator has a saving grace that makes this slowness almost acceptable. Whenever the screen is in this redraw mode, you can do other things. While your patterned, Filled object is redrawing, for example, Illustrator lets you go to the Type menu to change typefaces you've selected; when you are done selecting the type, the image finishes redrawing. This process is called *interruptable redraw,* and it is a godsend for Illustrator users.

Illustrator's Menus

Adobe's main products — Illustrator, Photoshop, Premiere, Dimensions, and Streamline — all have a fairly consistent interface, including menus, palettes, and dialog boxes. It appears that Adobe has listened carefully to their end users and made certain that Illustrator is not so *different* anymore in almost all respects.

Some general rules apply to Illustrator menus:

- To select a menu item, pull down to that item and release the mouse button. If the cursor is not on that item, but it is still highlighted, the command will not take effect.

- Whenever an *ellipsis* appears (three little dots that look like ...), choosing that menu item will bring up a dialog box where you must verify the current information by clicking an OK button or enter more information and then click OK. If there is no ellipsis, the action you select will take place right away.
- Anytime there is a *key command* listed on the right side — usually the Command (⌘) symbol and a character, sometimes the ⌘ symbol and other modifier keys and a character — instead of using the mouse to pull down this menu, you can type this key command. Using key commands for menu items works just like clicking the menu bar and pulling down to that item.
- If you see a little *triangle* next to a menu item, it means there is a *pop-up menu* associated with it. Items in the pop-up menu can be chosen by pulling over to the menu and then pulling up or down to select the menu item needed. Pop-up menus usually appear on the right side of the menu, but due to space limitations on your monitor, they may appear on the left side for certain menus.

Using Menus Effectively

If you can never remember what is on which menu, and you are constantly holding down the mouse button and slowly running along the menu bar, reading every menu item, looking for a certain command, you have a disease. Every year millions of people become afflicted with Menu Bar Scanning Syndrome (MBSS): the need to continually search and hunt for special menu items that they just can't remember the locations of. MBSS is a disease that can be treated fairly easily, but it wastes valuable production time, costing companies billions of dollars a year. Don't be surprised if the next time you flip to *60 Minutes,* Steve Kroft is doing an inside investigation into the mysteries of MBSS.

MBSS is deadly not only because it wastes time, but because the user is forced to read every single menu and pop-up menu. Sure, in the File menu you *know* that Page Setup is where to go to change the size of the page, but as you work your way over, things begin to get a little fuzzy. By the time you get to the Filter menu, your mind is mush. You see the Distort category and figure that all the pop-up menu items in there are legal functions. If you can manage to get to the Windows menu, thewordswouldjustruntogether, making no sense whatsoever. If Figure 1-23 looks familiar, then you're probably one of the millions of afflicted computer users.

Figure 1-23: MBSS

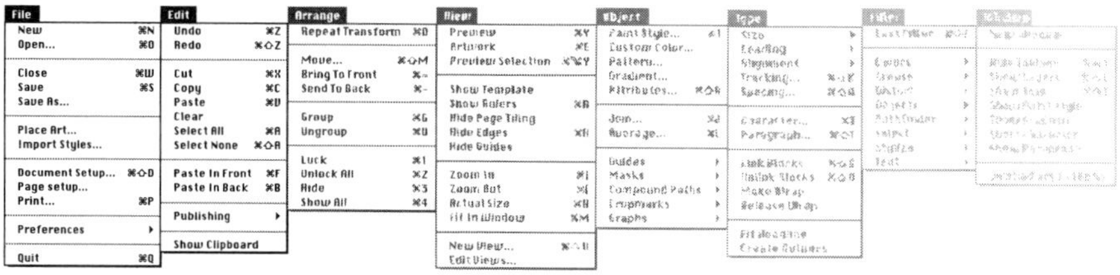

You can help prevent MBSS by doing two things:

- **Memorize what is in each menu.** This is the hardest thing to do, but a few hours spent memorizing each menu item and where it goes will eventually prevent countless MBSS-related searches. Make sentences out of the first letter of each menu item if it helps. The File menu is either "New, Old, Close, Save, Save As, Place Art, Import Styles, Document Setup, Page Setup, Print, Preferences, Quit" or "Nine Old Cats See Silly People Icing Danish Pieces of Prune Pit Quiche." (I know, I know. You're not supposed to put icing on prune pit quiche. That's why the people are *silly.*)
- **Use the menus as little as possible.** Instead, memorize key commands. Most of the menu items have them (if you don't include the Filter menu, more than half do), so now you only need to go up to the menu bar when a menu item doesn't have a key command.

Palettes Versus Windows

If there is a trend in graphics programs, it's the trend toward using palettes for everything possible. It started becoming noticeable with Fractal Design Painter, which has 12 palettes that can be on the screen at the same time. QuarkXPress soon followed with a half-dozen palettes, and Photoshop has scads of them. Illustrator 6 has a few more palettes than version 5, all of which can remain open while you work on your document (providing you can still see your document through all those palettes!).

Technically speaking, a palete is a window. Everything on the Mac is a window except (I think) the desktop. Movable Modeless Windows (palettes) are an *unsanctioned* variation on windows on the Mac.

In many respects, palettes are like windows. They have a title bar that can be clicked and dragged to move the palette. There is usually a close box in the upper-left corner of the palette, and in the upper-right corner there is often an auto-resize box, which makes the palette smaller or larger than its original size. Occasionally, a manual resize box will be located in the lower-right corner for dragging the palette to a new size. Options for hiding and showing palettes are even located under the Window menu. Figure 1-24 shows the Character palette with all its parts labeled.

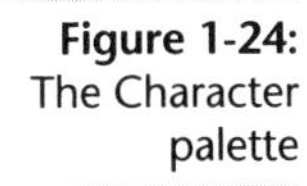

Figure 1-24: The Character palette

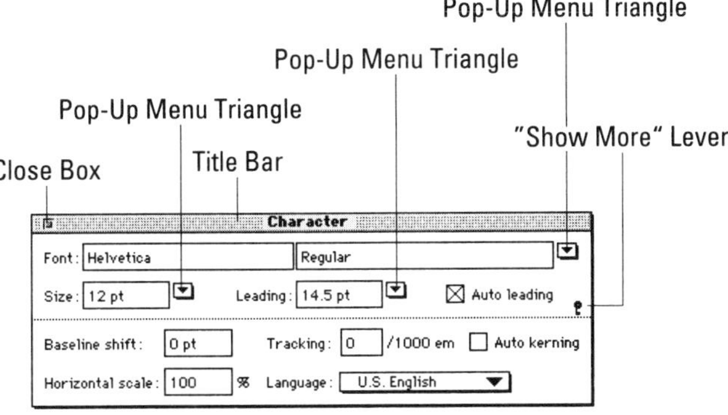

Palettes are unlike windows in several ways. Palettes seldom have scroll bars, although the Layers palette is an exception. When you hop from one program to another, palettes automatically hide, while windows remain visible.

The Toolbox in Illustrator is also a palette; it can be hidden by clicking the close box in the upper-left corner.

Unlike windows, palettes are never really "active." Instead, the one you are working in will be in the front, and if it has editable text fields, one will be highlighted or a blinking text cursor will appear. To bring a palette to the forefront — bring it into focus — simply click anywhere on it.

The Document Window

Getting around your documents in Illustrator can be a little confusing at first, especially if you have a monitor that is not the common 13-by-14-inch color monitor from Apple. If you have a larger monitor, the Illustrator window will initially take up about half of the available screen space. Clicking in the upper-right corner of the document window is a quick fix (for a permanent one, see Chapter 6).

The Pasteboard

Probably the worst thing that can possibly happen when you are using Illustrator is for you to lose everything you've worked on. "Where'd it all go?" you cry, along with the expected vulgarities. This can happen very easily in Illustrator, just by clicking a few times on the gray parts of the scroll bars at the bottom of the document window. When you click on those gray parts, you are moving about half the width (or height) of your window with every click, and three clicks later, your page and everything on it is no longer in front of you. Instead, you see the Pasteboard, a vast expanse of white nothingness.

The Pasteboard measures 120 x 120 inches, which works out to 100 square feet of drawing space. At actual size, you only see a very small section of the Pasteboard. A little letter-sized document looks extremely tiny on a Pasteboard that is this big. If you get lost on the Pasteboard, a quick way back is by choosing View⇨Actual Size. This puts your page in the center of the window at 100% view, at which time you should be able to see at least part of your drawing. To see the whole page quickly, choose View⇨Fit In Window, which resizes your page down to where you can see the entire page. To see the entire Pasteboard, press Option while double-clicking the Zoom tool.

Of course, if you've drawn your artwork somewhere besides the page, changing into the Fit in Window mode may not be that helpful at all. In this case, double-Click the Zoom tool to see everything.

This assumes of course that the user/artist has actually drawn there artwork on the defined page. I used to get frantic calls from people that had double clicked on the Zoom tool and all their artwork would disappear. It actually took me awhile (can you believe it!) to figure out that they had drawn their artwork way off on the side of the Pasteboard.

The Artboard

In the center of the Pasteboard is a black-bordered box called the Artboard. The Artboard represents the largest area that will actually print out of Illustrator. If you are taking your Illustrator artwork into another application, such as Photoshop or QuarkXPress, the size of the Artboard is irrelevant; your entire illustration will appear in most other software applications even if that artwork is larger than the Artboard.

The dotted lines on the Artboard represent which area will print and the size of your printer's paper, referencing the printer options you have chosen in Page Setup for this information. There are two sets of dotted lines on the Artboard, although you can normally only see the inside line. The inside line represents what will actually print; the outside line is the size of the paper you have chosen in Page Setup.

The dimensions of the Artboard can be changed by choosing File⇨Document Setup and typing in different values in the width and height text fields of the Document Setup dialog box.

The Page Tool

The Page tool changes how much of your document will print by moving the printable area of the document, without moving any of the printable objects in the document. Clicking and dragging the lower-left corner of the page relocates the page to the place where you release the mouse button.

This tool is useful when your document is larger than the biggest image area your printer can print. The tool allows you to *tile* several pages to create one large page out of several sheets of paper. *Tiling* is the process where the image consists of several pieces of paper, arranged in a grid formation. A portion of the image is on each page, and when fitted together, the image can be viewed in its entirety.

Miscellaneous Window Stuff

Illustrator windows act like windows in most other programs. The close box is in the upper-left corner, and the manual resize box is in the lower-right corner. The box in the upper-right corner will toggle between your current window size and full-screen size.

The title bar at the top of the window is used to move the window around your screen. On the title bar is the name of the document (if you have not yet saved your document, the name of the document is "Untitled Art 1," with the number changing for each new document you create). Next to the title of the document is the current viewing zoom percentage relative to actual size.

The scroll bars on the right side of the window allow you to see what is above and below the current viewing area. The scroll bars at the bottom of the window control panning from side to side. The arrows on each scroll bar let you see just a bit more with every click; holding down the mouse on an arrow slowly scrolls to other parts of the document. Dragging the elevator box takes you to another part of the document, relative to the direction you are dragging. Clicking either side of the elevator box in the gray bars changes your view by chunks of about half the width or height of your window.

In the lower-left corner is the status bar that tells you all sorts of neat information you just can't get anywhere else. The default is usually set to display the name of the tool you are working with.

The Toolbox

The Illustrator 6 Toolbox (see Figure 1-25) is identical to the Illustrator 5 Toolbox. However, the new Toolbox contains an additional the Plug-In Tools pallete.

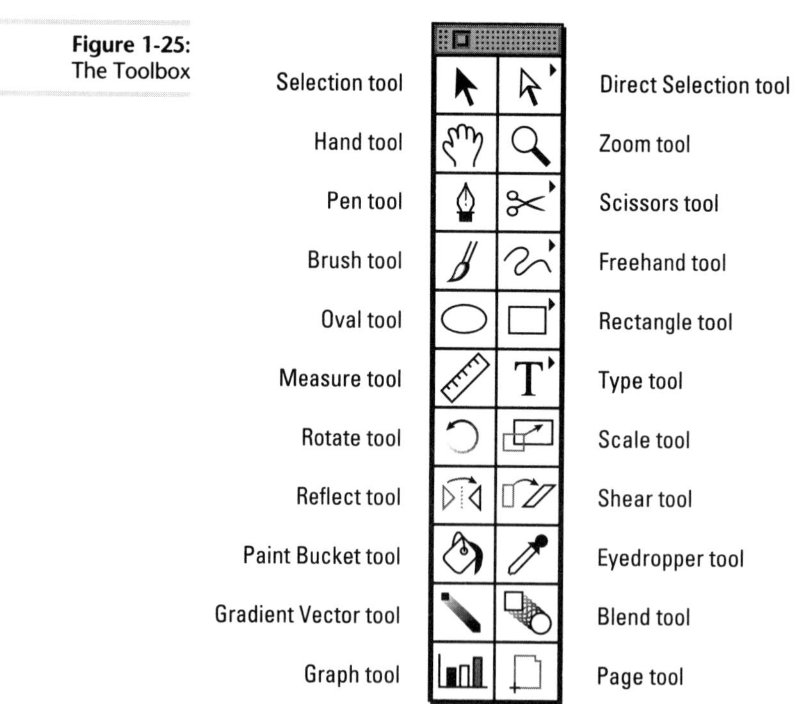

Figure 1-25: The Toolbox

The Toolbox appears on top of your document window, covering up part of your illustration in the upper-left corner. Clicking the close box in the upper-left corner of the Toolbox hides it from view; choosing Window⇨Show Toolbox causes it to appear in the same location it was before it was hidden. When the Toolbox is on-screen, the option under Window reads Hide Toolbox. Just as with most other palettes in Illustrator, you can use a key command, ⌘-Control-T, to show and hide the Toolbox.

The Toolbox has two columns of tools, with the tools on each row related to each other. The viewing tools — the Hand tool and the Zoom tool, for example — are next to each other. The Blend tool and the Gradient Vector tool are also side by side. In fact, only two sets of tools are *not* related on the Toolbar: the Measure tool and the Type tool, and the Graph tool and the Page tool.

To choose a tool, click the one you want to use in the Toolbox and release the mouse button. You can use this tool until you click another. Unlike most applications, Illustrator lets you click and drag from the tool of your choice across other tools while keeping selected the tool you initially clicked. But a better habit to develop is to just click the desired tool, release the mouse button, and use the tool in the document window.

Many tools have additional *pop-up tools*, tools that appear only when you click and hold down the mouse on the default tool. The default tools that have pop-ups are located in the right column and are indicated with a little triangle in the upper-right corner of the tool. To select a pop-up tool, click and hold on a tool with a triangle until the pop-up tools appear; then drag the pop-up tool you want over to the Toolbar. The new pop-up tool replaces the default tool in its slot. This procedure is demonstrated in Figure 1-26.

Figure 1-26: Selecting a pop-up tool

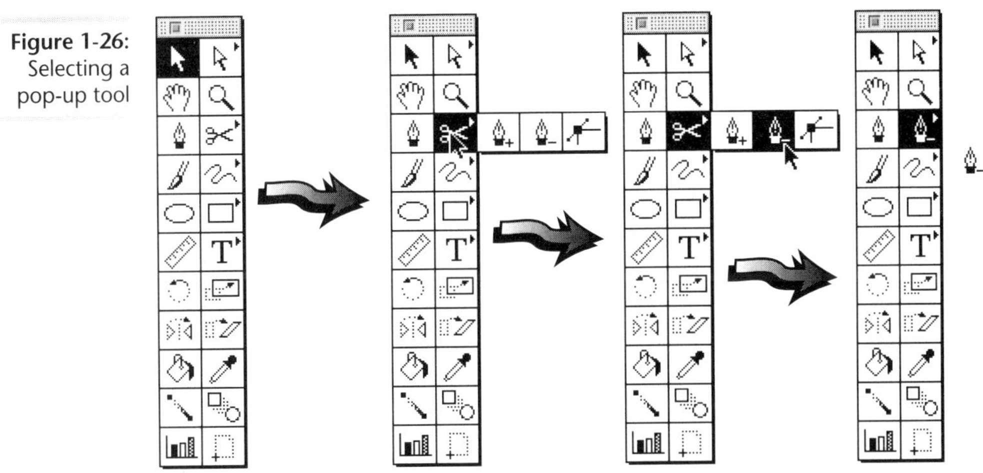

To change a pop-up tool back to its default, press Shift while you double-click the tool you want to reset. To change all the tools back to their defaults, even ones without pop-up tools, press ⌘-Shift while double-clicking any tool.

Where's That Tool?

The Fonz: I can't find the Convert Direction Point tool.

Toulouse: It's to the right of the Scissors tool.

The Fonz: I can't find my Scissors tool, either.

Toulouse: Are you sure you're using Illustrator?

The Fonz: Heeeeyyyyyy....

Toulouse: Just kidding. Someone (maybe Chachi?) might have been using another tool in that "slot."

The Fonz: Is there any way to reset all the tools back to the original ones?

Toulouse: Sure, Command-Shift double-click on any tool, and that'll reset the entire toolbox.

The Fonz: Coooollllll.

If you hide the Toolbox, you can still use whichever tool you last selected. By using different key commands, you can access even more tools. Most key commands let you use a certain tool while you hold down certain keys. For example, pressing ⌘-Spacebar activates the Zoom In tool, and pressing the Spacebar activates the Hand tool. After those keys are released, the tool originally selected becomes the active tool again.

The Plug-In Tools Palette

New to Illustrator 6 is the addition of another palette for tools. Choose Window⇨Plug-In Tools Palette and the Plug-In tools will appear, as shown in Figure 1-27.

The tools on this palette are:

- **Twirl,** for twirling selected artwork
- **Star,** for creating stars
- **Knife,** for slicing paths, even unselected ones
- **Spiral,** for creating spirals
- **Polygon,** for creating polygons

The Plug-In Tools palette can be resized by dragging on the Resize box in the lower-right corner of the palette. To close the palette, click the close box in the upper-left corner.

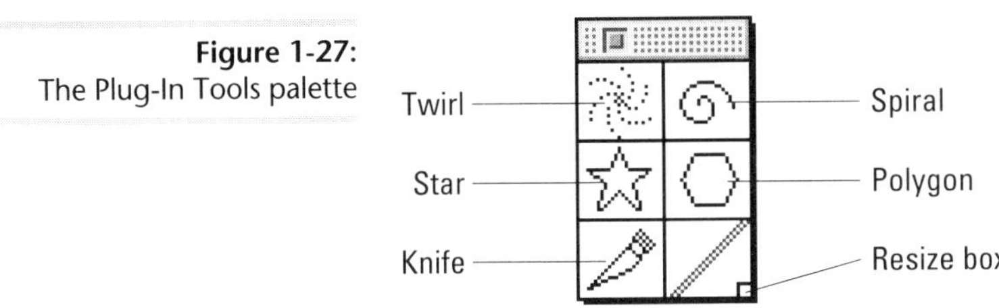

Figure 1-27: The Plug-In Tools palette

Summary

- Illustrator seems difficult to learn at first, but with this book and a bit of dedication, it can be mastered.
- Illustrator works best with PostScript fonts.
- Illustrator can be interpreted as a good front end for the PostScript page description language.
- There are four types of Anchor Points: Straight Corner Points, Smooth Points, Curved Corner Points, and Combination Corner Points.
- Curved paths in Illustrator are created with Bézier curves, named after the French mathematician Pierre Bézier.
- Curved segments are controlled by manipulating Control Handles, which extend from Anchor Points at either end of the segment.
- Illustrator has 200 available undos and redos.
- Access additional tools by choosing Window⇨Plug-In Tools.

Creating and Painting Shapes

CHAPTER 2

In This Chapter

- How to draw basic ovals and rectangles
- How to create polygons, stars, and spirals
- How to color paths with Fills and Strokes
- All about the Paint Style palette
- How to use the Paint Bucket and Eyedropper tools

Technically, the name of this section should really be "Placing and Sizing Preformatted Open and Closed Paths," but then no one would read it. And this is an important chapter because it introduces many concepts that are built upon in later chapters.

Shapes

Drawing the most basic shapes — rectangles, ovals, polygons, and stars — is precisely what a computer is for. Try drawing a perfect oval by hand. Troublesome, isn't it? How about a square that doesn't have ink bubbles or splotches at the corners? How about a nine-point star? Yuck. Drawing these objects and then coloring them in Illustrator is so easy and so basic that after a few weeks of using Illustrator, you'll never be able to draw a shape by hand again without wincing, maybe even shuddering. Figure 2-1 compares shapes drawn by hand with those drawn by a computer.

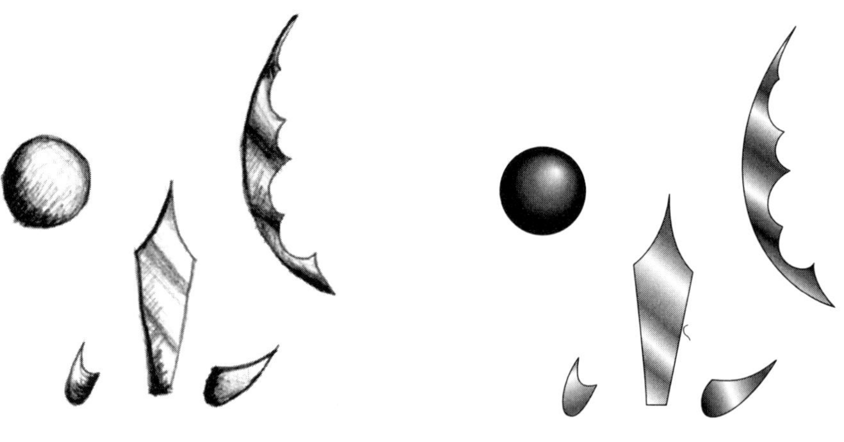

Figure 2-1: Hand-drawn shapes and their computer-drawn counterparts

Getting rid of the shape you've drawn is even easier than creating it in the first place. And after the shape is created, it can be moved, rotated, scaled, and manipulated in any way you like.

The true power of object-oriented drawing programs is exemplified in Illustrator. No matter what you draw, you can adjust and move each piece of the drawing independently until it's just right. Don't like the sun so high in your background? Pull it down and tuck it in just a bit behind those mountains. Is the tree too small for the house in your illustration? Scale it up a bit. This feature is great not only for artists, but also for your pesky client (or boss) who demands that everything be moved except that darned tree. Figure 2-2 shows an illustration drawn one way and then modified in a matter of seconds by moving and transforming existing elements.

A bitmap paint application does not have this capability to move pieces of a drawing (with the exception of the use of layers). After an image is moved in a bitmap program, a *hole* appears in the place where the section used to be. And if there is anything under the section where the image was moved to, that information is gone when the section is replaced with the new image.

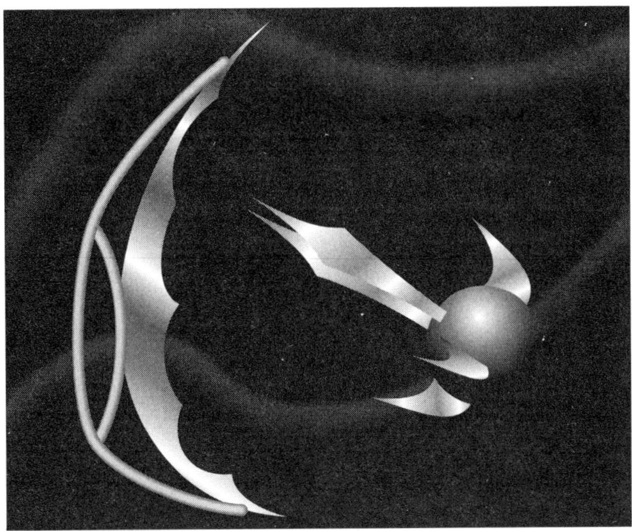

Figure 2-2: Illustrator objects moved from one drawing to the next

Drawing Rectangles

The most basic shape you can draw is a rectangle. The following steps, and the illustration of these steps in Figure 2-3, explain how to draw a simple rectangle.

STEPS: Drawing a Rectangle

Step 1. Select the Rectangle tool (highlighted in the Toolbox in Figure 2-3) by clicking it in the Toolbox. If the Toolbox is not visible, press ⌘-Control-T to display it.

Step 2. Click to set the origin while holding down the mouse button.

Step 3. Drag diagonally (down and to the right) to the size you desire.

Step 4. Release the mouse button. A rectangle is created. The farther the distance from the initial click until the point where you release the mouse button, the larger the rectangle.

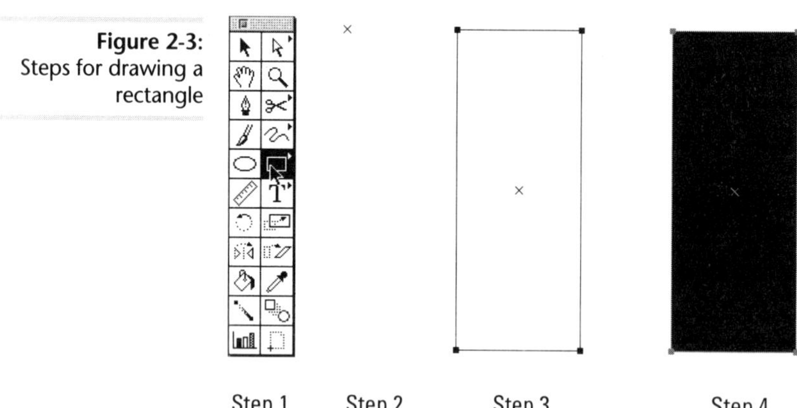

Figure 2-3: Steps for drawing a rectangle

After you release the mouse button, a Black rectangle appears with four Blue points in the corners and one Blue point in the center (if you are in Preview mode, the default viewing mode). The edge of the rectangle has thin Blue lines surrounding it. The Blue points in the corners are *Straight Corner Anchor Points.* The Blue point in the center is the *Center Point.* The Blue lines are *Straight Line Segments* that connect the Anchor Points of the rectangle. The Blue points and Blue lines together are considered a *path.* In Artwork mode, the rectangle has no Fill or Stroke, and the points and path appear Black.

If you aren't sure what View mode you're in, display the View menu (by clicking on "View" and keeping the mouse button down). Look for the check mark next to either Artwork or Preview.

The initial click you make with the Rectangle tool is called the *origin point.* While you drag a figure, the origin point never moves; however, the rest of the rectangle is fluid, changing shape as you drag in different directions and to different distances with your

mouse. Dragging horizontally with almost no vertical movement results in a long, flat rectangle. Dragging vertically with very little horizontal movement creates a rectangle that is tall and thin. Dragging at a 45° angle (diagonally) results in a squared rectangle.

Rectangles can be drawn from any corner by clicking and dragging in the opposite direction of where you want that corner to be. For instance, to draw a rectangle from the lower-right corner, click and drag up and to the left. As long as you have the Rectangle tool, dragging with it in the document window produces a new rectangle.

If you need to draw a rectangle that is an exact size, instead of dragging with the Rectangle tool, just click it once and release where you want the upper-left corner to be. The Rectangle dialog box appears, as shown in Figure 2-4. Type in the width and height, click OK, and the rectangle draws itself, becoming precisely the size that you specified.

The third text field in the Rectangle dialog box is for the size of the corner radius. This option makes the corners of the rectangle curved, although leaving the setting at a value of 0 keeps the corners straight. Rectangles whose sizes are specified in the Rectangle size dialog box are always drawn from the upper-left corner unless you press the Option key while drawing (see the next section, "Drawing Rectangles from Their Centers"). The largest rectangle you can draw is only 10 feet by 10 feet. It's a wonder you can get anything done at all with these limitations....

When the Rectangle dialog box appears, values are usually already inside the text fields. Those numbers correspond to the size of the rectangle you last drew. To create another rectangle the same size, just click OK (or press Return or Enter). To make the rectangle a different size, replace the values with your own measurements. If a text field is highlighted, typing replaces the text in the text field and deletes what had been highlighted. To highlight the next field in a dialog

Using the Rectangle Tool

Adama: I'm having trouble with the Rectangle tool.

Toulouse: What type of trouble?

Adama: My rectangles seem to have five sides. I guess they're overachievers.

Toulouse: Are you sure you have the Rectangle tool and not the Polygon tool? The Rectangle tool is the fifth tool down on the right side.

Adama: Wait, is it above or below the Spiral tool?

Toulouse: Actually, you're in the wrong Toolbox. Illustrator has two of them now.

Adama: I only see one. Its got a knife, a star....

Toulouse: Okay, go to your Window menu and select Show Toolbox.

Adama: Wow! There's bunches of tools in this one! I see the Rectangle tool now. Thanks!

box, press the Tab key. You can also highlight the preceding field in a dialog box by pressing Shift-Tab. If you'd like to highlight any text field instantly, double-click the value, or click once the "label" next to that value. To accept the options in the dialog box, click OK or press Return or Enter.

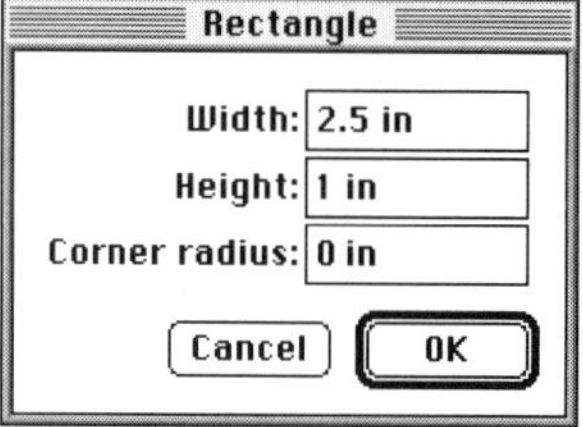

Figure 2-4: The Rectangle dialog box, used for specifying exact dimensions of a rectangle

When you first run Illustrator, all measurements are set to points and picas. This means that the values inside the Rectangle dialog box appear in so many points (12 points in a pica). You can work in inches in three ways. The first way, before you bring up the Rectangle dialog box, is to choose File⇨Preferences⇨General and choose inches as the measurement system. All dialog boxes in all new documents will then express their measurements in inches, not points. The second way is to choose File⇨Document Setup and choose inches in the Ruler Units pop-up menu, which will change the units to inches in that document *only.* The third way is to type either the inch symbol (") or **in** after the number, even though the text fields show points. Illustrator does conversions from points to inches and centimeters (and vice versa) on the fly, so after you enter a point value, the program converts the points into inches as soon as you press the Tab key. This little feature can be an excellent way for you to become more comfortable with points and picas.

To get out of the Rectangle dialog box without drawing a rectangle, click the Cancel button (or just press ⌘-Period). Anything you have typed in that dialog box is then forgotten; the next time the dialog box is opened, it still has the size of the previously drawn rectangle inside it.

STEPS: Creating a Basic Drop Shadow Box

Step 1. Using the Rectangle tool, draw a rectangle that is about 1 inch wide by 1 inch tall. If the rectangle is not black with no Stroke, choose Object⇨Paint Style, and in the Paint Style palette, click the Fill square and click the smaller black box below it. Then, click the Stroke square and click the box with a slash below it.

Step 2. Choose the Selection tool and drag up and to the right just a little while holding down the Option key. (The farther you drag, the greater the depth of the drop shadow.)

Step 3. After you release the mouse button, you should have two overlapping rectangles. Change the color of the top one by clicking the Fill square and changing the color in the first gray box to 25% Black. Put a border around the top box by clicking the Stroke square and clicking the black box below it. Your illstration should now look like Figure 2-5.

Figure 2-5: A basic drop shadow box

Drawing Rectangles from Their Centers

Instead of drawing a rectangle from a corner, you can also draw one from its center. Rectangles are often placed on top of or under certain other objects, and there needs to be an even amount of space between the rectangle and the object it is surrounding. Drawing from the corner forces you to "eyeball" the space around the object, while drawing from the center of the other object ensures that space surrounding the object is the same.

To draw a rectangle from its center, hold down the Option key, click, and drag. The origin point is now the center of the rectangle. The farther you drag in one direction, the farther the edges of the rectangle go out in the opposite direction. Drawing from the center of a rectangle lets you draw a rectangle twice as big as the one you can draw if you drag from a corner. As long as the Option key is pressed, the rectangle continues to be drawn from its center. If you release the Option key before you release the mouse button, the origin of the rectangle changes back to a corner. You can press and release the Option key at any time while drawing, toggling back and forth between drawing a corner rectangle and a centered rectangle.

If you click without dragging when the Option key is pressed, the Rectangle dialog box appears. The center of the rectangle is now where you clicked (normally, the corner of the rectangle is where you click). Unlike manually drawing (dragging) centered rectangles, the values you enter for the width and height are the actual width and height of the rectangle. The value is *not* doubled, as it is when you are dragging a centered rectangle.

You can also draw a rectangle from its center by double-clicking the Rectangle tool. The tool changes from the Corner Rectangle tool to the Centered Rectangle tool. Drawing with the Centered Rectangle tool automatically draws a rectangle from its center. Now the Option key toggles from drawing from the middle to drawing from the corner. So if you keep the Option key pressed until after you release the mouse button, the rectangle is drawn from the corner, not the center.

Drawing a Perfect Square

Few things in life really are perfect, but squares in Illustrator are pretty darn close.

When drawing, you can force Illustrator to create perfect squares by holding down the Shift key as you draw. When you press the Shift key while drawing a rectangle, it conforms to a square. (In review of your fourth grade math class, the difference between a square and a rectangle is that a square is a rectangle with four sides of exactly the same length.) You can also use the Rectangle dialog box to draw a perfect square by entering equal values for the width and height.

To draw a square from its center, hold down the Option and Shift keys while drawing. Make sure that *both* keys are still pressed when the mouse button is released. If you are using the Centered Rectangle tool (it has a little + in it) and you press Option-Shift, the square is drawn from a corner.

Drawing Rounded Rectangles and Squares

Sometimes, straight corners just aren't good enough. That's when it's time to create a rectangle with *rounded corners.* Why? Maybe you want your rectangles to look less "computery." A tiny bit of corner rounding (2 or 3 points) may be just what you need.

To draw a rectangle with rounded corners, choose the Rounded Rectangle tool, a pop-up tool that appears when you click on the Rectangle tool in the Toolbox and drag to the right. Click and drag with this tool as if you were drawing a standard rectangle; the only difference is that this rectangle has rounded corners. The point at which you clicked is where the corner would be — if there were a corner. Of course, with rounded corners, there is no real "corner," so the computer uses an imaginary point, called the *origin point*, as its on-screen corner reference.

The *corner radius* in Illustrator is the length from that imaginary corner (the origin point) to where the curve begins, as shown in Figure 2-6. The larger the value you enter in the Corner radius field of the Rectangle dialog box, the farther the rectangle starts from the imaginary corner, and the bigger the curve is. For example, if you set the corner radius at 1 inch, the edge of the rectangle would start curving 1 inch from where a "real" corner would normally appear.

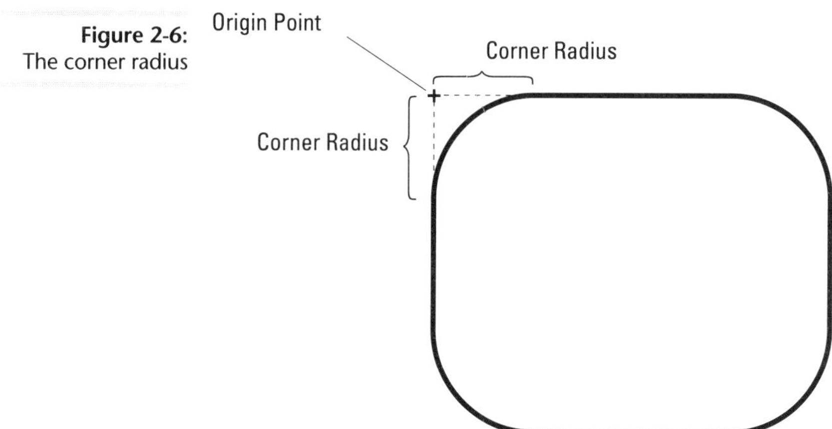

Figure 2-6: The corner radius

To draw a rounded rectangle from the center, press the Option key and keep it pressed until you release the mouse button. To draw a rounded square, hold the Shift key while dragging and do not release it until after you release the mouse button. Drawing a rounded square from its center requires that you press both the Option and Shift keys until you release the mouse button.

The *roundness* of the corners is determined by either the corner radius used by the most recent rounded-corner rectangle drawn or the radius set in the General Preferences dialog box (File⇨Preferences⇨General or ⌘-K). The corner radius in the General Preferences dialog box changes each time you change the radius with the Rounded Rectangle tool. To change the radius of the next rounded rectangle to be drawn, go to the General Preferences dialog box and enter the new corner radius value. All rounded rectangles are now drawn with this new corner radius until this value is changed.

The corner radius can also be changed by clicking once with the Rounded Rectangle tool anywhere in the document, which displays the Rectangle dialog box. Changing the value in the Corner radius field box not only changes the current rounded rectangle's corner radius, but also changes the radius in the General Preferences box. This corner radius is used for all subsequently drawn rounded rectangles until the radius value is changed again.

If the corner radius is more than one half the length of either the length or width of the rectangle, the rectangle will appear to have perfectly round ends on at least two sides. If the corner radius is more than one half the length of both the length or width of the rectangle, then the rectangle will be a circle!

You are limited to a maximum of a 4320-point corner radius, which works out to 5 feet. The largest rectangle you can create has a 10-foot length (the size of the Illustrator Pasteboard). So a 10-foot square with a 5-foot radius is another circle. (Those clever engineers...)

How the Corner Radius *Really* Works

For all you geometry buffs, this is the real way that this whole corner radius business works: The width of any circle is called the *diameter* of that circle. Half the diameter is the *radius* of the circle, as shown in the following figure.

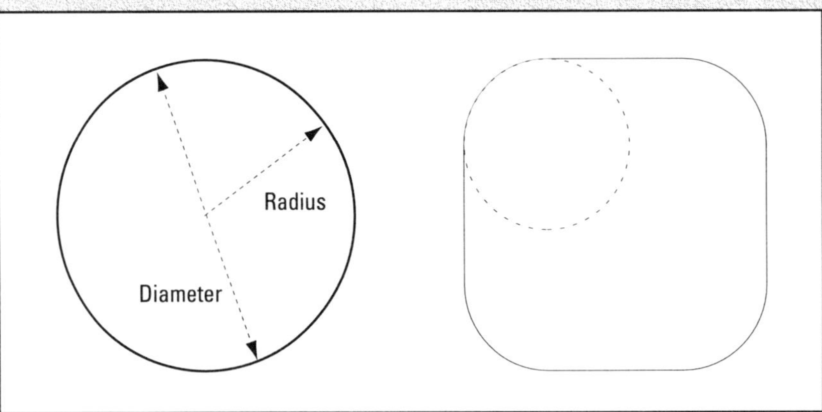

If you create a circle with a radius of 1 inch, the circle actually has a width (diameter) of 2 inches. Put this 2-inch circle into the corner of the rectangle, as in the figure above, and the curve of the circle matches the curve of the rounded rectangle that has a corner radius of 1inch. Huh?

To realistically determine the way a round corner will look, use the method that measures the distance from the imaginary corner to the place where the curve starts.

Artificial Intelligence in Illustrator: If you are in the Rectangle dialog box and enter a value of 0 in the Corner Radius field, the Rounded Rectangle tool is replaced by the standard Rectangle tool in the Toolbox. If you enter a value greater than 0, the Rounded Rectangle tool takes over that slot in the Toolbox.

Using the Round Corners Filter

If you have an existing rectangle with straight corners and you'd like to make the corners round, neither of the preceding methods will work. Instead, you must choose Filter⇨Stylize⇨Round Corners and enter the value of the corner radius you would like for the existing rectangle in the dialog box that appears. Using this filter allows you to change straight-corner rectangles to rounded-corner rectangles, not rounded-corner rectangles to straight-corner rectangles. Using this filter on rectangles that already have rounded corners isn't recommended, as it will usually result in an unsightly (ugly) distortion.

Furthermore, this filter cannot change corners that have been rounded with either the Rounded Rectangle tool or by previous use of the Round Corners dialog box. Using this dialog box affects corners that are *not* round. Figure 2-7 shows the Round Corners filter applied to various rectangles and the results.

Figure 2-7: Rounded corners on rectangles

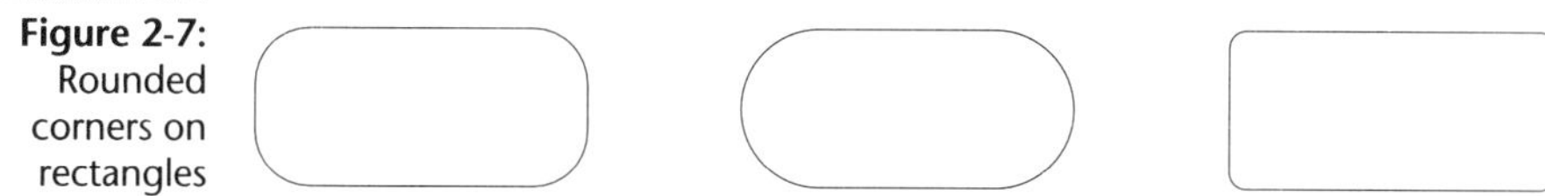

Rounding Corners Backwards

What if you want your corners to round "in" instead of out? Well, it would seem that you are initially out of luck, for Illustrator doesn't provide any way for you to enter a "negative" value for a corner radius. Instead, you need to manipulate the corners manually. The following steps, and the illustration of these steps in Figure 2-8, explain how to create a reverse rounded-corner rectangle.

Figure 2-8: Steps for creating "backwards" rounded corners on a rectangle

STEPS: Creating a Reverse Rounded-Corner Rectangle

Step 1. Choose File➪Preferences➪General and set the Corner radius to .25". Draw a rounded rectangle that is about 3-inches wide by 1-inch tall.

Step 2. Select the topmost point on the left side of the rounded rectangle with the Direct Selection tool (hollow arrow). One Control Handle appears, sticking out to the left.

Step 3. Using the Rotate tool, click the Anchor Point once to set the origin. Click the Control Handle again and drag it down below the Anchor Point. Press the Shift key to ensure that the Control Handle Line is perfectly vertical and then release the mouse button.

Step 4. Select the second point from the top on the left side with the Direct Selection tool. A Control Handle appears, sticking straight up out of this Anchor Point.

Step 5. Using the Rotate tool, click the Anchor Point once to set the origin. Click the Control Handle again and drag it to the right of the Anchor Point. Press the Shift key to ensure that the Control Handle line is perfectly horizontal and then release the mouse button.

Step 6. Repeat these steps for each of the corners. After you get the hang of it, the points start flying into position almost by themselves.

Drawing Ovals and Circles

Drawing ovals and circles is *almost* as easy as drawing rectangles and squares. You can create a wide variety of ovals and circles in Illustrator.

To draw an oval, choose the Oval tool, click, and drag diagonally. The outline of an oval forms, and when you release the mouse button, the oval itself appears on-screen. Ovals, like rectangles, have four Anchor Points, but the Anchor Points on an oval are at the top, bottom, left, and right of the oval.

Drawing an oval is harder than drawing a rectangle because the point of origin on an oval is outside the oval. With a rectangle, the point of origin corresponds to either a corner of the rectangle, which also happens to be an Anchor Point, or the center of the rectangle. On an oval, there are no corners. This means that clicking and dragging does not align the top or bottom, or left or right, but one of the 45° curves to the origin point (an *arc*). Figure 2-9 shows that the top of the curve extends above the origin point, the bottom of the curve extends below the origin point, the right edge extends to the right of the origin point, and the left edge extends to the left of the origin point. (More detailed — and largely unnecessary — math is available at the end of this section.)

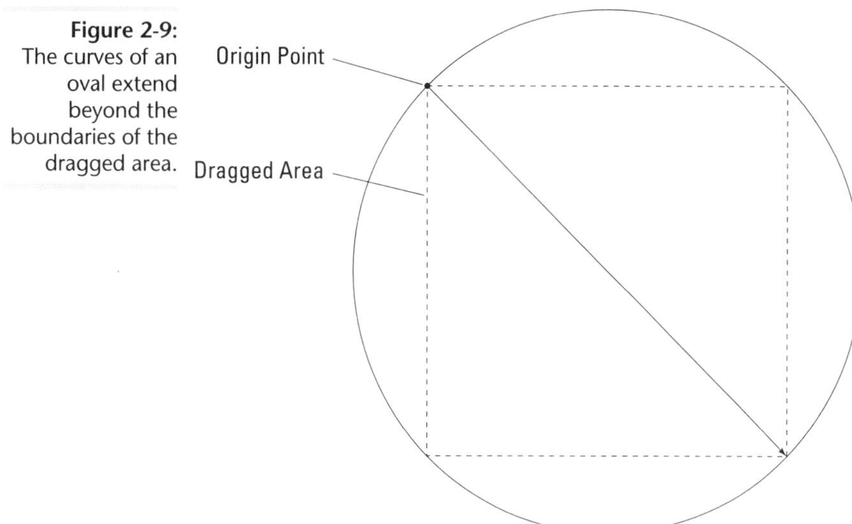

Figure 2-9: The curves of an oval extend beyond the boundaries of the dragged area.

Drawing an oval from its "corner" is a difficult task when the top, bottom, left, and right edges of the oval need to be at a specific location. On the other hand, tracing oval objects is easier because clicking and dragging on the edge of an existing oval object results in a close-to-perfect match, as shown in Figure 2-10.

Figure 2-10: Tracing a dimmed EPS image with the Rectangle and Oval tools

For easier tracing of circles, change the Constrain Angle value (File⇨General Preferences) to 45°. Now you can place the cursor on the top, bottom, or sides of the circle, and drag horizontally or vertically for a perfect fit. This technique doesn't work for ovals because the oval will be angled at 45° if drawn this way.

STEPS: Tracing an EPS Image with Basic Shapes

Step 1. Place the Horses/snowman file from the Artwork folder on the Macworld Illustrator Bible CD-ROM. Choose Window⇨Show Layers. In the Layers palette, double-click Layer 1 and check the Dim EPS images option.

Step 2. Use the Rectangle tool to trace the frame of the picture, the walls, and the pieces of the snowman's arms. Place the cursor in a corner of the object to be traced and drag towards the opposite corner. Use the Rotate tool to rotate the arms. For the hat, choose File⇨General Preferences (⌘-K) and change the Constrain Angle to 14°. Trace the hat and brim at this angle and then change the Constrain Angle back to 0°.

Step 3. Use the Oval tool in the same way as the Rectangle tool to trace the snowman circles, eyes, nose, mouth, snowballs, and snow drifts. If you can't see an entire circle, as is the case with most of the snow drifts and the bottom section of the snowman, just estimate.

To draw from the center of an oval, press the Option key and drag. As long as you are holding down the Option key when you release the mouse button, the oval uses the initial click as the origin point and is drawn from the center.

To change the Oval tool so that it *always* draws ovals from the center, double-click the Oval tool to change it to the Centered Oval Tool (an oval with a plus sign in its center). Double-clicking the tool again transforms it back to the standard Oval tool.

Clicking without dragging with the Oval tool brings up the Oval dialog box, where you can enter any value for the width and height of your oval. The oval is drawn from the upper-left arc. Entering identical values results in a circle. Option-clicking brings up the same dialog box, but the oval is now drawn from the center instead of the left arc.

To draw a perfect circle, hold down the Shift key as you drag. The oval now has equal width and height, making it a circle. Make sure that you keep pressing the Shift key until you release the mouse button; otherwise, the oval loses its equal proportions. To draw a circle from the center with the Oval tool, hold down both the Option and Shift keys and drag diagonally.

Ovals are drawn from the upper-left corner and extend about 20 percent of the total height above the origin point and about 20 percent of the total width to the left of the origin point. It's not just a coincidence that the right edge and bottom also extend 20 percent past the release point. The way this works out in mathematics (numerophobics should skip ahead to the next paragraph now) is that the height and width of the oval will be the square root of 2 (about 1.414) times the height and width of the "box" that is dragged from corner to corner.

Only rectangles and ovals were used to create the illustration in Figure 2-11. Through a creative use of Fills, the illustration comes alive.

Figure 2-11: An illustration drawn with only rectangles and ovals

STEPS: Drawing the Juggler with Rectangles and Ovals

Step 1. Change the Paint Style to a Fill of None and a Stroke of 1 point Black in the Paint Style palette.

Step 2. Using the Oval tool, drag to create the juggler's body and then his head, as shown in Figure 2-12.

Figure 2-12: Ovals and circles

Step 3. To tilt back the juggler's head, select the "head" oval and double-click the Rotate tool. Then enter a value of 30°, which angles the head back.

Step 4. Next, create one of the rings by pressing the Shift key and dragging to create a perfect circle.

Step 5. Duplicate the circles by pressing the Option key and dragging one of the circles to a new location. As long as the Option key is pressed when you release the mouse button, the circle is duplicated rather than moved.

Step 6. Draw a much smaller circle for one of the balls the juggler is balancing on his head. Option-copy the balls in the same way you copied the rings.

Step 7. Option-copy two more ball-sized circles to create hands, the white area of the eye, and the mouth.

Step 8. Choose File⇨General Preferences (⌘-K) and change the Constrain Angle to 45°.

Step 9. Using the Rectangle tool, create first the top part of the hat and then the rim of the hat, as shown in Figure 2-13. The pieces will automatically be angled at 45°.

Step 10. Change the Constrain Angle back to 0° and draw both arms. They may need to be rotated individually, depending on the location of the rings.

Step 11. Draw the rectangular background and choose Arrange⇨Send to Back (⌘-minus sign).

Step 12. Select individual paths and Fill them with different colors and gradients.

Creating Cool Shapes

Although it is just loads of fun to create more and more ovals, rectangles, and rounded rectangles, sooner or later you're gonna get bored. There are other, dare I say, *more interesting* shapes that you can create automatically by using some of the Plug-In tools that come with Illustrator.

New to Illustrator 6 are Plug-In tools, some of which are the Polygon, Spiral, and Star tools. These "tools" were filters in version 5 (Filter⇨Create).

Figure 2-13: Rectangles are added to the illustration.

Creating Polygons

To create a polygon, select the Polygon tool (shown in Figure 2-14) and click and drag in a document. As you drag, the polygon will grow from its center and get larger and larger.

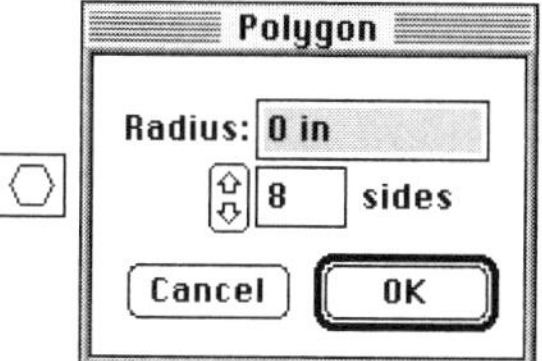

Figure 2-14: The Polygon tool and the Polygon Tool dialog box

To specify the number of sides for your polygon *before* you draw the polygon, Option-click with the Polygon tool. That will bring up the Polygon Tool dialog box, where you can specify both the number of sides and the size of the polygon.

The radius is the distance from the center of the polygon to the corners of the polygon. For even-sided shapes (4, 6, 8, 10 sides and so on), the radius is half the width of the object, from one corner to the opposite corner. For odd sided shapes, the radius is *not* half the width of the object, but instead, can *only* be measured by going from one corner point to the center.

When drawing a polygon, you can change the number of sides "on the fly." To increase the number of sides, press the Up Arrow. To decrease the number of sides, press the Down Arrow.

Creating Stars and Spirals

To create stars, select the Star tool from the Plug-In Tools palette, and click and drag. Like the Polygon tool, you can increase or decrease the number of points on the star by using the Up and Down Arrows. Press Control to constrain the inner radius to the current size. Press Option to make ever other side parallel.

To create spirals, select the Spiral tool from the Plug-In Tools palette and drag in the document. Increase the number of winds with the Up Arrow and decrease them with the Down Arrow. Figure 2-15 shows several stars and spirals drawn with the Star and Spiral tools.

Figure 2-15: Stars and spirals drawn with the Star and Spiral tools

Drawing Shapes at an Angle

Normally, when you draw a shape with a tool, it appears to be oriented with the document and the document window. For instance, the bottom of a rectangle is parallel to the bottom of the document window.

But what if you want to draw shapes that are all angled at 45° on the page? Well, one possibility is to rotate them after they are drawn using the Transform Each command or the Rotate tool. Better than this alternative, however, is to set up your document so that every new shape is automatically angled.

The angle of the shapes is dependent on the *constrain angle*. Normally, the constrain angle is 0°, where all shapes appear to align evenly with the borders of the document. To change the constrain angle, choose File⇨Preferences⇨General and enter a new value in the Constrain Angle text field inside the General Preferences dialog box.

When you are done drawing these angled shapes, make sure that you change the Constrain Angle setting back to 0°, or all new shapes will be created at the altered constrain angle.

The constrain angle affects not only shapes, but other objects created in Illustrator, such as type. In addition, dragging objects with the Shift key pressed will constrain them to the current constrain angle, or a 45° or 90° variation of it.

Filling and Stroking Shapes

One of the most powerful capabilities of Illustrator is its capability to color objects. In Adobe Illustrator, you can color both the Fill and the Stroke of the paths you have created.

Fills

The *Fill* of an object is the color inside the shape. If a path is closed, the Fill exists only on the inside of the path. If the path is open (meaning that it has two end points), the Fill exists between an imaginary line drawn from end point to end point and the path itself. Fills in open paths can provide some very interesting results when the path crosses itself, or the imaginary line crosses the path. Figure 2-16 shows an example of Fills in open and closed paths and how the paths appear in Artwork mode. For text, the Fill is the color of the text. Fills do not appear in Artwork mode, only in Preview mode. Depending on the complexity of the path and the type of Fill, Illustrator may refuse to preview the Fill and will automatically switch to Artwork mode.

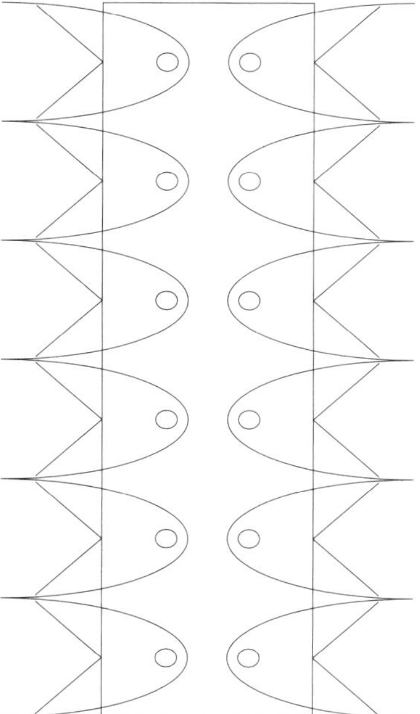

Figure 2-16: Open and closed paths in both Artwork mode (left) and Preview mode (right)

The Fill color options include White, Black, a tint of Black, Process Colors, Custom Colors, Patterns, and Gradients. The Fill option for an object can also be set to None, where the Fill is transparent. This allows you to see behind a path to what is underneath it when the Stroke of an object is the visible part.

Strokes

The *Stroke* of an object is made up of three parts: its color, weight, and style. Strokes appear where there are paths, or around the edges of type. Like Fills, any one path or object may have only one type of Stroke on it; the color, weight, and style of the Stroke are consistent throughout the length of the path or the entire text object. (Individual characters in a text object can have different Strokes if they are selected with the Type tool when the Stroke attributes are applied.)

The Stroke color options are White, Black, a tint of Black, Process Colors, Custom Colors, Patterns, and None (the Stroke is transparent). When the Stroke color option is set to None, then the object is said to have no Stroke. Strokes cannot display patterns in Preview mode, nor can they be Filled with gradients.

Preference Practical Jokes: Part 27

Apollo: So, I want to play a practical joke on my buddy Boomer.

Toulouse: Good man. I've got a great Illustrator one for you.

Apollo: Okay, hit me.

Toulouse: Change the General Preference setting called Constrain Angle to 180 degrees.

Apollo: What'll that do?

Toulouse: At first, everything will seem perfectly normal. But then....

Apollo: His computer'll explode, right?

Toulouse: Not quite. Actually, everything will work normally except type, which will appear upside down. All the time.

Apollo: Ha! That's great.

Toulouse: There's a worse one, you know.

Apollo: Would Boomer get really mad at this one?

Toulouse: Depends. Then again, with a name like Boomer, I wouldn't go making him upset. For a really good practical joke that Boomer probably won't even discover until he prints, set the Constrain Angle to .2 degrees.

The weight of a Stroke is how thick it is. On a path, the Stroke is centered on that path, with half the thickness of the Stroke on one side of the path and half the thickness on the other side of the path. Strokes can be anywhere from 0 to 1000 points thick.

The style of a Stroke consists of several parts, including the cap style, join style, miter limit, and dash pattern (see "The Stroke Attributes Panel" later in this chapter). The *cap style* is the way that the ends of a Stroke look and can be either butt cap, rounded cap, or projected cap. The *join style* is the way that Corner Points on paths appear when stroked and can be either mitered join, rounded join, or beveled join. Figure 2-17 shows examples of the cap styles and join styles.

The *miter limit* is the length at which miter joins are cropped. Normally, the dash pattern for a Stroke is solid, but various dash patterns can be created for different effects. Figure 2-18 shows different miter limits on different corners.

Combining Strokes with Fills

Many times, paths in Illustrator require both Fills and Strokes. When you give both a Fill and a Stroke to a single path, the Stroke knocks out the Fill at the edges of the path by one half the weight of the Stroke. Figure 2-19 demonstrates this.

A method for fixing this problem is to copy the path and paste it in front, removing the frontmost path's Stroke. The Filled path, on top of the Stroked path, knocks out the "inner" half of the Stroke. This technique is discussed in detail in Chapter 19.

Figure 2-17: The three different cap and join styles for Strokes

Figure 2-18: A sampling of all the different cap styles, join styles, miter limits, and dash patterns for Strokes

Figure 2-19: A Stroke knocks out a Fill by one-half the weight of the stroke.

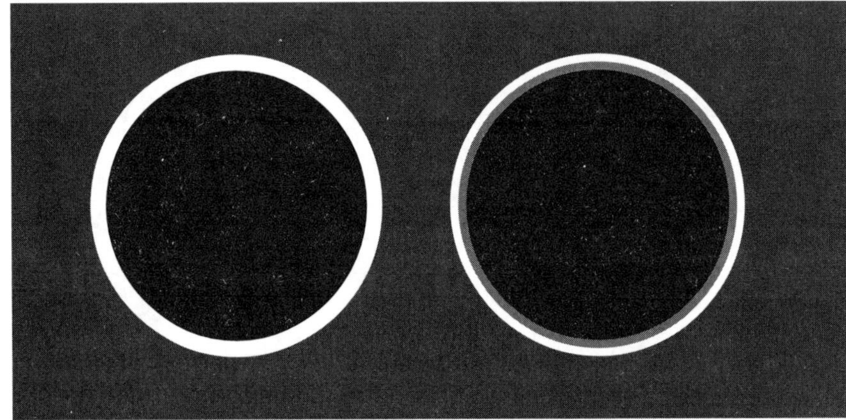

Original object with a 6-point Stroke and a Black Fill

How the Stroke knocks out the Fill by half of the weight of the Stroke

The Paint Style Palette

You use the Paint Style palette, shown in Figure 2-20, to give objects in Illustrator Fills and Strokes. The Paint Style palette has two main functions: It can be used to change the current Paint Style attributes of selected objects to something else, and it lists the current Paint Style attributes of an object.

To view the Paint Style palette, choose Object⇨Paint Style (⌘-I) or choose Window⇨Show Paint Style. If the Paint Style palette is behind other palettes, choosing Paint Style from the Object menu or clicking anywhere on the palette brings it to the forefront.

To hide the Paint Style palette, click the close box in the upper-left corner of the palette or choose Window⇨Hide Paint Style. When the Paint Style palette is visible and no text fields in it are selected, ⌘-I also hides the Paint Style palette. The Paint Style palette can be moved around your screen by clicking the title bar and dragging. The Paint Style palette cannot be dragged off the screen.

In the Paint Style palette, you may change the Paint Style attributes of selected objects, including the Fill (White, Black, Process Color, Custom Color, Pattern, and Gradient) and Stroke (White, Black, Process Color, Custom Color, and Pattern). This is also where you specify whether Fills and Strokes overprint and what, if any, dash patterns are within strokes.

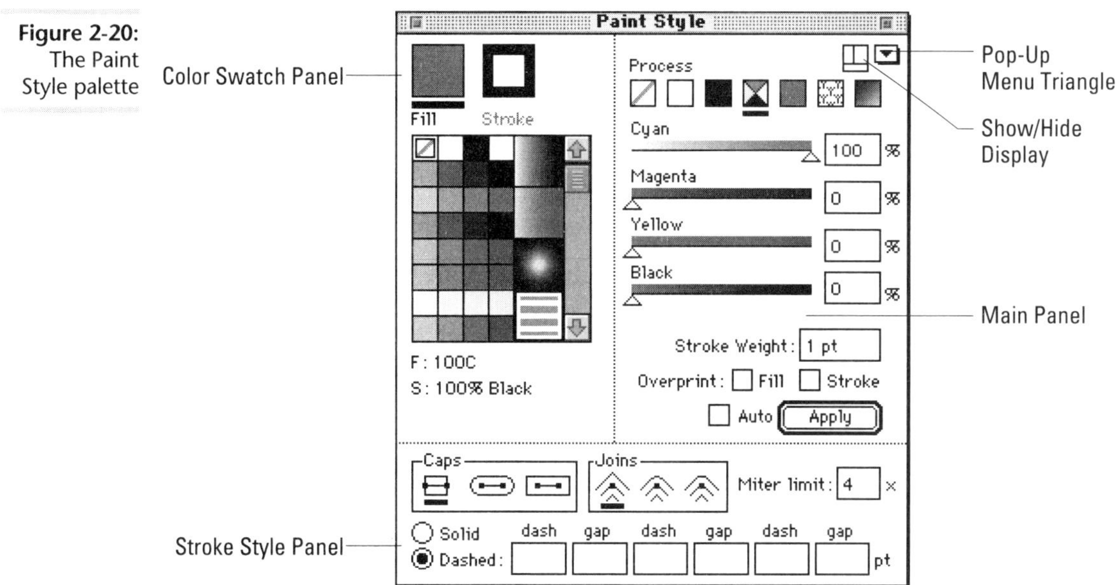

Figure 2-20: The Paint Style palette

To change the Paint Style attributes of an object, first select it and then make the changes in the Paint Style palette. To change the Fill of an object, click on the Fill square (the underline will move to the Fill square if it isn't already there) and then click the color you want to use. To change the Stroke, click on the Stroke square and then click the color you want to use. (The width of the Stroke is always 1 point by default.) If the Auto checkbox is checked, the changes you make in the Paint Style palette occur automatically; if it is not, you must click the Apply button.

To view the current Paint Style attributes of an object, select the object. The Paint Style palette's information changes to accurately reflect how the object is "painted." Figure 2-21 shows three different paths with different Paint Style attributes. The fourth illustration at the right of the figure has different paths with different Fills and Strokes, so question marks appear in the Fill and Stroke squares. If either the Fill or Stroke squares are changed at this point, all objects selected will have the new Fill or Stroke. Changing the Fill for several objects does not affect the Stroke on any of them; likewise, changing the Stroke for several objects does not affect the Fill on any of them.

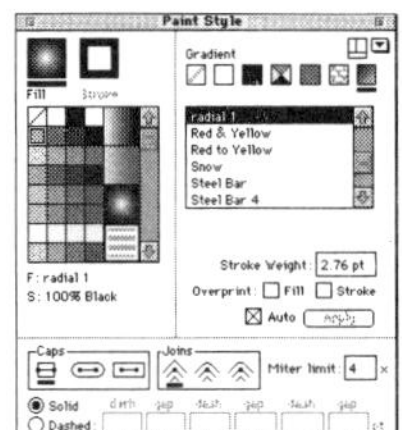

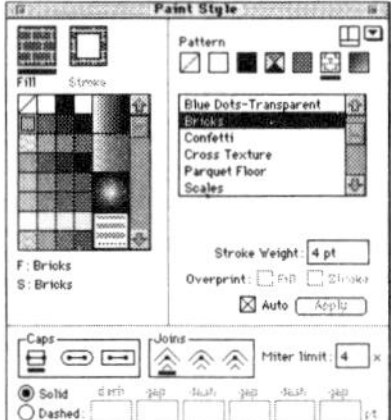

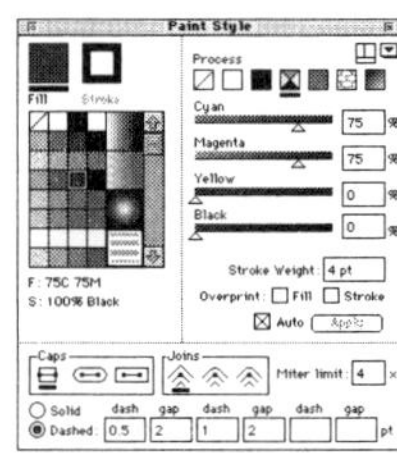

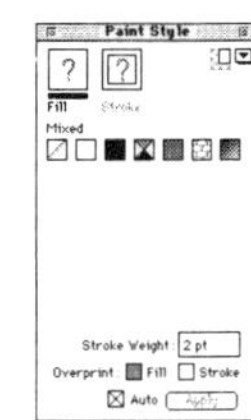

Figure 2-21: Paths and their Paint Style attributes

Customizing the Paint Style Palette

The Paint Style palette is the most flexible palette you'll find in Illustrator. You can view the palette in four different ways, depending on which of the three Paint Style panels you want to see.

The left panel is the Color Swatch panel, where different preset color swatches are available. The right panel is the Main Attributes panel, where most choices for Color, Fill, and Stroke options are available. The bottom panel is the Stroke Attributes panel, where the different options for Stroke attributes are available.

The default view of the Paint Style palette is the Three-panel view, where all three panels of the Paint Style palette are visible. This view takes up the most space on-screen, and it is the only view where you can see the Stroke Attributes panel. The Two-panel view displays the Color Swatch panel and the Main Attributes panel. The third view is the Color Swatch panel view, which shows only the Color Swatch panel. The last view is the Main Attributes panel view, which displays only the Main Attributes panel.

To change the views of the panels, click and hold the little triangle in the upper-right corner of the palette and then drag over and out to the right, where a pop-up menu appears. On this pop-up menu, you can choose any one of the four available views.

You can also choose different views by clicking different sections of the Show/Hide display to the left of the pop-up menu triangle. The current view is made of white boxes with black outlines. Any areas that are currently not being displayed are shown as gray boxes with darker gray borders.

When the Paint Style palette is displayed, it always appears the way it was viewed last. For instance, if you were viewing the Paint Style palette in the Two-panel view and closed it (hid it), then the next time it was opened, even if the computer was shut down between sessions, the Paint Style palette would be displayed in Two-panel view.

The Stroke and Fill Squares

When using the Paint Style palette, you can make changes to either the Stroke or Fill, but not to both at the same time.

In the top section of the Color Swatch panel, there are two squares, the Fill square and the Stroke square. The Stroke square has a heavy stroke around it, with an empty middle. There is an underline under the square that is currently being used. To change from Fill to Stroke, click the Stroke square. To change from Stroke to Fill, click the Fill square.

No matter which view you use, the Fill and Stroke squares are always visible. If the Main Attributes panel is the only panel visible, the Fill and Stroke squares are at the top of it. Every view also has the Stroke Weight text field. Although it normally appears in the Main Attributes panel, if only the Color Swatch panel is showing, the Stroke Weight text field also appears at the bottom of that field.

The panel selectors, the pop-up menu, and the diagram of the displayed panels appear in all views of the Paint Style palette, as well.

You can quickly use the Fill as the Stroke, or the Stroke as the Fill by dragging the color from one square to another. When you do this, the original square doesn't change, so both squares will have the same color attributes.

The Apply Button and the Auto Checkbox

In the lower-right corner of the Paint Style palette is the Auto checkbox. When this checkbox is checked, any changes in the Paint Style palette take place instantly to any selected objects (entries to text fields require a Tab or Return/Enter to be applied). When the Auto checkbox is selected (it has an *X* inside it), the Apply button remains dimmed.

When Auto is not checked, the Apply button becomes available. Changes in the Paint Style palette do not affect selected objects until the Apply button is clicked. You can also achieve the results of the Apply button by pressing Return or Enter on the keyboard. The Apply button can be clicked only when changes have been made to options in the Paint Style palette. Most users of Illustrator find that the Apply button isn't needed, and that having to click it can really slow them down.

The Main Attributes Panel

The Main Attributes panel of the Paint Style palette contains all the major options for Fill and Stroke colors. Along the top of the Main Attributes panel are seven boxes, shown in Figure 2-22, each with a different type of color for Fills and Strokes. When the Stroke option is chosen, there are only six boxes because Strokes can't have gradients. The box that is currently selected has an underline under it, similar to the underlines under the Stroke and Fill squares. Only one of the seven boxes can be chosen at one time.

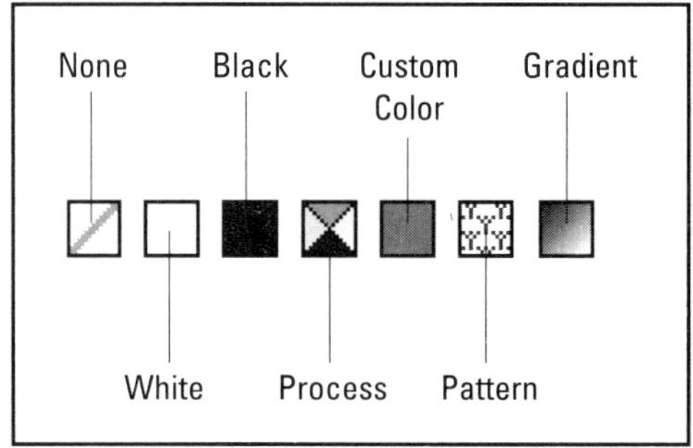

Figure 2-22: The seven color attributes boxes in the Paint Style palette

The first box has a slash in it, which corresponds to None. Fills painted with the None option are transparent, while Strokes painted with None are considered to have "no stroke." Objects and paths can have both no Stroke and no Fill and still exist in your illustration (of course, they won't print). Paths with no Fill or Stroke are used for several different things, including masks, pattern and graph design borders, and Pathfinder shapes.

The second box is the White option. When this box is chosen for either a Fill or a Stroke, the result is 0% color in that area. White is different from None in that anything colored with white is opaque. When an object with a White Fill is placed on top of any other object, the white object obscures anything underneath it. Also, an object with a Fill has the Fill reduced by half the width of a White Stroke on that object. When the White box is chosen, a *slider bar* appears, allowing you to make... well... a darker white. A triangle (*slider*) is at the far left of the bar, and the number to the right in the text field is 0%. Any number greater than 0 results in a shade of black, even though you initially chose the White square. If you deselect the object after changing the slider to a higher position, the next time the object is selected, the Black box will be underlined, not the White box. When entering a value in the text field, you must press Return or Enter for the value to be accepted. Moving the sliders, though, is instantaneous.

The following steps show you how to add color to the snowman in the winter scene.

STEPS: Coloring the Snow and the Snowman

Step 1. To color the snow and the snowman, select the snowman and the round drifts of snow with the Selection tool.

Step 2. Choose the Fill square and click the White box in the Main Attributes panel.

Step 3. Select the Stroke square and click the None box in the Main Attributes panel.

The third box is the Black option, and choosing this box allows you to specify exactly what tint of Black (Gray) you would like, from 0% (which happens to be White) to 100%. When the box is first selected, the slider on this slider bar is at the far right, and the text field reads 100%. Entering a value less than 100 results in that particular tint. If the value entered is 0, then the next time the object is selected, the White box is highlighted. When more than one object is selected and all have a tint of Black, the triangle slider does not show up, and the text field will be empty. In this case, the Stroke or Fill square, whichever is underlined, has a question mark inside it. This happens only because some of the objects selected have *different* tints of Black. Entering a value in the text field changes all selected objects to that tint. Clicking once on the left end of the slider bar places the triangle at the left end of the slider bar and changes the number in the text field to 0%, transforming all selected objects to White Strokes or Fills, whichever is chosen. Another click repositions the slider to a different location.

Now you can add more color to the winter scene with the following steps.

STEPS: Coloring the Hat and the Barn

Step 1. Select the two pieces of the hat with the Selection tool and move them on to the head of the snowman.

Step 2. Press the Shift key and select the barn, the eyes, and the mouth.

Step 3. Change the Fill to Black, and the Stroke to None.

The fourth box is made of four different triangles, each a different color. This is the Process box, with four different slider bars. Each of the slider bars represents a different process color: Cyan, Magenta, Yellow, and Black. These four process colors correspond to the four process colors used in printing. Different combinations of these four colors result in a large variety of colors, covering about half the colors that the human

The Color Purple

Cassiopeia: How can I make a purple color with the CMYK sliders?

Toulouse: Try 50% Cyan and 100% Magenta.

Cassiopeia: Wow, that was easy. How'd you know that?

Toulouse: Well, I sorta cheated. All the sliders in the Paint Style palette are interactive.

Cassiopeia: They provide a real-to-life multimedia experience?

Toulouse: Not exactly. But the sliders change color relative to what the current color is. For instance, when I set magenta to 100%, I looked at the other sliders, and saw there was purple in the middle of the cyan slider bar. So I dragged the Cyan slider to 50% and voilà!

Cassiopeia: Voilà, indeed. You know, someone should stick that in a book somewhere....

Toulouse: Good idea....

eye can see. Various combinations of these colors can closely represent Pantone colors, a spot color system that is widely used in the printing industry. For instance, to get a bright red color, set the Cyan and Black settings to 0%, and the Magenta and Yellow settings to 100%. For a dark forest green, change the Cyan setting to 100%, the Magenta setting to 0%, and the Yellow and Black settings to 50%. Setting all four Process Colors to 0% results in process white, which is different than regular white mainly through how it relates to other colors, especially in the areas of blends, gradients, and color adjustments through the color filters.

The fifth box is the Custom Color box. A *custom color* is a color that is set up to print as either a spot color, a color on a separate plate, or a color to be split into process colors when printed. If process-color printing is to be used, the advantage to using custom colors instead of process colors is that colors can remain much more consistent throughout the illustration. When the Custom Color box is selected (underlined), a scroll box appears, listing all the custom colors in the document. To choose a custom color, click the color of your choice with the cursor or type the first few letters of the custom color option to select it. When a custom color is chosen, a triangle appears on the slider bar beneath the scroll box. The position of the triangle represents the *tint* of the custom color. At 0%, the color resembles White, in that it will look White and will be opaque, but according to Illustrator, the color is still just the selected custom color with a tint of 0%. Double-clicking a custom color brings up the Custom Color dialog box.

To quickly make a custom color out of any process color, create your process color using the CMYK sliders, and then drag the color from the Fill (or Stroke) square to the Custom Color square. The Custom Color dialog box will appear where you can name your color, click OK, and get back to work in seconds.

The following steps show you how to add color to the stars in the winter scene.

STEPS: Coloring the Stars

Step 1. Select all the stars with the Selection tool.

Step 2. Change the Fill square to the Gold Custom Color and the Stroke square to None.

The sixth box is the Pattern box, used for giving a pattern to a Stroke or a Fill. Patterns given to Strokes appear in Preview mode as solid gray, although the width of the Stroke is represented accurately. After you select the Pattern box, a scroll box appears, listing all the patterns in the document. To choose a pattern, click the pattern name of your choice with the cursor or type the first few letters of the name to select it. There are no tint options for patterns; the tint of the pattern is determined when it is created. (Creating and modifying patterns is covered in depth in Chapter 11.)

The following steps show you how to add color to your barn.

STEPS: Coloring the Walls

Step 1. Select the two walls of the barn with the Selection tool.

Step 2. Change the Fill square to the Brick Pattern and the Stroke square to None.

Step 3. Deselect the top wall by Shift-clicking it with the Selection tool.

Step 4. Double-click the Scale tool. In the Scale dialog box, type **300** in the Uniform text field. Uncheck the Object checkbox and click OK. This step changes the size of the bricks in the lower wall so that they are three times the size of the ones in the back, producing the illusion that the lower wall is closer.

The seventh box is the Gradient box. Only Fills — not Strokes — of objects can have gradients as attributes. (After the Stroke option is chosen, only six boxes appear, all except the Gradient box.) After the Gradient box is selected for a Fill, a list of gradients appears in a scroll box. Select a gradient by clicking its name or typing the first few letters of the gradient. You cannot change the tint of a gradient; instead you must change the gradient itself in the Gradient palette. Double-click the gradient you want to modify and the Gradient palette appears with that gradient selected. (Gradients are explained in detail in Chapter 10.)

STEPS: Coloring the Background and the Sign

Step 1. Select the background rectangle with the Selection tool.

Step 2. Change the Fill square to the Black-and-White Gradient, change the angle to 90°, and change the Stroke square to None.

Step 3. Select the sign and change the Fill square to the Steel Bar Gradient with an angle of 160°.

STEPS: Finishing Touches

Step 1. Select the snow drift ovals, and choose Arrange⇨Bring To Front (⌘-plus sign).

Step 2. Select the three snowman circles, and choose Arrange⇨Bring to Front (⌘-plus sign).

Step 3. Select the brick wall, the hat, and the sign, and choose Arrange⇨Bring to Front (⌘-plus sign).

Step 4. Select the horizontal path and choose Filter⇨Stylize⇨Add Arrowheads. Click OK.

Step 5. Press the Option key and choose Filter⇨Add Arrowheads. In the Add Arrowheads dialog box, check the Start button and select arrowhead number 19.

Step 6. To make the illustration more interesting, add some custom gradients to the background and White radial gradients to the snow.

Overprinting options are available only in the Main Attributes panel. If these boxes are available, you may choose to overprint a Stroke, a Fill, or both. Overprint is available only when the Black, Process, Custom Color, or Gradient boxes are selected. When Overprint is checked, the object does not knock out anything directly under or above it but, instead, mixes with anything it overlaps. Overprinting is mostly useful for trapping (see Chapter 20 for more information).

Slider Magic

Moving the sliders around can be done in so many different ways that I've devoted a section to it. If you thought all you could do with the little triangles on the slider bars was drag them to different places, you'll be astounded by the next few paragraphs.

The most basic way to move the sliders around is by dragging them. Clicking a triangle and dragging it is beneficial because you actually see the Stroke or Fill square (whichever you have chosen) on the Paint Style palette change as you drag.

After you stop dragging the slider, you can drag the others (if you have chosen the Process box) to see what changes occur if you adjust the other sliders. Just watch the Fill or Stroke square. This process allows for much less guesswork than in previous versions of Illustrator.

When a value is entered in the text field to the right of each slider bar, the slider moves to that position. In the Process area, with its four slider bars, you can press Tab to move to the next slider bar text field and Shift-Tab to move to the preceding one.

You can move a slider much faster by clicking the slider bar where you want the slider to be. The slider instantly relocates to the position you clicked and shows the appropriate value in the text field. The drawback to this method of adjusting sliders is that you can't watch the Fill or Stroke squares change color as you drag.

To move a slider in *tiny* increments, hold down the Option key and click either side of the triangle. The triangle moves along the slider bar in 1% increments for every click. To move a slider in *small* increments, press Shift-Option and click either side of the triangle. The triangle moves along the slider bar in 5% increments for every click made with the Option and Shift keys pressed.

Tinting Process Colors

Starbuck: Why isn't there a tint control for Process Colors?

Toulouse: That would be too confusing; you'd have a 50% tint of 20% cyan, 50% magenta and 10% black, which would really be 10% Cyan, 25% Magenta, and 5% Black.

Starbuck: So, I have to do all that math each time I want to change a process tint?

Toulouse: You can, but there's a shortcut....

Starbuck: I thought all the letters on the keyboard were used up, but go ahead, tell me.

Toulouse: All you do is press Shift before you drag a slider, and all the sliders with values move along with the one you're dragging.

Starbuck: Wow! Great! Wait, it goes too fast, much too hard to control....

Toulouse: When adjusting the tint this way, be sure to move the slider with the largest percentage, as it gives you more control. The other sliders will move proportionately with that one.

The Color Swatch Panel

The Color Swatch panel, shown in detail in Figure 2-23, is made up mainly of little squares that have *color swatches* in them. In each color swatch is a color that was created in the Main Attributes panel. Color swatches can be made from any of the seven boxes in the Main Attributes panel and from any options in those boxes. Overprinting is not part of a color swatch, nor are any Stroke attributes.

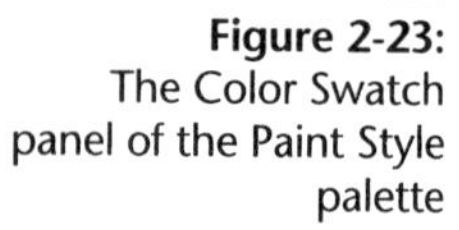

Figure 2-23: The Color Swatch panel of the Paint Style palette

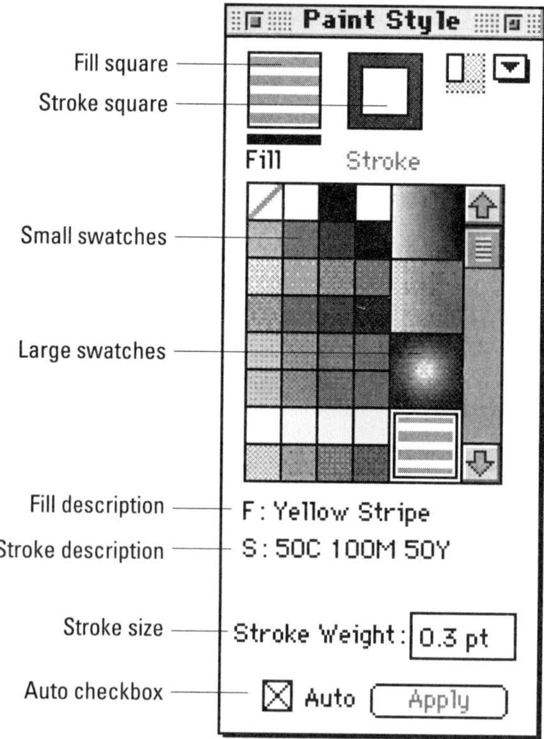

There are two different types of color swatch boxes: little ones and big ones. Large boxes are good for patterns and gradients because they show more detail than the smaller boxes. You *can* put patterns and gradients in the little boxes, though only slight details in patterns and two-color gradients will be clear.

To use the color swatches, first click either the Stroke or Fill square. Then, as you pass the cursor over the color swatches, the cursor changes into an eyedropper. Clicking a color swatch changes the selected square (Fill or Stroke) to that color. You can also move color swatches up to the "other" square (say, Fill, if the Stroke square was underlined), by clicking and dragging it up onto that square.

To add a new color swatch to the existing color swatches, set up the color by using the Main Attributes panel and then drag the new color from the appropriate square, either Fill or Stroke, to an empty (White) color swatch box at the bottom of the color swatches. To see empty color swatch boxes, you may have to scroll down in the swatch listing. Technically, the swatch boxes are really never "empty"; instead, they have, at the very least, the White process color in them.

To replace an existing color swatch with a new color, drag the new color from the Fill or Stroke square to an existing color. The new color replaces the existing color.

To remove a color, hold down the ⌘ key as you pass over the color swatches. The cursor turns into a scissors. Clicking a color swatch allows you to delete that swatch, after clicking OK in one of those annoying "Are you sure?" dialog boxes. You can delete a swatch without seeing a dialog box by pressing ⌘-Option and then clicking. To delete several colors at once, click and drag with the ⌘ key pressed. To delete several colors without a warning dialog box, press ⌘-Option and drag across the color swatches you wish to delete. To reset the Paint Style color swatches, press ⌘-Shift and click any color swatch.

Underneath the color swatch boxes are color information lines. The (F:) line tells you exactly what your Fill is, and the (S:) line tells you what your Stroke is. Process colors are specified by percentages and the first letter of the color. For instance, 100% cyan, 50% Magenta, 50% yellow, and 0% black would be: 100C 50M 50Y. If a process color has a value of 0%, it does not appear in the color information line. Custom colors, gradients, and patterns are displayed by name.

The Stroke Attributes Panel

At the bottom of the Three-panel view of the Paint Style palette (and visible only in this view, no others) is the Stroke Attributes panel (shown in Figure 2-24), which contains information about the Stroke attributes for the selected paths and objects.

The weight of the Stroke is always changed at either the bottom of the Main Attributes panel or, if that is not visible, in the Color Swatch panel. Everything else relevant to Strokes is changed in the Stroke Attributes panel.

In the Caps box, there are three different types of end caps. Caps apply only to the end points on open paths. The first cap is a butt cap (wouldn't a pair of modest boxers have been just as suitable?), which is a flat end of the Stroke, cut off perpendicularly to the direction the path is traveling at its end point. The second type of cap is a rounded cap, which is a smooth, round cap whose farthest distance from the end point is half the

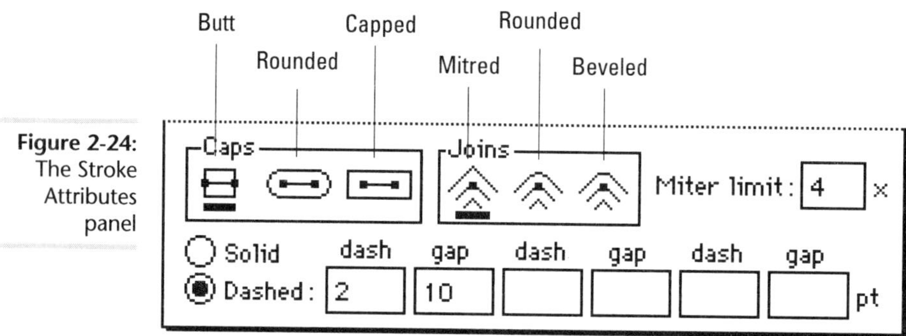

Figure 2-24: The Stroke Attributes panel

weight of the Stroke. The last type of cap is the projected cap, named so because the end of the cap projects from the end point half the width of the stroke and is squared off. Each path can have only one type of end cap on both ends.

There are three different types of joins in the Join box. Joins apply to corner Anchor Points *only.* The first type of join is a mitered join, where the edges of the Stroke meet at a point. The next type of join is a rounded join, where instead of meeting in a point, Stroked edges meet in a smooth curve. The last type of join is the beveled join, where the edges appear to have been mitered but then chopped off. Each path can have only one type of miter for all its joins. Caps and joins are shown in Figure 2-25.

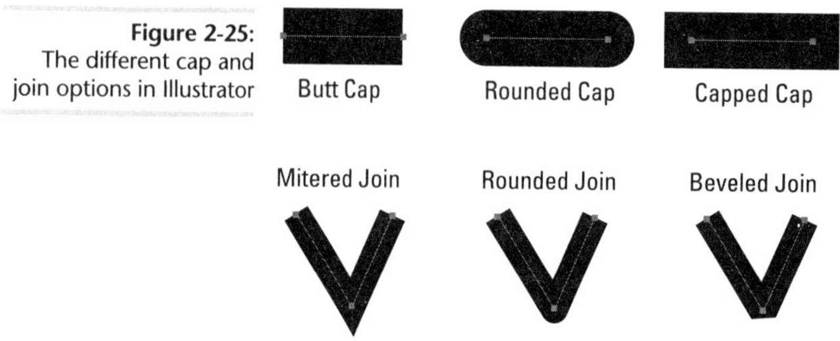

Figure 2-25: The different cap and join options in Illustrator

The Miter limit text field shows how far a miter can go past its corner point, relative to the width of the corner point. If the end of the miter exceeds the set miter limit, the miter is cropped off near the corner point. The Miter limit setting can never be more than 500, and the Stroke width times the Miter limit can never exceed 1800 points. The miter limit affects all the corner points on an entire path.

The bottom of the Stroke Attributes panel contains information about whether the Stroke is solid or dashed. If dashed, the length of the dashes and the Strokes can be specified. (Strokes are covered completely in Chapter 19.)

The Eyedropper and Paint Bucket Tools

The Paint Bucket and Eyedropper tools are lifesavers for those of us who are constantly using up notes to jot down what the percentages of CMYK (cyan, magenta, yellow, and black) are in one path so that we can apply those same amounts to another path. Double-clicking on either tool brings up the Paintbucket/Eyedropper dialog box (shown in Figure 2-26), where you can select or deselect multiple options regarding paint style information.

Figure 2-26: The Paintbucket/ Eyedropper dialog box

Paintbucket/Eyedropper

Paintbucket applies:	Eyedropper picks up:
☐ Fill	☒ Fill
☐ Color	☒ Color
☐ Overprint	☒ Overprint
☒ Stroke	☒ Stroke
☒ Color	☒ Color
☐ Overprint	☒ Overprint
☒ Weight	☐ Weight
☒ Cap	☒ Cap
☒ Join	☐ Join
☐ Miter limit	☒ Miter limit
☐ Dash pattern	☐ Dash pattern

Cancel OK

The Eyedropper Tool

The Eyedropper tool, shown with the Paint Bucket tool in Figure 2-27, samples paint style information from a path or a placed image and stores it in the Paint Style palette, without selecting that path. The information stays in the Paint Style palette until you change the information in the palette itself, select another path with different paint style information, or click any other path or placed image with a different paint style.

Why Use the Eyedropper and Paint Bucket Tools?

Baltazar: Why should I use the Paint Bucket and Eyedropper tools? It seems like a lot of work.

Toulouse: One reason is that you can be assured that your colors are consistent throughout the illustration. So if you used a custom color somewhere, you don't try to duplicate it with a CMYK mix somewhere else, for instance. And you don't have to select the objects you're clicking with the Paint Bucket tool.

Baltazar: What's all this nonsense about sampling colors from pixel-based images?

Toulouse: That's something new to version 6 of Illustrator. You can now sample colors from any placed image. And that's not all.

Baltazar: It's not?

Toulouse: You can sample colors right on your desktop or from within a Photoshop document that's open in the background.

(continued)

(continued)

Baltazar: Wow. Does the Eyedropper sample an average color, like that "other" Illustration program?

Toulouse: No, it samples the exact pixel you click on.

Baltazar: Thanks for the info. I won't tell the Cylons, honest.

Toulouse: Oh, sure, rat out your race but keep quiet about graphics applications...I believe you.

Figure 2-27: The Eyedropper and Paint Bucket tools

If you double-click the Eyedropper tool on any path, all selected objects in the document are changed to the paint style of the path that you double-clicked.

If you hold down the Option key and click the Eyedropper tool, it toggles to the Paint Bucket tool

The Paint Bucket Tool

The Paint Bucket tool is used for applying the paint style that is currently in the Paint Style palette to both paths and 1-bit TIFF images.

Holding down the Shift key when clicking a path fills the Paint Bucket tool with the current paint style and also selects that path. If the path was already selected, a Shift-click deselects it. Pressing the Option key toggles from the Paint Bucket tool to the Eyedropper tool.

Summary

- Illustrator provides basic drawing capabilities by allowing you to quickly draw basic objects with specialized tools, like the Rectangle, Oval, Star, Polygon, and Spiral tools.
- Painting objects is done by selecting them and then changing the Fill and Stroke Attributes in the Paint Style Palette.
- Paths can be colored quickly by using the Eyedropper tool (to sample colors from paths or placed images) and the Paint Bucket tool (to apply those sampled colors).

Drawing and Manipulating Paths

3 CHAPTER

In This Chapter

- Drawing with the Brush tool
- Drawing with the Freehand tool
- Using the Pen tool
- Learning the laws of the Pen tool
- Selecting, moving, and deleting entire paths
- Selecting, moving, and deleting portions of paths
- Understanding the concept of foreground and background
- Grouping and ungrouping paths
- Using the Group Selection tool

The most effective (and challenging) way to create paths is to draw them with one of the drawing tools. The Brush tool, the Freehand tool, and the Pen tool are Illustrator's primary drawing tools. These tools are shown in Figure 3-1.

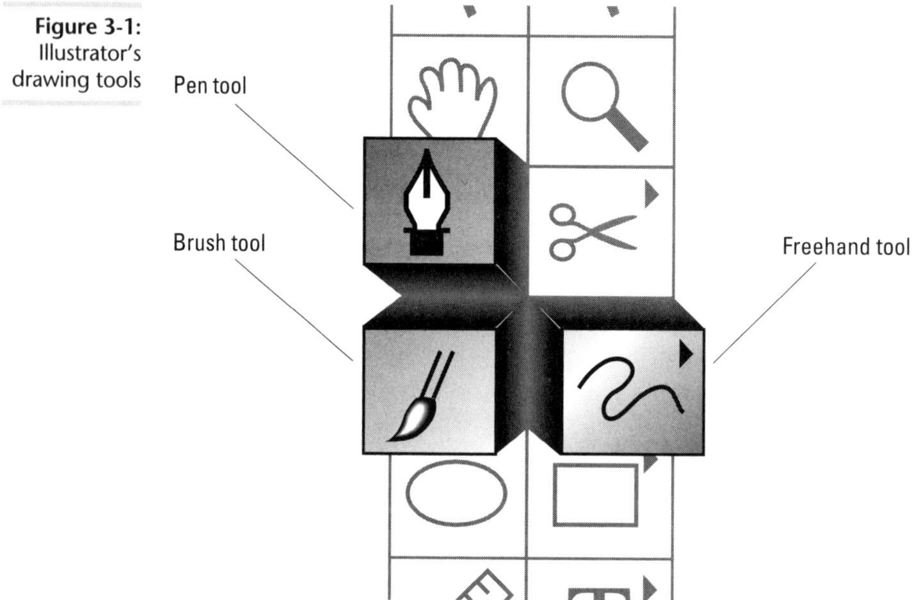

Figure 3-1: Illustrator's drawing tools

Drawing Paths in Illustrator

Using the Brush tool is the easiest way to create paths, but also the most limiting unless you use it with a pressure-sensitive tablet. The Freehand tool is simple to use to create paths, but the results can be questionable. The Pen tool is the most difficult to use, but the results from it can be better than from either the Brush or the Freehand tool.

Each drawing tool does something better than the others, as well as having its own limitations. However tempting it may be, don't ignore any one of these tools because you think that another tool can perform the same function.

If I were a gambling man, I'd bet that the one tool that you want to avoid is the Pen tool. Unfortunately, mastering Illustrator becomes impossible if you avoid learning how to use this tool. Hey, I won't kid you — mastering the Pen tool is like mastering calculus: it makes no sense at first and even less sense when people explain it to you. But, like calculus, the more you use the Pen tool, the more you like it, and the more technically amazing things you can do with it. (Personally, I think the Pen tool is easier to learn than calculus, and fortunately, the analogy ends here.)

Understanding how the Pen tool works helps you understand not only how Illustrator works but also how PostScript and many other tools in other programs work. Adobe Photoshop has a Path tool, which is virtually identical to Illustrator's Pen tool; so by understanding and using the Pen tool in Illustrator, you've already learned one of the most difficult tools to use in Photoshop.

Figure 3-2 was drawn with a combination of all three drawing tools. Throughout this chapter, I'll explain how the various parts of this illustration were drawn and how they were manipulated to produce the final drawing.

Figure 3-2: This illustration was drawn using a combination of the Brush, Freehand, and Pen tools.

About the Brush Tool

The Brush tool is more like the Rectangle and Oval tools than it is the Pen or Freehand tool because it draws closed paths, and closed paths only.

The Brush tool is similar to brush-type tools in painting programs; the brush has a certain width, and you can paint with this brush at this width anywhere in your document. The big difference between paint programs' brushes and Illustrator's brush is that when you finish drawing with Illustrator's Brush tool, a filled, outlined area has been created.

To use the Brush tool, just choose the tool and start drawing. A freeform path appears wherever you drag. That's all there is to it. Kinda. Figure 3-3 shows a drawing that was created with the Brush tool set to a variable width with a pressure-sensitive stylus.

Figure 3-3: A drawing created with the Brush tool

Drawing with the Brush tool is a bit more complicated than I just explained. The most important consideration is the width of the brush stroke. The brush stroke can be as narrow as 0 points and as wide as 1,296 points (that's 18 inches to you and me).

Although 0 is the smallest width, a brush stroke drawn with a width of 0 points actually has a width bigger than 0 points. To change the brush stroke width (the default is 9 points), double-click the Brush tool and enter a number in the Width text field.

The term *Stroke* in Illustrator and *brush strokes* drawn with the Brush tool are entirely different critters. In fact, brush strokes are usually Filled, not Stroked. Brush strokes are made of paths that surround the edges of the stroke, and the width of the brush stroke is the distance between the path on either side of the brush stroke. Brush strokes created with the Brush tool are always closed paths. After you release the mouse button, several Anchor Points appear. These Anchor Points and their corresponding Control Handles shape the path.

Results achieved with the Brush tool vary depending on two very important characteristics: your artistic ability and your ability to control the mouse. If you can't draw with a pencil or other forms of traditional media, there is very little possibility that using a mouse will turn you into a Michelangelo (the artist, not the turtle). If Michelangelo had to use a mouse to draw, he probably would have become a philosopher or sunk so low as to be an editor for a Mac magazine, constantly complaining about the inefficient means by which cursors are controlled.

A mouse is *not* an intuitive drawing tool, and not being able to draw in the first place makes it even more difficult to draw with the Brush tool. So if artists have trouble with the mouse, what's the point of having the Brush tool at all? Well, instead of a mouse, you can use several types of alternative drawing devices. The best of these is a pressure-sensitive tablet. Trackballs with locking buttons are also good for drawing with the Brush tool (this allows more control over the direction and speed of the brush).

When you're drawing with any of the tools in Illustrator, dragging off the edge of the window causes the window to scroll, which creates a frightening effect for the uninitiated. If you don't want the window to remain where it scrolled to, don't let go of the mouse button, but instead just drag in the opposite direction until the window returns to the original position. To scroll the other way while still using a tool, drag off the other side of the window.

To help you draw more precisely, you have the option of changing the cursor shape from the cute little brush into a crosshair. Press the Caps Lock key (to engage it), and the cursor changes into the crosshair with a dot in the center. Press the Caps Lock key again (to release it), and the cursor returns to the brush shape. The dot at the center of the crosshair is the center of any brush stroke drawn with the Brush tool. Normally, when the cursor is in the shape of a brush, the tip is the center of the brush stroke. Some people find it easier to draw when the brush cursor is replaced with the precise crosshair.

The best and, at the same time, the most limiting capability of the Brush tool is its consistency of width. If you make the width 18 points, the brush creates a brush stroke that is 18 points wide for the length you draw it. No other tool in Illustrator can be this precise, even the Pen tool with all its precision capabilities. Unfortunately, the Shift key doesn't constrain the Brush tool to 45° angles like it does for most of the other tools.

Problems with Corners and the Brush Tool

Gabe: I'm having trouble with the Brush tool...I'm getting....

Toulouse: Overlapping paths whenever you make a sharp corner?

Gabe: Yeah! How'd you guess?

Toulouse: Unfortunately, it's a common problem when using the Brush tool. Paths at sharp turns and corners overlap each other, sometimes extensively.

Gabe: You know, I didn't even notice it before, and I've been using Illustrator forever.

Toulouse: That's because if the brush stroke is just Filled, this usually isn't much of a problem. But if you give the brush stroke a regular Stroke, the Stroke goes into the middle of the brush stroke and looks, well, bad.

Gabe: You're telling me. Any way around it?

Toulouse: Sure. Use the Unite filter on individual brush strokes that have overlapping pieces.

Gabe: You know, we haven't gotten that far in the book...to filters, that is.

(continued)

(continued)
Toulouse: It's easy. To use the Unite filter on brush strokes, draw your brush stroke with the Brush tool and then immediately select Filter⇨Pathfinder⇨Unite. All the overlapping paths magically disappear. Make sure that only one path is selected when you apply the Unite filter, or any intersecting brush strokes will be joined.

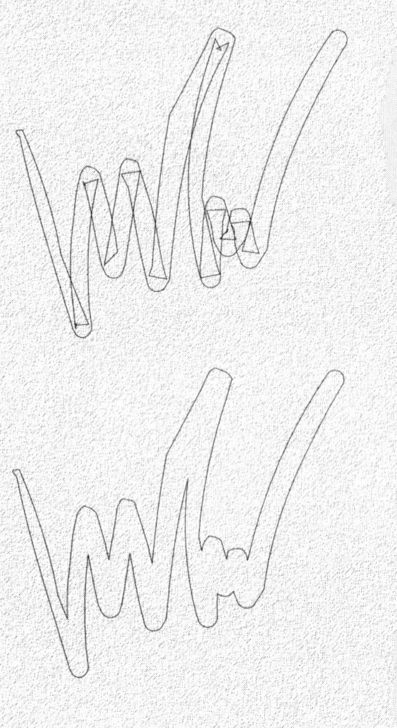

Drawing with the Brush Tool

In this section, you will create the grass and the horse outlines previously shown in Figure 3-2. Both can be drawn with or without a pressure-sensitive tablet (discussed in detail in "Variable Widths and Pressure-Sensitive Tablets" later in this chapter), although you can achieve better effects if you use a tablet.

STEPS: Drawing the Horse and Tall Grass Outlines

Step 1. Double-click the Brush tool and set the width to 3 points. If the Variable option can be checked (it can if you have a pressure-sensitive tablet), make the minimum 1 point and the maximum 10 points. Change your Paint Style to a Fill of Black and a Stroke of None in the Paint Style palette.

Step 2. Using the Brush tool, draw each piece of the basic shape of the horses, as shown in Figure 3-4. The more individual pieces you draw, the easier it is to use the Brush tool. Long strokes are difficult to produce and aren't as appealing as shorter strokes. Don't worry about filling in the horses with color at this point. You are using the Brush tool only to create the smoothly flowing outlines of the horses. If you make a mistake while drawing, choose Edit⇨Undo (⌘-Z).

Step 3. To draw the tall blades of grass, just draw a few select blade outlines to create a "clump" of grass. For the best effects, drag the Anchor Points from the base of the clump up and outward with the Scale tool and the Option key pressed.

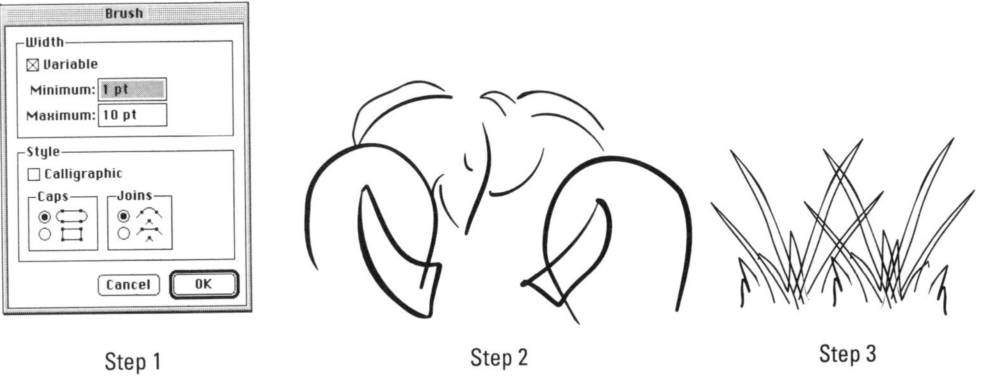

Figure 3-4: Horse and grass outlines created with the Brush tool

The Calligraphy Angle

Double-clicking the Brush tool brings up the Brush dialog box, in which the little Calligraphic checkbox appears. If this box is checked, the Brush tool no longer creates brush strokes with even widths; instead, it creates brush strokes that vary according to the angle that they are drawn.

When the Calligraphic box is checked, another box appears where you can set the angle of the Calligraphic brush. The angle you should choose depends on what is going to be drawn. To mimic hand-drawn lettering in a calligraphic style, the angle should be set to 45° (or if you're left-handed, it should be set to –45°).

You can also use the Calligraphy filter in the Stylize option of the Filters menu. However, the result achieved with the Brush tool and the Calligraphic option is much better than any possible result obtained from using the filter.

Bends and Ends

You can specify how the joins and caps appear when drawing brush strokes.

Caps are the way the ends of each brush stroke should appear — either rounded (the default) or straight. If you choose Straight, the ends appear perpendicular to the direction of the brush stroke at its ends — which can be a little disconcerting because the ends appear rounded while you are drawing the brush stroke, but the ends are promptly cut off after the mouse button is released.

Joins can be made round (default) or straight. When the joins are set to Straight, the width of the brush is usually much less at the point where the corner is straightened out.

The difference between the types of brush stroke caps and joins is shown in Figure 3-5.

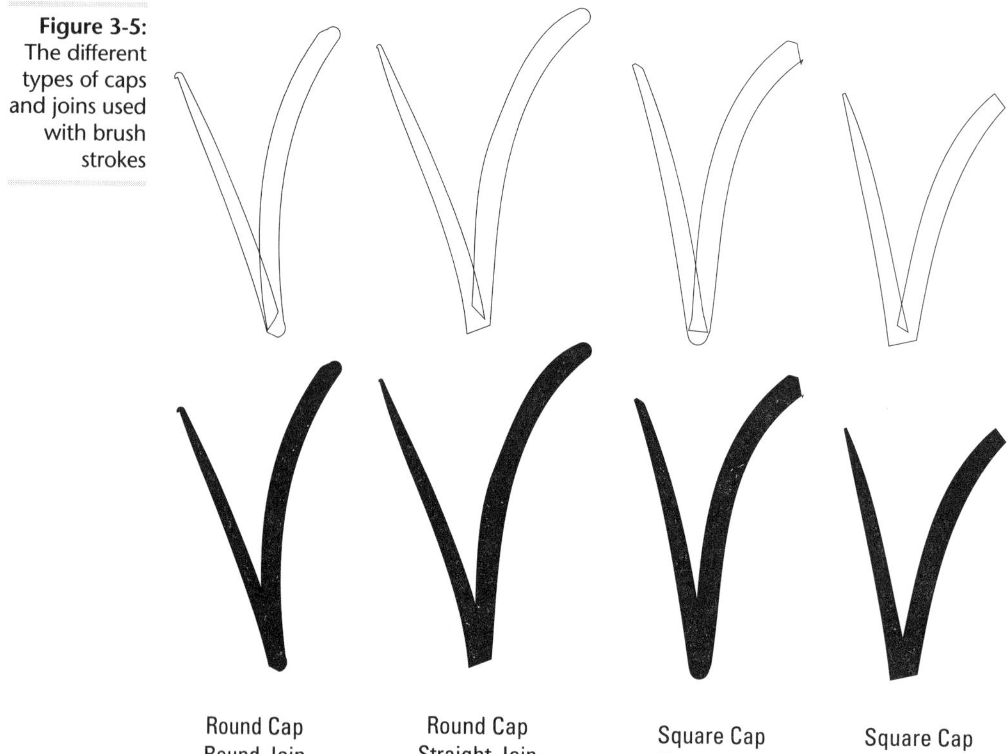

Figure 3-5: The different types of caps and joins used with brush strokes

Variable Widths and Pressure-Sensitive Tablets

If you have a pressure-sensitive tablet — a Wacom (pronounced "walk 'em") tablet, some call them, because a large majority tend to be made by Wacom — you can select the Variable checkbox in the Brush dialog box (accessed by double-clicking the Brush tool). If you don't have a pressure-sensitive tablet, this option is grayed out.

A *pressure-sensitive tablet* is a flat, rectangular device over which you pass a special stylus. The more pressure exerted by the stylus on the tablet, the wider a brush stroke will be, providing the Variable option in the Brush dialog box is checked. When using the Variable option, try to set the minimum and maximum widths fairly close to get the most realistic brush look for your drawings.

After you check the Variable option, two new text fields appear, giving you an option to specify the minimum and maximum width of the brush stroke as it is drawn. The minimum width is as narrow as the stroke can appear when you are pressing the pen as lightly as possible; the maximum width is as wide as the stroke can appear when you are pressing the pen as hard as possible.

Drawing Loosely with the Freehand Tool

The Freehand tool initially seems to be a primitive version of the Brush tool. Like the Brush tool, the Freehand tool draws a freeform path wherever the cursor is dragged, but instead of creating a closed path that is a certain width, the result is a single path following approximately the route you've taken with the cursor. You can get the resulting path to follow your cursor-drawn line exactly by lowering the freehand tolerance.

When you need to draw rough edges or realistic illustrations that don't look "computery," the Freehand tool is the tool to use. It draws a path wherever you drag the tool with the mouse, creating Smooth Points and corner Anchor Points relative to how you draw. Although the Pen tool is the tool to use to get precise, super-straight lines, it is difficult to use. The Freehand tool is much easier to use, but it draws lines that are far from perfect.

The Freehand tool has the unique capability to make the lines you draw with the cursor look...well...good. A swooping, uneven, jagged line that looks terrible as it is being drawn can be instantly transformed into a beautifully curved piece of artwork reminiscent of lines drawn traditionally with a French curve.

Still, the Freehand tool has some limitations. The main limitation is that, unlike the Pen tool, it is an *imprecise* path-drawing tool. It is difficult to draw a straight line with the Freehand tool. It is even more difficult to draw a shape with precise curves. The location of a path drawn with the Freehand tool is directly relevant to the direction and speed that the cursor is moving.

Using the Freehand Tool

Before you use the Freehand tool for the first time, it's a good idea to change the Paint Style attributes in the Paint Style palette to a Fill of None and a Stroke of Black, 1 point. Having a Fill other than None while drawing with the Freehand tool often results in bizarre looking shapes.

What's This Tool Again??

Arnold: Excuse me, Mr. Toulouse, but aren't we using Illustrator?

Toulouse: Yeah...

Arnold: Well, why is there a tool called the FreeHand tool?

Toulouse: It's the "Freehand" tool. No capital H.

Arnold: Aren't the Adobe people just asking for a lawsuit from Aldus?

Toulouse: Actually, MacroMedia distributes FreeHand now, and no, the lawsuit stuff is over, but they still hate each other.

Arnold: I'm a little confused.

Toulouse: Join the crowd. Here goes. Altsys Corp. created FreeHand, Aldus distributed it up through version 4.0. Then Adobe bought Aldus, Altsys sued Adobe for FreeHand, got it back, and then Altsys got sucked up by MacroMedia, which used to be Macromind, then Macromind-Paracomp. Like Melrose Place without the sex.

Arnold: And FreeHand tolerance is...?

Toulouse: (aside) How much patience can you have before you start swatting your overzealous FreeHand-using buddies?

To use the Freehand tool, select it from the Toolbox, click in the document window, and begin dragging the mouse. As you drag, you see a series of dots following the cursor. These dots show the approximate location of the path you have drawn. After you release the mouse button, the path of dots is transformed into a path with Anchor Points, all with Control Handle Lines and Control Handles shooting off from them. The faster you draw with the Freehand tool, the fewer points are created. The slower you draw, the more points are used to define the path.

STEPS: Drawing Grass and a Tree with the Freehand Tool

Step 1. Choose File⇨Preferences⇨General (⌘-K) and set the Freehand tolerance setting to 2, which allows for detail in the paths without making all the segments straight lines. Set the Paint Style to a Fill of C100 Y70 and a Stroke of Black, 1 point in the Paint Style palette.

Step 2. You can create the short grass by drawing three different clumps of grass (see the top of Figure 3-6) and then duplicating the clumps to create the appearance of random blades. To do this, select the Freehand tool and drag up and down to create the blades; then drag across under the blades to connect the bottom to form a closed path. Repeat this procedure to create three or four clumps of different sizes. Be sure to change the Fill color to a slightly different greenish color each time.

Step 3. Using the Selection tool, click the clumps of grass and Option-drag them side by side, overlapping them slightly. (Pressing the Option key duplicates the dragged clumps.) Repeat this process until there are enough clumps to resemble a grassy area.

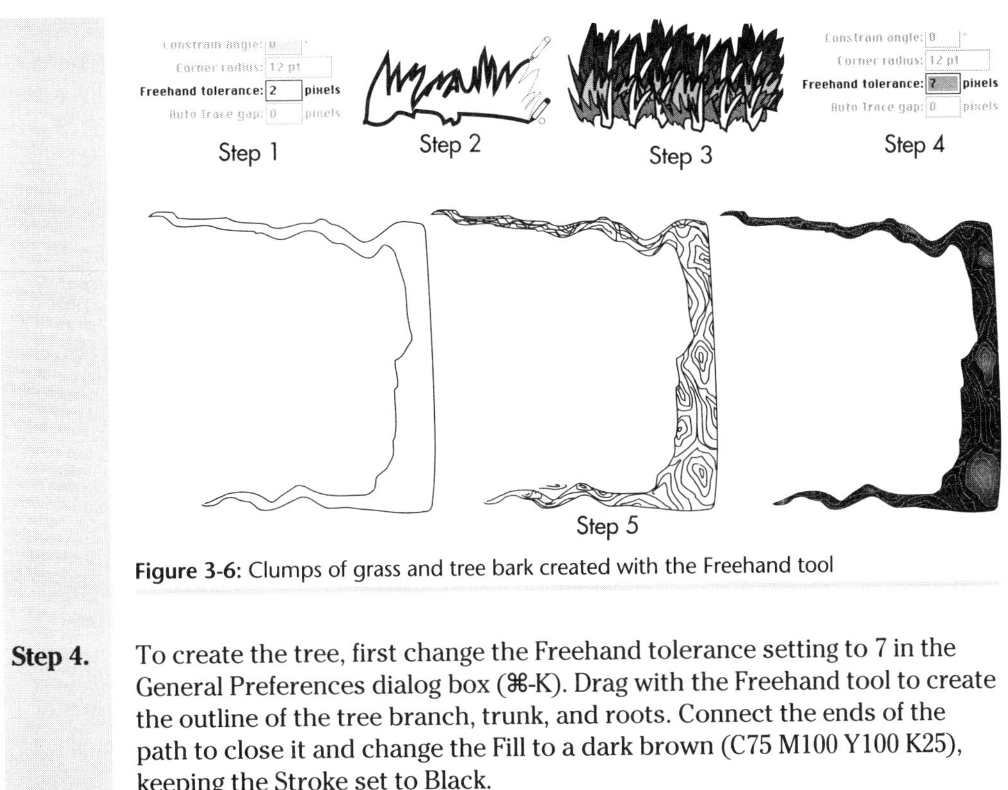

Figure 3-6: Clumps of grass and tree bark created with the Freehand tool

Step 4. To create the tree, first change the Freehand tolerance setting to 7 in the General Preferences dialog box (⌘-K). Drag with the Freehand tool to create the outline of the tree branch, trunk, and roots. Connect the ends of the path to close it and change the Fill to a dark brown (C75 M100 Y100 K25), keeping the Stroke set to Black.

Step 5. To create the textured areas of the bark on the tree, change the Fill to None and the Stroke to a dark shade of gray. Drag along the contours of the tree, which creates circles and wavy patterns.

Every Anchor Point created with the Freehand tool has two Control Handles shooting out of it; this means that Straight Corner Points cannot be drawn with the Freehand tool. This lack of Straight Corner Points makes constructing precise objects not only difficult, but impossible. Also, though they may appear to exist at first glance, smooth Anchor Points are also not created with the Freehand tool, which can be especially deceiving when the Freehand tolerance option is set to a high number, and all the Anchor Points look like they have to be Smooth Points. This is *not* the case. In fact, most Anchor Points created with the Freehand tool — except for its End Points — are *Curved Corner Points*, which are Anchor Points with two independent Control Handles shooting out. If the Freehand tolerance setting is high enough, you'll get Smooth Points as well. (See "Jagged Paths Versus Smooth Paths" later in this chapter for more information.)

Normally, the Freehand tool resembles a little pencil when you are drawing, which is far better than having to draw with the little squiggle that appears in the Toolbox. The line of dots that are drawn comes directly from the point (tip) of the pencil cursor. Pressing the Caps Lock key (engaging it) changes the cursor from the pencil shape to a crosshair, which looks suspiciously like the crosshair from the Brush tool. The line of points comes from the dot in the center of the crosshair.

If you like using the crosshair cursors all the time, but get really mad that every time you start typing you forget to take off the Caps Lock key, you've got short-term memory problems. To fix this, you might need brain surgery. Fortunately, you can set your cursors to *always* be "crosshair style" just by going to General Preferences (⌘-K) and checking the Use Precise Cursors checkbox.

Drawing Open Paths and Closed Paths

You can draw both open and closed paths with the Freehand tool. An *open path* has two separate, distinct End Points. A *closed path* has no End Points. To change an open path into a closed path, the End Points must be joined together. (Joining is discussed in Chapter 7.)

Paths in Illustrator may cross themselves (no, not to protect against vampires). When these paths cross, the Fills may look a little unusual. Strokes look normal; they just overlap where paths cross.

To create an open path, draw a path with the Freehand tool, but make sure that the beginning and end of the path are two separate points at different locations. Open paths with Fills may look a little bizarre because Illustrator automatically fills in between the End Points on the path, even if the imaginary line between the End Points crosses the path itself. Figure 3-7 shows both open and closed paths drawn with the Freehand tool.

Figure 3-7: Paths drawn with the Freehand tool

Imaginary Lines

Open Paths

Closed Path

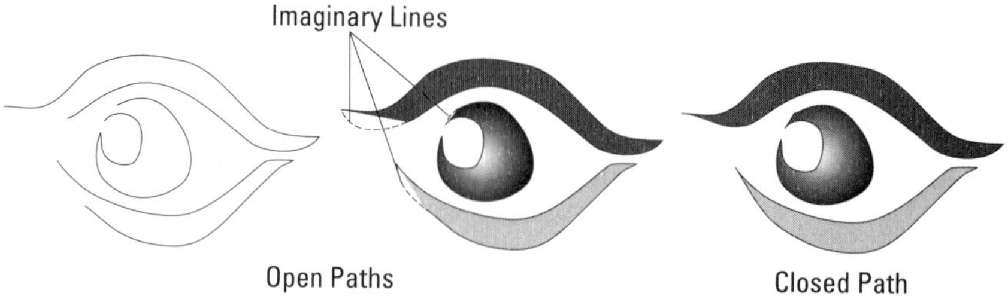

To create a closed path, end your path at the same place that you started the path. When the pencil cursor is directly over the location where the line begins, the eraser end of the pencil (at the opposite end from the tip) turns black, and a little circle appears to the lower right of the pencil. This change means that the path is a closed path if you release the mouse button when that particular cursor is showing.

Drawing Semistraight Segments

You can draw semistraight segments — that is, segments that look straight but, upon closer inspection, are really just a teeny bit curved — with the Freehand tool. To draw these segments, start drawing with the Freehand tool and press the ⌘ key at the point where you want the semistraight segment to begin. The cursor changes to an eraser (see the next section for details on erasing). Keep dragging to where you want the semistraight segment to end and release the ⌘ key to continue drawing with the Freehand tool.

Notice that the dots that normally appear along the path that the Freehand tool takes do not appear between the area where you first pressed the ⌘ key and where you released the ⌘ key; this is normal. After you are done drawing, release the mouse button and a semistraight line segment appears between the locations where you pressed and then released the ⌘ key. Upon further inspection with the Direct Selection tool, you will notice that Control Handles extend out from the Anchor Points on either side of the semistraight segment.

One of the important things to remember in this process is that you should never release the mouse button while pressing the ⌘ key. You can create as many semistraight segments in a path drawn with the Freehand tool as you like by pressing and holding the ⌘ key for each of them. Keep in mind, however, that when drawing multiple semistraight segments, there must be some movement of the mouse between drawing the semistraight segments. After you press the ⌘ key, move the mouse, and then release the ⌘ key, you *must* move the mouse before you press the ⌘ key again to create a new segment. If the mouse is not moved between ⌘-key presses, only one segment is drawn, from the location where the ⌘ key is initially pressed to the location where it is ultimately released.

A problem with drawing semistraight segments is that it is difficult to see exactly where to place the endpoint of the segment because the cursor looks like a huge eraser (the type you were given in first grade that you needed two hands to hold onto and use properly and that always seemed to take the varnish right off the desk after they tore through that wonderful Grade Triple Z paper that still had tree bark in it). If you press the Caps Lock key before the ⌘ key, the big fat eraser cursor becomes the suave dotted crosshair cursor.

Of course, it is my belief that the ⌘ key was never intended to be used with the Freehand tool to draw these semistraight lines. In fact, the only real reason the ⌘ key does anything like this at all is because it is used for erasing.

Erasing in Real Time

The Freehand tool has a capability not found in any of Illustrator's other tools: the capability to erase itself right away while being drawn. Some people think they are erasing when they draw a rectangle or oval and then decide they don't want the figure, so they make it so tiny that it seems to disappear. Of course, the shape isn't erased; instead, a tiny rectangle or oval is created, which is visible only in Artwork mode and on final output. The Brush tool doesn't erase, nor does the Pen tool.

To erase a path as it is being drawn with the Freehand tool, press the ⌘ key (that's right, the ⌘ key again) and while still pressing the mouse button, retrace over the line of dots that you just drew. The dots that the cursor, now an eraser shape, passes over are deleted. After you release the ⌘ key (still pressing the mouse button), the dots again begin to form wherever the cursor is being dragged. While the ⌘ key is pressed, the cursor appears as an eraser — a big ugly eraser, but an eraser nonetheless. If the Caps Lock key was engaged first, the cursor appears not as an eraser but as a dotted crosshair, which I find much easier to use than the big fat eraser when I'm drawing semistraight segments.

Erasing works *only* if you haven't let go of the mouse button yet. Releasing the mouse button results in a path with points that can't be erased with the ⌘ key and the Freehand tool, you can only delete selected Anchor Points.

Jagged Paths Versus Smooth Paths

Because drawing nice-looking paths with the Freehand tool and a mouse is just a tad difficult and frustrating ("Really?" you ask sarcastically...), Illustrator provides a way to determine how rough or smooth your path will be *before* you draw it.

Normally, paths that appear from the dotted lines created with the Freehand tool are fairly similar to those dotted lines in direction and curves and such. When lines are being drawn, though, human error can cause all sorts of little bumps and "skiddles" (a *skiddle* is a little round misdrawn section resembling a small fruit-flavored candy) to appear, making the path look lumpy. In some cases, lumpy is good. More often than not, though, lumpy is an undesirable state for your illustrations.

The smoothness of the resulting paths drawn with the Freehand tool relies on the Freehand tolerance option in the General Preferences dialog box (⌘-K), which determines how jagged or smooth each section will appear from the dotted line to the path.

Freehand tolerance is a value, between 0 and 10, that determines the smoothness of the paths drawn, with 0 being rough, and 10 being really smooth. To change the Freehand tolerance, choose File⇨Preferences⇨General (⌘-K) and enter a number between 0 and 10 in the Freehand tolerance text field. Figure 3-8 shows the same clump of grass created with different freehand tolerance settings. After the number is changed, the new setting affects all paths drawn *after* the new value has been entered. Previously drawn freehand paths are not affected by a change in the Freehand tolerance setting. The default value is 2, which is a good all-around value, supplying partially smooth curves and some detail.

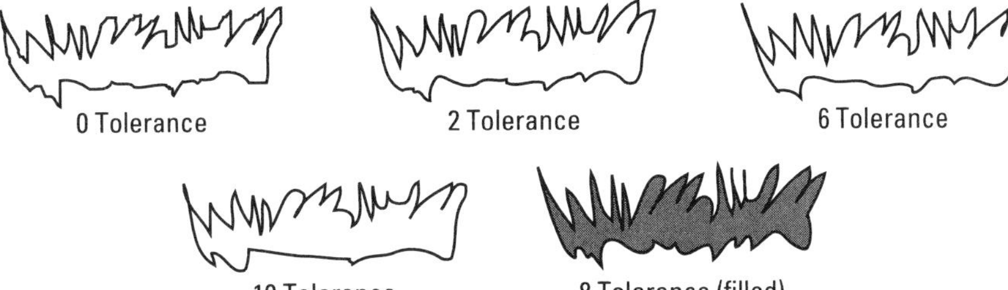

Figure 3-8: The result of different Freehand tolerance values

At a Freehand tolerance setting of 0, paths appear jagged and rough. Also, many more Anchor Points are present, although there are still no Straight Corner Points. A setting of 0 is great for creating some photo-realistic illustrations of complex, detailed objects, such as tree leaves and textures. When the setting is this low, the resulting path follows the dotted line as closely as possible.

When the Freehand tolerance option is set to 10, paths created with the Freehand tool appear extremely smooth. The smallest number of Anchor Points are used, and the curve of the line appears to be very graceful. Because so few Anchor Points are used, much detail is lost, and the path wavers from the original dotted line of the Freehand tool by a significant amount. Even though it appears that all the Anchor Points are Smooth Points, they are actually Curved Corner Points, with two independent Control Handles.

Because the Freehand tolerance setting is changed in the General Preferences dialog box, it retains its current value until it is changed, even if you quit Illustrator or restart the entire system.

Freehand tolerance affects the way the Auto Trace tool (discussed in more detail in the next chapter) works in the same way as it affects the Freehand tool (higher numbers for smooth paths with few Anchor Points and lower numbers for jagged paths with many Anchor Points).

Adding to an Existing Open Path

To continue drawing on an existing path (which could have been drawn with the Pen tool or the Freehand tool), the existing path must first be an open path with two distinct End Points. After you pass your drawing tool over one end of the path with the Freehand tool, the pencil cursor changes into a pencil with a black eraser. This action means that if you click and drag, you can now extend the path with the Freehand tool. If the Caps Lock key is engaged, the cursor looks like a crosshair with a hollow box in the center.

Although you are continuing with the same path, you may not erase that part of the path that was in place before you added to it. You may, however, press the ⌘ key and erase any part of the dotted line that appears from the new add-on segment.

So far, all the points in paths drawn with the Freehand tool have been Curved Corner Points. This changes when you add to an existing path with the Freehand tool. The point that connects the existing path to the newly drawn path is a Smooth Point. No matter which way you drag, the point always is a Smooth Point. However, you can force a Curved Corner Point in place of the Smooth Point by pressing the Option key while clicking the end of the existing path.

If you drag to the other open end of the existing path, you have the opportunity to make the path into a closed path. This point will also be a Smooth Point — unless you press the Option key, at which time it changes into a Curved Corner Point.

You can add on only to End Points on an existing path. Anchor Points that are within paths cannot be connected to new (or existing, for that matter) segments. If you attempt to draw from an Anchor Point that is not an End Point, you create an End Point for the path you are drawing that is overlapping but not connected to the Anchor Point you clicked above.

Illustrator's pencil cursor changes the eraser to black whenever the pencil tip passes over any Anchor Point, not just End Points on open paths. This change can be a little confusing at first, so try to remember that you *absolutely cannot* add a new path to an existing path on an Anchor Point that is not an End Point.

Precision Drawing with the Pen Tool

The Pen tool is the most powerful tool in Illustrator's arsenal because you are dealing more directly with Bézier curves than with any other tool. It's one thing to adjust paths, Anchor Points, and Control Handles with the Direct Selection tool, but using the Pen tool to create paths out of nothing is dumbfounding.

For the first several months of my experience using Illustrator, I avoided the Pen tool like the plague. Then I slowly worked up to where I could draw straight lines with it comfortably, and finally curved segments. Even after I had been drawing curved segments for a while, I really didn't understand how the tool worked, and I was missing out on a lot of its capabilities because of that lack of knowledge. The manuals for Illustrator really weren't very clear on how to use the Pen tool, and no one I knew could do any better. To learn how to use it, I forced myself to use the Pen tool to draw objects that I could've just traced with the Auto Trace tool.

While practicing with the Pen tool, I necessarily learned about the four types of Anchor Points — Smooth Points, Straight Corner Points, Curved Corner Points, and Combination Corner Points — because the key to using the Pen tool is understanding how Anchor Points work (see Figure 3-8).

Why Use the Pen Tool?

Vinnie: Why should I use the Pen tool instead of the other drawing tools?

Toulouse: The Pen draws paths *exactly* where you want them.

Vinnie: Yeah....that's it?

Toulouse: For instance, you can draw perfectly straight paths with the Pen tool just by clicking at the corner of each line.

Vinnie: Doesn't the Line Segment tool already do that?

Toulouse: Yes, but the Pen tool also draws curves.

Vinnie: I thought that's what the Freehand tool was for.

Toulouse: Yes, but the Pen draws *precise, perfect* curves.

Vinnie: Like the Oval tool.

Toulouse: Ah, here's a difference: the Pen draws curves one line segment at a time.

Vinnie: It sounds like a lot of work.

Toulouse: No, you just click and drag for each point. Once you get the hang of it, you'll be amazed that you ever used Illustrator without it.

The Pen tool draws points one at a time. The first click of the Pen tool produces one Anchor Point. The second click (usually in a different location) creates a second Anchor Point that is joined to the first Anchor Point by a line segment. Clicking without dragging produces a Straight Corner Point.

After you get the hang of it, the Pen tool isn't so bad. Go ahead, ask anyone who has been using Illustrator for, say, two years or longer. They like the Pen tool. I use the Pen tool more than the Brush, Auto Trace, and Freehand tools combined.

I have approached this tool delicately because, although it is a little frustrating and confusing to use well, it is the most important tool to learn, and this is the one section of this book that you should really read well. (On the enclosed CD-ROM, there are several examples that should help to clarify the Pen tool's use.)

In our sample illustration from Figure 3-2, the weeds in the upper-right corner were created with the Pen tool. The weeds are composed entirely out of straight lines and were duplicated in clumps, just as the long and short grasses were. Figure 3-9 shows the process used for creating the mass of weeds in the illustration.

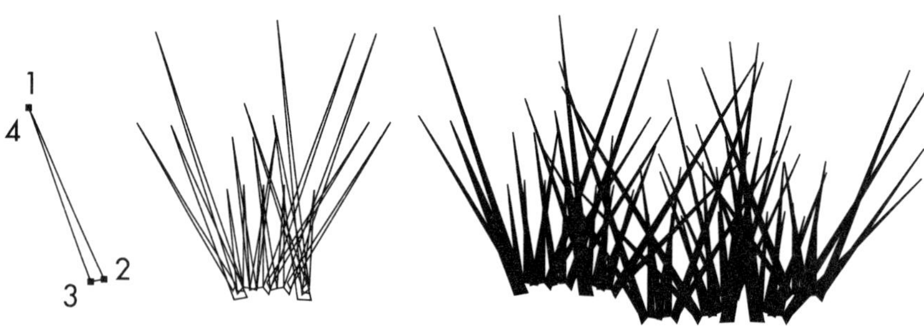

Figure 3-9: A clump of weeds as drawn with the Pen tool

STEPS: Drawing Weeds with the Pen Tool

Step 1. Change the Paint Style to a Fill of Black and a Stroke of None. Using the Pen tool, click (don't drag!) at the top of the first weed (1). Then click lower at the bottom right of the first weed (2). Click to the right (3) and click back at the start point (4) to complete the weed. When the last weed in the clump has been finished, click the first Anchor Point to close the path.

Step 2. Repeat Step 1 to create additional weeds, making clumps of them like the one in Figure 3-9.

Step 3. With the Selection tool, Option-drag the clumps a few times to create a mass of weeds.

When drawing straight lines with the Pen tool, never drag the mouse while pressing the button. Doing so results in at least one curved segment.

The Pen tool draws precise lines, both curved and straight. With a little practice and with using the tips given in these pages, you can master the tool. In the process, you will understand Illustrator much better than is possible otherwise.

It would be really simple if the Pen tool did *all* the work, but you do have to do some of the labor involved in creating curves and straight lines yourself. Actually, using the Pen tool is easier than I have been letting on. All you have to do is place Anchor Points where you want the path to go.

OK, I've oversimplified it just a bit. Drawing with the Pen tool isn't *just* placing Anchor Points. The first obstacle is to figure out where the heck those Anchor Points are going to go. Two drawings with the same number of Anchor Points can look totally different depending on where they're placed. You have to think ahead to determine what the path will look like before you draw it.

Points should always be located where there is a change in the path. That change can be a different curve or a corner. The three changes to look for are:

- A corner of any type
- The point where a curve changes from clockwise to counterclockwise or vice versa
- The point where a curve changes *intensity:* from tight to loose or loose to tight (by far, the hardest change to judge)

The second obstacle is to decide what type of Anchor Point you want to use. Remember, there are four different Anchor Points to choose from when drawing with the Pen tool:

- **Smooth Points** are Anchor Points with two connected Control Handles sticking out, resulting in a path that moves smoothly through the Anchor Point. Changing the angle of one Control Handle changes the angle of the other Control Handle. Changing the length of the Control Handle Line does not affect the other Control Handle. A Smooth Point guides the path along its journey but doesn't severely or suddenly alter that path's direction.
- **Straight Corner Points** are Anchor Points where two line segments meet in a corner. The line segments are not curved where they reach the Anchor Point, and there are no Control Handles. Straight Corner Points usually, but not always, distinctly change the direction of the path at the location where it passes through the Anchor Point.

- **Curved Corner Points** are Anchor Points where two different curved segments meet in a corner. There are two Control Handles coming out of a Curved Corner Point, but the Control Handles are independent of each other. Moving one Control Handle does not affect the other.
- **Combination Corner Points** are Anchor Points where two segments meet, one curved and one straight. There is one Control Handle on a Combination Corner Point. That Control Handle affects only the curved segment, not the straight segment.

If the path is smoothly curving, you use a Smooth Point. If there is a corner, use one of the Corner Points.

Figure 3-10 shows each of the Anchor Point types.

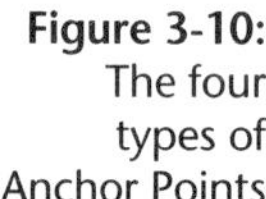
Figure 3-10: The four types of Anchor Points

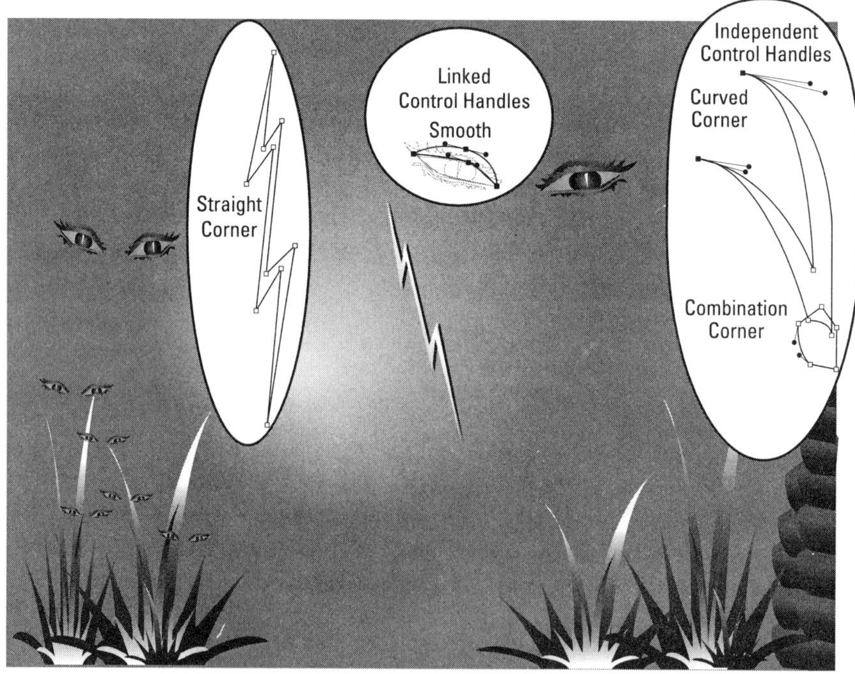

The third obstacle arises when you decide that the Anchor Point should be anything but a Straight Corner Point. All the other Anchor Points have Control Handles, you see. The obstacle is figuring out how to drag the Control Handles, how far to drag them, and which direction to drag them.

Drawing Straight Lines

The easiest way to start learning to use the Pen tool is by drawing straight lines. The lightning bolt in Figure 3-11 was created entirely with straight lines. The great thing about straight lines drawn with the Pen tool is that there are no Control Handles to worry about or fuss over.

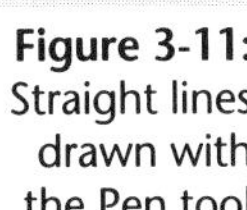

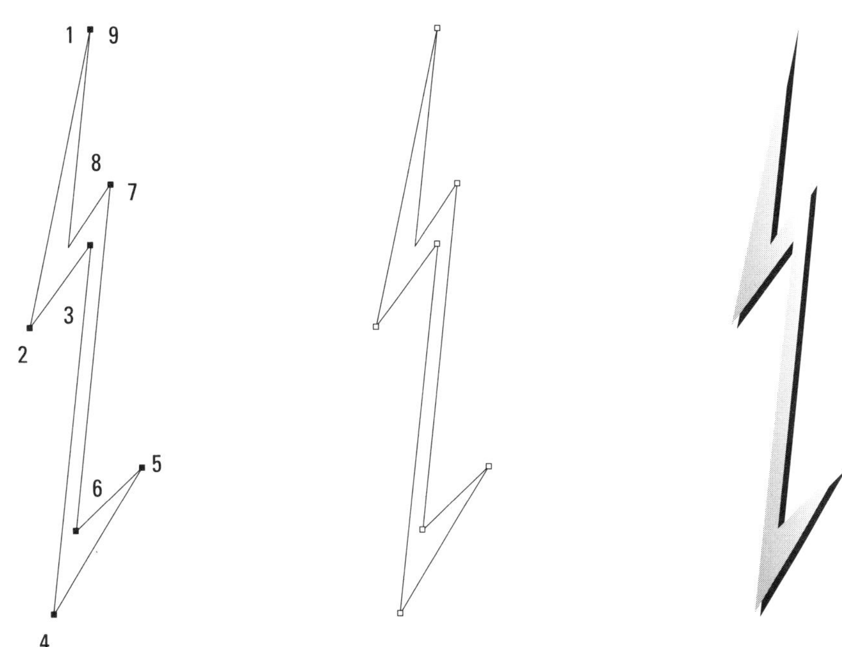

Figure 3-11: Straight lines drawn with the Pen tool

To draw the lightning bolt in Figure 3-11, click at each number with the Pen tool in order. Before you click at number 9, the Pen tool changes to a pen cursor with a little circle in the lower-right corner. This change signifies that the path is going to close when you click this point.

The simplest straight line is a line drawn with only two Anchor Points. To draw a line like this, select the Pen tool and click and release where you want the first End Point (the beginning of the line) to appear. Then click and release where you want the second End Point (the end of the line) to appear. A line appears between the two points. Too easy, isn't it?

Hold down the Shift key to keep the line straight.

To draw another separate line, first click the Pen tool in the Toolbox or hold down the ⌘ key and click. Either action tells Illustrator that you are done drawing the first line. Clicking and releasing again in one spot and then another draws a second line with two End Points. Be careful not to drag when clicking the Pen tool to form straight lines.

Paths drawn with the Pen tool, like the Freehand tool, may cross themselves. The only strange result you may see involves the Fills for objects whose paths cross. In open paths created with the Pen tool, Fills may look unusual because of the imaginary line between the two End Points and any paths that the imaginary line crosses.

To draw a straight segment that is angled at 0°, 45°, 90°, and so on, press Shift before you click. The segment drawn will be at the closest 45° angle possible.

Closing Paths

If you want to create a closed path (one with no End Points), return to the first Anchor Point in that segment and click. As the Pen tool crosses over the beginning Anchor Point, the cursor changes to a pen with a circle in the lower-right corner. After you have created a closed path, there is no need to click the Pen tool again. Instead, the next click of the Pen tool in the document automatically begins a new path.

You must have at least two Anchor Points to create a closed path with straight lines, but the irony is that a path with two Straight Corner Points is a line. You can change the identity of one of these points to a different type of Anchor Point by curving one of the segments and giving the closed path some substance.

Drawing Curves

Initially, the worst thing about drawing curves with the Pen tool is that the whole process is rather disorienting. You actually have to think differently to grasp what the Pen tool is doing. The difference that you notice right away between drawing straight lines and drawing curves is that to draw a curve, you need to drag with the Pen tool; whereas, when drawing straight lines, you click and release.

The most basic of curves is the bump (a curved segment between just two points). A bump was used to create a path to fill the horses' rears (previously shown in Figure 3-2). Use the following steps to create the bump that is illustrated in Figure 3-12.

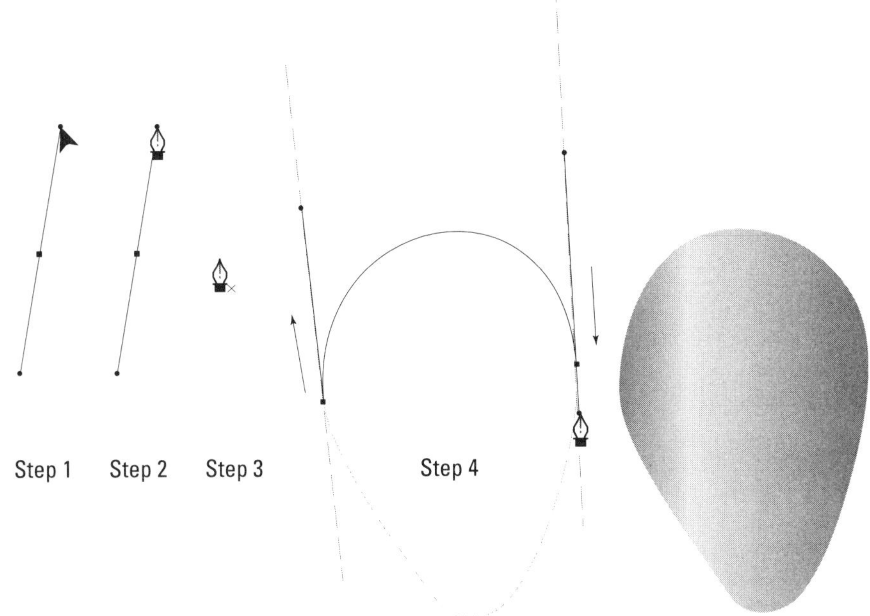

Figure 3-12: The four steps for creating a basic bump curve

STEPS:	**Creating a Basic Curve**
Step 1.	Click with the Pen tool and drag up about 1/2 inch. You'll see an Anchor Point and a line extending from it as you drag.
Step 2.	When you release the mouse button, you see the Anchor Point and a line extending to where you dragged, with a Control Handle at its end.
Step 3.	Position the cursor about 1 inch to the right of the place you first clicked.
Step 4.	Click with the mouse and drag down about 1/2 inch. As you drag, you see a curve forming that resembles a bump. When you release the mouse, the curve is filled with the current Fill color. You see the Control Handle you just dragged.

Before you try to draw another curve, remember that the Pen tool is still in a mode that continues the current path; it does not start a new one. To start a new path, click the Pen tool once or hold down ⌘ and click an empty spot. The next time you use the Pen tool, you will draw a separate path.

To create an S shape, one more step is needed. The steps for creating the S shape are illustrated in Figure 3-13.

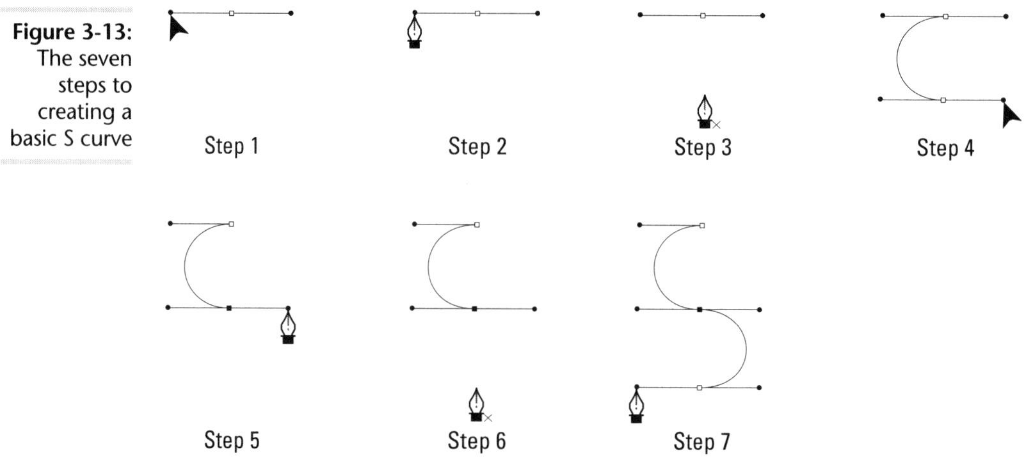

Figure 3-13: The seven steps to creating a basic S curve

STEPS: Creating a Basic S Curve

Step 1. Click and drag with the Pen tool about $^1/_2$ inch to the left.

Step 2. Release the mouse button. You should see the Anchor Point and the Control Handle that you just drew, with a Control Handle Line between them.

Step 3. Position the cursor about 1 inch below where you first clicked.

Step 4. Click and drag to the right about $^1/_2$ inch.

Step 5. Release the mouse button.

Step 6. Position the cursor about $^1/_2$ inch below the last point you clicked.

Step 7. Click and drag to the left, about $^1/_2$ inch. Now you have an S shape. To make the S look more like a real S, change the Fill to None and the Stroke to Black, 1 pt in the Paint Style palette.

All the Anchor Points we have created in these two examples are Smooth Points. The Control Handles were dragged in the direction of the next curve to be drawn, and the lengths of the Control Handle Lines on either side of the Anchor Point were the same.

The lengths of the Control Handle Lines on either side of the Smooth Point do not have to be the same. Instead, a Smooth Point may have both long and short Control Handle Lines coming out of it. The length of the Control Handle Line affects the curve, as shown on the S curve in Figure 3-14.

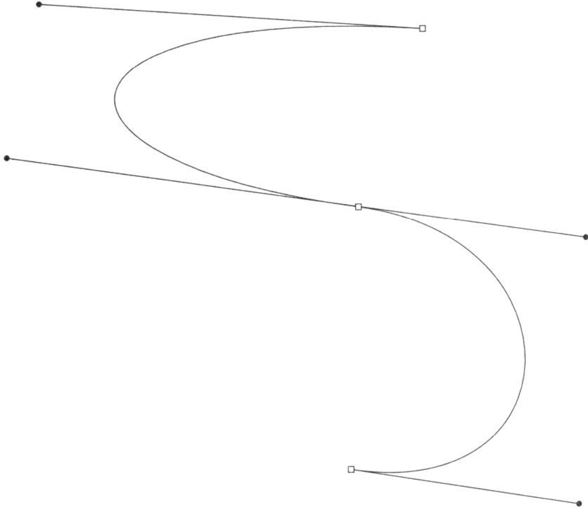

Figure 3-14: The length of the Control Handle Lines controls the shape of the curve.

To create a Smooth Point with two Control Handle Lines of different lengths, first create a Smooth Point along a path. Go back to this point after it has been created and click and drag it again. You can adjust the angle for both Control Handle Lines and the length for the new Control Handle Line that you are dragging. Note that as you are dragging out this Control Handle Line, the other Control Handle Line wobbles to the angle that you are dragging. This happens because on any Smooth Point, the Control Handle Lines *must* be at the same angle, and as you drag out the new Control Handle Line, you are changing the angle for both Control Handle Lines simultaneously.

Making Bad Waves with the Pen

Boom-Boom Washington: I'm having loads of trouble with my paths and the Pen tool.

Toulouse: What sort of trouble? Lines not connecting? Lumps everywhere? Pen running out of ink?

Boom-Boom Washington: Actually, I'm getting the "wave" thing happening ...except my waves have —

Toulouse: — Curved tips. I've been there. It isn't pretty.

Boom-Boom Washington: Wow, it's like you're in my head, looking out....

Toulouse: The wave effect you're describing usually happens when you click and drag with the Pen tool....

Boom-Boom Washington: Uh-huh....

Toulouse: And then let go, and the next click is right on top of the Control Handle you've dragged out. You drag out again, the next click is on the handle you've dragged out...and so on.

Boom-Boom Washington: So...how do I prevent it?

Toulouse: Just remember that each time you drag, you're setting the location of the Control Handle, not

(continued)

(continued)

the path itself. Don't click on the Control Handle, click far away from it.

Boom-Boom Washington: Like, if the first click is right in the middle of the page, the next click should be in, what, Jersey?

Toulouse: Not quite that far away. Now I know why you were 28 and still in 11th grade...you never did graduate, did you?

Knowing the Pen Commandments

The Pen Commandments are laws to live by — or, at least, to draw by — as shown dramatically in Figure 3-15.

The commandments are:

- **Thou shalt drag approximately one third of the length of the next curved segment.** What this means, as shown at the bottom of Figure 3-16, is that the Control Handle you drag from the Anchor Point should be about one third of the distance between this Anchor Point and the next one you click. (This technique takes some planning ahead.) In fact, you have to be aware of where the next Anchor Point is going to be located before you can determine the length of the Control Handle Line you are dragging. Dragging by one third is always an approximation — a little more or a little less doesn't hurt and, in fact, is sometimes quite necessary. You might run into trouble when the Control Handle Line is more than 1/2 or less than 1/4 of the next segment.

  If your Control Handle Line too long or too short, chances are the line will curve erratically. Remember not to drag where the next point will be placed, just one third of that distance.

- **Thou shalt remember that Control Handle Lines are always tangent to the curved segment they are guiding.** Tangent? Well, a simpler way of putting this commandment may be that Control Handle Lines go in the same direction as the curve and that they are always outside of the curve, as previously shown in Step 4 of Figure 3-13. Don't get the outside of the curve and the outside of the shape you are drawing confused — they may well be two different things. If your Control Handle lies inside the curve you are drawing, it will be too short and overpowered by the next Anchor Point. Control Handles *pull* the curve toward themselves; this

Figure 3-15: The Pen Commandments

Figure 3-16: Handles used for curving segments should be approximately 1/3 of the length of the curved segment.

makes them naturally curve out toward the Control Handle Lines. If you fight this natural pull, your illustrations can look loopy and silly.

- **Thou shalt always drag the Control Handle in the direction that you want the curve to travel at that Anchor Point.** Once again, the Control Handle pulls the curve toward itself by its very nature; doing otherwise will certainly cause some trouble. If you drag backwards toward the preceding segment, you will create a little curved spike that sticks out from the Anchor Point. This commandment applies *only* to Smooth Points, as shown in Step 4 of Figure 3-13. If the Anchor Point is to be a Curved Corner Point, then the initial drag should be in the direction the curve was traveling, and the next drag (an Option-drag) should go in the direction that the curve is going to travel. If the Anchor Point is a Combination Curve Point and the next segment is straight, then the dragging motion should be in the direction that the curve was traveling; then the Anchor Point should be clicked and released. If the Combination Curve Point's next segment is curved, the first click should be clicked and released, and the second click should be dragged in the direction of the next curve.

- **Thou shalt make segments as long as possible.** If your illustration calls for smooth, flowing curves, use very few Anchor Points. If, on the other hand, your illustration should be rough and gritty, use more Anchor Points. The fewer Anchor Points you have, the smoother the final result, as demonstrated in Figure 3-17. When there are only a few Anchor Points on a path, changing its shape is easier and faster. More Anchor Points means a bigger file and longer printing times, as well. If you're not sure if you need more Anchor Points, don't add them. You can always add them later with the Add Anchor Point tool.

Figure 3-17: The path on the left was created with 12 Anchor Points; the one on the right, with 60.

- **Thou shalt place Anchor Points at the beginning of each "different" curve.** Anchor Points should be used as *transitional* points, where the curve either changes direction or increases or decreases in size dramatically. If it looks as though the curve will change from one type of curve to another, then the location to place an Anchor Point is in the middle of that transitional section. The top drawing in Figure 3-18 shows good locations to place Anchor Points on a curved path.

- **Thou shalt not overcompensate for a previously misdrawn curve.** If you really screw up on the last Anchor Point you've drawn, don't panic and try to undo the mistake by dragging in the wrong direction or by dragging the Control Handle out to some ridiculous length. Doing either of these two things may temporarily fix the preceding curve but usually wrecks the next curve, causing you to have to overcompensate yet again. The results of just minor overcompensation are shown in the bottom drawing in Figure 3-18.

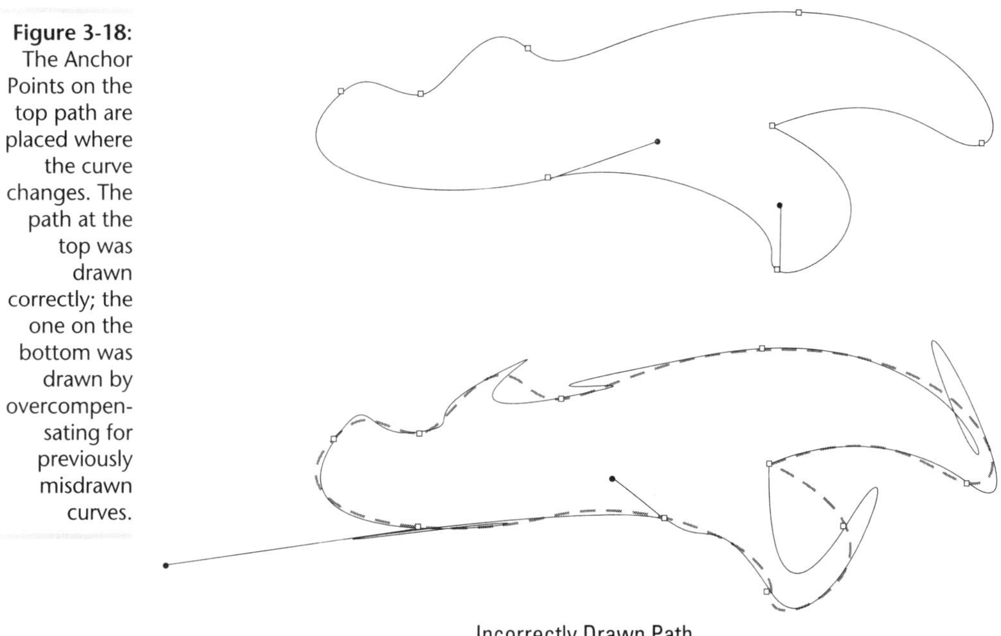

Figure 3-18: The Anchor Points on the top path are placed where the curve changes. The path at the top was drawn correctly; the one on the bottom was drawn by overcompensating for previously misdrawn curves.

Closing Curved Paths with the Pen Tool

The majority of the paths you draw with the Pen tool will be closed paths, not the open ones we've drawn so far. Like open curved paths, any closed curved path must have at least two Anchor Points, just as paths with Straight Corner Points need three distinct points to create a closed path.

When the Pen tool is placed over the starting point of the path while you draw, a little circle appears to the right of the pen shape. This is an indicator that the path will become a closed path if you click this Anchor Point.

Points on a Path to Make a Figure 8

How few points does it take to create a basic curved shape? This is a good test of your capabilities. The following infinity shape was drawn with the least amount of Anchor Points possible.

The number of points used to draw this shape was a number something less than infinity.

After you've tried to do this a few times, look at the next page see at some of the different ways it can be done.

Of course, to ensure that the initial Anchor Point remains a Smooth Point, you need to click and drag on the initial Anchor Point. Simply clicking produces a Combination Corner Point, which only has one Control Handle associated with it.

Curved Corner Points

Curved Corner Points are points where two different, usually distinct, curved segments meet at an Anchor Point. Because the two curves meet this way, a Smooth Point does not provide the means for their joining correctly. Instead, a Smooth Point would make the two different curves blend into each other smoothly.

The main difference between a Curved Corner Point and a Smooth Point is that a Smooth Point has two linked Control Handle Lines with Control Handles on their ends; a Curved Corner Point has two *independent* Control Handles. Like the word indicates, the Control Handles and their associated Control Handle Lines move independently of each other, enabling two different, distinct types of curves to come from the same Anchor Point.

To create a Curved Corner Point, create a Smooth Point in a path and then Option-drag on that same Anchor Point. As you Option-drag from the Anchor Point, you are creating a new, independent Control Handles. The next segment will curve as controlled by this Control Handle, not by the original one.

Option-dragging on a Control Handle attached to a Curved Corner Point changes the Anchor Point back to a Smooth Point, where the Control Handle Lines and Control Handles are linked once again.

The clumps of grass from Figure 3-2 were created by using Curved Corner Points. The process is explained in the following steps.

STEPS: Creating Paths with Curved Corner Points

Step 1. As shown in Figure 3-19, click the first point (1) and drag up and to the left. Try to duplicate the locations of all the points for the best results.

Step 2. Click at (2) and drag left and down just a little bit, which creates the curved segment between (1) and (2). You won't see the Control Handle you are dragging on the figure on the right because Step 3 replaces it.

Step 3. To create the first Curved Corner Point, Option-click on (2) and drag up and to the right.

Step 4. Click at (3) and drag to the lower right.

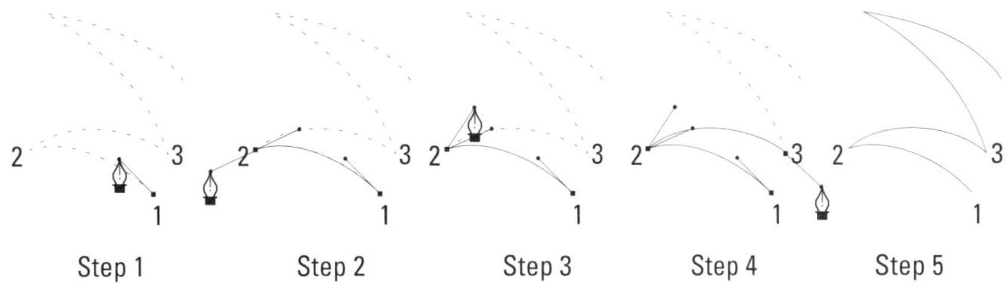

Figure 3-19: How to create paths with Curved Corner Points

Step 5. Continue to Option-click when starting to draw a new segment, effectively creating independent Control Handles until you have created a clump of grass.

Step 6. Option-copy and transform the clumps to create several clumps of grass.

When creating Curved Corner Points, you can press the Option key (to create independent points) all the time, not just when starting a new segment.

Points on a Path to Make a Figure 8: The Answers

There are several ways to make a figure 8, as shown by the following figures.

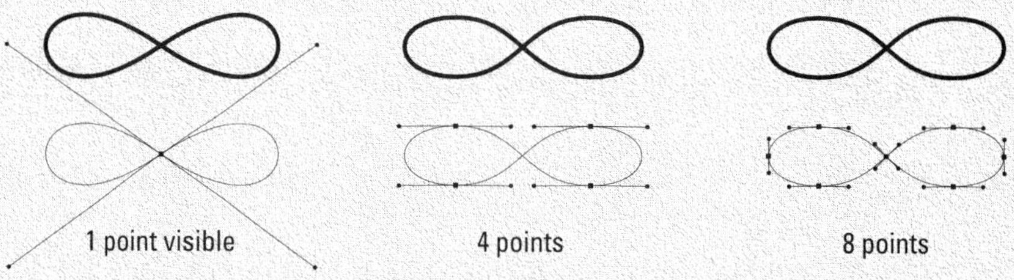

1 point visible

4 points

8 points

Compare these figures to the one you've drawn.

Your score is as follows:

1 visible point (really 2 overlapping): PenMaster

2 points, both visible: Lots of Pentential

3-4 points: ApPentice

6 or more points: The sword is still mightier

Combination Corner Points

A Combination Corner Point is a point where a curved segment and a straight segment meet each other. At this corner point, there is one Control Handle coming from the Anchor Point from the side where the curved segment is located and, on the other side, there is no Control Handle, indicating a straight segment.

To create a Combination Corner Point with the Pen tool, draw a few curved segments and then go back to the last Anchor Point. There should be two linked Control Handles displayed at this point. Simply click once on the Anchor Point, and one of the two Control Handles will disappear. The next segment then starts out straight.

You can change existing Smooth and Curved Corner Points into Combination Corner Points simply by dragging one of the Control Handles into the Anchor Points.

Using the Pen Tool

In the sample illustration previously shown in Figure 3-2, the Pen tool was used not only to draw the spiky weeds, but also to draw the horses on the hill and the Fill shapes for the hill. The horse outlines and the blade outlines were created with the Brush tool.

To Fill the hillside, click where the left edge of the hill should begin and drag down and to the right about 1/2 inch. Next, click at the top of the hill and drag just a tiny bit (less than 1/4 inch) to the right. Click again at about halfway down the hill and drag at about the same angle as the hill. Click again at the base of the hill and drag to the right 1 inch. Click without dragging on the far side of the illustration. To finish off the hillside Fill, click the lower-right and lower-left corners and then click the starting point. Fill the path with a gradient that complements a hillside and change the Stroke to None.

To create the horse Fill shape, create a path with the Pen tool by using mostly Smooth Points that go right through the center of the horse outlines. Make separate shapes for the head area, manes, body area, and the tails. Fill the paths with gradients or solid colors and choose a Stroke of None.

To create the long grass blade Fills, use the Pen tool to draw paths that go right through the center of the blades of grass. Create separate paths for each blade, and Fill the blades with a green linear gradient.

Selection Tools

If there is one group of tools in Illustrator you absolutely *must* have, it is the set of three selection tools. As in most Macintosh applications, to change or alter something (move, transform, and so on), you must first select it. When you draw a new path or when you paste in Illustrator, the program automatically selects the object you're working on; however, as soon as you draw another path, the preceding object is deselected and Illustrator automatically selects the object with the new path. The selection tools allow you to select paths and perform additional manipulations on them. Illustrator has three selection tools: the Selection tool, the Direct Selection tool, and the Group Selection tool, as shown in Figure 3-20.

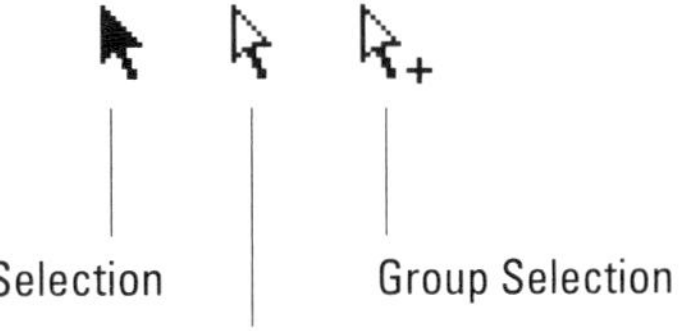

Figure 3-20: The Selection tools. The Group Selection tool is accessed by clicking and holding on the Direct Selection tool slot in the Toolbox.

There are several different ways to select a path in Illustrator, depending on what you wish to change:

- **InterPath selecting:** *InterPath selecting* means at least one point or segment within a path is selected, usually with the Direct Selection tool. InterPath selecting is used to adjust individual points, segments, and series of points.

  Even though just a portion of the path is selected, many changes will affect the entire path — not just the selected points. For example, most of the attributes available in the Object menu (including Paint Style, Masking, and Compound Paths) will affect the entire path even when only a point or segment is selected.

  InterPath selecting also allows you to use most of the functions in the Arrange menu, such as hiding, locking, or grouping. But these options lock, hide, or group the entire path.

  Selected Anchor Points on InterPath selected paths are solid squares; unselected points are hollow squares. Selected segments are indicated by visible Control Handles and Control Handle Lines on either side of the segment if the selected segment is curved. If the selected segment is not curved, no indication that the segment is selected appears on-screen. If you delete a segment or point, the entire remaining path becomes selected at the second level.

  Figure 3-21 shows InterPath selection.

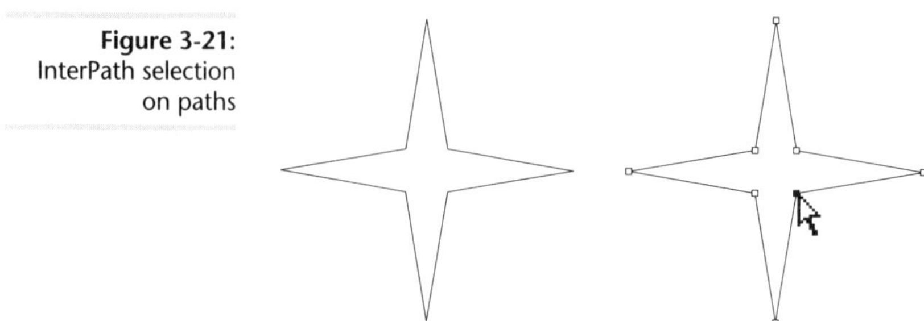

Figure 3-21: InterPath selection on paths

- **Path selecting:** *Path selecting* means that all points and segments on a path are selected. When a path is clicked by using the Group Selection tool or the Selection tool, the entire path will automatically be selected. (Drawing a marquee entirely around a path with the Direct Selection tool will also select the entire path.)

  All the capabilities from InterPath selecting are available, such as the entire Object menu and the Arrange menu and most of the functions in the Filter menu.

  After you select a path on the second level, the entire path is affected by moving, transforming, cutting, copying and pasting, and deleting. An example of Path selecting is shown in Figure 3-22.

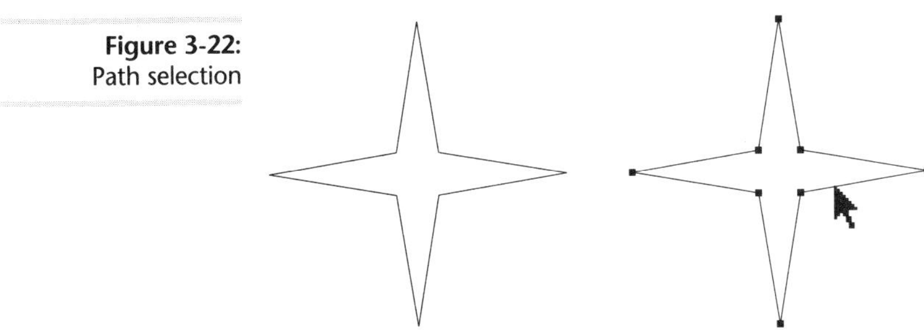

Figure 3-22: Path selection

- **Group selecting:** You can select and affect any series of grouped paths as one path using *Group selecting*. All paths in the group are affected in the same way as paths that you select with path selection. The Selection tool will select entire grouped paths at once. If you use the Group Selection tool instead, you will need a series of clicks to select a group of paths. Refer to Figure 3-23 to see what you can accomplish with Group selecting.

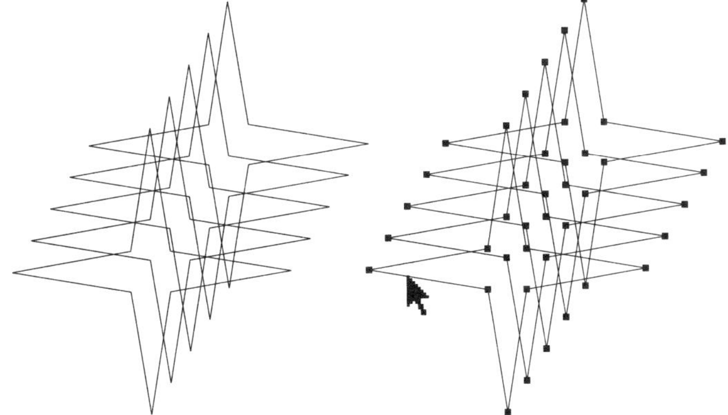

Figure 3-23: Group selection

- **InterGroup selecting:** You can select and affect groups of paths within other groups by using *InterGroup selecting*. All paths in the group are affected in the same way as paths that you select with path selection. Use the Group Selection tool to select a group of paths at once. Each successive click on the same path will select another "set" of grouped paths that the initial path is within. InterGroup selecting is demonstrated in Figure 3-24.

To select everything in your document that hasn't been hidden or locked, choose Edit⇨Select All (⌘-A), which selects all the points and segments on every path in the document. You can also select everything in the document by drawing a marquee around all the paths with any selection tool.

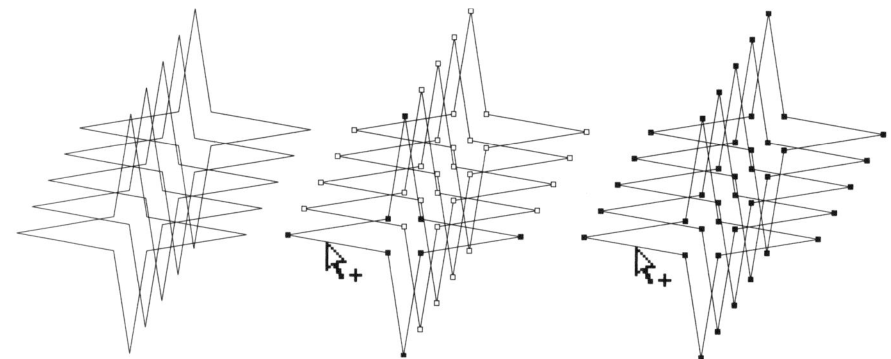

Figure 3-24: InterGroup selection

Normally, after you select something new, everything that you have previously selected becomes *deselected.* To continue to select additional points, paths, or segments, you must hold down the Shift key while clicking and dragging.

The Shift key normally works as a toggle when used with a selection tool, selecting anything that is not selected and deselecting anything that is currently selected. Each selection tool works with the Shift key a little differently, as described in the following sections.

To deselect everything that is selected, click a part of the document that is empty (where you can see the Pasteboard or Artboard) without using the Shift key. You also can deselect everything by choosing Edit⇨Deselect All (⌘-Shift-A).

You can use the selection tools for manually moving selected points, segments, and paths. Personally, the thought of manual labor terrifies me, but when I do something *manually* in Illustrator, I am usually referring to the process of dragging or clicking with the mouse. You use *automatic* or *computer-assisted manipulations* when you type in specific values in the Move dialog box (Arrange⇨Move or ⌘-Shift-M), for example. The Move Dialog box can also be accessed by Option-clicking the Selection tool. The next few sections cover the selection tools and their functions.

Using the Selection Tool

The Selection tool selects entire paths or complete groups at one time. You can't select just one point or a few points on a path with the Selection tool. Instead, the entire path on which that point lies is selected (all the Anchor Points turn black). Drawing a marquee (clicking and dragging as a box forms behind the cursor) around parts of paths or entire paths also selects those entire paths.

If you press the Shift key, the Selection tool works as a toggle between selecting and deselecting paths. While you hold down the Shift key and click on paths that are not selected, they become selected. When paths that are selected are Shift-clicked, they become deselected. The Shift key can be used in this way to add to or subtract from a series of selected paths.

Using the Direct Selection Tool

To select individual points, line segments, or a series of specific points within a path, you need to use the Direct Selection tool. It is the *only* tool that allows you to select something less than an entire path. You can also draw a marquee over a portion of a path to select only those points and segments within the area of the marquee. If the marquee surrounds an entire path, the entire path is selected. Individual points or a series of points on different paths can also be selected by drawing a marquee around just those points.

The Shift key is used with the Direct Selection tool to select additional points or segments or to deselect previously selected points. If only one segment or point on a path is selected and you Shift-click on that segment or point with the Direct Selection tool, the entire path is deselected.

Selecting items with the Direct Selection tool can be a little intimidating because Anchor Points show up as *solid* when selected and *hollow* when deselected. Furthermore, a selected segment does not have any Anchor Points selected; instead, any Control Handles and Control Handle Lines associated with that segment become selected. If there are no Control Handles associated with a segment, such as a segment that is in between two Straight Corner Points, then it is difficult to tell which segment is selected.

Too Many Selection Tools?

Marcia: I'm getting mouse wrist because of all these different selection tools.

Toulouse: How so?

Marcia: It's such a pain to keep going up to the Toolbox to select different selection tools. And then there are the other tools as well....

Toulouse: You use the Toolbox to access the selection tools?

Marcia: No, I have them flown in from Hackensack when I wanna use them. Of *course* I use the toolbox.

Toulouse: Actually, you can use the keyboard to jump around each of the selection tools.

Marcia: I have a keyboard. Tell me more.

Toulouse: No matter what tool is selected in the Toolbox, pressing Command will select the Selection tool.

Marcia: Wow! This is great!

Toulouse: You can toggle between the regular Selection tool and the Direct Selection tool by pressing Command-Tab.

Marcia: No kidding.

Toulouse: When you have the Direct Selection tool, press Option, and you'll access the Group Selection tool!

Marcia: You should really write a book on this stuff....

After you select a point or series of points, those selected points can be manipulated in a number of ways, including being moved and transformed (via the transformation tools) and having certain filters applied to them. Individual segments and series of segments can be selected and modified in the same way points are transformed.

The Group Selection Tool

The Group Selection tool is driven by a very cool concept: it first selects a path, then the group that the path is in, then the group that the other group with the path is in, and so on.

For the Group Selection tool to work properly, the first path or paths can be chosen by either clicking them or drawing a marquee around them. To select the group that a particular path is in, however, requires you to click one of the initially selected paths. To select the next group also requires a click; if you drag at any point, only the paths you drag over are selected.

This process may seem a little fuzzy at first, but it will get easier the more you use the Group Selection tool. Remember, the first time you select something with the Group Selection tool, you select only the paths you click or drag over. The next time you click an already selected path, all the paths in its group will be selected.

Still confused about how the Shift key selects and deselects paths? I can make it worse. The Shift key is an odd duck when used with the Group Selection tool. What happens when you click an unselected path with this tool while holding down the Shift key? The path is selected. But what happens when you click a selected path? The process deselects *just one path*. What makes more sense to me is if you would click again with the Shift key, and it then would deselect the entire group. Nope. Ain't gonna happen. The Shift key works as a toggle between the one path you are clicking on: selecting it, deselecting it, and so on.

Dragging a marquee around paths with the Group Selection tool works only for the first series of clicks; dragging another marquee, even over the already selected paths, just reselects those paths.

If you have selected several paths at once, clicking a selected path will select only the group that the selected path is in. If other selected paths are in different groups, those groups will not be selected until you click those paths with the Group Selection tool. However, clicking multiple times on any of the paths in the selected group continues to select "up" in the group that the selected path is part of.

The Group Selection tool is the most useful when dealing with graphs and blends, but it can be used in a number of other situations to greatly enhance your control of what is and is not selected. People who are always ungrouping and regrouping paths (groupies) can greatly benefit from using the Group Selection tool. In fact, proper use of this tool prevents you from ever having to ungroup and regroup objects for cosmetic (that is, paint style) reasons.

You can access the Group Selection tool when the Direct Selection tool is selected by holding down the Option key. If the Direct Selection tool is not chosen, then select it by holding down the ⌘ key (you may have to press ⌘-Tab to toggle from the Selection tool to the Direct Selection tool) and pressing the Option key at the same time.

Selecting, Moving, and Deleting Entire Paths

Usually, the best way to select a path that is not currently selected is by clicking it with the regular Selection tool, which highlights all the points on the path and allows you to move, transform, or delete that entire path.

To select more than one path, you can use a number of different methods. The most basic method is to hold down the Shift key and click the successive paths with the Selection tool, selecting one more path with each Shift-click. Shift-clicking a selected path with the Selection tool deselects that particular path. Drawing a marquee around paths with the Selection tool selects all paths that at least partially fall into the area drawn by the marquee. When drawing a marquee, be sure to place the cursor in an area where there is nothing. Finding an empty spot may be difficult to do in Preview mode because Fills from various paths may cover any white space available. Drawing a marquee with the Selection tool when the Shift key is depressed selects nonselected paths and deselects currently selected paths.

If paths are part of either a compound path or a group, all other paths in that compound path or group are also selected.

To move a path, click the path and drag (in one motion) with the Selection tool. To move several paths, select the paths and then click a selected path with the regular Selection tool or the Direct Selection tool and drag.

If you have been selecting multiple paths by using the Shift key, be sure to release it before clicking and dragging on the selected paths. If the Shift key is still pressed, the clicked path becomes deselected, and no paths move. If this does happen, just Shift-click the paths that were deselected and drag.

To delete an entire path, select it with the Selection tool and press the Delete key. To delete multiple paths, select them and press the Delete key.

In my sample illustrations, many of the objects needed to be moved and duplicated. To duplicate paths when moving them, press the Option key while the mouse button is released.

Duplicate the spiky weeds by clicking them and dragging to the left or right. When the weeds are at a visually good distance, press Option and release the mouse button. Choose Arrange➪Repeat Transform to create another set of weeds at the same distance, if necessary.

The short grass, long grass, and silhouetted horses can be duplicated the same way, by choosing one and dragging it to the left or right and pressing Option while the mouse button is released.

Choosing Select All (⌘-A or ⌘-period when the screen is not redrawing) from the Edit menu selects all paths in the active document. If a type tool is selected and there is an insertion point in the text, all the type in that story will be selected.

Choosing Select None (⌘-Shift-A) from the Edit menu deselects all selected objects. Select None does *not* work with type selected with a type tool.

Selecting, Moving and Deleting Portions of Paths

To select just a portion of a path, you *must* use the Direct Selection tool. To select an Anchor Point or a line segment, simply click it. To select several individual points or paths, click the points or paths to be selected while holding down the Shift key. Series of points and paths can be selected by dragging a marquee across the paths that are to be selected.

Individual points that are selected become solid squares. If these points are Smooth, Curved Corner, or Combination Corner Points, Control Handles appear from the selected Anchor Point.

Line segments that have at least one Anchor Point that is either a Smooth, Curved Corner, or Combination Corner Point may display a Control Handle Line and Control Handle coming out from that Anchor Point. Samples of each of these selected types of Anchor Points are shown in Figure 3-25.

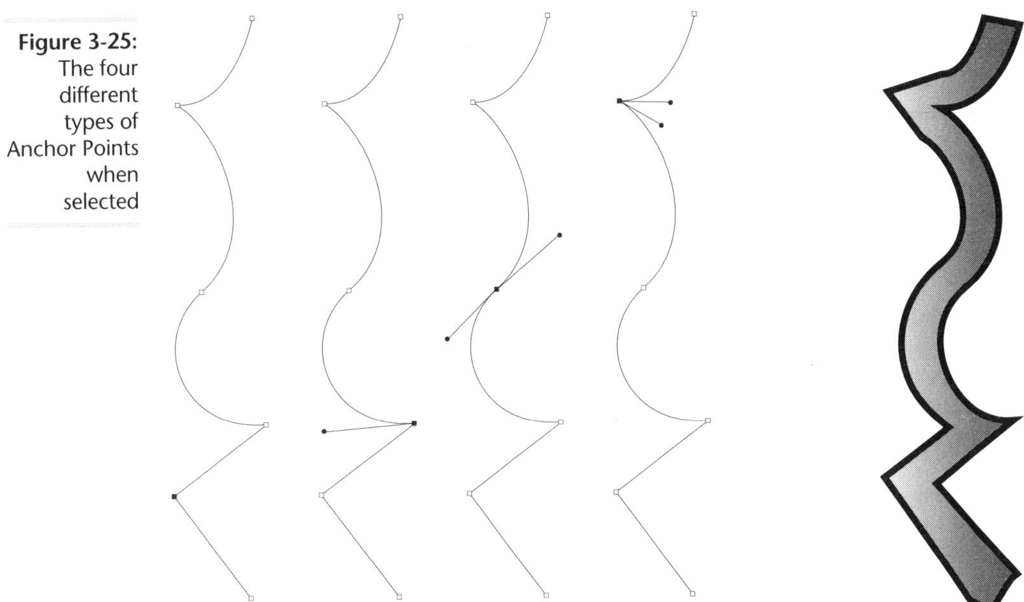

Figure 3-25: The four different types of Anchor Points when selected

To move these selected points or paths, release the Shift key and click a selected path or point and drag.

Illustrator doesn't tell you when a straight line segment is selected or which one is selected. The first time you click a straight line segment, all the Anchor Points on the path appear as hollow squares, which is just telling you that something on that path is selected. Selected points turn black, and curved line segments have one or more Control Handles and Control Handle Lines sticking out from the ending Anchor Points, but straight line segments don't do anything when selected. The inventive side of you may think that you can get around this problem by dragging the selected segments to a new location or by copying and pasting them and then undoing — but this solution doesn't work because of Illustrator's habit of selecting all points on paths when undoing operations on those paths.

When you run into this problem of not knowing if a straight segment is selected, do the following: Instead of moving, copying, or pasting, simply whack the good ol' Delete key, and whatever disappears is what you had selected. Now when you undo, just the segments that were selected before the deletion are still selected, not the entire path.

To delete points and segments, select them as described previously and then press Delete. Remember that line segments exist only when there is one point on either side of the segment. Even if the line segment is not selected, if one of its Anchor Points is deleted, the line segment is deleted, as well. A path is made up of points, and those points are connected via segments. If the points are gone, the paths disappear along with them. But if you delete all the segments, all the points remain.

Portions of paths can be duplicated when pressing the Option key while the mouse button is being released. Duplicating segments also duplicates the Anchor Points on either side of that segment.

Locking and Hiding Objects

All objects in Illustrator (except PICT templates, which always seem to be locked) can be locked or hidden — including guides. Locking and hiding work about the same, and the results are only marginally different, but you can move objects in Illustrator in several ways.

Locking

To lock an object, select it and choose Arrange⇨Lock (⌘-1). The selected object is not only locked but also deselected. In fact, an object is unselectable when locked. Locked objects cannot be moved or changed, but they are always visible and will always print (locked objects cannot be hidden). Because a locked object can't be selected, it can't be changed, and in Illustrator, as in most Macintosh applications, objects can be modified only when selected.

A locked object remains locked when the document is saved and closed. As a result, locked objects are still locked the next time the document is opened. Locked objects print with no indication whether they are locked or not.

Holding down Option and choosing Arrange⇨Lock or typing ⌘-Option-1 will lock all the objects that are not selected.

To change a locked object, choose Arrange⇨Unlock (⌘-2), unlocking (and selecting) all objects. There is no way to unlock just a few objects locked with the Lock command.

A tricky way to invisibly "copyright" your illustration is to create a small text box in a far corner of the pasteboard with your copyright information in it, color the text white, and lock the text box. No one will know it is there, and it can't be easily selected. In fact, it'll even print if it is placed on top of a background in another program.

I like to lock objects under the following circumstances:

- When the document is full of complex artwork, so I can do a Select All and not have to wait forever for the selection to finish
- When I don't want to accidentally move or change certain artwork
- When I can't easily select paths that are under other paths (in which case, I lock the ones on top)
- When I have to fit an illustration into a certain area (in which case, I'll create a box that size and lock it so I have an instant boundary to work with)

Hiding

Sometimes, you don't want to see certain objects on your document page — perhaps because they obstruct your view of other objects or they take a long time to redraw. In these cases, it's a good idea to hide the objects in question. To do so, select them and then choose Arrange⇨Hide (⌘-3).

Hidden objects are invisible and unselectable; they still exist in the document, but they do not print. When a document is reopened, hidden objects reappear.

Holding down Option and choosing Arrange⇨Hide or typing ⌘-Option-3 will hide all the objects that are *not* selected.

To show (and select) all hidden objects, choose Arrange⇨Show All (⌘-4). Think of it as "unhide." There is no way to show just a few of the hidden objects when using the Show All command.

Object Information

Choosing Object⇨Attributes (Ctrl-A) brings up the Attributes dialog box. In this box, notes can be added to any selected object, the path direction can be reversed (if the object is part of a compound path), the center point of the object can be made to display or hide, and the flatness characteristics (output dpi) can be changed. At least one object must be selected in order to choose Attributes.

Another useful way to "copyprotect" your artwork is to select all the objects, go to the Attributes dialog box and enter your copyright information within the dialog box.

Stacking Order

One of the crucial concepts that you'll need to understand in the world of Adobe Illustrator is that of stacking order. This concept is not the same as the layer concept that is discussed in Chapter 7, but it is rather the forward/backward relationship between objects within each layer.

After you create the first object in Illustrator, the next object is created *above* the first object, or on top of it. The third object is created above both the first and second objects. This cycle continues indefinitely, with objects being stacked on top of one another.

A great deal of planning goes into creating an illustration so that the object you draw first is on the bottom of the pile, and the last thing you draw ends up on the top. To make your life much more pleasant, Illustrator has the capability to move objects up and down (forward or backward) through the stack of objects. In fact, Illustrator's method of moving objects up and down is so simplistic and basic that it is also quite limiting.

You can change the stacking order of objects in Illustrator relative to foreground and background either all the way to the bottom or all the way to the top. You may not move an object up a bit or down just a little; you can move the objects only to the extremes. Figure 3-26 shows the same illustration after various objects were moved in the stacking order.

To move an object to the front, choose Arrange⇨Bring to Front (⌘-=). The selected object is brought forward so that it is in front of every other object (but only in that layer — Chapter 7 explains how layers work). If more than one object is selected, the topmost object of the selected group will be at the very top and the bottommost object of the selected group will be beneath all the other selected objects — but all the selected objects will be on top of all the nonselected objects. Bring To Front is not available when no objects are selected. Multiple-selected paths and grouped paths still retain their front/back position relative to each other.

To move an object to the back, choose Arrange⇨Send to Back (⌘--). The selected object is sent backwards so that it is behind every other object. Send To Back is not available when there are no objects selected. Multiple selected paths and grouped paths still retain their front/back position relative to each other.

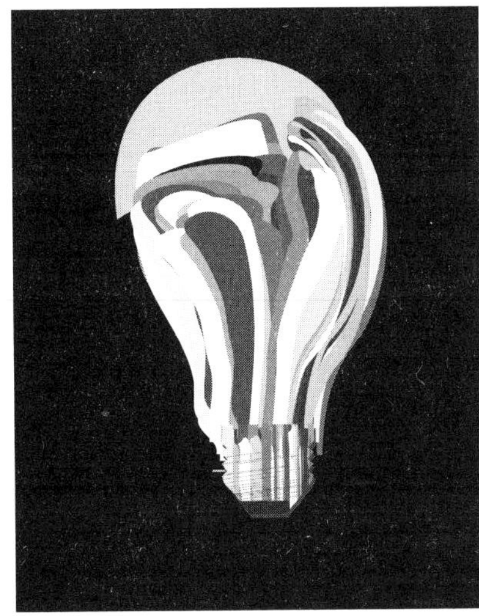

Figure 3-26: The original art (left) and after the stacking order of various pieces has changed (right)

Individual characters in a string of text work in a similar manner to their object cousins when it comes to front/back placement. The first character typed is placed at the bottom of the text block, and the last character typed is placed at the top, as shown in Figure 3-27. To move individual characters forward or backward, you must first choose Type⇨Create Outline and select the outline of the character you wish to arrange.

Figure 3-27: Text characters that overlap each other

Try as you might, you cannot change the forward/backward relationship of Strokes and Fills. Strokes are always in front of Fills for the same path. To get the Fill to cover or overlap the Stroke, you must copy the path, use the Paste In Front command (choose Edit⇨Paste In Front or press ⌘-F), and then remove the stroke from the path you just pasted.

Pasting Objects In Front of and Behind Selected Objects

Choosing Paste In Front (⌘-F) from the Edit menu pastes any objects on the Clipboard on top of any selected objects, or on the top of the current layer if no objects are selected.

Choosing Paste In Back (⌘-B) from the Edit menu pastes any objects on the Clipboard behind any selected objects, or on the bottom of the current layer if no objects are selected.

In addition, both Paste In Front and Paste In Back paste objects *in the same* location as the copied object, even from document to document. If the documents are different sizes, Illustrator pastes them in the same location relative to the center of each document. If the Clipboard is empty, or if type selected with a type tool is on the Clipboard, these options are not available.

Grouping and Ungrouping

Grouping is the process of putting together a series of objects that need to remain spatially constant in relationship to each other. Groups can be made up of as little as one path, and they may contain an unlimited number of objects.

To group objects together, they should first be selected with any of the selection tools. After you select the objects, choose Arrange⇨Group (⌘-G) to make the separate objects stay together when selected.

Selecting any object in a group with the regular Selection tool selects all the objects in that group and makes all the points in a path solid (selected). To see how the Group Selection tool works with selecting groups, see "Using the Group Selection Tool," at the end of this chapter.

Not only can several objects be grouped together, but groups can be grouped together to form a "group of groups," in which there is a hierarchical series of grouped groups. In addition, groups can be grouped to individual objects or to several other objects.

After a set of objects or groups is grouped together, grouping it again produces no effect. The computer does not beep at you, display a dialog box, or otherwise indicate that the objects or groups you are attempting to group together are already grouped. Of

course, it never or hurts to choose Arrange⇨Group (⌘-G) again if you are not sure if they are grouped. If they weren't grouped before, they now are, and if they were grouped before, nothing unusual or unexpected happens. If you choose Group again after the selected objects have already been grouped, nothing will happen.

In our example illustration shown in Figure 3-2, the objects will be much easier to manipulate if they are grouped. Group the short grass together as one group, the long grass as one group, the horse outlines and Fills as one group, and the hillside outline and Fills as one group. The tree outline and bark detail should be one group as well.

If you are having trouble selecting all the objects for each type in a group, choose Filter⇨Select⇨Same Paint Style after one object is selected. This process usually (but not always) selects all the objects of one type.

Grouping similar areas is helpful for moving entire areas forward or backward as well as doing any type of horizontal or vertical movement or transformation upon a set of objects.

Grouping is also helpful for controlling blends.

Ungrouping

To ungroup groups (separate them into standalone paths and objects), choose Arrange⇨Ungroup (⌘-U), and any selected groups become ungrouped. Ungrouping, like grouping, works on one set of groups at a time. For example, if you have two groups that are grouped together, ungrouping that group results in the two original groups. (Don't worry, I'm just as confused as you are in this area. It makes my head do the "Linda Blair.") If Ungroup is chosen again, those two groups will also become ungrouped.

Moving Objects Through the Stacking Order

Epstein: I really hate having to Send to Back and Bring to Front several times to position artwork the way I want it. For example, If I have 600 objects, and I want to place one of them right in the middle, I have to send it to the back, then select and send the 300 bottommost objects to the back. What a pain.

Toulouse: There's an easier way.

Epstein: Trade you my pick if you show me how to do it.

Toulouse: Deal. Select the object you want stuck in the middle.

Epstein: Done. Nothing happened.

Toulouse: Just wait. Then choose Cut, or press Command-X.

Epstein: It's GONE! Hey!

Toulouse: Calm down. Select the object in the middle of all those objects that you want the original object in front of. Then choose Paste in Front.

Epstein: It's in the middle! That's great.

Toulouse: Thanks. Your pick, please?

When you absolutely do not want anything in a group grouped with anything else — and you suspect that there may be several minigroups within the group you have selected — simply press ⌘-U several times. You do not need to select the subgroups individually to ungroup them. To get rid of all the groups in your illustration, choose Edit⇨Select All (⌘-A) and then proceed to ungroup (⌘-U) several times. To remove certain objects from a group or compound path, select just these objects, cut and Paste in Front (or in Back).

When you're ungrouping, groups must be selected with either the Group Selection tool or the regular Selection tool.

Using the Group Selection Tool

The Group Selection tool is used primarily to select groups within other groups or individual paths within groups. To access the Group Selection tool, click the Direct Selection tool in the Toolbox and drag to the right to the Group Selection tool. Clicking once with the Group Selection tool on any path selects that particular path. Clicking again with the Group Selection tool on the same path selects the group that path is in. Clicking yet again selects the group that the previously selected group is in.

To move a path that is part of a group, do not ungroup the path; instead, select the path with the Group Selection tool and move it.

If you select a path in a group with the Group Selection tool and then click the same path again to move it, the group that path is in will be selected instead. To avoid this problem, either select and move at one time or use the Direct Selection tool for moving.

If several different paths are selected with the Group Selection tool either by dragging a marquee or Shift-clicking, clicking again on a selected path or object selects the group that object is in. If that object's group is already selected, then the group that the selected group is in will be selected.

The Group Selection tool also selects compound paths. One click selects an individual path within the compound path, and the second click selects the entire compound path.

Using the Shift key with the Group Selection tool on selected paths or objects deselects just one path at a time. Shift-clicking a path that has just been deselected reselects that path, it does not deselect the group that path is in.

For quick access to the Group Selection tool, press the Option key when the Direct Selection Tool is the active tool. But release the Option key before the mouse button is released, or you'll have a duplicated path or object. The Direct Selection tool can be selected by pressing the ⌘ key (⌘-Tab toggles between the Direct Selection and regular Selection tools). Pressing the ⌘ and Option keys together can be used to access the Group Selection tool, no matter which tool is selected in the Toolbox!

Summary

- Use a pressure-sensitive tablet with the Brush tool for the best results.
- The Brush tool creates closed paths.
- To get rid of overlapping inside corners within brush strokes, apply the Unite filter to the brush strokes.
- The Freehand tool creates single paths, open or closed, and is not related at all to that *other* drawing program.
- Erase Freehand tool paths while you're drawing them by pressing ⌘ and retracing your path.
- Control the roughness of Freehand-tool-generated paths by setting the Freehand tolerance *before* you draw with the Freehand tool.
- The Pen tool is the most powerful tool in Illustrator, allowing you to create perfectly formed curves and straight paths.
- Clicking with the Pen tool creates straight line segments; dragging with the Pen tool creates curved segments.
- Keep the distance of Control Handle Lines to about $^1/_3$ of the length of the affected curved line segment for the best results.
- The Selection tool selects entire paths or groups with one click.
- The Direct Selection tool will select individual points, segments, or portions of paths that are surrounded with a drag marquee.
- Quickly duplicate objects in Illustrator by dragging them, and releasing the mouse button while pressing the Option key.
- Locking objects prevents paths from being selected or altered in any way.

- Lock selected objects by pressing ⌘-1 or lock unselected objects by pressing ⌘-Option-1; unlock all locked objects by pressing ⌘-2.
- Group paths together by selecting more than one path and pressing ⌘-G; ungroup selected groups by pressing ⌘-U.
- Use the Group Selection tool to select paths and groups within other groups.

Tracing and Using Guides

4 CHAPTER

In This Chapter

- What templates are and how they are used
- Creating high-quality templates
- Manual tracing versus automatic tracing
- Measuring by using the Measure tool
- Measuring by using circles and using the Offset Path filter
- Creating and using guides
- How to measure for printing

It's often much easier to create artwork in Illustrator by starting with something to trace, whether it's a logo, a floorplan, or your cousin Fred's disproportionate profile. Even the best artists use some form of template when they draw, to keep proportions consistent, to get angles just right, and for other reasons that help them to achieve the best possible result.

This chapter discusses different methods and techniques for tracing different types of artwork within Illustrator (and even outside of Illustrator). Don't think of this as cheating, but instead, a way to do better, faster, and more accurate artwork.

Okay, it's cheating just a little bit....

Templates

An Illustrator template is a gray image that sits underneath the drawing plane — that is, a template is a background object — and serves as a model for your illustration. Using a template eliminates the guesswork and measuring usually needed when you want to re-create an image. With a template, you can easily match or even improve upon the original art.

The downside: Template quality is rather poor. Templates are always Gray with a resolution of 72 dpi at 100%; as a result, zooming in on a template does not display any more detail than you see at 100%. Templates with fine details appear as so much mush.

Nonetheless, a *template* enables you to quickly reconstruct an image that was created by other means. For example, a template can help you convert a scanned illustration or logo (see Figure 4-1) into Illustrator paths.

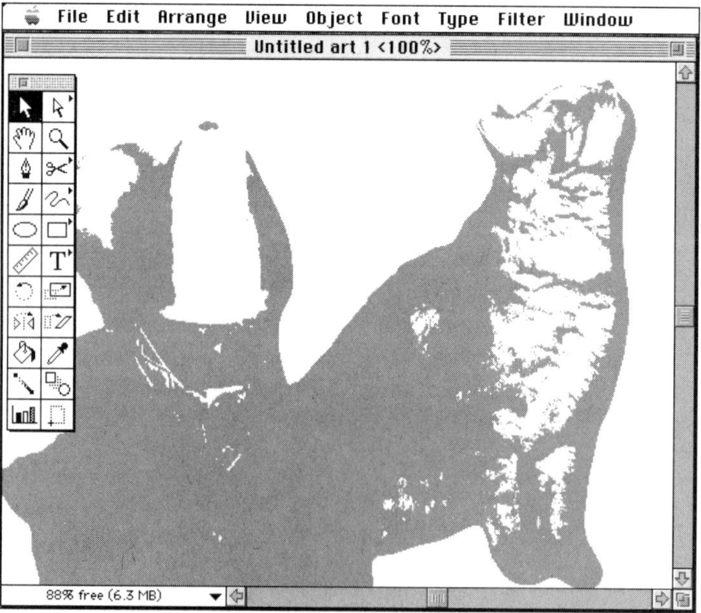

Figure 4-1: A template as it appears in Illustrator

Images used as templates do not print, nor are they saved inside the new Illustrator file. (Instead, Illustrator creates a link between the file and the template.)

Any illustration created in another application usually can be imported into Illustrator as a template. An Illustrator template can be one of two file formats: Paint or PICT. (The only difference between these formats is how other applications save them.) Paint images are often cropped, and PICT images are sometimes stretched, reducing their resolution, or even distorted, making them unusable as templates.

Much better clarity can be achieved in Illustrator by using an enlarged template, effectively increasing the detail available in the template. When creating a template, open an image in Photoshop and save it in either Paint or PICT format in bitmap mode at 75 dpi. For most images scanned at 300 dpi, this rule of thumb quadruples their relative size in Illustrator. After tracing the template, simply select the new image and scale it down to 25% to see it at the original size.

When Is a Template Not a Template?

The best Illustrator templates aren't templates; they're placed files that you've locked into place. If you don't have Photoshop, you can "dim" an EPS image (see Figure 4-2) by using the following the steps. (If you do have Photoshop, see the sidebar "Dimming Photoshop Images," later in this chapter.)

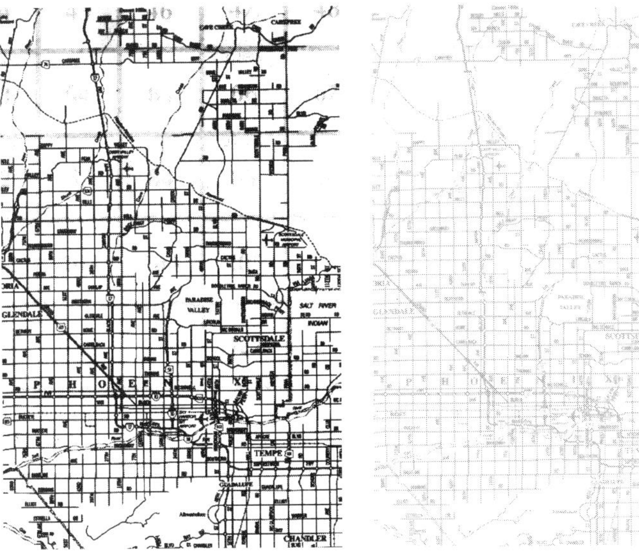

Figure 4-2: The original image (left) and after "dimming" (right)

Template Confusion

Janet: I'm going nuts here. I hate Illustrator.

Toulouse: Whoa. What's the problem?

Janet: Okay. I traced this logo in Illustrator. I tossed the PICT file, now I can't open the Illustrator document!!

Toulouse: Actually, you can. In the dialog box that appears, click None and the Illustrator document will open up with no template. Save it and you're in business.

Janet: Okay. That solves one problem. Now, how do I stick a template in an existing document?

Toulouse: Uh, heh...ya see, uh...

Janet: You can't, can you? I'm toast.

Toulouse: Well, there's an easy workaround.

Janet: If I ever see a "Life is a Workaround" bumper sticker on a VW van, I'll run it off the road.

Toulouse: Okay...To use a template in an existing document, open the document with the Option key pressed.

Janet: Should I be writing this down?

Toulouse. Harumph...Anyway, in the dialog box that appears, you'll be able to choose a new template for the existing document.

STEPS: Dimming an EPS Image for Tracing

Step 1. Place an EPS image into the document by choosing File⇨Place Art and selecting the EPS image.

Step 2. Move the EPS image into the proper position and transform it if necessary.

Step 3. Open the Layers palette by choosing Window⇨Show Layers (⌘-Control-L). In the Layers palette, double-click on Layer 1. In the Layer Options dialog box, select the Dim Placed Images checkbox and then click OK.

Dimming an EPS image in Illustrator causes severe performance problems in your documents. Oddly enough, it's the dimming of the image, and not the image itself, that causes the performance hit. Use the Levels setting in Photoshop to quickly lighten the image within Photoshop.

Placed images work well as templates because their resolution is independent of the Illustrator document. You can scale placed images up or down, *changing their on-screen resolution* as you change their size. For instance, if you scale a 72 dpi image down to one-fourth of its imported size (making the dpi of the placed image 4 × 72 dpi, or 288 dpi), you may zoom in on the image in Illustrator at 400%. At 400%, the placed EPS image still has a 72 dpi resolution because one-fourth of 288 dpi is 72 dpi. The more the placed image's dpi is increased by scaling it down, the more you may zoom in to see the details of the image. If the placed image's dpi is already higher than 72 dpi, you'll be able to zoom in to a certain amount and retain quite a bit of detail automatically.

Another plus: A placed image "template" is a full-color template (well, it's a 256 Color or 256 Gray template, which should be fine for most applications) while standard PICT and Paint templates are Black and White (and the black appears this questionable Gray color). Keeping all the shading and colors enables you to see all the fine details easily.

The one drawback: You can't use the Auto Trace tool with placed images because Illustrator doesn't consider them templates. Unless you constantly use the Auto Trace tool, though, this problem is just an oddity.

PICT Templates in Photoshop

A template's usefulness is directly related to the quality of its scan. You can scan any image and stick it in Illustrator as a template for you to trace, but the quality of your final image will be based on the way the scan looks in Illustrator.

To achieve the best results, try the following:

1. Scan the Black-and-White artwork as Grayscale.

   Yes, doing so takes up more memory (on average, Black-and-White bitmapped images take up 1/8 the space of their Grayscale counterparts), but only temporarily (until Step 5).

2. Open the scanned Grayscale image in an image editing program, such as Photoshop. In Photoshop, open the Levels dialog box (see the figure below) by choosing Image⇨Adjust⇨Levels (⌘-L).

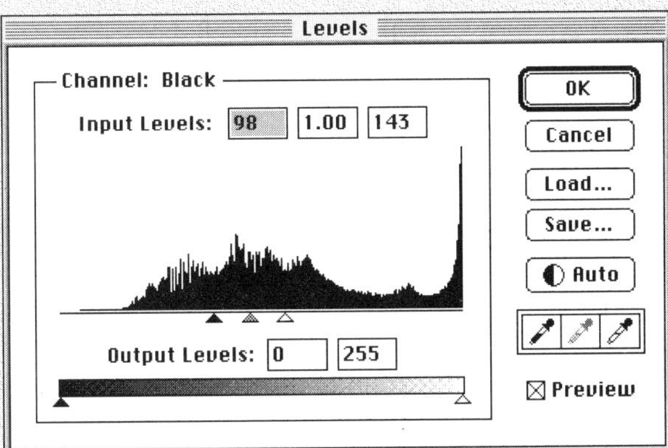

(continued)

(continued)

3. In this dialog box, you can adjust the appearance of the scanned grayscale image by moving the three triangle sliders. Move the three sliders so that they overlap, changing the Grayscale image into a Black-and-White image. Adjust the sliders as needed to achieve the most detail in your image.
4. After clicking OK in the Levels dialog box, choose Mode⇨Bitmap and make sure that the DPI is 75 and the Method is set to 50% Threshold. These settings eliminate any unsightly little stray pixels.
5. Save the image as a PICT file.
6. Open the bitmapped file in Illustrator. It appears as a template.

   The difference in quality between an original scan and one touched up in Photoshop is illustrated in the figure below. The top scanned image was opened directly in Illustrator as a template. The sharper scanned image was touched up in Photoshop and then brought into Illustrator as a template.

Dimming Photoshop Images

Since "dimming" images is problematic in Illustrator, you might want to dim your image *before* you place it into Illustrator, taking advantage of the "lightened" image while avoiding the slowdown that occurs with dimming an image right in Illustrator.

Open your image in Photoshop and go to the Levels dialog box (⌘-L). Drag the bottommost slider on the left (it's solid Black) to the right, until the left output level reads about 200, as shown below.

Copy and paste the image into Illustrator. (Or, if you can't run both Illustrator and Photoshop at the same time, save the image in Photoshop, close Photoshop, and then place the image in Illustrator.)

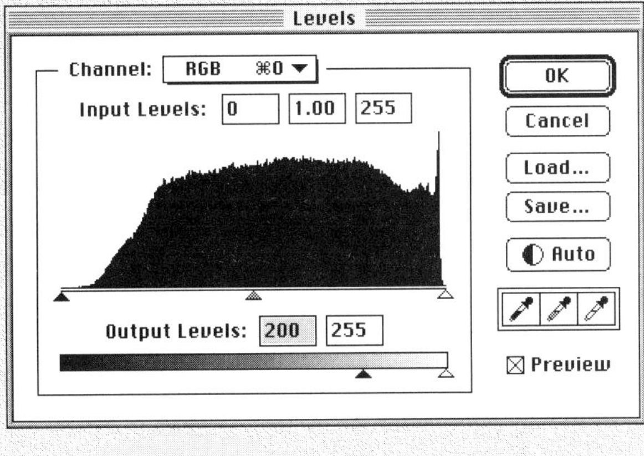

Tracing

Now that you've got your template (placed image) all set up, you're ready to trace it…or so you would think. There are lots of different ways to go about tracing, and I've included the "best of the best" techniques in this section to help you muddle through this mess.

You can trace templates in two ways: manually and automatically. Manually tracing consists of using the Freehand and Pen tools to tediously trace the edges of a template — often a very time-consuming task. Using the Auto Trace tool, though, speeds up the process.

Automatically Tracing Templates

The Auto Trace tool seems simple to use at first: clicking on the edge of the template pixels causes Illustrator to outline the template with a path. The Auto Trace tool appears to outline both White and Gray areas within the template, but it actually creates a path between the two contrasting areas. After all the paths have been drawn, the paths can be selected and transformed into a compound path. This process often automatically colors the alternating Black and White areas correctly (where Black is the "Fill" and White appears as the "holes").

Always use the Auto Trace tool from the outside in. This makes sure that bigger paths around the outside don't overlap the inside paths.

The Freehand Tolerance setting in the General Preferences dialog box (⌘-K) directly affects the Auto Trace tool much like it affects the Freehand tool — the higher the number, the less precise the tracing. A Freehand Tolerance setting of 2 or 3 works pretty well for automatically tracing templates, but neither setting enables the Auto Trace tool to follow the ridges created from the template's diagonal and curved edges.

Manual Tracing

Most designers prefer manually tracing templates. Using the Pen and Freehand tools provides illustrators with a level of precision not found with the Auto Trace tool. Furthermore, illustrators may add detail, remove oddities, and change curves, angles, and the like to their satisfaction (as opposed to an image that has been automatically traced, which gives it a "final" appearance with less "editability").

I've found that a combination of manual and automatic tracing works quite nicely for drawing fairly basic illustrations, especially those with type and straight lines. Automatically trace the basic shapes first and then use the path editing tools to add or remove Anchor Points and move paths so that the image has a consistent look. After fixing the traced section, use the Pen and Freehand tools to draw in the intricate shapes.

About Adobe Streamline

Adobe Streamline is the Auto Trace tool on a natural high (actually, it's more like a coke rush, I'm told, but I hate to equate software to drugs...though both can be addicting and expensive). Anyway, Streamline can automatically trace full-color images, *retaining their color* automatically.

Adobe Streamline is so cool that I've given it its own chapter, along with its big cousin Adobe Dimensions, later in the book. It takes tracing images to a whole 'nother plane, like… [yet another unsavory reference, this time deleted by a savory editor].

Using Layers for Tracing

You can use layers for more than just dimming EPS images for tracing. In fact, once I discovered the fact of the tremendous slowdown to Illustrator when images are dimmed, I stopped using that feature entirely, but I still needed the power of layers for tracing.

One of the unsung features of Illustrator's layers (more features are sung in Chapter 7) is the ability to show some layers in Preview mode, and others in Artwork mode.

This is great for tracing because now you can take any placed image, put it on a layer that is shown in Preview mode, lock that layer (so the "template" isn't moved), and then create a new layer *above* the existing one and set it to Artwork view. Not only will you be able to see the placed image in color, but the paths you draw will be outlines with the placed image visible below them.

Measuring

You can measure distances in Illustrator in three ways:

- Use the Measure tool
- Use the rulers along the side of the document window
- Place objects whose dimensions are known against the edges
- Eyeball it (popular since the first artist painted his recollections of the preceding day's battle with the saber-toothed animals of his time)

The Measure Tool

The fastest way to obtain a precise, exact measurement in Illustrator is to use the Measure tool (shown in Figure 4-3). As soon as you click an object with the Measure tool, the Info palette appears, showing the distance between the location first clicked and the next location clicked or the distance between where the tool was first clicked and where the mouse was released after being dragged.

Measuring Trouble

Jack: You know, my measurements never seem accurate.

Toulouse: Really? How far are they off?

Jack: It varies. Sometimes they'll be right on, other times they'll be half the size, twice as big...Once they were 1/16 of the actual size!

Toulouse: I hate to ask this, but what are you using to measure your on-screen objects?

Jack: The rulers on the monitor, of course.

Toulouse: Well, that's very weird. I've always found those rulers to be quite accurate.

Jack: You've used my computer?

Toulouse: No, but I have rulers on my system too.

Jack: But how do you know they're the same as mine?

Toulouse: You know, I'm thinking there's a lack of communication somewhere here...

Jack: The real problem was getting them to stay in place.

Toulouse: Huh?

Jack: Yeah, I ended up hot-gluing each ruler to the edges of the monitor. Duct tape would've been my next choice.

Toulouse: You know, there are rulers "within" Illustrator.

Jack: Yer kidding me.

Toulouse: Command-R. Check it out.

Figure 4-3: The Measure tool

If the Snap to point option in the General Preferences dialog box (⌘-K) is checked, the Measure tool automatically snaps to nearby paths and points.

As soon as the Measure tool measures a distance, it routes that information to the Move dialog box, shown in Figure 4-4. The next time you open the Move dialog box (by choosing Arrange⇨Move, Option-clicking the Selection tool, or pressing ⌘-Shift-M), it will hold the values sent by the Measure tool.

Figure 4-4: The Move dialog box

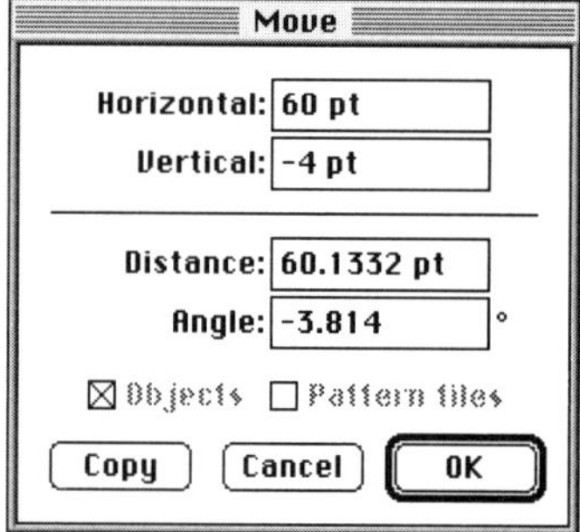

Know anything about PostScript? Well, one thing you absolutely have to know is that pages in PostScript are always measured from the lower-left corner of the page. That means moving something along the *Y* axis with a positive number will move it up, not down. It's a math thing. Your geometry teacher would've thought that's the way to measure things, while the rest of the world thinks it's stupid.

If you hold down the Shift key, you can constrain the movement of the measuring line to the following:

- In Preview mode, the measuring line defines a 45° or 90° angle if no paths or Filled parts of paths are under the cursor.

- In Artwork mode, your cursor snaps to the paths.
- In Preview mode, the cursor snaps to any Filled part of any path.

Sizing Up Objects with the Control Palette

The Control palette (choose Window⇨Show Control Palette) shows the height, width, and location of any select path or paths, as illustrated in Figure 4-5.

Figure 4-5: The Control palette

W is the width of the selected object (or the total width of the selected objects when more than one is selected), while *H* is the height or total height of the selected object or objects.

X and *Y* show the location of the object on the page, measured (as always) from the lower-left corner.

All these measurements will be in points…unless, of course, you know how to change the measurement units, which coincidentally, is the topic of my next section.

Changing the Measurement Units

When you first use Illustrator, you'll be faced with points. That's great for type and numbering star tips, but when was the last time your art director said, "I'd like you to design a 360 x 288 ad and make the logo at least 144 high." (Or your grandmother said to you, "Gosh, you must be at least 5600 tall, maybe taller. You've grown at least 100 since the last time I saw you. And does your mother let you wear *that* to school?!")

Points don't work for everything, so Adobe lets us change the Measurement Units to inches or millimeters. There are several ways to do this. The most basic way is to indicate a different unit of measurement each time you enter a value, by appending a character or two to the end of your numerical value. For instance, to enter two inches you'd type **2 inch, 2 in**, or **2"**. To enter two millimeters, you'd enter **2 mm**. To enter 2 points you'd enter **2 pt** or **p 2**. You can even enter picas by putting a *p* after the number, such as **2p** for 2 picas. You can also combine picas and points by sticking a *p* between them, as in **2p6** for two picas, six points.

To permanently alter your measurement units, choose File⇨Preferences⇨General and change the Measurement Units pop-up menu to the measurement system you want.

To quickly change Measurement Units, press ⌘-Control-U, which will cycle through all three different measurement unit settings. You can do this right in the document at any time.

Using Rulers

You can toggle rulers on and off by choosing View⇨Show/Hide Rulers (⌘-R). Normally, the rulers measure up and across from the document's lower-left corner; however, you can alter this orientation by dragging the ruler origin (where the zeros are) from its position in the lower-right corner, between where the two rulers meet. Because rulers take up valuable on-screen real estate, it's usually a good idea to leave them turned off unless you are constantly measuring things or you want to display your illustration at a higher magnification. Rulers are easy to show and hide: just press ⌘-R when you want to see them; press ⌘-R again to lose them.

One of the rulers' nicest features is the display of dotted lines corresponding to the cursor's position. And yet, at times, measuring with rulers works no better than eyeballing: Although the process requires precision, you are limited by the rulers' hash marks in pinpointing the cursor's exact position. The rulers are best suited for measuring when the document is at a very high zoom level.

Measuring with Objects

Using objects to compare distances can be more effective than using either the Measure tool or the rulers, especially when you need to place objects precisely — for example, when you want several objects to be the same distance from one another.

If you place a circle adjacent to an object (so that the objects' edges touch), you know that the second object is placed correctly when it's aligned to the circle's other side. (A circle is the object most commonly used because the diameter is constant.)

You can use other objects for measuring, including the following:

- Squares — when you need to measure horizontal and vertical distances
- Rectangles — when the horizontal and vertical distances are different
- Lines — when the distance applies to only one direction

To enable better precision, turn the measuring object into a guide. (Guides are discussed in more detail later.)

If you change the ruler origin to the middle of the document page, try to move it back to a corner when you are finished. When you zoom in, rulers may be your only indicator of your location within the document.

Using the Offset Path Filter (for Equidistant Measuring)

Sometimes, you may want to place several objects the same distance from a central object. Using any of the previously mentioned measuring techniques can be time-consuming and even inaccurate, especially when you deal with complex images. Illustrator's Offset Path filter, however, enables you to automatically align objects equidistantly from a central object.

First, select the central object. Then choose Filter⇨Object⇨Offset Path and enter the desired distance (in points, millimeters, or inches) in the Offset text field. After the new path is created, check the corner areas to see whether there are any overlapping areas that appear as loops. If so, use the Unite filter to eliminate these unsightly aberrations by choosing Filter⇨Pathfinder⇨Unite. Change the new path into a guide and align your objects to this guide.

Guides

Guides are teeny tiny little people that show you around Illustrator, as shown in Figure 4-6. The more of them you make, the easier it is to use the program. (Uh huh…I know, let you know when the shuttle lands…Sigh.)

Okay, actually, *guides* are dotted lines that help you align artwork. Guides will not print, and they will be saved with documents. In Illustrator and most desktop publishing software, guides are straight lines extending from one edge of a document to the other. But in Illustrator, you can also turn *any* path into a guide (see the following section).

More Measuring Woes

Furley: This isn't working. I'm no mathematician.

Toulouse: Trouble with rulers?

Furley: Yeah. I want to place objects at certain distances from the edges of different pieces of artwork.

Toulouse: Why's that a problem?

Furley: Well, my object is at about 2.3" across the page, and 6.7" from the bottom. I can't work this way.

Toulouse: You can reset the way the rulers measure, so you can measure from the top left of any artwork on the page.

Furley: Without doing the math?

Toulouse: No math. Just drag the origin (that's where the rulers meet at the bottom right of the page) to where you want to measure from.

Furley: Wow! This is great! I haven't been this excited since Stanley took off for his own show! Which then bombed, of course, leaving me on a top 10 show.

Toulouse: If I recall, wasn't the ratings high point *before* you came on the show?

Furley: I've never really done the math…

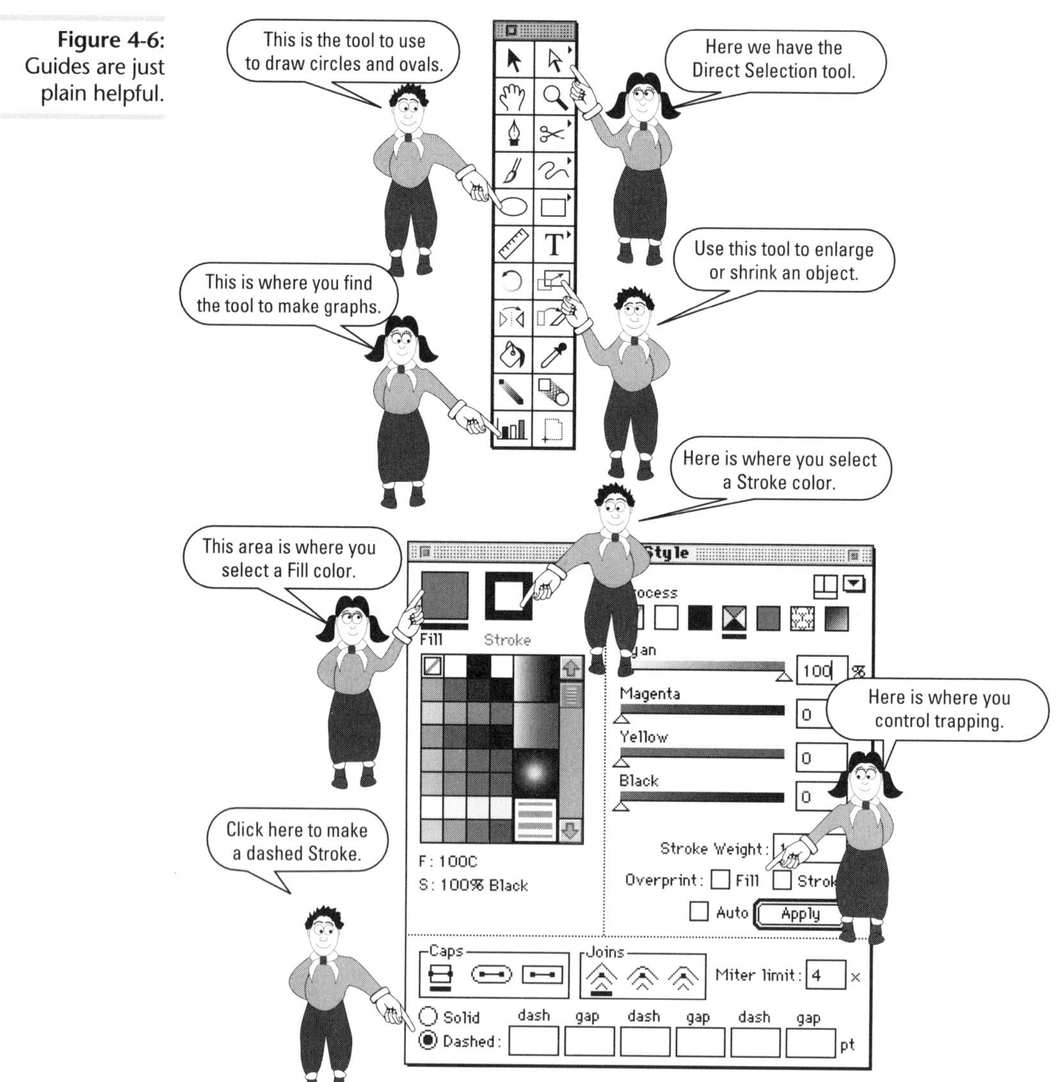

Figure 4-6: Guides are just plain helpful.

Creating Guides

You can create guides in two ways: by pulling them out from the rulers and by transforming paths into guides.

To pull a guide from a ruler, first make the vertical and horizontal rulers visible by choosing Objects⇨Show Rulers (⌘-R). To create guides that span the entire Pasteboard, click on the vertical or horizontal ruler and drag out.

To transform an existing path into a guide, select the path and choose Object⇨Guides⇨Make (⌘-5).

And now a word about the Magic Rotating Guide (possibly the coolest tip you'll ever learn): When you drag a guide out from the vertical ruler, hold down Option, and the vertical guide becomes a horizontal guide. And vice versa.

Moving Guides

Moving an unlocked guide is simple — click on it and drag. If the guide is locked, press Control-Shift and then click and drag.

If you aren't sure whether the guides in your document are locked or unlocked, choose Object⇨Guides. If you see a check mark next to Lock, the guides are locked (and all new guides will also be locked). To unlock all the document's guides, choose Object⇨Guides⇨Lock or press ⌘-7; to lock guides again, choose Object⇨Guides⇨Lock or press ⌘-7 again (yes, it's a toggle).

All guides in a document have a special status of "lockedness," where all guides are either locked or unlocked. Weirdly enough, however, guides can be locked and unlocked individually as well by selecting them and choosing Arrange⇨Lock (⌘-1).

Releasing Guides

To release a guide, or change it into a path, press Control-Shift and double-click the guide or select the guide and choose Object⇨Guides⇨Release (⌘-6).

To release multiple guides: First, make sure that the guides are unlocked; in other words, make sure that there's no check mark next to Lock in the Object@⇨Guides submenu. Then select the guides (in the same way you select multiple paths: either drag a marquee around the guides or Shift-click each guide) and choose Object⇨Guides⇨Release (⌘-6).

Selecting *all* guides — even those that are currently paths — by dragging a marquee or Shift-clicking can be a chore. Here's another way: Make sure that the guides are not locked and choose Edit@⇨Select All (⌘-A). Then select Object⇨Guides⇨Release (⌘-6). This releases all guides and, more importantly, selects all paths that were formerly guides (all other paths and objects are deselected). Then choose Object⇨Guides⇨Make (⌘-5) and all guides become guides again and are selected.

Picas ≠ Picas

Chrissy: I'm about to get fired.

Toulouse: I thought you had a stake in the Thighmaster thing...

Chrissy: No, things I print don't measure correctly.

Toulouse: How so?

Chrissy: Well, picas don't equal picas.

Toulouse: Actually, that's a common occurrence. But you're not doing anything wrong.

Chrissy: Pardon me for asking, but why the hell does it happen?

Toulouse: Well, when you measure, you're probably using one of those pica sticks, right?

Chrissy: Sure. It's *the* weapon of the graphic artist.

Toulouse: Okay. The problem is that until just recently, most pica sticks were "traditional picas," which aren't the same as "new picas," sometimes called "Adobe picas."

Chrissy: And traditional picas are different than Adobe picas?

Toulouse: Um, yeah...See, there are 72.27 points in an inch using traditional points

For the most part, guides behave exactly like their path counterparts. As long as guides are unlocked, you may select them, hide them, group them, and even paint them (although paint attributes will not be visible onscreen or on a printout until the guides are converted back into paths).

Measuring for Printing

Thinking ahead to the time your job will be printed is always a good thing, and one of the most important areas of printing is both the placement and sizing of your artwork within the Illustrator document. This section deals with production-oriented issues you might face while using Illustrator to create printable pieces.

Stepping

Oftentimes, you'll create something that's quite small and need to have several copies of the artwork on the page at once. Setting up your artwork for optimal spacing and printing is referred to as *stepping*.

Illustrator doesn't do stepping automatically, but it does provide the tools you need to step your artwork.

The best way to do step and repeat actions is with CSI's Socket Set 2, which includes a Step and Repeat filter with lots of flexibility. See Chapter 18 for a complete description of this amazing third-party filter.

STEPS: Creating Stepped Artwork

Step 1. Make sure the Control palette is open. Then select the finished artwork and open the Move dialog box (⌘-Shift-M, or Option-click on the Selection tool).

Step 2. Enter the width of the art (the *W* in the Control palette) in the Horizontal field. Enter **0** (zero) in the Vertical field. Click the Copy button (or press Option-Return).

Step 3. Choose Arrange⇨Repeat Transform (⌘-D) to create another duplicate of the artwork. Press ⌘-D until there are the right number of pieces across the page.

Step 4. Select the entire row of artwork, and open the Move dialog box again.

Step 5. Enter **0** (zero) in the Horizontal field, and enter the height of the art (the *H* in the Control palette) in the Vertical field. Click the Copy button (or press Option-Return).

Step 6. Choose Arrange⇨Repeat Transform (⌘-D) to create another duplicate of the row of artwork. Press ⌘-D until there are the right number of pieces down the page, as shown in Figure 4-7.

Creating Cropmarks

Cropmarks are little lines that are designed to help you cut (or crop) along the edges of your illustration after the document has been printed (see Figure 4-8). Crops (that's the slang term; if you're even half cool you won't say "cropmarks") don't intrude on the edges of the artwork, but instead are offset a bit from the corners of where the edges are.

and picas, and there are 72 points in an inch using Adobe points and picas. So picas, which are 12 points, are different sizes between the two systems.

Chrissy: So, which programs use Adobe picas, and which ones use traditional picas?

Toulouse: Actually, by default, "all" Mac software uses Adobe picas and points. Some programs, like QuarkXPress, let you switch between them.

Chrissy: How confusing.

Toulouse: It is. You know, we really should be talking about setting up artwork "step by step"...

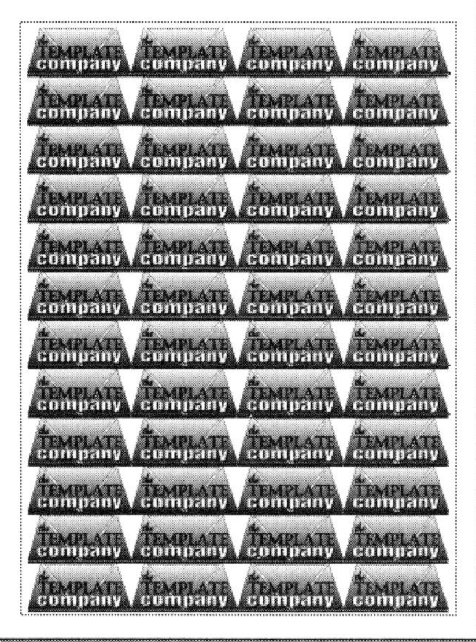

Figure 4-7: Artwork that has been stepped and repeated on a page

Figure 4-8: Cropmarks show where the edges of the artwork are.

Unfortunately, you can only create one set of cropmarks per document. Making multiple cropmarks by drawing them yourself or using the Trim Marks filter (Filter⇨Create⇨Trim Marks) isn't enough for color separations; black cropmarks that you create by drawing may be 100% of process colors but will not contain any other spot colors you may have in your illustration. (This problem is the result of a serious limitation in Illustrator: The program does not allow you to choose "registration" as a color, which would print on every different color plate.) Trim marks created with the Trim Marks filter are 100% black.

Here's a workaround: Choose the cropmarks and/or trim marks you created and Stroke them with 100% of all four process colors when you are printing out four-color separations. If you are printing out spot-color separations, you must copy the cropmarks, choose Edit⇨Paste in Front (⌘-F) or Edit⇨Paste in Back (⌘-B), and then color the Stroke of the crops with the spot color you are using, choosing the Overprint Strokes option in the Paint Style palette. Additional cropmarks need to be pasted in front or pasted in back for every additional color separation in your document.

To transform a selected rectangle drawn with the rectangle tool into cropmarks, choose Cropmarks⇨Make.

The rectangle can only be modified prior to becoming cropmarks by moving it or resizing it via the Scale tool. If any transformation is done to the rectangle, a message will appear saying that you can only make cropmarks out of a single rectangle. If a rectangle is drawn with a constrain angle set to an angle other than 0°, 90°, 180°, or 270° (–90°), you will not be able to make cropmarks out of that rectangle.

If you choose Cropmarks⇨Make when nothing is selected, cropmarks will appear around the edge of the single full page. If Tile Imageable Areas is enabled in Document Setup, the cropmarks will appear only around the first page. If crops are set to the size of the page and the page is moved with the Page tool, or if the document has been resized with the Document Setup dialog box, the cropmarks *will not move*.

To release selected cropmarks, choose Cropmarks⇨Release. If the cropmarks were created from a rectangle, then that rectangle is an editable path, that can be resized and changed back into cropmarks, deleted, or modified. Any rectangle that has been changed back from being a set of cropmarks will have a Fill and Stroke of None.

You cannot choose Cropmarks⇨Release when no cropmarks are in your document. In addition, Cropmarks⇨Release will not release trim marks made with the Filter⇨Create⇨Trim Marks command.

Summary

- Templates are used in Illustrator to make your drawing easier and more precise.
- Templates can be either 1-bit PICT or Paint template images, or they can be placed images.
- Avoid Illustrator's Dimming feature, as it drastically slows down Illustrator operations when active.
- The Auto Trace tool only works with PICT or Paint templates.
- Manual tracing will usually generate better results than using the Auto Trace tool.
- The Measure tool provides a quick way to measure distances in your Illustrator documents.
- Measurements generated by the Measure tool will appear in the Move dialog box the next time you open it.
- Guides can be created from any object by selecting the object and pressing ⌘-5.
- You can quickly create document high/wide guides by dragging out from the rulers.
- Use the Copy button within the Move dialog box to step and repeat artwork.

Working with Illustrator Files

CHAPTER 5

In This Chapter

- Setting up and viewing documents
- Managing files
- Opening and saving Illustrator files
- Importing and exporting files
- Setting up pages for printing
- Printing illustrations

Setting Up a New Document

Illustrator has a unique way of working, at least in the world of desktop publishing and graphics. As soon as you run the program, an empty document window appears, ready for you to begin drawing. No hassles. Just an instant drawing area. A new document window that is ready to use is shown in Figure 5-1.

Choosing New (⌘-N) from the File menu when you're already *in* Illustrator creates a brand new document and makes that new document the *active* document. In previous versions of Illustrator, users were hit with an evil dialog box, where they had to indicate which template they wanted to use. Because most users do not normally use templates, this command was altered to instantly create a new document with no questions asked.

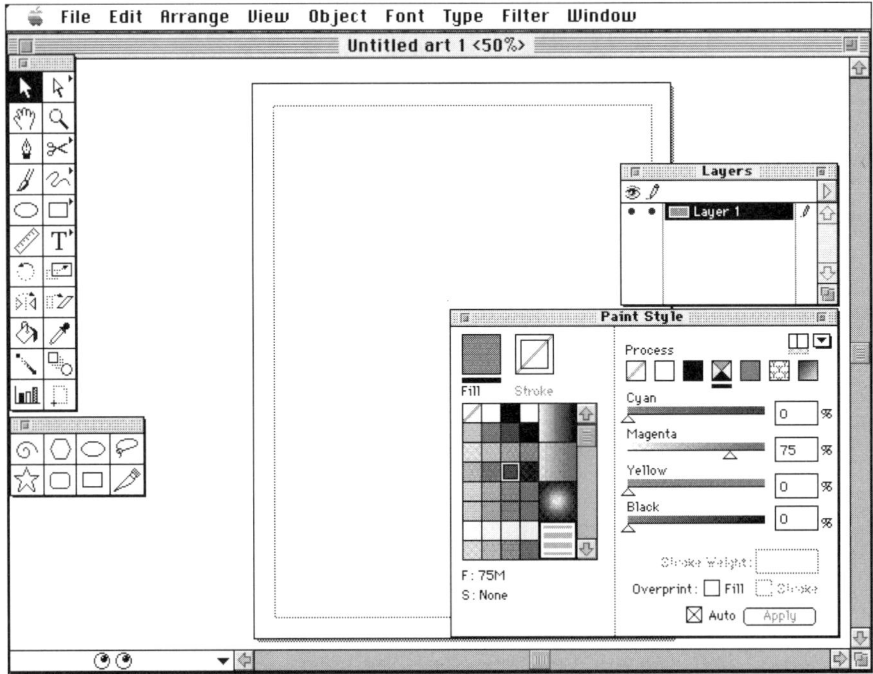

Figure 5-1: The new document window that appears when you first run Illustrator

The Dark Ages

Creating a new document hasn't always been easy. Back in the days of Illustrator 88, and even Illustrator 3 to some extent, creating new illustrations was rather annoying. Choosing New Document brought up a dialog box that politely yet sternly asked you to choose a template to trace in Illustrator. Most of the time, though, you didn't want a template, so you had to click the little None button in the dialog box. If you pressed Return, Illustrator would attempt to open a template.

Illustrator 3 was a little more flexible. It enabled you to create a new document without having to deal with the dialog box that asked you to choose a template. You could either press ⌘-Option-N or hold down the Option key when you chose File⇨New. If you forgot about the Option key, you had another chance. Pressing ⌘-N when you were in the dialog box would send the box away and create a new document with no template — as long as you didn't have Directory Assistance, Super Boomerang, or any other utilities that created a new folder open when you pressed ⌘-N.

Adobe slowly seemed to realize that you didn't want or need a template to do everything, and now, fortunately, "template forcing" is a thing of the past.

Everybody Else and Their Mother

In most graphics and desktop publishing software, the program opens to a splash screen, but no document appears. Choosing File⇨New results in a nasty dialog box with options for this, choices for that, conditions for certain occurrences, and confusing terms that seem to have been made up solely to intimidate you.

In these dialog boxes, you can specify page size, units of measurement, margins, columns, output resolution, number of pages, and whether you would like the document to vote Republican, Democratic, or Independent in the next major election. You must check the correct boxes, enter the right figures, and in some cases, pray that you aren't wrong about something, because making a change later can be a nightmare.

The nice thing about entering all of this information ahead of time is that you can set up the document just as you want it. The bad thing is that you get pummeled with having to enter lots of other information about the document that slows you down right off the bat.

Many other graphics and desktop publishing programs, including FreeHand, Photoshop, and QuarkXPress, all ask you to set up your document size before the document is created. When you create a new Illustrator document, it defaults to the size of the start-up document that is located in the Plug-Ins folder (see Chapter 6 for more information on altering the start-up document). By default, this document is 8.5 x 11 inches, and it is in the portrait orientation (meaning that the width is less than the height). The document window initially shows up at "actual size," which is supposedly the same size at which it will be printed. In the title bar at the top of the window, you see "Untitled Art 1 <100%>." As soon as you save the document, the title bar will contain the name of the document.

You cannot change the way that some things appear when you first start Illustrator. For example, the Selection tool is always selected in the Toolbox. Another unchangeable item is the initial Paint Style that you begin drawing with: a Fill of 100% Black, and a Stroke of None. The character attributes are always the same: 12-point Helvetica, Auto leading, Flush left. In addition, the layer color is always light blue (a color that is just dark enough so that it doesn't conflict with cyan).

Changing the Document Setup

To change almost anything about the document structure and how you work with that document, you need to go to the Document Setup dialog box (see Figure 5-2) by choosing File⇨Document Setup or pressing ⌘-Shift-D. In this dialog box, you can change the size of the Artboard, define how and when paths are split, change the ruler units, and change the way that printable page edges, patterns, and placed images are viewed.

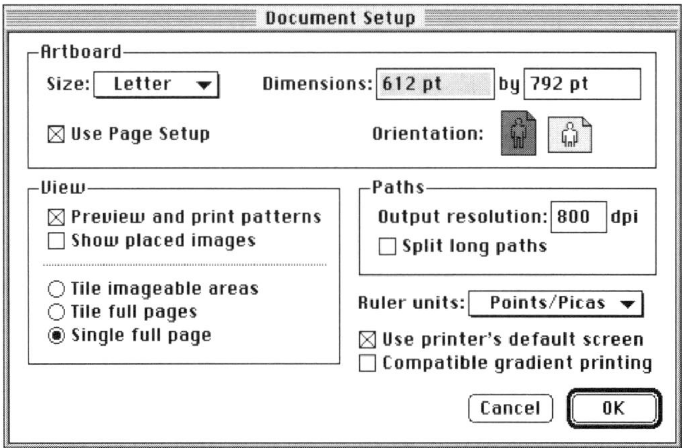

Figure5-2: The Document Setup dialog box

The following sections describe the various options that are available in the Document Setup dialog box. Any changes that you make to these options are saved with the document.

Artboard Options

In Illustrator, the *Artboard* defines the maximum drawing area that can be printed. The Artboard is useful as a guide for where the objects on a page belong. In older versions of Illustrator, the maximum printable size was 11 x 17 inches; in Version 6, it is 120 x 120 inches or 10 square feet (provided that you can find a printer that prints that big).

Adobe Separator (software included with Illustrator for printing out color separations of Illustrator documents) ignores the Artboard and places crop marks around the entire imagable area. The imagable area, according to Separator, is only the area where artwork exists. It may be within the Artboard, but it also may extend onto the Pasteboard. When you export an illustration to another program, such as QuarkXPress, the Artboard is ignored entirely.

To choose the size of the Artboard, you select from one of the following preset sizes on the Size pop-up menu:

- **Letter** is 8.5 x 11 inches.
- **Legal** is 8.5 x 14 inches.
- **Tabloid** is 11 x 17 inches.
- **A4** is 8.268 x 11.693 inches (21 x 29.7 centimeters).
- **A3** is 11.693 x 16.535 inches (29.7 x 42 centimeters).
- **B5** is 7.165 x 10 inches (18.2 x 25.4 centimeters).
- **B4** is 10.118 x 14.331 inches (55.7 x 36.4 centimeters).
- **Custom** is whatever size you type in the Dimensions text fields.

A4, A3, B5, and B4 are European paper sizes.

To define the orientation of your Artboard, you choose one of the two Orientation pages. On the left is the Portrait orientation, where the lesser of the two dimensions goes across the page from left to right, and the greater of the two dimensions goes from top to bottom. On the right is the Landscape orientation, where the greater of the two dimensions goes across the page from left to right, and the lesser of the two dimensions goes from top to bottom. You can put the lesser or the greater value in either of the two Dimensions text fields, but the next time you open the Document Setup box, the lesser of the two will always be on the left.

If you check the Use Page Setup box, then the Artboard will default to the page size and orientation that is selected in the Page Setup dialog box.

View Options

You can control how certain things in Illustrator are viewed by checking the appropriate boxes:

Multiple Pages in Illustrator?

Kate: I think my Illustrator is broken.

Toulouse: I doubt it, but why do you think that's the case?

Kate: I can't put anything on page 2.

Toulouse: That might be because there is no page 2.

Kate: Ha ha ha. Okay, so how do I create page 2?

Toulouse: Look, this isn't Word or XPress. There is no page 2.

Kate: Really?

Toulouse: Really. But you can kinda fudge it.

Kate: I'm trying to lose weight...I put on some pounds after the Scarecrow gig ended.

Toulouse: Sorry to hear that. You can set up Illustrator to have either one or nine pages.

Kate: One or Nine? Oh, that makes sense.

Toulouse: Good. Now, to get nine pages, go into Document Setup, and select the Tile Imageable areas option.

Kate: And where are pages 2 through 9?

(continued)

(continued)

Toulouse: Zoom out a few times, and you'll see all nine pages.

Kate: All I see is a big grid thing that divides my artboard into nine sections.

Toulouse: That's it!

Kate: You're kidding me.

Toulouse: Nope. And when you print, you can pick which pages to print. They're number 1, 2, and 3; then 4, 5, and 6; then 7, 8, and 9. So you normally start on page 5.

Kate: I think I'll wait for Illustrator 7.

Toulouse: Good idea.

- The **Preview and print patterns** option displays patterns that are used as Fills in objects when Illustrator is in Preview mode or selected objects that are Filled with patterns when Illustrator is in Preview Selection mode. Illustrator will also print patterns when this option is checked. If this option is not checked, it affects only the way that Illustrator sees and prints the pattern objects; it does not affect how other applications see and print them. Choosing this option can dramatically increase screen redraw times (Preview mode) and printing times. If this checkbox is not checked, patterns will not print or preview in Illustrator, but they will print in other software.

- The **Show placed images** option displays placed images in Artwork mode. It does not affect how placed artwork is viewed in Preview or Preview Selection (when the artwork is selected) modes. When the checkbox is not checked, placed artwork is represented as a box with an *X* inside it.

- The **Tile imageable areas** option creates a grid on the document, with the size of each *block* equal to the page size that is chosen in the Page Setup dialog box. Little page numbers appear in the lower-left corner of each block, representing the pages you page *x* to page *x* entered in the fields in the Print dialog box.

- The **Tile full pages** option creates as many page outlines (from Page Setup) as will completely print. For example, if the Artboard is landscape, 11 x 17 inches, and the selected page size in Page Setup is portrait, 8.5 x 11 inches, then two page outlines will appear side by side in the document.

- The **Single full page** option creates one Page Setup size outline on the page.

To move the page outlines, select the Page tool and click and drag in the Artboard. The click point of the page is always the lower lefthand corner.

Path Splitting Options

Robbie the Robot would be screaming his metal head off if Will Robinson ever thought about clicking the Split long paths check box. The checkbox looks friendly enough, but the results of checking it can be deadly. If you are quick enough, you can always undo the split paths function, but the actual splitting of paths doesn't always happen when and where you expect it to happen.

Instead, it happens only when you save or print a document. This feature presents some very interesting problems. First, if you save the document and close it right after you save it, the paths are split permanently, and you cannot undo the damage the next time you open the document. Second, after you print a document, saving and closing it is a very natural thing to do. But once again, you cannot get it back to normal. Another problem arises when you are working in Preview mode: if you forget whether you checked the option, sometimes you can't easily determine whether paths have been split.

The Split long paths function tries to fix paths that are too long or too complex for your laser printer to handle. By entering the final output resolution for the Illustrator document, you can ensure that it will have a better chance of printing than if paths were not split. Every curve in Illustrator is made of tiny straight segments. The higher the resolution of the output device, the more straight segments are needed to create the curve. The processing power of the laser printer limits how many little straight segments can be in one path. If you exceed that limit, Illustrator chops away at the paths, splitting them into several smaller sections. Because this problem occurs more with high-resolution devices, the greater the number you enter in the Output resolution field, the more paths will be split. Figure 5-3 shows an original document and several examples of path splitting.

The only reason to use the Split long paths function is if a document fails to print because of a PostScript error (usually a Limitcheck error). But instead of just checking the Split long paths checkbox, first make a copy of the entire document (doing a Save As with another name will do this quickly) and then split paths in the new document. Then the original file will not contain split paths. Split paths are extremely difficult to reassemble, and the results from split paths can be horrifying. Please use caution when you split paths.

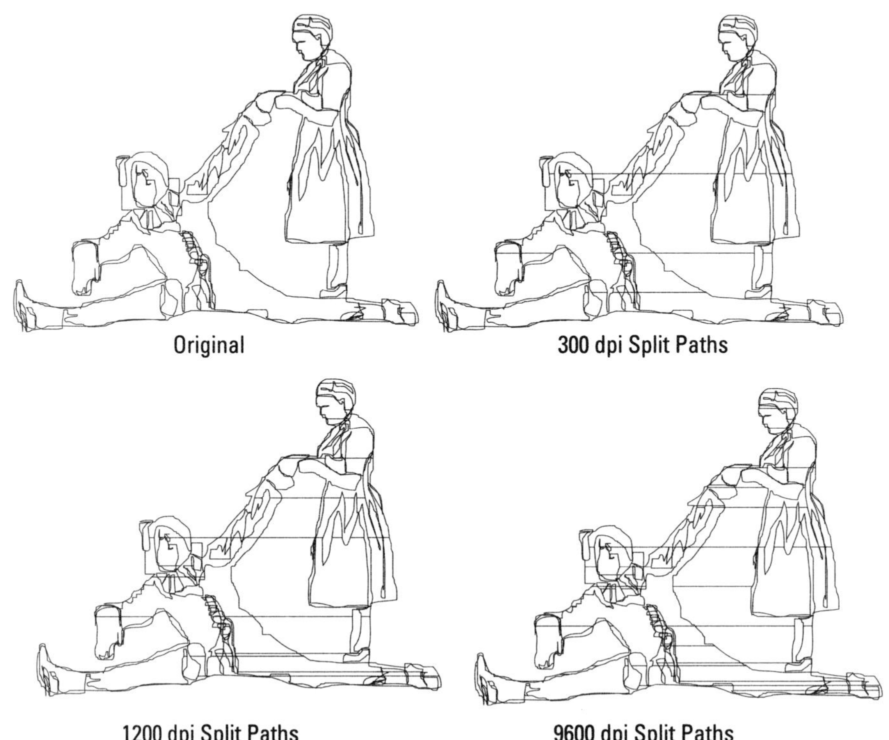

Figure 5-3: A document before and after path splitting at different output resolutions

Ruler Units

You can view a document in inches, points and picas, or centimeters. The measurement units affect the numbers on the rulers and the locations of the hatch marks on those same rulers. The measurement system also changes the way measurements are displayed in the Info palette and in all dialog boxes where you enter a measurement (other than a percentage).

The measurement system is changed in either the General Preferences dialog box (choose File⇨Preferences⇨General, or press ⌘-K) for all documents, or in the Document Setup dialog box (choose File⇨Document Setup, or press ⌘-Shift-D) for the currently active document.

To change the unit of measurement in Illustrator 6, press ⌘-Ctrl-U to cycle through the different available measurement systems.

Using the Printer's Default Screen

For gradients on low-resolution printers (600 dpi or less) when composite printing only, Illustrator uses a dither pattern called Adobe Screens (not to be confused with Adobe Accurate Screens) when Use Printer Default Screen is unchecked. This increases the apparent levels of gray by fracturing the halftone cells.

You'll notice when you first open a document that the Use Printer Default Screens checkbox is checked. But, the first time you Fill an object with a gradient, it automatically unchecks itself. Illustrator assumes when you use gradients that you want Adobe Screens turned on — if you don't want it on, you have to manually turn Use Printer Default Screen back on. When checking Use Printer Default Screens, you're just disabling Adobe Screens; you are *not* telling Illustrator to image the file at the printer's default line screen. Output software can still set the printer's line screen for the Illustrator file.

Navigating Through the Document

Being able to move through a document easily is a key skill in Illustrator. You rarely can fit the entire illustration in the document window at a magnification where you can see much of the detail of the image. Usually, you are zooming in, zooming out, or moving off to the side or above or below to focus in on certain areas of the document.

Who's Zoomin' Who?

The most basic of navigational concepts in Illustrator is the ability to zoom to different magnification levels. Illustrator's magnification levels work like a magnifying glass. In the real world, you use a magnifying glass to see details that aren't readily visible without it. In the Illustrator world, you use the different magnification levels to see details that aren't readily visible at 100% view. The magnification levels of Illustrator do not affect the illustration. If you zoom in to 200% and print, the illustration will be printed at the same size as it would if the view were 100%. It will *not* print twice as large.

The Zoom Tools

You use the two Zoom tools, Zoom In and Zoom Out, to magnify a certain area of artwork and then return to the standard view.

Zooming Out Wrong?

Charlie: You know, that marquee thing just isn't happening here.

Toulouse: I bet Joan Collins sabotaged your system.

Charlie: Uh, wrong show. Anyway, I drag and...nothing!

Toulouse: It doesn't zoom in? Maybe I should be calling you Blake?

Charlie: No, and no, it doesn't zoom out!

Toulouse: Well, it's supposed to zoom in, not out. I guess then it's only half broke.

Charlie: I thought the Zoom Out tool zoomed out. Hence the name.

Toulouse: You aren't trying to draw a marquee with the Zoom Out tool, are you?

Charlie: Sure. Is that a problem?

Toulouse: The Zoom Out tool doesn't work by drawing a marquee. You have to click with it. Drawing with a marquee is the same as clicking.

Charlie: But what if I want to zoom out really far, right away?

Toulouse: Double-click on the Hand tool to make the page fit in your window. Is that small enough?

Charlie: No...I want it smaller.

Toulouse: You can quickly go to 6.25% by Option-clicking on the Zoom tool.

To use the Zoom In tool, select it in the Toolbox or press ⌘-Spacebar. Either way, the Zoom In tool should appear. It looks like a magnifying glass with a plus sign in it. Clicking any spot in the illustration will enlarge that part of the illustration to the next magnification level. There are 17 different Zoom levels available within Illustrator. The highest magnification level is 1600%, which shows the illustration at 16 times the size of its original measurements. Of course, the Zoom In feature is not without its pitfall: The more you zoom in on an illustration, the less of that illustration you see at one time.

Where you click with the Zoom In tool is very important. Clicking the center of the window will enlarge the illustration to the next magnification level, but the edges (top, bottom, left, and right) will be cropped off as the magnification increases. Clicking the upper-right corner will crop off mostly the lower-left edges, and so forth. If you are interested in seeing a particular part of the illustration close up, click that part at each magnification level to ensure that it remains in the window.

If you zoom in to too high of a magnification level, you can use the Zoom Out tool to zoom out again. To access the Zoom Out tool, press Option while you click the Zoom In tool in the Toolbox or press ⌘-Option-Spacebar. Clicking with the Zoom Out tool reduces the magnification level to the next lowest level. You can zoom out to 6.25%, or 1/16 actual size.

When you use the Zoom tools, you change the size of everything in the document, not just the illustration. You change the size of all paths, objects, the Artboard, the Pasteboard, and the Page Setup boundaries relative to the current magnification level. However, the points and paths retain their shape and thickness at all times.

If you need to zoom in quite a bit, you can zoom in more easily by using the Zoom In tool to draw a marquee (by clicking and dragging diagonally) around the objects that you want to magnify. The area that is surrounded

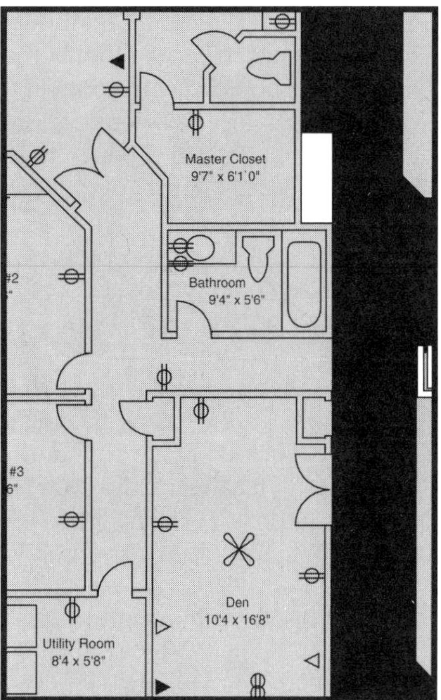

Figure 5-4: Zooming in to a certain area in the original image (left) results in the magnification and placement of the image on the right.

will magnify as much as possible so that everything inside the box just fits in the window that you have open, as shown in Figure 5-4. Dragging a box with the Zoom Out tool does nothing special; it works the same as if you had just clicked with the Zoom Out tool.

You can move a zoom marquee around *while you're drawing it* by pressing the Spacebar after you've drawn the marquee but before you release the mouse button.

Other Zooming Techniques

You also can zoom in and zoom out by using commands in the View menu. Choose View⇨Zoom In (⌘-]) to zoom in one level at a time until the magnification level is 1600%. The Zoom In feature zooms from the center out. Choose View⇨Zoom Out (⌘-[) to zoom out one level at a time until the magnification level is 6.25%.

You can use two different methods to automatically zoom to 100%. The first method is to double-click the Zoom tool in the Toolbox. This action changes the view to 100% instantly. A better way to zoom in to 100% is to choose View⇨ Actual Size (⌘-H), which not only changes the magnification level to 100% but also centers the page. At this view, an 8.5 x 11-inch piece of paper should fit squarely over an 8.5-x 11-inch document on your Illustrator screen. The accuracy of the fit depends on the pixels-per-inch of your monitor.

Choosing Actual Size also centers the document in your window (this is unlike double-clicking the Zoom tool, which resizes the page to 100% but brings the current center at the smaller or larger size to the center when resizing).

You can choose from two different methods to change the document view to the Fit in Window size. Fit in Window instantly changes the magnification level of the document so that the entire Artboard (not necessarily the artwork, if it isn't located on the page) fits in the window and is centered in it. One way to automatically change to the Fit in Window view is to choose View⇨Fit in Window (⌘-M). Another way is to double-click the Hand tool.

You can instantly zoom out to 6.25% by holding down Option while you double-click the Zoom tool. To instantly zoom in to 1600%, draw a tiny marquee with the Zoom In tool. At actual size, the marquee must be less than $^1/_2$ x $^1/_2$ inches for the magnification level to go instantly to 1600%. It may be necessary to draw more than one marquee if the current magnification level is less than 100%.

You can never undo any type of magnification level change. Choosing Edit⇨Undo after zooming will undo the last change you made to the document before you changed the magnification level.

Using the Scroll Bars

Sometimes after you zoom in to a high magnification, part of the drawing that you want to see is outside the window area. Instead of zooming in and out, you can use one of two different scrolling techniques to move around inside the document.

The scroll bar on the right side of the document window controls where you are vertically in the document. Clicking the up arrow displays what is above the window's boundaries by pushing everything in the window *down* in little increments. Clicking the down arrow displays what is below the window's boundaries by pushing the document *up* in little increments. Dragging the little elevator box up displays what is above the window's boundaries proportionately by whatever distance that you drag. Dragging the little elevator box down displays what is below the window's boundaries proportionately by whatever distance that you drag. Clicking on the gray bar above the little elevator box between the arrows displays what is above the window's boundaries in big chunks. Clicking on the gray bar below the little elevator box between the arrows displays what is below the window's boundaries in big chunks.

The gray area of the right scroll bar is proportionate to the size of the Pasteboard. If the little elevator box is at the top of the scroll bar, then you are viewing the top edge of the 120" x 120" Pasteboard. If it is centered, you are viewing the vertical center of the Pasteboard.

The scroll bar on the bottom of the document window controls where you are in the document horizontally. Clicking the left arrow displays what is to the left of the window's boundaries by pushing everything in the window *right* in little increments. Clicking on the right arrow displays what is to the right of the window's boundaries by pushing the document *left* in little increments. Dragging the little elevator box left displays what is left of the window's boundaries by whatever distance proportionately that you drag. Dragging the little *elevator box* right displays what is to the right of the window boundaries by whatever distance proportionately that you drag. Clicking on the gray bar between the arrows that is left of the little elevator box displays what is to the left of the window's boundaries in big chunks. Clicking on the gray bar between the arrows that is right of the little elevator box displays what is to the right of the window's boundaries in big chunks.

Scrolling with the Hand Tool

The Hand tool improves upon the scroll bars. Instead of being limited to only horizontal and vertical movement, you can use the Hand tool to scroll diagonally as well. It is especially useful for finding your way around a document when you are at a high magnification level. The higher the magnification level, the more you will end up using the Hand tool.

To use the Hand tool, either select it in the Toolbox or press the Spacebar. (If you are currently using the Type tool, press ⌘-Spacebar and then release ⌘, keeping the Spacebar pressed.) Clicking and dragging the page will move the document around inside the document window.

When you click with the document, be sure to click on the side that you want to see. Clicking at the top of the document and dragging down enables you to scroll down through almost an entire document at a height of one window. Clicking in the center and dragging enables you to scroll through only half a window size at a time. If the window of the document does not take up the entire screen space, you can continue to drag right off the window into the empty screen space. Just be sure that you first click within the document that you want to scroll.

The best thing about the Hand tool is that it works *live.* As you drag, the document moves under "your Hand." If you don't like where it is going, you can drag it back, still live. The second best thing is that to access it requires only one keystroke, a press of the spacebar.

You cannot use Undo (⌘-Z) to reverse scrolling that you have done with the scroll bars and the Hand tool.

Artwork Mode Versus Preview Mode

In the old days, everyone worked in Artwork mode. You could occasionally check work in progress to see what the illustration would look like by switching to Preview mode. Usually the preview was not quite what you had in mind while you were in Artwork mode, so it was back to Artwork mode to fix everything, and then to Preview again to check....

Illustrator 6 enables you to work in both Artwork and Preview modes. The mode that you are in when documents are printing does not matter. Illustrator will Fill and Stroke all paths and objects with the colors that are defined in the document, even if the document is in Artwork mode and those colors aren't visible. Saving the document while you are in Artwork mode will not affect anything in the document, but the next time you open it, it will be in Artwork mode. The same thing applies to Preview and Preview Selection modes: Whatever mode you are in will be saved with the artwork.

You cannot undo a Preview or Artwork mode change (going from Preview Selection to Artwork, for example). If you make a Preview or Artwork mode change and then close your document, Illustrator will ask you if you want to save changes, which in this case only refers to the view change.

Artwork (Only) Mode

To change the current document to Artwork mode, choose View⇨Artwork (⌘-E). In Artwork mode, the illustration will disappear and be replaced on-screen by outlines of all the Filled and Stroked paths. Text that has yet to be converted into outlines will look fine, although it will always be black. Depending on your choice in the Document Setup dialog box (choose File⇨Document Setup or press ⌘-Shift-D), a placed image will be displayed as a box with an *X* in it (if Show placed images is not checked) or as a black-and-white-only image, surrounded by a box with an *X* in it (if Show placed images is checked).

Working with a drawing in Artwork mode can be significantly faster than working with it in Preview mode. In more complex drawings, the difference between Artwork mode and Preview mode is significant; on very slow computers, working in Preview mode is next to impossible.

Artwork mode enables you to see every path that isn't directly overlapping another path; in Preview mode, many paths can be hidden. In addition, invisible masks are normally visible as paths in Artwork mode.

Placed artwork will be displayed in Black and White only, and templates will be grayer than before. The main advantage to working in Artwork mode is the speed increase over Preview mode. The speed that you gain is even greater when the artwork contains gradients, patterns, placed artwork, and blends. In addition, you can select paths that were hidden by the Fills of other objects.

If you have installed a Plug-In called Artwork Speedup (originally located in the Separator & Utilities folder), your Anchor Points, Control Handles points, and Control Handle Lines will be black in Artwork mode.

Artwork mode can take some getting used to. To select paths in Artwork mode, you must click the paths or draw a marquee across them.

Artwork mode can be better than Preview because it's faster, and also because your brain can learn to know what the drawing looks like from seeing just the outlines, which show *all* of the paths, including masks (masking paths cannot be viewed in Preview).

Preview Mode

Choosing View⇨Preview (⌘-Y) changes the view to Preview mode. In Preview mode, the document looks just the way it will look when you print it...sort of. Patterns in strokes and patterns in type show as gray areas, and you can't view overprinting.

Artwork Shmartwork

Farrah: You know how you keep saying artwork mode is so wonderful?

Toulouse: Well, it is.

Farrah: Then how come I still can't select certain paths?

Toulouse: Can you see the path you want to select?

Farrah: Sure, it's right next to the path that I keep selecting accidentally.

Toulouse: There's a couple things you can do.

Farrah: Great. And number one is....

Toulouse: First, you could zoom in really close, so the paths appear further apart. This allows for easier selecting.

Farrah: Makes sense. What if I don't feel like zooming in?

Toulouse: You know, I'm really not that surprised that you got dumped by the "fall guy."

Farrah: I dumped "him" you know.

(continued)

(continued)

Toulouse: Yeah, I can see that. Anyway, you could also select the path that keeps being selected and then press Shift and drag a marquee around both paths. That'll select the unselected path and deselect the selected path.

Farrah: That's it?

Toulouse: Since you asked, you could also lock the path you keep selecting, then the next click would select the other path.

In Preview mode, the color that you see on the screen represents only marginally what the actual output will be because of the differences between the way computer monitors work (red, green, and blue colors — the more of each color, the brighter each pixel will appear) and the way printing works (Cyan, Magenta, Yellow, and Black colors — the more of each color, the darker each area will appear). Monitor manufacturers make a number of calibration tools that decrease the difference between what you see on the monitor and the actual output. You can also use software solutions. One software solution, CIE calibration, is right in Adobe Illustrator (choose File⇨Preferences⇨Color Matching).

In Preview mode, you can see which objects overlap, which objects are in front and in back, where gradations begin and end, and how patterns are set up.

Sometimes previewing complex drawings on-screen can take a long time. Usually this problem occurs when you are displaying paths with patterns or a great number of blends. To stop an illustration from being redrawn in Preview mode, press ⌘-period to change the document to Artwork mode. If the redrawing has been completed before you press ⌘-period, everything will be selected. Objects that were unselected will be selected. This can be especially frustrating when you have spent a good deal of time selecting certain objects, but you didn't group these objects together. The selection or deselection of objects cannot be undone.

Preview Selection Mode

To change to Preview Selection mode, choose View⇨Preview Selection (⌘-Option-Y) to display all selected objects in Preview mode and all unselected objects in Artwork mode. Figure 5-5 shows an illustration in Preview Selection mode.

Figure 5-5: An image in Preview Selection mode

The Preview Selection mode can be useful in a complex illustration when you need to adjust a few object colors and want to see the results without waiting a long time. You can cancel redrawing in progress and return to Artwork mode by pressing ⌘-period. You can even create new paths and adjust existing ones while in Preview Selection mode.

Combining Artwork and Preview Modes

Using the Layers palette, you can easily combine Artwork and Preview or Artwork and Preview Selection modes. You can force individual layers to display in Preview mode while other layers remain in Artwork mode. This feature can be useful when you have a layer with a placed image, gradients, or patterns (or all three!) that would normally slow down the work flow. You can place those images on their own layer and set that layer to Artwork mode.

You also can view the same artwork in both Preview mode and Artwork mode at the same time by creating a new window for the current document. Choose Window⇨New Window to create a window that is the same size as the original window. You can manipulate these two windows so that they are next to each other, and each window can have different viewing characteristics. One window can be in Preview mode, and the other one can be in Artwork mode. One window can be at Fit in Window size, and you can zoom the other to any percentage.

Using multiple windows to show Artwork and Preview modes of the same drawing simultaneously was used mainly when Illustrator did not enable artists to edit and create in Preview mode. This function is no longer as helpful as it was before, but you can still use it to preview an illustration when you want to select artwork that is hidden by Fills and Strokes of other artwork in Preview mode. In addition, two windows can be used for viewing the entire artwork at a small size, while editing a blown up version in another.

Now You See It

Illustrator also provides options that enable you to show and hide various parts of an illustration:

- **Show Template** (choose View⇨Show Template) shows the document's template if it has one. When the template is showing, this menu item changes to Hide Template. If a template was hidden the last time you saved the document, it will be hidden the next time you open the document. If a template was showing when you saved the document, it will be visible the next time you open the document as well.

- **Show Rulers** (choose View⇨Show Rulers or press ⌘-R) displays rulers (in the current measurement system) on the right side of the document and on the bottom of the document window. By default, all rulers measure up and to the right from the lower-left corner of the Artboard.

  If you're confused about why the rulers in Illustrator are on the right side of the document window — but they measure up from the lower-left corner — you're not alone. Undoubtedly the Adobe engineers themselves are confused on this topic, so they set up the rulers this way to confuse the general public.

  To change the measurement system that is displayed on the rulers, choose File⇨Document Setup (⌘-Shift-D) and select the new measurement system. A quick way to instantly change ruler unit measurement systems is by pressing ⌘-Ctrl-U, which cycles through the three measurement systems.

  To change the origin of the rulers (0 across, 0 up), drag from the box where the rulers meet to the new intersection point.

Pressing ⌘-R toggles between showing and hiding rulers. If rulers are showing, the menu item is Hide Rulers. If rulers are displayed when you save the document, they will be displayed the next time you open it. If rulers are not showing when you save the document, the rulers will be hidden the next time you open the document.

- **Show Page Tiling** (choose View⇨Show Page Tiling) shows the outlines of the page guides from the Page Setup and Document Setup dialog boxes. When Page Tiling is visible, the menu item changes to Hide Page Tiling. The condition of Page Tiling is saved with the file.
- **Hide Edges** (choose View⇨Hide Edges or press ⌘-Shift-H) does not show paths, Anchor Points, Control Handles, or Control Handle Lines when it is selected in Preview mode and does not show Anchor Points, Control Handles, or Control Handle Lines in Artwork mode. When edges are hidden, the menu item reads Show Edges. Pressing ⌘-Shift-H toggles between showing and hiding edges. Edges are always visible when you open a file, regardless of whether they were visible or hidden when you saved it.

  Be careful to note when you have this feature enabled, as it can appear to the unwary that they are unable to select anything just because Hide Edges has been activated.
- **Show Guides** (choose View⇨Show Guides) shows all guides in your artwork, whether you created them by using rulers or by transforming paths into guides. Show Guides does not show guides that were hidden with the Hide (⌘-3) command. The alternate, Hide Guides, hides all guides in the document. Whether you save a document with guides visible or hidden, they are always visible when you open a document.

Remember when this function is on so that you don't unwittingly pull guide after guide onto your document, wondering why they don't show up. Or you may choose Make Guides and wonder if you accidentally chose Hide instead because paths changed into guides when Hide Guides is on simply disappear.

Using Custom Views

Illustrator has a special feature, called *custom views,* that enables you to save special views of an illustration. Custom views contain view information, including magnification, location, and whether the illustration is in Artwork or Preview mode. If you have various layers in Preview mode and others in Artwork mode, custom views can also save that information. However, custom views do not record whether templates, rulers, page tiling, edges, or guides are showing or hidden.

To create a new view, set up the document in the way that you would like to save the view. Then choose View➪New View (⌘-Ctrl-V) and name the view in the New View dialog box. Each of the first 10 views that you create is given a key command of ⌘-Ctrl-1, ⌘-Ctrl-2, and so on. You can create up to 25 custom views, but the last 15 will not have a key command. Custom views are saved with a document as long as you save it in Adobe Illustrator 5.x or Illustrator 6 format.

If you find yourself continuously going to a certain part of a document, zooming in or out, and changing back and forth between Preview and Artwork mode, that document is a prime candidate for creating custom views. Custom views are helpful when you show clients artwork that you created in Illustrator. Instead of fumbling around in the client's presence, you can, for example, instantly show the detail in a logo if you have preset the zoom factor and position and saved the image in a custom view.

The Window Menu

The Window menu contains the various options for displaying the different palettes available in Illustrator, as well as any documents that are currently open:

- **New Window** creates a new window that displays the current document, usually at a different viewing percentage or in a different mode. This new window will initially be the same size and have the same viewing options as the existing, frontmost window, but the viewing options can be changed without affecting the other window.
- **Hide/Show Toolbox** (⌘-Ctrl-T) hides the Toolbox from view. If the Toolbox is hidden, this command will read Show Toolbox.
- **Hide/Show Layers** (⌘-Ctrl-L) hides the Layers palette from view. If the Layers palette is hidden, this command will read Show Layers.
- **Hide/Show Info** (⌘-Ctrl-I) hides the Info palette from view. If the Info palette is hidden, this command will read Show Info. The Info palette appears automatically when the Measure tool is used.
- **Hide/Show Paint Style** (⌘-I) hides the Paint Style palette from view. If the Paint Style palette is hidden, this command will read Show Paint Style.
- **Hide/Show Gradient** hides the Gradient palette from view. If the Gradient palette is hidden, this command will read Show Gradient. The Gradient palette also appears automatically when the Gradient tool is clicked or if a gradient in the Paint Style box is double-clicked.

- **Hide/Show Character** (⌘-T) hides the Character palette from view. If the Character palette is hidden, this command will read Show Character. If any of the options for type are chosen that have to be entered through the keyboard (that is, leading, size, font, and so on), then the Character palette appears.
- **Hide/Show Paragraph** (⌘-Shift-P) hides the Paragraph palette from view. If the Paragraph palette is hidden, this command will read Show Paragraph.
- **Hide/Show Tab Ruler** (⌘-Shift-T) shows the Tab Ruler palette if it is hidden.
- **Hide/Show Align** hides the Align palette if it is displayed. If the Align palette is hidden, this command will read Show Align.
- **Hide/Show Shortcuts** hides the shortcuts palette if it is displayed. If the Shortcuts palette is hidden, this command will read Show Shortcuts.
- **Hide/Show Plug-In Tools** will hide the Plug-In Tools palette. If the Plug-In Tools palette is hidden, this command will read Show Plug-In tools.
- **Hide/Show Control Palette** will hide the Control palette. If the Control palette is hidden, this command will read Show Control Palette.
- The **Online Guide** submenu provides several options for online help.
- **Untitled Art 1** and all other titles below this dotted line are referencing the open Illustrator documents and duplicate document windows. A check mark appears in front of the title of the active document or window.

Managing Files

Controlling how files are saved in Illustrator can be a little daunting at first. Although you have many different options for saving file types, you need to follow one basic rule: Save as an EPS with a color preview if you are going to take the file into other applications. This type of file is not the smallest file type, but it is compatible with most software.

Opening files in Illustrator is fairly simple. Illustrator can open and manipulate only files that were created in Illustrator, Streamline, or Dimensions and files that were saved in an Illustrator format. It can open PICT files, but they will always be black-and-white bitmapped templates.

Files placed in Illustrator can be almost any raster file format. PostScript files that are printed to disk usually can't be placed in Illustrator.

Other important file issues: Illustrator opens pixel files as a new Illustrator document with the pixels inside. Arbitrary PostScript level one files can be opened with the built-in PostScript Interpreter. Illustrator files can now be saved directly into pixel formats.

The Unopenable File

Bosley: Well, I did as you asked, saving and all. But now I'm screwed.

Toulouse: You forgot the name of the file?

Bosley: No, I'm getting an error, something about operators making illegal calls to Texas.

Toulouse: Ah, the ole Illegal Operand 'TZ' error.

Bosley: That's it. It won't let me open my document.

Toulouse: There's a way to fix that.

Bosley: Cool. What causes it?

Toulouse: If you use a certain symbol in the first font after the Symbol font, you'll get this error. Usually the degree sign.

Bosley: Ick. But I can fix it, right?

Toulouse: Sure. Open the Illustrator document in a word processor.

Bosley: I can do that?

Toulouse: Yes, but you want to open it as a text file, not as a graphic.

Bosley: Done. What a mess.

Toulouse: Find the line: "/_Symbol_/Symbol 0 0 0 TZ" and add a "[" to the beginning of the line so it looks like this: "[/_Symbol_/Symbol 0 0 0 TZ." Save the document and open it in Illustrator. Voila.

Saving Files

Saving Illustrator documents is the most important Illustrator activity you do. Saving often prevents damage to your computer — by keeping you from picking it up and sending it flying across the room. Saving often makes your life less stressful, and backing up your saved files helps you sleep better.

The amount of space that a saved Illustrator file takes up on the hard drive depends on two things: the complexity of the drawing and the Preview option (if any) that you've selected. Tiny Illustrator files take up the smallest amount, about 10K or so. The biggest illustrations are limited only by your storage space, but they can regularly exceed 2MB. As a practice, when you are working on a drawing, save it to the hard drive, not to a floppy disk or a removable cartridge. Hard drives are faster and much more reliable. If you need to place a file on a floppy disk or Syquest cartridge, copy it there in the Finder by dragging the icon of the file from the hard drive to the disk or cartridge.

You should only save the file to another disk if you run out of room on the hard drive. To ensure that you never run out of room, always keep at least 10 percent of the hard drive space free. A hard drive that is too full can cause many problems that are more serious than being unable to save a file.

To save a file, choose File⇨Save (⌘-S). If you have previously saved the file, then updating the existing file with the changes that you have made will take just a fraction of a second. If you have not yet saved the file, the Save As dialog box will appear, as shown in Figure 5-6.

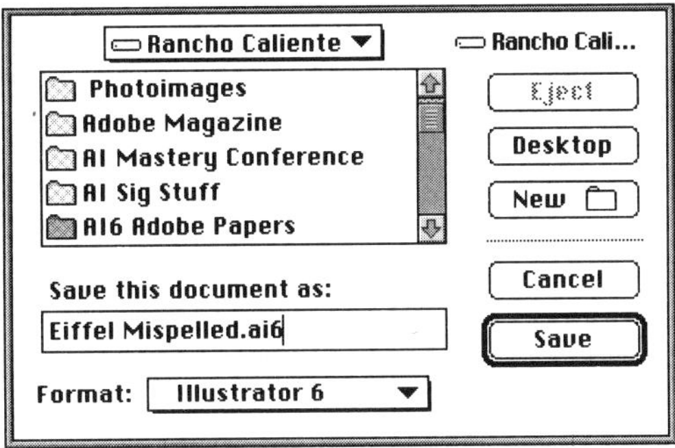

Figure 5-6: The Save As dialog box

STEPS: Saving Illustrator Documents

Step 1. Decide how you are going to save the file. Choose the correct Preview and Compatibility options for the file. (See the descriptions in the "EPS Preview Options" and "Compatibility Options" sections, later in this chapter.)

Step 2. Decide where you are going to save the file and make sure that the name of the folder that you want to save it in is at the top of the file list window. Saving your working files in a location other than the Illustrator folder is a good habit. Otherwise, you can have trouble figuring out which files are yours, which files are tutorial files, and so on.

Step 3. Name the file something distinctive so that if you look for it six months from now you will recognize it. Avoid using *Untitled Art 1, Untitled Art 2,* and so on. The names are nondescriptive, and besides, you can too easily accidentally replace the file at a later date with a file of the same name. For the same reasons, do not use *Document 1, Document 2,* and so on (QuarkXPress's default names). Also avoid using *Test1* (if I had a nickel for every *Test1* or *Test2* I've seen on people's hard drives, I'd have…well, I'd have a lot of nickels), *stuff, #$*&!!* (insert your favorite four-letter word here), *picture, drawing,* or your first name. A file name can have up to 32 characters, and you can use all the letters, numbers, and special characters (except a colon [:]), so make the most of them and *describe* the file.

When Should I Save?

You really can't save too often. Whenever I put off saving for "just a few minutes," that's when the system locks up, crashes, or gives me a Type 1 error. Depending on your work habits, you may need to save more frequently than other people do. Here are some golden rules about when to save:

- Save as soon as you create a new file. Get it out of the way. The toughest part of saving is deciding how and where you are going to save the file and naming it. If you get those things out of the way in the beginning, pressing ⌘-S later is fairly painless.
- Save before you print. For some reason, PrintMonitor and PostScript errors can crash a system faster than almost anything else.
- Save before you switch to another application. Jostling stuff around in a computer's RAM is an open invitation for the whole system to poop out.
- Save right after you do something that you never want to have to do again — such as getting the kerning "just right" on a logo or matching all of the colors in your gradients so that they meet seamlessly.
- Save after you use a filter that takes more than a few seconds to complete.
- Save before you create a new document or go to another document.
- Save before you go to any Apple menu item, including the Chooser and Control Panels folder (which are really parts of the Finder, another application).
- Save at least every 15 minutes.

The Save As Command

The Save As command (File⇨Save As) enables you to save multiple versions of the document at different stages of progress. If you choose Save As and do not rename the file or change the save location, you will be prompted to replace the existing file. If you choose Replace, the file that you saved before will be erased and replaced with the new file that you are saving. Most disk and trash recovery utilities cannot recover a file that you delete this way.

The Save As command is also useful for changing the Preview and Compatibility options (which are described in the "EPS Preview Options" and "Compatibility Options" sections, later in this chapter). If you have saved in Omit Header Preview and want to change to Color Preview, choose File⇨Save As, don't change the file name or file location, and choose Color from the Preview pop-up menu.

Reverting to the Last Saved Version

Choosing File⇨Revert To Saved is an option that automatically closes the document and opens the last saved version of it. This option will be grayed out if the file has not been saved yet. When it is selected, a dialog box appears, asking you to confirm that you *do* want to revert to the last saved version of the document.

A Revert To Saved action cannot be undone, and you won't be able to redo anything you've done up to that point with the document.

File Types

You can save Illustrator 6 files in several ways. Actually, you can save them in almost 30 different formats…though some formats just don't make any sense.

Saving an Illustrator file with the wrong options can dramatically affect whether that file can be opened or placed in other software, as well as what features are included with the file when it is reopened in Illustrator. For example, saving the file as anything but EPS makes it virtually useless to every piece of software but Illustrator. Saving a document as an older version of Illustrator may alter the document if the older version was missing features you used in your document.

As a rule, unless you're going to take your Illustrator document into another program, you can save it as Illustrator 6 without any problems. This will keep the file size down, and make saving and opening the file much quicker.

Compatibility Options

Illustrator is one of the few software programs that is almost fully backwards compatible. If you open a file in Illustrator 88 that you created in Illustrator 6, it looks almost exactly the same. Most software packages are forward compatible for one major version, but Illustrator is a novelty in that you can open an Illustrator 1.1 file in Version 6 of the software, even though more than seven years passed between those product versions.

There are a number of reasons to save illustrations in older versions of Illustrator. The following list provides information about saving files in each version:

- **Illustrator 6** saves the file in the Illustrator 6 format. The major file structure difference between Illustrator 6 and Illustrator 5.x is Illustrator 6's ability to import almost any type of raster image, while 5.x only supported EPS images. Other, not-so-obvious changes have to do with advanced object "labels" that plug-in developers use to achieve all sorts of effects.
- **Illustrator 5** saves the file in the Illustrator 5 format, which includes both Illustrator 5.0 and 5.5. The features added to Version 5.5 do not affect file content. Thus, files created in Version 5.5 have the same structure as files created in Version 5.0.
- **Illustrator 4** saves the file in the Illustrator 4 format, which is a version that is available only for Windows users. Saving a file in the Illustrator 4 format ensures that Illustrator 4 for Windows will open Illustrator files. Gradients, views, layers, and custom Artboard sizes are not supported by the Illustrator 4 format. Technically speaking, there is really no difference between the Illustrator 3 and 4 formats.
- **Illustrator 3** saves the file in the Illustrator 3 format, which is useful not only for taking files into the Illustrator 3 program, but also for taking Illustrator files into FreeHand. The Illustrator 3 format transforms gradients into masks with blends, which is useful when you want to open Illustrator files in Photoshop (Photoshop normally doesn't accept gradients) or other software that doesn't like Illustrator's use of blends. In fact, you can use the Illustrator 3 format for a lot of "cheating" — doing things that Illustrator normally doesn't enable you to do. For example, technically, you can't put gradients or masks into patterns. But if you save a gradient as an Illustrator 3 file and reopen it in Illustrator 6, the gradient becomes a blend, which you *can* use in a pattern. Also, FreeHand 5.x can import the Illustrator 5 format.
- **Illustrator 88** saves the file in the Illustrator 88 format, which, for about four years (1988 to 1991), was *the* Illustrator standard. Much clip art has been created and saved in the Illustrator 88 format. The main problem with saving in the Illustrator 88 format is that type changes occurred between Illustrator 88 and Illustrator 3. Illustrator 88 cannot handle type on a curve (called path type which it turns into individual segments), and it doesn't deal correctly with compound paths (type converted to outlines are made up of several compound paths, one for each character).
- **Illustrator 1.1** saves the file in the oldest of Adobe Illustrator formats, Version 1.1. Saving in the Illustrator 1.1 format is useful when you want to take files into older versions of Freehand and many other older draw programs. Illustrator 1.1 format doesn't support custom colors or masks.

Saving as EPS

If you *do* have to place your Illustrator document in another program, like QuarkXPress, you'll need to save the file as EPS. After you select the EPS option in the Save As box and name the file, clicking the Save button brings up yet another dialog box, shown in Figure 5-7.

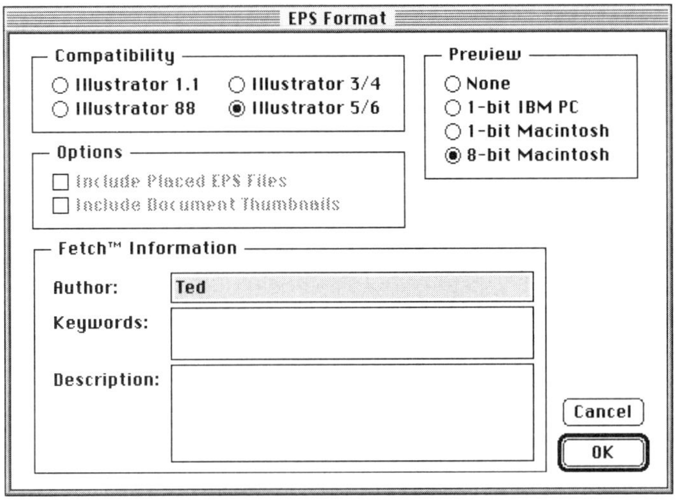

Figure 5-7: The EPS Format dialog box

EPS Format
Compatibility
Illustrator 1.1
Illustrator 3/4
Illustrator 88
Illustrator 5/6
Preview
None
1-bit IBM PC
1-bit Macintosh
8-bit Macintosh
Options
Include Placed EPS Files
Include Document Thumbnails
Fetch™ Information
Author: Ted
Keywords:
Description:
Cancel
OK

The multiple options that are available when saving a file as EPS are discussed in the following section.

EPS Preview Options

The following options in Illustrator 6 affect the way that other software programs see Illustrator files when they are saved as EPS files:

- **None** lets most software programs recognize the Illustrator document as an EPS file, but instead of viewing it in their software, you see a box with an *X* in it. Usually, this box is the same size as the illustration, includes any stray Anchor Points or Control Handles. The file will print fine from of other software.
- **1-bit Macintosh** saves the EPS file with a PICT file preview as part of the EPS file. A PICT image is embedded within the EPS file (technically, a PICT resource); you do not have two separate files. Page-layout and other software display this illustration in a black-and-white preview with no shades of gray in it. This file may

take up substantially more space than the Include EPSF Header file requires because of the PICT file. The larger the illustration measures, the more storage space the PICT file uses.

- **8-bit Macintosh** saves the file with a color preview that is an embedded PICT image. Page-layout and other software displays this file in 8-bit color (256 colors) when you place it in a document. An Illustrator file that you save with a color preview takes up more file space than a file saved with any other option.
- **1-bit IBM** saves the file with a preview for IBM systems. Page-layout or other software for PCs that can import EPS files can preview illustrations that you save with this option.

Saving Files in PDF Format

The PDF format option saves files in Adobe Acrobat-compatible *P*ortable *D*ocument *F*ormat. An Illustrator document saved as a PDF file will become a page when opened in Acrobat. Saving your Illustrator file this way removes several Illustrator attributes, like layers, gradients, patterns, and path type.

Acrobat Reader is free on most online services and is provided on the Illustrator 6 CD-ROM.

Opening and Closing Illustrator Files

You can open any Illustrator file from any version of Illustrator in Illustrator 6. Regardless of which Preview options you select, Illustrator 6 can still open the file. When you choose File⇨Open or press ⌘-O, the Open dialog box appears and asks you to find an Illustrator file. Find the file and double-click it to have it open into a document window on the screen.

To close the *active* Illustrator file, choose File⇨Close (⌘-W). The active document is the one that is in front of all other documents and has a title bar with lines on it and text in black. Nonactive documents don't display any lines in their title bar, and the text in the title bar is gray. Closing an Illustrator document does *not* "close" Illustrator; it continues running until you "Quit."

If you saved the file prior to closing it, it will just disappear. If you have modified the file since the last time you saved it, a box appears, asking whether you want to save changes before closing. If you press Return or Enter to save the file, it will be updated. If you have not saved the file at all, the Save As dialog box appears so that you can name the file, choose a location for it, and choose Preview and Compatibility options for the file. If you click the Don't Save button (⌘-D while the dialog box is showing), then any changes that you made to the document since you last saved it (or if you have never saved it, all the changes you made since you created it) are lost. Clicking Cancel (⌘-period) takes you back to the drawing, where you can continue to work on it.

Opening PICT Templates

You can bring any PICT image into Illustrator by simply opening it. Unfortunately, all PICT bitmapped images that are "opened" become templates, which cannot be printed. Instead, you can trace around them, either manually with the drawing tools or automatically with the Auto Trace tool. Only one template can be opened at a time. Templates are visible when you have selected the Show Template option in the View menu and hidden when you have selected the Hide Template option. Files that you save with Hide Template or Show Template will hide or show the template the next time the file is opened. Templates are discussed in more detail in Chapter 4.

EPS, TIFF, and Other Files

Files that you can place or import into Illustrator are EPS (*E*ncapsulated *P*ost*S*cript), TIFF (*T*agged *I*mage *F*ile *F*ormat), and most other bitmap file formats. To place files, you choose File⇨Place Art. A standard Open dialog box appears. Only files that can be placed or imported show up in the file window.

After you place art into Illustrator, you can transform it (move, scale, rotate, reflect, and shear it) in any way.

The quality of placed art is as good as the original; if the original file was bitmapped (created or saved in a paint program such as Photoshop), then the quality will lessen as the file is scaled up, and the quality will increase as the file is scaled down. If the file was in PostScript outline format (created in Illustrator or FreeHand, EPS only), then the quality will stay consistent as the file changes in size.

You can use placed raster images for tracing, similar to the way that you can use PICT images for tracing, except that the Auto Trace tool does not recognize EPS and will not automatically surround it. In addition, placed files usually have a 72-dpi preview, which can actually become a 144-dpi preview if the file is reduced to 50 percent of its imported size.

Illustrator shows placed art differently in Artwork mode and in Preview mode. In Artwork mode, placed art is in black and white, or just shows up as a box with an *X* inside of it.

When you save a document with placed art in it with a preview, you can link the placed art to Illustrator or include it in the Illustrator file. Normally, including the placed art within the Illustrator file is the better choice. This method prevents the two files from being separated; if you have one and not the other, you are out of luck. But you may want to link the file instead of including it for two reasons. First, placed art can be huge and may make your Illustrator file too large. Second, if you need to make changes to a placed art file that you have included in an Illustrator file that you have saved with a preview, you have to replace the placed art in the preview file with the new version. If you have linked the placed art, instead of including it, it is automatically updated when you make changes.

You may want to replace placed art with new versions or completely different artwork. Illustrator has made this process painless. If placed artwork is selected, a dialog box will appear asking if you would like to replace current artwork or place new artwork, not changing the selected artwork.

The really cool part about changing placed art this way is that if you have placed artwork that has been transformed, the artwork you exchange with it via the Place Art command will have the exact same transformation attributes! For example, if you scale down placed artwork to 50% and rotate it 45°, artwork that is exchanged with that artwork is also scaled down 50% and rotated 45°.

You can dim placed art by checking the Dim Placed Art checkbox from the Layer options on the Layers palette. If you dim placed art, then a ghost of the image appears instead of the solid image. This feature makes tracing placed art easy. Dimming placed art does not affect its printed output.

Placed EPS Options

Placed EPS images work differently than other types of raster images you can bring into Illustrator. The main difference is that EPS images are brought into Illustrator via the Place command in the File menu, rather than the Import⇨Art command.

Placed EPS Images can not have Photoshop-compatible filters applied to them, as can imported images.

Placed EPS images can be "dimmed" via the Layers palette.

Importing Styles

The ability to import styles from other documents can save you enormous amounts of time. Styles that you can import include gradients, patterns, custom colors, and graph designs. This feature is useful for maintaining consistency between illustrations that are related.

Different styles with the same name as styles in your current document get replaced with styles from the imported file. This can be a big problem if the currently open document has any paths with styles that are different in a document being imported. Import Styles cannot be undone, so Save before you use Import Styles. That way if there is a problem, you can close the file without saving and open it again, restoring the original styles. Another method is to change the names of all your styles to different names before importing other styles.

To import styles from another document, choose File⇨Import⇨Styles to see the Import Styles dialog box. In the dialog box, select the file from which you want to import styles. The styles that are different from the ones in your document will be imported.

You can use Import Styles to bring in Pantone Colors, Trumatch colors, and so on, by selecting files that include custom colors.

Publish and Subscribe

Publish and Subscribe is a convenient way to keep various elements in different documents "current" by updating affected documents when other related documents are changed.

The Edit menu contains the following Publish and Subscribe options:

- The **Publishing** option displays a category with four submenu items, all related to System 7's Publish and Subscribe feature. Publish and Subscribe allows certain users to publish documents that are subscribed to by others. As the Publisher changes its *edition*, the Subscriber receives updated information about that edition. You may neither publish nor subscribe text only, but you may publish and subscribe to entire type objects (such as a Area type or Path type).
- The **Create Publisher** option creates an edition file that other users can subscribe to (by choosing Subscribe in their application). The edition includes any selected objects at the time Create Publisher is chosen. After the edition is created, a light gray border appears around the edition's objects when one or more of those objects is selected. After you have created an edition using the Create Publisher command, it will be updated every time you save the file that contains the edition. An edition border is a fixed size and cannot be changed.
- The **Subscribe To** option lets your document subscribe to an edition. A dark gray border will appear around editions you have subscribed to if that edition is selected. Your document is updated instantly whenever the edition is updated, even if your document is open.
- The **Publisher Options** give you the ability to manually update the edition, even without saving your file. You can also choose to Unpublish your edition at this point.
- The **Show Borders** option always shows the borders of both the edition files you have published (light gray) and the edition files to which you have subscribed (darker gray).
- The **Hide Borders** option reverses the Show Borders option.

Document Info

You can use this feature in any document by choosing File⇨Document Info. A dialog box (shown in Figure 5-8) appears with a pop-up menu at the top.

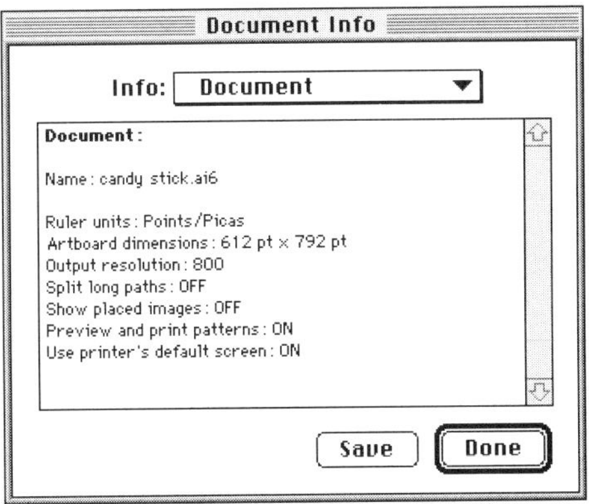

Figure 5-8: The Document Info dialog box

The pop-up menu consists of seven different ways to view information about the active document:

- The first option, **Document**, shows the document setup of the active document. All the relevant options from the Document Setup dialog box are shown, along with the name of the file.
- The second option is **Objects**, which lists how many paths, masks, compound paths, custom colors, patterns, gradients, fonts, and placed EPS artwork are used in the document. This can be used as a rudimentary guide to how long a file may take to print.

For instance, the puzzle pieces from the color insert (also available in Illustrator format on the CD-ROM) contain 4,394 paths, 6 masks, 141 compound paths, and 23 different gradients. These numbers give an indication that this file will take a bit of time to print. In fact, this file takes about 15 minutes to print to a low-end PostScript Level 2 printer at 300 dpi.

- The remaining options show the names of any enclosed custom colors, patterns, gradients, and fonts. The final option, **Placed Art**, lists not only the name of the placed art but the disk path that tells Illustrator where to find it.

If you have anything selected, the Document Info dialog box will contain only information about these selected objects.

At the bottom of the Document Info dialog box are two buttons: the Save button creates a TeachText format file with all eight categories of information about the document, while the Done button closes the dialog box.

TeachText format cannot be read in Illustrator. To view the saved Document Info file, you must double-click the file name or open it within a word processor.

Summary

- When you launch Illustrator, a new document automatically appears.
- New documents are based on the start-up file size and attributes, and are created as soon as you choose New Document from the File menu.
- The current document setup can be modified in the Document Setup dialog box, accessed by pressing ⌘-Shift-D or by choosing File⇨Document Setup.
- You can automatically use the current Page Setup as your artwork size by selecting the "Use Page Setup" checkbox in the Document Setup dialog box.
- Path splitting is useful if you have several long paths, and are getting PostScript Limitcheck errors when printing.
- You can quickly change ruler measurement systems by pressing ⌘-Ctrl-U to cycle through the Inches, Points/Picas, and Centimeters options.
- Zoom in by pressing ⌘-Spacebar to access the Zoom In tool, and then dragging a marquee around the area you wish to zoom into.
- You can zoom out rapidly by pressing ⌘-Option-Spacebar.
- Pan around your document by pressing Spacebar to access the Hand tool and then dragging the document around within its window.
- Artwork mode can be useful when drawing a complex piece of artwork, enabling Illustrator to operate quicker than in Preview mode, and letting you select points and paths that might have otherwise been obscured.
- Preview Selection mode is handy for when you'd like to see just a portion of your illustration without having to wait for the entire document to redraw.
- Using various options in the View menu, you can specify which elements you'd like to view and which ones you'd like to hide.
- The Window menu enables you to show and hide all the different palettes in Illustrator, as well as letting you arrange document windows.
- Unless you'll be taking files into another application, save them as Illustrator 6 files.
- If you'll be taking files into another application, you probably want to save them as EPS, with an 8-bit preview.
- You can place any EPS image, bitmap or vector, by using the Place Art command, located in the File menu.
- Bitmap formats other than EPS have to be brought into Illustrator through the Import⇨Art command.

Customizing Illustrator

6

CHAPTER

In This Chapter

- Personalizing Illustrator
- Modifying the Adobe Illustrator Startup file
- Setting preferences that affect all documents
- Setting document-specific preferences

Under the Apple menu (), you'll find a few useful items of information.

About Adobe Illustrator displays a dialog box with the user information and scrolling credits for everyone, absolutely everyone, who had any teeny tiny little thing to do with Illustrator. If nothing else, you'll become aware of the large numbers of people that are involved in creating the software.

About Plug-Ins displays a submenu that lists all the installed Plug-Ins. Choosing one of the items in the Plug-Ins submenu displays who made the Plug-In, and occasionally some useful or interesting information about that Plug-In.

About this Macintosh (in the Finder, while Illustrator is running) displays how much memory is allocated to Illustrator, and how much Illustrator is actually using of that allocated amount.

You can also determine how much memory is used and is currently available by clicking on the Info bar at the lower left of the Document window and selecting the Free Memory option from the pop-up menu. This will display how much memory is free both in megabytes and as a percentage of the total amount of memory.

Preferences

No two illustrators work the same. To accommodate the vast differences in styles, techniques, and habits, Illustrator provides many settings that each user can change to personalize the software.

Illustrator provides four major ways to change preferences. The most dramatic and difficult changes are to a small file called Adobe Illustrator Startup. The start-up file changes how new documents appear and which custom colors, patterns, and gradients are available.

You can also control how Illustrator works by accessing the Preferences submenu (choose File⇨Preferences). You make most of these changes in the General Preferences dialog box, which you access by choosing File⇨Preferences⇨General (⌘-K).

A third way to make changes is by changing preferences relative to each document. You usually make these changes in the Document Setup dialog box, but a few other options are available. See Chapter 5 for more information on document-specific preferences.

The fourth way that you can customize preferences happens pretty much automatically. When you quit Illustrator, it remembers many of the current settings until the next time you run it. These settings include palette placements and values in Toolbox settings.

Illustrator has a few settings that you cannot customize. These features can really get under your skin because most of them seem like things that you should be able to customize. See the "Things You Can't Customize" section later in this chapter for a list of these settings.

Modifying the Start-Up File

When you first run Illustrator, the program looks to the Illustrator start-up file to check a number of preferences. Those preferences include window size and placement, as well as custom colors, gradients, patterns, zoom levels, tiling options, and graph designs.

New documents (like the one created automatically when you first run the program) have all the attributes of the start-up file. Opened documents have all the gradients, custom colors, patterns, and graph designs of the start-up file.

STEPS: Changing the Start-Up File

Step 1. Open the start-up file. The start-up file, called Adobe Illustrator Startup, is located in the Plug-Ins folder in the Adobe Illustrator folder. The file is an Adobe Illustrator 6 document, so double-clicking the file opens Illustrator, as well.

Step 2. Figure 6-1 shows what the file looks like. Each square in the document contains a pattern, gradient, custom color, or color swatch square. Remove any square that contains patterns, gradients, or custom colors that you don't use. Then go to the Pattern dialog box, Gradient palette, and Custom Colors dialog box and delete those same patterns, gradients, and colors.

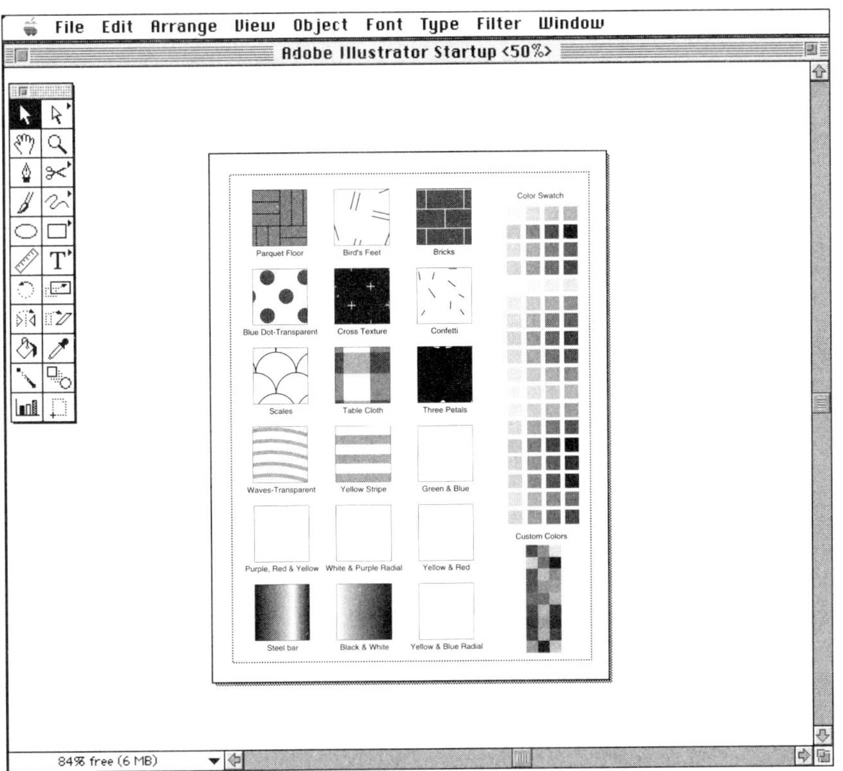

Figure 6-1: The Adobe Illustrator Startup document

If you remove a pattern, go to the Pattern dialog box (choose Object⇨Pattern) and delete the pattern. Do the same for gradients and custom colors and save the file.

If you delete a pattern, custom color, or gradient from the start-up file, it is gone. Kaput. The only way to get it back is to replace the start-up file from the original disks or CD-ROM.

Step 3. To add something to the start-up file, create a rectangle and fill it with a new pattern, custom color, or gradient. In order for a pattern, custom color, or gradient to appear for use in new documents, it has to be part of an object.

To add a graph design, create the graph design and apply it to a graph. Place the graph in the start-up file.

Step 4. To change the window size, just save the start-up file with the window size that you want new documents to have.

Step 5. To change the color swatches on the Paint Style palette, add, replace, or delete color swatches while the start-up file is open and then save the start-up file.

If you delete the Adobe Illustrator Startup file, most patterns, gradients, and custom colors will not be available until you create a new start-up file or place the original start-up file from the disks or CD-ROM in the Plug-Ins folder.

To check whether changes that you made in the start-up file will work, quit Illustrator and run the program again. You cannot tell whether the changes are in place until you quit and then reopen Illustrator.

You can change not only the window size of new documents, but also the viewing percentage. Most people like documents to fit in the window when it is created. For a 13-inch screen, use 50%; for a 16- or 17-inch screen, use 66%.

Changing General Preferences

General Preferences are preferences that affect the way the entire program works, regardless of which document you pull up. To alter application preferences, access the Preferences submenu (choose File⇨Preferences).

In most programs, "Preferences" is logically located on the Edit menu, not on the File menu. General Preferences, unlike everything else on the File menu, deals with the entire program rather than with a specific document.

The General Preferences Dialog Box

The General Preferences dialog box (choose File⇨Preferences⇨General or press ⌘-K) contains most of the "personalized" customizing options for Illustrator. The options in this box affect keyboard increments, measuring units, and the way that objects are drawn. These options are considered personalized options because they are specific to the way that each person uses the program. Few people have the same preference settings as others have (unless they never change the defaults). The General Preferences dialog box is shown in Figure 6-2.

General Preferences

Tool behavior
Constrain angle: 0 °
Corner radius: 12 pt
Freehand tolerance: 10 pixels
Auto Trace gap: 0 pixels
☒ Snap to point
☐ Transform pattern tiles
☐ Scale line weight
☒ Area select
☐ Use precise cursors

Keyboard increments
Cursor key: 1 pt
Size/leading: 2 pt
Baseline shift: 2 pt
Tracking: 20 /1000 em

Edit behavior
Undo levels: 10
☐ Paste remembers layers

Greek type limit: 6 pt
☐ Smart Punctuation

Ruler units: Points/Picas
Type units: Points/Picas

Cancel OK

Figure 6-2: The General Preferences dialog box

The Constrain Angle Option

The Constrain angle option controls the angle on which all objects are aligned. Rectangles are always drawn "flat," aligning themselves to the bottom, top, and sides of the document window. When you press the Shift key, lines that you draw with the Pen tool and objects that you move will align to the constrain angle, or 45°, 90°, 135°, or 180°, plus or minus this angle.

The constrain angle also affects how the four transformation tools transform objects. The Scale tool can be very hard to use when the constrain angle is not 0°, and the Shear tool becomes even more difficult to use than normal at different constrain angles.

Pressing Shift when you are using the Rotate tool constrains the rotational angle to 45° increments added to the constrain angle. Chapter 7 discusses the Rotate tool and other transformational tools.

In Illustrator, 0° is a horizontal line, and 90° is a vertical line. Figure 6-3 shows Illustrator angles.

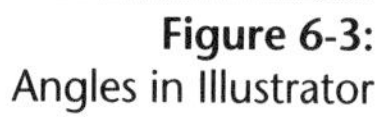
Figure 6-3: Angles in Illustrator

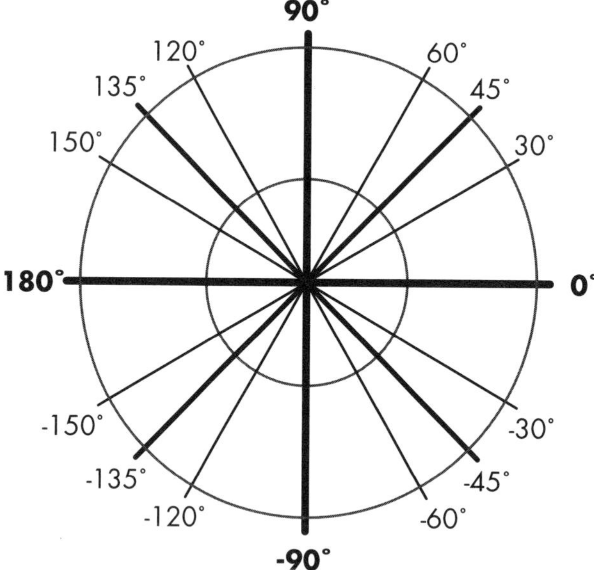

If you set the constrain angle at 20°, objects are constrained to movements of 20°, 65°, 110°, 155°, and 200°. Constrain angles of 90°, 180°, and –90° (270°) affect only type, patterns, gradients, and graphs; everything else works normally.

When Option-copying objects, you can use the Shift key in conjunction with a constrain angle to duplicate objects at a specific angle. Option-copy means press the Option key while dragging an object and then release the mouse button before releasing the Option key to produce a duplicate of the object at the new location.

The Corner Radius Option

The Corner radius option affects the size of the curved corners on a rounded rectangle. For a complete explanation of the corner radius and rounded rectangles, see Chapter 2.

The Corner radius value changes each time you enter a new value in the Rectangle dialog box. This dialog box appears when you click the Rectangle or Rounded Rectangle tools without dragging in a document. If, for example, you create one rounded rectangle with a rounded-corner radius of 24 points, all rounded rectangles that you create from that point forward will have a radius of 24 points. The only ways to change the corner radius are to click a rectangle tool without dragging in a document and then enter a new value in the Rectangle dialog box or to enter a new value in the Corner radius text field in the General Preferences dialog box.

The real advantage to changing the corner radius in the General Preferences box is that the corner radius will affect manually created (dragged with the Rounded Rectangle tool) rounded rectangles immediately. Changing the corner radius in the Rectangle dialog box requires that you know the exact dimensions of the rectangle or that you draw a rectangle by entering information in the Rectangle dialog box (clicking with the Rectangle tool without dragging) and specifying the corner radius. You must then delete the original rectangle in order to draw a rounded rectangle with the correct corner radius manually.

Because you can change the Corner radius setting easily, be sure to check it before you draw a series of rounded rectangles manually. There is no easy or automatic way to change the corner radius on existing rounded rectangles.

If you use 0 point as the Corner radius setting, the corners will not be rounded at all. If you click with the Rounded Rectangle tool and enter 0 point as the corner radius, the Corner radius setting in the General Preferences dialog box will change to 0 point.

The Freehand Tolerance Option

The Freehand tolerance setting controls how accurate the paths that Illustrator creates are when you compare them to the area dragged with the Freehand tool and to any templates being traced with the Auto Trace tool. Chapter 3 discusses Freehand tolerance settings and resulting paths.

The lower the Freehand tolerance setting, the more exact the resulting path. A higher setting results in smoother, less accurate paths. You can enter a value from 0 to 10, in increments of $^{1}/_{100}$ of a point (two decimal places).

The Freehand tolerance number is relative to the number of pixels on the screen that the resulting path may vary. A tolerance of 10 means that the resulting path may vary up to 10 pixels from the location of the actual dragged or traced area.

The Auto Trace Gap Option

When you use the Auto Trace tool to trace a template, the tool may encounter gaps, or white space, between solid areas. The Auto Trace gap option enables you to specify that if the Auto Trace tool runs into a white-space gap of 1 or 2 pixels, it can jump over the gap and continue tracing on the other side of it.

A value of 0 prevents the Auto Trace tool from tracing over gaps. If you use a value of 1, the Auto Trace tool will trace over gaps that are up to 1 pixel wide. If you use a value of 2 (the highest allowed), it will trace over gaps that are 2 pixels wide. The Auto Trace gap setting not only goes over gaps, it also adheres less closely to the original template.

I usually use a setting of 0 because when I bring any template into Illustrator, I examine it closely in Photoshop to make sure that it does not have any gaps. I can then be sure that the resulting paths will not be misshapen because of template-tracing inaccuracies.

The Snap to Point Option

You turn on the Snap to point feature in Illustrator to automatically align a point that you are dragging with another point that already exists within the illustration. As soon as the cursor is within 2 screen pixels of an anchor point, the cursor will become hollow. If you release the mouse button when the cursor is hollow, the new point will precisely overlap the existing point.

Be sure to click and drag on a *point* when you are dragging and using the Snap to point feature, or you may unintentionally align part of a line segment with the existing point.

I usually keep this feature on to make sure that my points always align; the only trouble that I have is accidentally clicking and dragging segments rather than points.

Never assume that Snap to point is on, unless you know that you have not changed it. Watch for those hollow arrows, and if you don't see them, check the General Preferences box to see whether the feature is turned on.

The Transform Pattern Tiles Option

Check the Transform pattern tiles option if you want patterns in paths to be moved, scaled, rotated, sheared, and reflected when you manually transform paths. When this option is checked, pulling up a transformation dialog box (either Move, Rotate, Scale, Reflect, or Shear) automatically checks the Pattern checkbox. When the option is not checked, the Pattern checkbox is not checked in the transformation dialog box.

I usually keep the Transform pattern tiles box checked, which sets all patterns to automatically transform and move with the objects that are being transformed and moved. This feature is especially useful when you want to create perspective in objects because the transformations of patterns can enhance the intended perspective.

The Scale Line Weight Option

When the Scale line weight feature is on, it automatically increases and reduces line weights relative to an object when you uniformly scale that object manually. For example, if a path has a Stroke weight of 1 point and you reduce the path uniformly by 50 percent, the Stroke weight will be .5 point.

Scaling objects nonuniformly (without the Shift key pressed) does not change the Stroke weight on an object, regardless of whether the Scale line weight feature is on or off.

If an object is scaled uniformly throughout the Scale dialog box, the Scale line weight option in the Scale dialog box will default to checked if the Scale line weight checkbox is checked in the General Preferences dialog box.

Unlike the Corner radius option, checking or unchecking the checkbox in the Scale dialog box for Scale line weight has no effect on the corresponding checkbox in the General Preferences dialog box.

The Area Select Option

When the Area select feature is on, you can select an object in Preview mode by clicking the object's Fill. If the Area select feature is not on, you select an object the same way that you select it in Artwork and Preview selection mode: by clicking paths or Anchor Points of objects. The Area select feature has no effect on selecting objects in Preview selection mode, but after you select them, you can move them by clicking a Filled area.

I have yet to have a good reason to turn this option off. The only reason that I can imagine for turning off this feature is if, for a particular illustration, I need to select specific paths from several overlapping, Filled objects. To be honest, I think that selecting individual paths in Preview would still be difficult because you can't see most of them.

The Area select feature does not enable you to select paths by clicking Strokes, unless you click the center of the Stroke where the path is (in which case you would be clicking the path anyway). In addition, you can't select "through" a compound path; instead, clicking in the empty areas of a compound path will result in selecting the compound path itself.

Use Precise Cursors Option

Precise cursors are cursors that appear as a variation of a crosshair instead of in the shape of a tool. Figure 6-4 shows cursors that are different when the Precise cursors feature is on.

Figure 6-4: The regular cursors are on the left, the precise cursors are on the right.

Name	Cursor	Precise Cursor or Cursor with Caps Lock
Pen tool		
Convert Direction Point with Pen tool		
Close path with Pen tool		
Add to existing path with Pen tool		
Connect to path with Pen tool		
Add Anchor Point tool		
Delete Anchor Point tool		
Eyedropper tool		
Select a Paint Style with Eyedropper tool		
Brush tool		
Freehand tool		
Paint Bucket tool		
Close open path with Freehand tool		
Connect an open path with Freehand tool		
Erase with Freehand tool		

The Caps Lock key toggles between standard cursors and precise cursors. When the Use precise cursors option is checked, the Caps Lock key makes the cursors standard. When the Use precise cursors option is not checked, Caps Lock activates the precise cursors.

I usually keep this option on and rarely engage the Caps Lock button to change the cursors back to normal. In particular, I've found the precise cursor for the Brush tool to be quite useful seeing as how the standard Brush cursor is one giant amorphous blob.

The Ruler Units Option

The pop-up menu for the Ruler units option changes the measurement system for the current document and all future new documents. This change affects most of the ways that dialog boxes, the Info palette, and the rulers display measurements.

Changing the Ruler units in the General Preferences dialog box changes the Ruler units in the Document Setup dialog box (choose File⇨Document Setup or press ⌘-Shift-D).

Being aware of which measurement system you are working in is important. When you enter a measurement in a dialog box, any numbers that are not measurement-system specific are applied to the current unit of measurement. For example, if you want to move something 1 inch and you open the Move dialog box (choose ArrangeÍMove, press ⌘-Shift-M, or Option-click on the Selection tool), you need to add either the inch symbol (") or the abbreviation *in* after you type a 1 in the dialog box if the measurement system is not inches. If the measurement system is points and picas, entering just a 1 moves the object one point, not one inch. If the measurement system is inches already, entering just the number 1 is fine.

Usually the measurement system is indicated by a corresponding letter or letters: *in* for inch, *pt* for points, and *cm* for centimeters.

You can change the Ruler units setting in the General Preferences dialog box without opening up the dialog box. Just press ⌘-Ctrl-U to toggle through inches, points/picas, and millimeters.

I use the points/picas system for several reasons. First, using points and picas is easier because you can specify smaller increments exactly (ever try to figure out what $^1/_{12}$ inch is in decimals?). Second, type is measured in points, not inches. Third, points and picas are the standard in measuring systems for designers and printers.

The default measurement is points and picas, so if you ever toss your preferences file or reinstall Illustrator, be aware that you might have to change the measurement system.

The Type Units Option

This option controls how type is measured, how keyboard increments are defined, and how paragraph indents are measured.

Chapter 8 explains type measurements, and why type is measured strangely, from ascender to descender, using points.

The Cursor Key Option

The increment that you specify in this setting controls how far an object moves when you select it and press the keyboard arrows.

I have this increment set to .5 point because this is the smallest amount that I usually need to move things. I make my increment smaller when I am working in 800% or 1600% views.

The Size/Leading Option

You can use the keyboard to increase and decrease type size by pressing ⌘-Shift- > and ⌘-Shift- <, respectively. You can increase and decrease leading by typing Option- ↑ and Option- ↓, respectively. In the Size/leading text box, you specify the increment by which the size and leading change.

You can increase or decrease the type size and leading only until you reach the upper and lower limits of each. The upper limit for type size and leading is 1296 points, and the lower limit for each is .1 point.

I keep my settings fairly high, at 10 points, because I have found that I require large point changes, usually quite a bit more than 10 points. If I need to do fine-tuning, I either type in the exact size that I want or use the Scale tool.

The Baseline Shift Option

The Baseline shift feature moves selected type up and down on the baseline, independent of the leading. The increment specified in this box is how much the type will be moved when you press the keyboard commands. To move type up one increment, press Option-Shift-Up Arrow. To move type down one increment, press Option-Shift-Down Arrow.

I keep the Baseline shift increment at 1 point so that I can adjust Path type better; specifically, I like to be able to adjust the baseline shift of type on a circle.

The Tracking Option

Tracking changes the amount of space between selected characters, and the setting in this text field represents the amount of space (measured in thousandths of an em space) that the keyboard command will add or remove. To increase tracking, you press ⌘-→; to decrease it, you press ⌘-←.

To increase the tracking by five times the increment in the General Preferences dialog box, press ⌘-Option-→. To decrease the tracking by five times the increment, press ⌘-Option-←.

The value in the Tracking text field also affects incremental changes in kerning. *Kerning* is the addition or removal of space between one pair of letters only. Kerning is done instead of tracking when a blinking insertion point is between two letters, as opposed to at least one selected character for tracking.

I have the Tracking increment set to 10 because it produces a result that corresponds to twice the tracking generated by the QuarkXPress key command. (In QuarkXPress, pressing ⌘-Option-Shift-[or ⌘-Option-Shift-] increases or decreases, respectively, tracking by 1⁄200 of an em space.)

The Undo Levels Option

The number that you specify in the Undo levels text field defines how many times you can undo. The maximum number is 200.

If you undo as far as you can, increasing the number of undo levels does not enable you to undo more.

The more undo levels you specify, the more memory the undos can eat up, taking away from Illustrator's application memory.

Memory Trouble

Starsky: I keep getting that terrible dialog box, telling me that I have to taper my undos.

Toulouse: Well, that always means there's a low memory situation.

Starsky: How can I avoid it?

Toulouse: If you can allocate more memory to Illustrator, that would be a good start. Also, what's your undo level set to?

Starsky: 200, like you say to do.

Toulouse: If your document is fairly complex, you might want to set the number of undos down as low as 2.

Starsky: Yikes.

Toulouse: If that still doesn't work, copy the section you are working with out of the document, and paste it in front in a new document. Then close the original document, and do the "thing" you were having trouble with in the new document.

Starsky: Sounds like a lot of trouble.

Toulouse: Desperate times call for desperate measures. After you're done, copy and paste in front in your original document.

I usually have Undo levels set to 200, the maximum number. If I run out of memory, a dialog box appears, asking whether I want to get rid of some of the oldest undos. Clicking the Always Discard option gets rid of them for me and frees up the necessary memory.

Change this setting to 200 right now so that you don't forget. This feature is one of the most powerful features of Illustrator, and the default is a measly 10 undos.

The Paste Remembers Layers Option

Checking the Paste remembers layers checkbox causes all objects to be pasted on the layer that they were copied from, regardless of which layer is currently active. Unchecking this box causes objects on the Clipboard to be pasted in the current layer.

This option is available in the Layers palette as well, and if it is on, a checkmark appears next to Paste Remembers Layers in the pop-up menu. When you turn the Paste Remembers Layers menu item on or off, the preference setting changes in the General Preferences dialog box.

One of the unheralded super features of the Paste remembers layers option is what happens when you paste in another document that doesn't contain that particular layer. A new layer with the same name as the one you copied the items from is created automatically. This is also a good way to quickly copy layers to another document…just delete the items after you've pasted them, and the new layers will remain.

The Greek Text Limit Option

The number that you enter in this field defines the point at which Illustrator begins to greek text. Illustrator *greeks text* — turns the letters into gray bars — when the text is so small that reading it on the screen would be hard or impossible. This change reduces screen-redraw time dramatically, especially when the document contains a great deal of text.

The size in this text field is relative to the viewing magnification of the document. At a limit of 6 points, 6-point type at 100%, 66%, 50%, 25%, or smaller will be greeked; but 6-point type at 150%, 200%, or larger will be readable. With the same limitations, 12-point type will be greeked at 50% and smaller, but it is readable at 66% and larger.

Other Application Preferences

The three other preference items in the File Preferences submenu deal with one issue apiece, as opposed to General Preferences, which is a catchall for most other preferences. By creating the submenu and these additional preference menu items, Illustrator's preference setup resembles Photoshop's preference setup. This similarity should make the transition between the two programs easier as both programs evolve.

Other preferences are set automatically by Illustrator as it tries to keep the program the way you had it last.

Practical Preference Joke #435

Hutch: I want to play a good practical joke on my partner.

Toulouse: Tell him he should start singing again.

Hutch: Heh. No, something on his Mac.

Toulouse: All right, here's one that'll have him uttering things that might not make it on NYPD Blue.

Hutch: And NYPD Blue is…?

Toulouse: Never mind. Go into his Illustrator General Preferences, and change the Greek text limit to 1296 points.

Hutch: What'll that do?

Toulouse: It'll make everything he types look like gray blocks.

Hutch: He carries a gun, you know.

Color Matching Dialog Box

Choose File⇨Preferences⇨Color Matching to bring up the Color Matching dialog box (shown in Figure 6-5). In this dialog box, you can specify how colors are to appear on the monitor. The way that colors appear on the monitor does not affect the output, but it may affect your perception of the colors on the screen. Changes that you make, based on what you see on the screen, may affect the output.

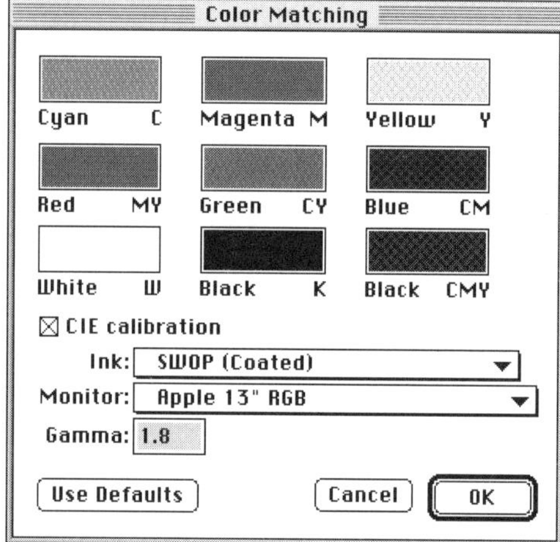

Figure 6-5: The Color Matching dialog box

The nine boxes at the top of the dialog box show each color as it will appear in Illustrator. These colors should be fairly close to the colors in the *Adobe Illustrator Manual.* If they are not, you can adjust them by clicking the mismatched colors and changing them so that they resemble the printed colors more closely.

Preference practical jokes, part 3. Switch black to white and white to black in the Color Matching dialog box. Turn that buddy's "negative" attitude into a positive one. Lots of fun for all! Clicking the Use Defaults button will reset all the colors back to normal. Remember, this change will not affect output but could cause an unsuspecting mark to make all black objects white and all white objects black. (Not to be used when the "buddy" has an important deadline or is going to send files to a service bureau.)

When you check the CIE calibration checkbox, the color in the color boxes is determined by the specifications that you enter in the Ink and Monitor text fields. You cannot change the color boxes manually when the CIE calibration checkbox is checked. The Gamma value is usually 1.8 for Macintosh monitors. Clicking the Use Defaults button automatically changes the options to the default values.

Because monitors and printed pieces are based on different display technologies, their colors are never exact matches. Certain monitors are better than others for color matching.

For more information on color matching and getting output to resemble what you see on-screen, see Chapter 20.

The Hyphenation Options Dialog Box

The Hyphenation Options dialog box (choose File⇨Preferences⇨Hyphenation Options) contains options for customizing the way Illustrator hyphenates words. At the top of the dialog box is a pop-up menu that lists various languages. Select the default language. At the bottom of the dialog box is an area where you can add to the list of hyphenation exceptions. These exceptions are words that you don't want Illustrator to hyphenate under any circumstances.

Practical Preference Joke #436

Starsky: Uh, I'm trying to come up with a good practical joke for my buddy Hutch.

Toulouse: Really? What'd he ever do to you?

Starsky: Nothing...well, a little thing with my type. Ticked me off pretty good.

Toulouse: Ah. You'll have to tell me about it.

Starsky: Yeah. I almost shot him. I carry a gun, you know.

Toulouse: I know. How about messing around with his colors?

Starsky: It's not like he's in a gang, but what the heck, I'll give it a shot.

Toulouse: All right. Go into the Color Matching dialog box, in the File Preferences submenu.

Starsky: Gotcha. Nice colors.

Toulouse: Change Black to White and White to Black. That's it.

Starsky: That's it? What'll it do?

(continued)

(continued)

Toulouse: Heh…It'll make everything on the screen look the opposite of what it is, at least for black and white. But it'll print fine. Of course, if your partner tries to compensate for the problem, it'll look fine on screen, but print reversed.

Starsky: I'll try it. If it doesn't work, I can always shoot him….

The Plug-Ins Folder Preference

The last preference item in the Preference submenu is a one-trick pony, the Plug-Ins Folder preference. This preference enables you to specify a folder in which Plug-Ins are located. The default is the folder called Plug-Ins in the Adobe Illustrator folder.

You can do all sorts of sorting and organizing for your Plug-Ins by using Cytopia Software's Socket Set 1, which contains a Plug-In Manager. More information on Socket Set filters is in Chapter 18.

Placement and Toolbox Value Preferences

Most Illustrator users take many preferences for granted. But if Illustrator didn't remember most preferences, most Illustrator users would be quite annoyed.

Palettes (including the Toolbox) remain where they were when you last used Illustrator. Illustrator remembers their size, and even whether they were open. Values in the Toolbox are still whatever you set them to last. For example, the options in the Paint Bucket/Eyedropper dialog box remain the same between Illustrator sessions.

Things You Can't Customize

There are a few things that you cannot customize in Illustrator, and they can be annoying:

- Type information always defaults to 12-point Helvetica, Auto leading, 100% Horizontal Scale, 0 tracking, Flush left, Hyphenation off. There is no easy way around this set of defaults.
- Layers for new documents are limited to one, which is colored light blue and called "Layer 1."
- When you create new objects, they are always 100% Black Fill and no Stroke.
- The Selection tool is always the "active" tool.

If any of these things, or anything else, annoys you too much, call Adobe Tech Support (206-628-2757) and tell them about it. Usually (when you can get a human on the line), they are receptive to hearing your problem, and they may have an easy way for you to do something that you thought the program couldn't do. In addition, if enough users complain about adding certain "missing" features (like TIFFs and integrated color separations), Adobe will undoubtedly listen and implement those features in new versions of their software.

Summary

- There are several different preferences that can be changed in Illustrator: General Preferences, the start-up file, and other application preferences.
- By changing the Adobe Illustrator Startup file, you can change the default colors, patterns, gradients, and zoom level of each new document created in Illustrator.
- Most preferences in Illustrator can be changed in the General Preferences dialog box.
- The Constrain angle option controls the angle at which objects are drawn and moved when the Shift key is pressed.
- The Freehand tolerance option controls the behavior of both the Freehand tool and the AutoTrace tool.
- The Ruler Units option controls how all measurements are controlled in Illustrator.

Putting Illustrator to Work

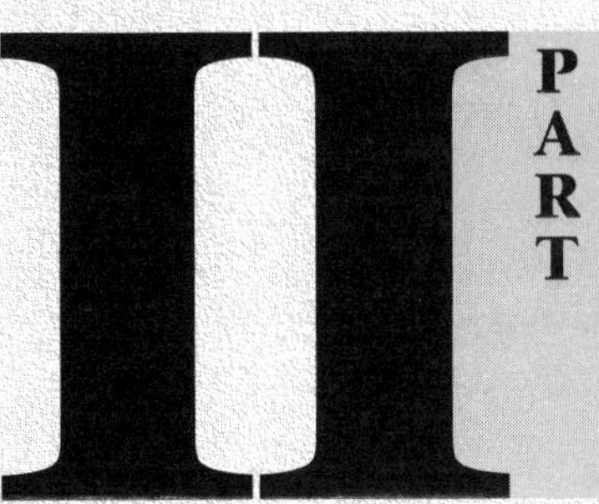

Now that you've learned the basics, it's time to start experimenting with some of the more interesting features in Illustrator. This part guides you through the steps of adjusting your artwork just so, adding type to illustrations, and taking advantage of some of the more advanced features of Illustrator such as compound paths, masks, blends, and patterns.

You'll have the most fun when you use Adobe Illustrator to achieve really incredible special effects. An illustration can come to life when you add exciting effects that give it a personality of its very own.

Fine-Tuning Illustrator Artwork

CHAPTER 7

In This Chapter

- Adding and removing Anchor Points from paths
- Cutting paths into separate paths
- Averaging points together
- Joining paths
- Changing Anchor Points into other types of Anchor Points
- Techniques for using the transformation tools
- Working with layers

Once you've created, traced, or even stolen someone else's artwork, there's always that period where you look at it and it just doesn't do it for you. That's where this chapter comes in. No, I won't do your finishing up for you, but I'll show you how to take advantage of Illustrator's many tools to get the best end result, from slight Control Handle manipulations to massive scalings and rotations.

This is the chapter that separates the men from the boys, but even so, my editor wouldn't let me name it "Chapter 7: Path Puberty." As I left my editor's office, I muttered "C'est la vie," but I swear to this day, my editor mumbled "la vee" right back. . . .

The Path Editing Tools

The path editing tools are the Scissors tool and its three pop-up tools: the Add Anchor Point, Delete Anchor Point, and Convert Direction Point tools. Clicking and holding down the Scissors tool (also known as the Split Paths tool) displays all four tools. Dragging out to a path editing tool replaces the default Scissors tool with the newly selected pop-up tool. If you press the Caps Lock key at the same time that you choose a path editing tool, the tools resemble crosshairs. The crosshair cursors enable precision positioning of cursors.

The purpose of each path editing tool is as follows:

- The **Scissors** tool is used for splitting paths. Clicking with the Scissors tool on a closed path makes that path an open path with the end points directly overlapping each other where the click occurred. Using the Scissors tool on an open path splits that open path into two separate open paths, each with an end point that overlaps the other open path's end point.
- The **Add Anchor Point** tool is used for adding Anchor Points to an existing path. If an Anchor Point is added to a straight segment (one that has no Control Handles on either end), then the Anchor Point will be a Straight Corner Point. If the segment is curved — meaning that you have at least one Control Handle for that segment — then the new Anchor Point will be a Smooth Point.
- The **Delete Anchor Point** tool gets rid of the Anchor Point that you click. A new segment is created between the Anchor Points that were on either side of the Anchor Point you clicked. If the Anchor Point you clicked on is an end point, no new segment is drawn; instead, the next Anchor Point on the path becomes the new end point.
- The **Convert Direction Point** tool has two functions. The first is to simply change an Anchor Point from its current type of Anchor Point to a Straight Corner Point by clicking and releasing it. You can also change the current type to Smooth by clicking and dragging on the Anchor Point. The second function is to move Control Handles individually by changing Smooth Points to Curved Corner Points and by changing Combination Corner Points and Curved Corner Points to Smooth Points. (Straight Corner Points don't have any Control Handles, so they can't be changed by using this method.)

You can add and remove Anchor Points in two different ways. I've already mentioned one of these methods in Chapters 2 and 3, where I demonstrated how to add Anchor Points with the drawing tools and remove them simply by selecting them and pressing the Delete key.

The techniques that I cover in this chapter are entirely unlike the method discussed previously. Instead of adding new points that create an extension to an existing path, you will learn how to add points in the middle of existing paths. Instead of deleting points and the line segments connected to them, you will discover how to remove points in between two Anchor Points and watch as those two Anchor Points are connected by a new line segment.

In Figure 7-1, the top row shows a drawing with a point added, resulting in a new curved section. The second row shows a point being removed and then re-added. Adding points, even to the same areas where they were removed, will not change the path back to the shape that it was before the points were removed. That path will have to be altered to resemble the original path. I will discuss these and other issues throughout this chapter.

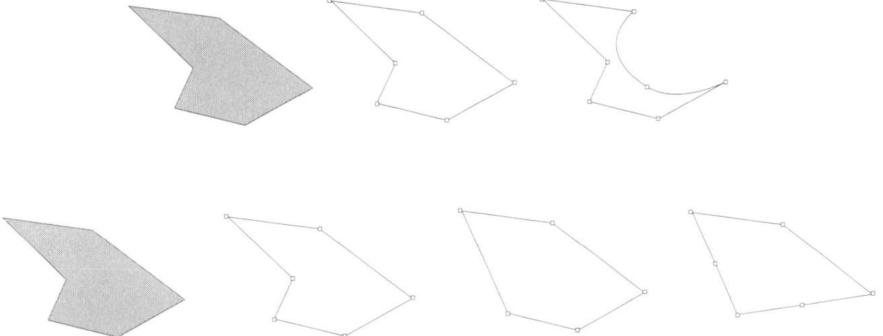

Figure 7-1: Adding Anchor Points after they've been removed will not readjust the shape back to its original shape.

Figure 7-1 shows a very simple example. The Delete Anchor Point tool is most often used to remove unnecessary points from overly complicated drawings.

Adding Anchor Points

To add an Anchor Point to an existing path, select the Add Anchor Point tool and click a line segment of a path. You may not place an Anchor Point directly on top of another Anchor Point, but you can get pretty darn close. Figure 7-2 shows a path before and after several Anchor Points are added to it.

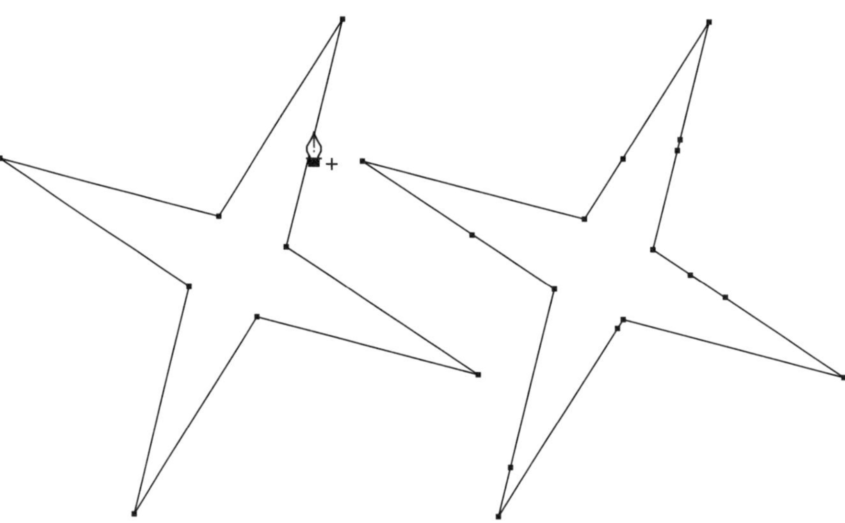

Figure 7-2: Adding Anchor Points to a path doesn't alter the shape of the path, but it *does* allow the path to be modified, more easily than if the points had not been added.

I like to select the paths to which I am adding Anchor Points before I start actually adding the points. This technique ensures that I don't accidentally get the annoying message "Can't Add Anchor Point. Please use the Add Anchor Point tool on a segment of a path." It seems that if there is just one point in the middle of a path, that's where I end up clicking to add the point. After I add one point, the path becomes selected automatically.

Anchor Points added to paths via the Add Anchor Point tool are either Smooth Points or Straight Corner Points, depending on the segment where the new Anchor Point is added. If the segment has two Straight Corner Points on either side of it, then the new Anchor Point will be a Straight Corner Point. If one of the Anchor Points is any other type of Anchor Point than a Straight Corner Point, the new Anchor Point will be a Smooth Point.

See Chapters 13 and 14, which discuss the Roughen and Add Anchor Points filters, respectively, for other ways to add Anchor Points to a path without adding length to it.

Removing Anchor Points

Removing Anchor Points is a little trickier than adding them. Depending on where you remove the Anchor Point, you may adversely change the flow of the line between the two Anchor Points on either side of it, as shown in Figure 7-3. If the point removed had any Control Handles, the removal will usually result in more of a drastic change than if the Anchor Point had been a Straight Corner Point. This situation occurs if Control Handles on the Anchor Point being removed controlled at least half the aspect of the curve. A Straight Corner Point would affect only the location of the line, not the shape of its curve.

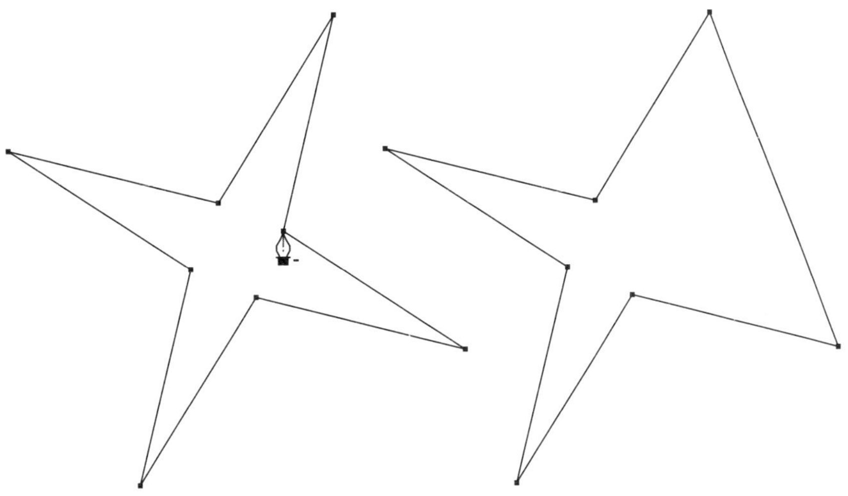

Figure 7-3: Removing an Anchor Point can dramatically alter the shape of the path.

To remove an Anchor Point, click an existing Anchor Point with the Delete Anchor Point tool. Like the Add Anchor Point tool, you can remove points without first selecting the path, but, of course, if the path is not selected, you can't see it or the points that you want to remove. If you miss and don't click an Anchor Point, you will get a message informing you that to remove an Anchor Point, you must click one.

After you remove Anchor Points, you cannot usually just add them back with the Add Anchor Point tool. Considering that the flow of the path will change when you remove a point, adding a point — even the correct type of point — will not give the same result as just undoing the point deletion.

If there are only two points on an *open* path, the Anchor Point you click is deleted and so is the segment connecting it to the sole remaining Anchor Point. If there are only two points on a *closed* path, both line segments from the Anchor Point you click are deleted along with that point, leaving only one Anchor Point remaining.

Splitting Paths

To change a single path into two separate paths that together make up a path equal in length to the original, you must use the Scissors tool. You can also split paths by selecting and deleting Anchor Points or line segments, although this method shortens the overall length of the two paths.

To split a path with the Scissors tool, click anywhere on a path. Initially, it doesn't seem like much happens. If you clicked in the middle of a line segment, a new Anchor Point will appear. (Actually, two will appear, but they are directly on top of one another, so you see only one.) If you click directly on top of an existing Anchor Point, nothing at all seems to happen, but Illustrator actually creates another Anchor Point on top of the one that you clicked.

After clicking with the Scissors tool, you have separated the path into two separate sections, but it will appear that there is still only one path because the two sections are both selected. To see the individual paths, deselect them (⌘-Shift-A) and select just one side with the Selection tool. After a path has been split, one half may be moved independently of the other half, as shown in Figure 7-4.

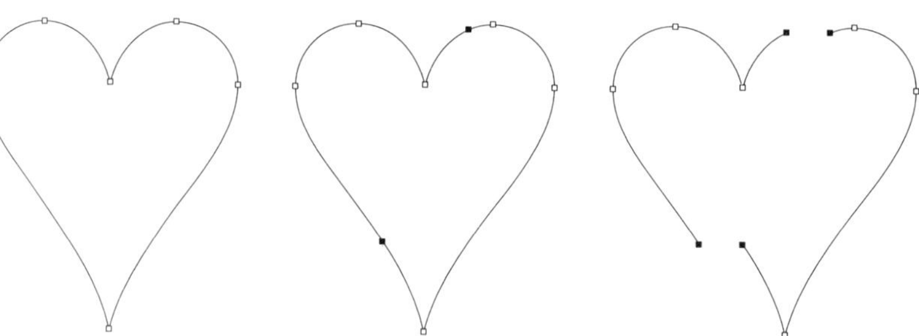

Figure 7-4: The original path (left), after splitting (center), and after the three pieces have been moved apart

The Anchor Points created with the Scissors tool will be either Smooth Points or Straight Corner Points, depending on the type of Anchor Point that is next along the path. If the line segment to the next Anchor Point has a Control Handle coming out of that Anchor Point that affects the line segment, then the new end point will be a Smooth Point. If there is no Control Handle for the line segment, the end point will be a Straight Corner Point.

You cannot use the Scissors tool on an end point of a line — only on segments and Anchor Points that are not end points.

Dividing and Duplicating Paths

Illustrator 6 provides several new capabilities that allow for multiple types of dividing and duplicating of paths, even paths that aren't selected. This section discusses those different features, as well as the tools that make this possible: the Knife tool and the Divide tool.

The Knife Tool

The Knife tool is found on the Plug-in Tools palette. To see the Plug-In Tools palette, choose Window⇨Show Plug-In Tools. The Knife tool divides paths into smaller sections as it slices through them. Those sections are initially selected, but they're not grouped. Figure 7-5 shows a path before and after it "crosses paths" with the Knife.

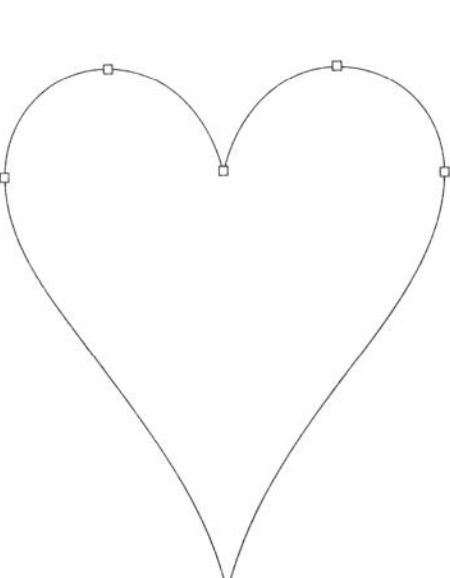
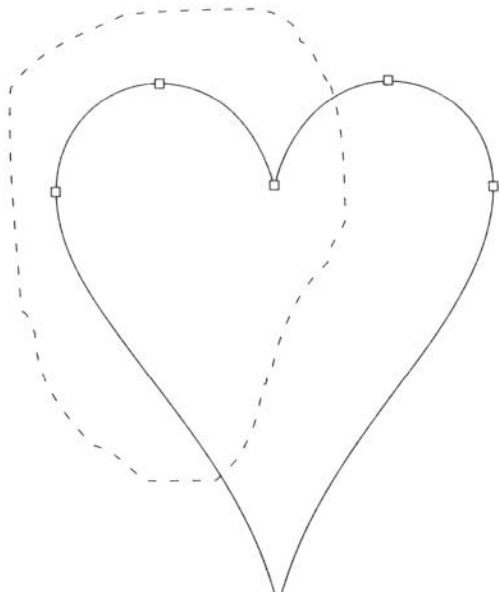
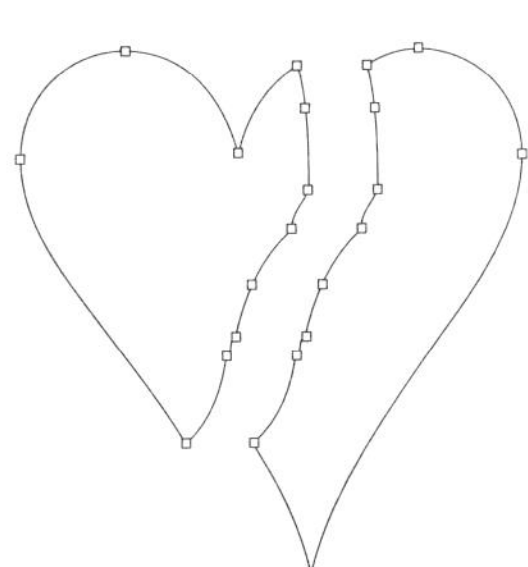

Figure 7-5: The original path (left), the path of the Knife tool (center), and the resulting paths (right), all shown in Artwork mode

The Lasso Tool

The Lasso is the Knife tool on a good day. Instead of tearing the paths into pieces, it duplicates the areas it's been dragged across. Figure 7-6 shows what happens with the same path from the previous example when the Lasso tool is used.

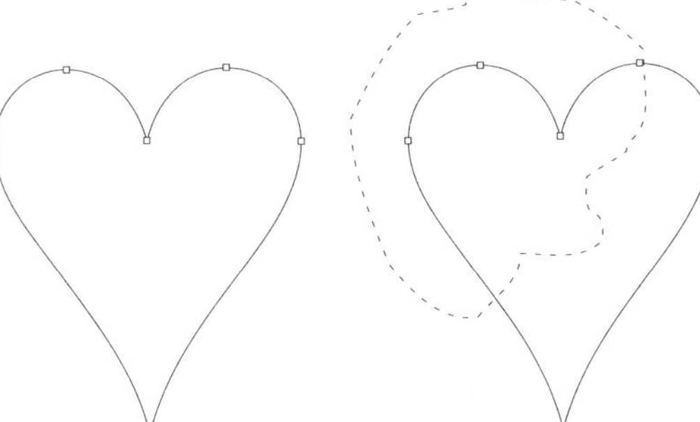
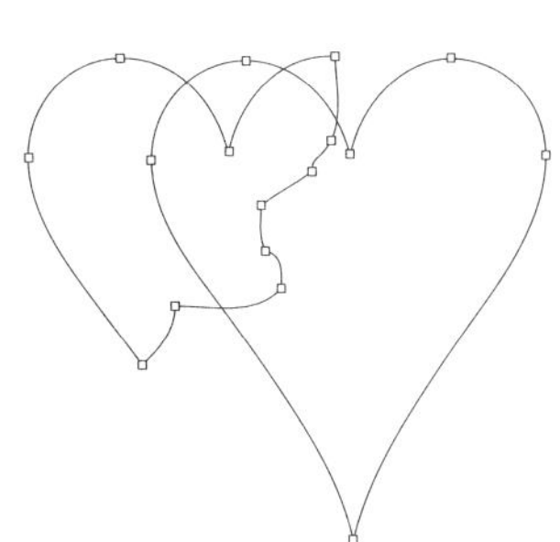

Figure 7-6: The original path (left), the path of the Lasso tool (center), and the resulting paths (right), all shown in Artwork mode

Remember that the Lasso and the Knife work on all paths that are under the existing path, selected or not.

Applying Knives

The Knife tool is useful, but sometimes you might want to divide or duplicate a portion of existing paths without having to draw them (maybe you need perfectly sized cuts or duplicates in the shape of text). That's where Apply Knife comes in. It takes any selected path and turns it into the Knife.

Averaging Points and Joining

Averaging points is the process in which Illustrator determines the location of the points and figures out where the center of all the points will be on a mean basis. *Joining* is the process in which either a line segment is drawn between two end points, or two end points are merged into a single Anchor Point.

Averaging and joining are done together when two end points need to change location to be on top of one another and then merged into one point. You can perform these steps one at a time, or you can have Illustrator do both of them automatically; just press ⌘-Option-J or ⌘-Option-L.

Averaging Points

To line up a series of points either horizontally or vertically, use the Average command. The Average command also works to place selected points directly on top of one another. Figure 7-7 shows the different types of averaging.

Figure 7-7: Different types of averaging

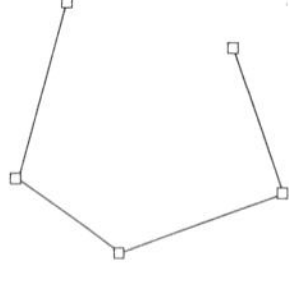

Horizontal

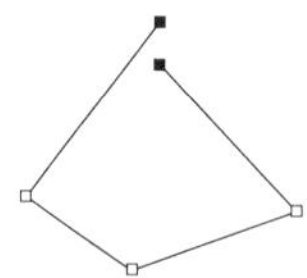

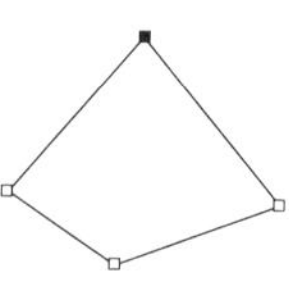

To average points horizontally, select the points to be averaged with the Direct Selection tool and choose Object⇨Average (⌘-L). The Average dialog box appears, asking which type of averaging you would like to do. In this case, choose Horizontal, which will move selected points only up and down.

Be sure to select the points to be averaged with the Direct Selection tool. If you select a path with either the Group Selection tool or the regular Selection tool, every point in the path will be averaged! This mistake can do quite a bit of damage when averaging both horizontally and vertically.

To average points vertically, choose the Vertical option in the Average dialog box. To average points both vertically and horizontally, choose Both. The Both option will place all selected points on top of each other.

When averaging points, Illustrator uses the mean method to determine the center. No, Illustrator isn't nasty to the points that it averages; rather, Illustrator adds together the locations of the points and then divides by the number of points, which provides the mean location of the center of the points.

Joining

Joining is a tricky area to define. Illustrator's Join feature does two entirely different things: It joins two end points at different locations with a line segment, and it also combines two Anchor Points into one when they are placed directly on top of each other.

To join two end points with a line segment, select just two end points in different locations (not on top of each other) with the Direct Selection tool and choose Object⇨Join (⌘-J). A line segment will be formed between the two points, as shown in Figure 7-8.

Join Trouble

Mary: I can't join my two paths.

Toulouse: They're both open paths?

Mary: Yep.

Toulouse: You've selected just the end points you want to join?

Mary: Yep.

Toulouse: You're choosing Join from the Arrange menu?

Mary: Yep.

Toulouse: Are both paths ungrouped?

Mary: Yep. Uh...I mean...I'm not sure.

Toulouse: Select them both and Ungroup. Then try.

Mary: That was it!

Toulouse: Keep in mind you can't join paths when they're part of different groups.

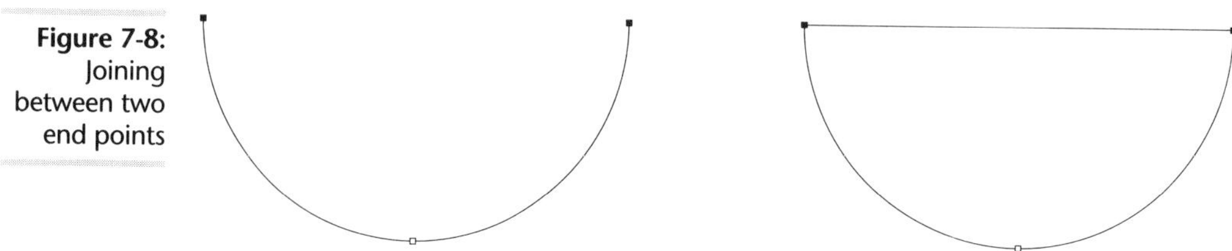

Figure 7-8: Joining between two end points

To combine two end points into a single Anchor Point, select the two points that are *directly* over one another and choose Object⇨Join (⌘-J). The Join dialog box appears, asking what type of point should be created when the two end points become one Anchor Point. If you choose Smooth Point, then the point will become a Smooth Point with two linked Control Handles. If you choose Corner Point, the point will retain any Control Handle position that is part of it. And if no Control Handle is on the line, there will be no Control Handle on that side of the Anchor Point.

Not only can you join two separate paths, but you can also join together the end points on the same open path (overlapping end points) to create a closed path in the same way that two end points from different paths are joined (see Figure 7-9).

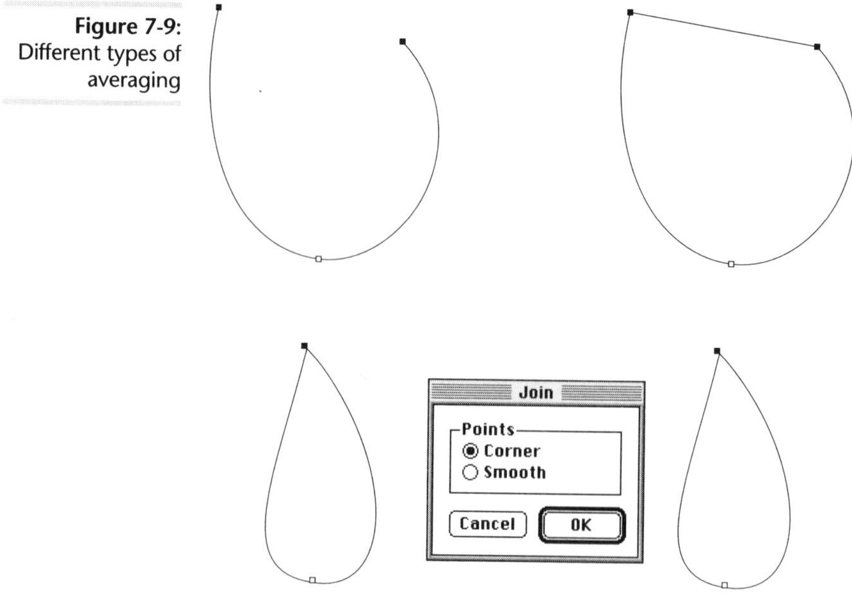

Figure 7-9: Different types of averaging

To make sure that end points are overlapping, turn on the Snap to Point feature in General Preferences and drag one end point to the other with a selection tool. When the two points are close enough, the arrowhead cursor (normally black) will become hollow. Release the mouse button when the arrowhead is hollow, and the two points will be directly above one another.

Another way to ensure that the end points are overlapping is to select them, choose Object⇨Average (⌘-L), and select the Both option in the Average dialog box.

When creating an Anchor Point out of two overlapping end points, make sure that the two points are precisely overlapping. If they are even the smallest distance apart, a line segment will be drawn between the two points instead of transforming the two end points into a single Anchor Point. You can tell immediately whether the points are overlapping correctly when you select Join. If a dialog box appears, the points are overlapping. If no dialog box appears, the points were not overlapping, and it is best to undo the join.

To make the points overlap and join at once, press ⌘-Option-L or ⌘-Option-J, which will both average and join the selected end points. This method works only on end points. The end points are averaged both horizontally and vertically and are also joined into an Anchor Point that is a Corner Point, with Control Handle Lines and Control Handles unchanged.

You have the following limitations when joining:

- Joins may not take place when one path is part of a different group than the other path.

If the two paths are in the same base group (that is, not in any other groups before being grouped to the other path, even grouped by themselves), the end points can be joined.

- If one path is grouped to another object and the other object has not been previously grouped to the path, the end points will not join.
- The end points on text paths cannot be joined.
- The end points of guides cannot be joined.

If all the points in an open path are selected (as if the path has been selected with the regular Selection tool), then choosing Object⇨Join (⌘-J) will automatically join the end points. If the two end points are located directly over one another, the Join dialog box appears, asking whether the new Anchor Point should be a Smooth Point or a Corner Point.

Joining is also useful for determining the location of end points when the end points are overlapping. Select the entire path, choose Object⇨Join (⌘-J), and choose Smooth Point. These steps will usually alter one of the two segments on either side of the new Anchor Point. Undo the join, and you will know the location of the overlapping end points.

Aligning and Distributing Objects

In version 5.x of Illustrator, aligning and distributing objects was done with one of the three Align and Distribute filters: Align and Distribute, Distribute Horizontally, and Distribute Vertically. In Illustrator 6, these filters have been replaced with an Align palette, which includes all the functionality of those filters in one handy palette, as shown in Figure 7-10.

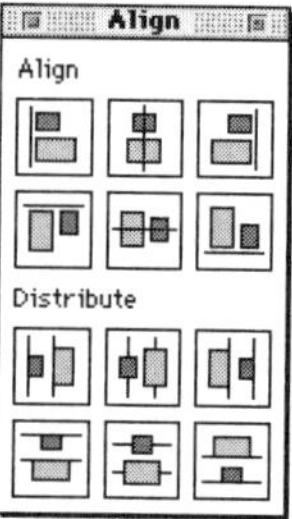

Figure 7-10: The Align palette

The Distribute functions of the Align palette work the same way as they did in version 5.x of Illustrator: They distribute along the edges or the center only. There is no "reset" button on the palette (a most unfortunate oversight), so you'll have to undo if you click the wrong button.

Once again, Cytopia Software comes to the rescue. In their Socket Set 2, they've included an Alignment filter (Space and Align) that does much more than the Adobe Align palette, and does it better. You can control how much space is between the objects, and where that space is measured from. (More information about Space and Align can be found in Chapter 18.)

To use the Align palette, select the objects you wish to align and/or distribute, and click the appropriate button in the palette. Each click in the palette counts as a "change" in Illustrator, meaning that if you click around 20 times, you'll need to undo 20 times in order to get back where you started.

Converting Anchor Points

The title of this section should probably have been "Converting Direction Points" because this section deals with the Convert Direction Point tool, but since the Convert Direction Point tool only converts Anchor Points by adjusting Control Handles, the use of the term "direction points" is a bit obscure.

The Convert Direction Point tool works differently with each type of Anchor Point. The different types of Anchor Points are shown in Figure 7-11. (See Chapter 3 for detailed definitions of the four different types of Anchor Points in Illustrator, and how they're drawn with the Pen tool.)

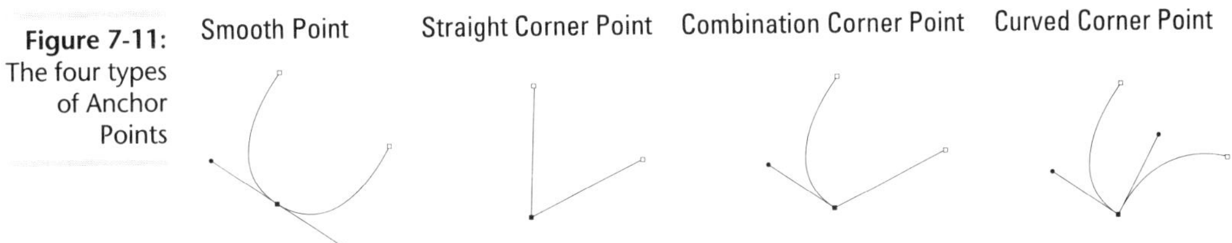

Figure 7-11: The four types of Anchor Points

You can use the Convert Direction Point tool on either extended Control Handles or on Anchor Points. When there are two Control Handles on an Anchor Point, clicking either Control Handle with the Convert Direction Point tool will toggle the Control Handles from being linked (so that when the angle of one is changed, the other is changed as well) to being independent (the Control Handle's length from the Anchor Point and the angle can be altered individually). It is generally a good idea to use the Direct Selection tool to move Control Handles unless you want to toggle between linked and independent points.

Converting Smooth Points

Smooth Points can be changed into the other three types of Anchor Points by using both the Direct Selection tool and the Convert Direction Point tool as follows:

- To convert Smooth Points into Straight Corner Points, use the Direct Selection tool to drag the Control Handles on both sides of the Anchor Point into the Anchor Point; then release the mouse button.
- To convert Smooth Points into Combination Corner Points, use the Direct Selection tool to drag one Control Handle into the Anchor Point.

Trouble with Control Handles

Lou: My Control Handles are really giving me trouble.

Toulouse: What sorts of trouble?

Lou: Every time I readjust them, they snap back into place. It's really annoying.

Toulouse: You're using the Convert Direction Point tool?

Lou: Yeah. I click and drag, and the Control Handles move independently; but then when I adjust the other side. . . .

Toulouse: Uh, you wouldn't be using the Convert Direction Point tool to adjust the other side, would you now?

Lou: Sure. What of it?

Toulouse: Each click with the Convert Direction Point tool toggles between linked and unlinked Control Handles.

Lou: So, what can I do?

Toulouse: Click once to unlink, and then switch to the Direct Selection tool.

- To convert Smooth Points into Curved Corner Points, use the Convert Direction Point tool to drag one of the Control Handles. After being dragged with the Convert Direction Point tool, the two Control Handles become independent of each other (the movement of one will not affect the other).

The following steps show you how you can use the Direct Selection tool and the Convert Direction Point tool to change shapes — in this case, from a circle to a diamond.

STEPS: Changing a Circle into a Diamond

Step 1. Draw a circle with the Oval tool. Remember to keep the Shift key pressed so you end up with a perfect circle.

Step 2. Select the Convert Direction Point tool.

Step 3. Click on each of the Anchor Points and release. The diamond should look like the illustration in Figure 7-12.

Converting Straight Corner Points

You can change Straight Corner Points into the other three types of Anchor Points by using both the Convert Direction Point tool and the Direct Selection tool as follows:

- To convert Straight Corner Points into Smooth Points, use the Convert Direction Point tool to click and drag on the Anchor Point. As you drag, linked Control Handles will appear on both sides of the Anchor Point.

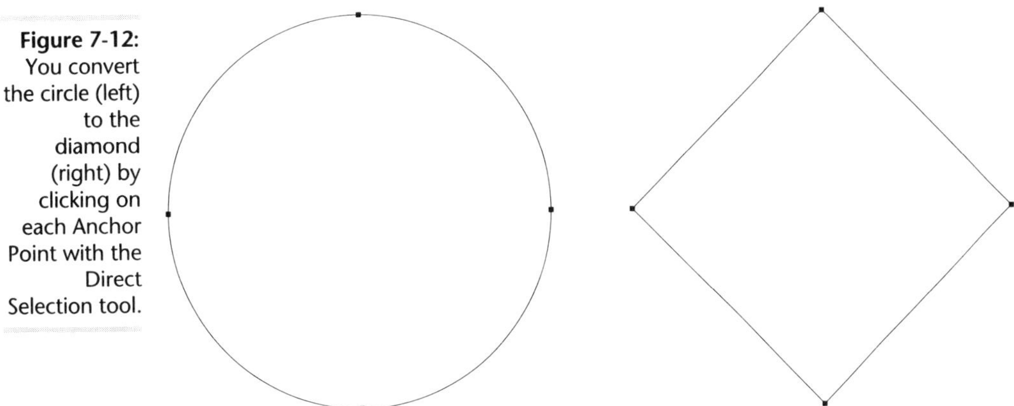

Figure 7-12: You convert the circle (left) to the diamond (right) by clicking on each Anchor Point with the Direct Selection tool.

- To convert Straight Corner points into Combination Corner points, use the Convert Direction Point tool to click and drag on the Anchor Point. As you drag, linked Control Handles appear on both sides of the Anchor Point. Select one of the Control Handles with the Direct Selection tool and drag it toward the Anchor Point until it disappears.
- To convert Straight Corner points into Curved Corner points, use the Convert Direction Point tool to click and drag on the Anchor Point. As you drag, linked Control Handles appear on both sides of the Anchor Point. Then use the Convert Direction Point tool to drag one of the Control Handles. After being dragged with the Convert Direction Point tool, the two Control Handles become independent of each other.

Converting Combination Corner Points

You can change Combination Corner Points into the other three types of Anchor Points by using both the Convert Direction Point tool and the Direct Selection tool as follows:

- To convert Combination Corner Points into Smooth Points, use the Convert Direction Point tool to click and drag on the Anchor Point. As you drag, linked Control Handles appear on both sides of the Anchor Point.
- To convert Combination Corner Points into Straight Corner Points, use the Convert Direction Point tool to click once on the Anchor Point. The Control Handle disappears.
- To convert Combination Corner Points into Curved Corner Points, use the Convert Direction Point tool to click and drag on the Anchor Point. As you drag, linked Control

Handles appear on both sides of the Anchor Point. Then use the Convert Direction Point tool to drag one of the Control Handles. After being dragged with the Convert Direction Point tool, the two Control Handles become independent of each other.

The following steps are another example of how you can change shapes using the Direct Selection tool and the Convert Direction Point tool — this time, from a circle to a heart.

STEPS: Changing a Circle into a Heart

Step 1. Draw a circle with the Oval tool. Remember to keep the Shift key pressed so you end up with a perfect circle.

Step 2. Click on the lowest point on the circle with the Direct Selection tool.

Step 3. Click on the right Control Handle of that Anchor Point and drag it up, as shown in Figure 7-13.

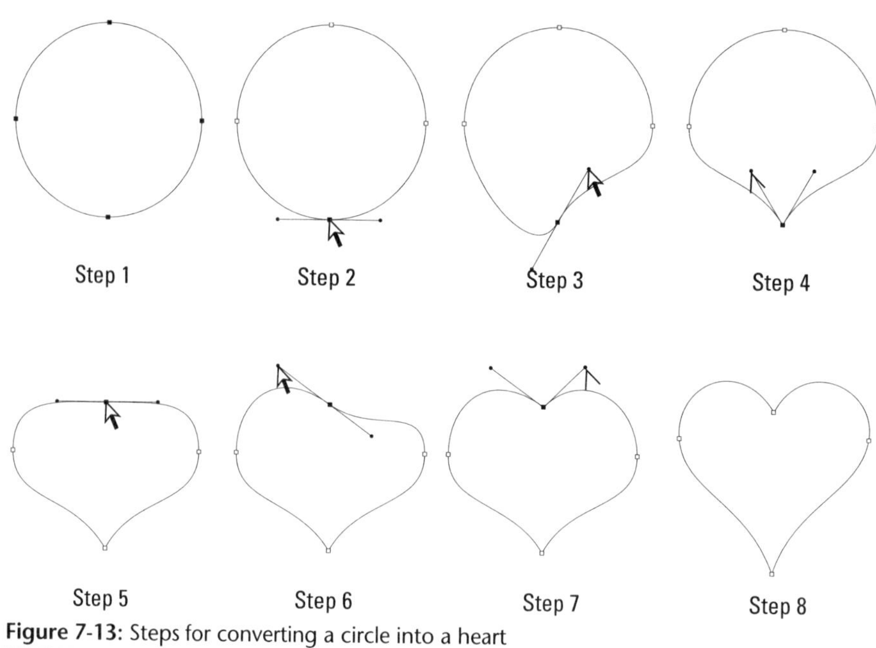

Figure 7-13: Steps for converting a circle into a heart

Step 4. With the Convert Direction Point tool, click on the left Control Handle of that point and drag it up. Be careful not to click more than once on the handle.

Step 5. Click on the Anchor Point at the top of the circle and drag it down a little.

Step 6. With the Direct Selection tool, click on the left Control Handle of the topmost point and drag it up.

Step 7. Click on the right Control Handle with the Convert Direction Point tool and drag it down.

Step 8. Adjust the Anchor Points and Control Handles until the heart looks really...well...nice.

Converting Curved Corner Points

You can change Curved Corner Points into the other three types of Anchor Points by using both the Convert Direction Point tool and the Direct Selection tool as follows:

- To convert Curved Corner Points into Smooth Points, use the Convert Direction Point tool to click or drag one of the Control Handles. You can then use the Direct Selection tool to adjust the angle of both Control Handles at once.
- To convert Curved Corner Points into Straight Corner Points, use the Convert Direction Point tool to click once on the Anchor Point. The Control Handles disappear.
- To convert Curved Corner Points into Combination Corner Points, use the Direct Selection tool to drag one Control Handle into the Anchor Point.

Transforming Objects

PostScript has the capability to transform any PostScript object by scaling it, rotating it, reflecting it, and shearing it. Illustrator takes this power and enhances it by providing you the flexibility of using certain tools, each of which does one of those transformations.

The following four tools in the Illustrator Toolbox have been a staple of PostScript drawing applications for years because they address four fundamental functions: the Rotate tool, the Scale tool, the Reflect tool, and the Shear tool. Before any of these tools can be used, one or more objects (including paths, points, and segments) must be selected. The selected paths are the paths that are transformed.

There are four ways to transform selected objects:

- Click with the transformation tool to set an origin point and then drag from a different location. (This is called a *manual transformation.*)
- Click and drag in one motion to transform the object from its center point.
- Option-click to set the origin and then enter exact information in the tool's transformation dialog box. (This method is more precise than manually transforming.)
- Double-click a transformation tool to set the origin in the center of the selected object; then you can enter information in the tool's transformation dialog box.

All the transformation tools work on a relative basis. For instance, if an object is scaled to 150% and then is scaled again to 150%, the object is now 225% of its original size (150% x 150% = 225%). If the object is initially scaled to 150% of its original size, and you want to take it back to that original size, you must do the math and figure out what percentage is needed to resize it — in this case, 66.7% (100% ÷ 150% = 66.7%). Entering 100% in the Scale dialog box leaves the selected objects unchanged.

When manually transforming objects, you can make a copy of the selected object (and thus leave the original untransformed) by holding down the Option key before and after releasing the mouse button. In a transformation dialog box, you can make a copy by clicking the Copy button, pressing Option-Return, or Option-clicking OK.

If the Pattern Tiles checkbox is available (you must have a pattern for the option not to be grayed out) inside any of the transformation dialog boxes, you can check its option box to transform your pattern along with the object. You can also transform the pattern only, leaving the object untransformed, by unchecking the Objects box.

Manually transforming objects is fairly simple if you keep in mind that the first place you click (the point of origin) and the second place should be a fair distance apart. The further your second click is from the point of origin, the more control you have when dragging to transform. The Shear tool is an exception — although it does matter where you click — because you can lose control of your shape anywhere.

All the transformation tools perform certain operations that rely on the Constrain Angle setting as a point of reference. Normally, this setting is set to 0°, which makes your Illustrator world act normally. You can change the setting by choosing File⇨Preferences⇨General (⌘-K) and entering a new value.

The Rotate Tool

The Rotate tool rotates selected objects within a document. Double-clicking the Rotate tool displays the Rotate Tool dialog box, where the precise angle of the selected item's rotation can be entered in the Angle box. The object rotates around its mathematical center. A positive number between 0 and 180 rotates the object counterclockwise that many degrees. A negative number between 0 and –180 rotates the selected object clockwise. The Rotate tool works on a standard 360° circle of rotation, although it is usually easier to type in numbers between 0 and 180 or 0 and –180 than numbers like 270, which is the same as –90°.

Holding down the Option key and clicking somewhere in the document also brings up the Rotate Tool dialog box; however, the object now rotates around the point where the Rotate tool was clicked. This point can be on or off the selected object. Be careful because it is quite easy to rotate an object right out of your viewing area! Illustrator has many precautions, however, that prevent you from transforming or moving an object off the Pasteboard.

Click once to set the origin point from where the object's center of rotation should be and then click fairly far from the origin and drag in a circle. The selected object spins along with the cursor. To constrain the angle to 45° or 90° as you are dragging, hold down the Shift key. This angle is dependent on the Constrain Angle box (File➪Preferences➪General or ⌘-K), and is 45° or 90° plus the angle in this box. Figure 7-14 shows an illustration before and after being rotated.

Old Math

Rhoda: I've just upgraded to Illustrator 6, and I'm a bit concerned about the Rotate thing.

Toulouse: The Rotate thing?

Rhoda: You know. On my Power Mac, when I rotated something 180 degrees in Illustrator 5.x, it was more like 179.97.

Toulouse: That was an Illustrator math thing. It's been taken care of.

Rhoda: So something that was rotated 180 degrees is rotated...?

Toulouse: Oddly enough, 180 degrees. Exactly.

Figure 7-14: An illustration before (left) and after (right) being rotated

The Scale Tool

The Scale tool resizes objects both proportionally and nonproportionally. You can also use the Scale tool to "flip" objects, but without the precision of the Reflect tool. (It is impossible to keep both the size and proportions of an object constant while flipping and scaling.)

Double-clicking on the Scale tool brings up the Scale dialog box, shown in Figure 7-15. All selected objects are scaled from the mathematical center of the objects. If the Uniform button is checked, numbers typed into the text field result in proportionately scaled objects (where the width and height of the object remain proportional to each other). Numbers less than 100% shrink the object; numbers greater than 100% enlarge it. When the Uniform button is checked, you may also check the box called Scale line weight (this option is grayed out if nonproportional scaling is used).

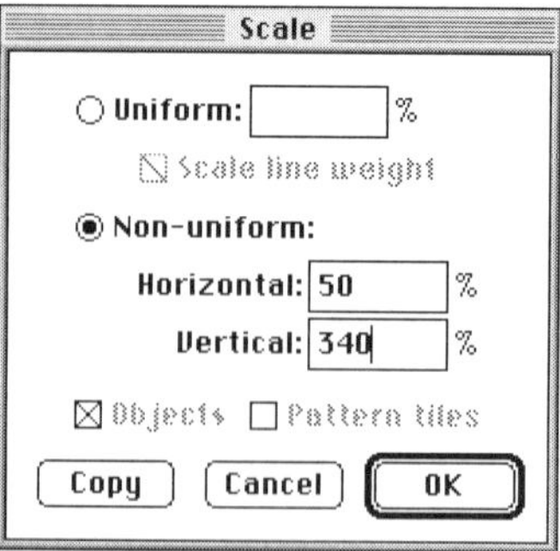

Figure 7-15: The Scale dialog box

Nonproportional scaling resizes the horizontal and vertical dimensions of the selected objects separately, distorting the image. The way nonproportional scaling works is related to the Constrain Angle box (File⇨Preferences⇨General or ⌘-K), where the angle is the horizontal scaling, and the vertical scaling is 90° from that angle.

Pressing the Option key and clicking in the document window also brings up the Scale dialog box, but now the objects are scaled from the location in the document that was Option-clicked.

Manual resizing is achieved by clicking your point of origin and then clicking away and dragging to scale. If you cross the horizontal or vertical axis of the point of origin, the selected object flips over in that direction. Holding down the Shift key constrains the objects to equal proportions (if the cursor is dragged at approximately 45° from the point of origin) or constrains the scaling to either horizontal or vertical scaling only (providing the cursor is being dragged along at about a 90° angle from the point of origin relative to the constrain angle).

The Reflect Tool

The Reflect tool makes a mirror image of the selected objects, reflected across an axis of reflection. Double-clicking on the Reflect tool reflects selected objects across an axis of reflection that runs through the center of the selected objects. In the Reflect dialog box, you can enter the axis of rotation. If you want to rotate the object along either the horizontal or vertical axis, click the appropriate button.

Option-clicking in the document window also brings up the Reflect dialog box, but the axis of reflection is now not in the center of the selected object, but in the location in the document where you Option-clicked.

Manual reflecting is done by clicking once to set the origin point (the center of the axis of reflection) and again somewhere along the axis of reflection. If you click and drag after setting your origin point, you can rotate the axis of reflection and see what your objects look like reflected across various axes. The Shift key constrains the axis of reflection to 90° angles, relative to the constrain angle (File⇨Preferences⇨General or ⌘-K). Holding down the Option key during the release of the click leaves a copy of the original object. Figure 7-16 shows an illustration before and after being reflected.

Figure 7-16: An illustration before (left) and after (right) being reflected across the vertical axis

The Shear Tool

This tool should actually be called the "Swear" tool since it causes more cursing (no, not cursoring; that's different) than any other tool (except perhaps for the mighty Pen tool). Another good name for the Shear tool (one that I have heard many people use) is the "Stupid" tool because that's usually how you feel when trying to get good results from its use. It's a terrifying feeling to see the artwork you spent an hour touching up until it's just right go zinging off the screen, seemingly all by itself.

The Shear tool is rightfully distrusted because using it manually is usually a quick lesson in futility. Double-clicking on the Shear tool brings up the Shear dialog box, shown in Figure 7-17, which is much more controllable. Double-clicking causes the origin to be in the center of the selected object. The Angle box is simple enough; in its text box, you enter the angle amount the object should shear. Any amount over 75° or less than –75° renders the object into an indecipherable mess. The Shear tool reverses the positive-numbers-are-counterclockwise rule: To shear an object clockwise, enter a positive number; to shear counterclockwise, enter a negative number. The Axis Angle box is for shearing an object along a specified axis.

Figure 7-17: The Shear dialog box

Option-clicking in the document window also brings up the Shear dialog box, with the origin of the shear being the location of the preceding Option-click.

Manual shearing is something else again because you are doing two things at once: changing both the angle of shearing (the distance from the beginning of the second click until it is released) and the angle of the axis of shearing (the angle the mouse is dragged during the second click). Usually, it's best to start your second click fairly far away from the point of origin. Holding down the Shift key constrains the axis of shearing to a 45° angle, relative to the constraining angle. Figure 7-18 shows an illustration before and after being sheared.

Figure 7-18: An illustration before (left) and after (right) being sheared

Moving

The most common way to move an object is to use a selection tool and drag the selected points, segments, and paths from one location to another.

The precise way to move an object is to use the Move dialog box. Select the object you want to move and then choose Arrange➪Move (⌘-Shift-M). The Move dialog box appears, and you can enter the appropriate values in either the horizontal or vertical text fields. If you want to move an object diagonally, enter a number in the Distance text field and then enter the angle of movement direction in the Angle text field.

Any selected object (except for text selected with a type tool) can be moved via the Move dialog box, including individual Anchor Points and line segments.

By default, the Move dialog box contains the distance and angle that you last moved an object, whether manually (with a Selection tool) or in the Move dialog box. If you have used the Measure tool prior to using the Move dialog box, the numbers in the Move dialog box correspond to the numbers that appeared in the Info palette when you used the Measure tool.

In the Move dialog box, positive numbers in the horizontal text field move an object from left to right, while negative numbers move an object from right to left. Positive numbers in the vertical text field move an object from bottom to top, while negative numbers move an object from top to bottom. Negative numbers in the Distance text field move an object in the opposite direction of the Angle text field. The Angle text field works a bit differently. Negative numbers in the Angle text field move the angle in the opposite direction from 0° (so entering –45° is the same as entering 315° and entering –180° is the same as entering 180°).

The measurement system in the Move dialog box matches the system set in the General Preferences dialog box. To enter a measurement different from the current measurement system, use the following indicators:

- For inches: 1" or 1in (one inch)
- For picas: 1p or 1pica (one pica)
- For points: 1pt or 0p1 (one point)
- For picas/points: 1p1 (one pica, one point)
- For millimeters : 1mm (one millimeter)
- For centimeters: 1cm (one centimeter)

The Horizontal and Vertical text fields are linked to the Distance and Angle text fields; when one of the fields is changed, the others are altered accordingly.

Pressing the Copy button duplicates selected objects in the direction and distance indicated, just as holding down Option when dragging duplicates the selected objects.

The Move dialog box is a great place to enter everything via the keyboard. Press Tab to move from text field to text field, press Return to push the OK button, and press ⌘-Period or Esc to push the Cancel button. Pressing Option-Return or pressing Option while clicking OK pushes the Copy button.

Transform Each

A pseudo-new feature in Illustrator 6 is Transform Each. Actually, it's a delightful combination of several of the "each" filters from version 5.x: Move Each, Scale Each, and Rotate Each. The new dialog box (shown in Figure 7-19) combines the filter dialog boxes, including the useful Random checkbox.

The unique thing about Transform Each is that each selected object is transformed independently, as opposed to having all the selected objects moved together. Figure 7-20 shows the difference between "normal" rotating and scaling, and the Rotate and Scale functions in Transform Each.

But of all things, the randomize function of Transform Each is its most powerful asset. Checking the Random checkbox can turn a grid into a distinct random texture, as shown in Figure 7-21.

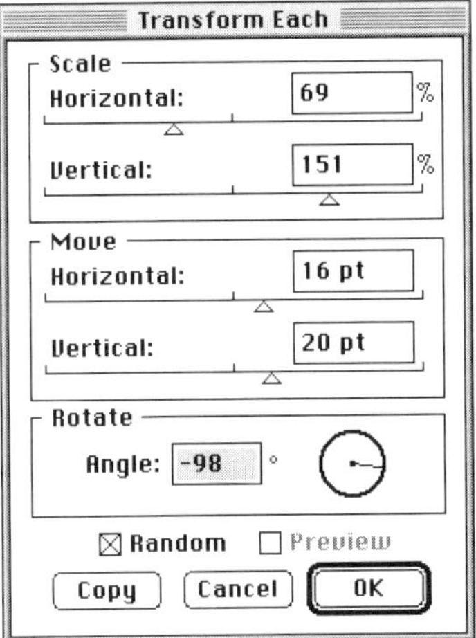

Figure 7-19: The Transform Each dialog box

Figure 7-20: An illustration (left) after being rotated and scaled, and then after using the Rotate and Scale functions via Transform Each

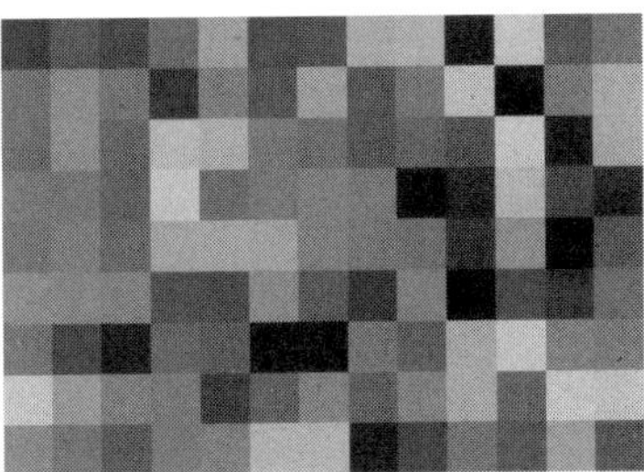

Figure 7-21: Transform Each's randomize function applied to a checkerboard of colored squares

Transformation Effects

The transformation tools open up a world of possibilities within Illustrator. The following tips and ideas should give you a head start in exploring the amazing power of transformations.

Choosing Repeat Transform (⌘-D) from the Arrange menu redoes the last transformation that was done to a selected object. Transformations include Move, Rotate, Scale, Reflect, Shear, and Transform Each. Repeat Transform also makes a transformed copy if a copy was made either manually or by clicking the Copy button in a transformation dialog box.

Repeat Transform remembers the last transformation, no matter what else you do, and it can apply that same transformation to other objects, or reapply it to the existing transformed objects.

Creating Shadows

You can create all sorts of shadows by using the Scale, Reflect, and Shear tools, as shown in the illustrations in Figure 7-22.

Figure 7-22: Creating shadows with the transformation tools

STEPS: Creating a Shadow with Transformation Tools

Step 1. Select the path where you want apply the shadow and click the bottom of the path once with the Reflect tool. This action sets the origin of reflection at the base of the image. Drag down while pressing the Shift key. The image flips over, creating a mirror image under the original. Press the Option key (keeping the Shift key pressed) before and during the release of the mouse button.

Step 2. Using the Shear tool, click the base of the reflected copy to set the origin. Click and drag left or right at the other side of the reflection to set the angle of the reflection.

Step 3. Using the Scale tool, click once again on the base of the reflected copy to set the origin. Click and drag up or down at the other side of the reflection.

Step 4. Color the shadow darker than its background.

To create a shadow for type, you must first vertically scale a copy of the type. Hold down the Option key when you release the mouse button to make the copy, and hold down the Shift key to constrain the scaling to vertical as you drag the mouse up or down. Setting the origin of the scale to the baseline of the type helps, as does using all caps or type with no descenders.

Send the copy to the back (⌘-Hyphen) and shear the shadow off to one side or the other, once again setting the origin at the baseline of the type. Holding down Shift as you shear prevents the baseline of the copy from angling up or down.

If you want the shadow in front of the type (making it appear as if the light source is coming from behind the type), use the Reflect tool to flip the copy of the type across the baseline of the type.

Transforming Gradients

You can transform gradients in the same way that you transform objects that are colored by gradients. All of the transformation tools affect gradients, but the best effects are achieved by scaling and shearing gradients, especially radial gradients, as shown in Figure 7-23.

To create an effect similar to that of Figure 7-23, create a radial gradient inside a circle with no Stroke. (Use a circle so that no portions of it are cropped outside of the shape when it is distorted.) Scale and shear the circle with the radial gradient, and the radial gradient becomes scaled and sheared as well.

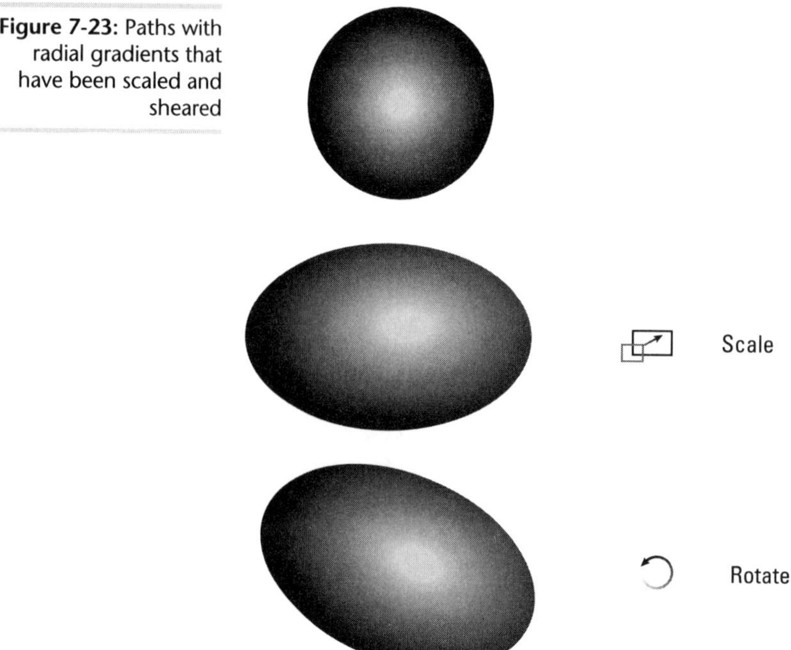

Figure 7-23: Paths with radial gradients that have been scaled and sheared

Rotating into a Path

Clever use of the Rotate tool can create a realistic, winding path by duplicating the same object at different rotational intervals, rotated from different origins.

Start by creating an object of some sort. (The illustration in Figure 7-24 uses paw prints.) Select the objects (I've found it best to group them together) and choose the Rotate tool. Click to set an origin a little distance from the side of the object. Click the other side of the object and drag. As you drag, you will see the outline of the shape of the object that you are dragging. When the object is a good distance away, press the Option key (to copy) and release the mouse button; then release the Option key. A copy of the object appears. Press ⌘-D (Repeat Transform) to create *another* object the same distance away.

After using the Repeat Transform command (⌘-D) a few times, click with the Rotate tool on the other side of the object to set another origin. Click and drag the outline of the object about the same distance; then press the Option key and release the mouse button. Use the Repeat Transform command a few more times.

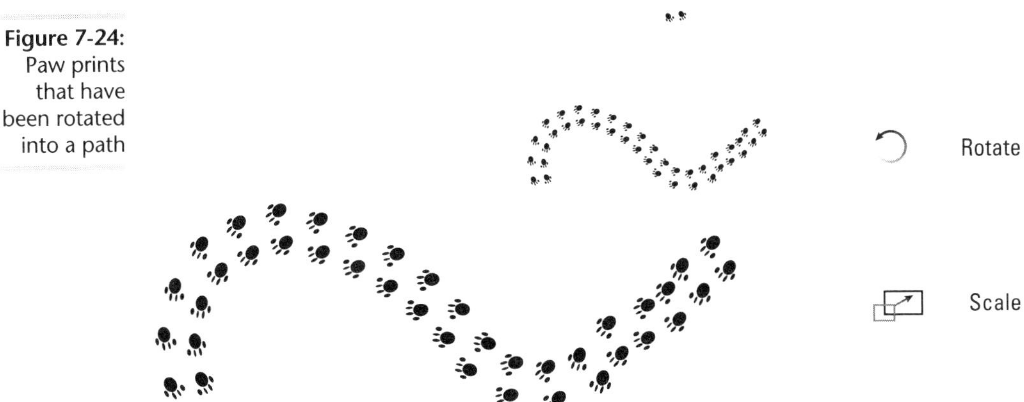

Figure 7-24: Paw prints that have been rotated into a path

The farther you click from the objects to set the origin, the smaller the curve of the path of objects. Clicking right next to the objects causes them to turn sharply.

Making Tiles Using the Reflect Tool

You can make symmetrical tiles with the Reflect tool. You can use a set of four differently positioned yet identical objects to create artwork with a "floor tile" look, as shown in Figure 7-25.

STEPS: Creating Symmetrical Tiles with the Reflect Tool

Step 1. Create the path (or paths) that you will make into the symmetrical tile. Group the artwork together.

Step 2. Take the Reflect tool and click off to the right of it to set the origin. Click and drag on the left edge of the object and drag to the right while pressing the Shift and Option keys. (Using the Shift key reflects the image at only 45° angles.) When the object has been reflected to the right side, let go of the mouse button, still pressing the Option key. Release the Option key. You now have two versions of the object.

Step 3. Select the original and reflected object and reflect again, this time across the bottom of the objects. There are now four objects, each mirrored a little differently, that make up a tile. You can now use this tile to create symmetrical patterns.

Figure 7-25: Creating tiles with the Reflect tool

Using Transformation Tools on Portions of Paths

When using the transformation tools, you don't need to select an entire path. Instead, try experimenting with other effects by selecting single Anchor Points, line segments, and combinations of selected Anchor Points and segments. Another idea is to select portions of paths on different objects.

When you're working with portions of paths, one of the most useful transformation tool procedures is to select a Smooth Point with the Direct Selection tool and then choose a transformation tool.

You can achieve precise control with the Rotate tool. Click the center of the Anchor Point and drag around the Anchor Point. Both Control Handles move, but the distance from the Control Handles to the Anchor Point remains the same. This task is very difficult to perform with just the Direct Selection tool, which you can also use to accomplish the same task.

You can accomplish the exact lengthening of Control Handle Lines by using the Scale tool. Click the Anchor Point to set the origin and then drag out from one of the Control Handles. Both Control Handles will grow from the Anchor Point in equal proportions.

When working on a Smooth Point, you can use the Reflect tool to switch lengths and angles between the two Control Handles.

The following are some more portion-of-path transformation ideas:

- Select all the points in an open path except for the end points and use all the different transformation tools on the selected areas.
- Select the bottommost or topmost Anchor Point in text converted to outlines and scale, rotate, and shear for interesting effects.
- Select two Anchor Points on a rectangle and scale and skew copies into a cube.
- Select just the inside Anchor Points on a star and scale to make the arms of the star wider and thinner. Use the Rotate tool to create Chinese throwing stars. Use the Shear tool to take the "computery" (precise) look away from the star.

Rotating into Kaleidoscopes

By rotating and duplicating objects that have strokes, you can make kaleidoscopic illustrations, such as the one in Figure 7-26. You may have trouble working with the last two or three objects, but this section shows you how to work through any difficulties.

First, select the object that you wish to rotate and duplicate. Choose the Rotate tool and Option-click at one end or corner of the object. In the Rotate dialog box, enter an angle that goes into 360 evenly, such as 18 (20x18=360), and press the Copy button (Option-Return). Choose Repeat Transform (⌘-D) until the object circles around the origin back to the beginning.

Figure 7-26: Objects that have been rotated into kaleidoscopes

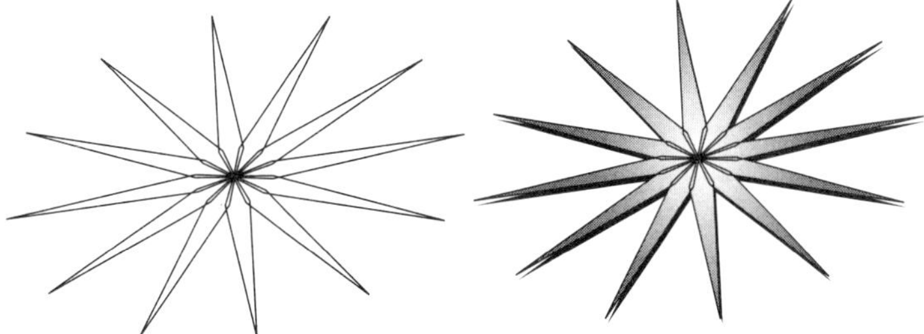

The trouble that you run into here is that if the objects have a Fill and they overlap at all, the last object looks as if it's on the top, and the original object looks as if it's on the bottom, which destroys the perspective of the kaleidoscope. So either the original or the last object has to be fixed. It is generally easier to fix the original (bottommost) object.

Start by selecting the bottommost (original) object. Copy (⌘-C) it and paste it in front (⌘-F). Then create two breaks in the path of the object with the Scissors tool, one on either side of the area where the two objects overlap. Remove that portion of the path by deselecting all (⌘-Shift-A) and selecting it, and then delete just that portion. Many times this step alone will fix the path. If there is a Fill and a Stroke, however, your problems may not work out quite so easily. Copy the remaining piece of the copied object, choose Paste in Front (⌘-F) again, and change the Fill to None. This procedure will correct any Stroke deficiencies from the first copy.

Transforming Patterns

The option in all transformation dialog boxes (and the Move dialog box) to apply transformations to patterns can produce some very interesting results, as shown in Figure 7-27.

Figure 7-27: A pattern that has been scaled up inside text and rotated

One of the most interesting effects results from using patterns that have transparent Fills. Select an object that has a pattern Fill and double-click a transformation tool. Enter a value, check the Pattern tiles box, uncheck the Objects box, and then click Copy. A new object (which is unchanged) will overlap the original object, but the pattern in the new object will have changed. If desired, use the Repeat Transform command (⌘-D) to create additional copies with patterns that have been transformed even more.

Layers

The layering feature of Illustrator provides an easy and powerful way to separate artwork into individual sections. A layer is a separate section of the document that is on its own level, above, under, or in between other layers, but never on the same level as another layer. You can view these sections separately, locked, hidden, and rearranged around each other.

You create, control, and manipulate layers by using the Layers palette. Each layer can have its own color, and that color will show up when all paths and points of objects are selected.

You can create as many layers as you want, up to the limitations of application memory. To make sure that the Adobe people were on the up-and-up about this, I set up a QuicKey to create 4,500 layers on my Quadra 800. The project took about 10 hours, but Illustrator created 4,500 usable layers. Why would you need 4,500 layers? I hope you wouldn't. But you shouldn't have any fears that you will not be able to create enough layers for an illustration. Of course, having 4,500 layers to work with slowed the operation of Illustrator to a crawl. I had to click the mouse button and hold on the menu bar for about 10 seconds before the menu appeared. Suffice to say, the more layers you create, the slower Illustrator will run.

Getting Started with Layers

After you realize that you need to use layers, what do you do? The only way to manipulate, create, and delete layers is by using the Layers palette.

STEPS: Creating and Customizing New Layers

Step 1. If the Layers palette is not showing, choose Window⇨Show Layers (⌘-Control-L). When you open the Layers palette for the first time in a new document, you see only Layer 1 listed.

Step 2. To create a new layer, click the triangle in the upper-right of the palette to display a pop-up menu. Drag over to the first item, New Layer, to see the New Layer dialog box.

Step 3. In the New Layer dialog box, the name of the new layer, Layer 2, is highlighted. To change this name, type a new name, and it will replace the generic name.

Step 4. The options below the name affect how the layer works and is viewed. The first option is the color of the paths and points when objects on that layer are selected. Choose one of the preset colors from the pop-up menu or select the Other option to use a Custom Color.

The preset colors are faded colors that can easily blend into an illustration. For the most vibrant colors, use colors that you have picked from the color wheel at its outermost edges, where the brightness is as high as possible.

Step 5. Select any of the options that you want for this layer. Show makes the objects in the layer visible. Print enables you to print objects that are on this layer. Preview makes the objects on this layer preview. Lock prevents objects on this layer from being selected and prevents any objects from being put on this layer. Dim Placed EPS dims any EPS images on the layer, making them about 50 percent lighter than normal.

Step 6. Click OK after you have chosen all the options you want. The new layer appears above the existing layer in the Layers palette. If you want the objects on the new layer to appear below the objects on the existing layer, click the name of the new layer and drag it under Layer 1.

Step 7. To modify the existing layer, double-click it. You see the Layer Options dialog box, which looks just like the New Layer dialog box. Make the changes and choose the options that you want for this layer and then click OK.

Using the Layers Palette

The Layers palette (shown in Figure 7-28) is the control center where all layer-related activities take place. Most activities take place on the main section of the Layers palette, which is always visible when the Layers palette is on-screen. Other activities take place in the pop-up menu that appears when you press the triangle in the upper right of the palette.

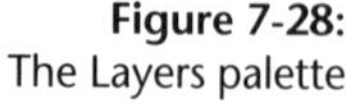

Figure 7-28: The Layers palette

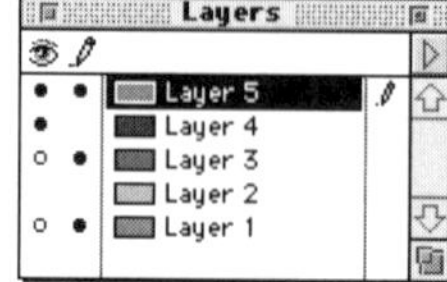

The Main Section of the Layers Palette

Clicking the close box in the upper-left corner closes the Layers palette. Another way to close the Layers palette is to choose Window⇨Hide Layers (⌘-Control-L).To bring the Layers palette back to the screen, choose Window⇨Show Layers (⌘-Control-L).

Clicking the resize box in the upper-right corner of the Layers palette resizes the palette to as large as it needs to be to show all the layers and all the layer names in the document. The resize box never makes the Layers palette smaller than the one previously shown in Figure 7-28, and it does not make it taller than the height of the screen.

The eye in the upper left is above the Show/Hide Column. Clicking the eye toggles between showing only the active layer (the one that is highlighted, which is Layer 5 in Figure 7-28) and showing all the layers. Option-clicking the eye toggles between previewing all layers and previewing only the selected layer, changing the other layers to Artwork mode.

The bullets (circles) below the eye signify different things. Solid bullets represent a layer that is in Preview mode. Hollow bullets mean that the layer is in Artwork mode. No bullet means that the layer is hidden. Clicking a solid or hollow bullet toggles it from showing to hidden. Clicking in the Show/Hide Column when no bullet is present shows the layer. Option-clicking the bullet changes it from solid (Preview mode) to hollow (Artwork mode).

The pencil in the upper left is above the Lock/Unlock Column. Clicking the pencil toggles between unlocking all the layers and locking all the layers but the active one.

The bullets under the pencil signify whether each layer is locked or unlocked. A solid bullet means that the layer is not locked. No bullet means that the layer is locked from use. A light gray bullet means that the layer is hidden, but that when the layer is shown it will not be locked. You can move items to hidden layers as long as those layers are not locked, but you cannot change anything that is already on a hidden layer.

The column in the center of the palette lists all the layers in the document. When no documents are open, no layers are listed. If one layer is highlighted, it is the active layer. You create all new objects on the active layer. You can select more than one layer by Shift-clicking each layer to be selected. To deselect a layer, Shift-click it while it is selected. One layer must always be selected.

The layer at the top of the column is the layer that is on top of all the other layers. The layer at the bottom of the column is at the bottom of all the other layers. To move a layer, click it and drag it up or down. As you drag, a triangle pointer indicates where the layer will be placed when you release the mouse button.

You can undo all layer changes by choosing Edit⇨Undo (⌘-Z).

To the right of the layer names is a column that shows the object status of the layer. If a square appears in that column, at least one object on that layer is selected. If a pencil is in the column, that layer is active, and it is not locked. If a pencil with a slash through it is in that column, then that layer is active, and it is locked.

STEPS: Moving Objects from Layer to Layer

Step 1. Select the objects that you want to move from one layer to another. If the objects are on one layer, group them together so that you can reselect them easily.

Do not group objects from different layers together, or all objects will be placed on the topmost layer.

Step 2. Open the Layers palette by choosing Window⇨Show Layers. A square should appear next to one of the layers. The square represents the selected objects.

If you select objects on more than one layer, a square appears on each of the layers that has a selected object.

Step 3. Drag the square from its current layer to the target layer. The objects do not move left, right, up, or down, but now they may be in front of or behind other objects, depending on the layer that they are now upon.

Figure 7-29 shows an object that's been given the "layered-look."

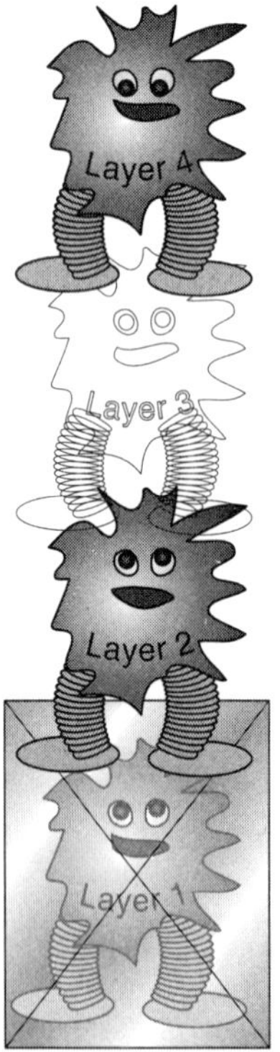

The Paths and Points and Handles
All of them wearing open-toed sandals
Had a dilemma, a confusing vector problem
That stumped even the most brightest of them
(Editors noted that this rhyming was sad
"It's unbalanced and ugly and just plain bad")

W'ever objects would meet, yet stay separated
They'd still be intermingled and some even dated
Groups were formed with a hierarchical slant
"We paths stick together" was their war cry and chant
Yet that wasn't enough, grouping groups was confusing
After keeping score for a while, the users were losing

Adobe Techs fielded support calls by the hundred zillions
So busy their Sega scores never made it to the millions
Suddenly the engineers assigned to make vectors better
Thought "We'll make layers, and make them to the letter"
Layers were magic and frosting and sugar and spice
The things of calories, tooth decay, and Disney mice

Vector objects rejoiced and cheered and screamed in glee,
"This is how life in a PostScript application should be"
Layers could be moved and previewed and printed
They could be colored and of course the fonts were still hinted
When the Paths and Points and Handles heard this great news
They ditched those open-toed sandals and bought leather dress shoes....

Figure 7-29: A Layers Seussian story

Clicking the triangle in the upper-right of the Layers palette displays a pop-up menu that shows different options that are available relative to the selected layers.

The first option, New Layer, creates a new layer at the top of the list. When New Layer is selected, the New Layer dialog box appears, which is the same as the Layer Options dialog box, except for the title. When a new layer is created with Illustrator 6, it is automatically assigned the next color in the color list.

If you press the Option key before you click the pop-up menu triangle, the first menu item will read New Layer Above First Layer or New Layer Above whatever the name of the active layer is.

The next option is Delete, which will delete the layer and any artwork on the layer. If the layer to be deleted contains artwork, a dialog box will warn you that you are about to delete it. If several layers are selected, the entry reads Delete Layers, and all selected layers will be deleted. You can undo layer deletions.

The third menu item is Layer Options for Layer 1 (or Layer Options for whatever the name of the active layer is) — the menu item will read Layers Options if more than one layer is selected. Selecting Layer Options displays the Layer Options dialog box, in which you can choose a number of different options. If more than one layer is selected, the layer options will affect all selected layers.

Double-clicking a layer name also brings up the Layer Options dialog box.

The next three options are different ways of changing the locking and viewing options. Hide Others/Show All does the same as clicking the eye. Artwork Others/Preview All is the same as Option-clicking the eye, and Lock Others/Unlock All is the same as clicking the pencil.

Checking the Paste Remembers Layers option causes all objects to be pasted on the layer they were copied from, regardless of which layer is currently active. Unchecking this menu item causes objects on the Clipboard to be pasted on the current layer.

Layer Advice and Strategies

Layers take up RAM and computer power, and the more layers you have, the slower your system will be.

Do create layers when you believe that they will help you organize an illustration better. Even setting up one additional layer can dramatically ease selection and moving problems. One of the best uses for layers is for tracing EPS images. To learn exactly how to perform this procedure, see Chapter 4.

Use vivid, distinct colors for each layer. Using the same colors for all layers makes you miss out on half the power of layers. If you can't tell which layer an object is on, what good is it?

Summary

- Path editing is done in Illustrator by using the Direct Selection, Scissors, and Convert Direction Point tools.
- Adding Anchor Points alone never changes the shape of a path.
- Removing Anchor Points can drastically change the shape of a path.
- Paths can be split one at a time with the Scissors tool.
- You can slice through paths with the Knife tool.
- Quickly make duplicates of certain sections of paths with the Lasso tool.
- Selected points can be aligned using the Average command.
- Any two selected end points can be joined by using the Join command.
- Entire objects can be aligned by using the Align palette.
- The Convert Direction Point tool changes the Anchor Point type.
- The five major types of PostScript transformations are represented by four tools, Rotate, Scale, Reflect, and Shear, and the Move dialog box.
- Transform Each combines Illustrator 5.x's "each" filters and incorporates the Move, Scale, and Rotate functions that work on selected objects independently.
- Layers can be used to effectively separate different sections of your artwork.

Type

CHAPTER 8

In This Chapter

- Methods of entering type in a document
- Creating Point type
- Creating Rectangle type
- Placing type within areas
- How to create type on a path
- Selecting type and changing type attributes
- Importing type
- Converting type into editable outlines
- Designing with the Type tool
- Special characters
- Avoiding type compatibility problems
- Creating custom fonts

Type is a huge part of Illustrator. In previous versions of this book, I split type between several different chapters, in different areas of the *Macworld Illustrator 6 Bible*. But this time, I've packed this one chapter full of everything I could about type, to the point where this version of the Illustrator Bible is a little type-heavy, and severely off balance.

But then, when I talk to Illustrator users, from vets to those who are wet behind the ears, and even those users that have just started using Illustrator, they all tell me one thing: "Yer really tall, Ted." And a lot of them tell me that the main thing they use Illustrator for is manipulating type. So here's what could be the most important chapter in the book (and, by last count, it's the biggest).

The Type Menu

If you have a 12" or smaller monitor, you only have one menu with type information on it, called the Type menu. If you have a larger monitor, though, you will have two type menus: the Font menu and the Type menu. The Font menu lists all the fonts that you currently have installed on your computer, while the Type menu contains all sorts of cool menu items that affect type on your system. But don't be too concerned if you have a smaller monitor; fonts are available by pulling down the Font submenu from the Type menu.

Most of the Type options can be changed in the Character palette (choose Type⇨Character or press ⌘-T), which is discussed later in this chapter.

Type is set in Illustrator in *stories.* A story is a set of continuous, linked text. When the term *paragraph* is mentioned, it is usually referring to the characters that are between Returns. If there are no Returns in a story, then that story is said to have one paragraph. Returns end paragraphs and begin new ones. There is always exactly one more paragraph in a story than there are Returns.

The following sections describe each of the Type menu options.

The Font Option

The Font option (⌘-Shift-F or ⌘-Option-Shift-M) displays a submenu with all the fonts that are currently installed on the Macintosh you are using. Pressing ⌘-Shift-F or ⌘-Option-Shift-M automatically highlights the Font field on the Character palette. A check mark appears next to the font that is currently selected. If no check mark appears next to any of the fonts, more than one font is currently selected.

If you are wondering why the folks at Adobe chose such an odd combination of keys and commands, you probably don't use QuarkXPress too much. Quark's key command for highlighting the font field in its measurement palette is ⌘-Option-Shift-M.

The Size Option

The Size option (⌘-Shift-S) displays a submenu with "Other" listed and various point sizes. When Other is chosen, the Character palette appears with the Size field highlighted. You can type any point size from .1 to 1296 in this field.

Type created in Illustrator may be scaled to any size, but to go beyond the size limits, you must convert the type into outline paths by using the Create Outlines command.

A check mark appears next to the point size that is currently selected. If the point size currently selected does not correspond to a point size in the Size submenu, a check mark appears next to the Other menu item. Point size for type is measured from the top of the ascenders (like the top of a capital letter *T*) to the bottom of the descenders (like the bottom of a lowercase *g*). If no check mark appears next to any of the sizes, more than one size is currently selected (even if the different sizes are all Other sizes).

You can also increase and decrease the point size of type by using the keyboard shortcut ⌘-Shift->, which increases the point size by the amount specified in General Preferences, and ⌘-Shift-<, which decreases the point size by the amount specified in General Preferences.

Yet another way to change point size is to use the Scale tool. Using the Scale tool to change point size lets you change to any size; that size is displayed in the Character palette as soon as you are done scaling. Once again, keep in mind that the limit in scaling type is 1296 points, and you cannot exceed that even with the Scale tool (unless, of course, the type is already outlined paths).

The Leading Option

The Leading option displays a pop-up menu with leading sizes that correspond to the point sizes for type, along with an Auto item and an option called Other. *Leading* is the distance between the baseline of one line of type and the baseline of the preceding line of type, as illustrated in Figure 8-1.

When you are changing the leading option, you are affecting an entire paragraph at once — not just a word or a sentence, but the entire paragraph. In fact, with the type tools being used to select type, you must actually triple-click or drag over all the characters in the entire paragraph, including the Return at the end, for the leading to be decreased.

The leading for the entire paragraph is always the greatest leading within that paragraph. When you choose Auto, the leading is always 20% greater than the point size of the type. If you choose Other, the Character palette is displayed with the Leading field highlighted.

Let me start by saying that I am able to type this because my fingers are the only section of my body which is still functional. After this afternoon's practice, my knees are torn up, the balls of my feet are covered by blisters, my shoulders ache, those wonderful pedals have turned my shins to crushed bone and the muscles behind them to lifeless jelly, brushburns cover my palms, arms, left side of my face, and of course the sides of my legs.

} 11 Points baseline to baseline

I doubt I will be allowed back onto the tennis courts where I practice riding, for the blood that continuously spurted from my elbows has considerably darkened the out-of-bounds lines. But I have emerged alive. And most importantly, triumphant. For now I can ride backwards on my unicycle. Well, at least for about ten feet, until gravity takes control of the situation.

} 16 Points baseline to baseline

Figure 8-1: Two paragraphs with different leading

Technically, you cannot enter in a number in the Leading field that is less than .1 point or greater than 1296 points. But if you check the Auto leading box or choose Auto in the Leading submenu, the leading can go as high as 1555 points!

Unfortunately, when you take off Auto leading, the leading automatically changes back to 1296. Once again, if you convert your type to outlined paths, you can choose any leading you desire merely by dragging the lines apart. If no check mark appears next to any of the leading sizes, more than one leading size is currently selected (even if the different leading sizes are all Other sizes).

The Alignment Option

The Alignment option displays a pop-up menu with five different choices. *Alignment* refers to the horizontal positioning of type in relation to the point position in Point type, the Path Bar in Path type, or the left and right edges in Rectangle type and Area type.

Alignment always affects an entire paragraph if the following conditions are met:

- At least one character is selected with a type tool.
- An insertion point is blinking in that paragraph or the type is chosen with a selection tool.

Alignment directions are always relevant to the direction the type is rotated. For example, Rectangle type rotated 90° (it would read from bottom to top) and aligned flush left would be flush at the bottom of the rectangle.

A check mark appears next to the alignment that is currently chosen. If no check mark appears next to any of the alignments, more than one alignment is currently selected. The five different types of alignment are shown in Figure 8-2.

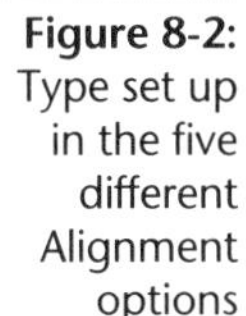

Figure 8-2: Type set up in the five different Alignment options

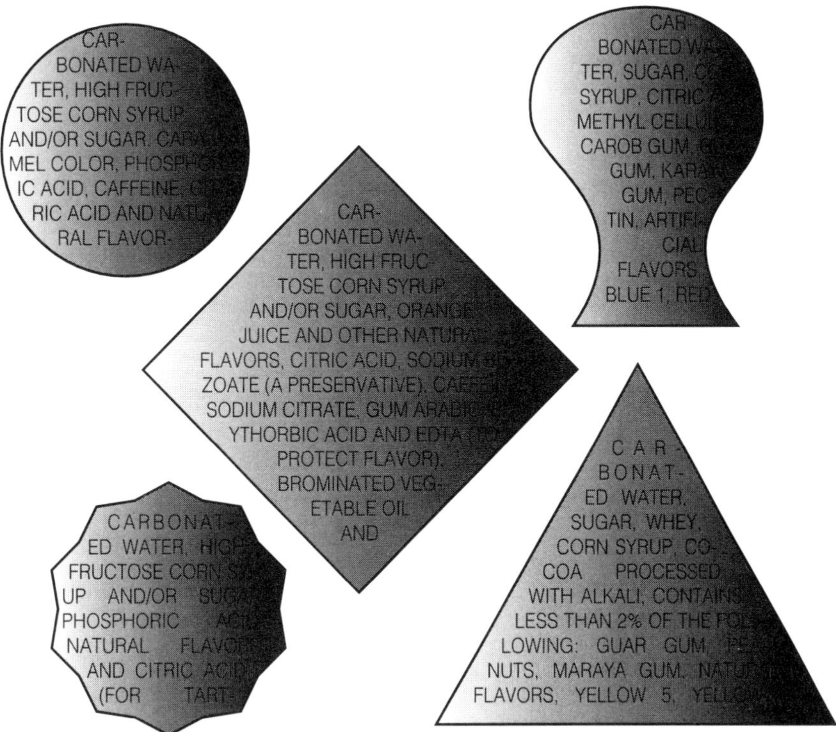

The function of each Alignment option is as follows:

- **Alignment⇨Left** (⌘-Shift-L) makes selected type *flush left.* Point type will align to the right of the point, and successive lines will be placed evenly on the left side of the type. Path type will align to the right of the Path Bar. Rectangle type and Area type will align as far as possible to the leftmost edge of the shape the type is within.
- **Alignment⇨Center** (⌘-Shift-C) makes selected type *centered.* Point type will align at the center of the point, and successive lines will be centered in relation to the first line. Path type will be centered on the Path Bar. Rectangle type and

Area type will be centered in their respective shapes. Flush-left type is sometimes referred to as ragged right because the left side is smooth and straight, while the right side is uneven.

- **Alignment⇨Right** (⌘-Shift-R) makes all selected type *flush right.* Point type will align to the left of the point, and successive lines will be even on the right side of the type. Path type will align to the left of the Path Bar. Rectangle type and Area type will align as far as possible to the rightmost edge of the shape the type is within. Flush-right type is often referred to as ragged left because the right side is smooth and straight, while the left side is uneven.
- **Alignment⇨Justified** (⌘-Shift-J) makes all selected type *justified.* In justified type, words are evenly spaced out in all lines in a paragraph — except the last line, which is flush left. The type can be considered to be both left and right justified. Justified type only works with Rectangle type and Area type. Choosing Alignment⇨Justified for Point type or Path type will result in no activity taking place.

  If a justified paragraph has only one line of type, that line is the last line in the paragraph and so will appear flush left.
- **Alignment⇨Justify Last Line** (⌘-Shift-B) makes all selected type *justified,* even the last line of a paragraph. Justify Last Line only works with Rectangle type and Area type. Choosing Alignment⇨Justify Last Line for Point type or Path type will result in no activity taking place.

  Justify Last Line will usually put extra space between words, not letters, when justifying. To put space evenly between letters as well as words, use the Fit Headline command.

The Character Option

The Character option (⌘-T) brings up the Character palette with the Font field highlighted. In the Character palette, you can change fonts, styles, point size, leading, baseline shift, horizontal scale, and tracking/kerning values, all at one time!

If the Character palette is currently open, choosing the Character option will close (hide) it.

The Paragraph Option

The Paragraph option (⌘-Shift-P) displays the Paragraph palette with the Left Indentation field highlighted (see Figure 8-3). You can use this palette to change the left, right, and first line indents, and change the alignment by clicking different alignment boxes. In addition, the Leading before ¶ (a fancy name for "space before paragraph"), Hang punctuation, and Auto hyphenate options are available. In the bottom part of the palette (click the little lever in the lower-right corner of the palette to see the bottom part), you can set hyphenation and spacing limitations and guidelines.

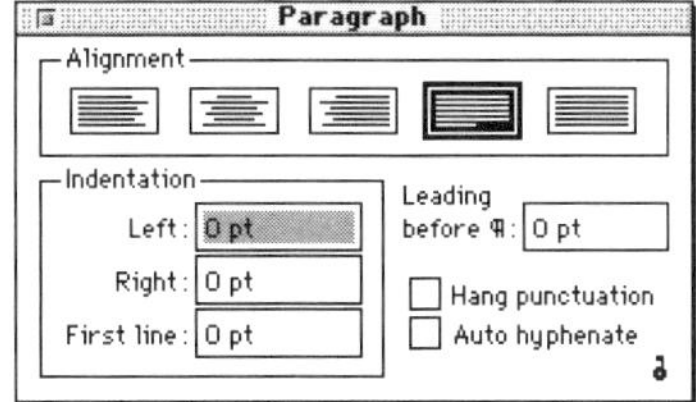

Figure 8-3: The Paragraph palette

If the Paragraph palette is currently open, choosing the Paragraph command will close (hide) it.

The Link Blocks Option

The Link Blocks option (⌘-Shift-G) links text from one area or rectangle to another, continuing a story from one area or rectangle to another (see Figure 8-4). Linked blocks act like groups, enabling you to use the regular Selection tool and click on just one area in order to select all areas. (Individual blocks can still be selected with the Direct Selection tool.) Whenever more text is available than can fit into a text area, a tiny little plus sign in a box appears, alerting you that there is more text in the box than you see.

To use Link Blocks, select a text area or rectangle and any other shapes, even text rectangles and areas, and choose Link Blocks. Text will flow from the backmost shape to the frontmost in any group of linked blocks, so be careful to order your boxes correctly when setting up linked text. In fact, if you send a box to the back, that will be where the text starts from, going to the next box forward, and then the next, and so on. You cannot select Link Blocks if at least one text area and one other path or text area is not selected.

The Unlink Blocks Option

The Unlink Blocks option (⌘-Shift-U) destroys the links made with the Link Blocks command. Blocks can only be unlinked when all boxes linked together are chosen. This is done quite easily with the regular Selection tool. When blocks are unlinked, the text inside them is split into several stories, one for each block. If the boxes are later relinked with the Link Blocks command, they will be separated by paragraph returns.

Figure 8-4: Text blocks linked together in the order of the arrows

I looked at the instruction sheet, but after seeing that they wanted me to hold onto the wall for support to get started, like I was a little kid or something, I threw it out. Three seconds later, after the unicycle had, under its own power, flown out from under me towards the dog (he's still in therapy), I crawled over to

the trash can and grabbed the instructions out with the arm that hadn't been crushed beneath my body. Hours later, I was clawing my way around the apartment walls, one revolution at a time. There was no stopping me now. It was time to let go of the wall. Reading the instructions further I

discovered that to go forward a rider leans and pedals forward to prevent falling forward. If you feel you are falling forward, the instructions said, pedal faster. Sure, that

makes sense, I thought. There is one problem with this method of riding. The faster I felt I was falling, the faster I pedalled, and soon I couldn't pedal fast enough to prevent myself from falling. To make a long story shorter, my face hit the floor at about sixty miles an hour, and as my nose was shoved through the back of my head, I watched the unicycle fly over my crumpled body, almost

The Make Wrap Option

The Make Wrap option wraps text around any paths, as shown in Figure 8-5. To use Make Wrap, select both the type and the paths you want the type to wrap around. The paths that the type wraps around must be in front of the type in order for them to wrap around the paths. The objects then act like a grouped object; you can use the regular Selection tool to select all objects in a Make Wrap area.

Make Wrap only works with Area type and Rectangle type (the option is dimmed for Path type and Point type). You can choose Make Wrap if no object is selected, but choosing Make Wrap at this point will display an error message.

Make Wrap works in levels: You can Make Wrap with one type area or rectangle to a path and then Make Path again with the same type area or rectangle to another path, and the type will wrap around both paths.

Remember that Make Wrap only wraps around paths; regardless of how thick the Stroke on your path is, the wrap will not change. This can cause the wrapping object to run into the text if the object has a heavy Stroke.

The Release Wrap Option

The Release Wrap option releases any text wraps that are selected, all at one time. Release Wrap does *not* release wraps in the order that they were created. Because paths wrapped to type areas and rectangles do not lose or change attributes when they become wrapped paths, those paths retain their original Paint Style attributes when released.

The Fit Headline Option

The Fit Headline option is designed to automatically increase the weight and width of type using Multiple Master fonts in order to fit type perfectly from the left side of a type area or rectangle to the right side of that same type area or rectangle. Of course, for this to work, you must have Multiple Master typefaces. Personally, I think this feature would have been great if it just increased the point size of any type, Multiple Master or not, so that the type fit from left to right.

If you don't have Multiple Master typefaces, you can still use Fit Headline. Although the command only increases the tracking of the type until it is justified, it actually does a lot better job than the Type⇨Alignment⇨Justify Last Line command, which only puts space in between words.

Figure 8-5: Text wrapped around different objects

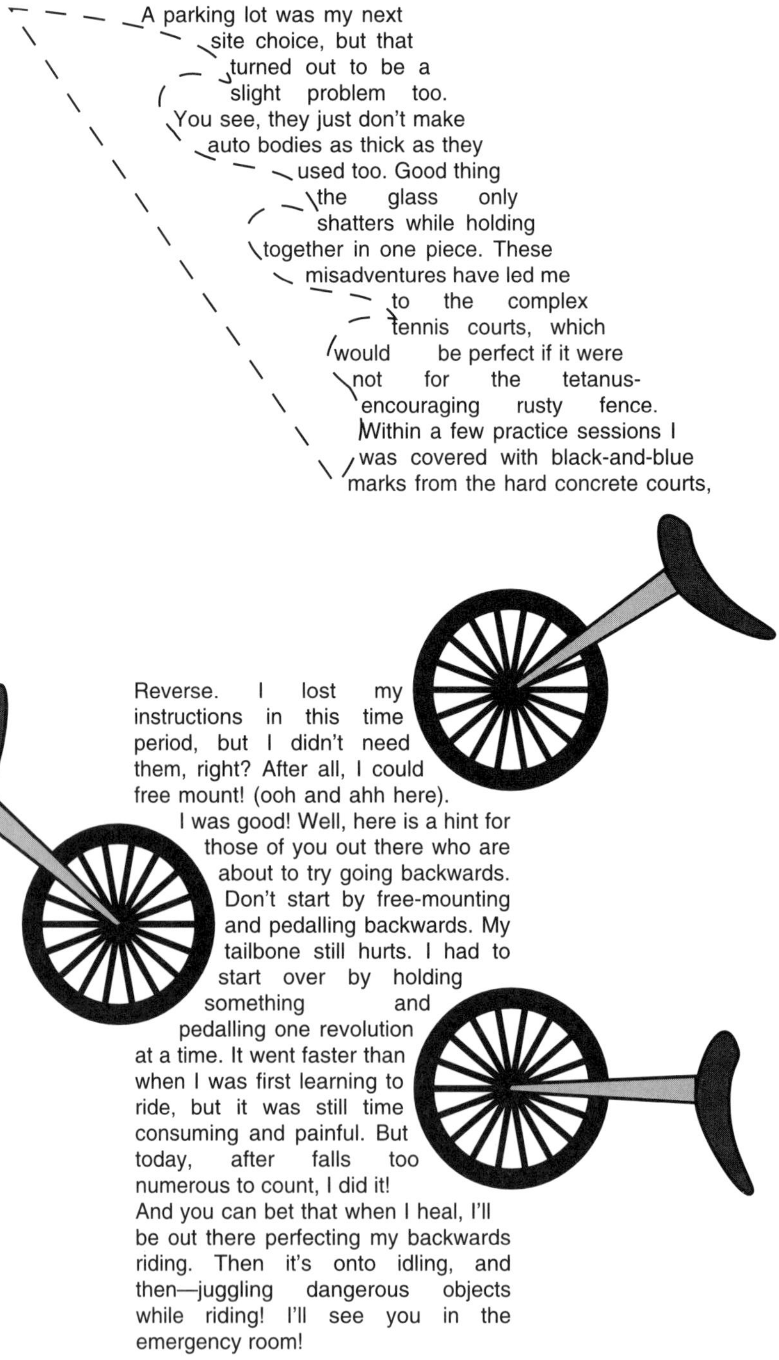

A parking lot was my next site choice, but that turned out to be a slight problem too. You see, they just don't make auto bodies as thick as they used too. Good thing the glass only shatters while holding together in one piece. These misadventures have led me to the complex tennis courts, which would be perfect if it were not for the tetanus-encouraging rusty fence. Within a few practice sessions I was covered with black-and-blue marks from the hard concrete courts,

Reverse. I lost my instructions in this time period, but I didn't need them, right? After all, I could free mount! (ooh and ahh here).

I was good! Well, here is a hint for those of you out there who are about to try going backwards. Don't start by free-mounting and pedalling backwards. My tailbone still hurts. I had to start over by holding something and pedalling one revolution at a time. It went faster than when I was first learning to ride, but it was still time consuming and painful. But today, after falls too numerous to count, I did it! And you can bet that when I heal, I'll be out there perfecting my backwards riding. Then it's onto idling, and then—juggling dangerous objects while riding! I'll see you in the emergency room!

The Create Outlines Option

This option needs a key command (alas, it currently has none) because it is one of the handiest capabilities of Illustrator. (To compensate for this lack of a command-key shortcut, I used QuicKeys and assigned F4 the function of creating outlines from type.)

After your type is set (and spelled correctly), choose Create Outlines and the type selected is converted into *editable paths* (see Figure 8-6). To convert type to outlines, the type needs to be selected with a selection tool, not a type tool. Each letter is its own compound path, and each path can be edited with the Direct Selection tool.

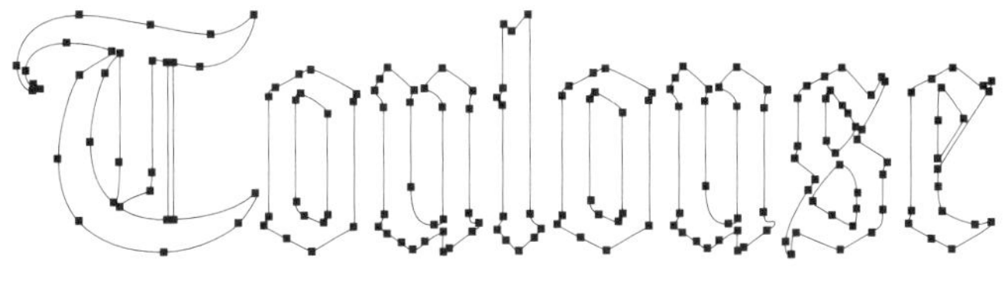

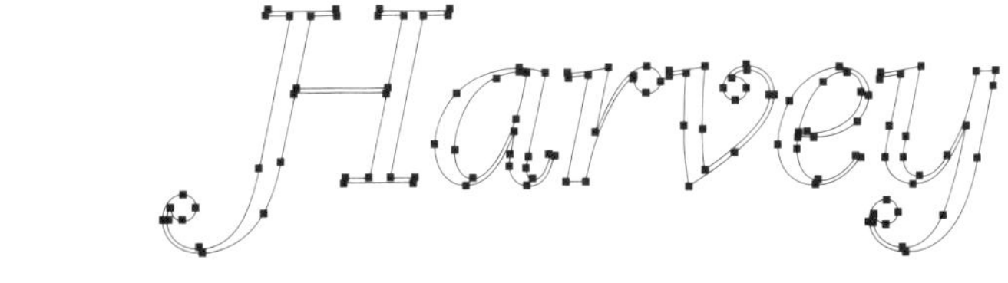

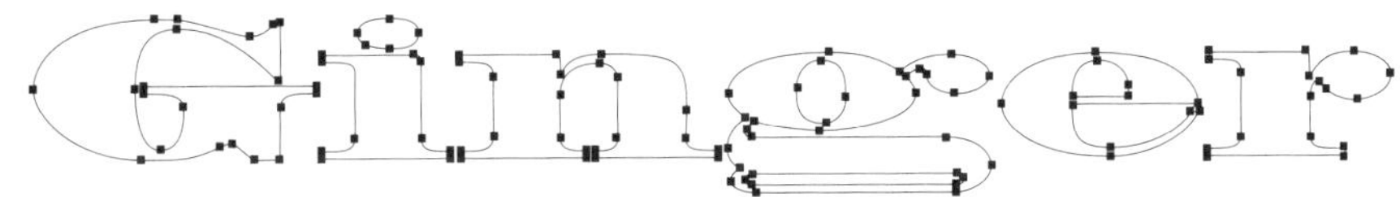

Figure 8-6: Type converted into outlines with the Create Outlines command

Create Outlines only works with Type 1 PostScript and TrueType fonts, not bitmapped or Type 3 PostScript fonts. For Create Outlines to work with PostScript Type 1 fonts, you must have Adobe Type Manager (ATM) installed and active (with the extensions on), and you must have both the screen and printer fonts for those fonts. (TrueType combines the screen and printer fonts into one piece — If you can choose a TrueType font, you can create outlines with it, regardless of whether ATM is installed or not.)

When type has been converted to outlines, you can apply gradients to its Fill, as well as apply patterns to its Fill that you can preview on-screen. (Patterns can be applied to non-outline type, but you cannot see those patterns in the type; instead, the type becomes a dingy gray color.)

While you can undo Create Outlines, be forewarned that there is no way to convert back to type in case you made a spelling error or wish to change the font or any other type attributes.

All forms of type, including Point type, Path type, Area type, and Rectangle type, may be converted to outlines.

Creating outlines out of type is also very useful when you want to send the file to be output and the person doing the output does not have the font you are using. Simply use the Create Outlines option before you send the file, and it will print just fine.

Hinting

Most Type 1 fonts have something called "hinting" built into them. Hinting is a method for adjusting type at small point sizes, especially at low resolutions. While hinting is built into several fonts, when those fonts are converted into paths via the Create Outlines command, the hinting is gone. This is part of the reason that type converted to outlines can look heavier than otherwise.

Creating outlines shouldn't cause that much of a problem when the type will be output to an imagesetter, because the high resolution of the imagesetter makes up for the loss of hinting.

Type Areas

In order for type to exist in Illustrator, there must first be a *type area* defined. Type can never be outside these areas because type is treated very differently than any other object in Illustrator.

There are four different kinds of type areas: Point type, Rectangle type, Area type, and Path type. Point type exists around a single point clicked with the standard Type tool. Rectangle type is type constricted to a rectangular area — also drawn with the standard Type tool. Area type is type that flows within a specific open or closed path. Path type is type whose baseline is attached to a specific open or closed path.

Figure 8-7 shows the same sentence as Point type, Rectangle type, Area type, and Path type.

These are the days you'll remember. Never before and never since, I promise, will the whole world be warm as this.

These are the days you'll remember. Never before and never since, I promise, will the whole world be warm as this.

These are the days you'll remember. Never before and never since, I promise, will the whole world be warm as this.

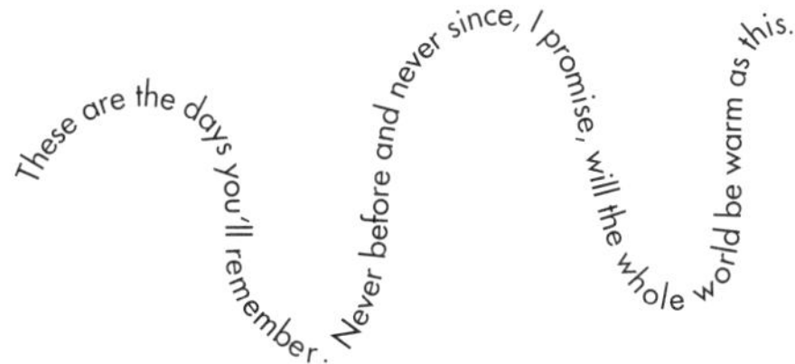

Figure 8-7: The same sentence as it appears in Point type, Rectangle type, Area type, and Path type

Using Type Tools

Initially, the three type tools are used to create type, and then later they can be used to edit that very same type. The default tool is the standard Type tool, which creates both Point type and Rectangle type. The two pop-up tools are the Area Type tool and the Path Type tool. (All of these tools are explained in detail in the following sections.)

Each of the type tools displays a different cursor, as shown in Figure 8-8.

Type

Area Type

Path Type

Figure 8-8: The Type cursors. The top cursor is present when creating Point or Rectangle type. The second cursor is for Area type, and the bottom cursor is for Path type.

You can select type in Illustrator with the Selection tool, in which case *all* the type in the *story* (a contiguous set of type in either Point type, Rectangle type, Area type, or Path type) is modified.

Selecting type with a type tool is done either by dragging across characters or lines — every character from the initial click until the release of the mouse button is selected. Double-clicking with a type tool selects the entire word you clicked, including the space after it. Triple-clicking (clicking three times in the same place) selects an entire paragraph.

You can enter new type into an existing story by clicking with a type tool where you want the new type to begin and then typing. If type is highlighted when you begin typing, the highlighted type is replaced with the new type.

The Type Tool

With the Type tool, you can do everything you need to do with type. Clicking in any empty part of your document creates Point type, an Anchor Point to which the type aligns. Type created as Point type does not wrap automatically; instead, you must manually press the Return key and start typing the next line. Point type is usually used for creating smaller portions of type, like labels and headlines.

Clicking and dragging with the Type tool creates Rectangle type — type that is bordered by a box, which you create when you click and drag the Type tool.

As the Type tool is passed over a closed path, it changes automatically into the Area Type tool. Clicking a closed path results in type that fills the shape of the area you clicked. Holding down the Option key as you pass over a closed path changes the tool into the Path Type tool. This "intelligent" switching of type tools by Illustrator prevents you from having to choose different type tools when you want a different kind of type.

If the Type tool crosses over an open path, it becomes the Path Type tool. Clicking an open path places type *on the path,* with the baseline of the type aligning along the curves and angles of the path. Holding down the Option key when the Type tool is over an open path changes it into the Area Type tool.

The Area Type Tool

The Area Type tool is used for filling closed or open paths with type. Even compound paths can be filled in Illustrator.

You can toggle between the Area Type tool and the Path Type tool by pressing the Option key. Pressing the Control key changes the Area Type tool to the standard Type tool.

The Path Type Tool

The Path Type tool is used for running type along any path in Illustrator. This is a great tool for putting type on the edges of a circle.

You can toggle between the Path Type tool and the Area Type tool by pressing the Option key. Pressing the Control key changes the Path Type tool to the standard Type tool.

Point Type

To create type with a single point defining its location, use the Type tool and click on one single location within the document window where there are no paths. A blinking *insertion point* appears, signifying that type will appear where that point is located (see Figure 8-9). By typing on the keyboard, text will now appear in the document at that insertion point. Type cannot be entered when a selection tool is being used. Type selected with a selection tool appears at the bottom of Figure 8-9.

Figure 8-9: Point type with an insertion point at the end of the line, and the same line of type selected with a selection tool

When the Illustrator program is first booted, text defaults into the following values: 12 Helvetica, Flush left, Auto Leading on, Spacing 0, Baseline Shift 0, Tracking/Kerning 0, Horizontal Scale 100%, Auto Kerning off, no indentation or paragraph spacing. There is no method within Illustrator to automatically change this default upon startup of the program.

Point type that is flush left will have its left side flush against the vertical location of the point initially clicked. Centered type will be centered left to right on the vertical location of the point. Flush right type will have its right edge flush with the vertical location of the point. Point type cannot be justified with either of the two methods available.

When creating Point type, keep in mind that only hard Returns will force a new line of text to be created. If no Returns are used, text will eventually run right off the document. When importing text, be sure that the text contains these hard Returns, or the text will run into oblivion. Hard Returns can be added after importing, but it may be difficult to do so.

Rectangle Type

There are two ways to create Rectangle type (see Figure 8-10). The easiest way is by clicking and dragging the Type tool diagonally, which creates a rectangle as you drag. The blinking insertion point appears in the top row of text, with its horizontal location dependent on the text alignment choice. Choosing flush right forces the insertion point to appear in the upper-right corner; centered puts the insertion point in the center of the row; and flush left or one of the justification methods makes the insertion point appear in the upper-left corner.

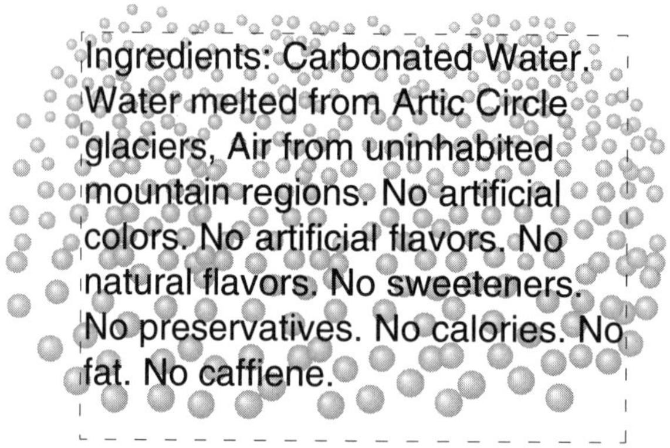

Figure 8-10: Rectangle Type (the dotted line is the border of the rectangle)

If you press the Shift key while drawing the rectangle, the rectangle is constrained to a perfect square. There is no need to drag from upper left to lower right — you can drag from any corner to its opposite — whichever way is most convenient.

STEPS: Creating Rectangle Type in an Area of Specific Proportions

Step 1. Using the Rectangle tool, click without dragging to get the Rectangle dialog box. Enter the exact dimensions of the type area.

Step 2. Choose the Type tool and click the Type cursor on the edge of the rectangle. Any type entered into this box will be constrained to that particular rectangle.

Once a rectangle has been used as a type rectangle, it is always a type rectangle, even if the text is removed. You can convert the type rectangle back to a normal rectangle by selecting it (when no text is in it) and choosing Revert Text Path from the Text filter submenu in the Filter menu. Revert Text Path can be installed into Illustrator by dragging the Revert Text Path Plug-In from the Optional Plug-Ins folder and the Plug-Ins folder.

To create type in a rectangle of specific proportions, draw a rectangle with the Rectangle tool by clicking once in the document window. The Rectangle Size dialog box appears, where you can enter the information needed. Then choose the Area Type tool and click on the edge of the rectangle. The type will fill the rectangle as you type.

If you need to create a Rectangle type area that is a precise size but don't want to draw a rectangle first, open the Info palette by choosing Window⇨Show Info (⌘-Control-I) and as you drag the type cursor, watch the information in the Info palette, which will display the dimensions of the type area. When the *W* field is the width you want, and the *H* field is the height you want, release the mouse button.

I Can't Select My Type!

Frank: I'm getting really mad.

Toulouse: Any particular reason for that?

Frank: I can't select my type.

Toulouse: Which tool are you using to select?

Frank: The Type tool, you ninny.

Toulouse: Okay. Do you see an insertion point blinking anywhere else?

Frank: I'm zoomed in pretty far.

Toulouse: Well, if you accidentally selected another text area first, you might not be able to select the one you want.

Frank: So, what can I do?

Toulouse: Try deselecting everything. The quickest way to do this is by pressing ⌘-Shift-A, which is the key command for Select None.

Frank: It worked!

Area Type

The capability of placing type within any area is one of the "cooler" features of Illustrator, right up there with the fact that the program comes in a hip, 90s looking box.

To create type within an area, first create the path that will be the area that confines the type. The path can be closed or open and any size. Keep in mind that the area of the path should be close to the size needed for the amount of text (at the point size that it needs to fit). After the path has been created, choose the Area Type tool and position the type cursor over the edge of the path and click.

The type in Figure 8-11 has been flowed into the outline of the CHO logo. Using text wraps, the type exists only inside the letters yet reads across all of them.

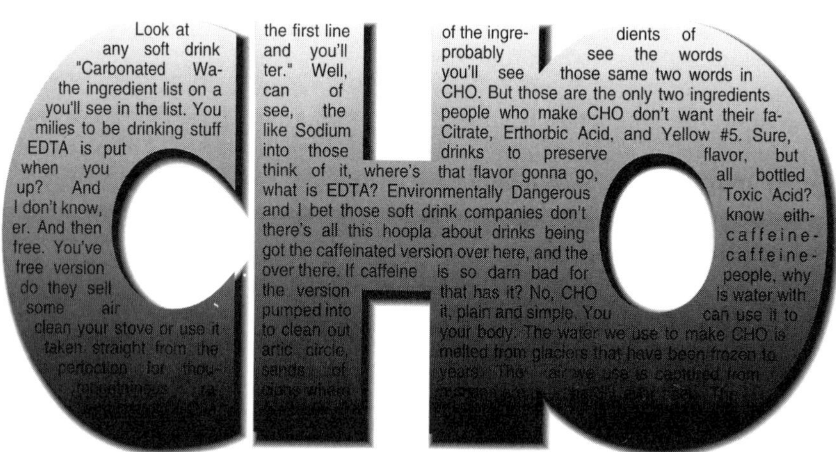

Figure 8-11: Area type created so that the text flows inside the outlines of the word "CHO"

Choosing the Good Shapes for Area Type

What exactly constitutes a "good" shape to be used for Area type? As a rule of thumb, gently curved shapes are better than harsh, jagged ones. Type tends to flow better into the larger lumps created by smoothly curving paths.

Try to avoid creating paths with wild or tight curves. Other designs that can cause problems are "hourglass" shapes or any closed path that has an area where the sides are almost touching. Figure 8-12 shows how type flows into a smoothly curved area and how it has trouble flowing into a sharp, spiky shape.

Figure 8-12: Type flows much better into a smoothly curved area (left) than a sharp, spiky one.

Try to make the top and bottom boundaries of the path have less "bumpiness" than the sides. This will reduce the number of times that type jumps from one area across another.

For the best results with Area type, make the type small and justify it (⌘-Shift-J). This will ensure that the type flows up against the edges of the path.

Outlining Areas of Area Type

Placing a Stroke on the path surrounding Area type can be a great visual effect, but doing so and getting good results can be a bit tricky.

If the Stroke is thicker than a point or two, and you don't want the type to run into the edges of the Stroke, there are a few things you can do.

The fastest way to do this (although it requires a bit of math) is to copy the Stroked path that contains the type and paste it in front. Fill the shape with the background color and a Stroke equal to twice the amount of white space you would like between the Stroke and the text. Then hide the path and the type, and select the original path. Delete the text from this path and use the following formula to calculate the correct Stroke width:

(Desired Width + White Space size) × 2 = Bottom layer Stroke weight

For example, if you want a Stroke that is 6 points wide on a shape and has 3 points of white space between the Stroke and the text, the bottom shape will have a Stroke of (6 + 3) X 2 = 18. The top layer will have a "white" Stroke of 6, with a Fill the same color as the Stroke.

The second way to do this is by using the Offset Path filter. This is better for two reasons: first, it requires much less math, and second, you don't have to worry about background color (especially if the background is a bunch of other objects or a placed raster image). Of course, there is a catch: The path cannot be turned into a text area boundary before the Offset Path filter is applied to it.

STEPS: Creating Inset Type Areas with the Offset Path Filter

Step 1. Create a path for your Area type with any drawing tool. Close the path for the best results when using the Offset Path filter.

Step 2. Do *not* make the path into a type area by clicking on the path with a type tool at this point. Select the path you wish to use for Area type with the Selection tool and then choose Filter⇨Object⇨Offset Path.

Step 3. Determine the distance that you wish your text to be from the edge of the real path. If there is a Stroke on the edge of the real path, add half the width of the Stroke to your distance. In the Offset field, enter this distance in negative form. For example, if you want the distance from the edge of the path to be 6 points and the width of the Stroke is 10 points, you would enter **–11** points in the Offset field (6+10/2).

Step 4. After you click OK, a new path is created inside the original. Click on this path with the Area Type tool; the text appears "inside" the edge, with a buffer (see Figure 8-13).

Doing Bizarre Things with Area Type

Probably the most overlooked rule when it comes to manipulating Area type and the paths that create the type boundaries is the simple fact that the path and the type are treated equally, unless the path is chosen with the Direct Selection (or Group Selection) tool. Area type is selected when there is an underline under all the characters in the area.

When using the transformation tools, be sure that if you don't want to change any of the characteristics of the type, you select just the path. Use the Group Selection tool to click once on the deselected path, and only the path is selected, not the type.

If the type is selected as well as the path, then the transformations will affect both the type and the path. Figure 8-14 shows transformations taking place to both type and its surrounding path as opposed to transformations taking place to just the surrounding path.

Figure 8-13: Steps to create Area type with a buffer between the type and the edge

Coloring Type That Is Anchored to a Path

When type is anchored to a path, either as Area type or Path type, there are some important considerations to think of before Filling and Stroking the type.

First, if just the type or just the path is selected with the regular Selection tool, the other (path or type) will be selected as well. Do you want to put a Stroke along that path that surrounds your type? If you select the path with the regular Selection tool, then the type will be selected as well, and each character in the type area will have the same Stroke you meant to apply to the path.

For changing just the path's Paint Style attributes, be sure to use the Direct Selection tool to select the path. If no underlines appear under the text, then the text is *not* selected. To change all the text, you must choose a type tool, click within the text area, and then use the Select All command (⌘-A). Only then will just the text be affected.

Figure 8-14: The original (left) after both the type and the path have been transformed (top right) and after only the path has been transformed (bottom right)

Changing the Area, Not the Type

Many times, you'll need to adjust the path that makes up the area of the Area type, like scaling that path up or down so that the text flows better. The trick here is to make sure the entire path is selected without selecting any of the characters. To do this, deselect the type and select the path with the Group Selection tool (the hollow arrow with the plus sign).

Now any changes you make will only affect the path, so you can scale it, rotate it, or change its Paint Style attributes without directly affecting the text within it. Figure 8-15 shows a path that has been transformed, allowing the text inside to flow differently.

Area Type

All sorts of nifty things can be done with type that has been flowed into areas — from unusual column designs to fascinating shapes.

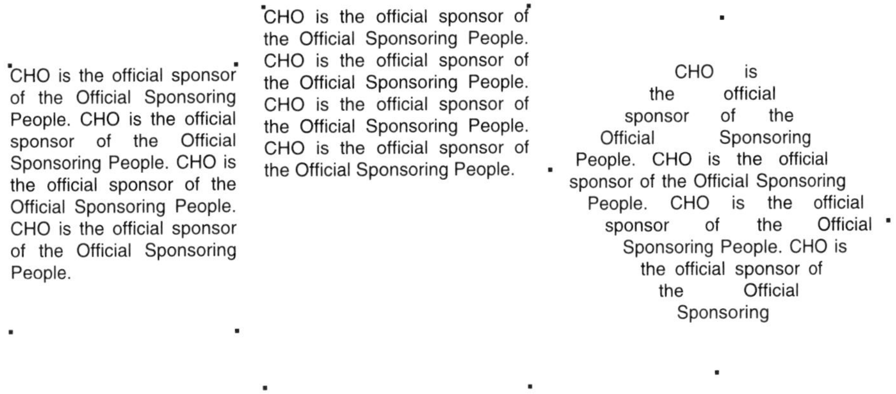

Figure 8-15: Changing the size (middle) and rotation (right) of the original path (left) only affects the text flow, not the text itself.

CHO is the official sponsor of the Official Sponsoring People. CHO is the official sponsor of the Official Sponsoring People. CHO is the official sponsor of the Official Sponsoring People. CHO is the official sponsor of the Official Sponsoring People.

CHO is the official sponsor of the Official Sponsoring People. CHO is the official sponsor of the Official Sponsoring People. CHO is the official sponsor of the Official Sponsoring People. CHO is the official sponsor of the Official Sponsoring People.

CHO is the official sponsor of the Official Sponsoring People. CHO is the official sponsor of the Official Sponsoring People. CHO is the official sponsor of the Official Sponsoring People. CHO is the official sponsor of the Official Sponsoring

A publication can be livened up quite easily by using nonrectangular columns. *Mondo 2000* magazine uses curved columns that are easy to read and lend a futuristic, hip look to the publication. Angled and curved columns are simple to create in Illustrator by creating the shape of the column and flowing Area type from one shape to the next.

Traditionally, forcing type into an irregular (nonrectangular) area was quite a task. The typesetter had to set several individual lines of type, each specced by the art director or client to be a certain specific length so that when all the text was put together, the text formed the shape (see Figure 8-16). This is probably the main reason the world has not seen too much of this, except in overly zealous art students' portfolios.

For example, you can give a report on toxic waste in New Jersey more impact by shaping the text into the form of a hypodermic needle. Or you can make a seasonal ad in the shape of a Christmas tree. Look at some of the Absolut Vodka ads to see what they've done to flow text into that all-too-familiar bottle.

Path Type

The unique thing about type on a path is that when the path is not visible, the type *becomes* the path, as shown in Figure 8-17. This can produce some really fascinating results, especially when combined with various fonts of different weights, styles, colors, and special characters.

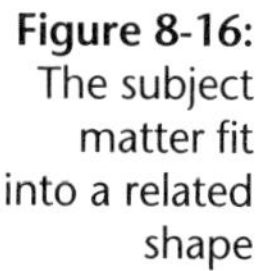

Figure 8-16: The subject matter fit into a related shape

To create Path type, first create a path in your document. Then click on the path with the Path Type tool to create an insertion point along the path. This will work whether the path is a closed path or an open path.

Type aligns to the insertion point; if the type is set to flush left, the left edge of the type will align to the location where the Path Type tool was first clicked. Unlike Point type, where a hard Return sent the type to the next line, hard Returns work just like spaces.

Figure 8-17: Type, when set on a path, can actually *become* the path.

You can flow Path type along the path to which it is aligned by clicking on the Insertion bar (which resembles a little "I" beam) with any selection tool and dragging along the path. If the I-bar is dragged to the other side of the path, then the type will flip over in the direction of the bar. For this reason, it is a good idea to click on the topmost part of the Insertion bar before dragging.

As with other objects in Illustrator that can be moved by dragging, pressing the Option key before releasing the mouse will cause the object being dragged to duplicate instead of just move. This works with the Type I-bar, as well.

If you would like the type you are dragging to appear below the path but not get flipped upside down and change direction, use baseline shift (found in the Character palette) to raise and lower the type to your liking. The key commands for baseline shift are Option-↑ and Option-↓ to move up and down by increments set in the General Preferences dialog box. These commands are particularly useful when adjusting Path type.

Even though there are three different type tools, you only need to choose one. If you have the standard Type tool, it will change into the Area Type tool when you pass over a closed path and will change into a Path Type tool when the cursor passes over an open path.

Type Color *and* the Color of Type

There is a difference between the *color of type* and *type's color.* Type can be painted in Illustrator to be any one of millions of different shades, which determines the color we normally think of.

The color of type, on the other hand, is the way the type appears in the document and is more indicative of the light or dark attributes of the text. The actual red-green-blue colors of the type do work into this appearance, but many times, the weight of the type and the tracking and kerning have a much more profound effect on color.

To easily see the color of type, unfocus your eyes as you look at your document, or turn the page upside down. This works better on a printed area than on-screen, but you can still get the gist of the way it will appear when viewing it on your monitor. Dark and light areas become much more apparent when you can't read the actual words on the path. This method of unfocusing your eyes to look at a page also works well when trying to see the "look" of a page and how it was designed. Many times, unfocusing or turning the page upside down will emphasize the fact that you don't have enough white space or that all the copy seems to blend together.

Heavy type weights, such as bold, heavy, and black, make type appear darker on a page. Type kerned and tracked very tightly also seems to give the type a darker feel.

The x-height of type (the height to which the lowercase letters, such as an *x,* rise) is another factor that determines the color of type. Certain italic versions of typefaces can make the text seem lighter, although a few make text look darker because of the additional area that the thin strokes of the italic type covers.

Combined with red-green-blue colors, type can be made to stand out by appearing darker, or blend into the page when lighter. When you add smartly placed images near the type, your page can come alive with color.

Type on the Top and Bottom of a Circle

Everyone's doing it. Peer pressure is going to make you succumb as well. If you can put type on the top and the bottom of a circle so that it runs along the same path, you are quite the designer, or so thinks the average guy on the street. The simple "Type On A Circle" shown in Figure 8-18 can be created quite easily.

Figure 8-18: Type on the top and bottom of a circle

Follow these steps (which are also illustrated in Figure 8-19 at the end of this procedure), and with a little practice, you can create type on a circle in under 15 seconds. Pretty impressive to even those who understand how it's done.

STEPS: Creating Type on the Top and Bottom of a Circle

Step 1. Draw a circle with the Oval tool (hold down the Shift key to make sure it is a perfect circle). Then choose the Path Type tool and click on the top center of the circle. The blinking insertion point appears at that point on the circle.

Step 2. Type the text that is to appear at the top of the circle and press ⌘-Shift-C (or choose Type⇨Alignment⇨Centered), which centers the type at the top of the circle.

Step 3. Choose the Selection tool and click on the top of the I-bar marker, dragging it down to the bottom center of the circle. Before letting go of the mouse button, center the type, making sure that it is readable from left to right, and press the Option key. When you do release the mouse button, there will be type along the top *and* the bottom of the circle, but the type on the bottom will be *inside* the circle.

The key here is that the Option key is pressed. The Option key *duplicates* the text and circle, moving them both to a new location in the process. If the Option key were not pressed, the type would have just moved to the bottom of the circle.

Step 4. Select the bottom text with the Type tool and slowly "scoot" the type down below the baseline by pressing Option-Shift-↓. This pushes the type down the baseline in the increments set in the General Preferences dialog box (the default is 2). Keep pressing the key combination until the type is vertically positioned to mimic the type on the top of the circle.

Step 5. Select the text along the bottom of the circle with the Type tool. Type in the text that is to appear at the bottom of the circle. It replaces the selected text.

You're finished. Amazing, isn't it? Just remember that you now have *two* circles with type on them, not one circle with two type paths (that can't happen).

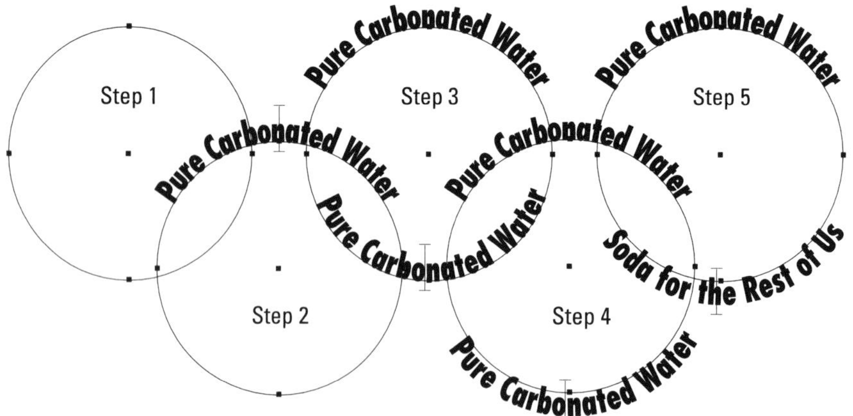

Figure 8-19: Steps for creating type on the top and bottom of a circle

Avoiding Path Type Trouble

The most common trouble with Path type usually occurs when the path has either corner Anchor Points or very sharp curves. Letters will often crash (run into one another) when this occurs.

Besides the most obvious way to avoid this problem, which is to not use paths with corner Anchor Points and sharp curves, the areas where the letters crash can sometimes be kerned apart until they aren't touching anymore.

When kerning Path type, be sure to kern from the "flush" side first. For instance, if the type is flush left, start your kerning from the left side and work to the right. If you start on the wrong end, the letters you kern apart will move along the path until they aren't in an area that needs kerning, but instead, other letters will appear there.

Another method of fixing crashed letters is to "tweak" the path with the Direct Selection tool. Careful adjusting of both Anchor Points and Control Handles can easily fix crashes and letters that have huge amounts of space between them.

If the path that is the base of the letters doesn't need to be directly under the letters, use the baseline shift keyboard commands (Option-Shift-↓ and Option-Shift-↑) to move the type until the path runs through the center of the text. This can automatically fix the spacing problems encountered by text that crashes over sharp turns and corners.

Path Type

One of the most desirable effects with Path type (and, in my opinion, much cooler than type on a circle) is Path type that is reversed, as shown in Figure 8-20.

STEPS: Creating Reversed Path Type

Step 1. Create the path you want to use for the Path type. In my example, I used a rounded rectangle. Your path can be open or closed.

Step 2. Click on the path with the Path Type tool and type in the text for the path. Type with no descenders works better than type with descenders.

Trouble with Path Type

Trapper: I'm having all sorts of trouble with Path type.

Toulouse: Aren't we all. Anything in particular?

Trapper: Well, for starters, I'm having a dickens of a time trying to move the little I-bar marker along the path.

Toulouse: The key to moving the I-bar marker is to click right at the top of it.

Trapper: Thanks. Also, it seems to flip over all the time.

Toulouse: Actually, grabbing the I-bar at the top will fix this as well.

Trapper: How come sometimes my type is below the path and sometimes above, but it reads the right way?

Toulouse: This usually happens after you've done something like type on a circle, where you've last changed the baseline shift to something less than 0. Change the baseline shift back to 0 and all will be well.

Step 3. Vertically center the type on the path by adjusting the baseline shift (Option-Shift-↑ or -↓). If there are descenders, make sure the type is centered from ascender to descender.

Step 4. Select the type with a type tool and change the Fill to White. Select the path with the Direct Selection tool and change the Fill to None and the Stroke of the path to Black. Make the weight of the Stroke just greater than the point size of the type.

Figure 8-20: Steps for creating type reversed on a path

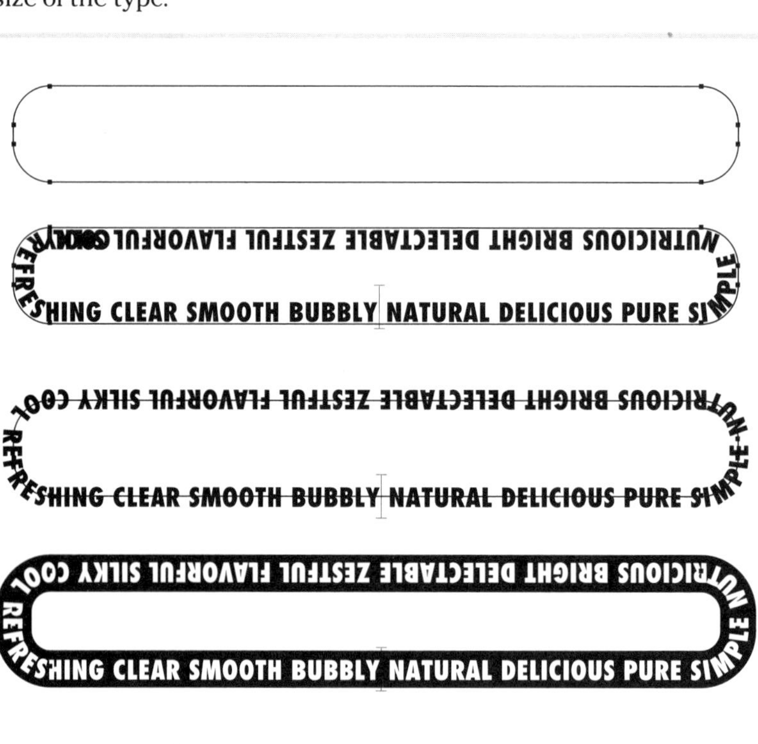

Selecting Type

Before you can make changes to text, you must first select it. There are two ways of selecting type: You can select type areas with a selection tool, which selects every character in the type area, or you can select characters individually or in groups with any of the type tools.

To select the entire type area or multiple type areas, click on the baseline of a line of type within the type area you want to select. Any changes made in the Type menu, Font menu, Character palette, or Paragraph palette affects every character in the selected type areas.

If there are blank fields in any of the palettes or no check marks next to some of the menu items (for instance, no font is checked) when type areas are selected, that means that there are different options for each of those fields or menu items within the type area (for instance, Helvetica for some characters, Times for others). Changing a blank field or unchecked menu item after a type area is selected will affect all characters in that area.

To select characters within a type area, you must use a type tool. As you near text that has been typed in the document, the dotted lines surrounding the cursor disappear. The "hot" point of the type cursor is the place where the short horizontal bar crosses the vertical bar (see Figure 8-21). It is this hot point that you should use when clicking with the type cursor.

Figure 8-21: The "hot" point of the type cursor

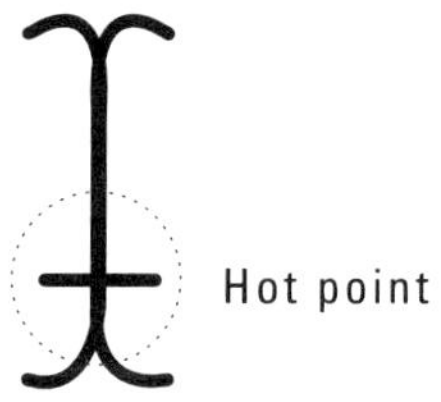

To select an individual character, drag across the character to be selected. As a character is selected, it is reversed (or highlighted, depending on the highlight color in the Colors control panel). To select more than one character, drag left or right across multiple characters; all characters from the location you originally clicked to the current location of the cursor are highlighted. If you drag up with the cursor over straight text, you select all the characters to the left and all the characters to the right of the cursor's current location. Dragging down does the reverse. The more lines you drag up or down, the more lines will be selected.

To select one word at a time (and the space that follows it), double-click on the word to be selected. The word and the space after it are reversed. The reason that the space following the word is selected is mainly due to the times you copy, cut, and paste words from within sentences. For example, to remove the word *Lazy* in the phrase "The Lazy Boy," you double-click on the word *Lazy* and press Delete. The phrase is then "The Boy," which only has one space where the word *Lazy* used to be. To select several words, double-click and drag the Type cursor across the words you want to select. Each word you touch with the cursor is selected, from the location initially double-clicked to the current location. Dragging to the previous or next line selects additional lines, with at least a word on the first line double-clicked and one word on the "dragged-to" line.

For the nimble-fingered clickers, you may also click three times to select a paragraph. Triple-click anywhere inside the paragraph and the entire paragraph is selected, including the hard Return at the end of the paragraph (if there is one). Triple-clicking and dragging selects successive paragraphs if the cursor is moved up or down while the mouse button is still pressed following the third click.

To select all the text within a type area with a type tool, click once in the type area and choose Edit⇨Select All (⌘-A). All the text in the type area is reversed. As in most other Macintosh programs, text can only be selected in contiguous blocks. There is no way to select two words in two different locations of the same type area without selecting all the text between them.

Type can also be selected through the use of the Shift key. Click in one spot (we'll call it the beginning) and then Shift-click in another spot. The characters between the beginning and the Shift-click are selected. Successive Shift-clicks will select characters from the beginning to the current location of the most recent Shift-click.

Editing Type

Text editing features in Illustrator are available on a limited scale. By clicking once within a type area, a blinking insertion point appears. If you begin typing, characters appear where the blinking insertion point is. If you press Delete, you will delete the previous character (if there is one).

The arrow keys on your keyboard move the blinking insertion point around in the direction of the arrow. The right arrow moves the insertion point one character to the right, and the left arrow moves the insertion point one character to the left. The up arrow moves the insertion point to the previous line, while the down arrow moves the insertion point to the next line.

Pressing the ⌘ key speeds up the movement of the insertion point. ⌘-← or -→ moves the insertion point to the preceding or next word, while ⌘-↑ or -↓ moves the insertion point to the preceding or next paragraph.

Pressing the Shift key while moving the insertion point around with the arrows selects all the characters that the insertion point passes over. This works for the ⌘-arrow movements as well.

When you select characters with a type tool, typing anything deletes the selected characters and replaces them with what is currently being typed. Pressing the Delete key when characters are selected deletes all the selected characters. If you paste type (⌘-V) when characters are selected, the selected characters are replaced with the pasted characters.

Character Attributes

The easiest way to change the attributes of characters is by using the Character palette, shown in Figure 8-22. Most of the changes in the Character palette are available as options in the Type menu and the Font menu, but on a limited scale. As a rule, if you have more than one change to make, it is better to do it in the Character palette than the menu, if just for the simple fact that everything you need will be in one place.

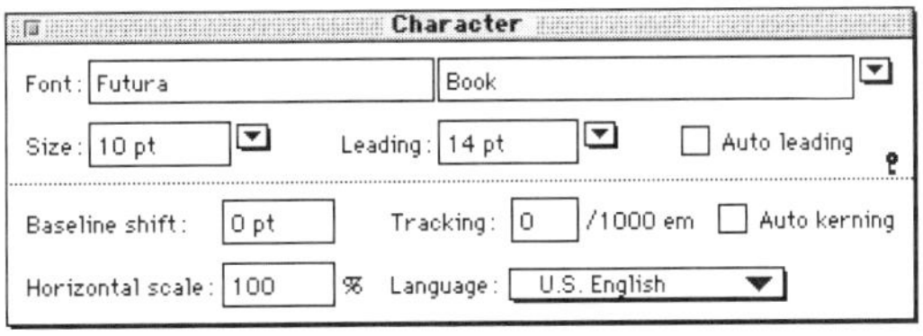

Figure 8-22: The Character palette

Character-attribute changes affect only the letters that are selected, with the exception of leading (explained later), which should really be in the Paragraph palette.

You can change several character attributes by increments. The increments are set in the General Preferences dialog box (choose File⇨Preferences⇨General, or press ⌘-K). Increments can be changed for point size, leading, baseline shift, and tracking/kerning values. Where appropriate, the key commands for each attribute change are listed in the following sections.

The Character Palette

The Character palette can be displayed in a number of different ways. Choosing any of the following menu items will display it or, when displayed, bring it in front of any other palettes: Type⇨Size⇨Other, Type⇨Leading⇨Other, Type⇨Kern, Type⇨Character, and Window⇨Show Character. The following key commands also display the Character palette: ⌘-T, ⌘-Shift-F, ⌘-Shift-S, ⌘-Shift-K, and ⌘-Option-Shift-M.

The Character palette can be displayed in two different modes: full palette or partial palette. Clicking the lever (it looks like a key) in the lower right of the partial palette (top half) displays and hides the rest of the palette. The Character palette remembers which mode the palette was in the last time it was displayed and shows that view the next time you display it. If it is in partial-palette mode, choosing Type⇨Kern (⌘-Shift-K) will display the full palette.

The Tab key can be used to tab across the different text fields. When in partial display palette mode, the Tab key works only in the partial palette; when the last field (Leading) is selected, the Tab key then goes back to the Font field. If a field in the lower part of the palette is highlighted when the palette is closed, the Font field will be highlighted. When the palette is in full view, tabbing past the last field (Tracking/Kerning) will highlight the Font field as well. In addition to the Tab key tabbing forward through the text fields, pressing Shift-Tab will tab backward through the text fields.

Choosing Edit⇨Undo (⌘-Z) will *not* undo items typed in the Character palette while you are still in the text field. To undo something, you must first move along (Tab) to the next field and then undo, and then Shift-Tab back. Canceling (⌘-period or Esc) will not cancel what you have typed but instead will highlight the field.

Font and Style Changes

The first field on the Character palette (in the upper-left corner) is the Font family field. When you type the first couple of letters of the font you want to use, Illustrator fills in the rest of the name for you. What happens if you type in a font that you don't have? Illustrator just ignores you, for the most part. In a nice touch, you don't get silly dialog boxes appearing telling you that there is no such typeface (à la QuarkXPress), but instead, the blinking insertion point remains in the same location until a letter that works is typed. The Font field can be automatically highlighted (and the Character palette displayed if it is not) by pressing either ⌘-T, ⌘-Shift-F, or ⌘-Option-Shift-M.

To close the Character or Paragraph palettes, press ⌘-Return after you enter your last entry in a text field on the palette. To exit the palette without closing it, press Shift-Return.

The field in the upper right, next to the Font field, is the Style field of the font family. The same rules as entering text for the Font field apply here. Type in the first couple letters of the style, and Illustrator fills in the rest for you. Only if you have the font style installed on your system will you be able to type it in. Illustrator is very strict when it comes to bold and italic versions of typefaces. If there is not a specific type style for what you want, you will *not* be able to type it in, unlike most software, which have "bold" and "italic" checkboxes.

For every text field, the information entered may be applied by either tabbing to the next or preceding text field, or by pressing Enter or Return.

In the upper-right corner is a little pop-up menu triangle, which when pressed displays a list of all the typefaces installed on your system. The families are displayed in the main list, and arrows show which families have different styles. To select a font, drag the cursor over it until it is highlighted. To select a specific style of a font family, drag the cursor to the font family name, and then drag to the right to select the style name. The fields to the pop-up menu's left are updated instantly.

Size Changes

The field directly below the Font field is the Size field. Type in the desired point size (from .1 of a point to 1296 of a point, in increments of 1/10,000 point) and any selected characters will increase or decrease to that particular point size. Next to the Size field is a pop-up menu triangle, which lists the standard point sizes available. Point size for type is always measured from the top of the ascenders to the bottom of the descenders. Type point size can be increased and decreased from the keyboard by typing ⌘-Shift-→ to increase and ⌘-Shift-← to decrease the point size by the increment specified in the General Preferences dialog box.

The keyboard commands for increasing and decreasing typographic attributes, such as point size, leading, baseline shift, and tracking are more than just another way to change those attributes. Instead, they are invaluable to making changes when the selected type has more than one different value of that attribute within it. For example, if some of the characters have a point size of 10 and some of them have a point size of 20, using the keyboard command (with an increment set to 2 points) will change the type to 12 and 22 points. This would be tedious to do separately, especially if there are multiple sizes or just a few sizes scattered widely about.

Measuring Type

So, you've finally mastered this whole silly point/pica concept, know that there are 72 points in an inch, and you think you're ready to conquer the world. And you are, as long as no one asks you to spec type.

At 72 points, the letter *I* is about 50 points tall. In inches that would be just under 3/4". To get better results for specially sized capital letters, a good rule of thumb is that every 100 points is about a 1-inch capital letter. This works for most typefaces, and only for the first several inches, but it is a good start to getting capital letters that are sized pretty accurately.

Curves in capital letters are yet another wrench thrown into the equation. In many typefaces, the bottom and top of the letter *O* will go beneath the baseline and above the ascender height of most squared letters (see the following figure). Serifs on certain typefaces may also cross these lines.

Type is one of those oddities that is measured from the top of the ascenders (like the top of a capital *T*) to the bottom of the descender (like the bottom of a lowercase *j*) as shown in the figure. So when people tell you they want a capital *I* that is 1-inch high, you can't just say, "Oh, there are 72 points in an inch, so I will create a 72-point *I* for them."

Next to the Size field is the Leading text field. Enter the desired leading value (between .1 of a point and 1296 of a point, in increments of 1/1000 point). To the right of the leading field is a pop-up menu triangle, from which common leading values can be chosen. In Illustrator, leading is measured from the baseline of the current line up to the baseline of the preceding line, as shown in Figure 8-23. The distance between these two baselines is the amount of leading.

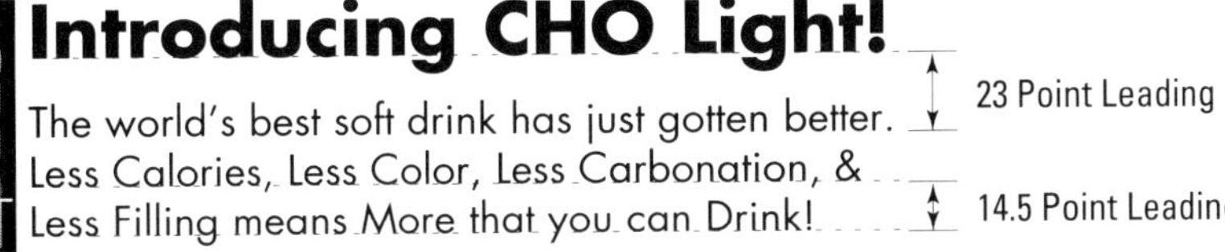

Figure 8-23: Leading is measured from baseline to baseline. The 23-point leading was set by selecting the second line and changing the leading. The 14.5-point leading was set by selecting the third and fourth lines and changing the leading.

Unlike every other character attribute in the Character palette, leading actually works on entire paragraphs, not just on individual characters. So if one letter in a 12-line paragraph is selected, and the leading for that character is changed, the distance between the lines of every line in that entire paragraph is changed to reflect the new leading value.

If the Leading field is changed from the number that displays there by default, the box to the Leading field's right will become unchecked. This box is the Auto leading box, which when checked makes the leading exactly 120% of the point size. This is just great when the type is 10 points because the leading is 12 points, a common point size-to-leading relationship. But as point size goes up, leading should become proportionately less, until, at around 72 points, it is less than the point size. Instead, when Auto leading is checked, 72-point type will have 86.5-point leading. That's a lot of unsightly white space.

Leading increments can be set in the General Preferences dialog box (⌘-K). Press Option-↑ to increase the leading (which pushes lines farther apart) and Option-↓ to decrease the leading.

The bottom portion of the Character palette contains the Baseline shift field, which, unlike leading, moves individual characters up and down relative to their baseline (from leading). Positive numbers move the selected characters up, and negative numbers move the characters down by the amount specified. The maximum amount of baseline shift is 1296 points in either direction. Baseline shift is especially useful for Path type.

Those *&@#$!!! Palettes

HotLips: I keep typing in my Character and Paragraph palettes. It's driving me to drink.

Toulouse: Hopefully not that still-brewed stuff.

HotLips: Why does this happen?

Toulouse: Well, when you enter a value in the Character or Paragraph palette by typing it in, Illustrator highlights that text field in the palette.

HotLips: Yeah, so the next time I type, it's in those text fields, not in the document where it belongs. What can I do?

Toulouse: The easiest thing to do is to press Shift-Return after you enter your values. That jumps you "out" of the palette and back to your document.

HotLips: That'll work.

Toulouse: Or, if you won't be needing that palette again, press Command-Return. That'll enter the value and close the palette. Keeps your screen nice and tidy.

Baseline shift can be changed via the keyboard by pressing Option-Shift-↑ to increase and Option-Shift-↓ to decrease the baseline shift in the increment specified in the General Preferences dialog box.

Directly under the Baseline shift field is the Horizontal scale field. Horizontal scale controls the width of the type, causing it to become expanded or condensed horizontally. Values from 1% to 10000% can be entered in this field. Like most other fields in the Character palette, the values entered are absolute values, so whatever the horizontal scale is, changing it back to 100% will return the type to its original proportions.

Tracking and Kerning

To the right of the Baseline Shift field is the Tracking/Kerning field. The field will read either Tracking or Kerning depending on what is selected in the type area. If the type area is selected with a selection tool, or if one or more characters in the type are selected, then the field will read *Tracking*. If there is a blinking insertion point placed between two characters, the field will read *Kerning*.

Tracking is the amount of space between all the letters currently selected. If the type area is selected with a selection tool, then it refers to all the space between all the characters in the entire type area. If characters are selected with a type tool, tracking only affects the space between the specific letters selected.

Kerning is the amount of space between any specific pair of letters. Kerning can only be changed when there is a blinking insertion point between two characters.

Although they are related, and appear to do basically the same thing, tracking and kerning actually work quite independently of each other. They only *look* like they are affecting each other; they never actually change the amount of one if the other is altered.

Figure 8-24 shows tracking and kerning examples.

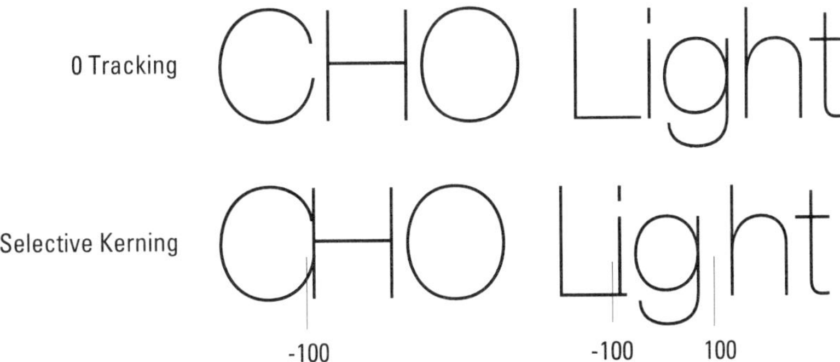

Figure 8-24: Examples of tracking and kerning

To highlight the Tracking/Kerning field and show the Character dialog box, choose Type⇨Track or Kern (⌘-Shift-K). To increase or decrease the tracking or kerning by the increments specified in the General Preferences dialog box, press Option-← or Option-→. To increase or decrease the tracking or kerning by a factor of five times the amount in the General Preferences dialog box, press ⌘-Option-→ or ⌘-Option-←.

For those QuarkXPress users who have already memorized a slate of key commands, Illustrator makes it easy to remember tracking and kerning increase and decrease commands by adding secondary commands. To increase and decrease the tracking or kerning by the amount set in the General Preferences dialog box, press ⌘-Shift-] and ⌘-Shift-[. In addition, another QuarkXPress-based keyboard command is ⌘-Option-Shift-M to highlight the Font field. These key commands work the same way in QuarkXPress as they do in Illustrator.

The space between letters is normally defined by the typeface designer; different typefaces look like they have different amounts of space between letters. If the Auto kerning checkbox is checked, then preset kerning values will go into effect for certain letter pairs. There are usually a couple hundred preset kerning pairs for common Adobe typefaces, although their "expert" sets have quite a few more. When the Auto kerning checkbox is checked, those preset kerning values can be seen by clicking between kerned letter pairs (capital *T* with most vowels is a good one to check) and reading the value in the Kerning field. Different typefaces have different kerning pairs, and kerning pairs don't only change from typeface to typeface, but even from weight to weight and style to style.

Kerning and tracking values are based on 1/1000 of an *em space*. An *em space* is the width of two numbers (think of two zeros — they tend to be the widest-looking numbers) at that particular point size.

The values entered for tracking and kerning must be between –1000 and 10,000. A value of –1000 will result in stacked letters. A value of 10,000 will make enough space between letters for 10 em spaces, or 20 numbers. That's a *lot* of space.

Different software works with kerning and tracking differently. In those programs that *do* offer numerical tracking, it is usually represented in some form of a fraction of an em space, but the denominator varies from software to software. In QuarkXPress, for example, tracking and kerning is measured in 1/200 of an em space. Check the documentation that came with your software to determine the denominator in other software. This can get a little confusing when going from program to program, although the transformation from QuarkXPress to Illustrator is quite simple: to get the same tracking and kerning values in Quark that you used in Illustrator, divide the number you used in Illustrator by 5 (1000/200=5).

The Language pop-up menu allows you to choose which language your system is native to. This is in support of Apple System 7.x's "World Ready" architecture, which makes it easily adaptable to different languages.

Paragraph Attributes

There are some changes that can be made to text that affect entire paragraphs at the same time. We've already talked about leading, which does this, but there are a number of other areas that are paragraph-specific. Unlike the Character palette, most of the options in the Paragraph palette are available only through the palette, and not through a menu choice. The obvious exception to this is Alignment, which you can access by choosing Type⇨Alignment and then choosing the alignment desired.

Type the "Right Way"

Although at first it seems quite simple to outline characters of type using the Stroke option in the Paint Style palette, just slapping on a Stroke of a weight that seems to look good on the screen and changing the Fill to None or White is technically incorrect.

The right way to outline type is only a little bit more involved. First, select the type that you want outlined and give the type a Stroke that is twice the weight you want on the printed piece. Then Copy, Paste in Front, and give the new type a Stroke of None and a Fill of White. The White Fill will knock out the inside half of the Stroke, leaving the Stroke one-half the width you specified, which is what you really want.

The following Figure shows both the right way and the wrong way to outline type. The top line is the original type. The middle line is outlined the wrong way with a 1-point Stroke and a Fill of White. The bottom part of the figure shows "100% Natural" outlined correctly, first with a white Fill and no Stroke, and then with a 2-point Stroke.

100% Natural

100% Natural

100% Natural

"Serif preservation," as it's known to a select few, requires a teeny bit of math, but it's worth the effort. The white area inside the Stroke is exactly the size of the character when done this way, as opposed to being smaller by half the width of the Stroke when done normally.

Paragraph attributes include alignment, indentation, leading before paragraphs (other programs usually refer to this as space between paragraphs), hanging punctuation, hyphenation, and spacing.

You can change paragraph attributes if you first select a type area using a selection tool, in which case, the changes will affect every paragraph within the entire type area. If you use the Type tool to select one or more characters, changes made to paragraph attributes will affect the entire paragraphs of each of the selected characters.

The Paragraph Palette

To display the Paragraph palette (see Figure 8-25) using menu commands, choose Type⇨Paragraph, Type⇨Spacing, or Window⇨Show Paragraph. To display the Paragraph palette with key commands, type ⌘-Shift-P (previously ⌘-Shift-T in Illustrator 5.0) or ⌘-Shift-O.

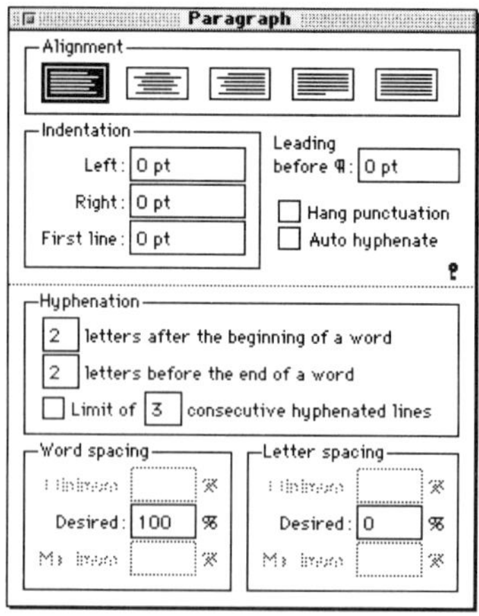

Figure 8-25: The Paragraph palette

Pressing Tab will tab forward through the text fields, while Shift-Tab will tab backwards through the same text fields. Press Enter or Return to apply the changes that were made.

To close the Paragraph palette, press ⌘-Return or ⌘-Enter after you enter your last entry in a text field on the palette.

The bottom part of the Paragraph palette contains information that doesn't get changed too often, so for the most part, it doesn't need to be displayed. If you wish to display it, click on the small lever on the lower right once to show the bottom portion, and again to hide it.

Alignment

There are five different types of paragraph alignment (see Figure 8-26). Each of them is represented by a graphical representation of what multiple lines of type look like when that particular alignment is applied.

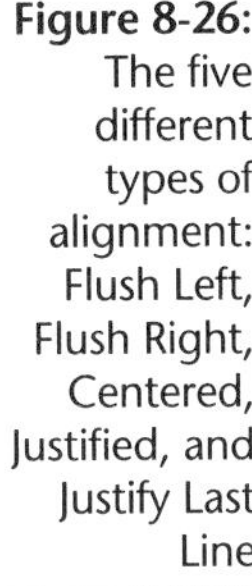

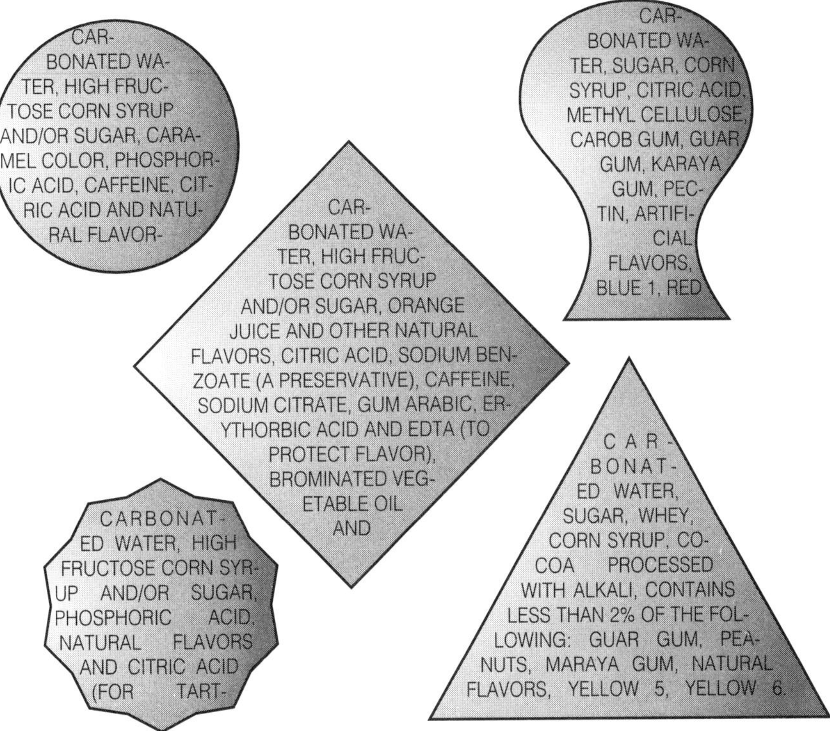

Figure 8-26: The five different types of alignment: Flush Left, Flush Right, Centered, Justified, and Justify Last Line

The first alignment type is the most common: Flush Left, which experienced typesetters often refer to as "ragged right" due to the uneven right side of the text. You can also apply this type of alignment by choosing Type⇨Alignment⇨Flush Left (⌘-Shift-L).

The next type of alignment is Centered, where all lines of type in the paragraph are centered relative to each other, to the point clicked, or to the location of the I-bar in Path type. You can also apply this type of alignment by choosing Type⇨Alignment⇨Centered (⌘-Shift-C).

The middle alignment choice is Flush Right, in which type has a smooth, even right side and an uneven left side (no, "ragged left" isn't really a correct term). You can also apply this type of alignment by choosing Type⇨Alignment⇨Flush Right (⌘-Shift-R).

The fourth type of alignment is Justified, where both the left and right sides appear smooth and even. Extra space is added between letters and words, as defined in the "Spacing" secion later in this chapter. The last line in a justified paragraph appears to be flush left. You can also apply this type of alignment by choosing Type⇨Alignment⇨Justify (⌘-Shift-J).

The last alignment is called Justify Last Line, which is the same as Justify except that the last line of every paragraph is justified along with the other lines of the paragraph. This can create some really *awful* looking paragraphs, and is done mainly for artistic emphasis, not as a proper way to justify type. Justify Last Line is particularly useful for stretching a single line of type across a certain width. You can also apply this type of alignment by choosing Type⇨Alignment⇨Justify Last Line (⌘-Shift-B).

Justification only works on Area type and Rectangle type. Illustrator will not allow you to select Justify or Justify Last Line for Path type or Point type.

Indentation, Paragraph Spacing, and Hanging Punctuation

Paragraphs can be indented within the Paragraph palette by choosing different amounts of indentation for the left edge, right edge, and first line of each paragraph. The maximum indentation for all three fields is 1296 points, and the minimum is –1296 points.

Using indents is a great way to offset type, such as quotes, that have smaller margins than the rest of the type surrounding the quote. Changing the indentation values is also useful for creating hanging indents, such as numbered or bulleted text.

To create hanging indents easily, make the left indent as large as the width of a bullet or a number and a space, and then make the first line value the negative value of that. If the left indent were 2 picas, the first line would be –2 picas. This will create great hanging indents every time.

Illustrator allows you to place additional space between paragraphs by entering a number in the Leading before ¶ text field. This measurement is added to the leading to determine the distance from baseline to baseline before the selected paragraphs. You can also enter a negative number to decrease space between paragraphs, if necessary. Values for Leading before ¶ can be between –1296 and 1296 points.

If Hang punctuation is checked, punctuation at the left edge of a Flush Left, Justified, or Justified Last Line paragraph will appear outside the type area, as shown in Figure 8-27. Punctuation on the right edge of a Flush Right, Justified, or Justified Last Line paragraph will also appear outside the type area. Strangely enough, Illustrator is one of the few Macintosh programs that supports this very hip feature.

Figure 8-27: When the Hang punctuation box is checked, quotes, periods, commas and hyphens will fall outside the boundary of the type area. ?'s and !'s will not hang, however.

"CHO is the best thing to hap-
pen to American soft drinks
since the aluminum can."

Hyphenation

Hyphenation? In a drawing program? I couldn't believe it either, but there it was staring me in the face. A nice addition to Illustrator's text-handling capabilities, hyphenation works in the background, silently hyphenating when necessary.

To use Illustrator's hyphenation, you must check the Auto hyphenate box in the lower-right corner of the top half of the Paragraph palette. After this is checked for selected text, that text will hyphenate fairly well.

Hyphenation in Illustrator works from a set of hyphenation rules, which you define in the bottom of the Paragraph palette. You can specify how many letters must fall before the hyphen can appear and how many letters must fall after the hyphen. You can also limit the number of hyphens in a row to avoid the "ladder look" of multiple hyphens.

When you need to hyphenate a word at a place where Illustrator doesn't seem to want to hyphenate it, you can create a discretionary hyphen. A discretionary hyphen is created by placing the blinking insertion point where the word should break and typing ⌘-Shift-Hyphen. This will cause the word to hyphenate at a

I Can't Select My Type!

Winchester: This is really annoying. Everytime I select my type, nothing happens.

Toulouse: Nothing's supposed to happen. Selecting doesn't "do" anything.

Winchester: I know that, but my type isn't being selected.

Toulouse: Have you talked to Frank?

Winchester: Yes, but I don't have any other text areas in the document. It can't be that.

Toulouse: Well, it might be...

Winchester: And the really spooky thing is, that sometimes, when the type isn't selected, I can change the font, and other type attributes.

Toulouse: Actually, the type is selected...You just can't see it.

Winchester: I've been meaning to update my eyeglasses prescription.

Toulouse: Actually, you probably have the Hide Edges option selected in the View menu.

Winchester: Whataya know, it *is* selected. But what does that have to do with my type?

(continued)

(continued)

Toulouse: Hide Edges doesn't just hide path edges and points, it hides the selection area when text is selected.

Winchester: That's silly.

Toulouse: Maybe, but it's a good way to change attributes of a few characters in a text story without having to see them in reverse.

certain part of the word only if that word has to be hyphenated. If the word doesn't have to be hyphenated, no hyphen will appear. This is much better than just typing a normal hyphen, which will work temporarily, but if the manually hyphenated word is moved from the edge of the line, the hyphen will remain within it.

Spacing

Illustrator allows you to control the spacing of letters and words in text by editing the Spacing fields at the bottom of the Paragraph palette.

Spacing affects the space between letters and words regardless of the alignment, although Justified text has even more spacing control than Flush Left, Flush Right, and Centered text.

When Flush Left, Flush Right, and Centered alignment are chosen, the only text fields that can be changed are the Desired fields for Letter spacing and Word spacing.

You can enter values between 0% and 1000% for Word spacing. The Minimum must be less than the amount in the Desired box, and the Maximum must be more than the amount in the Desired box. At 100%, the word space is normal; at less than 100%, the word space is reduced; and at a number greater than 100%, the word space is increased.

The values for Letter spacing must be between –50% and 500%. The Minimum must be less than the amount in the Desired box, and the Maximum must be more than the amount in the Desired box. At 0%, the letter space is normal; at less than 0%, the letter space is reduced; and at a number greater than 0%, the letter space is increased.

The Minimum and Maximum boxes in the Word spacing and Letter spacing areas are mainly used to control where the extra space goes and is removed from when stretching out and compressing the lines of text.

Changing the Flow of Type

Type can be steered around Illustrator in a number of different ways. In a previous section, "Area Type," I discussed how to make type adhere to specific shapes. In this section, I'll take a look at some other ways to control where type goes.

There are four basic ways to control the flow of type: creating specific areas out of paths in which the type flows, forcing type to wrap around other Illustrator objects, making type jump from one type area to another (text block links), and internal adjustments (indentations, space before paragraphs, and tabs).

Text Wrapping

Using text wraps in Illustrator is in some ways the opposite of using type areas. Instead of defining paths for the type to flow through, you define areas that the type cannot flow through. For example, Figure 8-28 shows type wrapped around small bubbles.

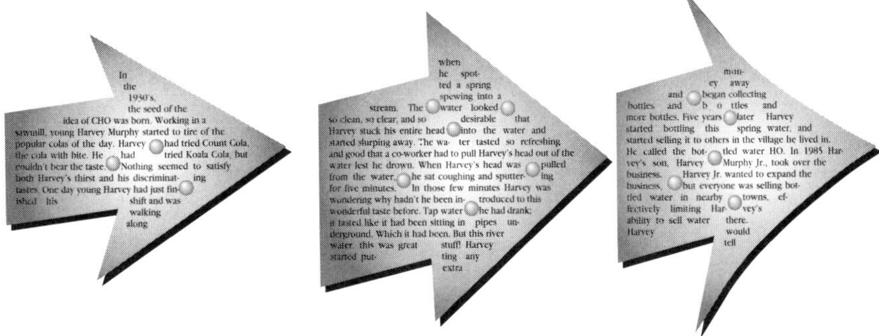

Figure 8-28: Type linked through the arrows and wrapped around the small bubbles

To create wrapped type, first create a block of type anywhere in your document. Then draw the path that you wish your type to wrap around. The object that the text will wrap around must be closed, and the wrapping object must be in front of the text. Select both the wrapping object and the text area with any selection tool, and choose Type➪Make Wrap. The text will flow around the wrapping object.

Additional objects can be used to wrap. Just place them in front of the type area, select both the type area and the new wrapping object, and choose Type➪Make Wrap.

Text wrapping objects need no Fill or Stroke, but they do need to be closed. If you want to use an existing path, but that path is not closed, simply copy the path, choose Edit➪Paste In Front (⌘-F), and change the Fill and Stroke to None.

Text Linking

Text can be linked in Illustrator quite easily, although the program does not give you much feedback about which type areas are linked and what the path of linked blocks is. Text linking is telling Illustrator that, while there isn't enough room in one particular text block for the amount of type you have placed there, the type can continue (be "linked") to another text area within the same document, as previously shown in Figure 8-28.

Text linking is done most often to link columns of text together. Because Illustrator does not have any other method of creating columns, text linking is often used for this purpose.

Text linking only works for Area type and Rectangle type. If more type is inside a type area than can be displayed, a small square with a plus sign in it appears. This is an indicator to you that there is more text to be seen in this text area.

To create a link between an overstuffed type area and a nice, new, empty one, select both the type area and the closed path or text area you wish to link to and then choose Type⇨Link Blocks (⌘-Shift-G). The text will flow from the first type area into the second. To continue the link, select another closed path or type area along with the current type area and select Link Blocks again.

Type in linked blocks can be selected with any type tool by dragging from one type area into another. Choosing Edit⇨Select All (⌘-A) while working with a type tool in a linked type area will select all the type throughout all type areas linked to the one the insertion point is currently in. All other editing and attribute changes will affect type throughout the entire story.

To change the flow of type from one box to another, select individual type areas with the Direct Selection tool and choose Send to Back or Bring to Front. Type will begin in the rearmost type area and end in the frontmost type area.

Graphical Tabs

Graphical tabs are tabs that flow around objects (paths) in Illustrator automatically. The following steps show you how to use graphical tabs.

STEPS: Creating Graphical Tabs

Step 1. Create a Rectangle type area and type in five words separated by tabs. (Yes, each word will go to the next line — we'll fix that shortly.) Press Return after the last word entered.

Step 2. Select All (⌘-A) and Copy (⌘-C). Then click the last line of type (it should be blank) and paste it a few times (⌘-V, ⌘-V, ⌘-V, ⌘-V).

Step 3. Using the Freehand tool, draw a series of four straight or curved vertical lines that extend above the top and below the bottom of the type area. Select the lines and the type area and choose Type⇨Make Wrap. The type should be tabbed to the lines that you drew.

Tabs will tab to the other side of text wrap objects. Play with this a little, and you'll discover that this method is much more flexible than standard word processing tab stops.

The Tab Ruler Palette

The Tab Ruler palette is used to set tabs the same way you would in your word processing or page layout software. To access the Tab Ruler palette, choose Window⇨Show Tab Ruler or press ⌘-Shift-T. The Tab Ruler palette is shown in Figure 8-29.

Figure 8-29: The Tab Ruler palette

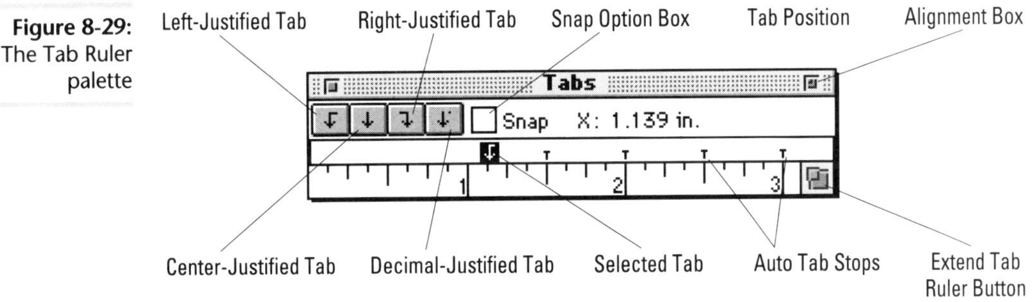

To set tabs for type, select the type and choose Window⇨Show Tab Ruler or press ⌘-Shift-T. The Tab Ruler palette appears above the type you have selected and automatically assumes the width of the type area.

Tab Problems with 5.5

Radar: Is it fixed?

Toulouse: What, that occasional helicopter noise in your ears?

Radar: No, all the tab problems that I had in version 5.5.

Toulouse: There were problems, huh?

Radar: Not according to Adobe. Just according to us users.

Toulouse: Well, I have it on good authority that if indeed there were any problems with tabs in 5.5...

Radar: There were.

Toulouse: ...and of course I'm only speculating that there might have been problems, you know...

Radar: I have the cold hard facts to prove it.

Toulouse: ...that those problems do not exist in Version 6 of Illustrator.

Radar: This "good authority" wouldn't be the Adobe Company Spokesman, would it?

Toulouse: No, heh... whatever gave you that idea...heh...

To change the width of the Tab Ruler palette, click and drag on the Extend Tab Ruler button in the lower-right corner of the palette. The Tab Ruler palette can be made wider or thinner, but not taller. To reset the Tab Ruler palette back to the exact size of the type area, click on the Alignment box in the upper-right corner of the palette.

The Alignment box will move the Tab Ruler palette to make it flush left with the type and move it up or down so that it is right above the selected text area.

Before you set any tabs, tabs are automatically set at every half inch. These are called *Auto tab* stops. Once you set a tab, all the Auto tab stops to the left of the tab you have set will disappear. The Auto tab stops work like left-justified tabs.

If the Snap option box is checked, tab stops will correspond to ruler tick marks.

The measurement system shown on the ruler is the same system that is used by the rest of the document and can be changed in the General Preferences dialog box or by cycling through the different measurement systems by pressing ⌘-Control-U until the proper measurement system is displayed.

To set a tab, select a tab from the four Tab Style buttons on the upper left of the Tab Ruler palette and click on the ruler below to set exactly where you would like the new tab. Once the tab has been set, you can move it by dragging it along the ruler or remove it by dragging it off the top or left edge of the ruler.

You *cannot* remove tabs by dragging them off the bottom of the palette, like in most word processing programs and page layout software.

There are four types of tabs you can set:

- **Left-justified tabs** make type align to the right side of the tab, with the leftmost character aligning with the tab stop.
- **Center-justified tabs** make type align to the center of the tab, with the center character aligning with the tab stop.
- **Right-justified tabs** make type align to the left side of the tab, with the rightmost character aligning with the tab stop.
- **Decimal-justified tabs** make type align to the left side of the tab, with a decimal or the rightmost character aligning with the tab stop.

To change a tab from one style to another, select a tab stop and click on the Tab style button that you wish to change to. To deselect all tabs, click in the area to the right of the Tab position box. It is a good idea to get in the habit of deselecting tabs after they are set so that defining a new tab style for the next tab stop does not change the tab stop that was just set.

There is no way to create dot leader tabs automatically by using the Tab Ruler palette. We may have to wait for Version 7 of Illustrator for this feature to be incorporated. As always, if you think this feature or any other feature that Illustrator lacks would be useful, send them a note (a "feature request") and it *will* be considered. After all, why do you think the Tab Ruler palette was incorporated into Version 5.5?

Type Outlines

The process of creating editable type outlines has many uses, the main one that I have seen being the ability to distort mild-mannered characters into grotesque letters. More practical uses for editable type outlines include the following: making type-based logos unique, arcing type (where one side is flat and the other is curved), special effects and masking, and avoiding font compatibility problems.

To change type from being editable text into an Illustrator path (for that is what an editable type outline really is), select the type with a selection tool, not a type tool. Choose Type⇨Create Outlines, and the type changes into paths that you can edit. Figure 8-30 shows the "CHO" logo before and after being converted into outlines.

Figure 8-30: Type that has been converted to outlines and united via the Unite filter

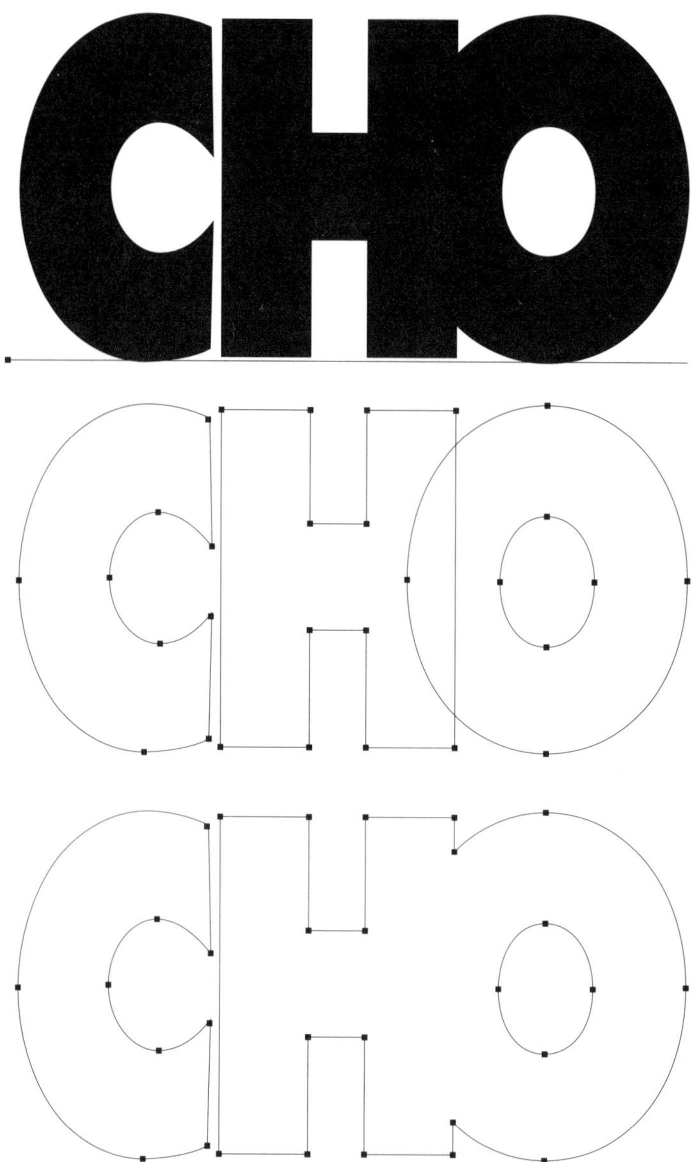

After type has been changed into Illustrator paths using Create Outlines, the only way back is to use the Undo command (⌘-Z). There is no "Convert from Paths to Type" function. Type cannot be edited in Outline mode. That means if you misspell somthing, it will remain misspelled.

Initially, when type is converted into outlines, individual characters are turned into compound paths. This ensures that holes in letters such as in a lowercase *a*, *b*, or *d* are see-through, and not just White-Filled paths placed on top of the original objects. (See Chapter 11 for an in-depth discussion of compound paths.)

Making Letters That Normally Appear in Your Worst Nightmares

After letters have been turned into outlines, there is nothing stopping you from distorting them into shapes that only resemble letters in the most simplistic sense of the word, and even then it takes some imagination.

The results of letter distortion usually aren't all that eye-pleasing, but they can be *fun*. Few things in life are as pleasing as taking a boring letter *Q* and twisting it into "the letter that time forgot." Or fiddling around with your boss's name until the letters look as evil as he does. Or adding pointed ears and whiskers to a random array of letters and numbers and printing out several sheets of them with the words "Mutant kittens for sale." Some of these samples are shown in Figure 8-31.

When modifying existing letters, use the Direct Selection tool. Select the points or segments you wish to move and drag them around to your heart's content. This can be great practice for adjusting paths, and you might accidentally stumble onto some really cool designs.

Creating Logos from Type Outlines

Type outlines provide you with the flexibility to manipulate letters to turn an ordinary, boring, letters-only logo into a distinct symbol embodying the company's image.

Outlines are flexible enough that there really are no limits to what can be done with something as simple as a word of type.

The examples in Figure 8-32 show some logos that have been "touched up" by changing them into outlines and moving around the paths that comprise them.

Figure 8-31: Fun with type outlines

Arcing Words and Phrases

The difference between arced words and type on a circle is that while the letters in type on a circle are rotated individually, making each letter line up with one part of the circle; the letters in arced type are not rotated, but instead either the top or bottom of them is stretched to fit to a circular curve, as in the examples previously shown on the right side of Figure 8-32.

Arcing type is easier and creates better results when the type is created as all capital letters, especially when the tops of the letters are being curved to fit a circle.

Figure 8-32: Type converted to outlines, edited, and ready to be used for logos

To arc type, first convert it into outlines, and then create an oval or circle above or below the outlines. As an example, the following steps arc type using the "circle-below" method.

STEPS: Arcing Type by Creating a Circle Below Outlines

Step 1. Make sure that the tip of the top of the circle touches the center letters in the word so that these letters don't need to be changed. Always adjust the horizontal scaling prior to aligning the circle to the outlined type, as this will prevent unnecessary adjustments.

Step 2. Using the Scale tool, scale the first letter vertically only (hold down the Shift key) and drag until either the left or right side is even with the path of the circle. Do the same for the remaining letters.

Step 3. After the letters are the correct approximate height, use the Direct Selection tool to adjust the bottoms of the letters to fit the curve well. This can take some time and a bit of practice to get the technique correct, but the results can be outstanding.

The best way to arc type is by using a third-party filter, such as the KPT Warp Frame in the KPT Vector Effects set of filters.

Arcing curved letters is much more difficult than arcing straight ones, and arcing letters with serifs is slightly more difficult than arcing letters that are sans serif.

Arcing letters just on one side of a curve can be started easily by selecting just those letters on that half and using the Free Distort filter (choose Filter⇨Distort⇨Free Distort). This does the scaling even more accurately than with the Scale tool because the letters aren't just scaled proportionately but angled automatically as well.

Masking and Other Effects

After type has been converted into outlines, it can then be used as a mask or Filled with gradients or patterns, as shown in Figure 8-33. (Standard type cannot be used as a mask, Filled with gradients, or Filled with patterns.)

Figure 8-33: Type that has been converted to outlines and is now Filled with a pattern (left) and used as a masking path (right)

In order for words to work as a single mask, they must first be changed into a compound path. Usually, individual letters of converted type are changed into individual compound paths, whether the letter has a "hole" in it or not. In order for masks to work properly, you must select the entire word or words you want to use as a mask and then choose Object⇨Compound Path⇨Make (⌘-8). This changes all the selected letters into one compound path.

In some third-party (non-Adobe) and shareware typefaces, making a compound path out of a series of letters can produce results where the "holes" are not transparent at all. This issue is usually one of path direction, which can be corrected by selecting the inner shape (the "hole") and choosing Object⇨Attributes (⌘-Control-A), and then checking or unchecking the Reverse Path checkbox.

After the words are a compound path, place them in front of the objects to be masked, select both the words and the masked objects, and then choose Object⇨Mask⇨Make.

Avoiding Font Conflicts by Creating Outlines

If you ever give your files to a service bureau or to clients, you've probably already run into some font compatibility problems. A font compatibility problem usually means that the place you gave your file doesn't have a typeface that you've used within your Illustrator document.

This is a problem that there is no great solution to, and if nothing else, the trouble seems to be worsening as more font manufacturers spring up — TrueType fonts being the Windows standard, and PostScript Type 1 fonts being the Mac standard. And then there are shareware typefaces, some of which resemble Adobe originals to an uncanny degree of accuracy. All this leads to a great deal of confusion and frustration for the average Illustrator user.

But there is a way around this problem, at least most of the time. Convert your typefaces into outlines *before* you send them to other people with other systems — they don't need your typefaces for the letters to print correctly. In fact, converted letters aren't really considered type anymore, just outlines.

Save your file before converting the text to outlines and then save as a different file name after converting the text to outlines. This will allow you to do text editing later on the original file, if necessary.

Converting typefaces to outlines removes the hinting system that Adobe has implemented. This hinting system makes small letters on low-resolution (less than 600 dpi) devices print more accurately, controlling the placement

Masking Type Mishaps

Klinger: I can't get masking with text to work right.

Toulouse: What's happening?

Klinger: Well, only the last letter in the word I'm using as a mask is working like a mask. The other letters disappear.

Toulouse: Did you make a compound path out of all the letters in your word *before* you masked?

Klinger: Uh, no. That's bad, huh?

Toulouse: Actually, yes. What's happening now is that the last letter in the word, which is in front of all the other objects that are selected, is trying to mask everything else that's selected.

Klinger: Ah. Including the other letters.

Toulouse: Exactly. Illustrator has to see the word as *one* path, which is what making a compound path out of the entire word does.

Klinger: So to fix it?

Toulouse: First, release the mask, select just the letters, and make them a compound. Then select everything and Make Mask.

and visibility of serifs and other small, thin strokes in characters. Type at small point sizes will look quite different on laser printers, although it will retain its shape and consistency when it is output to an imagesetter or an output scanner system.

Amazing Type (and Path) Effects

Typefaces edited in Illustrator and certain paths can be given three-dimensional attributes by using KPT Vector Effects, like the example shown in Figure 8-34. Chapter 18 discusses some of the various ways that Vector Effects can spiff up your type-based artwork. Another way to soup up your type is to take it into Adobe Dimensions, which comes on the *Macworld Illustrator 6 Bible CD-ROM.* The Dimensions program is discussed in Chapter 22.

Figure 8-34: Type effects with KPT Vector Effects

Special Characters

On a Macintosh, there are many special characters available besides the standard letters, numbers, and symbols that appear on your keyboard. To see these special characters, Apple includes a desk accessory called KeyCaps, which displays the keyboard you are using and shows what each character will look like in the typeface you choose.

There are some other popular desk accessories (Apple Menu Items) that allow you to view the character set of each typeface. PopChar is a very popular shareware one, and KeyFinder from Symantec (Part of Norton Utilities) is a good one as well. Both of these have a bit more flexibility than KeyCaps, but all do basically the same thing: They tell you which characters are available in each font and which key combination will result in that character.

There are essentially four sets of characters in each font. The first set is reached by normal typing of the keyboard keys, which include numbers, lowercase letters, and a few symbols. The second set is reached by pressing the Shift key prior to pressing the keyboard key and includes capital letters and symbols that appear on the top half of the keyboard keys. The third set reached by pressing the Option key before pressing a keyboard key. This set consists primarily of the common special symbols, such as bullets (•), the cents symbol (¢), an ellipsis (…), and the pi symbol (π). The fourth set of characters can only be reached when both the Option and Shift keys are pressed before a keyboard key is pressed and includes less common symbols, like f-ligatures (fi, fl), the double dagger (‡), and the Apple symbol ().

While almost all typefaces have the first and second sets, many typefaces do not contain very many characters in the third and fourth sets. The list in Figure 8-35 shows the common symbols and their keyboard equivalents, but not all typefaces have all the symbols, and some of the symbols in some of the typefaces may have different keyboard commands.

Be careful when you use special characters if you'll be taking files onto the PC platform, as some fonts have characters that aren't available with PC systems.

Symbol Typefaces

There are several symbol typefaces available that contain symbols in place of letters and numbers. The most popular of these is the Symbol typeface, which has Greek letters and mathematical operands and symbols. The next most popular symbol font would have to be Zapf Dingbats, which contains a wide variety of different symbols, as shown in Figure 8-36.

Figure 8-35: The standard keyboard set for most fonts

1st set	2nd set + Shift	3rd set + Option	4th set +Option–Shift
`	~	`	`
1	!	¡	⁄
2	@	™	¤
3	#	£	‹
4	$	¢	›
5	%	∞	ﬁ
6	^	§	ﬂ
7	&	¶	‡
8	*	•	°
9	(	ª	·
0	)	º	‚
-	_	–	—
=	+	≠	±
q	Q	œ	Œ
w	W	Σ	„
e	E	´	
r	R	®	‰
t	T	†	ˇ
y	Y	¥	Á
u	U	¨	¨
i	I	ˆ	ˆ
o	O	ø	Ø
p	P	π	∏
[	{	"	"
]	}	'	'
\	|	«	»
a	A	å	Å
s	S	ß	Í
d	D	∂	Î
f	F	ƒ	Ï
g	G	©	˝
h	H	˙	Ó
j	J	∆	Ô
k	K	˚	
l	L	¬	Ò
;	:	…	Ú
'	"	æ	Æ
z	Z	Ω	¸
x	X	≈	˛
c	C	ç	Ç
v	V	√	◊
b	B	∫	ı
n	N	˜	˜
m	M	µ	Â
,	<	≤	¯
.	>	≥	˘
/	?	÷	¿

Some other typefaces that contain primarily symbols are Carta, the map symbol typeface; Bill's Dingbats, a shareware set of symbols that nicely complements Zapf Dingbats; and Mathematical Pi, a math font containing math symbols.

One of the great things about Symbol typefaces is that individual characters can be turned into outline characters and edited to create different illustrations.

Figure 8-36: The character set of Zapf Dingbats

Key	1st set	2nd set + Shift	3rd set + Option	4th set + Option–Shift
`	❀	❞	❀	❀
1	✑	✁	➁	➚
2	✒	✠	♥	➛
3	✓	✃	❣	➜
4	✔	✄	❢	➝
5	✕	☎	⑤	➞
6	✖	✾	❤	➟
7	✗	✆	❦	➠
8	✘	☛	❥	❡
9	✙	✈	❻	➡
0	✐	✉	❼	➢
-	✍	✿	➐	➑
=	✝	☞	②	⑥
q	❑	✱	➏	➎
w	◗	✷	❷	➣
e	❅	✥	♠	♠
r	❒	✲	♣	➤
t	▼	✴		
y	❙	✹	⑨	➧
u	◆	✵	①	①
i	❉	✩	➶	➶
o	❏	✯	❿	④
p	❐	✰	❹	❸
[	✻	❛	➒	➓
]	✽	❝	➔	→
\	✼	❜	➇	➈
a	❁	✡	❴	❩
s	▲	✳	❧	➪
d	❄	✤	❶	➫
f	❆	✦	➄	➬
g	❇	✧	♦	➽
h	❈	★	➺	➮
j	❊	✪	➆	➯
k	❋	✫	➻	
l	●	✬	➂	➱
;	✛	✚	➉	➲
'	✇	✂	❾	③
z	❚	✺	❽	➼
x	❘	✸	➅	➾
c	❃	✣	❵	❪
v	❖	✶	➃	↕
b	❂	✢	❺	➵
n	■	✮	➷	➷
m	❍	✭	⑩	➥
,	✌	✜	⑦	➸
.	✎	✞	⑧	➹
/	✏	✟	↔	➀

Customizing Fonts

Typefaces can be created and modified right on your Macintosh, with tools very similar to the ones in Adobe Illustrator. Creating fonts is, in a way, the reverse process of outlining existing fonts because you are taking outlines and turning them into characters in typefaces. Figure 8-37 shows two of the most popular shareware fonts created through a combination of Illustrator and Fontographer: Lefty Casual and Ransom Note.

Figure 8-37: Lefty Casual and Ransom Note

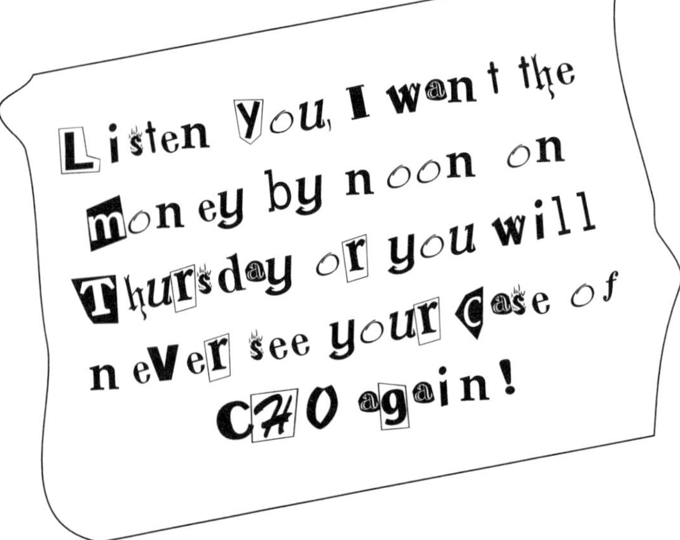

By taking existing typefaces, you can customize the characters, creating a unique typeface. In a typeface you create, all the special characters can be ones you've designed especially for that face.

Check with the original typeface manufacturer before customizing to ensure that you will not be violating any copyright laws for that particular font vendor.

MacroMedia Fontographer is the most popular of the font-creation software currently available, boasting Multiple Master capabilities and very precise Bézier control tools.

Additional Text Functions

The following sections describe the functions that appear at the bottom of the Type menu or in the Text Filters submenu. These functions add various capabilities to Illustrator's type-handling capabilities.

The Export Filter

To export text, choose Type⇨Export. A Save dialog box appears, asking in what format and where you want to save the text.

To use the Export filter, you need to have the Claris XTND folder in your System Folder, which is automatically installed with Illustrator.

You can save text in most of the common formats, and you can import it back into Illustrator with the Import Text command (choose File⇨Import Text when a text area is active with a Type tool). Word processing software, page layout software, or any other software that can read text files can open and use text that you saved in Illustrator.

The Find Filter

The Find filter (Filters⇨Text ⇨Find) uses the Text Find dialog box that is shown in Figure 8-38 to search for and, if necessary, replace certain letters, words, or character combinations.

Figure 8-38: The Text Find dialog box

Text Find

Find what: | Replace with:

☒ Whole Word ☒ Case Sensitive ☒ Search Backward ☒ Wrap Around

Find Next | Replace, then Find | Replace | Replace All

STEPS: Finding and Replacing Text

Step 1. Choose Filters⇨Text⇨Find. The Text Find dialog box appears.

Step 2. Type the word, phrase, or characters that you want to find in the Find what text field.

You do not need to select areas of type with the Selection or Type tools. All that is necessary is that the document that you want to search be the active document.

Step 3. Check the appropriate options:

- **Whole Word:** Tells Illustrator that the characters you type in the Find what box are an entire word, not part of a word.

- **Case Sensitive:** Selects the characters only if they have the same uppercase and lowercase attributes as the characters you type in the Find what text field.
- **Search Backward:** Tells Illustrator to look before the current word for the next instance of the characters, instead of using the default, which is to look after the current word.
- **Wrap Around:** Keeps Illustrator going through all the text blocks and makes Illustrator continue looking and finding the next occurrence throughout each text block. When it reaches the last text block, it starts where it originally began and continues finding the word or characters that you specified in the Find what box.

Step 4. Click the Find Next button to find the first occurrence of the word or characters.

Step 5. In the Replace with box, type the word or characters that you want to use to replace the text that Illustrator found.

Step 6. Click the Replace button to replace the selected text. Click the Replace button and then the Find button to replace the selected text and automatically highlight the next matching word or characters. Click the Replace All button to replace all occurrences of the word or characters throughout the document.

Illustrator cannot find words or characters that you have converted to outlines.

The Change Case Filter

The Change Case filter converts selected text to a variety of case options. To use this filter, select type with a type tool and then choose Filter⇨Text⇨Change Case. The Change Case dialog box appears, as shown in Figure 8-39.

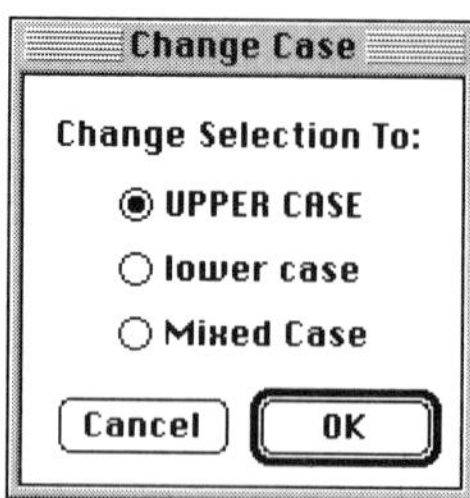

Figure 8-39: The Change Case dialog box

Type *must* be selected with the Type tool (characters must be highlighted) to use the Change Case filter. If type is selected with a Selection tool, then the filter will not work, and a dialog box stating this will be displayed.

The three Change Case options affect only letters, not numbers, symbols, or punctuation. The options are as follows:

- **UPPER CASE** converts all selected letters into uppercase, regardless if any letters were uppercase or lowercase.
- **lower case** converts all selected letters into lowercase, regardless if any letters were uppercase or lowercase. It also doesn't matter if the letters were originally uppercase because they were typed with the Caps Lock key engaged, or if the uppercase letters were uppercase because of a style format.
- **Mixed Case** converts all selected words into lowercase, with the first letter of each word becoming uppercase, regardless if any letters were originally uppercase or lowercase. It also doesn't matter if the letters were originally uppercase because they were typed with the Caps Lock key engaged, or if the uppercase letters were uppercase because of a style format. The Mixed Case option separates words by making *any* character that is between letters end one word and begin another. At the time of this writing, even apostrophes in contractions caused words like "don't" and "can't" to display as "Don'T" and "Can'T".

The Check Spelling Filter

The Check Spelling filter checks all text in a document to see if it is spelled (and capitalized) correctly. To use this filter, choose Filter⇨Text⇨Check Spelling. The Check Spelling dialog box appears, as shown in Figure 8-40.

But My Insertion Point Is Waaayyy Over There

Hawkeye: My insertion point is posessed.

Toulouse: Possesed, eh?

Hawkeye: When I enter text using the Text tool, my cursor floats 2-6 spaces to the right of its actual position in the line of text.

Toulouse: This usually happens when you have both TrueType and Type 1 versions of the same fonts installed.

Hawkeye: How can I fix it?

Toulouse: Just remove one or the other. I'd recommend keeping the PostScript Type 1 version.

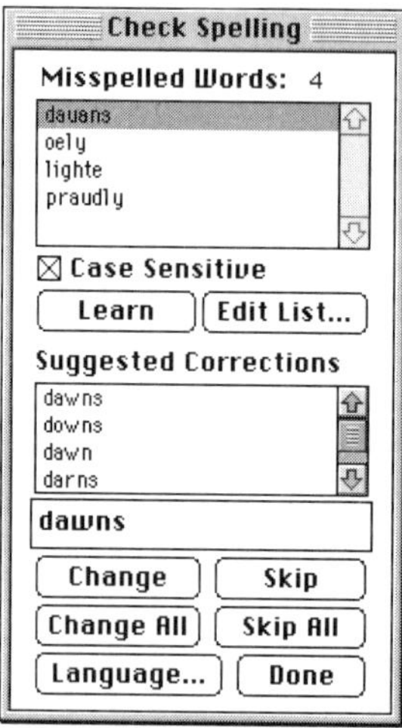

Figure 8-40: The Check Spelling dialog box

If all words are spelled correctly, a congratulatory message appears telling you that your spelling is "excellent."

If you are having a bad day and want some instant encouragement, there is no better way to get it than by creating a new document with no text and selecting the Check Spelling filter. The "Your spelling is excellent" message will appear, making you feel just dandy.

If you have any misspelled words or words that are not in the spelling dictionaries, those words will be listed at the top of the Check Spelling dialog box in the Misspelled Words window. Selecting a word in this list will display similar words below in the window titled Suggested Corrections.

If the Case Sensitive option is checked, the capitalization of words must match the words in the spell checker's dictionary, or they will appear as misspelled words.

Under the Case Sensitive checkbox are two buttons. The button on the left, Learn, is used when you would like to add the selected "misspelled" word to your custom dictionary. Clicking the Edit List button displays the Learned Words dialog box (on the right side of Figure 8-40), showing you which words are currently in the user dictionary. The Learned Words dialog box enables you to add, remove, or change entries in the user dictionary.

STEPS: Adding Words to the User Dictionary

Step 1: To add a new entry to the user dictionary, select the Edit List button in the Check Spelling dialog box, which displays the Learned Words dialog box.

Step 2: Type in the word that you would like to add to the user dictionary. Click the Add button, and the word is added to the list of words in the user dictionary.

Capitalization is very important when adding words, so be sure to place initial caps on proper nouns and to use correct capitalization on all words that require it.

If the word you are trying to add exists in the user dictionary or the main dictionary, a dialog box appears telling you that it is already a dictionary entry.

Step 3. Repeat Step 2 until all the words have been added.

Step 4. If at any time you make a mistake, you may change the spelling of an entered word by selecting it in the window above, typing in the correct spelling, and then clicking the Change button. If you wish to delete an entry that exists in the Learned Words window, select that word and click the Remove button.

Step 5. When you are finished, click the Done button.

The user dictionary words are saved in a file called "AI User Dictionary," which is stored in the Plug-Ins folder. The file is in TeachText-compatible format, but the character that separates the words is indistinguishable (it appears as an open rectangle, the symbol for a symbol that is not available in that typeface), so there is no way to add words to the dictionary by using TeachText or another word processor.

Be careful not to delete or remove the AI User Dictionary file when reinstalling the software or moving the files in the Plug-Ins folder. Doing so will cause Illustrator to create a new user dictionary file with no words in it. There is no way to combine two different user dictionary files.

While you're checking your spelling in the Check Spelling dialog box, clicking the Change button changes the misspelled word with the highlighted word in the Suggested Corrections list. Clicking the Change All button replaces all misspelled occurrences of that word throughout the entire document with the correctly spelled word.

Clicking the Skip button ignores that occurrence of the misspelled word. Clicking Skip All skips all occurrences of that word in the document.

Clicking the Language button uses a dictionary for the language you specify. Illustrator supplies dictionaries for the United States and the United Kingdom, both located in the Plug-In filters files.

Oddly enough, dictionaries for other languages are not available through Adobe, even though there are Hyphenation dictionaries available for several different languages, including Danish, Dutch, Finnish, French, German, Hungarian, Italian, Norwegian, Spanish, Swedish and many more (several are located in the Goodies folder on the *Macworld Illustrator 6 Bible CD-ROM*).

Clicking the Done button closes the Check Spelling dialog box.

The Find Font Filter

The Find Font filter looks for certain fonts in a document and replaces them with fonts you specify.

Select type with either a selection tool or with a type tool. Then choose Filter⇨Text⇨ Find Font to use this filter. The Find Font dialog box appears, as shown in Figure 8-41.

Figure 8-41: The Find Font dialog box

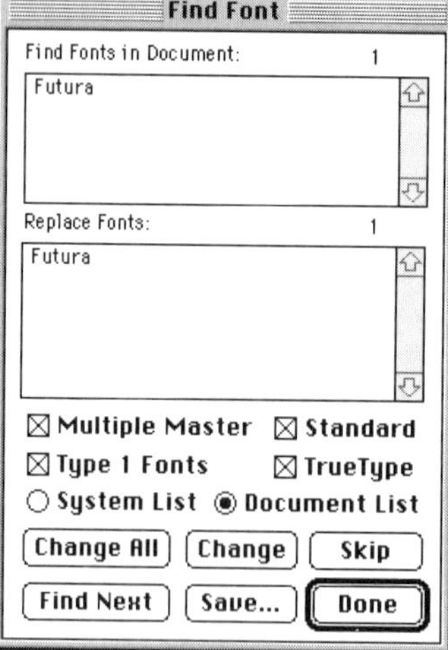

To change all occurrences of a certain font to another font, select the font to be changed in the top window, titled "Find Fonts in Document." Then select a font in the Replace Fonts window and click the Change All button. To change one particular instance, click the Change button. To find the next occurrence of that font, select Find Next. The Skip button skips over the currently selected text and finds the next occurrence of that font.

Pressing the Save button will allow you to save your font list as a text file. After the fonts are found, you have to select type with the Type tool, no matter how it was selected before the Find Font filter was used.

The Revert Text Paths Filter

The Revert Text Paths filter converts selected text paths into standard Illustrator paths. This is useful for working with paths that have had text on them but don't work like normal paths anymore. Revert Text Path isn't normally installed with Illustrator. To install it, drag it into the Illustrator Plug-Ins folder from the Optional Plug-Ins folder.

Before you use this filter, the text path to be converted must contain *no* text. If it does contain text, click on the text path with a type tool, choose Edit⇨Select All (⌘-A), and press Delete. Select the type path with a selection tool. Then choose Filter⇨Text⇨Revert Text Path. The Revert Text Path dialog box appears.

You have one choice in the Revert Text Path dialog box: whether or not to delete the original text path. If you check the checkbox, the original text path will be converted into an Illustrator path. If you do *not* check the checkbox, the original text path will remain, and a new Illustrator path of the exact same size will be placed directly on top of the original path.

This filter works for Path type, Area type, and Rectangle type.

The Rows & Columns Filter

The Rows & Columns filter divides rectangular paths (text or standard Illustrator rectangles) into even sections. This is as close to a "grid" feature as Illustrator gets.

To use the Rows & Columns filter, select a path and choose Filter⇨Text⇨Rows & Columns. The Rows & Columns dialog box appears, as shown in Figure 8-42.

Figure 8-42: The Rows & Columns dialog box

Any path, open or closed, can be selected and divided into rows and columns, with one catch: The object will become a rectangular shape, the size of the original path's *bounding box* (the smallest box that could completely contain the path). There is no way to divide a nonrectangular path automatically. See the steps in the next selection for a way to do this without Illustrator knowing about it.

The Rows & Columns Dialog Box

The left side of the Rows & Columns dialog box determines the width of the columns. The right side determines the height of the rows. At the bottom of the dialog box is a Preview checkbox; checking this will display changes as you make them in the Rows & Columns dialog box.

All measurements in the Rows & Columns dialog box are displayed in the current measurement system.

The first text field, Columns, determines how many columns the selected path will be cut into. Below that, the Column Width text field determines the width of the columns. The Column Width must be less than the Total Width (fourth field) divided by the number of columns. The third text field is Gutter, which is the space between columns. The Total Width is how wide the entire rectangle is.

As the Column Width is increased, the Gutter will decrease. When Column Width is decreased, the Gutter will increase. Likewise, as the Gutter is increased, the Column Width will decrease. When the Gutter is decreased, the Column Width will increase.

On the right side, the first text field is the number of Rows that the original path will be divided into. The second text field, Row Height, is the height of each of the rows. The Row Height must be less than the Total Height (the fourth field on right) divided by the number of rows. The third text field on the right is Gutter, which is the space between rows. The Total Height is how high the entire rectangle is.

As the Row Height is increased, the Gutter will decrease. When Row Height is decreased, the Gutter will increase. Likewise, as the Gutter is increased, the Row Height will decrease. When the Gutter is decreased, the Row Height will increase.

Remember that using the Rows & Columns filter actually divides the selected rectangle into several pieces.

The Text Flow option determines the direction of text as it flows from one section to the next. You may choose between text that starts along the top row and flows from left to right, and then goes to the next lowest row, flowing from left to right, and so on. The other option is to have text start in the left column, flowing from top to bottom, and then to the next column to the right, flowing from top to bottom. The Text Flow is changed by clicking once on the graphic that is next to the words "Text Flow."

The Add Guides checkbox will create guides that extend off each edge of the page. These guides align with the edges of each of the boxes created from the Rows & Columns filter.

The following steps describe how to create rows and columns in a nonrectangular object.

STEPS: Creating Rows and Columns in a Nonrectangular Object

Step 1. Create the object that you wish to divide into rows and columns. (In Figure 8-43, I used type converted into outlines and made the entire word one compound path.)

Step 2. Copy the object to the Clipboard (choose Edit⇨Copy, or press ⌘-C).

Step 3. Choose Filter⇨Text⇨Rows & Columns and divide the object into the number of rows and columns desired. Click OK. The object becomes rectangular.

Step 4: Paste in Front. The original object appears in front of the rectangle that is divided into rows and columns.

Step 5: Select all objects and choose Filter⇨Pathfinder⇨Crop. The result is a nonrectangular shape that has been divided into rows and columns.

Figure 8-43: Steps for creating non-rectangular columns and rows

Step 1

Step 2

Step 3

Step 4

These steps show how to create angled rows and columns.

STEPS: Creating Angled Rows and Columns

Step 1. Create an oversized object that will become the rows and columns.

Step 2. Choose Filter⇨Text⇨Rows & Columns and divide the object into the rows and columns, but this time specify the size of the rows and columns, not how many you want. Click OK.

Step 3. Rotate the columns and rows you have just created.

Step 4. Create the object that will contain the angled rows and columns, and place it in front of the rows and columns. (In Figure 8-44, I used a plain rectangle.)

Step 5. Select all objects and choose Filter⇨Pathfinder⇨Crop. The result is an object with angled rows and columns within it.

Smart Punctuation

The Smart Punctuation filter looks for certain fonts in a document and replaces them with fonts you specify. To use this filter, select type with either a selection tool or with a type tool. Then choose Filter⇨Text⇨Smart Punctuation. The Smart Punctuation dialog box appears, as shown in Figure 8-45.

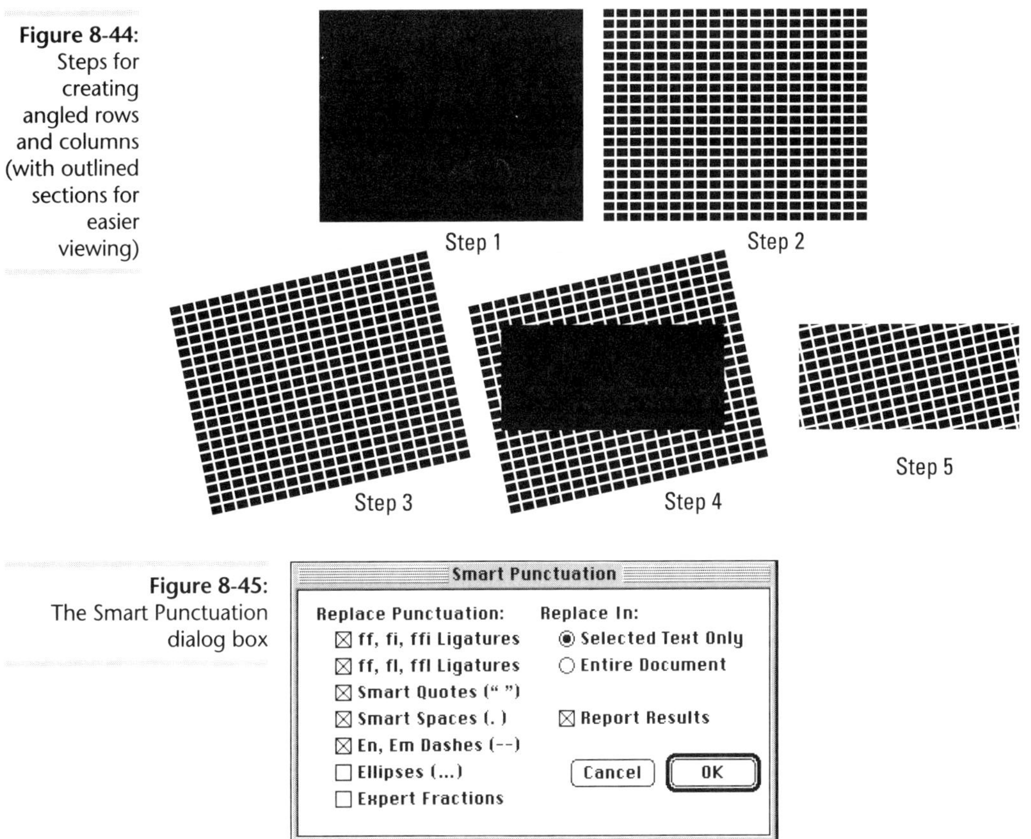

Figure 8-44: Steps for creating angled rows and columns (with outlined sections for easier viewing)

Figure 8-45: The Smart Punctuation dialog box

The Smart Punctuation filter works “after the fact,” making changes to text already in the Illustrator document. There are no settings, for instance, to convert quotes to curved quotes as you are typing them. The types of punctuation to be changed are determined by a set of checkboxes in the Smart Punctuation dialog box. A checked box means that Illustrator will look for these certain instances and, if it finds them, correct them with the proper punctuation.

The first two options are used for replacing ff, fi (or fl), and ffi (or ffl) with *ligatures.* Ligatures are characters that represent several characters with one character that is designed to let those characters appear nicer when placed next to each other. Most fonts have fi and fl ligatures, which look like ﬁ and ﬂ, respectively.

The remaining Smart Punctuation options work as follows:

- **Smart Quotes** replaces straight quotes (" " and ' ') with curly quotes, known as typesetter's quotes or printer's quotes (“ ” and ‘ ’).
- **Smart Spaces** replaces multiple spaces after a period with one space. (In typesetting, there should only be one space following a period.)
- **En, Em Dashes** replaces hyphens (-) with en dashes (–) and double hyphens (- -) with em dashes (—).
- **Ellipses** replaces three periods (...) with an ellipsis (…).
- **Expert Fractions** replaces fractions with expert fractions if you have the expert fractions available in the font family you are using. Adobe sells “Expert Collection” fonts that contain these fractions. If you do *not* have expert fractions, your fractions remain unchanged.

Checking the Report Results box displays a dialog box when the filter is finished, telling you how many of the punctuation changes were made, divided into several categories.

Other Type Considerations

When you're using type in Illustrator, there are a number of things to keep in mind to get good results:

- Make sure that the person you are sending the Illustrator file to has the same fonts you have. It isn't enough just to have the same name of a font; you'll need the exact font that was created by the same manufacturer.
- Try not to mix TrueType fonts with PostScript fonts. This usually ends up confusing everyone involved.
- If the person you are sending Illustrator files to does *not* have your typeface, select the type in that font and choose Type➪Create Outlines.
- When you're printing an Illustrator file that has been placed in other software, missing typestyles may go unnoticed until after the job has printed. Be doubly sure that the person outputting the file has all the fonts in the embedded Illustrator file.

Summary

- Most of the options used to control type can be found in the Type menu.
- There are four different ways to put type on a page: Point type, Rectangle type, Area type, and Path type.
- Point type has one point as its "anchor" and the type is aligned to that point.
- Rectangle type exists within a rectangle drawn with the Type tool.
- Area type is type that exists within the confines of any path.
- Path type is type that runs along the edge of a path.
- Type can be selected all at once by clicking on the path (or point) of the type with the Selection tool.
- Individual characters, words, and paragraphs can be selected by using any of the type tools.
- The Character palette (accessed by pressing ⌘-T) contains all the character-specific information about selected type, and can be used to change that information.
- There are no "styles" in Illustrator with regard to type; instead, you must select the exact font you wish to use.
- Tracking and kerning remove or add space between groups or pairs of letters, respectively.
- The Paragraph palette (accessed by pressing ⌘-Shift-P) contains all the paragraph-specific information about selected type, and can be used to change that information.
- Type can be set to wrap around selected paths by using the Text Wrapping feature.
- Type can be set to jump from text block to text block by linking text blocks together.
- The Tab Ruler palette is used to set tabs for text areas.
- If you have both the screen font and the printer font of a Type 1 typeface, or if you have a TrueType font installed, you can convert the font into outlines via the Create Outlines command.
- Once type has been changed to outlines, you may use those outlines as a mask, or Fill those outlines with gradients or patterns.
- Many special characters can be accessed in each font by pressing the Option key.
- Illustrator includes many specialized text functions in the Text Filter submenu.

Masks and Compound Paths

9 CHAPTER

In This Chapter

- Understanding compound paths
- The difference between a Fill of None and a hole
- How paths travel in directions, and reversing those directions
- Type and compound paths
- Faking a compound path
- Understanding masks
- Putting Strokes and Fills on masks
- Printing problems with masks
- Compound masks: an output nightmare

Compound Paths

Compound paths are one of the least-understood areas of Illustrator, but after you understand a few simple guidelines and rules, manipulating and using them correctly is simple.

Compound paths are paths made up of two or more open or closed paths. Where the paths cross or every other Fill area exists is a "hole," which is transparent. You can specify which paths create the holes by changing the direction of the paths via the Reverse option in Object⇨Attributes. The general rule is that holes are formed by paths traveling in the opposite direction of any adjoining paths. Compound paths can be fun or frustrating, depending on the location of Pluto relative to Saturn, Jupiter, and Mickey.

Creating Compound Paths

Compound paths of all sorts can be created by following the next steps. It is a good idea to make sure that none of the paths are currently compound paths or grouped paths before creating a new compound path.

STEPS: Creating a Compound Path

Step 1. Create all the paths that you need for the compound path, including the outside path and the holes.

Step 2. Select all the paths and choose Object⇨Compound Paths⇨Make (⌘-8). The paths will now be treated as one path by Illustrator. When you click one of the paths with the Selection tool, the other paths in the compound path will be selected as well. Fill the object with any Fill. (I used a custom radial gradient for the illustration in Figure 9-1.)

Figure 9-1: The frame of this window is a compound path with several "holes" in it.

Step 3. Place the compound path over any other object. (I used a placed EPS image for this example.) The inner paths act like holes that enable you to see the object underneath.

Figure 9-2 shows these three steps.

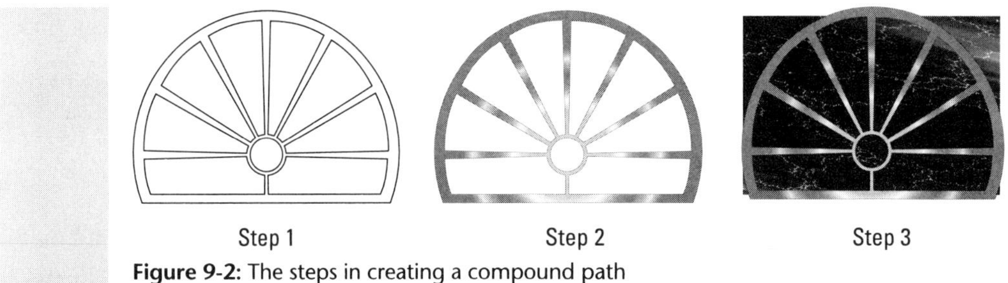

Figure 9-2: The steps in creating a compound path

You can select individual paths by clicking them once with the Group Selection tool. As always, you can select points and segments within each path by using the Direct Selection tool.

Clicking only once with the Group Selection tool on paths that you wish to select is important. Clicking those paths more than once with the Group Selection tool will select all the other paths in the compound path. To click (for moving or copying purposes) the selected individual paths after they have been clicked by the Group Selection tool once, click them with the Direct Selection tool.

Paths belonging to different groups cannot be made into a compound path unless all paths in all the groups are selected.

When you create a compound path, it takes on the Paint Style attributes of the bottommost path of all the paths that were selected and have become part of that compound path.

You can create a compound path that is only one path, though there are very few reasons to do so. If the singular compound path is selected as part of a larger compound path (with either the Direct Selection tool or Group Selection tool), the path directions may be altered. If you aren't sure whether an individual path is a compound path, select the path and choose Object⇨Compound Path. If the Release option is available, the path is a compound path; if it is not available, the path is not a compound path.

Compound paths do not work in a hierarchical process as groups do. If a path is part of a compound path, it is part of that compound path only. If a compound path becomes part of another compound path, the paths in the original compound path are compounded only with the new compound path.

You cannot blend between multiple-path compound paths. Only the individual paths that you click with the Blend tool will be blended. You can blend each of the paths in a compound path separately; however, the blend step paths will not be compound paths.

Blending Compounds

Mindy: I can't blend my compound paths right.

Toulouse: Actually, the Blend tool only works with a single path at a time.

Mindy: So I'm out of luck?

Toulouse: Not really. There's two different options available.

Mindy: And they are…?

Toulouse: Well, what are you trying to do with the blend?

Mindy: I'm trying to make zooming text.

Toulouse: Ah. Well, instead of blending, you could use KPT Vector Effects. Some of the filters, ShadowLand specifically, does some amazing things with compound blends.

Mindy: Okay. The other way?

Toulouse: Change your compounds to "fake compounds," making them consist of truly one path.

Mindy: How could I do that?

Toulouse: It involves quite a bit of splitting paths and joining. But there's a catch.

Mindy: As long as it doesn't involve stalking…

Toulouse: No…actually, you just can't use Strokes, which would appear in the seams.

Mindy: Sounds fair, I'll try it.

Releasing Compound Paths

When you want to release a compound path, select the path and choose Object⇨Compound Path⇨Release (⌘-9). The path changes into regular paths.

If any of the paths appeared as holes, they will, instead, be Filled with the Fill of the rest of the compound path. The results might be a little confusing because these holes then seem to blend right into the outer shape of the compound paths, as shown in Figure 9-3.

If the compound path that you are releasing contains other compound paths, they will be released as well because Illustrator doesn't recognize compound paths that are within other compound paths.

Understanding Holes

Holes for donuts, Life Savers, and rings are quite simple to create. Just select two circles, one smaller than, and totally within, a larger circle, and choose Compound Path⇨Make (⌘-8). The inside circle is then a hole.

Holes in Illustrator really aren't holes at all. Instead, a compound path considers every path within it to lie along the borders of the compound path. Path edges within an object appear to you to be on the inside of an object, but they appear to Illustrator to be just another edge of the path.

With this concept in mind, you can create a compound path that has several holes, such as a slice of Swiss cheese or a snowflake. Just create the outermost paths and the paths that will be holes, select all the paths, and then select Compound Path⇨Make.

You aren't limited to one set of holes. You can create a compound path with a hole that has an object inside it with a hole. In that hole can be an object with a hole, and so on.

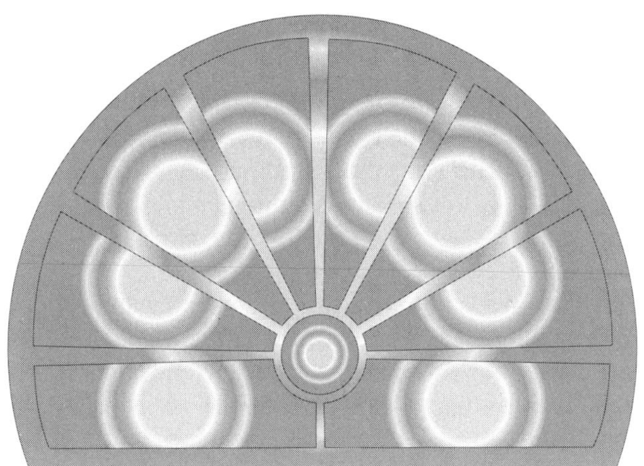

Figure 9-3: The compound path from Figure 9-1, after you release the path. The circles are the radial gradients that the compound path uses.

Overlapping Holes

Holes, if they really are paths that are supposed to be empty areas of an object, should not overlap. If anything, you can combine multiple holes that are overlapping into one larger hole, possibly by using the Unite filter.

If holes within a compound path do overlap, the result is a solid area with the same Fill color as the rest of the object. If multiple holes overlap, the results can be quite unusual, as shown in Figure 9-4. (See "Reversing Path Directions" later in this chapter to learn more about multiple overlapping holes.)

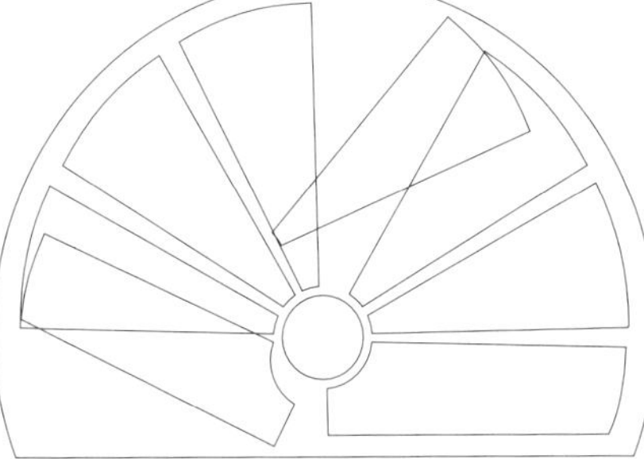

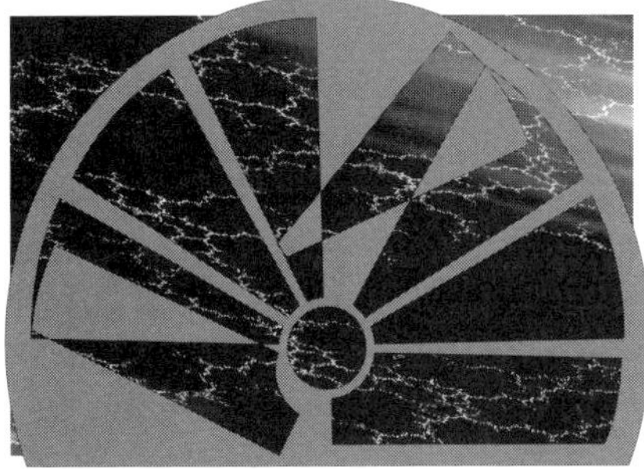

Figure 9-4: Overlapping holes in compound paths, in Artwork mode (left) and Preview mode (right)

In most cases, you will get the desired results with holes only if the outermost path is under all the holes. As a rule, Illustrator uses the topmost objects to "poke" holes out of the bottommost objects. If you want holes to overlap, make sure that the holes are above the outside border.

Creating Compound Paths from Separate Sets of Paths

Compound paths are very flexible. You can choose two sets of paths, each with an outline and a hole, and make them into one compound path. This technique is especially useful for making masks, but you also can use it to alleviate the repetition of creating several compound paths and selecting one of them at a time.

For example, if you have two shapes, a square and a circle, and want a round hole in each of them, you draw two smaller circles and put them into place. After you position the two shapes in the correct locations, you select them and the round paths inside each of them, and then you choose Object⇨Compound Path⇨Make (⌘-8). Each of the objects will have a hole, and they will act as if they are grouped.

To move separate objects that are part of the same compound path, select each object with the Group Selection tool, which selects an entire path at a time, and then move them. Remember that once selected, you should use the Direct Selection tool to move the selected portions of a compound path.

Type and Compound Paths

You have been using compound paths as long as you have been using a Mac with PostScript typefaces. All PostScript typefaces are made of characters that are compound paths. Letters that have holes, such as uppercase *B, D,* and *P* and lowercase *a, b,* and *d,* benefit from being compound paths. When you place them in front of other objects, you can see through the empty areas to objects behind them that are visible in those holes.

Each character in a PostScript typeface is a compound path. When you convert characters to editable outlines in Illustrator, each character is still a compound path. If you release the compound paths, the characters with empty areas appear to fill with the same color as the rest of the character, as shown in Figure 9-5, because the holes are no longer knocked out of the letters.

Many times, type is used as a mask, but all the letters used in the mask need to be one compound path. Simply select all the letters and choose Object⇨Compound Path⇨Make (⌘-8). This action creates a compound path in which all of the letters form the compound path. Usually, all the holes stay the same as they were as separate compound paths.

Figure 9-5: Type as it normally appears after you convert it to outlines (top) and after you release compound paths (bottom)

Any letters that overlap in a word that you make into a compound path can change path directions and thus affect the "emptiness" of some paths. If letters have to overlap, use the Unite filter on them first and then select all the letters and choose Object⇨Compound Path⇨ Make (⌘-8).

Path Directions

Each path in Illustrator has a direction. For paths that you draw with the Pen or Free-hand tools, the direction of the path is the direction in which you draw the path. When Illustrator creates an oval or a rectangle, the direction of the path is counterclockwise.

If you're curious about which way a path travels, click any spot of the path with the Scissors tool and then choose Filter⇨Stylize⇨Add Arrowheads. In the Add Arrowheads dialog box, make sure that the End button is selected and click OK. An arrowhead appears, going in the direction of the path. (Figure 9-6 shows several paths and arrowheads appearing for each path.) If the path is Filled and not Stroked, you see only half the arrowhead in Preview mode. Choose the Undo command twice (once for the arrowhead and once for the path splitting) to go back to where you started.

Paths have directions for one purpose (one purpose that you need to know about, anyway), and that is to determine what the solid areas of a compound path will be and what the empty areas will be. The individual paths in a compound path that create holes from solid paths go in opposite directions.

Create a large circle and put a smaller circle within it. Both circles are traveling in the same direction — counterclockwise. Select both of them and choose Object⇨ Compound Path⇨Make (⌘-8). The outside circle changes its direction to clockwise so that the two circles can work together to form a doughnut-like shape.

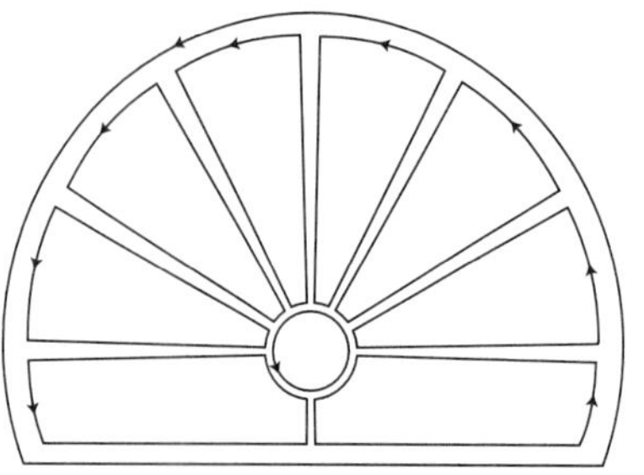

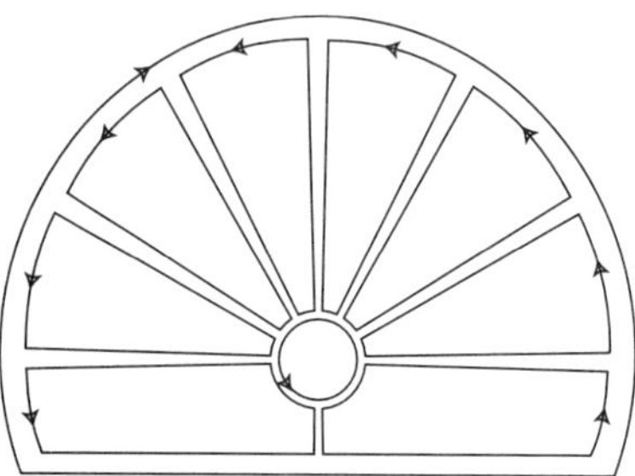

Figure 9-6: The paths on the left are individual paths. The paths on the right make up a compound path. The arrows represent the direction of the paths. Notice that the only difference in direction is on the outermost path.

If two smaller circles are inside the larger circle, they still punch holes in the larger circle because both of them are traveling in the same direction. But what happens when the two inside circles are overlapping? The area where they overlap is inside the empty areas, but both holes go in the same direction. The intersection of the two holes is solid because of the winding path rule.

The Winding Numbers Rule, or What Happened to My Fills?

Understanding the Winding Numbers Rule is helpful when you are dealing with compound paths. The Winding Numbers Rule counts surrounded areas, starting with 0 (outside the outermost edge) and working its way in. Any area with an odd number is Filled, and any area with an even number (such as 0, the outside of the path) is empty, or a hole.

You can apply this rule to most compound paths — although taking the time to diagram the paths you've drawn and place little numbers in them to figure out what is going to be Filled and what isn't is usually more time consuming than doing it wrong, undoing it, and doing it right. I've done the work for you in Figure 9-7.

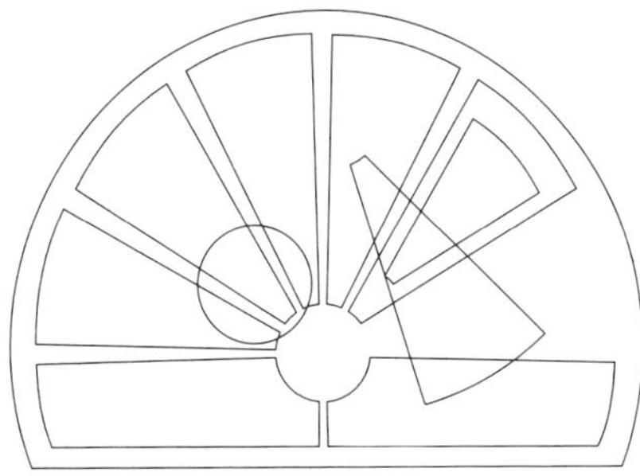

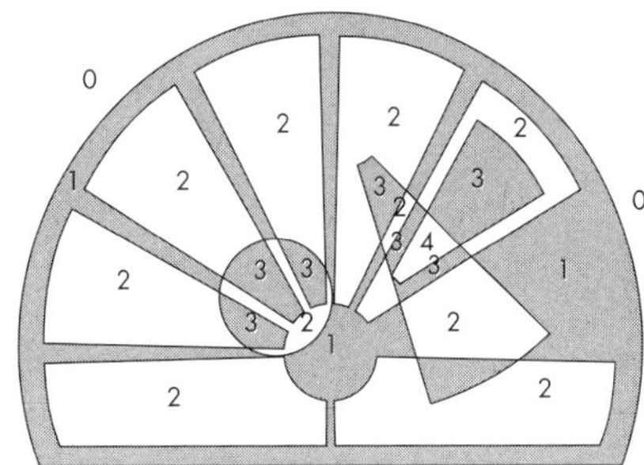

Figure 9-7: As the paths wind in from the outside, odd-numbered areas are Filled and even-numbered areas are empty.

Reversing Path Directions

To change the direction of a path, select just that path (you may need to use the Group Selection tool) and choose Object⇨Attributes (⌘-Ctrl-A). In the Object Attributes dialog box, check the Reverse Path Direction checkbox.

When paths are changed into compound paths, their direction may change. The strange thing about this is that the Reverse Path Direction box is usually checked for objects that are traveling counterclockwise. The outermost path does not change direction from counterclockwise to clockwise until more than one overlapping path is made into a compound path. The paths that make up the holes don't change direction. They're still counterclockwise, but when you look at their Object Attributes, Reverse Path Direction is checked.

One thing that is consistent when dealing with path directions is that holes must travel in the opposite direction from the outside path. As a result, if the Reverse Path Direction checkbox is checked for the holes, it is not checked for the outside path. That scenario is the normal one when you create compound paths with holes. You can, if you so desire, check the Reverse Path Direction checkbox for the outside path and uncheck it for the inside paths. The resulting image will have the same holes as produced by the reverse. Figure 9-8 shows a compound path and its path directions before and after four of the paths were reversed.

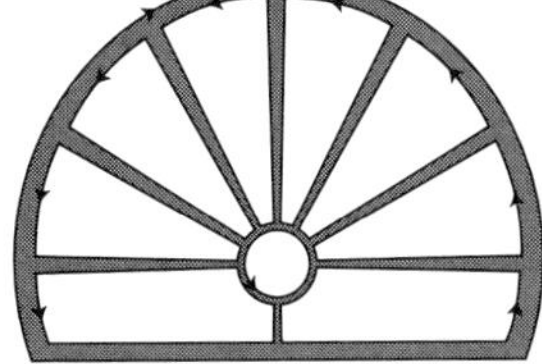

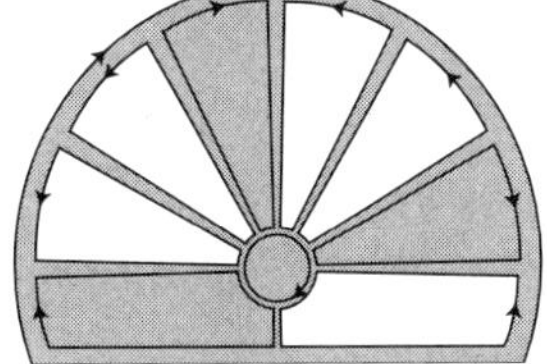

Figure 9-8: Reversing the direction of the four paths in the illustration on the left Fills those holes

Can't Make a Compound

Mork: I can't make a compound out of my selected paths!

Toulouse: That often happens when one or more of the paths is already a compound path.

Mork: Huh. How would I find out if that's the case?

Toulouse: Well, you can check and fix it at the same time. First, select the paths you'd like to make into a compound path.

Mork: Got it.

Toulouse: Then, go under Object to Compound Path and hold.

Mork: Okay.

Toulouse: Is Release gray or black?

Mork: Black.

Toulouse: That means at least one of the selected paths is already a compound. Drag over to release.

Mork: Done.

Toulouse: Then choose Object⇨Compound Paths⇨Make.

Mork: It worked!

Toulouse: And what did you learn this week...?

Never, never, never choose Object⇨Attributes (⌘-Control-A) to change path direction when all paths of a compound path are selected. Doing so will display a gray box in the Reverse Path Direction checkbox in the Object Attributes dialog box. Clicking once on this gray checkbox will make it an empty box. Clicking twice on this box will change it to a Filled (with an *X*) checkbox. Either way, all the paths in the compound path will be going in the same direction at this point, meaning that no holes will appear.

Using Unite to Create Compound Paths

Another way to make compound paths is by using the Unite filter. The Unite filter works a little differently than the Make Compound Path command. All the selected paths become a single compound path, but none of the path directions are reversed. This means that no "holes" will be created when the Unite filter is applied.

Unite is quite useful for creating compound paths when there are overlapping pieces of paths that you don't want to create holes between accidentally, such as text converted to outlines.

In addition, Unite removes any overlapping path areas where Filled areas or "holes" are, so if you Stroke the object, you'll get a much better result than if the object was just a plain compound path.

Faking a Compound Path

At times, using a compound path just doesn't work. You may need to cheat a little. Except in the most extreme circumstances, you can fake compound paths, but you need to make quite an effort.

If the background is part of a gradient, select the hole and the object that is painted with the gradient, apply the gradient, and use the Gradient Vector tool to make the gradient spread across both objects in exactly the same way. This trick can fool even the experts.

One way to fake a compound path is by selecting the background, making a copy of it, making the hole a mask of the background area, and grouping the mask to the copy of the background.

Masks

In Illustrator, you use masks to mask out parts of underlying objects that you don't want to see. The shape of the mask is defined by a path that you draw in Illustrator. Anything outside the mask is hidden from view in Preview mode and does not print.

Masks are objects that *mask* out everything but the paths made up by the mask (see Figure 9-9). Masks can be open, closed, or compound paths. The masking object is the object whose paths make up the mask, and this object must be in front of all the objects that are being masked.

Figure 9-9: An object, its mask, and the resulting masked object

You can make masks from any path, including compound paths and text. You can use masks to view portions of multiple objects, individual objects, and placed EPS images.

Creating Masks

In order for you to create a mask, the masking object (the path that is in the shape of the mask) has to be in front of the objects that you want it to mask. You select the masking object and the objects that you want to mask. Then you choose Object⇨Mask⇨Make. In Preview mode, any areas of the objects that were outside the mask vanish, but the parts of the objects that are inside the mask remain the same. Figure 9-10 shows an illustration with masks and without them.

Figure 9-10: The image on the left uses masks to hide portions of objects. The image on the right is the result of releasing those masks.

Masks are much easier to use and understand in Preview mode than in Artwork mode.

If you want to mask an object that is not currently being masked, you need to select the new object and all the objects in the mask, including the masking object. You then choose Object⇨Mask⇨Make. The mask then applies to the new object as well as to the objects that were previously masked. The new object, like all others being masked, must be behind the masking object.

Like compound paths, masking does not work in hierarchical levels. Each time you add an object to a mask, the old mask that didn't have that object is released, and a new mask is made that contains all of the original mask objects as well as the new object. Releasing a mask affects every object in the mask, as described in "Releasing Masks" later in this chapter.

Usually, grouping all the objects in a mask is a good idea, but group them only after you have created the mask. Having the objects grouped facilitates moving the mask and its objects and selecting them when you want to add other objects to the mask.

Masking Raster Images

There are two different ways to mask raster images. The first method is done in Photoshop by creating a *clipping path* and saving it as an EPS image. The second method is to use a mask in Illustrator.

The two methods have their strengths and weaknesses, with the best solution being a combination of both methods. The main advantage to creating a clipping path in Photoshop is that the path can be adjusted while viewing the image clearly at 16:1. (Viewing an EPS image at 1600% in Illustrator displays chunky, unrecognizable blocks of color.) In this manner, the path can be precisely positioned over the correct pixels so that the right ones are selected to be masked. One disadvantage to using Photoshop's clipping path is that the Path tool and path-editing controls in Photoshop are a limited version of Illustrator's Pen tool and path-editing controls, making it more difficult to create and edit a path. The second disadvantage to using a clipping path is that compound paths in Photoshop adhere to one of two different Fill rules, which control the way holes appear for differing path directions. Illustrator is much more flexible in this respect because you are able to change the path direction of each individual path with the Reverse Path Direction checkbox in the Object Attributes dialog box.

The best solution is to create the clipping path in Photoshop, and then, when the clipping path is selected, choose File⇨Export⇨Paths to Illustrator, which saves an Illustrator-compatible file with the clipping path intact. Save the Photoshop image as an EPS and place it in Illustrator (File⇨Place Art). Then open the Illustrator file (that was created by Paths to Illustrator) and copy the path to the document with the raster image. The path is sized to fit directly onto the raster image.

Copying the selected path in Photoshop will allow you to paste it directly in Illustrator, even if you can run only one of those programs at a time. Just copy, quit Photoshop, run Illustrator, and paste it into the Illustrator document. This will work when going from Illustrator to Photoshop (paths only) as well.

Masking Blends and Other Masks

You can mask objects that are masking other objects. Just make sure that you select all the objects in each mask and that, as with other objects, they are behind the path that you want to use for a masking object. You also can mask blends, as described in Chapter 12.

Stroking and Filling Masking Objects

Creating a basic mask requires four steps.

STEPS: Creating a Mask and Stroking It

Step 1. Select the path that you want to use as a mask and bring it to the front.

Step 2. Select the mask and any objects that you want to mask and then choose Object⇨Masks⇨Make. Group the masked objects with the mask for easier selecting in the future.

Step 3. Using the Group Selection tool, select the mask. Then change the Stroke to 1-point Black. Nothing will happen in Preview mode.

Step 4. Choose Filters⇨Stroke & Fill for Mask. A dialog box appears; click OK. The mask now has a 1-point Black Stroke. The result should resemble Step 4 in Figure 9-11.

You cannot Stroke or Fill masking objects. Any Paint Style attributes that you applied to the masking object prior to transforming it into a mask are replaced by a Fill and Stroke of None. If you release the mask, the path that was the masking object continues to have a Fill and Stroke of None. You can, however, use two other methods to create a Stroke or Fill on a duplicate path of the masking object:

- The first method is to copy the masking object before you turn it into a masking object so that you can paste the copy onto the mask after you create it. To save a step, you can Fill and Stroke the masking object before you copy it. After you create the mask, choose Edit⇨Paste in Front (⌘-F) to put a Stroke on the mask (remove the Fill or it will obscure all the objects that you are masking). Choose Edit⇨Paste in Back (⌘-B) and Arrange⇨Send to Back (⌘-hyphen) if you want the object to have a Fill. If the object in the back has a Stroke, the masking object will obscure half of it; the other objects in the mask may obscure other parts of it. If you want both a Stroke and a Fill, you need to paste two copies, one in front and one in back, to see both the Fill and Stroke accurately.
- The second method is to select the masking object and then from the Paint Style palette, choose the Paint Style attributes that you want for the masking object (it won't change in color, but you can change the attributes). Then choose Filter⇨Create⇨Fill & Stroke for Mask to create two more copies of the mask. Finally, paste the Filled copy behind the mask's objects and the Stroked copy in front of the masking object.

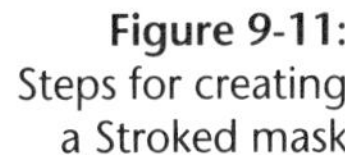

Figure 9-11: Steps for creating a Stroked mask

Step 1

Step 2

Step 3

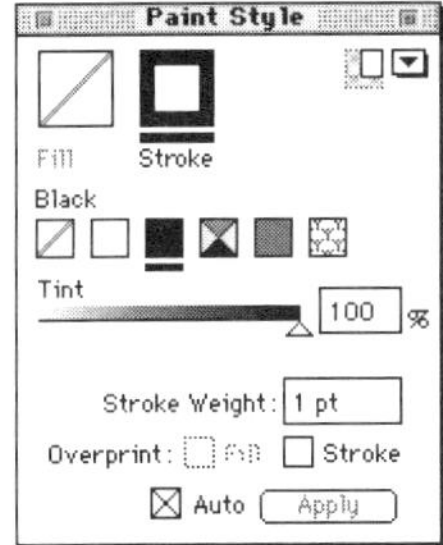

Step 4

Releasing Masks

To release a mask, first select the masking object (you may select other objects as well). Then choose Object➪Mask➪Release, and the masking object will no longer be a mask.

Masking vs. Cropping

Mearth: Should I mask, or should I crop?

Toulouse: You mean with the Pathfinder Crop filter?

Mearth: No, I'm considering a career change in the direction of shucking corn.

Toulouse: I take it you're being sarcastic.

Mearth: Harumph.

Toulouse: It really depends. Cropping has two serious advantages over masking.

Mearth: And those are...?

Toulouse: First, unnecessary paths are deleted, and second, potential printing problems that might occur when a mask is being used are eliminated.

Mearth: So I should crop.

Toulouse: Actually, there's more in favor of masking.

Mearth: Ah ha!

Toulouse: Yep. Masking allows you to edit the artwork in the future.

Mearth: That's a big one.

Toulouse: Real big. You can change the shape, size, whatever, of the mask and the masked objects.

Mearth: Good points.

Toulouse: And, you can mask raster images and non-outlined text.

Mearth: I'm sold.

If you aren't sure which object is the masking object or if you are having trouble selecting the masking object, choose Edit⇨Select All (⌘-A) and choose Object⇨Mask⇨ Release. Of course, this action releases any other masks that are in the document — unless they were separate masks that were being masked by other masks — got that?

To release all the masks in the document, even those masks that are being masked by other masks, Select All (⌘-A) and choose Release Mask repeatedly. Usually, three Release Masks gets everything, unless you went mask-happy in that particular document. You can also use the Select Masks filter to check if there are any remaining masks.

Masks and Printing

As a rule, PostScript printers don't care too much for masks. They care even less for masks that mask other masks. And they really don't like masks that are compound paths.

Unfortunately, because of the way that Illustrator works, every part of every object in a mask is sent to the printer, even if only a tiny piece of an object will be used. In addition, controlling where objects are sliced by the masking object requires a great deal of computing power and memory. You can have a problem, for example, when you have more stuff to mask than the printer can handle.

More importantly than any other issue involved with masks and printing is the length and complexity of the masking path.

The more objects in a mask, the more complex it is. The more Anchor Points, the more complex it is. The more direction points coming off those Anchor Points, the more complex the mask is. In other words, your printer would enjoy a mask if the masking object were a rectangle and no objects were being masked.

Masks are usually incredibly complex. This complexity causes many problems for printers (especially ones equipped with PostScript Level 1 and PostScript clones) and quite often results in PostScript printing errors. In addition, be careful not to go mask-crazy (using hundreds of masks), or your document may never see toner.

Masks and Compound Paths

Creating masks from compound paths is especially useful when you are working with text and want several separate letters to mask a placed EPS image or a series of pictures that you created in Illustrator.

The reason that you need to transform separate objects into compound paths is that a masking object can only be one path. The topmost object of the selected objects will become the masking object, and the others will be objects within the mask. Creating a compound path from several paths makes the masking feature treat all the objects as one path and makes a masking object out of the entire compound path.

You can use compound paths for masking when you are working with objects that need to have "holes" as well as when you are working with text and other separate objects. Figure 9-12 was created by making one compound path from all of the parts of the window frame and using that compound path as a mask for the space scene.

Figure 9-12: Creating a compound path out of all of the parts of the window frame made the window frame a mask for the space scene.

Using Compound Paths and Masks in an Illustration

I used several compound paths and masks to achieve the effects in Figure 9-13. The compound paths are the word *Tropical* and the large strips of film across the lower half of the illustration. The masks are the word *Tropical,* the binocular shape, and the outside frame of the poster.

Figure 9-13: This poster was created by using several different compound paths and masks.

The first set of steps explains how to create the strip of film and place the island pictures into the film. You do not use masks in this process. I make this point so that you don't think that you always have to use masks, especially when another method is easier.

STEPS: Creating Complex Compound Paths

Step 1. To create the film shape, draw a long, horizontal rectangle with the Rectangle tool and place five rounded-corner rectangles inside the long rectangle.

Step 2. To create the sprocket holes in the film, place a right-side-up triangle next to an upside-down triangle and continue placing triangles until you have a row of triangles across the top of the film.

Step 3. After you group all the triangles together, Option-copy them (drag the triangles with the Option key pressed, releasing the mouse button before releasing the Option key) to create a second row of triangles along the bottom of the film.

Step 4. Select all of the pieces of the film and choose Object⇨Compound Paths⇨Make (⌘-8). Fill the compound path with a dark purple color that is not quite black.

Step 5. This part looks as if you use a mask, but you don't need to do any masking here. Instead, place one EPS image, size it so that it just covers the hole, and Option-copy it across the remaining holes. Select each image in turn, choose File⇨Change Placed Art, and select a different image for each square. To complete the effect, simply bring the strip of film to the front.

Step 6. Before you place the film into the poster, group the images and the film and rotate them slightly. Grouping them prevents the hassle of selecting each one later if you need to move or transform them.

Figure 9-14 illustrates each of these steps.

Instead of making the film a compound path, you could mask each of the photos and place each masked photo on top of the film. The method described in the preceding steps makes changing photos easier and takes less of a toll on the output device.

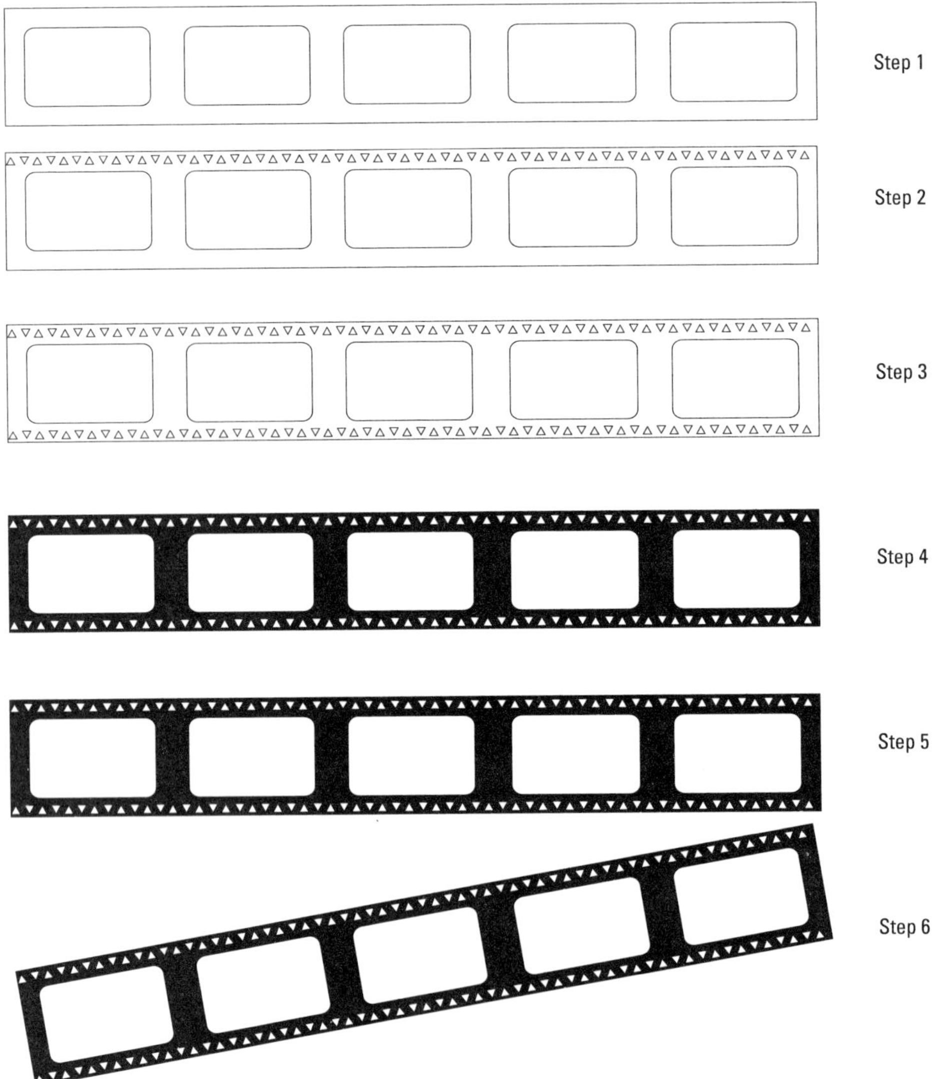

Figure 9-14: Steps for creating a complex compound path to achieve a masking effect

The next set of steps describes how to use the word *Tropical* to show the tropical island.

STEPS: Using Slightly Altered EPS Images with Masks

Step 1. Place an EPS image in the document and create a masking path for the top of it. Before you make the objects into a mask, select the EPS image and choose Edit⇨Copy (⌘-C). (You use this copy in Step 3.)

Step 2. Select both the masking path and the EPS image and choose Object⇨Mask⇨Make.

You can use the outline of the masking path as a shadow by Option-copying it before you perform Steps 1 and 2. Change the Fill in the copy to Black and place the copy below and to the right of the original.

Step 3. Choose Edit⇨Paste in Back (⌘-B) to position the EPS image directly underneath the original image. Choose File⇨Change Placed Art and substitute a slightly varied version of the original EPS image. The letters stand out decisively, as the third image in Figure 9-15 shows. The EPS image behind the word *Tropical* has been changed in Photoshop by using a Mosaic filter.

Figure 9-15: Using dissimilar raster images as masked objects makes the word *Tropical* stand out in the image.

Summary

- Compound paths are one or more paths that Illustrator treats as a single path.
- Compound paths give you the ability to put "holes" in your paths.
- Changing the direction of a path via Object Attributes can change the holes in the compound path.
- Each character of type converted to outlines consists of a compound path.
- Masks are paths that overlay other Illustrator objects, showing the objects only through the masking path.
- When using text outlines as a mask, make sure all the paths comprising the text outlines are a single compound path.

Blends and Gradients

CHAPTER 10

In This Chapter

- Comparing blends to gradients
- Creating blends of color
- Creating shape blends
- Understanding complex shape blends
- Using blends created in dimensions
- The magic of stroke blending
- Creating airbrush effects
- Understanding radial and linear gradients
- Creating gradients
- Using the Gradient Vector tool
- Using the Gradient palette
- Using gradients in software that doesn't like gradients

In Illustrator, a blend is a series of paths that Illustrator creates based on two other paths. The series of paths transforms from the first path into the second path, changing Paint Style attributes as it moves. Gradients are Fills that change from one color to another in either linear or radial form.

Understanding Blends and Gradients

Blends and gradients, at first glance, seem to do the same things but in different ways — so why have both? The Blend tool, moreover, seems to be much harder to use than the Gradient Vector tool. On the surface, it seems that more can be done with gradients than with blends. Blends are limited to two colors; gradients can have tons of colors. Blends take a long time to redraw; gradients take a fraction of the time.

After all, if gradients are so much easier to use and produce so much better results, is it really necessary to have a Blend tool? I've been asked this question quite often by students, clients, and the occasional passerby, and they seem to have a good point at first. Upon further study, however, it becomes apparent that blends are quite different from gradients, both in form and function.

Gradients are used only as Fills for paths. Gradients can be either linear or radial, meaning that color can change from side to side, top to bottom, or from the center to the outside. Every gradient can have up to 32 distinct colors in it.

Blends, on the other hand, are series of transformed paths between two *end paths.* The paths between the end paths mutate from one end path into the other. All the attributes of the end paths change throughout the transformed paths, including shape, size, and all Paint Style attributes. The major drawback is that you can only blend two colors at a time. Of course, you can blend between 34 different pairs of end paths, but that would be a little time-consuming, especially when you can use gradients to make the task much easier and quicker.

To summarize, gradients are an easier way to create blends that change only in color, not in shape or size. Figure 10-1 shows how you can use blends and gradients to create a similar result.

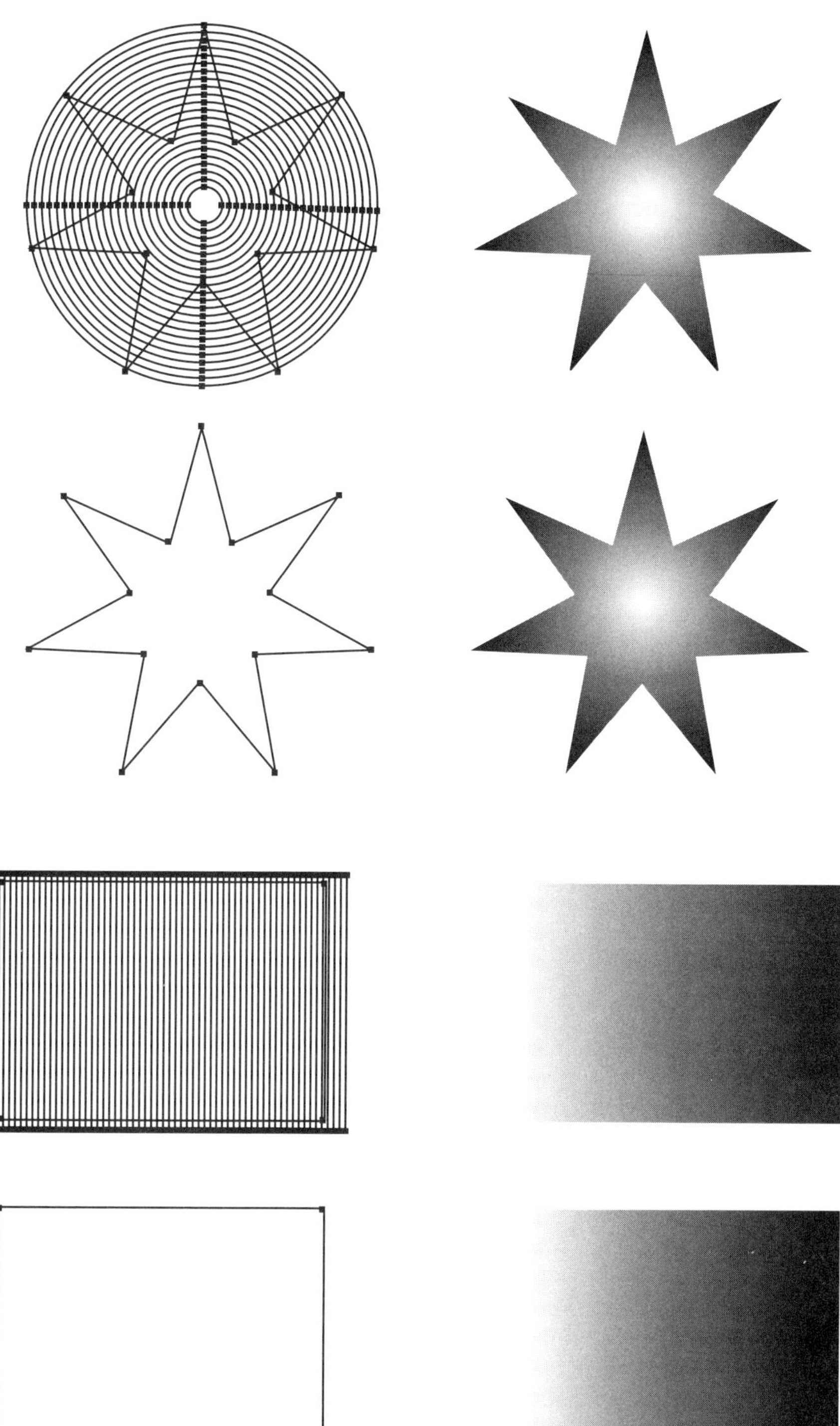

Figure 10-1: Each example uses a blend or a gradient. The left side shows the image in Artwork mode; the right side shows the Preview mode.

If you keep in mind that gradients work only with color, not with shapes, you should already have an idea of when to use which function. Linear and radial gradients usually look better than their blended counterparts because the quality is better and more colors can be added and manipulated. Changes to color are also more easily accomplished with gradients than with blends. In addition, changes to angles and the placements of the gradients are much easier to make than analogous position changes with blends.

One drawback to using gradients is their "computery" look. Gradients are exact blends that are even from start to finish. Of course, with a little practice, additional colors or tints can be added, and the midpoint balance between two adjacent colors can be offset, giving the blend a more natural look. In general, though, realistic effects aren't all that easy to achieve with gradients.

Blends, on the other hand, can be incredibly flexible when it comes to creating photorealistic changes in color, if you plan ahead. Changes to blends aren't really changes at all; instead, they are deletions of the transformed objects and changes in the attributes of the end paths. If you know what you want, blending colors can take on an incredibly "real" look by changing the shapes of the blend's end paths just slightly.

But even more useful than creating realistic changes in color is blending's capability to transform shapes from one shape to another, as shown in the examples in Figure 10-2. With a bit of practice (and the information in this chapter), you can transform any illustration into another illustration. There is a limit to the complexity of the illustrations that can be transformed, but the limit is due more to the time it takes to create the blends than to limitations inherent in Illustrator.

Figure 10-2: Blending to transform a shape

Because blends work on both Stroke and Fill attributes of objects, some really exciting effects can be created that aren't possible by using any other technique, electronic or traditional.

Blends

In past versions of Illustrator, blends were used predominantly for what gradients are used for now: to blend between different colors, normally just two different colors. But some artists took it upon themselves to stretch the capabilities of the Blend tool to create fantastic effects that amazed even the creators of the tool.

Originally, Adobe marketed the Blend tool (new to Version 88) as a tool with the primary purpose of transforming shapes, not blending colors. Yeah, that's cool, designers said, but instead they used the tool for blending colors to create what were known as vignettes, or what traditional artists called gradients.

The Blend tool creates in-between steps in the area between two paths, where the paint style and shape of one path transform themselves into the paint style and shape of the second path.

For the most part, the blending function really hasn't changed since Version 88 was released more than six years ago. Unfortunately, Adobe (or MacroMedia, which has a similar tool in FreeHand) never emphasized the incredible variations of effects that can be achieved with the Blend tool. In combination with some of the filters available in Illustrator, some pretty amazing effects are now possible.

The most noticeable change to the way the Blend tool works was in Version 3, when Illustrator began to calculate blend steps automatically and put the best number relative to color changes in the Steps field. This change was an indication that Adobe realized more people were using the blending function for color blends than shape blends. In Version 5 of Illustrator, instead of making the Blend tool better, Adobe opted to create the Gradient feature, which does what most people were using the Blend tool for in previous versions. Once again, the emphasis on the Blend tool is on shape transformation, rather than as a way to create gradients.

Although any blend takes into account both color and shape, in this chapter I treat color and shape separately because people using the Blend tool are often trying to obtain *either* a color effect *or* a shape effect, rather than both at once.

The Blend tool is the tool used to create blends, which are a group of paths (commonly referred to as *blend steps)* that change in shape and color as each path is created closer to the opposite *end path.*

STEPS: Creating a Basic Blend

Step 1. Using the Rectangle tool, create a small (1") vertical rectangle. With the Selection tool, Option-copy the path a few inches to the side. Press Shift as you drag horizontally to constrain the movement of the path.

Step 2. On the left rectangle, change the Fill to Black and the Stroke to None. Change the right rectangle to a Fill of White and a Stroke of None.

Step 3. Select both paths and choose the Blend tool. Click the top-left point of the left path and then the top-left point of the right path. This step tells Illustrator to blend between these two paths, and it uses the two Anchor Points as reference. The Blend dialog box appears after the second click.

Step 4. Click OK in the Blend dialog box. A mass of paths is created between the two end paths, all of them selected. Press ⌘-Shift-A to deselect all selected paths. The blend is made up of a total of 256 paths, including the two end paths. Each path is a slightly different tint of black.

You must use the Blend tool to click one point on each of two different paths, and those points must have been previously selected. Both paths must be open paths or closed paths. If the paths are open paths, only End Points can be clicked.

You should always click the corresponding points on both end paths. Figure 10-3 shows what can happen when opposite points are selected.

Before you click any paths, the cursor looks like a crosshair. After the first click of the Blend tool, the cursor looks like a crosshair with three dots after it. After the second point has been clicked, the Blend dialog box appears.

There is no key command that accesses the Blend tool from any other tool.

Creating Linear Blends

Color blends are made by creating two end paths, usually identical in shape and size, giving each path different Paint Style attributes, and creating a series of steps between them with the Blend tool. The more end paths that are created, the more colors that you can create. Figure 10-4 shows the steps needed to create a basic linear blend.

Figure 10-3: Selecting the correct points (middle) and the wrong points (bottom) to create a blend

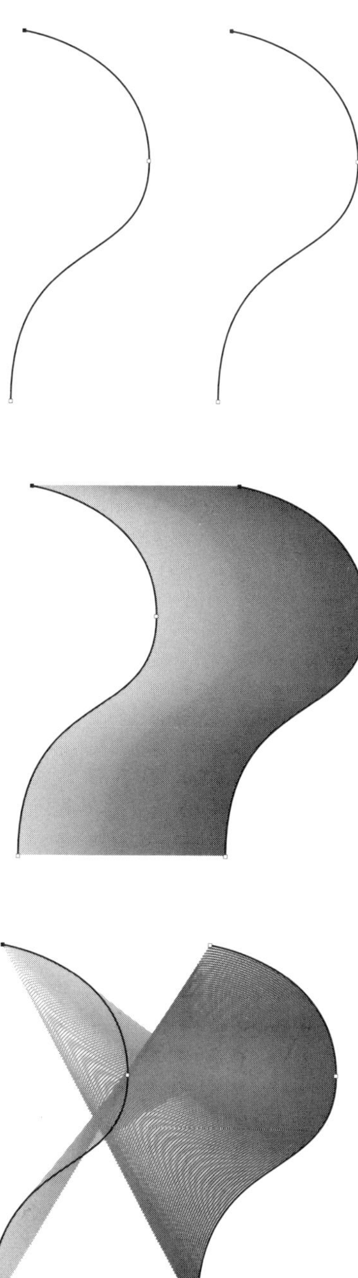

Figure 10-4: The steps needed to create a linear blend

The examples in this chapter are easier to understand when you are working in Preview mode.

STEPS: Creating a Basic Linear Blend

Step 1. Draw a vertical path with the Pen tool. Give it a Fill of None and a Stroke of 2 points Black in the Paint Style palette.

Step 2. Option-copy the path to the right. Give the new path a Stroke of 2 points White.

Step 3. Select both paths. With the Blend tool, click the top point on the left path and then the top point on the right path. When the Blend dialog box appears, click OK.

Step 4. Deselect all (⌘-Shift-A) to see the result.

Whenever you create a blend, stop and select the blend steps (which are already grouped together) and the two end paths, and group them all together. This step makes selecting the blend easier in the future, especially if you use the Group Selection tool.

Multiple Colors with Linear Blends

To create linear blends that have multiple colors, you must create intermediate end paths, one for each additional color within the blend.

STEPS: Creating Multiple Color Blends

Step 1. Create two end paths at the edges of where you want the entire blend to begin and end. Don't worry about colors at this time.

Step 2. Select the two end paths and click the top point in each of them. In the Step field in the Blend dialog box, enter the number of additional colors you will be adding to the blend and click OK. For instance, if you want a blend to go Blue, Yellow, Red, Black, Green, you would enter **3** in the Step field because there are three colors between the two end colors. For my example, I entered 3 to create three evenly spaced paths between the two end paths.

Step 3. Ungroup the newly created Strokes, color each of the Strokes of the paths differently, and give them a weight of 2 points. Select the first two paths and blend them together.

Step 4. Select the next pair and blend the next pair together. Continue blending until all the paths have been blended together. The result should look like the blend of colors at the bottom of Figure 10-5.

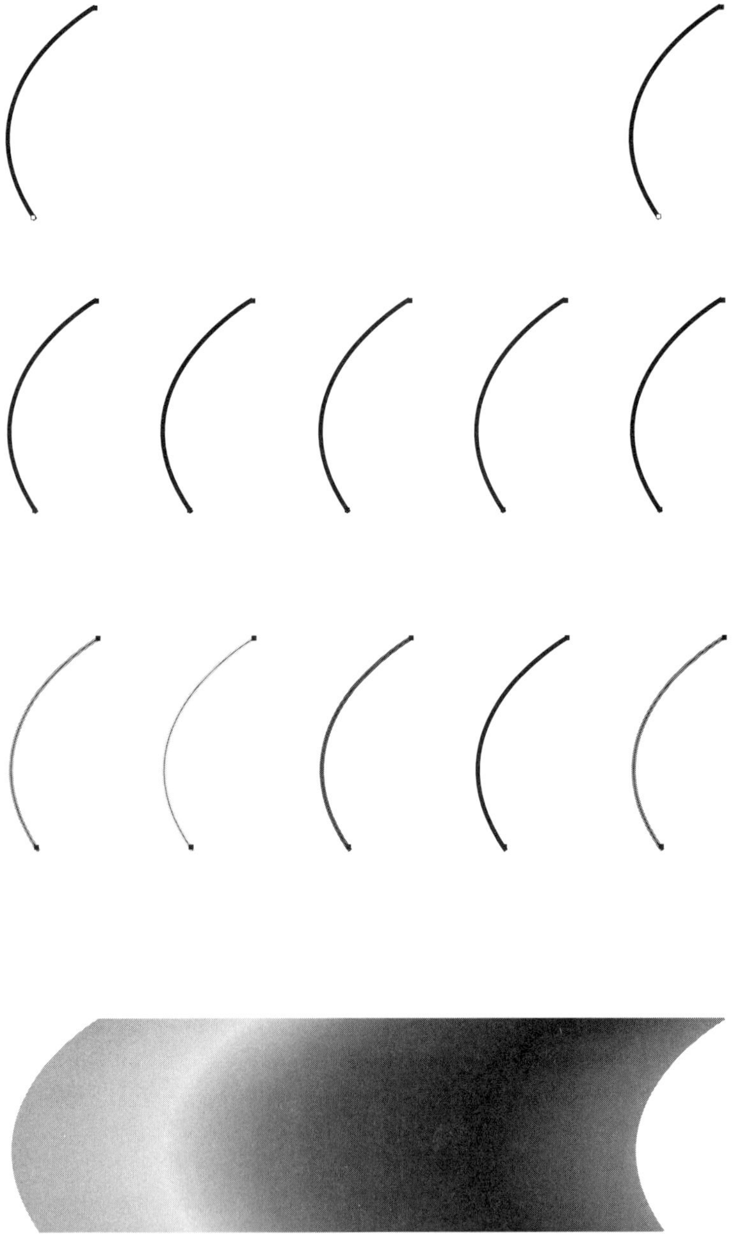

Figure 10-5: The steps to create a multiple-color linear blend

Group all the end paths to all the blends after creating them. This step makes selecting the multiple color blend easy with the Group Selection tool.

Nonlinear Blends

End paths created with two End Points that make up blends don't have to be just horizontal or vertical. And when you create multiple color blends, the intermediate End Paths don't have to be aligned in the same way as the end paths are aligned.

Careful setup of intermediate blends can create many interesting effects, such as circular and wavy appearances, all created with straight paths.

End paths that cross usually produce undesirable effects. If carefully constructed, however, the resulting blends can be quite intriguing. Blending crossed end paths creates the appearance of a three-dimensional blend, where one of the end paths blends "up" into the other.

To create nonlinear blends, set up the end paths and either rotate them or change their orientation by using the Direct Selection tool on one of the End Points. Then blend from one end path to the intermediate end paths and then to the other end path. Figure 10-6 shows two examples of nonlinear blends.

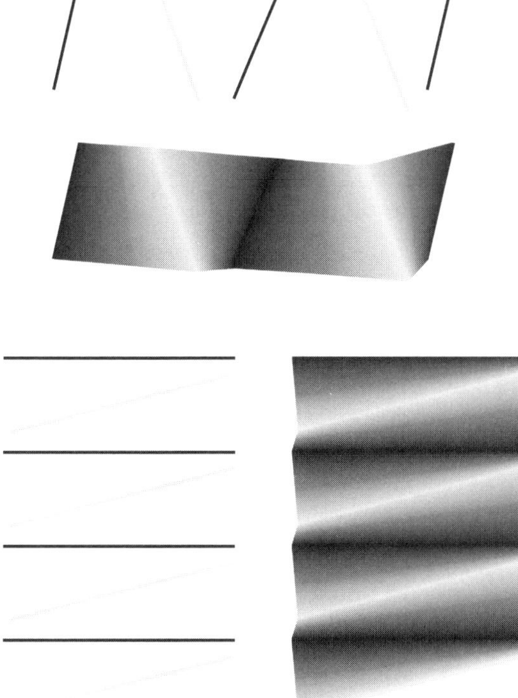

Figure 10-6: Blending end paths together to create a nonlinear blend

Masking Blends

Blends by themselves are great, but when masked by other paths, they can really take on a life of their own. To illustrate this concept, use the following steps to create a color wheel (refer to Figure 10-7).

STEPS: Creating a Color Wheel

Step 1. Using the Pen tool, draw a straight segment and give it a 2-point Green (100% Cyan, 100% Yellow) Stroke and a Fill of None in the Paint Style palette.

Step 2. Choose the Rotate tool, press Option, and click one End Point of the path to set the origin. Type in 60° for the angle in the Rotate dialog box and press the Copy button (Option-Return). This procedure creates a copy of the Stroke at a 60° angle, with one End Point directly on top of one of the existing ones.

Step 3. Choose Arrange⇨Repeat Transform (⌘-D). Another Stroke is created at a 60° angle from the second. Continue to Repeat Transform until there are six Strokes. Each of these Strokes is used as an end path.

Step 4. Color each Stroke as follows, moving clockwise: 1. Green (100% Cyan, 100% Yellow); 2. Yellow (100% Yellow); 3. Red (100% Magenta, 100% Yellow); 4. Magenta (100% Magenta); 5. Blue (100% Cyan, 100% Magenta); 6. Cyan (100% Cyan).

Step 5. Blend each pair of end paths together, a pair at a time. Click the outermost points to get the best results. When you are finished blending all the end paths together, the result is a beautifully colored hexagon. Because of the shape, the end paths really stand out as points on the hexagon.

Step 6. To complete the illusion of a perfect color wheel, the blend needs to be in the shape of a circle. Using the Oval tool, draw a circle so that the edges are just inside the flat sides of the hexagon, with its center corresponding to the center of the hexagon. This process is easiest to do by Option-clicking with the Oval tool at the center of the hexagon and pressing the Shift key as the oval is being drawn. Select the circle, the blend steps, and the end paths, and choose Object⇨Masks⇨Make.

Step 7. For a more realistic color-wheel effect (one that resembles Apple's color wheel), create a Black Stroke on the mask and a small circle at the center that has a Fill of White and a Stroke of Black.

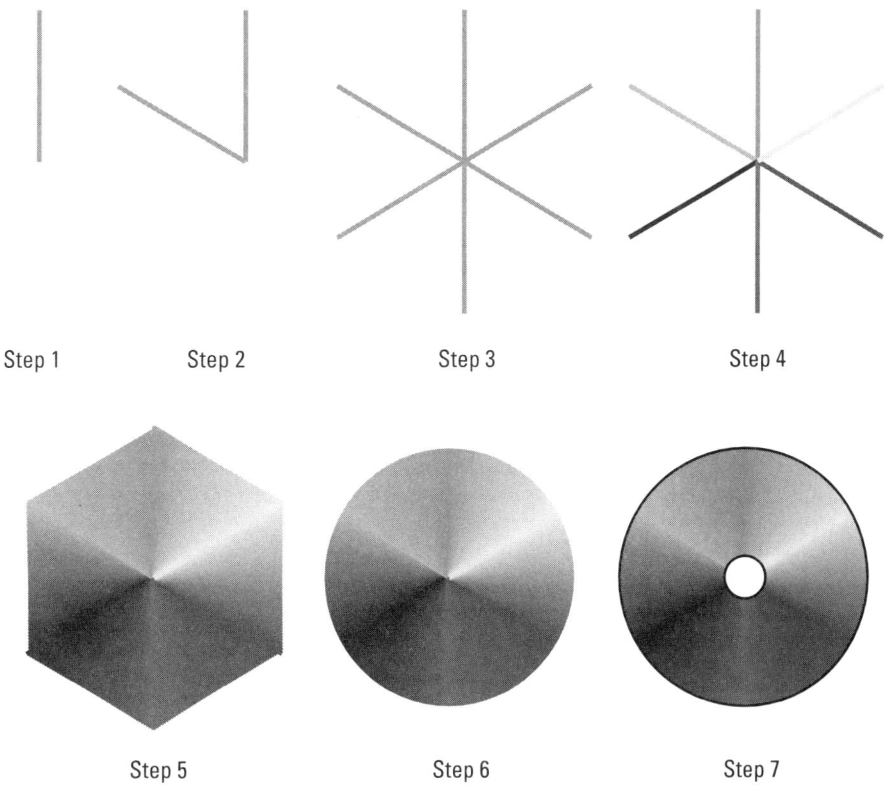

Figure 10-7: Creating a Black and White color wheel

Blends can be masked with any object. For some really great effects, mask your blends with text (converted to outlines).

New and Improved Pseudolinear Blends

There is very little difference in the end product of straight-line linear blends and linear gradients. Both are very "computery" looking, but gradients are easier to create. The important thing about blends is that the end paths of linear blends *don't have to be straight lines.* This blend capability makes all the difference in the world and is why using linear blends takes on a "really cool" aspect.

Twisted Blends

Daphne: My blends are really strange.

Toulouse: How so?

Daphne: Well, they keep bunching up and twisting.

Toulouse: What are you blending from and to?

Daphne: Two different paths.

Toulouse: But they have the same number of points, right?

Daphne: Uh...heh...

Toulouse: You need either (1) the same number of points on your end paths or (2) the same number of points selected on those end paths.

Daphne: Or they'll twist. Gotcha.

By using a smoothly curving line, the blend takes on a fluidity and life of its own, gently caressing the objects it is behind, next to, or masked by. The curves (especially if the end paths are masked off) are not always visible to the eye, and this creates an effect that is both realistic and surreal, giving depth to your illustration in a way that flat linear blends can't.

Instead of smoothly curving lines, try broken, jagged paths, which can add fierce highlights to a blend. Once again, this type of blend is even more effective when the end paths are masked off. Figure 10-8 shows two examples of masked pseudolinear blends.

Figure 10-8: Masked pseudolinear blends

When using end paths that have more than two Anchor Points, be sure to click the same End Point on each path. Clicking an Anchor Point that is not an End Point results in a dialog box telling you to . . . click an End Point. If you click different End Points, the result resembles an *X* shape, which is usually undesirable (as previously shown in Figure 10-3).

Guidelines for Creating Color Linear Blends

Although the preceding procedure should have gone nice and smoothly with no problems, you should follow these guidelines when creating blends to get good results each time you print:

- For linear blends, use rectangles with only four Anchor Points. If you use a shape with any more Anchor Points or if you use a curved shape with any paths that aren't perfectly straight, you'll get extra information that isn't needed to create the blend, and printing will take much longer than usual. You *can* use basic 2-point paths, but printing could take longer than if you use rectangles.
- When creating linear blends, use one rectangle per end path and color the Fills of the paths, not the Strokes. Coloring the Strokes may appear to work, but it usually results in a moiré pattern when printed. Make sure that the Stroke is set to None, regardless of what the Fill is.
- Don't change the number that appears in the Steps text field in the Blend dialog box. Making the number higher creates additional paths that can't be printed; making the number lower can result in banding when printed (see the "Avoiding Banding" sidebar).

End Paths for Linear Blends

In the previous linear blend example, I used lines with Stroke weights to create the blend. You can also use rectangles with Fills and no Strokes and achieve pretty much the same printed result. Figure 10-9 shows both lines and rectangles used for end paths.

There is no good reason to use a rectangle as an end path instead of a single line with two End Points (at least, none that I can dig up). In fact, lines are better than rectangles for three reasons: First, lines use half as much information as rectangles because there are two Anchor Points on a line while there are four on a rectangle. Second, the width of a line (Stroke weight) is much easier to change after the blend has been created (just select the lines and enter a new weight in the Paint Style palette) than the width of rectangles (you would have to use the Scale Each filter). Third, creating a linear blend with lines (Strokes) creates a thick mess of paths, but creating a linear blend with rectangles creates a thicker mess, so much so that it is difficult to select specific rectangles.

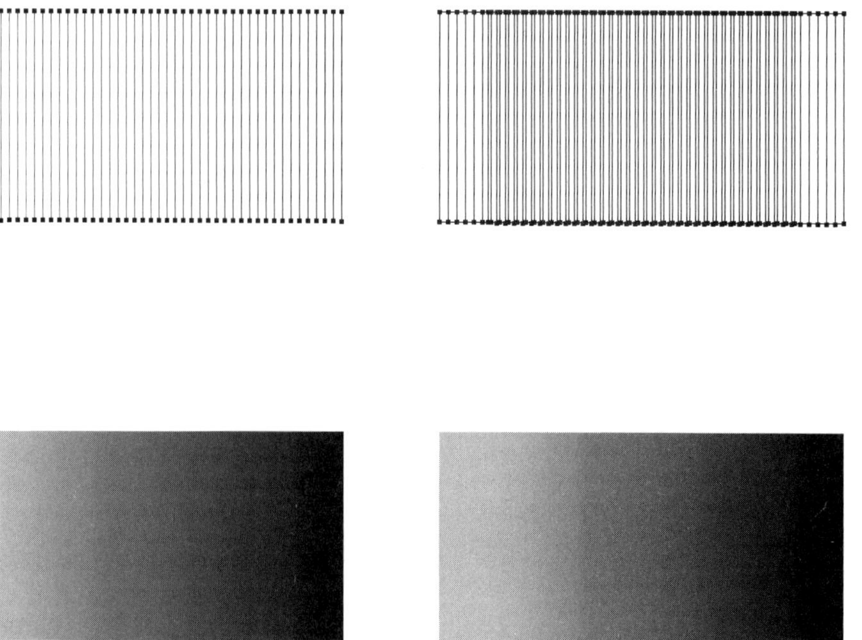

Figure 10-9: Lines (left) and rectangles (right) used for end paths in both artwork and final output

An open path cannot be blended with a closed path and vice versa. Open paths can be blended to other open paths, as long as you click an End Point on each with the Blend tool. Closed paths can be blended with another closed path.

Avoiding Banding

The graphic artist's worst nightmare: Smooth blends and gradations turn into large chunks of tints, as shown in the accompanying figure, and suddenly get darker or lighter instead of staying nice and smooth. *Banding,* as this nightmare is called, is an area of a blend where the difference from one tint to the next changes abruptly and displays a defining line showing the difference between the two tints. Individual tints appear as solid areas called *bands*.

Avoiding banding is easier when you know what is causing it. Usually one of three things in Illustrator is the cause: too few blend steps, too much of a distance between end paths, or too little variation in the colors of the end paths. Preventing banding due to any of these causes depends on the line screen setting and the capability of your printer to print it.

These causes make pretty much sense. Take the linear blend example in a previous section. If there are only three intermediate steps between end paths, there will be only five colors in the blend, thus creating five bands. If the end paths are each on one side of a 17-inch span, each blend step created would take up the 5 points of width of the Stroke, making each shade of gray 5-points wide, a noticeable size. If the color on the left were 10% Black instead of 100% Black, there would be only 26 color steps between the two end paths.

So to avoid banding, use the recommended number of steps over a short area with a great variation of color.

If you find it hard to fix the banding problem and the blend is made of process colors, try adding a small amount of an unused color (Black, for instance) to cover up the banding breaks. A 5- to 30-percent change over distances may provide just enough dots to hide those bands. Keeping this in mind, there is more chance for banding if you use the same tints for different process colors. Alter the tint values for one of the colors at one of the end paths just a little, and this alteration will stagger the bands enough to remove them from sight.

See "Calculating the Number of Steps" in this chapter for more information on banding.

Calculating the Number of Steps

Whenever you create a blend, Illustrator provides a default value in the Steps text field that assumes you are going to be printing your illustration to an Imagesetter or other high-resolution device capable of printing all 256 levels of gray that PostScript allows.

The formula Illustrator uses is quite simple. It takes the largest change that any one color goes through from end path to end path and multiplies that percentage by 256. The formula looks like this: (256 x largest color change %) = the number of steps to be created.

For instance, using our linear blend example, the difference in tint values is 100% (100% – 0% = 100%). Multiply 100% by 256, and you get 256. Because the total number of grays must be 256 or fewer, only 254 were created. When added to the two ends, there are 256 tints.

In the second example, where the first line was changed to a 10% Stroke, the difference in tint values is 10% (10% – 0% = 10%). 10% x 256 is 26, the number of steps Illustrator calculates.

In a process color example, if the first end path is 20% Cyan, 100% Magenta, and 40% Yellow, and the second end path is 60% Cyan, 50% Magenta, and 0% Yellow, the largest difference in any one color is Cyan (100% – 50% = 50%). 50% x 256 is 128, the number of steps created.

But, of course, not everything you create is output on an imagesetter. Your laser printer, for example, cannot print out 256 grays, unless the line screen is set extremely low. To determine how many grays your laser printer can produce, you need to know both the dpi and the line screen. In some software packages, you can specify the line screen, but unless the printer is a high-end model, it is usually difficult to specify or change the dpi. Use the following formula to find out how many grays your printer can produce:

```
(dpi/line screen) x (dpi/line screen) = number of grays
```

For a 300-dpi printer with a typical (for 300 dpi) line screen of 53, the formula looks like this:

```
(300/53) x (300/53) = 5.66 x 5.66 = 32
```

A 400-dpi printer at a line screen of 71 has the following formula:

```
(400/65) x (400/65) = 6.15 x 6.14 = 38
```

A 600-dpi printer at 75 lines per inch uses this formula:

```
(600/75) x (600/75) = 8 x 8 = 64
```

Sometimes you may want to reduce the number of blend steps in a blend from the default because either your printer can't display that many grays or the distance from one end path to another is extremely small (see "Airbrushing and the Magic of Stroke Blends" later in this chapter).

When reducing the number of blends, start by dividing the default by 2 and then continue dividing by 2 until you have a number of steps that you are comfortable with. If you aren't sure how many steps you need, do a quick test of just that blend with different numbers of steps specified and print it out. If you are going to an Imagesetter, don't divide by 2 more than twice, or banding (oh no!) can occur.

Creating Radial Blends

To create a radial blend, make a circle about 2 inches in diameter, Filled with 100% Black. Make a smaller circle inside the larger circle and Fill it with White. Select both shapes, click the point at the top of the larger circle, and then click on the point at the top of the smaller circle. Click OK in the Blend dialog box and deselect.

Radial blends can be created with objects other than circles. In Figure 10-10, the radial blend was created with a star.

As with most other blends, when blending from two identically shaped end paths, always click the Anchor Point in the same position on each object. Figure 10-10 shows the difference between clicking the Anchor Points in the same position and those that are not in the same position.

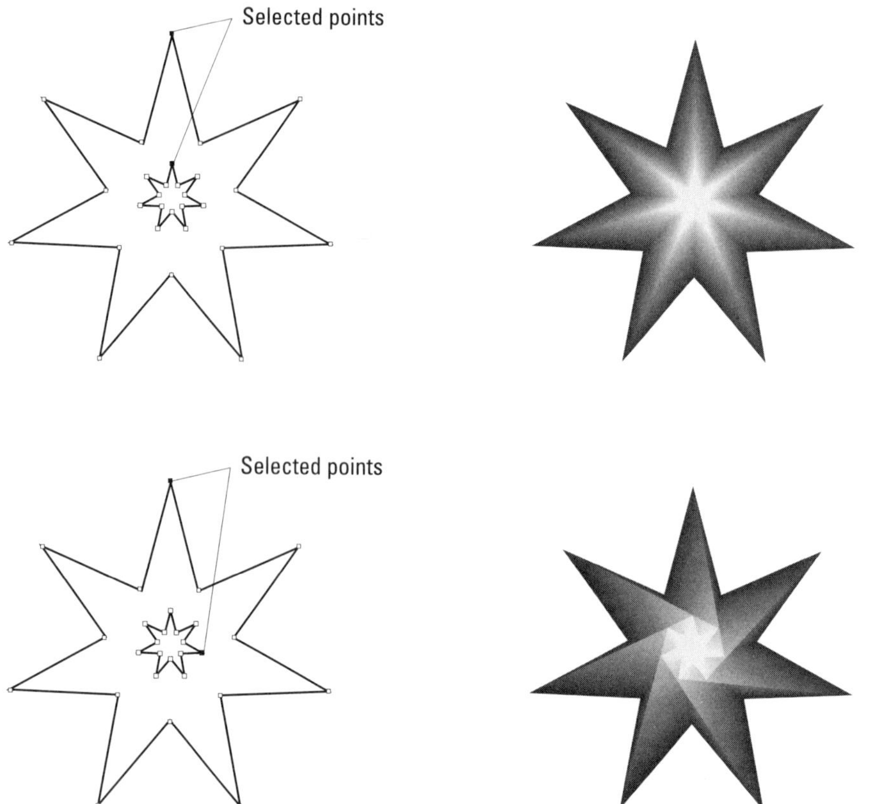

Figure 10-10: Each example uses a blend or a gradient. The left side shows the image in Artwork mode; the right side shows the Preview mode.

One of the nice things about creating radial blends manually (not using the gradient feature) is that by changing the location and the size of the inner object, the gradient can look vastly different. The larger the inner object, the smaller the blended area.

The Gradient feature allows you to change the highlight point on a radial Gradient without changing the source, or angle, of the highlight.

Creating Shape Blends

The difference between color blends and shape blends is in their emphasis. Color blends emphasize a color change; shape blends emphasize blending between different shapes.

There are a number of things to keep in mind when creating the end paths that form a shape blend. Both paths must be either open or closed. If open, only End Points can be clicked to blend between the two paths. If the shapes also change color, be sure to follow the guidelines in the preceding section related to color blends.

For best results, both paths should have the same number of Anchor Points selected before blending, and the selected points should be in a relatively similar location. Illustrator pairs up points on end paths and the segments between them so that when it creates the blend steps, the lines are in about the same position.

Shape Blend #1: Computer Vents

Look on the side of your monitor or on the side of a computer or hard drive case. You will undoubtedly see vents or simulated vents used for design purposes running back along these items. This type of blend (changing the angle of straight lines) is the most basic of shape blends and is rather easy to create, so I've added an extra tip at the end of this section to make these blends more realistic. Figure 10-11 shows the process for creating computer vents.

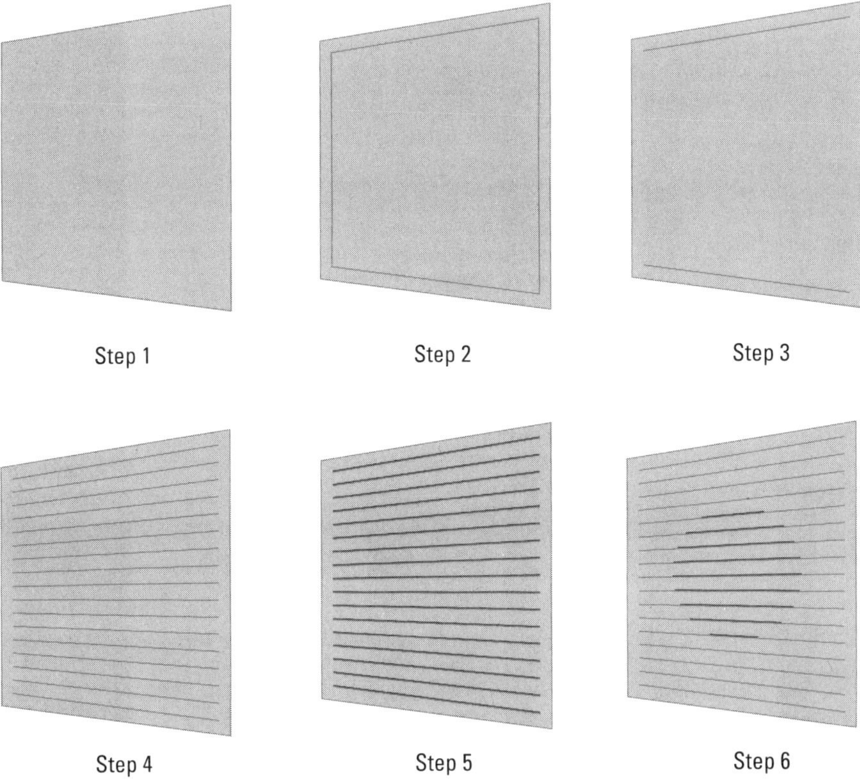

Figure 10-11: A computer vent blend

STEPS: Creating Computer Vents

Step 1. Draw a rectangular shape that has been distorted to appear like the side of your monitor (use the Pen tool). Choose a Fill of 25% Black and a Stroke of 1/2 point, 50% Black in the Paint Style palette.

Step 2. Select the shape and double-click the Scale tool. Enter 90% in the Uniform field of the Scale dialog box and click Copy (Option-Return).

Step 3. With the Direct Selection tool, select and delete the two vertical segments of the shape. Select both of the horizontal segments and change the Fill to None.

Step 4. Blend the two paths together with 15 steps. One side of a monitor is now complete.

Step 5. Select all the paths and copy them up 1/2 point by using the Copy button in the Move dialog box. Group the paths and change the Stroke to 75% gray.

Step 6. Draw a circle over the center of the group and select the group and the circle. Choose Object⇨Mask⇨Make, and you will have a "real" vent in the simulated one.

Shape Blend #2: Circle to Star

The preceding blend slowly transformed one path to another, but the paths were basically the same. The real power of the Blend tool is evident when it is used to generate intermediate paths between two totally different, distinct paths, as in the following example.

STEPS: Blending a Circle to a Star

Step 1. Create a 1-inch circle with the Oval tool. Create a 5-point star by choosing Filter⇨Create⇨Star and entering **5** in the Points text field. Enter **.19"** in the First Radius text field and **.5"** in the Second Radius text field.

Step 2. Fill both shapes with a color (I used light gray) and give each of them a 2-point Stroke of another color. Change the view to Fit In Window (⌘⌘-M) and place the two objects as far apart on-screen as possible.

Step 3. Choose the Direct Selection tool and select the entire circle. Press the Shift key and click four points on the star that closely match the four on the circle. If you accidentally click a point that you decide should not be selected, just click it again with the Direct Selection tool. As long as the Shift key is pressed, the tool deselects only that point while all the other points remain selected.

Step 4. After four points are selected on both the circle and the star, blend them together with the Blend tool. Click the corresponding points on each, such as the topmost point, and enter **7** in the Steps dialog box.

Step 5. To see what happens if a different number of points are selected on each path, select both paths with the Selection tool. Click the topmost point of the circle with the Blend tool and then click the topmost point of the star. In the Blend dialog box, enter **7** in the Steps text field and then click OK. The star appears to work its way out of a growth on the circle. Figure 10-12 shows the difference between blending without corresponding Anchor Points selected and with corresponding Anchor Points selected.

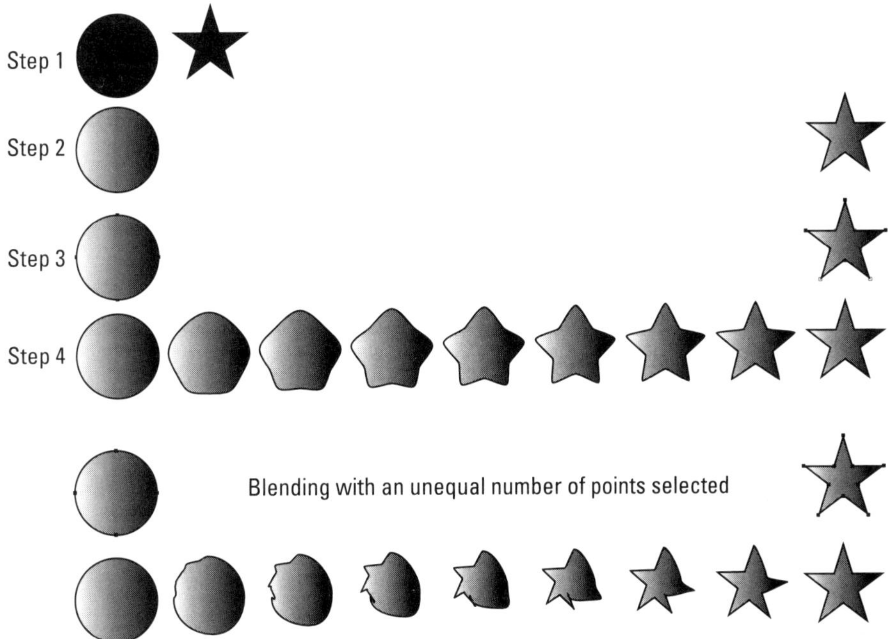

Figure 10-12: The difference between selecting the same number of Anchor Points on each path in a shape blend (top) and selecting a different number of Anchor Points on each path (bottom)

Another way to get a smooth transformation between two paths with different numbers of Anchor Points is to add Anchor Points strategically to the path with fewer points. By selecting both of the paths with the Selection tool, you can get results that are similar to selecting similarly positioned points. The results can actually be better when Anchor Points are added because they can be added in positions that correspond to the Anchor Points on the other path.

Complex-Shape Blending

Whenever a shape is complex (it isn't a perfectly symmetrical shape, such as a circle or a star), a number of things may have to be done to create realistic and eye-pleasing effects. Figure 10-13 shows a complex-shape blend.

Figure 10-13: Complex shape blending

One thing you can do to make the blend better is to add or remove anchor Points from the end paths. Even if the same number of points are selected and those points are in similar areas on each path, the results can be anything but acceptable.

The Add Anchor Point and Delete Anchor Point tools become quite useful here. By adding points in strategic locations, you can often fool Illustrator into creating an accurate blend; otherwise, the blend steps can *resemble* a total disaster.

As a general rule, it is less disturbing to the composition of the graphic to add Anchor Points than to remove them. On most paths, removing any Anchor Points changes the shape of the path dramatically.

Another method of getting the paths to blend more accurately is to shorten them by splitting a long, complex path into one or two smaller sections that aren't nearly as complex. After the blends are finished — each path has to be blended separately and can't all be done at once — it takes just a few seconds to go through and Average or Join (⌘-Option-L or ⌘-Option-J) the paths back together.

And then there is the third method to blend paths, which is described in the next section.

Shape Blend #3: Cheating

There are times when blending together two different shapes produces results that end up being just plain grotesque no matter what you do with the Anchor Points. In these cases, a little fixing (which I will call "cheating") is in order: The more blend steps you need, the more you benefit from this method.

To get more aesthetically pleasing results from shape blending, it is sometimes easier to create one or more intermediate (middle) end paths. Instead of blending from end to end, you blend from end to middle and then middle to end. Keep in mind that the middle should contain aspects of both end paths. Figure 10-14 shows how a blend would naturally appear (Steps 1 and 2) and how it appears after cheating (Steps 3 through 7).

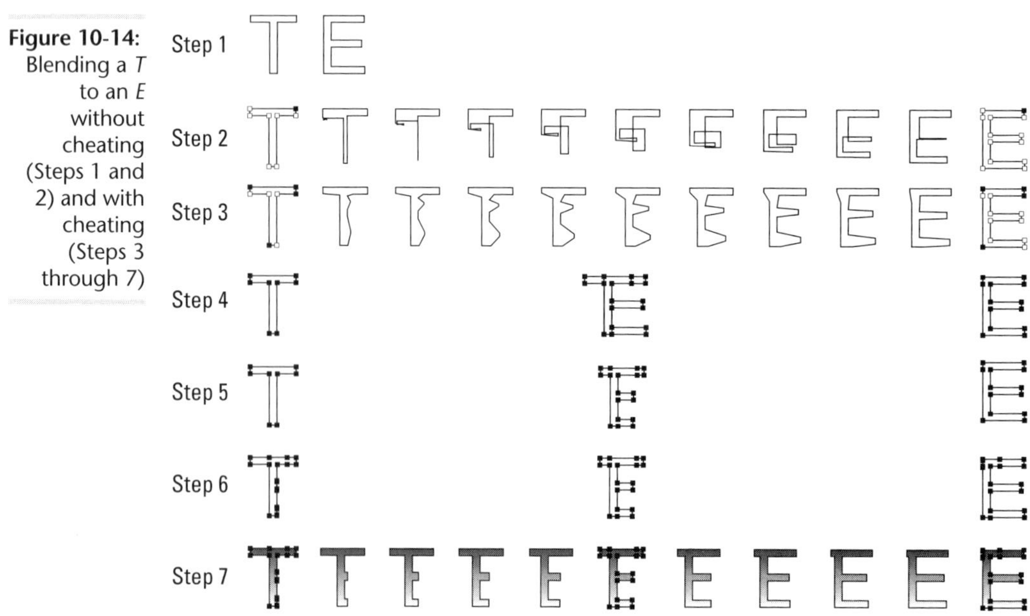

Figure 10-14: Blending a *T* to an *E* without cheating (Steps 1 and 2) and with cheating (Steps 3 through 7)

Remember, "cheating" is apparent only to you. The client or your boss will never know from seeing the final output that the results were "forced." Surprisingly, many illustrators actually feel guilty about creating another end path by using this method. If you can't live with yourself, by all means continue trying to select just the right points. However, I'll let you in on a secret: Adobe cheats too. In one of the original ads for

Illustrator 88 and in the accompanying videotape (watch it and check for the poor splicing!), you see an *S* transformed into a swan. Of course, in Adobe's case, it was misrepresenting the capabilities of the Blend tool by making it look like the tool automatically made eye-pleasing middle paths when, in reality, the "blended" paths were only loosely based on the real blends.

STEPS: Creating Complex Shape Blends by Cheating

Step 1. In this example, create a text area with a 100-point T and E in any font, (a sans serif font, such as Helvetica, is easier than a serif one, such as Times). Select the type with a Selection tool and choose Type⇨Create Outlines. You are blending between these two letters. Change the Fill to None and the Stroke to 1-point Black in the Paint Style palette.

Step 2. Choose View⇨Fit in Window (⌘-M) and put each letter on either side of the document. Select both of them with the regular Selection tool and then blend them together with 10 steps by choosing the upper-right point in each object. The results are quite ugly. A common shape-blending problem, called *blend arcing,* occurs when you choose very few or no Anchor Points on either the top or bottom of end paths. In this case, you selected an Anchor Point along the top and no Anchor Points along the bottom, so the blend arc formed along the bottom of the letters.

Step 3. Undo the blend. A better blending effect can be achieved by selecting the two upper-right points, the upper-left point, and the lower left point of the *T* and the *E* (previously shown in Figure 10-14), but then the blend takes on an ugly, lumpy look.

Step 4. Undo the blend again. The best thing to do in this case is to create an intermediate end path. Copy the *E* and *T* and place them over the top of each other between the two original letters.

Step 5. Select the overlapping letters and choose Filter⇨Pathfinder⇨Unite. The two paths merge into one. Bring in the horizontal bars about halfway by using the Direct Selection tool.

Step 6. Select both the *T* and the merged letters. Make sure that there are corresponding points for each path by adding Anchor Points to the *T* with the Add Anchor Point tool. Both paths should have the same number of Anchor Points. Add corresponding Anchor Points to the *E,* as well.

Step 7. Blend the *T* to the merged path with the Blend tool by clicking the lower-right point of each and creating four steps. Blend the *E* to the merged path by clicking the lower-right point of each and creating four steps. The transformation should be almost perfect. If necessary, individual points can be touched up with the Direct Selection tool.

Some really interesting effects can be achieved by using the Rotate tool or the Rotate Each filter, which makes the paths appear to spin as they are transforming from one shape into another. Using these tools also serves to mask any anomalies in the blend steps.

Creating Realism with Shape Blends

To create a realistic effect with shape blends, the paths used to create the blends need to resemble objects you see in life. Take a look around you and try to find any solid-colored object…Doesn't the color appear to change from one part of the object to another? Shadows and reflections are everywhere. Colors change gradually from light to dark, not in straight lines but in smooth, rounded curves.

Complex Realistic Blends

Freddy: My blends aren't...well, they look fake.

Toulouse: So, they don't look like real blends?

Freddy: No, they don't look *real*.

Toulouse: An important key to getting shape blends to look really good is to blend from the background color of the shape to the first blend, or to make that first blend the background color.

Freddy: What'll that do?

Toulouse: That'll flow the blend smoothly into the background, so you can't tell exactly where the blend starts and stops.

Blends can be used to simulate reflections and shadows. Reflections are usually created with shape blends; shadows are usually created with Stroke blends.

In the following example, I show you how to simulate reflections with shape blends. This procedure is a little tricky for any artist because a reflection is determined by the environment. The artwork you create will be viewed in any number of environments, so the reflections have to compensate for these differences. Fortunately, unless you are creating a mirror angled directly at the viewer (impossible, even if you know who the viewer is in advance), you can get the person seeing the artwork to perceive reflection without really being aware of it.

The chrome-like type in the word "DON'T" in Figure 10-15 was created by masking shape blends designed to look like a reflective surface.

STEPS: Creating Muted Reflective Surfaces in Type

Step 1. Type the word or words you want to use for masking the reflective surface. The typeface and the word itself have an impact on how the finished artwork is perceived. I chose the word *DON'T* and the typeface Madrone. I also did a great deal of tracking and kerning so that all the letters touched, which makes the word look like one piece of material. In addition, I used baseline shift to move the apostrophe up several points.

Step 2. Choose Type➪Convert Outlines. Choose a Fill of White for the text and a Stroke of Black. At this point, most of the serifs on the letters overlap.

Step 3. Select all the letters and choose Filter➪Pathfinder➪Unite. This command gets rid of any unsightly seams between the letters. Create a rectangle and place it behind the letters.

Figure 10-15: Steps for creating type with a reflective surface

Step 4. Set the Freehand tolerance option to 2 in the General Preferences dialog box (File⇨Preferences⇨General, ⌘-K). Using the Freehand tool, draw a horizontal line from left to right across the rectangle. With a low Freehand tolerance setting, this step should result in a path with many points.

Step 5. Option-copy several paths from the original down to the bottom of the rectangle. An easy way to copy the paths is to Option-drag down just a bit and then choose Arrange⇨Repeat Transform (⌘-D) several times. In my example, I created five more paths. With the Direct Selection tool, randomly move around individual Anchor Points and direction points on each path, but try to avoid overlapping paths. I left the third and fourth paths virtually identical and kept them close together so that there would be a swift change in color that brings out a "shine." Color the Stroke of each path differently, going from dark to light to dark. In my example, I went from dark to light to dark to light and back to dark again.

Step 6. Blend the Stroked paths together and mask them with the type outlines. In my example, I did this step twice. The first time, I created the front piece; the second time, I used lighter colored Strokes for a highlight, which I offset slightly up and to the left and placed behind the original type.

In the preceding steps, I Option-copied the path not only because it was easy, but also to ensure that the end paths in the blends would have the same points in the same locations. This technique is much more effective than adding or deleting points from one path or another.

With slight transformations, you can use the same reflection blend for other objects in the same illustration, and no one will being the wiser. A method that I often use is to reflect the original, scale it to 200%, and then use only a portion of the blend in the next mask.

In the next example, I use shape blends to create the glowing surface of a light bulb (see Figure 10-16). The key to achieving this effect successfully is to draw the light bulb first and then use a copy of exactly the same path for the highlights. The relative locations of Anchor Points stay the same, and the number of Anchor Points never changes.

Figure 10-16: Steps for creating real surfaces of a light bulb

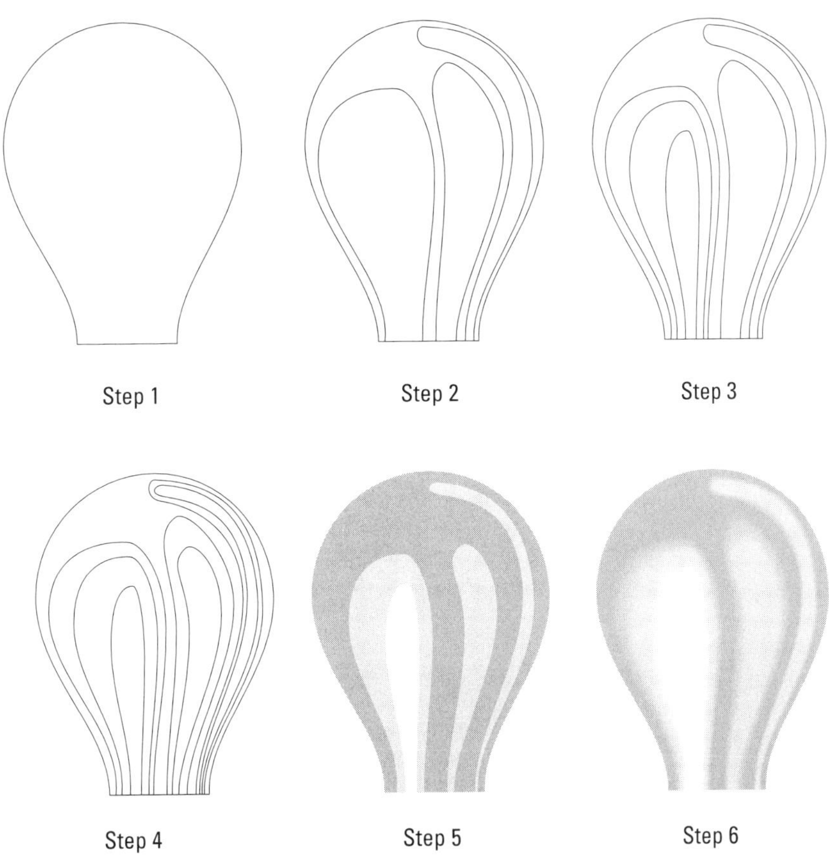

STEPS: Blending to Simulate Real Surfaces

Step 1. Draw a light bulb. Take your time and get it exactly the way you want it because this path is the basis for everything else in this example. Fill the light bulb with 30% Magenta, 80% Yellow, and a Stroke of None. The first four steps in Figure 10-16 show the light bulb in Artwork mode.

Step 2. Option-scale the light bulb down just a little bit, setting the origin on the base of the bulb. Option-scale two more copies of the light bulb. Use the Direct Selection tool to change the shape of the paths until they resemble the paths in Step 2 of Figure 10-16. These paths are the basis for blends within the light bulb. Don't change the color of these paths.

Step 3. Option-scale down three copies of the path on the left and shape them to resemble the paths in Figure 10-16. While your paths do not have to be exactly like the ones in the picture, be sure that each smaller path does not overlap the larger path. Color the paths as follows, from inside out: Color the first (inside) path as 5% Magenta, 10% Yellow; the next path as 10% Magenta, 30% Yellow and the last path as 15% Magenta, 40% Yellow. The outermost path should still be 30% Magenta, 80% Yellow.

Step 4. Option-scale one copy of each of the other two outermost paths and reshape them. Color the new paths 5% Magenta and 10% Yellow.

Step 5. The paths should be in the correct top-to-bottom order, but if they are not, fix them. To see if they are in the correct order, go to Preview mode. If the smaller paths are not visible, then send the outer paths to the back.

Step 6. Blend the paths together by selecting similar Anchor-Point locations on each step.

Airbrushing and the Magic of Stroke Blends

After wading through all the technical mumbo jumbo about blending information, you are ready to enjoy your newfound blending powers. Blending can create effects that are usually reserved for bitmap graphics software, such as Fractal Design Painter and Adobe Photoshop.

Most of the effects described in this section are created by blending identical overlapping paths together and varying their Stroke weights and colors. This technique can provide some of the best effects that Illustrator has to offer.

Usually, the bottommost Stroke has a heavier weight than the topmost Stroke, and as the color changes from bottom Stroke to top Stroke, the colors appear to blend in from the outside.

Tubular Blends

Creating tubular blends with the Blend tool is quite often easier than creating any other type of Stroke blend for one simple reason: the two paths, while identical, are not placed *directly* over each other, but instead are offset just slightly, giving the tube a three-dimensional appearance.

STEPS: Creating Tubular Blends

Step 1. Draw a path with the Freehand tool. Smooth curves work better than corners, so make the Freehand tolerance high (7 to 10) in the General Preferences dialog box before drawing the curves. Change the Fill to None and the Stroke to 50% Yellow, with a weight of 1/4 point in the Paint Style palette. The path may cross itself.

Step 2. Copy the path and Paste In Back (⌘-B). Offset the copy about 1/2 point up and to the right by selecting Arrange⇨Move (⌘-Shift-M) and entering the appropriate values in the text fields. Change the stroke on the copy to 50% Yellow and 100% Black and a weight of 4 points.

Step 3. Blend the two paths together. Create a Black rectangle and send it to the back. The result should look similar to the tube in Figure 10-17.

Figure 10-17: Creating a basic tubular blend

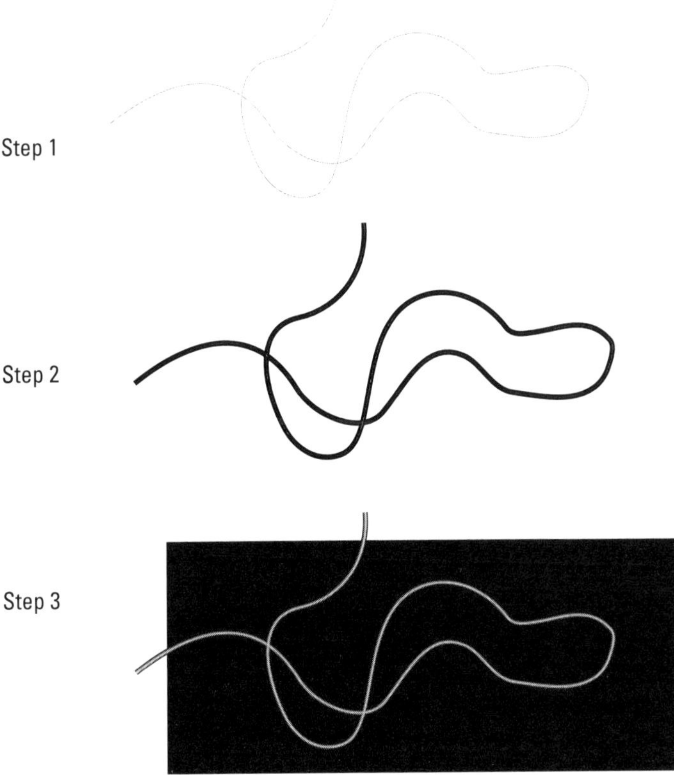

When you're creating Stroke blends, the number of steps usually doesn't need to exceed 100. If the default is more than 100, divide it by 2 (as explained in section, "Calculating the Number of Steps" earlier in this chapter) until the number is less than 100.

In order to see the End Points better on Stroke blend end paths, draw a tiny marquee around one of the ends with the Zoom tool. If you still can't see the End Points, switch to Artwork mode while creating the blend.

To create a Stroke blend that has more "shine" to it, make the Stroke lighter and thinner and do not offset it as far as in the preceding example.

To create a color Stroke blend that has more depth, make two end paths and color the bottom darker and wider and the top lighter and thinner. Then blend the paths together with one step between the end paths. Add a bit of Black (20% to 40%) to the bottom-most Stroke and then blend from the bottom to the middle and from the middle to the top. The extra Black usually creates a much more realistic appearance of depth than using just two colors, and it keeps Black from being in the upper-half of the tube.

Try not to use White as your topmost path when creating tubes because White not only looks bad, but can also cause problems when you print. The more subtle your color change, the more realistic your results. If necessary, you can always add highlights of much lighter colors after the Stroke has been blended.

There are many shapes besides free-flowing tubes that benefit from this type of Stroke effect, including stars, spirals, and line drawings. Objects that appear in everyday life that can be created with tube-like Stroke blends include wires, rods, paper clips, hangers, antennas, pins, and needles. The next section explains how to make one of the most confusing types of objects with blends — the spring tube.

Spring-Tube Blends

To create the curly section of a telephone cord (a spring tube), create a spiral with two winds (Filter⇨Create⇨Spiral) and get rid of the inner spiral. Select the outer spiral and go through the steps to create a tube. Make this particular tube look like a section of a telephone cord, as shown in Figure 10-18.

After the spring tube has been created, group the entire tube together and Option-copy it down until the one side of the spiral lines up with the other side of the spiral. Choose Arrange⇨Repeat Transform (⌘-D) until the telephone cord is the desired length. To curve the phone cord, draw a marquee around one of the ends with the Direct Selection tool and move it, if necessary. Then use the Rotate tool to change the direction of the curve. Option-copy the next section and rotate that section into place.

Figure 10-18: A telephone cord created with tubular blends

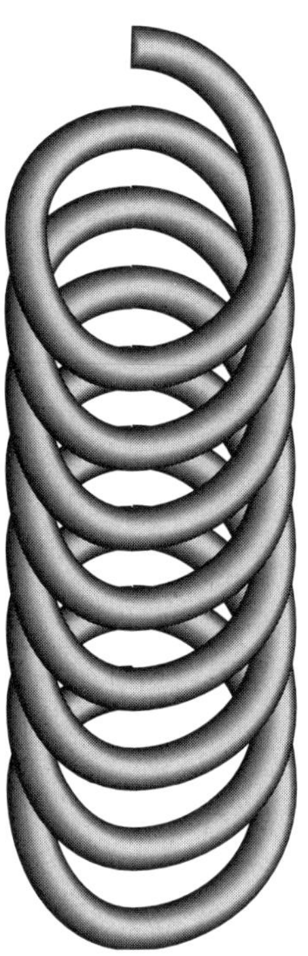

For quicker but less effective changes in direction, select a small section of the telephone cord and just rotate that section.

Airbrushed Shadows

To create a realistic shadow effect, the edges of an object must be a little fuzzy. The amount of fuzziness on the edges of the path is relative to the distance of the object from its shadow and the strength of the light source. These two areas also affect how dark the shadow is.

To make really cool shadows, you can use either the Pathfinder filter called Mix Soft, which can be used to darken areas, or the Color Adjust filter, which can be used to change the types of color in a selected area. The Drop Shadow filter creates hard-edged shadows, which are usually good only for creating text shadows quickly.

A second way to create cool shadows is to use Stroke blends. Stroke blends can allow the shadows to fade smoothly into the background with a Gaussian blur-like effect. You can combine Stroke blends with the Mix Soft filter for even better effects. For information on using the Mix Soft filter to create shadows, see Chapter 18.

STEPS: Creating Airbrushed Shadows

Step 1. Create a path (or copy it from an original object) for which you want to create a shadow. At this point, you may want to hide the object from which the shadow is being made so that it doesn't get in your way, especially if this object is right above where the shadow will be. Fill the shadowed path with the color you want the shadow to be and then make the Stroke the same color, with a 1/2-point Stroke weight.

Step 2. Copy the shadow, choose Edit⇨Paste In Back (⌘-B), and then change the Stroke color to whatever the background color is (usually White, unless something else is under the shadow). Make the Stroke weight twice the distance you want the shadow to fade out to. In my example, I made the Stroke 12 points.

Step 3. The hard part now is blending these two paths together (because they overlap each other). The easiest way to fix this problem is to offset the two paths by 1/2 point and then Zoom in to 1600% and blend them together. The shadow slowly fades in from the background color to the shadow color. Show the hidden objects (you may have to bring them to the front), and your shadow effect has been created (see Figure 10-19).

Figure 10-19: Steps for creating airbrushed shadows with linear blends

Be careful not to overlap shadows. Because all the steps of a blend are grouped together, the steps should all be above or behind neighboring blends.

Creating Glows

Glows are very similar to soft-edged shadows, but instead of a dark area fading into the background, a lighter area fades into the background. Using the light bulb from Figure 12-16, you now can create a glow for that light bulb by using Stroke blending.

STEPS: Creating Glows with Stroke Blends

Step 1. Select the edge of the object on which you want to create the glow. In my example, I use the light bulb previously shown in Figure 12-16. Copy the edge, Paste in Back (⌘-B), and press ⌘-Option-1. These steps lock everything that is not selected. Give the copied edge a stroke of 6% Magenta and 62% Yellow and a weight of 1 point.

Step 2. Draw a Black rectangle around the outside edge of the object and send it to the back. Copy the edge of the light bulb and Paste in Back (⌘-B) again. Change the Stroke to 6% Magenta, 60% Yellow, and 100% Black and make the Stroke about 40-points wide. Move this path about 1/2 point to the right and up.

Step 3. Blend the two edge paths together, which creates the glow of the light bulb (see Figure 10-20). The larger the weight of the second copied path from Step 2, the bigger the glow.

Clicking Trouble

Shaggy: I can't handle it any more. No pun intended.

Toulouse: What's your point? Pun intended.

Shaggy: Everytime I click to blend I miss and I have to start over again.

Toulouse: Have you tried zooming in?

Shaggy: Uh, no. But the points don't get any bigger on-screen then, do they?

Toulouse: No, but the paths they're on get further and further apart.

Shaggy: Big deal.

Toulouse: That makes them easier to click on.

Shaggy: Zoinks!

Toulouse: Exactly.

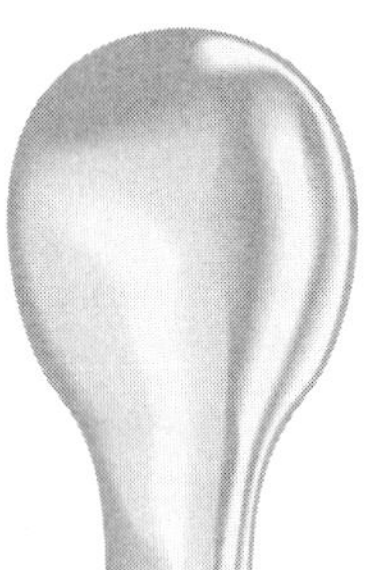
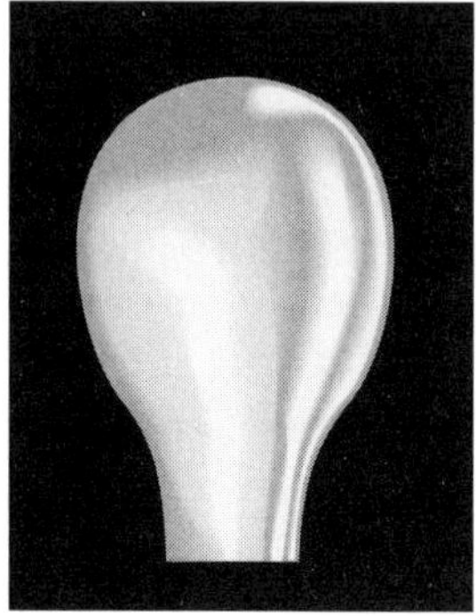
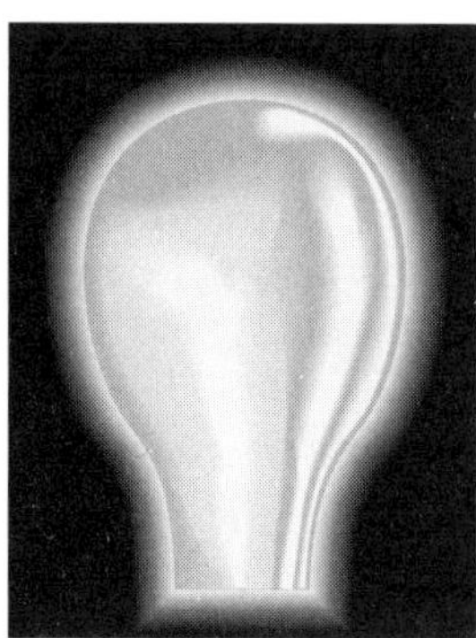

Figure 10-20: Creating a glow around the light bulb

When creating glows, make the initial glow area (around the edge of the object) *lighter* than the object edges if there are bright highlights in the object. Make the initial glow *darker* than the edges if the edges of the object are the brightest part of the object.

Softening Edges

Edges of objects can be softened in a manner very similar to that of creating shadows. The reason that edges are softened is to remove the hard, computer-like edges from objects in your illustration. Softening edges can be done to an extreme measure so that the object appears out of focus or just a tiny bit for an almost imperceptible change.

When determining how much of a distance should be softened, look at the whole illustration, not just that one piece. Usually, the softening area is no more than 1 or 2 points (unless the object is being blurred).

To soften edges on an object, select the object, copy, and hide the original object. Choose Edit⇨Paste in Back (⌘-B) and then make the Stroke on the object .1 point, the same color as the Fill. Copy again, Paste in Back, make the Stroke the color of the background, and make the weight 2 points (which makes the "softening" edge 1-point thick).

When softening objects, rather than moving the entire path in the background, try moving one Anchor Point out just far enough to be able to click it. Blend the two paths together and then show the original object (it may have to be brought to the front).

To blur an object, just make the bottom layer Stroke extremely wide (12 to 20 points or more, depending on the size of the illustration) and blend as described in the preceding paragraphs.

Neon Effects

To create neon effects with Stroke blends, you need to create two distinct parts. Part one is the neon tubing, which by itself is nice, but it doesn't really have a neon effect. The second part is the tubing's reflection off the background, which usually appears as a glowing area. These two separate blends give the illusion of lit neon.

Neon effects work much better when the background is very dark, though some interesting effects can be achieved with light backgrounds.

STEPS: Creating Neon Tubing

Step 1. To make the tubing, create a path that will be the neon. In Figure 10-21, I used two paths: a candle and a flame. Give the Stroke of the paths a weight of 4 and color them 100% Yellow. Make sure that the Fill is set to None. Change the cap of the Stroke to round and the join of the Stroke to curved.

Step 2. Create a rectangle that is larger than the area of the path. Send it to the back and set the Fill to Black.

Step 3. Select the neon path, copy it, and choose Arrange⇨Paste in Front (⌘-F). Offset the copy by .25 points and change the weight of the copy to .25 points. Hold down the Shift key and change the color of the Stroke by dragging the sliders to the left to make the color lighter. Do not make the copy White, but make it noticeably lighter than the neon color.

Step 4. Blend the two paths together and then group the two end paths with the blend. This is the neon tube part of the illustration. Hide this tube.

Step 5. To create the reflected area of the background, choose Arrange⇨Paste in Back (⌘-B). This step pastes a copy of the original path behind the bottom part of the existing neon tube. Give the path a Stroke of 4 and change the color to 100% Yellow and 75% Black.

Step 6. Copy the Stroke and Paste in Back (⌘-B) again, changing the color of the Stroke to the same as the background and then making the weight of the Stroke 24 points. Offset this copy by .25 points and blend the two together.

Step 7. Choose Arrange⇨Show All (⌘-4). Your result should now look similar to Figure 10-21.

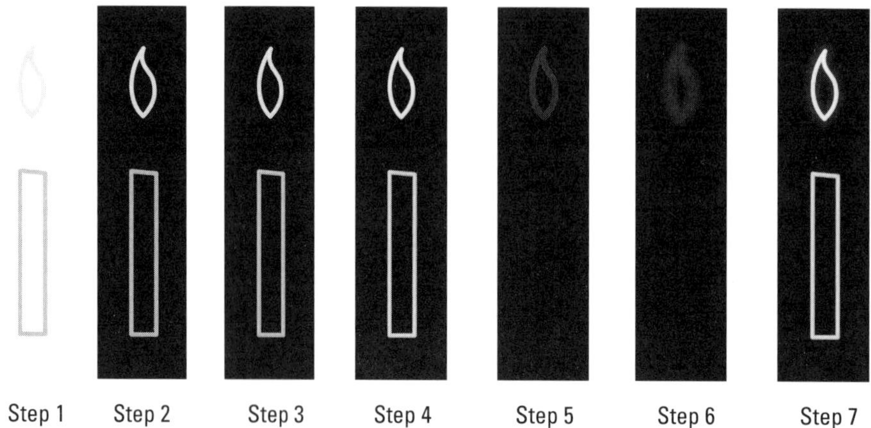

Figure 10-21: Neon candles

Try crossing paths with neon or, for an even more realistic look, create "unlit" portions of neon by using darker shading with no reflective glow.

Backlighting

Backlighting effects can be accomplished by simply creating a glow for an object and then placing that same object on top of the glow. By making the topmost object Filled with Black or another dark color, a backlit effect is produced, as shown in Figure 10-22.

Figure 10-22: Backlighting the word *dark*

Gradients

Adobe has finally succumbed to the pressure from Illustrator users who have been asking why, since Version 88 of Illustrator, their drawing software didn't have a way to make gradient Fills. "FreeHand users point at us and laugh," they said.

The Gradient feature now has no rivals. It is by far the most powerful gradient-creating mechanism available for PostScript drawing programs. Gradients in Adobe Illustrator can have 32 different colors, from end to end in a linear gradient, and from center to outside in a radial Gradient. Gradients can consist of custom colors, process colors, or just plain Black and White. The midpoint of two adjacent colors can be adjusted smoothly and easily toward either color. The Gradient palette can be made available at all times because it is a floating palette, although it cannot be accessed or viewed with a key command, like all other palettes in Illustrator. And, for what they do, gradients are easier to use than blends.

Gradients can only be applied to the Fills of paths, not to Strokes or text objects. Gradients cannot be used in patterns, either.

Checking the Compatible Gradients check-box in the Document Setup box will prevent most gradient problems from occurring. When you're printing to PostScript Level 1 printers, checking this box will speed up gradient printing dramatically. Compatible gradients bypass a high-level imaging system within Illustrator that older printers and printers without genuine Adobe PostScript (commonly referred to as "PostScript clones") cannot understand. Checking this box may cause documents to print slower on printers that would ordinarily be able to print those documents.

The Gradient Vector Tool

The Gradient Vector tool is used to change the angle and the starting and ending points for a linear gradient as well as the location of the center and edges of a radial gradient. The tool is also used to offset the "highlight" on a radial gradient.

Unlike blends, which can be created only with the Blend tool, gradients can survive quite nicely without the Gradient Vector tool. Gradients are created with the Gradient palette and applied from the Paint Style palette. Double-clicking the Gradient Vector tool displays the Gradient palette.

To use the Gradient Vector tool, at least one path that is Filled with a Gradient must be selected. By dragging with the Gradient Vector tool on linear gradients, the angle and

Multiple Gradients

Velma: There aren't enough color stops in my gradients.

Toulouse: What? Not enough color stops?

Velma: Do I stutter?

Toulouse: No, it's just that...there's 32!

Velma: And I want more.

Toulouse: Okay, you can do that...

Velma: How?

Toulouse: For a linear gradient, divide the path the gradient is applied to into two (or more) sections, and give each a different gradient. Make sure the ends match up.

Velma: And for a radial gradient?

Toulouse: A little trickier. You'll need to split the path up into concentric circles.

Velma: Via Divide. Got it.

Toulouse: Then make the gradient on the outside start with the color the inside gradient finishes with, and set the first two stops the same and apart. That's it!

Velma: Thanks! I knew old Mr. Warnock was behind it all the time...he didn't fool me...

the length of the gradient can be changed as well as the start and end points. By dragging with the Gradient Vector tool on radial gradients, the start position and end position of the gradient is determined. By clicking with the Gradient Vector tool, the highlight is reset to a new location.

Using Preset Gradients

There are eight preset gradients in Illustrator; six of them are linear, and two are radial. The linear ones are Black & 50% Gray; Black & White; Green & Blue; Purple, Red, & Yellow; Red & Yellow; and Steel Bar. The radial gradients are White & Purple Radial and Yellow & Blue Radial.

To choose a preset gradient, select a path and make sure the Fill box is underlined in the Paint palette. On the right side of the Paint palette, click the seventh box along the top, which is the Gradient Fill box. The eight default Gradient presets appear below the row of boxes. None of the options is selected until you click one of them.

Do you think it's strange that Illustrator doesn't have a preset radial fill that goes from White to Black? You're not alone. This is one of the great mysteries of modern times, right up there with "Why is the # symbol on a phone called the *pound* key?"

These preset gradients appear in Illustrator because they exist in the Illustrator start-up file, which is discussed in Chapter 14.

Using the Gradient Palette

The Gradient palette, if nothing else, is really *neat* looking, with all sorts of nifty little controls at your disposal for creating and modifying gradients, as shown in Figure 10-23.

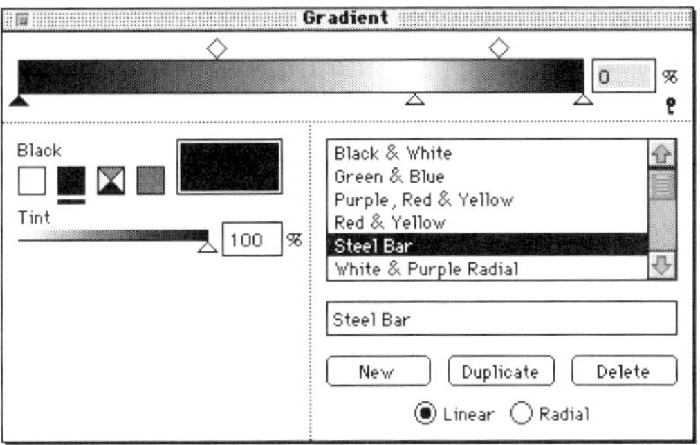

Figure 10-23: The Gradient palette

On the right side of the palette is a list of all the gradients that have been created, including the presets. Under the list is a group of buttons for creating new gradients, duplicating existing gradients, and deleting gradients.

On the left side of the Gradient palette is the area where you may choose colors and tints for individual Gradient steps. The boxes across the top are White, Black, Process, and Custom and correspond to the same boxes in the Paint Style palette.

The top of the Gradient palette is where you control what colors are in the gradient and where the colors are in relation to each other.

To add a new color to the bar, click below the bar where you want the new color to appear. Then change the lower-left side of the palette to create the color you want for that *color stop* in the same way that colors are created in the Paint Style palette. You can enter up to 32 color stops between the two end colors. When a color stop is selected, entering a different percentage in the text field on the right changes the color stop's position.

The diamonds at the top of the color bar show where the midpoint between two color stops is. By moving the midpoint left or right, you alter the halfway color between two color stops. When a diamond is selected, entering a different percentage in the text field on the right changes the diamond's position.

The lever under the percentage text field changes the size of the palette from full size to just big enough to see the top section. Unfortunately, in this small position, you can't do much except alter existing gradients' color stops, moving them back and forth.

STEPS: Using Custom Gradients to Create a Cityscape

Step 1. Draw a series of vertical rectangles, some overlapping, with their bases horizontally even. In my example (Figure 10-24), I angled the top of one of the rectangles.

Step 2. Fill the rectangles with the Black & White Gradient and be sure that the Gradient angle in the Paint Style palette is 0°.

Step 3. In the Gradient palette, duplicate the Black & White Gradient and name the copy "Buildings." Enter a new color stop at 31% across and make the color 70% Black. Change the color of the leftmost color stop to 85% Black. Apply the Gradient "Buildings" to the rectangles.

Step 4. Draw a rectangle and send it behind the buildings. Change the fill to the Black & White Gradient and change the Gradient angle to 90°.

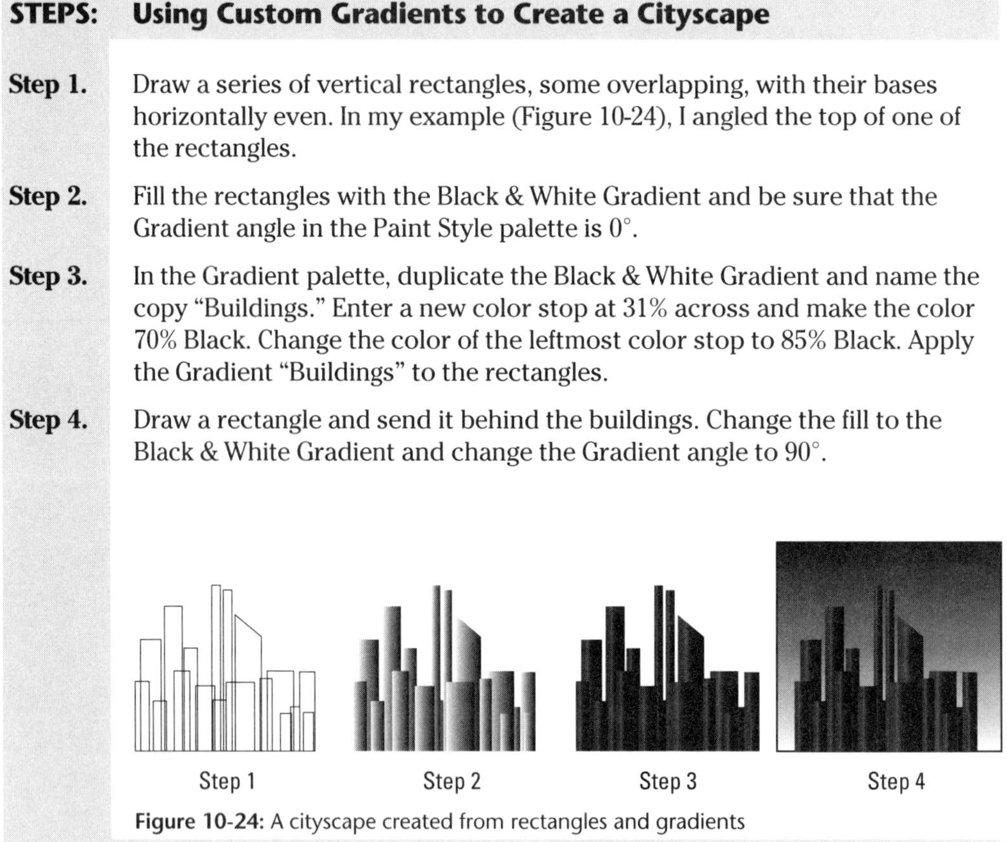

Figure 10-24: A cityscape created from rectangles and gradients

For added dramatic impact in a cityscape, copy the buildings one by one and Paste in Front (⌘-F). Fill the front copies with a Custom pattern of lights with a transparent background.

Shadows, Highlights, Ghosting, and Embossing

Gradients can be used to simulate special effects by either duplicating and altering a gradient or by using the Gradient Vector tool on similar gradients.

Ghosting can be simulated by using the Gradient Vector tool to slightly alter the starting and ending locations of the gradient.

STEPS: Creating Ghosting Effects with Gradients

Step 1. Ghosting effects are easiest to see on text, so create a rectangle and then create large text on top of the rectangle.

Step 2. Convert the type into outlines and position the type outline just to the right and below the center of the rectangle.

Step 3. Select both the type and rectangle and apply a Gradient Fill to them. For Figure 10-25, I used the Red & Yellow Gradient at 90°.

Step 4. Move the type to the center of the rectangle. The type appears to be "ghosted" there, as in Figure 10-25.

Step 1

FIRE

Step 2

FIRE

Step 3

Step 4

Figure 10-25: Ghosting with gradients

Embossed gradient images are created by offsetting two copies of the original graduated image. In one offset image, the gradient is lightened; in the other, the gradient is darkened.

STEPS: Embossing Text

Step 1. Create text and convert it to outlines.

Step 2. Select the outlined type and choose Filter⇨Pathfinder⇨Unite. Draw a rectangle around the type and send it to the back.

Step 3. Select both the type outline and the rectangle and Fill them with a Gradient. Use a process gradient for this example. Drag the Gradient Vector tool across the rectangle (keeping both objects selected) to set the gradient length and angle.

Step 4. In the Gradient palette, select the gradient used for both the rectangle and type outlines, and make two duplicates of it. Make one duplicate lighter by selecting each color stop and moving it to the left. Create one gradient darker than the original by moving each color stop to the right.

Step 5. Using the Move dialog box, create a copy of the path offset a few points up and to the left. Create another copy offset a few points down and to the right.

Step 6. Fill the upper-left path with the lighter duplicate and the lower-right path with the darker duplicate.

Step 7. Select the middle type path and choose Arrange⇨Bring to Front (⌘-Plus). The type appears embossed, as shown in Figure 10-26.

To make embossed images seem sunken rather than raised, make the lighter image below and to the right and the darker image above and to the left. To make the image seem further raised or recessed, increase the distance between the original path and the offset images.

Figure 10-26: Steps for making embossed type

Step 1

Step 2

Step 3

Step 4

Step 5

Step 6

Shadows can be simulated by creating darker gradients based on an existing Gradient. The new, darker Gradient is created in a path that is the same shape as the object causing the shadow.

STEPS: Creating Shadows with Gradients

Step 1. For this example, use the cityscape created in Figure 12-24. Create a rectangle at the bottom of the city and give it a blend from light to dark. Send the rectangle behind the city. In the Gradient palette, duplicate the Gradient and add some Black to the color stops in the duplicate.

Step 2. Select the city and choose the Reflect tool. Reflect a copy of the city across the base of the city.

Step 3. Unite the city buildings with the Unite filter (Filter⇨Pathfinder⇨Unite). Fill the united city with the darker Gradient.

Step 4. Select both the background and the city, and draw the Gradient Vector tool across both paths. The shadow is automatically created.

Step 5. Using the Scale and Rotate tools, adjust the shadow to more accurately resemble the light source. The result should resemble Figure 10-27.

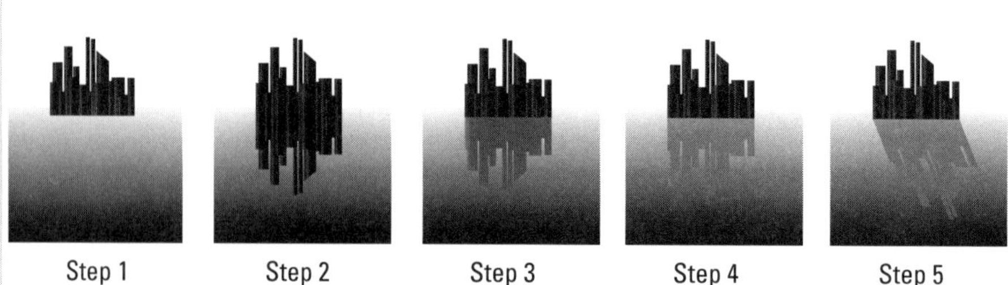

Figure 10-27: Creating a shadow on a gradient

Taking Gradients Where Gradients Fear to Go

There are many pieces of software that accept Illustrator files but don't care for gradients very much. Photoshop, for instance, will replace gradients with Black areas. Dimensions 1.0 just ignores them. And even Illustrator says "uh-uh" when you try to use a gradient in a pattern.

The solution to this problem is to save your Illustrator file with the gradient that has Illustrator 3 compatibility and then reopen it in Illustrator 5.0. All gradients in Illustrator 5.0 are changed into blends automatically.

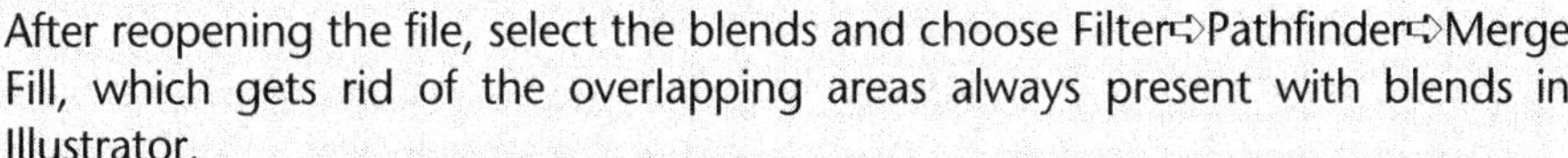

After reopening the file, select the blends and choose Filter⇨Pathfinder⇨Merge Fill, which gets rid of the overlapping areas always present with blends in Illustrator.

In addition, gradients cannot be used in Strokes of paths. To get around this limitation, select the path, make the Stroke the correct weight, and choose Filter⇨Object⇨Outline Stroked Path. The Stroke is transformed into a closed path, which can then be Filled with a Gradient.

Before using the Outline Stroked Path filter, be sure that the weight of the Stroke on the path to be outlined is the correct weight; otherwise, there is no way short of undoing the whole thing to convert outlined Strokes back into a single path.

Gradients to Paths

In Illustrator 6.0, you can automatically change gradients into blends by selecting the Gradient you wish to change, and then choosing Gradients to Paths. A dialog box appears like the one shown in Figure 10-28.

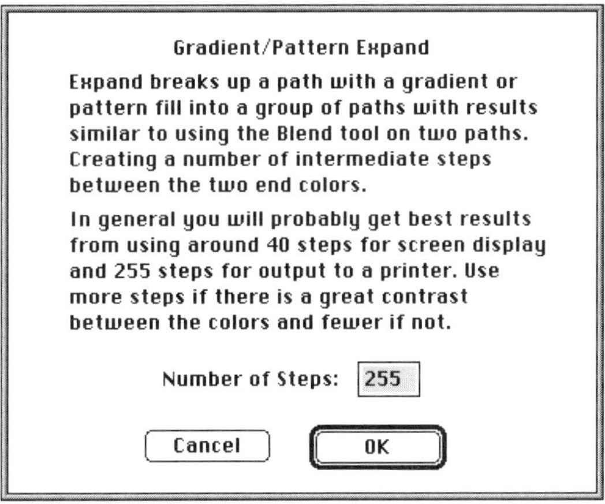

Figure 10-28: The Gradients to Paths dialog box

In the dialog box, you can specify how many blend steps there should be in the blend.

Summary

- Blends and gradients may resemble each other on the surface, but they are both quite different in their capabilities and functionality.
- Blends can be created between any two open or 2 closed paths.
- Blends can be masked so that a blend can be used as a Fill.
- Shape blends can be created to transform from one shape to another.
- Blends can be used to create smooth airbrushing effects.
- Gradients can be much easier to use than blends.
- You can quickly turn gradients into blends by selecting the gradient and applying the Gradients to Paths option.

Patterns, Graphs, and Textures

11 CHAPTER

In This Chapter

- Using the default patterns
- Creating your own patterns
- Making patterns seamless
- Understanding how transparency works with patterns
- Modifying existing patterns
- Putting patterns and gradients into patterns
- Transforming patterns
- Creating graphs
- Entering information into graphs
- Working with different types of graphs
- Modifying existing graphs
- Using marker and column designs

Patterns

"The Perfect Pattern is one in which you cannot determine the borders of its tiles," so saith the Chinese *Book of Patterns*. If that is the case, you can use Adobe Illustrator to create perfect patterns.

The Pattern function in Illustrator is twofold. First, you can Fill or Stroke any path with a pattern, although Strokes are not visible on-screen. Second, you can edit existing patterns or create new ones from Illustrator objects. The real strength of Illustrator's pattern features is that you can create patterns as well as apply them on-screen in almost any way imaginable.

A pattern in Illustrator is a series of objects within a rectangle that is commonly referred to as a *pattern tile*. When you choose the Pattern option in the Paint Style palette, the selected pattern is repeated on each of the four sides of the rectangle as well as in the four corners, as shown in Figure 11-1.

Figure 11-1: The area inside the solid rectangular outline in the center of the figure is the original pattern tile. The dotted line rectangles represent additional pattern tiles that are aligned with the original to create the pattern and fill up the object.

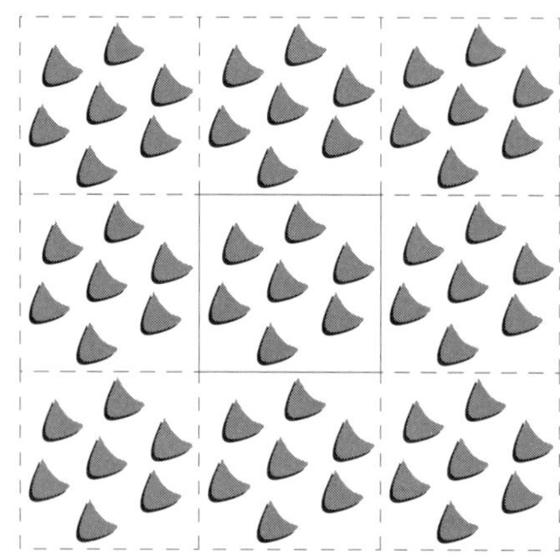

Illustrator places the pattern tiles together for you. After you apply a pattern to an object, you can use any of the transformation tools to transform it, and you can move within the object by using the Move command. You can move and transform patterns with or without the objects they are within.

Tile patterns can have a background color, or they can be transparent. Transparent patterns can overlay other objects, including objects Filled with patterns.

Using the Default Patterns

Eleven default, ready-made patterns are available all the time in Illustrator. You choose Object⇨Pattern to see a list of the default patterns. If a pattern in the scrolling list is selected, the box to the right of the list is Filled with that pattern.

To Fill or Stroke an object with a pattern, select the object and click on the sixth box (Pattern) in the Paint Style palette. A list of the available patterns appears, though none is selected yet. To select a pattern, click it, and it will Fill or Stroke the object that is selected in the document. Figure 11-2 shows the Paint Style palette when the Pattern option is checked, as well as samples of each of the patterns.

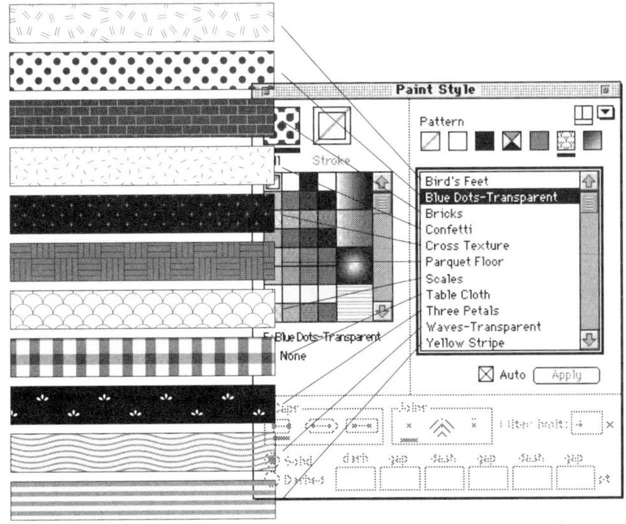

Figure 11-2: The Paint Style palette with the Pattern square selected, and samples of each of the default patterns

To some people, eleven patterns may seem like quite a few. To others, eleven patterns may seem like hardly any. The amazing thing about the few supplied patterns is that you can use them to create a great number of different effects, and you can use the pattern tiles to create new patterns that have even more exciting effects. Figure 11-3 shows patterns that were created by using just five of the default patterns.

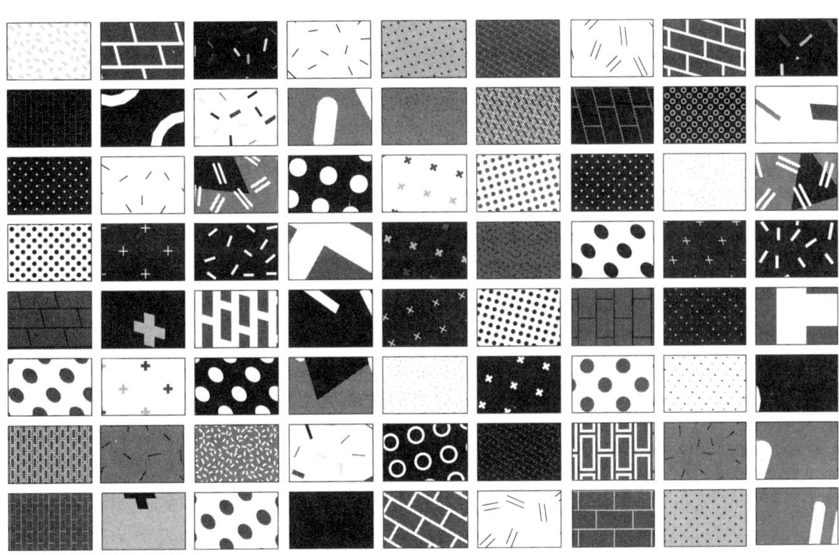

Figure 11-3: These patterns are based on the Bird's Feet, Blue Dots, Bricks, Confetti, and Cross Texture patterns. I created all of these variations from the five basic patterns in about 10 minutes.

In Preview mode, patterns that are applied to Fills appear, but patterns that are applied to Strokes do not. Instead of the latter patterns, you see a Gray Stroke. When you print the illustration, however, patterns will appear in strokes. If you want to see a pattern in a Stroke on-screen, apply the Outline Path filter (Filter➪Object➪Outline Path) to convert a Stroke into outlines and Fill the outlines with the pattern.

Patterns used as Strokes can send your printer to a crashing halt. A Pattern-Filled object has the object's path to figure out where to put the pattern when it is printed. The Stroke command in PostScript is a one shot command that follows the path with thickness and a line join attribute. With a pattern in a Stroke, the PostScript interpreter must figure out where the Stroke should be and then Fill it with a pattern.

After you select a pattern, you can see the pattern in the Fill of selected objects if you are in Preview mode. Text with patterns appears only as gray text. To see patterns in text, you need to convert the text to outlines by choosing Type➪Convert to Outlines.

If you see just a gray area in place of the pattern, you may not have the Preview and Print Patterns option selected in the Document Setup dialog box. This option is usually on by default.

In addition to the default patterns, you can choose from an incredibly wide variety of patterns that are in the Collector's Edition folder on the Illustrator CD-ROM. This folder contains borders and clip art as well as patterns. Open the pattern file to see large blocks that contain the patterns as well as the art that was used to create the patterns.

The default patterns are stored in the Adobe Illustrator Startup file. To learn how to modify the start-up file to have a specific set of patterns available every time you use Illustrator, see Chapter 6.

Creating Custom Patterns

In addition to using the patterns provided with Illustrator, you can create custom patterns by following the steps shown in Figure 11-4 and described below the figure.

Step 1

Step 2

Step 3

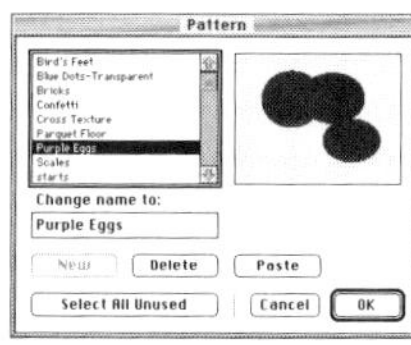

Step 4

Step 5

Figure 11-4: The steps for creating and using a basic pattern

STEPS: Creating a Basic Pattern Tile

Step 1. Using the Rectangle tool, draw the rectangle that will be the boundary of the pattern tile.

You must use a rectangle that you have drawn with the Rectangle tool. You cannot transform the rectangle, except to scale it to any percentage, mirror it, or rotate it in an increment of 90°. You cannot use rectangles that you have created with the Pen tool, even if they are perfect. On the same note, if the constraining angle is not an increment of 90° when the rectangle is drawn, you have to rotate it to an increment of 90°.

Step 2. Create any shapes or objects that you want to make up the pattern. Make sure that the objects do not overlap the outside edge.

Step 3. Change the Fill of the boundary rectangle to the color that you want to have for the background color of the pattern tile. If you put a Stroke on the rectangle, each tile will have a Stroke with the same color and weight on it.

Step 4. Select all of the objects — both the boundary rectangle and the objects in the rectangle. Choose Object⇨Pattern. Click the New button and type a name for the new pattern. The words *New Pattern 1* normally appear in the text field, but I recommend that you use a more descriptive name. The name of the new pattern then appears in the list of patterns in the Paint Style palette.

Step 5. Select an object to apply the pattern to and select that pattern from the Paint Style palette.

Why Patterns Aren't Always Seamless

In order for patterns to appear seamless, the edges of the rectangle cannot be apparent. Avoiding this problem sounds rather easy: You just avoid creating any objects that touch the edges of the rectangle. Well, that technique will do it, but when you use such a pattern, the pattern tiles become evident because of the lack of any objects along the borders.

So, then, you do want objects to cross the edges of the pattern rectangle. The catch is that those objects cannot appear to be broken. Doing an illustration the wrong way can help you understand this principle.

Start by drawing a background rectangle with a Fill of None. Draw a 1-point Black Stroked wavy path from left to right, overlapping both edges. Draw a circle, Filled with 50% Gray, that overlaps the bottom of the rectangle. Select all the objects and choose Object⇨Pattern. Click the New button and then the OK button.

When you Fill an object with the new pattern, the edges of the pattern will be very noticeable because the wavy path and the circle will both be cut at the edges of the pattern boundary. The figure shows the pattern tile and the original objects that formed the pattern.

Making Seamless Patterns

In order to make patterns seamless, you need to remember that objects that lie across the edge of the pattern border will be cut into two sections, one of which will be invisible. You also need to make sure that lines that stretch from one edge of a pattern border to the other side connect to another line on the opposite edge of the boundary. The second problem is more difficult to deal with than the first one. To make a line match well from one side to the other, you usually have to move one or both of the ends up or down slightly.

Use the following steps to fix objects that get sliced apart at the edges of the pattern tile boundary.

STEPS: Making Seamless Patterns, Part 1

Step 1. Create the boundary and the pattern tile objects. The objects may overlap any of the edges, including the corners. In the example that I created (see Figure 11-5), the stones overlap all four sides as well as one of the corners. I gave the edges of the pattern a Stroke so that you can see the boundary clearly.

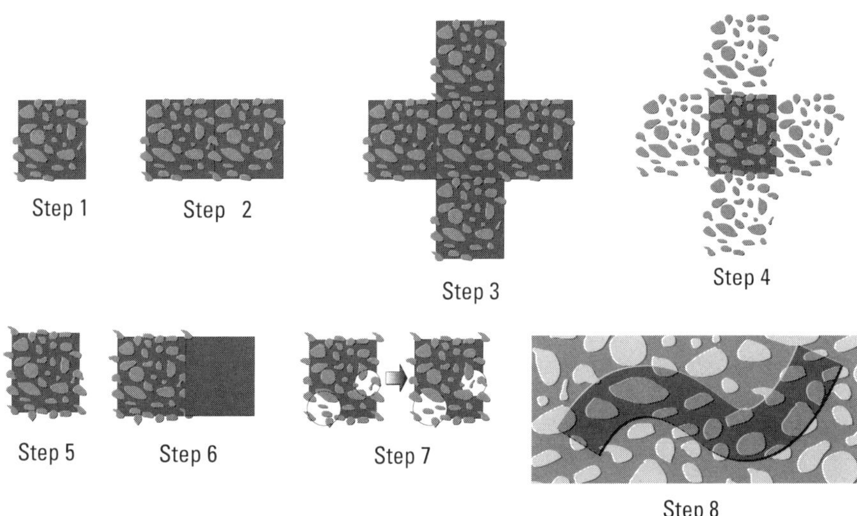

Figure 11-5: Steps for creating a seamless pattern

Step 2. Select all of the objects, including the pattern boundary, and group them. Click the upper-left corner of the pattern and drag to the right until the arrow pointer is directly over the upper-right corner (it will turn hollow at this point). Press Option and release the mouse button. A copy of the tile will be created to the right of the original.

Step 3. Repeat the process in Step 2 until all four sides have copies of the pattern up against them.

Step 4. Select all five sections and ungroup them. Select the boundary rectangles on the four copied sections and delete them.

Step 5. Delete all the paths (stones, in the example) that don't cross the border of the rectangle.

Changing Pattern Color

Julie: I can't change the color of the background of my pattern.

Toulouse: There are two ways you can do this.

Julie: Tell me the easiest way first.

Toulouse: OK, the first way is to Duplicate the pattern, and change the color.

Julie: Take me through it step by step.

Toulouse: First, go to the Patterns dialog box. Select the pattern you want to change. Click the Paste button and close the Pattern dialog box.

Julie: What does the Paste button do?

Toulouse: It puts a copy of the original pattern artwork in your document.

Julie: Cool.

Toulouse: Then select the background rectangle of the pattern, and change its color. Then select the pattern and the rectangle, and go back to the Pattern dialog box. Click New, and you have the same pattern with a different color!

Step 6. Look at the corners of the rectangle. If an object overlaps any of the corners at all, it should overlap the other three corners. If it doesn't overlap the other three (as in the upper-right corner in the example), Option-copy (drag the selected object, pressing the Option key, and release the mouse button *before* the Option key) that piece and the boundary to cover the empty corners. Move the boundary with a corner as before so that the piece lines up perfectly. Delete the rectangle after you finish.

Step 7. Look for any overlapping pieces of art in the artwork, including areas of objects that are "too close" for your liking. Move any pieces of art that are not overlapping a boundary.

Step 8. Make the boundary and objects into a pattern (Object ⇨Pattern); apply it to a shape and check the seams to make sure that it is correct. (If I am even the least bit doubtful that a pattern may be showing seams, I zoom in to 1600% to examine the questionable area.)

If you deleted the original pattern artwork, choose Object⇨Pattern. In the Pattern dialog box, select the pattern that was just created and click the Paste button to place a copy of the original artwork on the screen.

To fix lines that cross the edges of the pattern tile boundary, you need to adjust both the lines and the boundary rectangle itself.

STEPS: Making Seamless Patterns, Part 2

Step 1. Create the artwork that you will use in the pattern.

Step 2. Option-copy all of the artwork to the right. At a few points inside the original tile boundary, use the Scissors tool to cut along each path in order to prevent any change to the location and angle of the lines as they meet the opposite edge. You must cut the paths *inside* the original boundary, not outside. Join the paths together, moving only the End Point of the path in the original tile boundary.

Step 3. Option-copy both the original and the copied artwork down. Use the Scissors tool to cut along the inside bottom edge of the tile boundary and join the pieces, moving only the End Point of the paths inside the original tile boundary.

Step 4. Using the Scissors tool again, click about 1/2 inch down the outside right and bottom edges of the tile boundary. Select all paths that do not go into the tile boundary and delete them.

Step 5. Select the tile boundary rectangle and move it 1/8 inch down and to the right. Make sure that no new paths are overlapped on the top and left edges; if they are, do not move the rectangle so far.

Step 6. If you plan to use a blended line or a series of lines placed on top of each other, you may want to join the ends of the paths outside the rectangle to make blends merge together and keep layers of paths separate. I joined such ends in the example; if I hadn't, the pattern edges would not have lined up directly.

Step 7. Add any other elements of the pattern and change the background color if necessary. In the example, I added meatballs and a sauce-colored background. Select all the elements and make them into a pattern.

Step 8. Fill a path with the pattern. Three variations on the pattern appear at the top of Figure 11-6.

Julie: And the other way?

Toulouse: If you'll be changing colors all the time, or you want to use a gradient or another pattern for your background...

Julie: I thought you couldn't do that with patterns.

Toulouse: That's why you need to know this workaround.

Julie: Gotcha.

Toulouse: Go ahead and paste a pattern like before, but this time, make the background rectangle Filled with None.

Julie: Ahhhhh...

Toulouse: Yes, now the new pattern won't have any background, and you can paste a background behind the copy of the path that has the pattern.

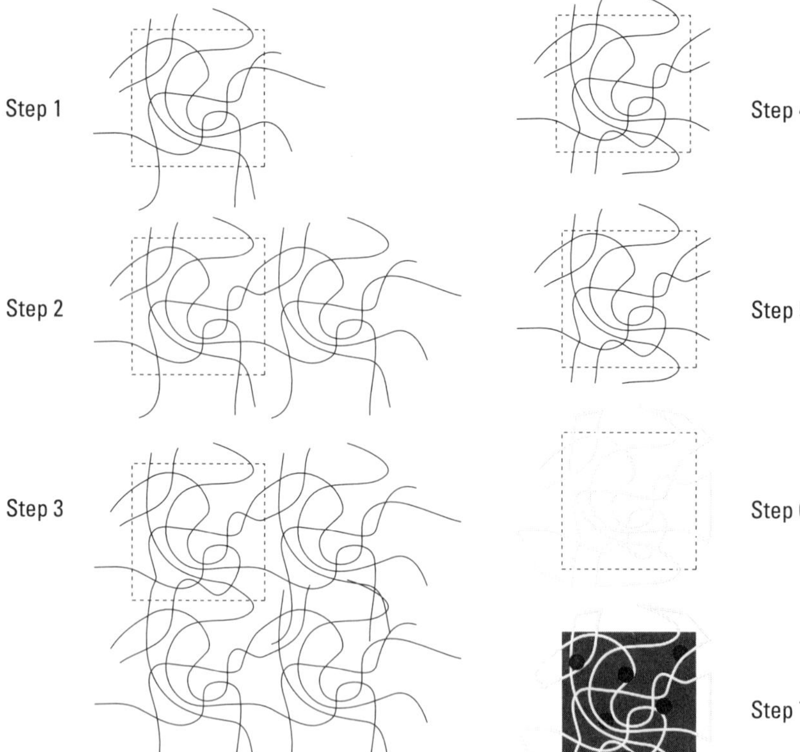

Figure 11-6: Steps for creating seamless patterns with continuous paths

Symmetrical Patterns

You can easily create symmetrical patterns in Illustrator. The key to creating them is to draw the bounding rectangle after you create the rest of the objects, drawing outward from the center point of one of the objects.

When you are creating symmetrical patterns, the main difficulty is judging the space between the objects in the pattern. Objects always seem too close together or too far apart, especially in patterns that have different amounts of space between the objects horizontally and vertically.

To have an equal amount of space from the center of one object to the center of the next object both vertically and horizontally, use a square as the pattern tile boundary.

Using the method described in the following steps (and illustrated in Figure 11-7), you can visually adjust the amount of space between objects before you make the objects a pattern.

STEPS: Making Symmetrical Patterns

Step 1. Create the artwork to use in the pattern.

Step 2. Draw a rectangle from the center of the object so that the object is in the upper-left corner of the rectangle.

Step 3. Option-copy the object and the rectangle across and down. Delete the extra rectangles.

Step 4. Using the Direct Selection tool, drag to select the objects on the right and Shift-drag (move the object with the Shift key pressed, releasing the mouse button before the Shift key) them left or right to change the horizontal spacing.

Step 5. Drag the Direct Selection tool to select the objects on the bottom and Shift-drag up or down to adjust the vertical spacing.

Step 6. Move the rectangle so that it surrounds only the initial object and delete the other three objects.

Step 7. Make the objects into a pattern and apply them to a path. The pattern is the background for Figure 11-7.

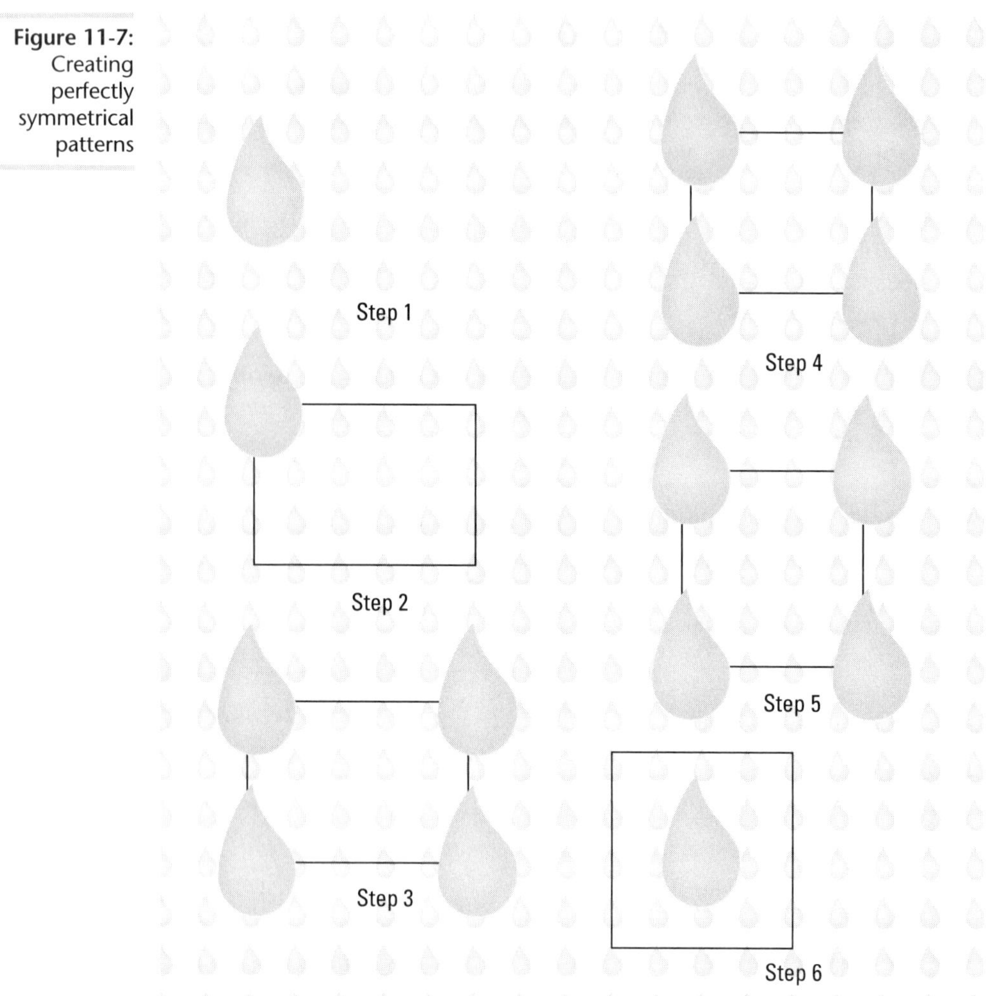

Figure 11-7: Creating perfectly symmetrical patterns

Line Patterns and Grids

Using lines and grids for patterns is ideal because they are so easy to create. The key in both types of patterns is the size of the bounding rectangle.

To create a line pattern with horizontal 1-point lines that are aligned on every $^1/_2$ inch, do the following: Draw a rectangle that is exactly $^1/_2$ inch tall, at any width, with a Fill and Stroke of None. Draw a horizontal line from outside the left edge of the rectangle to outside the right edge of the rectangle, with a Fill of None and a Stroke of 1 point.

Creating grids is even easier than creating evenly spaced lines. Create a rectangle that is the size of the grid "holes" (for a 1/4 inch grid, the rectangle would be 1/4 x 1/4 inch) and apply a Stroke to the object. Make the Stroke the weight that you want the grid lines to be. Make that rectangle into a pattern. That's it. You now have a pattern grid that is as precise as possible.

Make a pattern out of the two objects. The new pattern will consist of 1-point horizontal Strokes that are spaced 1/2 inch apart.

You can use this technique with vertical lines, as well. Just make the bounding rectangle the width of the distance from line to line.

If you want the space between gridlines to be an exact measurement, make the rectangle bigger by the stroke weight. A 1/4 inch grid (18 points) with 1-point grid lines requires a rectangle that is 19 points by 19 points. Remember that four of these grids don't equal an inch; instead, they equal 4 points more than an inch.

Diagonal-Line and Grid Patterns

Creating diagonal-line and grid patterns can be difficult if you try to make a rectangle, draw a path at an angle, and then use the rectangle with the path in it as a pattern. Joining diagonal lines at the edges of the pattern is nearly impossible.

A better method is to create line and grid patterns in horizontal or vertical alignment and then double-click on the Rotate tool. In the Rotate dialog box, enter the angle to change the lines and uncheck the Object checkbox. The pattern will rotate to the desired angle inside the path.

Patterns to Paths

Isaac: Is there an easy way to convert patterns to paths that really works?

Toulouse: Well, there are several options. The Expand option in the Object menu, KPT Gradients/Patterns to Paths (included on the Macworld Illustrator Bible CD-ROM) and CSI Patterns to Paths.

Isaac: Which works the best?

Toulouse: Well, CSI gives you the option of keeping any transformations that were done to the patterns before they're converted.

Isaac: I sometimes get bad results with patterns to paths.

Toulouse: Actually, because of the way Illustrator Patterns work, the patterns are always offset a little bit.

Isaac: Any way to fix this?

Toulouse: Just manually. :(

Using this technique is also a great way to avoid making several patterns when you need line patterns that are set at different angles. Just make one horizontal line pattern and rotate the patterns within the paths.

Transparency and Patterns

To make the background of a pattern transparent, give the bounding rectangle a Fill of None. Only the other objects in the pattern will be opaque.

To make the objects in a pattern transparent, copy the rectangle and then make the rectangle and the other objects into a compound path. Paste the copy of the rectangle in the back (choose Edit⇨Paste In Back or press ⌘-B) and give the copy no Fill or Stroke. Select the compound path and the copy of the rectangle and make the objects into a pattern. You can achieve some fascinating effects by using the transformation tools to make transformed copies of patterns on top of themselves.

When you make the bounding rectangle part of a compound path, it is no longer a rectangle, and you cannot use it as the bounding rectangle. Always copy the rectangle before you make the objects and the rectangle into a compound path.

Another way to achieve interesting effects is by making a copy of the object behind the original. Select the object, choose Edit⇨Copy (⌘-C), and then choose Edit⇨Paste In Back (⌘-B). Change the Fill in the copy of the object to a solid or a gradient or change it to another Pattern. Chapter 16 describes a technique for creating a "hollow honeycomb" effect.

Modifying Existing Patterns

To change an existing pattern, choose Object⇨Pattern with no object selected. In the Pattern dialog box, select the pattern to change and press the Paste button. Then press the OK button. A copy of the original artwork will be placed in the document.

Select individual parts with any of the selection tools and change Paint Style attributes or change the shape of any of the objects with selection or transformation tools.

After modifying the artwork, select all the pattern-related objects and choose Object⇨Pattern. Click the New button and name the pattern something close to but not exactly the same name as the original. Click OK to exit the Pattern dialog box.

Select one of the objects that contains the original pattern as a Fill and choose Filter⇨Select⇨Same Paint Style. All the objects that have that pattern as a Fill will be selected. Change the Fill pattern from the old pattern to the new one that is in the Paint Style palette. If any objects have that pattern as a Stroke, repeat the procedure for them.

Return to the Pattern dialog box and select the original pattern. Click the Delete button to remove that version of the pattern from the scrolling list.

Putting Patterns and Gradients into Patterns

Under normal circumstances, you cannot put gradients into patterns or patterns into other patterns. But if Illustrator doesn't think of the objects as patterns or gradients, you can put patterns and gradients into patterns.

To put a pattern into another pattern, choose Object⇨Pattern and select the pattern that you want to put into the new pattern. Click the Paste button and click OK to exit the Pattern dialog box. Group the pattern artwork and Option-copy several squares. Draw a rectangle around the squares and add any additional artwork for the new pattern. Choose Object⇨Pattern and click the New button.

Including gradients in patterns is not quite so simple. First, create the object in the shape of the gradient and Fill it with the Gradient. Expand the gradient with the Object⇨Expand command. You can then use the blended object in any pattern.

When you transform gradients into blends via Expand for placement in a pattern, check for masked areas. You cannot use masks in patterns, so you need to release the mask before you incorporate the blend into the pattern. Also, try to keep the number of blend steps to a minimum.

Technical overkill: Patterns in Illustrator are actually saved as Type 3 fonts into your Illustrator file. Remember how long it takes some of those fancy Berthold fonts to print? Imagine stuffing hundreds of colored, tinted, twisted, turned objects into a font....

Pattern Printing Problems

CptnStubing: Why does it take so long to print patterns?

Toulouse: Well, if you think of what patterns actually are, you'll know.

CptnStubing: If I knew, would I be asking?

Toulouse: It's just that patterns are really bunches of masked sections of — get this — Type 3 fonts.. The masks are rectangles.

CptnStubing: Which means...?

Toulouse: Masks can always cause printing problems, as can Type 3 fonts, but if you do complex transformations to complex patterns, you're asking for trouble.

Transforming Patterns

After you create patterns and place them within paths, they may be too big or at the wrong angle, or they may start in an awkward location. You can use the transformation tools and the Move command to resolve these problems.

To transform a pattern inside a path, select the path and double-click on the transformation tool that corresponds to the change that you want to make to the pattern. In the transformation tool's dialog box, uncheck the Object checkbox. The Pattern Tiles and Objects checkboxes will be grayed out if the selected object does not contain a pattern.

Any changes that you make in the transformation tool's dialog box when only the Pattern checkbox is checked will affect only the pattern, not the outside shape. The default (which cannot be changed) is for both checkboxes to remain checked always.

If you are using any of the transformation tools manually, the pattern inside the selected object will transform with the object only if the Transform pattern tiles option in the General Preferences dialog box is checked.

To move a pattern within a path, choose Arrange➪Move (press ⌘-Shift-M or Option-click on the Selection tool). The Move dialog box also contains Pattern and Objects checkboxes. If you uncheck the Objects checkbox, only the pattern will be moved.

Graphs

The Graphs feature seems to be one of the most underused features in Illustrator.

All the graph tools work in a similar manner as the shape creation tools: click and drag to set the size of the graph, or click to display the Graph Size dialog box and then enter the size information. If you press the Shift key while you drag, the graph is constrained to a perfect square (or circle, if it's a pie graph). If you press the Option key while you drag, you will drag from the center of the graph out. If you Option-click, the graph you create is centered at the point you Option-clicked. That's it. That's all you have to do to use the graph tools. Neat, huh?

Double-clicking on the Graph tool brings up the Graph Style dialog box, shown in Figure 11-8. Choosing a different graph style at this point and clicking OK changes the tool to represent the type of graph you selected. You can choose from six graph styles; the grouped-column graph is the default.

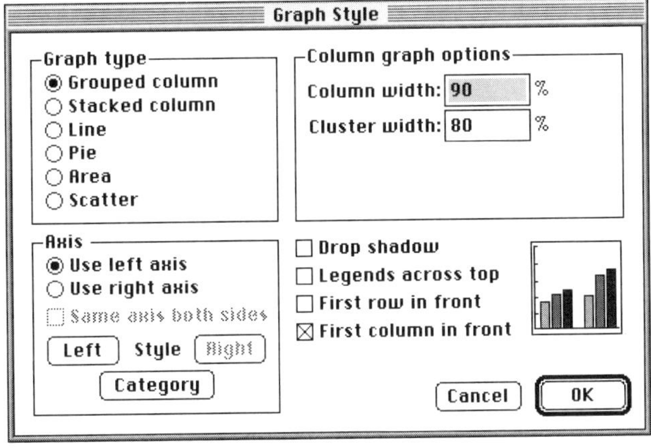

Figure 11-8: The Paint Style palette with the Pattern square selected, and samples of each of the default patterns

One of the most exciting things about graphs in Illustrator is their fluidity. Not only can you create graphs easily, but after you create them, you can change them easily. In addition, if the data that you used to create a graph changes, you can enter the new data and have it show up in the graph instantaneously.

Figure 11-9 and the steps that follow describe the basics of creating and modifying a graph. The type of graph in this example is a grouped column graph, which is commonly used to compare quantities over time or between different categories.

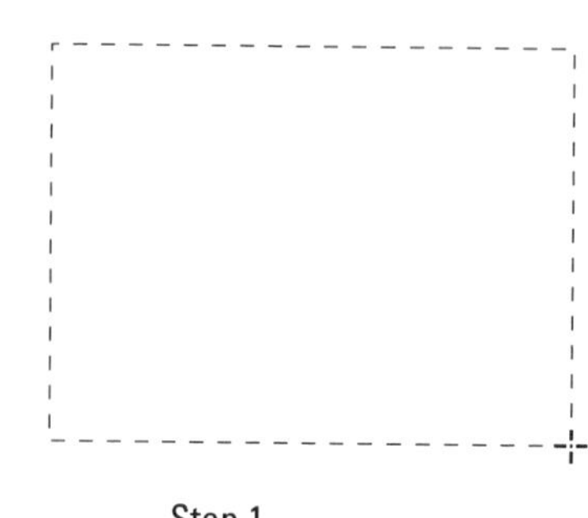

Step 1

	Me	World	Record
Balls	7	11	
Rings	6	12	
Plates	3	8	
Clubs	5	9	
Torches		4 7	
Bowling Balls		3 5	
Knives	4	7	

Step 2

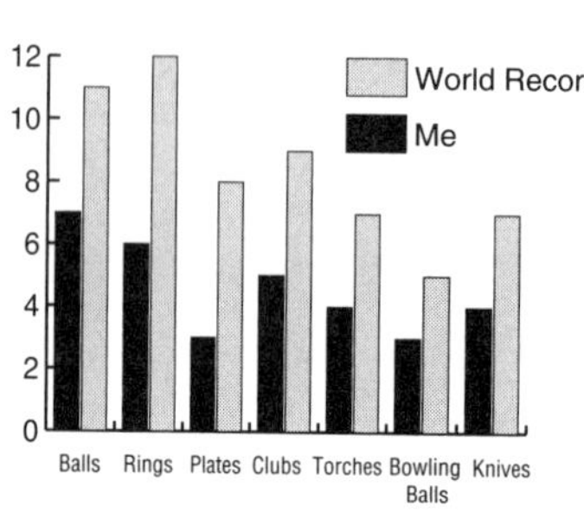

Step 3

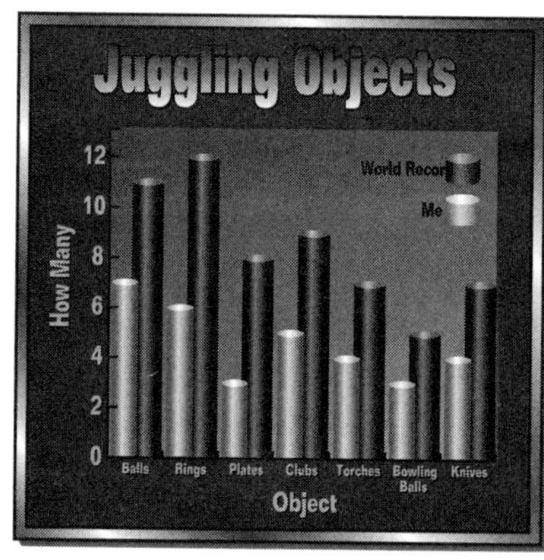

Step 4

Figure 11-9: The basic steps for creating a graph in Illustrator: dragging to set the size of the graph, entering the graph data, and touching up the final graph

STEPS: Creating a Graph

Step 1. Select the Graph tool and click and drag to form a rectangular area, similar to the way that you use the Rectangle tool. The size of the rectangle that you create will be the size of the graph.

Step 2. As soon as you release the mouse button, the Graph Data dialog box appears. Information that you enter in the Graph Data dialog box becomes formatted into graph form.

The top row in the Graph Data dialog box worksheet area should contain the labels for comparison within the same set. In the example, I compared how many things I can juggle to what the current world records are for juggling those particular objects. The items in the top row appear as *legends* outside the graph area.

In the leftmost column, you can enter labels that appear at the bottom of the grouped column graph as *categories*. I entered the types of objects that are to be compared in the graph.

In the remaining *cells,* enter the pertinent information.

Step 3. Click OK to have all the data that you entered used in the graph. The graph appears, and it should look something like the one in step 3 of Figure 11-9.

Step 4. After I created the graph, I edited it by changing the paint style of the bars and legends, adding a background, changing the point sizes and font of the type in the graph, and adding the lightened circles at the top of each bar and legend to make the elements in the graph look more three-dimensional.

When to Use Graphs

Graphs are most useful when they show numerical information that would normally take several paragraphs to explain or that can't be expressed easily in words. Furthermore, you can express numerical information easily in graphs, and using graphs makes finding and understanding information easier than when the same information is in lines of text.

Numbers are fascinating concepts that most people have a good grasp of, but you can overlook their significance, especially when you are comparing different numbers. The numbers *2* and *9* are the same size when you type them; however, when you use them in a graph, they can represent a drastic difference.

Of course, although graphs are normally used to educate and inform, they are also suited very well for misinforming. Stretching or crushing a graph can cause a great difference in the way the information appears. Even worse is the ability to stretch or compress information in one part of the graph. The figure shows the same information in two radically different graphs.

The information for the top graph, created by the Smitty's people, shows them to be even with their competitors. The text for the numbers, the column drop shadows, and the distracting images cause the data to make less impact on the reader than it does in the graph below. Dublin's graph indicates that Dublin is doing substantially better than Smitty's. The vast difference in the length of the bars is one way to show the difference, as is the numbering scheme, which starts at 20250, making the first Smitty's bar appear to be a negative number.

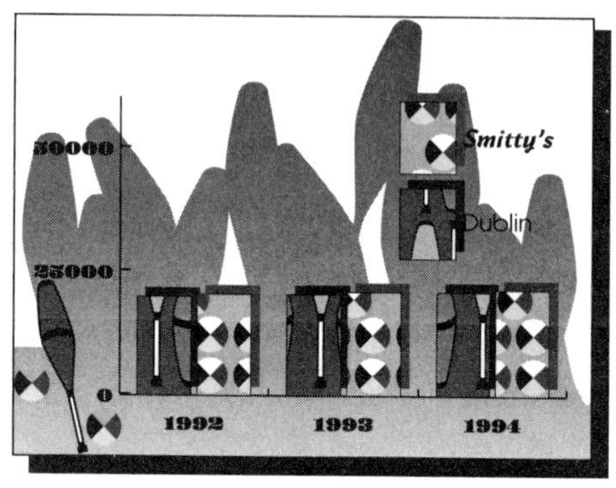

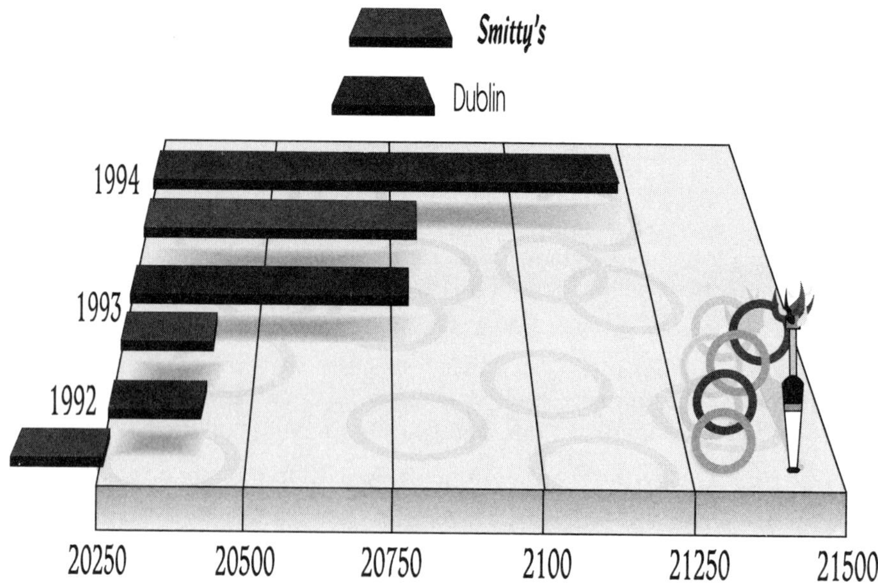

The Six Types of Graphs

You can choose from six different types of graphs in Illustrator. Each type gives a specific kind of information to the reader. Certain graphs are better for comparisons, others for growth, and so on. The following sections describe the graphs, explain how to create them, and tell how you can use them.

Grouped-Column Graphs

You primarily use grouped-column graphs to show how something changes over time. Often, they are referred to as bar graphs because the columns that make up the graphs resemble bars.

Step 3 of Figure 11-9 showed a grouped column graph as created in Illustrator. This graph contains seven categories, and each of the seven categories is represented by two different totals. The height of the bars represents the number in each case, with higher bars representing higher values.

The real strength of a grouped-column graph is that it provides for the direct comparison of different types of statistics in the same graph. In the sample graph, the number of rings that I can juggle is compared to the bowling ball juggling world record by the height of the bars.

Both column and cluster width are two customizable options for grouped-column graphs and stacked-column graphs. Column width refers to the width of individual columns, with 100% being wide enough to butt up against other columns in the cluster. Cluster width refers to how much of the available cluster space is taken up by the columns in the cluster. At 80% (the default), 20% of the available space is empty, leaving room between clusters.

Making the columns or clusters wider than 100% can have a dramatic impact on the appearance of the column graph because the columns will then overlap each other just a bit, giving the graph depth.

You can widen columns and clusters to 1,000% of their size and condense them to 1% of the width of the original column or cluster.

Stacked-Column Graphs

Stacked-column graphs are good graphs for presenting the total of a category and the contributing portions of each category. In Figure 11-10, I used objects once again as categories and split each object into the number of those objects being juggled. The total of the time it takes (in weeks) to learn to juggle that number of objects is the height of the object's bar. The time for each number of objects juggled represents a certain portion of the entire time, reflected in each of the smaller sections of the bars.

Figure 11-10: Data for a stacked-column graph, how the graph appears when it is first created in Illustrator, and the graph after it is altered

	"3"	"4"	"5"	"6"	"7"	"8"	"9"	
Balls	1	6	28	32	40	38	72	
Rings	2	8	42	10	35	14	34	
Clubs	4	38	50	75	140			

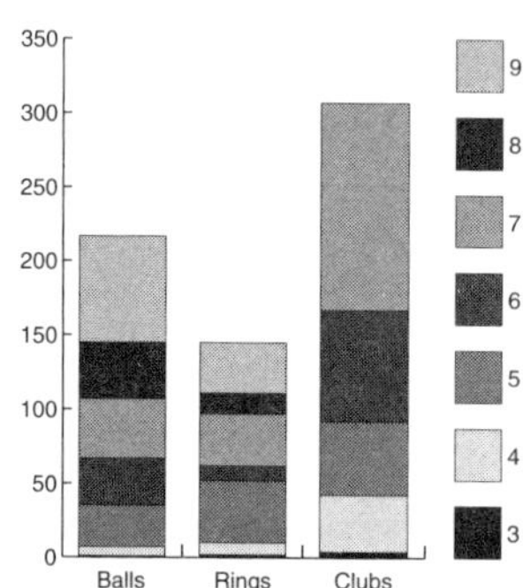

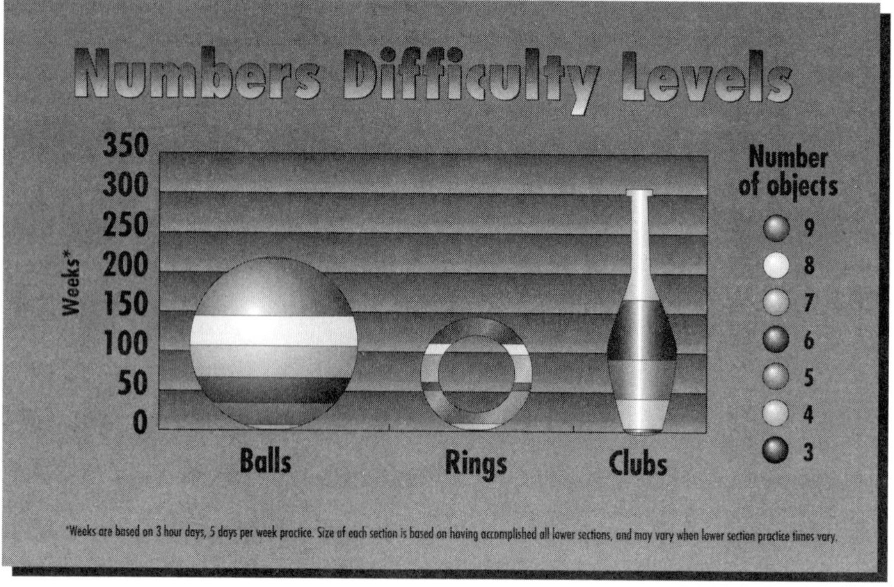

To get the labels on the legends to read numbers only, I had to put quotation marks (" ") around each of the numbers. If I had not used quotation marks, the numbers would have been considered data, not labels.

This graph shows the same amount of information as the grouped column graph, but the information is organized differently. The stacked-column graph is designed to display a total of all the legends, and the grouped-column graph is designed to aid comparison of all individual legends in each category.

Line Graphs

Line graphs (also known as line charts) show trends over time. They are especially useful for determining progress and identifying radical changes. For example, the line graph in Figure 11-11 shows the average income of three street performers on successive weeks throughout the summer.

The Mark Data Points option in the Line graphs area of the Graph Style dialog box (Object⇨Graphs⇨Style) forces data points to appear as squares. If this box is not checked, the data points are visible only as direction changes in lines between the data points.

If the Connect Data Points option is checked, lines will be drawn between each pair of data points.

The Fill Lines option and the corresponding text box for line width create a line that is Filled with the data point legend color and is outlined with Black. The Fill Lines option changes the line from a single path with a Stroke weight into a Filled path with a Black Stroke.

The Edge to Edge lines option stretches the lines out to the left and right edges of the graph. Although the result is technically incorrect, you can achieve better visual impact by using this feature.

Graph Trouble

Doc: Sometimes my data values change when I close a document and open it later.

Toulouse: Really?

Doc: Yeah, it's very annoying.

Toulouse: I'm just fooling with you. That's a problem within Illustrator.

Doc: What can I do to fix it?

Toulouse: The best thing to do is to change the graph into plain Illustrator artwork.

Doc: Done. Wait. How do I do that?

Toulouse: Select the graph and ungroup it.

Doc: But I get a message saying it won't work as a graph anymore.

Toulouse: That's the downfall, unfortunately.

Figure 11-11: Line graph data (top), the graph as it first appears in Illustrator (center), and the graph after it has been redesigned (bottom)

	Animated Suspension	The Flying Linguini	Disoriented Convolution
May	300 220 145		
	240 190 120		
	260 260 140		
	320 300 200		
June	380 360 150		
	400 350 195		
	395 320 230		
	435 420 190		
July	520 190 200		
	600 290 195		
	440 405 240		
	380 340 150		
August	300 210 200		
	275 250 240		
	360 280 230		
	300 290 210		
September	420 280 170		
	220 140 110		

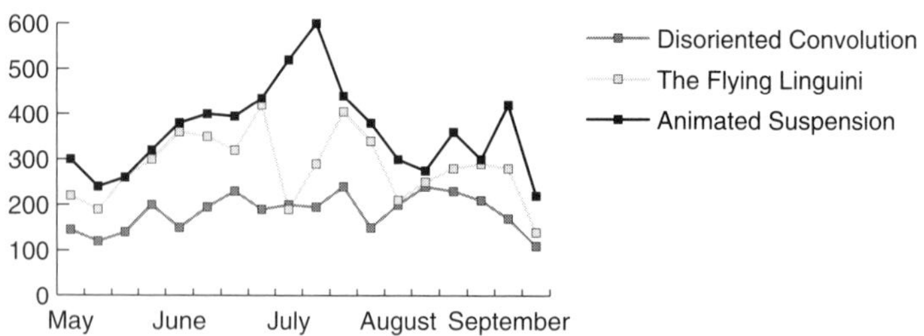

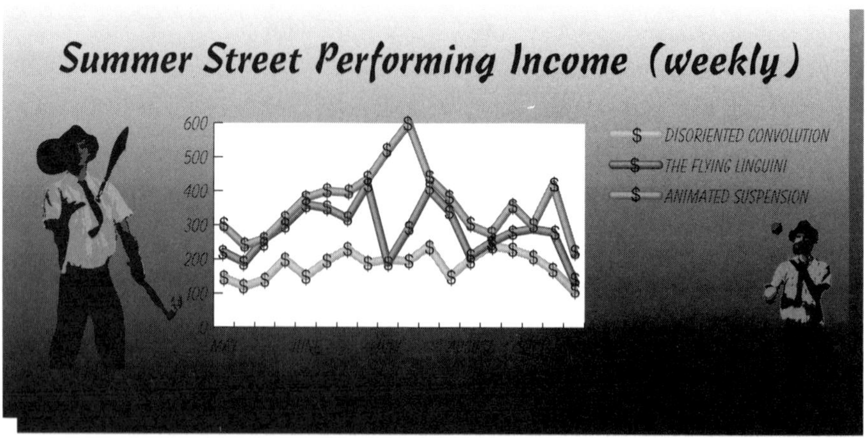

Pie Graphs

Pie graphs are great for comparing percentages of the portions of a whole. In Figure 11-12, pie graphs show how much of a juggling performance was spent doing particular activities. The higher the percentage for a certain activity, the larger its wedge.

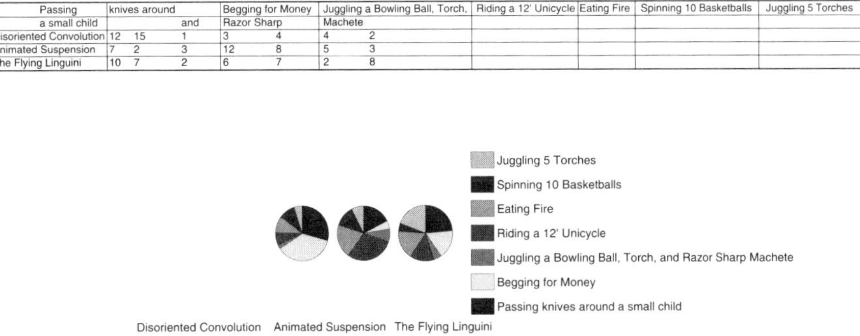

Passing	knives around	Begging for Money	Juggling a Bowling Ball, Torch,	Riding a 12' Unicycle	Eating Fire	Spinning 10 Basketballs	Juggling 5 Torches
a small child	and	Razor Sharp	Machete				
Disoriented Convolution	12 15 1	3 4	4 2				
Animated Suspension	7 2 3	12 8	5 3				
The Flying Linguini	10 7 2	6 7	2 8				

Figure 11-12: A pie graph showing how much time each performer spent on certain activities

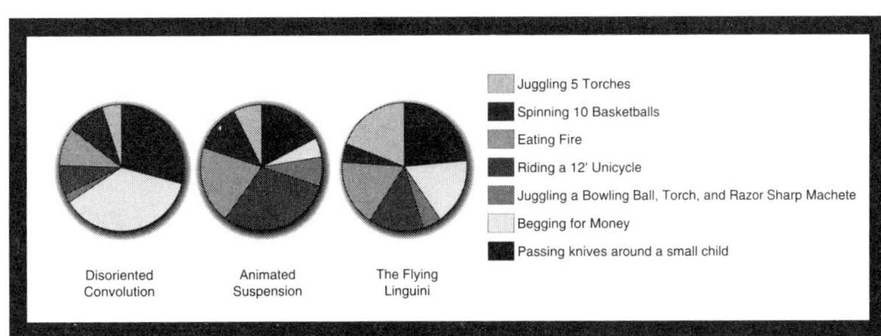

When you create pie graphs, you can remove the individual wedges from the central pie with the Group Selection tool to achieve an exploding pie effect.

The Legends in wedges option is the only option in the Graph Style dialog box that is specifically for pie graphs. If Legends in wedges is selected, the name of each wedge will be centered within that wedge. Illustrator doesn't do a very good job of placing the legend names, many times overlapping neighboring names. In addition, the letters in the legend names are black, which can make reading some of the names difficult or impossible.

Area Graphs

Upon first glance, area graphs may appear to be just like line graphs that are Filled. Like line graphs, area graphs show data points that are connected, but area graphs are stacked upon each other to show the total area of the legend subject in the graph.

Scatter Graphs

Scatter graphs, which are primarily used for scientific charting purposes, are quite different from all the other types of graphs. Each data point is given a location by x-y coordinates instead of by category and label. The points are connected, as are the points in line graphs, but the line created by the data point locations can cross itself and does not go in any specific direction. Scatter graphs have the same customization options as line graphs.

Customizing Graphs

When a graph is selected and the Graph Style dialog box is displayed, a number of options become available for most graphs:

- The Left or Right axis options will display the vertical values on either the left side (the default) or the right side. The Same axis both sides option will put the same axis on both sides. Clicking the Left or Right button displays options for customizing axes.
- Checking the Drop shadow option will place a black shadow behind the graph objects. The shadow will be offset up and to the right.
- The Legends on top option will make existing legends (if any) appear across the top of the graph, instead of being grouped together on the right side of the graph.
- The First row in front option will place overlapping rows in order from left to right, wherever columns, clusters, or other objects overlap.

Each type of graph has its own customization options. The preceding sections that describe each type of graph explain those options. It is usually quicker to press Apply and then (if necessary) move the Graph Data dialog box out of the way than it is to press OK and have to reopen the Graph Data dialog box.

To make visually striking graphs, use a combination of graph types. Simply use the Group Selection tool to select all the objects that are one legend type and then choose Object⇨Graphs⇨Graph Style and enter the new graph type for that legend.

Using the Graph Data Dialog Box

You can change the numbers and the text in the Graph Data dialog box at any time by selecting the graph and choosing Object⇨Graphs⇨Data. Illustrator will recreate the graph to reflect the changes you make. If you have moved some of the graph objects around, they may revert to their original locations when Illustrator recreates the graph. If a number does not have quotation marks around it, Illustrator assumes that you want the number to be entered as a value in the graph.

Make sure that the graph is never ungrouped, at least not until you have finished making all graph data and graph style changes. If you ungroup the graph, you will not be able to use any of the graph options to change the ex-graph because it will be just a set of paths and text in Illustrator's view.

You can import graph data in tab-delimited word processing files. *Tab-delimited files* are text and numbers that are separated by tabs and returns. To import data from another file, click the Import button or click the Import button while you are in the Graph Data dialog box.

Illustrator is not really a graphing or spreadsheet program, so many of the controls for arranging data are not available, including inserting rows and columns and creating formulas.

The Cut, Copy, and Paste functions work within the Graph Data dialog box, so you can move and duplicate information on a very basic level.

One very useful feature in the Graph Data dialog box is the Transverse button. This function switches the X and Y axes of the data, reversing everything that you have entered.

Using Marker and Column Designs

The most exciting part about the graphing functions in Illustrator is the capability to give column, line, and area graphs special icons to indicate values on the graphs.

On line and area graphs, marker designs are created, which you can use in place of the standard markers. For each value in the graph, the marker design is placed, adding visual impact to the graph.

Column designs are created for grouped-column graphs and stacked-column graphs. The strength of using column designs is most evident in grouped-column graphs, where images are placed side by side (see Figure 11-13).

Figure 11-13: Creating a column design and using it in four different grouped column graphs.

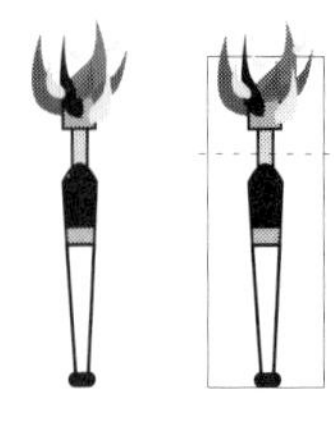

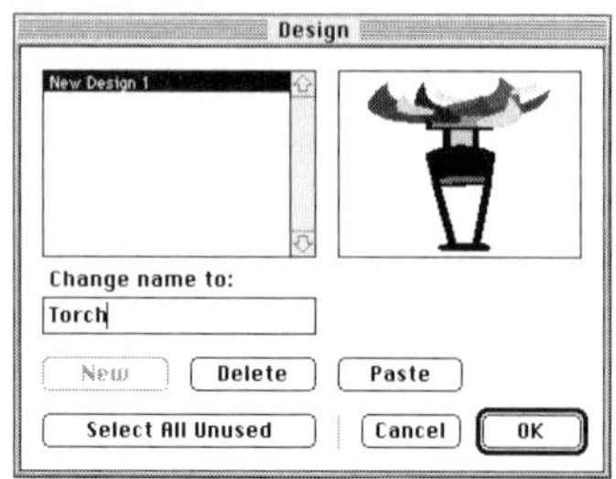

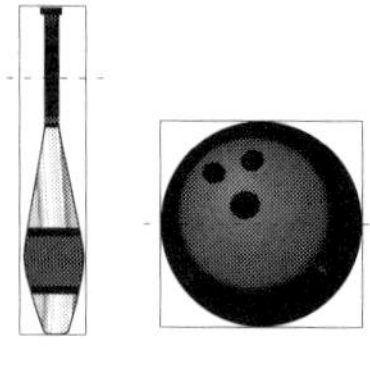

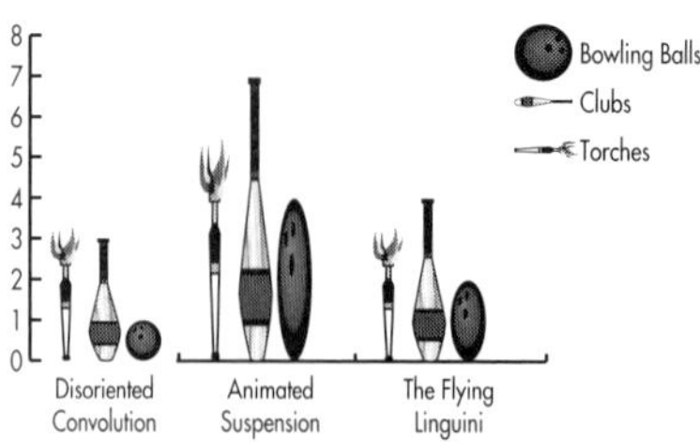

Vertically Scaled

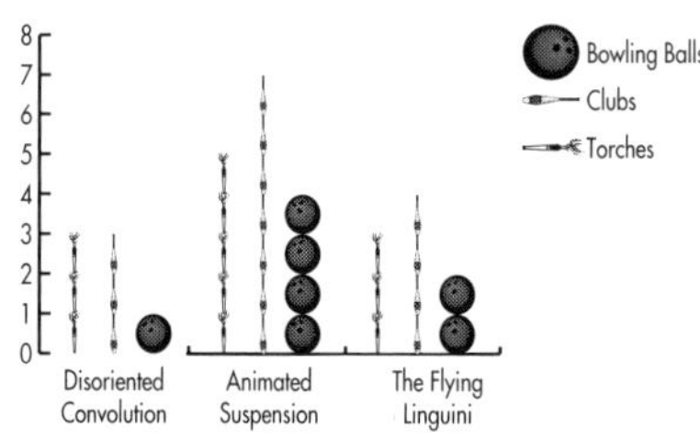

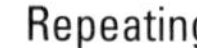

Repeating

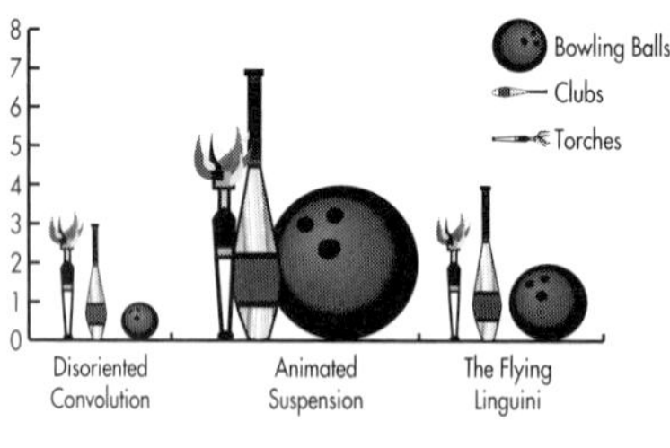

Uniformly Scaled

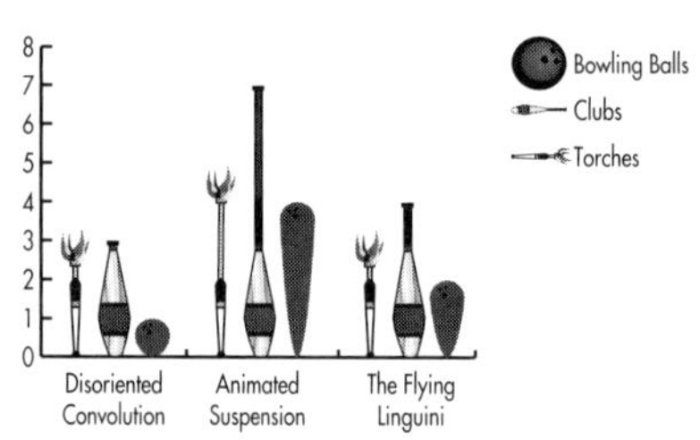

Sliding

STEPS: Creating and Using a Column Design

Step 1. Create the graphic object in Illustrator.

Step 2. Draw a rectangle around the border of the object. Illustrator will use this border to determine the area of the object relative to the values entered for the graph.

Step 3. Draw a horizontal line across the rectangle at a good place for the image to stretch. Make the horizontal line into a guide (choose Object⇨Guides⇨Make or press ⌘-5).

(Step 3 is necessary only if you use the column design as a sliding design.)

Step 4. Select the rectangle, object, and guide, and choose Object⇨Graphs⇨Design. Click the New button to make the selected object appear in the window. Name the design and click the OK button.

Step 5. Select just one legend type by clicking twice on the legend graphic with the Group Selection tool. Choose Object⇨Graphs⇨Column Design and select the design from the list. Choose the column design type (see Figure 11-13 for examples of each type). Repeat this step for each legend.

You can combine column-design types by selecting a different type for each legend.

Texture Generation

One of the newest, niftiest features in Illustrator 6.0 is a Fill called Ink Pen. Ink Pen takes basic Illustrator paths and turns them into random textures that you can control and manipulate through a variety of options.

To create a texture, select any path or paths and choose Object⇨Ink Pen Edit. The Ink Pen Edit dialog box will appear, as shown in Figure 11-14.

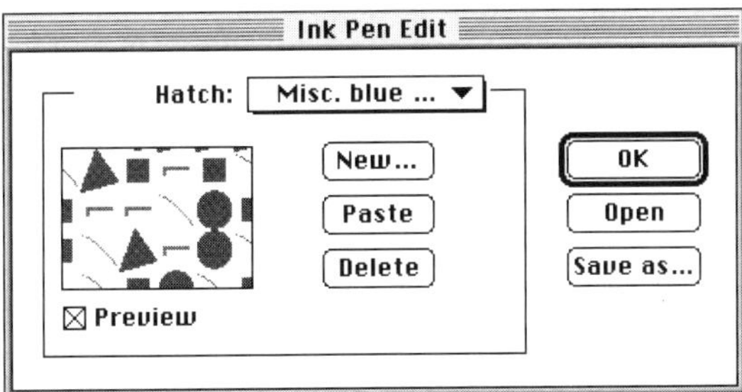

Figure 11-14: The Ink Pen Edit dialog box

Click the New button and name your hatch. Click OK, and you'll be able to use that hatch as an Ink Pen Fill.

Ink Pen Color Change

Gopher: I want to change the color of my hatch style.

Toulouse: After it's applied or before?

Gopher: Before, since I'm using the Fade to White option.

Toulouse: Okay. Open the Ink Pen Edit dialog box.

Gopher: Done.

Toulouse: Then select the hatch style you wish to re-color.

Gopher: Done again.

Toulouse: Then click the Paste button.

Gopher: Paste does what?

Toulouse: Paste puts a copy of the hatch art in your document. Then change the color, go back to Ink Pen Edit, click New, and name your new hatch style something else.

After the hatch has been created, you're ready to apply it as a Fill for any selected path. To do so, select the path you wish to fill and choose➪Object➪Ink Pen Fill. The Ink Pen Fill dialog box will appear, as shown in Figure 11-15.

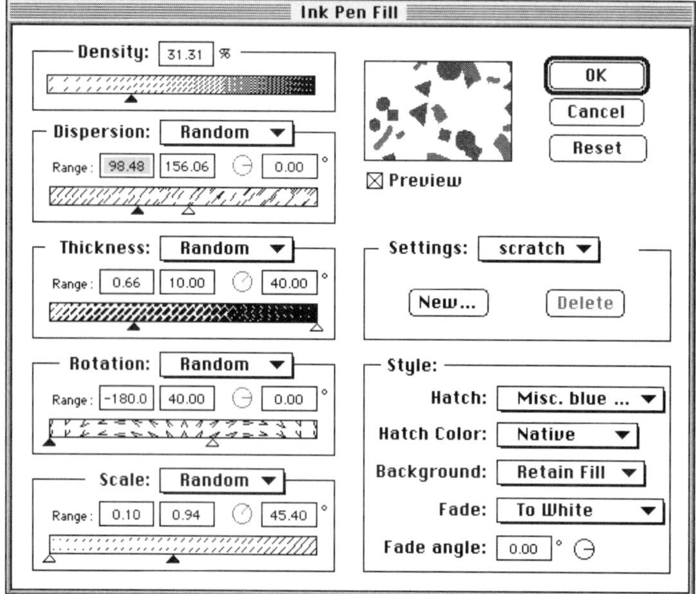

Figure 11-15: The Ink Pen Fill dialog box

Inside the Ink Pen Fill dialog box, you have an infinite amount of combinations of various properties to apply to the hatch style. The effects are listed, with figures showing the effects of various property setting.

The texture that is created is actually a grouped mask of several paths. This allows you to change the paint attributes of the texture after it has been applied. In addition, you can then modify the individual paths just like you would any other path in Illustrator.

Remember that the paths you use in a hatch style can have both Fills and Strokes, but the "thickness" property only affects Stroke width.

Ink Pen Density

Density is how closely packed together the elements of the hatch style are. The closer together the pieces, the "darker" or "thicker" the texture will be. You can adjust the density by dragging the Density slider to the left and right; left is less dense, right is more dense. Figure 11-16 shows various amounts of density.

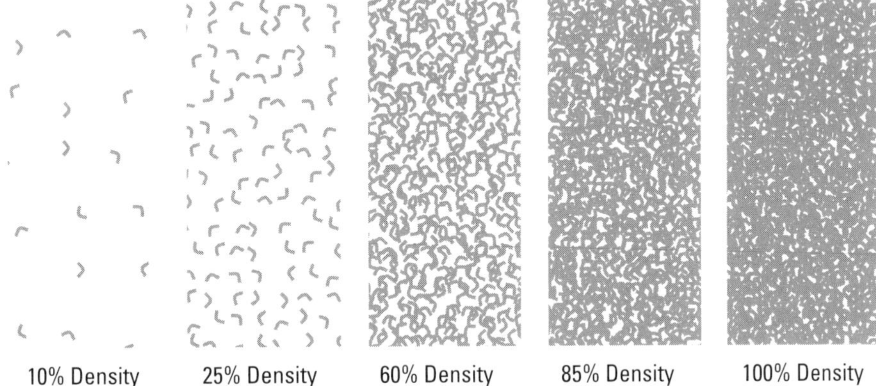

Figure 11-16: Different amounts of density for a hatch style

Ink-Pen Dispersion

Dispersion controls how evenly the texture elements are spread within the Fill. Setting the dispersion to None results in a pattern-tile appearance that is very uniform, while increasing it randomizes the location and grouping of the pieces of the hatch style. Figure 11-17 shows various settings of the Dispersion slider.

Each of the lower four settings in the Ink Pen Fill dialog box have different ways of creating each parameter. For instance, instead of a Constant dispersion, you can choose from Linear, Symmetrical, Reflected, or Random dispersion. Each of the other properties (with the exception of Density) have these same controls.

The Ink Pen Fill option work as follows:

- **Constant** keeps the setting the same throughout the entire Fill shape.
- **Linear** changes the amount of the effect across the Fill shape. The angle at which this is applied is changed in each effect section, either by moving the angle indicator or by entering a different angle in the Rotate field. There are two sliders to adjust, controlling the maximum and minimum amount of the effect.
- **Reflect** increases and decreases the amount of the effect (somewhat like a double-linear effect). The angle and minimum and maximum amounts are controlled in the same way as Linear.
- **Symmetric** creates a symmetric pattern of the effect. The angle and amounts are adjusted in the same way as they are in Linear and Reflect.
- **Random** generates random amounts of the effect, between the minimum and maximum amount that you specify.

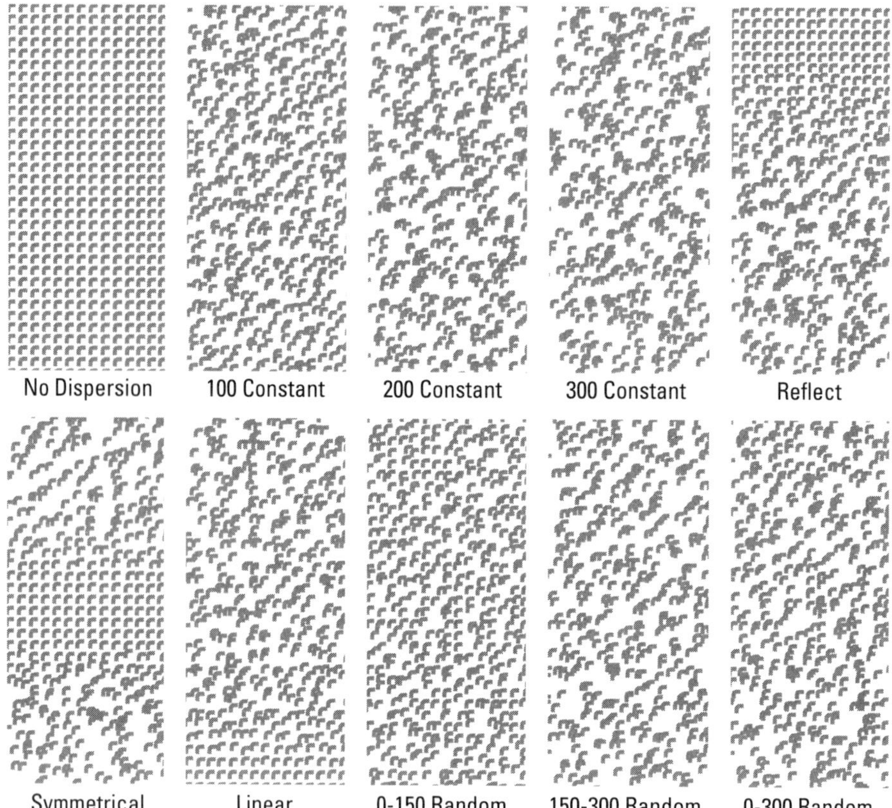

Figure 11-17: Different amounts of dispersion for a hatch style

Thickness

Thickness controls the Stroke thickness of the paths in the hatch style. Some of the variations of Stroke thickness are shown in Figure 11-18.

Rotation

Rotation controls the angle of the pieces in the hatch style. A Constant amount of rotation will rotate each of the pieces in the hatch style the same amount. Other Rotation options vary the amount of rotation, as shown in Figure 11-19.

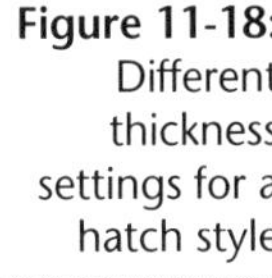

Figure 11-18: Different thickness settings for a hatch style

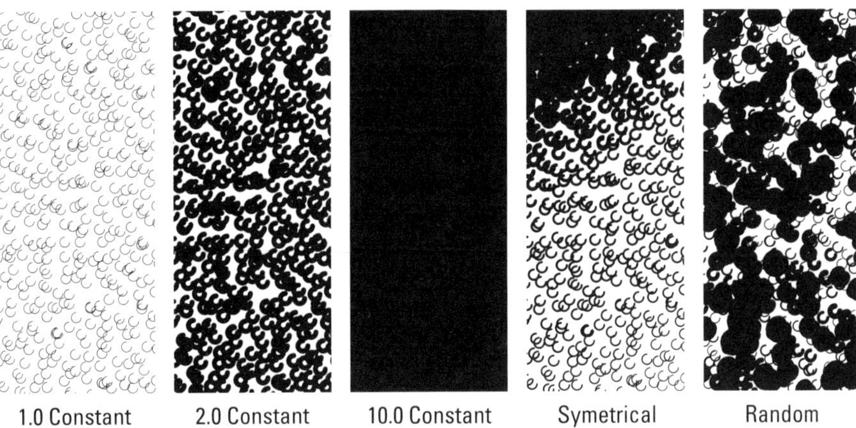

Figure 11-19: Different settings for the Rotation property

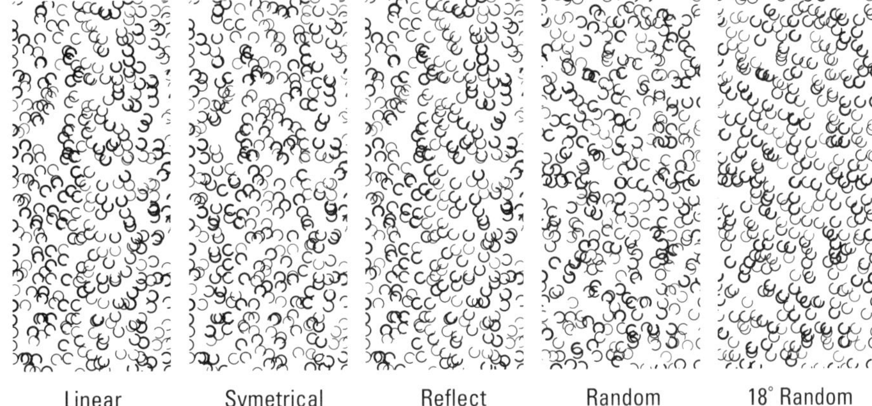

Steps: Creating Symmetrical Textures

Step 1. Start by creating the path you wish to Fill with the symmetrical texture.

Step 2. With the path selected, choose Object➪Ink Pen Fill, and select the Hatch Style to use.

Step 3. Change the Rotation to Linear, making the left and right sliders the same (for example 90, 90). Click the OK button to apply the texture to the path.

Step 4. Select the path and Rotate-copy the path 180°, so that it overlaps itself. The texture will be symmetrical.

Step 5. To finish up, you might want to place a gradient behind the image, like I did in Figure 11-20.

Figure 11-20: A symmetrical texture...don't stare at this too long, or it starts to look really gross....

Scale

The Scale property changes the size of the hatch style pieces. It does *not* change the Stroke weight, however, just the size of the paths. Figure 11-21 shows sample scale settings.

Figure 11-21: Different settings for the Scale property

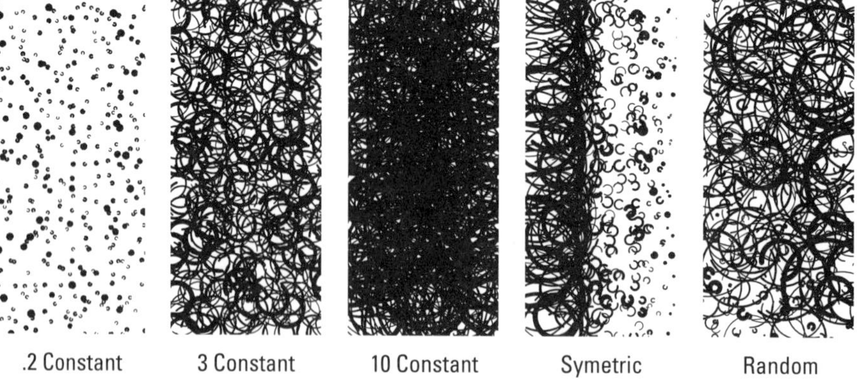

If you are going to be using "lines" that you'd like to scale uniformly (instead of just the length changing, you'd like the width to change as well), then create thin rectangles instead of single paths. That way, the width of the rectangle will increase with its length. However, the Thickness property will then have no effect on the hatch style.

Other Ink Pen Fill Controls

There are several other controls that determine how your Fill interacts with the background. These controls are located in the lower-right of the Ink Pen Fill dialog box.

Select the hatch style you'd like to use in the Hatch pop-up menu. The hatch color can be Native (the color of the original paths when they were created as a hatch) or the color of the Fill of the selected path. The Background color of the original object can be the color of the original path or a Fill of None by changing the Background pop-up menu. The Fade pop-up controls the fade of the hatch style. The Fade Angle option controls the angle of the fade.

Figure 11-22 shows two examples of the Fade to White option with the background (a gradient) and no background.

Figure 11-22: Fade to white with a gradient background and no background

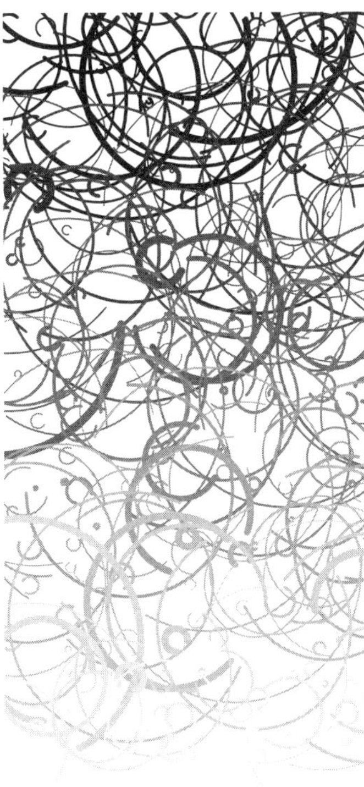

Summary

- Patterns are a type of fill that provides texture to any path.
- Several default patterns are supplied with Illustrator, and these patterns can be transformed in the same ways that other Illustrator objects can be transformed.
- Almost anything in Illustrator can be used as a pattern, with the exception of masks, gradients, placed images, and other patterns.
- Diagonal line patterns can be created by creating a horizontal line pattern and then rotating it by using the rotate tool while the pattern is filling a path.
- Graphs can be created in Illustrator just by entering the data.
- After a graph has been created, it can be adjusted and manipulated like any other path-based object.
- Textures can be created with the Ink Pen Fill command.

PART III

Filters

The Filter menu in Illustrator is unlike any menu in any other program. It can be remotely compared to the filters in Photoshop. However, because Illustrator is vector based, the comparison falls short.

This part will take you on a journey of discovery into all the filters that Illustrator has to offer. More importantly, you will understand how and when to use these filters, as well as which filters are really useful and which ones are just for "fun."

Filter Basics

CHAPTER 12

In This Chapter

- An overview of filters
- Filters in Illustrator compared to filters in Photoshop
- Moving and using the Plug-Ins folder
- FPUs and the special Pathfinder and object filters
- Using filter combinations
- The mysterious Last Filter option

Adobe introduced Illustrator filters back in Version 5.0. Most users of Illustrator expected Photoshop-type filters and were a little disappointed with the Illustrator filters. Actually, the only filters that are like Photoshop filters are the Distort filters and a few of the Stylize filters.

Filters in Illustrator

Instead of just changing the appearance of images, most of the filters in Illustrator perform tasks that took hours to do manually in previous versions of Illustrator. In a way, most of these filters work as intelligent macros, and they enable you to produce a variety of effects.

Some filters, such as the Unite filter, seem to perform quite simple tasks. In reality, however, these filters are complex, math-based programs that accomplish certain tasks faster than the fastest illustrator could dream of performing without them.

So why are all these functions in the Filter menu, and not just functions within the software? Because none of them are really integrated into Illustrator; instead, each filter is an individual file called a *Plug-In*, which resides in the Plug-Ins folder. For a filter to be available, the Plug-In must be in the Plug-Ins folder.

After using filters supplied with Illustrator, I can't imagine how I used Illustrator before they were part of the software package. I use the Select filters religiously, and the Pathfinder Divide Stroke filter enabled me to do trapping for color separations in Version 5.0 so fast that it was all a blur. Outline Stroked Path opens up a world of possibilities by enabling me to change Strokes into Filled paths. I use the Roughen filter to give Illustrator documents a bitmapped quality (I have my reasons). The Adjust Colors filter makes color adjustment incredibly simple.

Version 5.5 added several filters that I would now be hard-pressed to do without as well. Instead of the Divide Stroke filter, the Trap filter (along with the Overprint filter) automates all areas of trapping, providing a much-needed function to one of the few areas of Illustrator that had been sorely lacking. The Document Info filter makes it easier than ever to take Illustrator files from system to system, or to have those files output at a service bureau. The combination of new text filters makes Illustrator's text functions rival that of page layout software.

Adobe, in its marketing wisdom, initially pushed two filters with grunge-like names: Punk and Bloat. To be honest, I rarely use either of these filters, though I was quite intrigued the first time I saw them demonstrated. Cool names, little functionality. The same thing applies to the Twirl filter, which produces some really amazing effects. But once again, I don't use it very much (but I do use it more than the Punk and Bloat brothers). Yet I understand Adobe's marketing: I certainly wasn't that excited at first about the Select filters in comparison to these and other Distort filters.

New Filters in 6

There are several new filters in Illustrator 6 that add various new forms of functionality to Illustrator. Several of the 5.x filters have been combined and moved out of the filter menu into other menus. Some of the 5.x filters are now tools as well as filters.

New in version 6 are: Path Patterns, which places patterns on paths; Zig Zag, which transforms paths by zig zagging them; and Cleanup, which gets rid of annoying Illustrator elements.

Color Plate 3-1

This illustration was created out of many basic shapes. Only a few blends and gradients were used. Each shape was given a unique color in order to create highlights and detail. Several overlapping pieces were used for each section. Note the detail in the individual characters that surround the main character.

Step 1: The basic shapes for the character's head are drawn with the Pen tool. Slight curves are used so that the edges, while dramatic, don't appear too rigid.

Step 2: Additional pieces are added to enrich the shape of the character.

Step 3: Detail is added, still using the Pen tool. At this point many shapes will have to be moved forward or backward so that the smaller pieces are in front of the larger ones they overlap.

Step 4: The final rendering of the character in full color.

Step 1: Create two vertical rectangles. Use Option-Copy to make a duplicate of the rectangle on the left. Move the duplicate rectangle to the right.

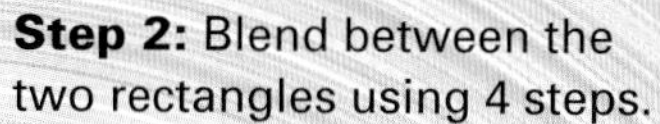

Step 2: Blend between the two rectangles using 4 steps.

Step 3: Color each of the rectangles differently. Make sure that there is a drastic color change between the side-by-side rectangles.

Step 4: Blend each set of rectangles together. Use 50 steps between each pair, regardless of what Illustrator recommends.

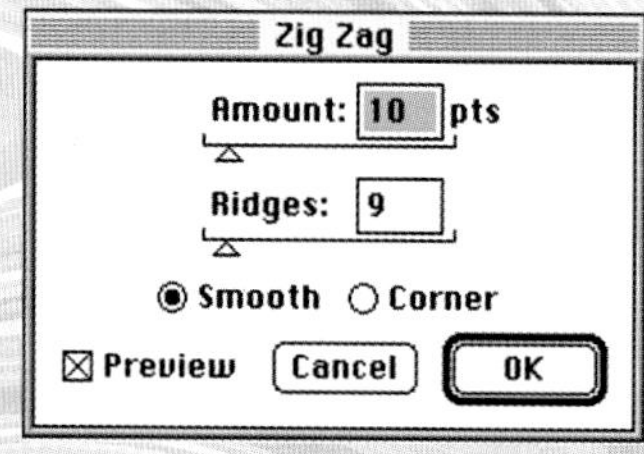

Step 5: Apply the Zig Zag filter, choosing the Smooth option.

Step 6: The result of Zig Zagging on the blend.

Step 7: Using KPT ColorTweak, change the Hue to 50%, and check the Randomize option.

Step 8: Create the mask object and position it over the blend.

Step 9: Select the masking object and the blend. From the Object menu, choose Masks and then Make.

Color Plate 14-1: Steps for creating a random wavy-colored gradient fill. The cards at the bottom show two different distortions applied to a blend. The card on the left uses the Zig Zag filter, while the card on the right uses the Twirl filter.

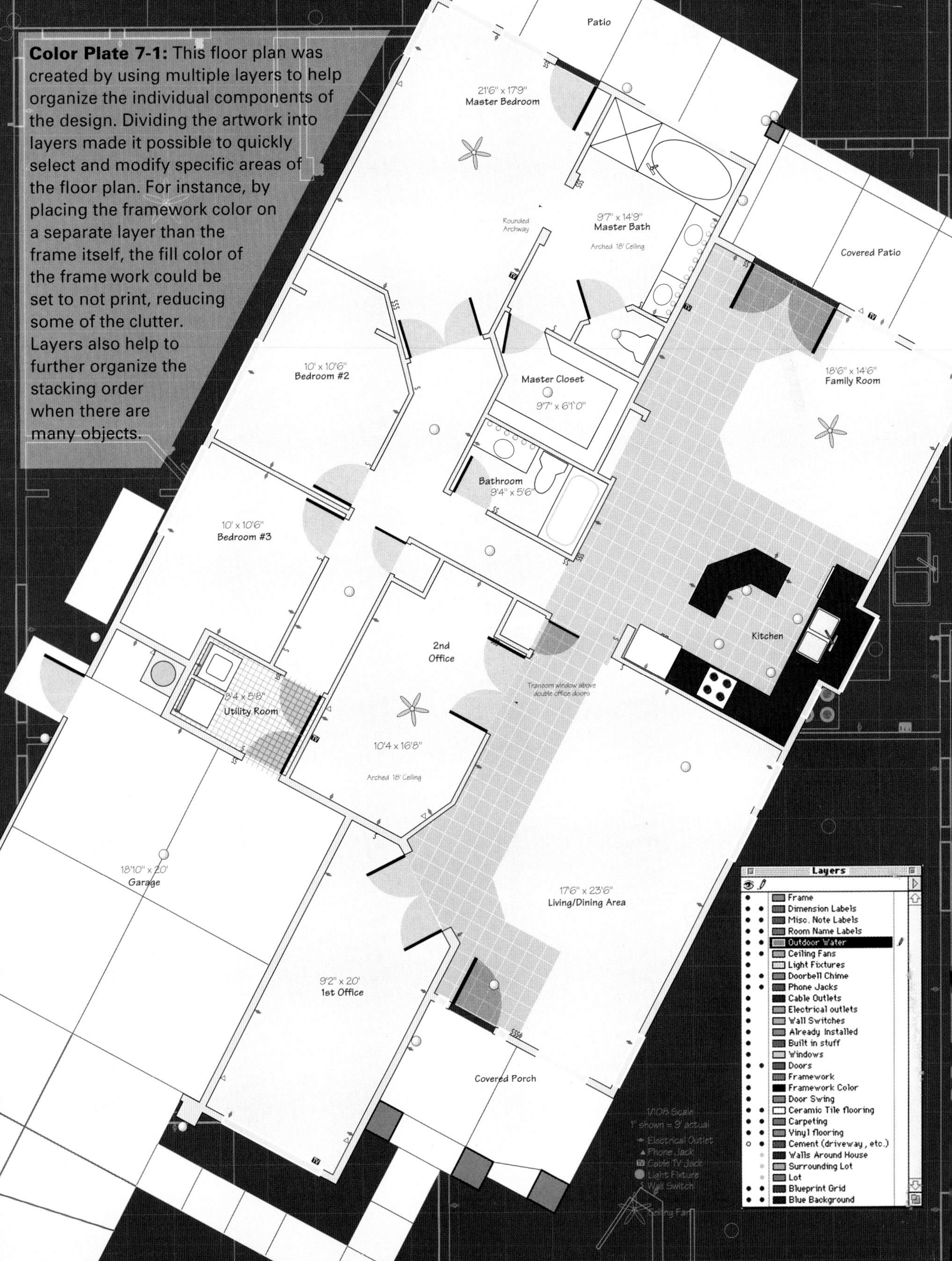

Color Plate 7-1: This floor plan was created by using multiple layers to help organize the individual components of the design. Dividing the artwork into layers made it possible to quickly select and modify specific areas of the floor plan. For instance, by placing the framework color on a separate layer than the frame itself, the fill color of the frame work could be set to not print, reducing some of the clutter. Layers also help to further organize the stacking order when there are many objects.

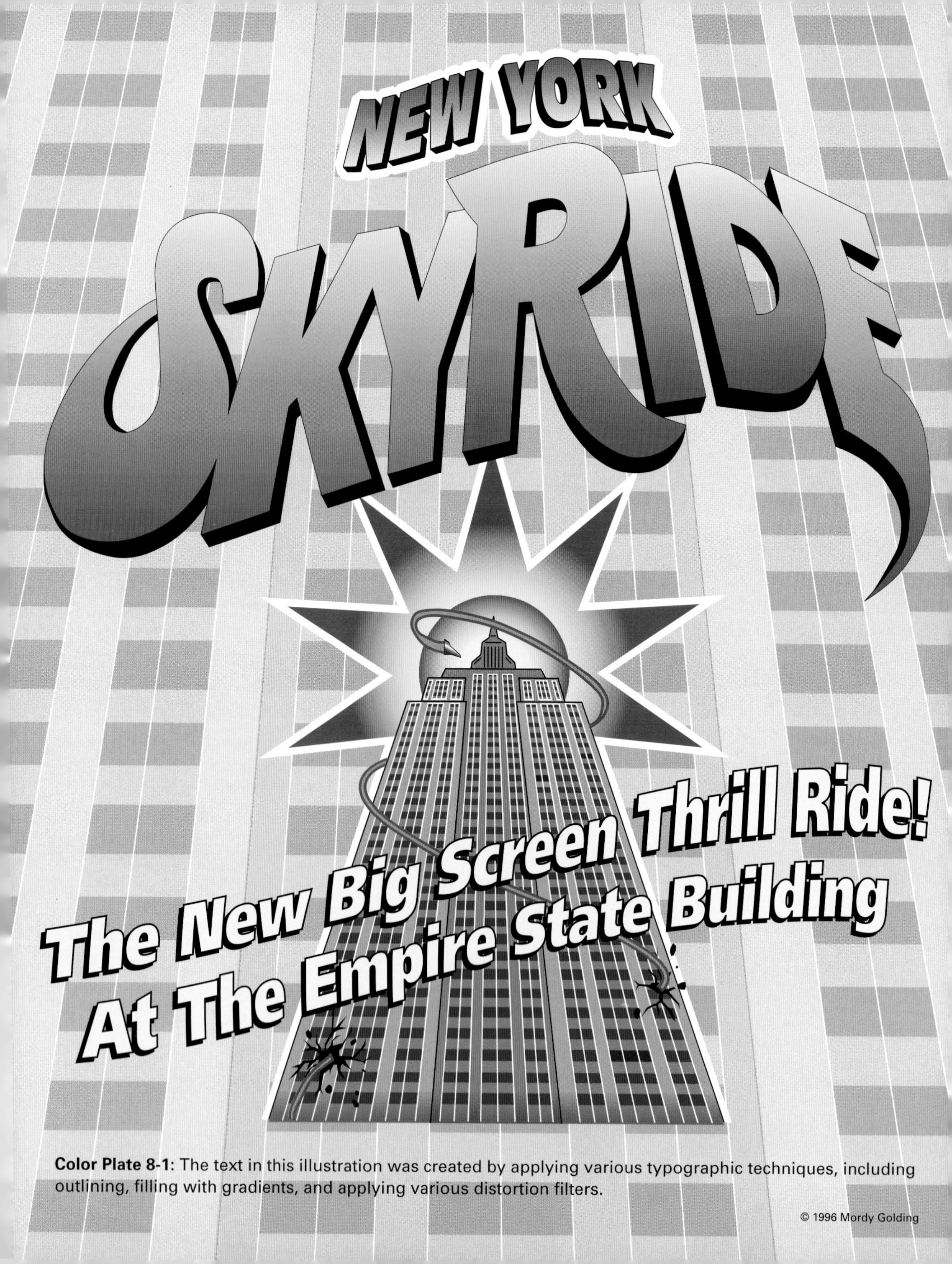

NEW YORK

SKYRIDE

The New Big Screen Thrill Ride!
At The Empire State Building

Color Plate 8-1: The text in this illustration was created by applying various typographic techniques, including outlining, filling with gradients, and applying various distortion filters.

Color Plate 8-2: This logo was created by rotating type around the path of a circle, as shown in the steps below. The bubbles in the "CHO" logo are custom radial gradients. The cans were revolved shapes from Adobe Dimensions. Artwork from Illustrator was applied to them in Dimensions. Afterwards, they were copied and pasted back into Illustrator.

Step 1: Draw a circle (use the Shift key).

Step 2: Click on the top of the circle with the Path Type tool, and type the text for the top of the circle.

Step 3: Press Ô-Shift-C to center the text at the top of the circle (or where you clicked).

Step 4: Click on the I-bar at the top of the circle and drag it to the bottom until the type looks exactly the same as the type above. Press and hold the Option key before releasing.

Step 5: Change the type on the bottom.

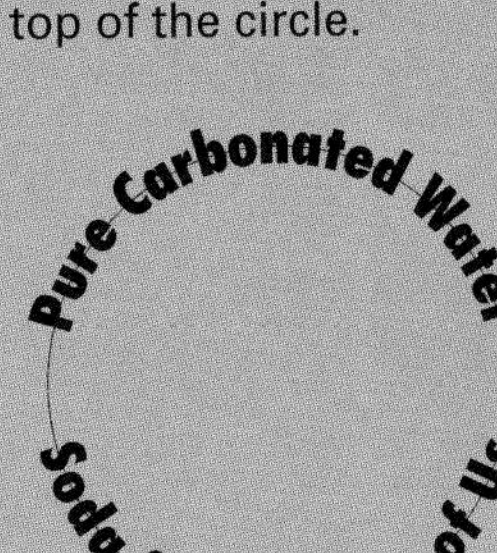

Step 6: Using Baseline Shift, move the type to the center of the path.

Step 7: Rotate both text paths if necessary.

Step 8: Draw another circle the same size as the text circles, and stroke it with a color.

Color Plate 9-1: The "Cactus Race" portion was created by overlapping text outlines onto a rectangle and then making a compound path out of both outlines and rectangle. The center logo was then added. To simulate the flag motion, KPT Warp Frame was applied to the flag. An additional gradient was created for the white flag background to add depth to the flag.

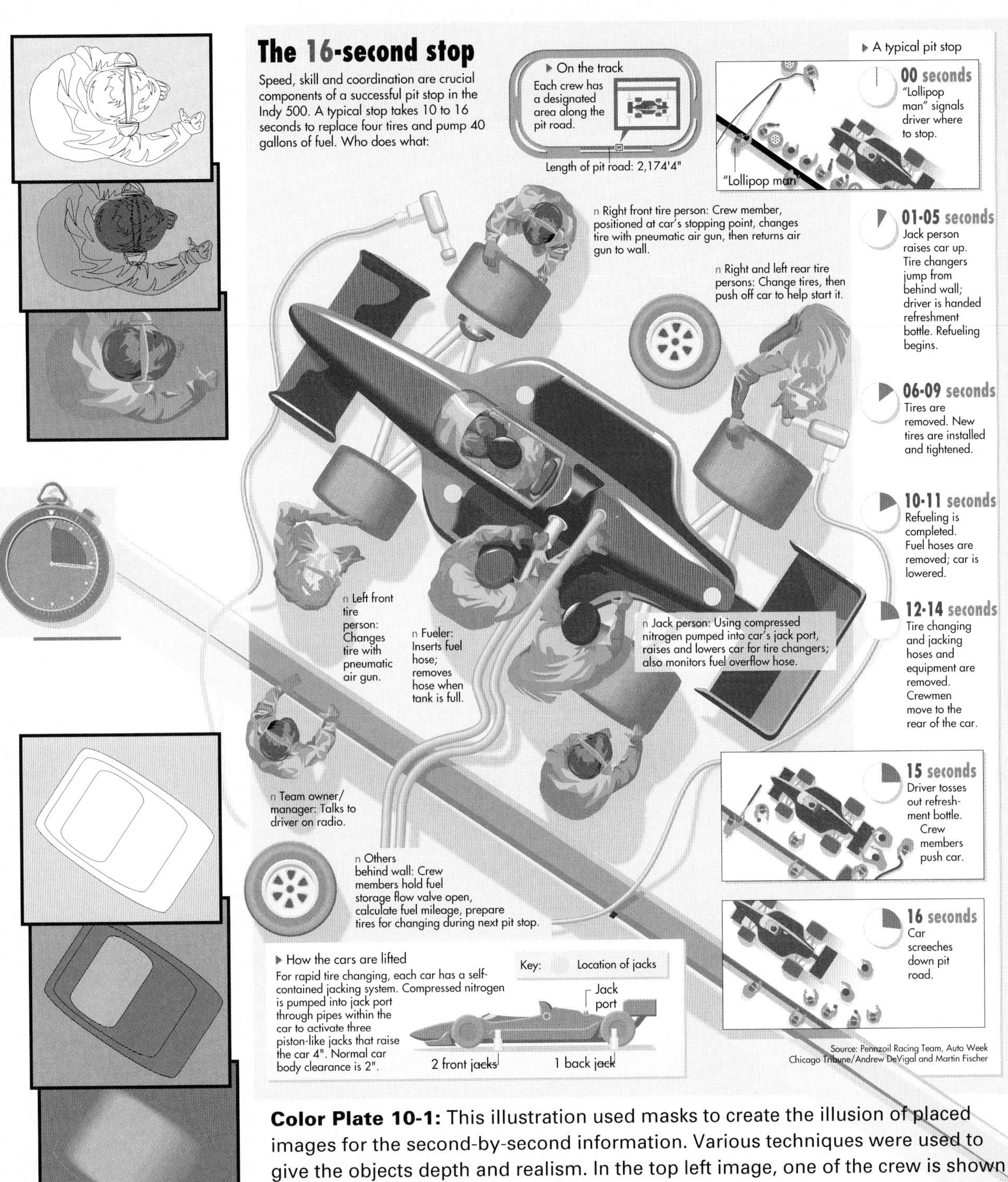

Color Plate 10-1: This illustration used masks to create the illusion of placed images for the second-by-second information. Various techniques were used to give the objects depth and realism. In the top left image, one of the crew is shown in artwork mode, after the outer edges have been filled in and the detail has been colored. The lower left image shows how the tires were blended together to create the illusion of a smoothly curving tire.

Illustration by Andrew DeVigal

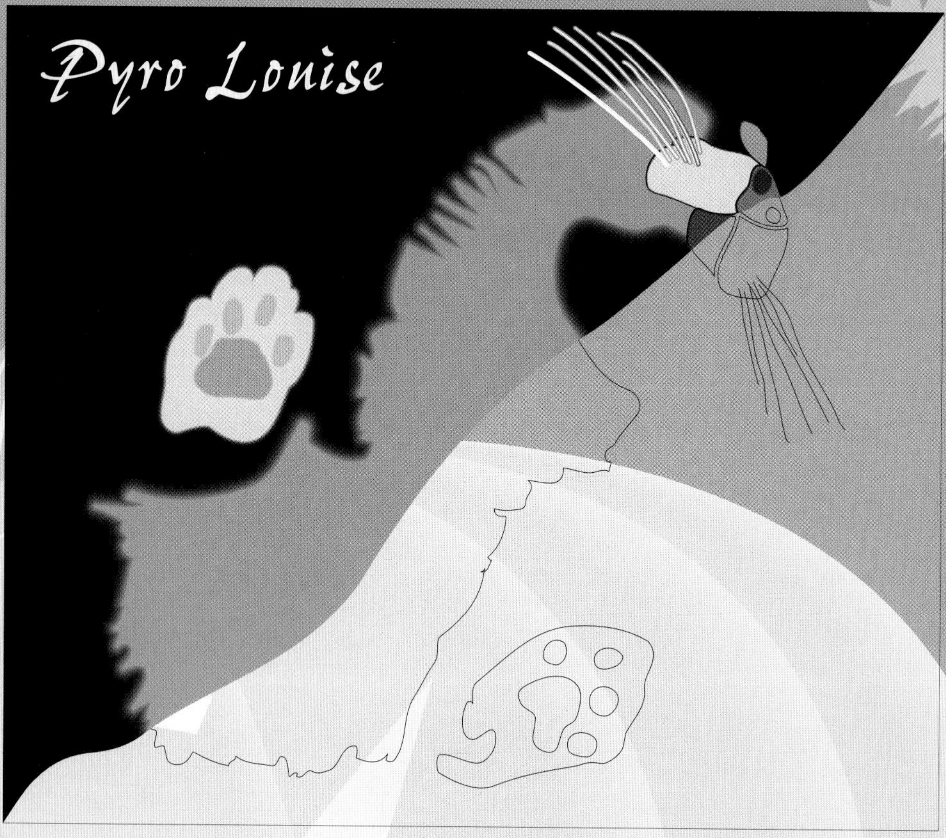

Color Plate 10-2

"Catscan" uses various stroke blends to achieve a natural, almost fuzzy look. The cutaway section (lower right) shows the paths in Artwork mode. Note how the stroke blends perfectly overlap each other, keeping the artwork tidy.

The neon whiskers were created with KPT Neon.

Color Plate 10-3

This image (which was originally intended for a holiday greeting card for...maybe Christmas?) consists entirely of blends, but no gradients, to achieve the effect. Artwork view (not shown) reveals an opaque mess of paths. Even the background is a blend from one rectangle to another.

Color Plate 21-1

"Lucy" was created by converting a PhotoCD image into a TIFF file in Photoshop, then taking that image and streamlining it with Adobe Streamline. After opening the file in Illustrator, highlights were added to the white, blown-out areas to give them more visual interest. The brightest colors were tinted with a bit of Cyan and Magenta, giving Lucy a purplish hue.

Color Plate 21-2

"Linus" was created in a manner similar to Lucy, except that the number of colors was limited to 16. After the outlined image was brought into Illustrator, each color was selected. Next, the Select Same Fill Color filter was applied, and the selected paths were grouped and locked. Each set of same-colored paths were grouped as well. Finally, each group was selected and then a different pastel color was applied.

Color Plate 10-5

These images use multiple gradients to achieve a glowing ethereal effect (above) and a shiny metallic effect (left). Different gradients, including radial and linear, were used with similar but different values to give the artwork a sense of texture. Chapter 8 discusses gradients in detail.

© 1996 Mordy Golding

Step 1: Type Option-Shift-K.

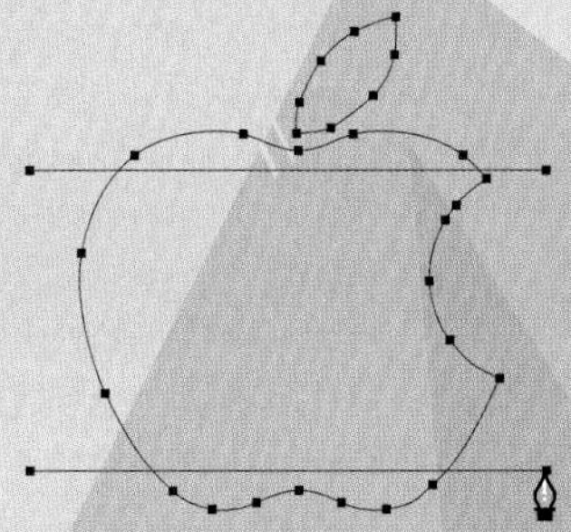

Step 2: Create Outlines, then draw two horizontal paths.

Step 3: Blend between paths.

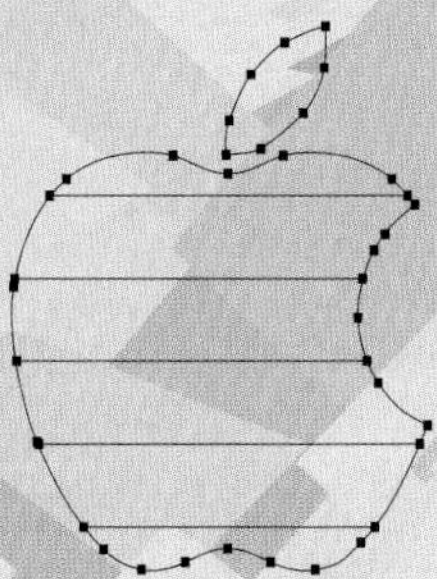

Step 4: Divide.

Color Plate 15-1: This apple was created by following the steps on this page. Substitute drawing several paths and using the Divide filter if you don't have KPT Shatterbox.

Step 5: Ungroup and then paint.

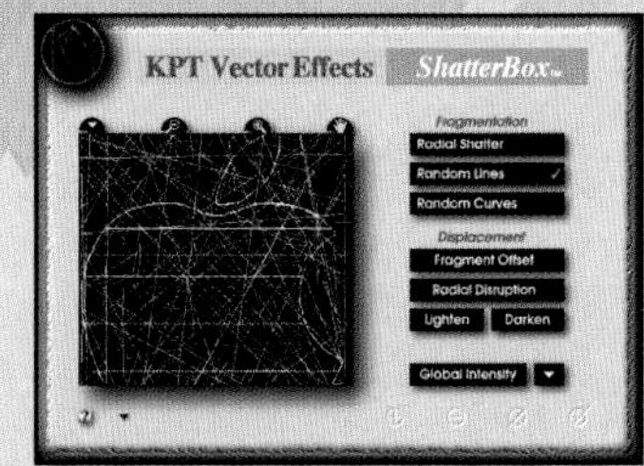

Step 6: Use KPT ShatterBox or Divide filter.

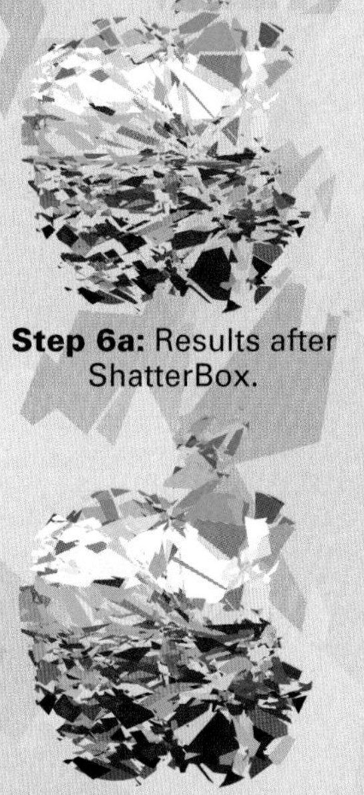

Step 6a: Results after ShatterBox.

Step 7: Transform each path with Scale and Rotate.

Step 8: Apply Mix Soft at 100%.

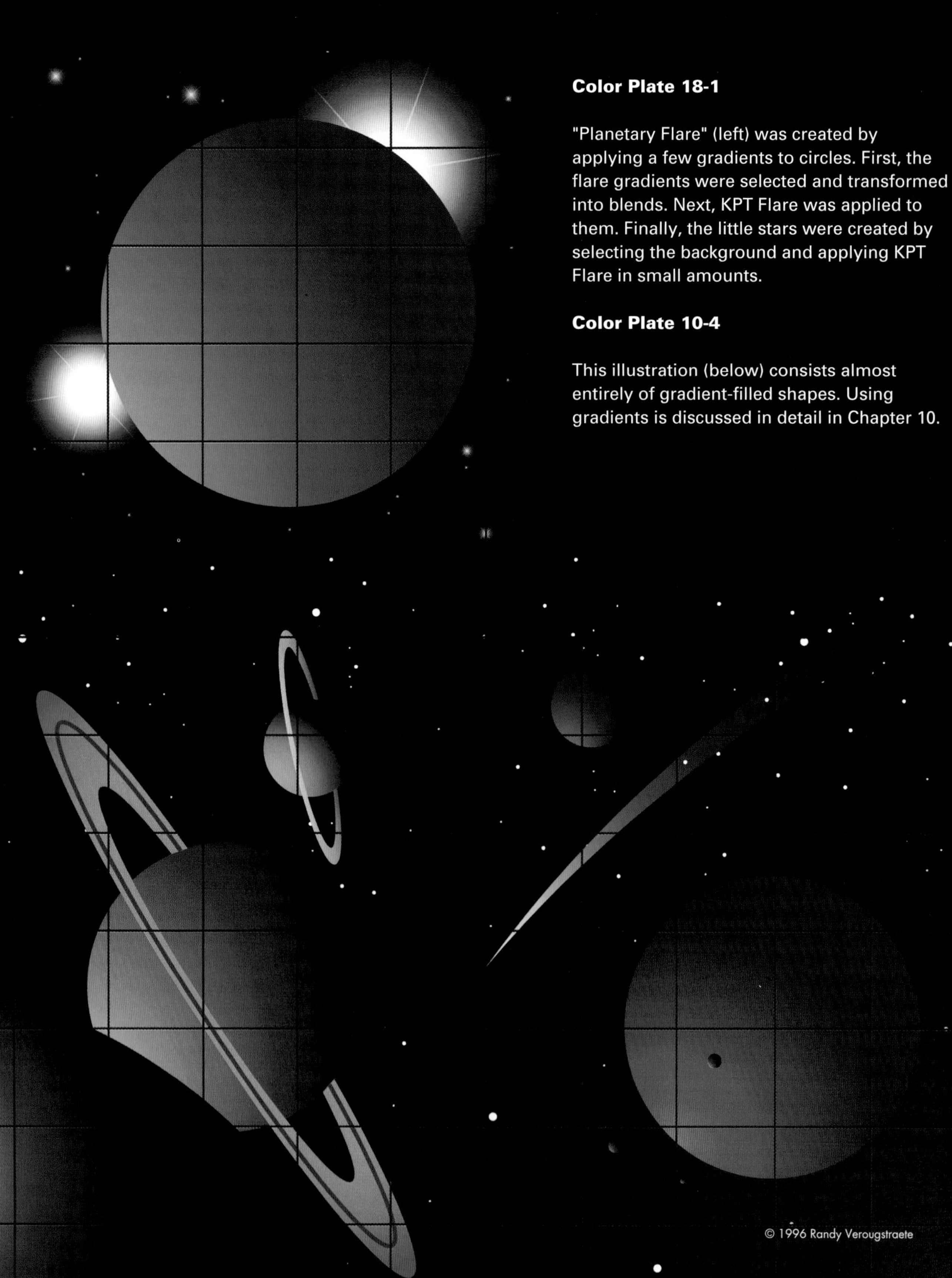

Color Plate 18-1

"Planetary Flare" (left) was created by applying a few gradients to circles. First, the flare gradients were selected and transformed into blends. Next, KPT Flare was applied to them. Finally, the little stars were created by selecting the background and applying KPT Flare in small amounts.

Color Plate 10-4

This illustration (below) consists almost entirely of gradient-filled shapes. Using gradients is discussed in detail in Chapter 10.

Color Plate 7-2 (top six images): These images compare the differences between Illustrator format (left), Photoshop without anti-aliasing (center), and Photoshop with anti-aliasing (right).

Color Plate 17-1 (left): Type was created in Illustrator, changed to outlines, manipulated, and copied. The original paths were turned into pixel-based objects with the Rasterize command. Kai's Power Tools 3.0 Texture Explorer was then used to create the textures within the letter shapes. Finally, the Rasterized artwork was dragged into a Photoshop document and touched up.

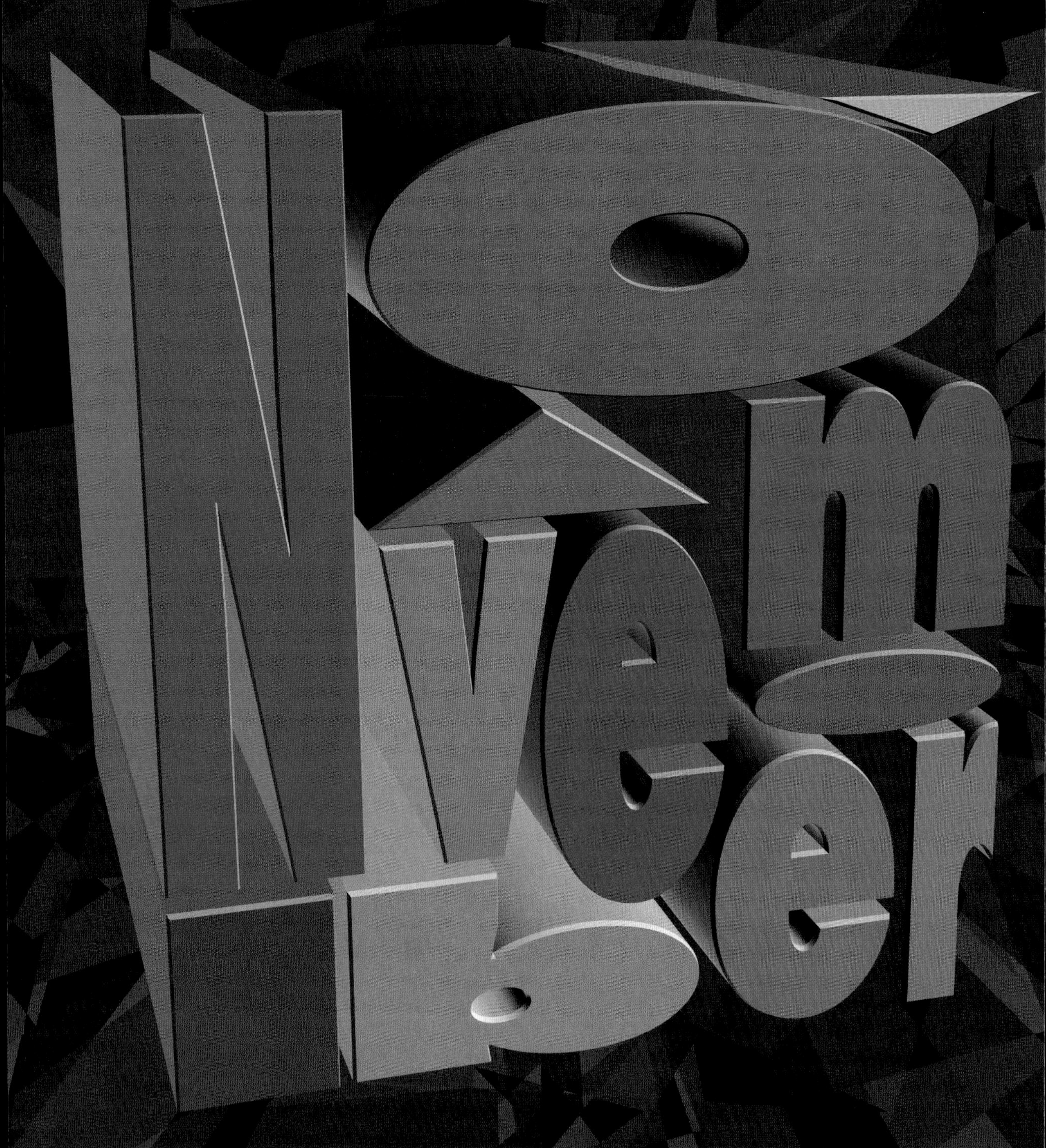

Color Plate 18-2: The word "November" was created in a large bold font and then converted to outlines. Each of the letters was scaled and moved into position. Extra shapes were added to fill in larger empty areas. After the text outlines and shapes were selected, the Round Corners filter was applied at 6 points, giving the corners a nice smooth look. The outlines and shapes were extruded in KPT 3D Transform with a 70% perspective. A small bevel was applied to further enhance the "soft" look of the letters. The background was created by applying a 200 Straightline shatter from KPT ShatterBox. To make the size of the file more manageable, the middle shattered paths were selected and removed, reducing the file size from over 5MB to just over 1.5MB.

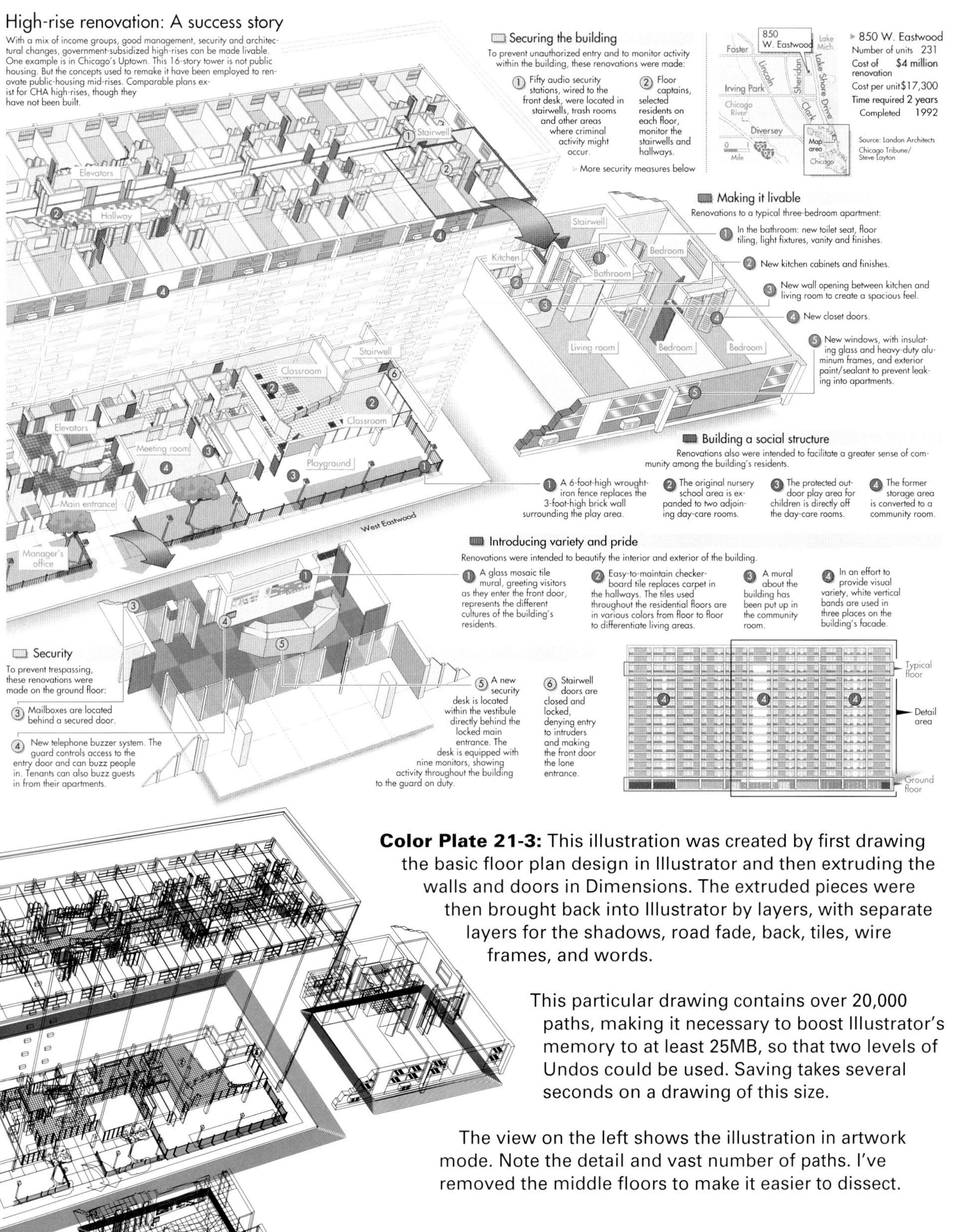

Color Plate 21-3: This illustration was created by first drawing the basic floor plan design in Illustrator and then extruding the walls and doors in Dimensions. The extruded pieces were then brought back into Illustrator by layers, with separate layers for the shadows, road fade, back, tiles, wire frames, and words.

This particular drawing contains over 20,000 paths, making it necessary to boost Illustrator's memory to at least 25MB, so that two levels of Undos could be used. Saving takes several seconds on a drawing of this size.

The view on the left shows the illustration in artwork mode. Note the detail and vast number of paths. I've removed the middle floors to make it easier to dissect.

Illustration by Steve Layton

Color Plate 10-6: It's hard to believe that this athletic shoe was created using only Illustrator, but that's the sort of magic that only the wizards at Thomas Bradley Illustration and Design can create. The lower half of the page consists of six steps for creating the fabric texture that surrounds the heel of the sneaker. To give this portion of the shoe some depth, a shape blend was created within itself, consisting of three basic shades and five shapes. The blends were created with less than the "recommended" number of steps to keep the file size down; because of the overlapping texture, additional steps would be overkill. The texture was created by placing criss-crossed dashed strokes above the blend, then masking out the edges with the copy of the original shape.

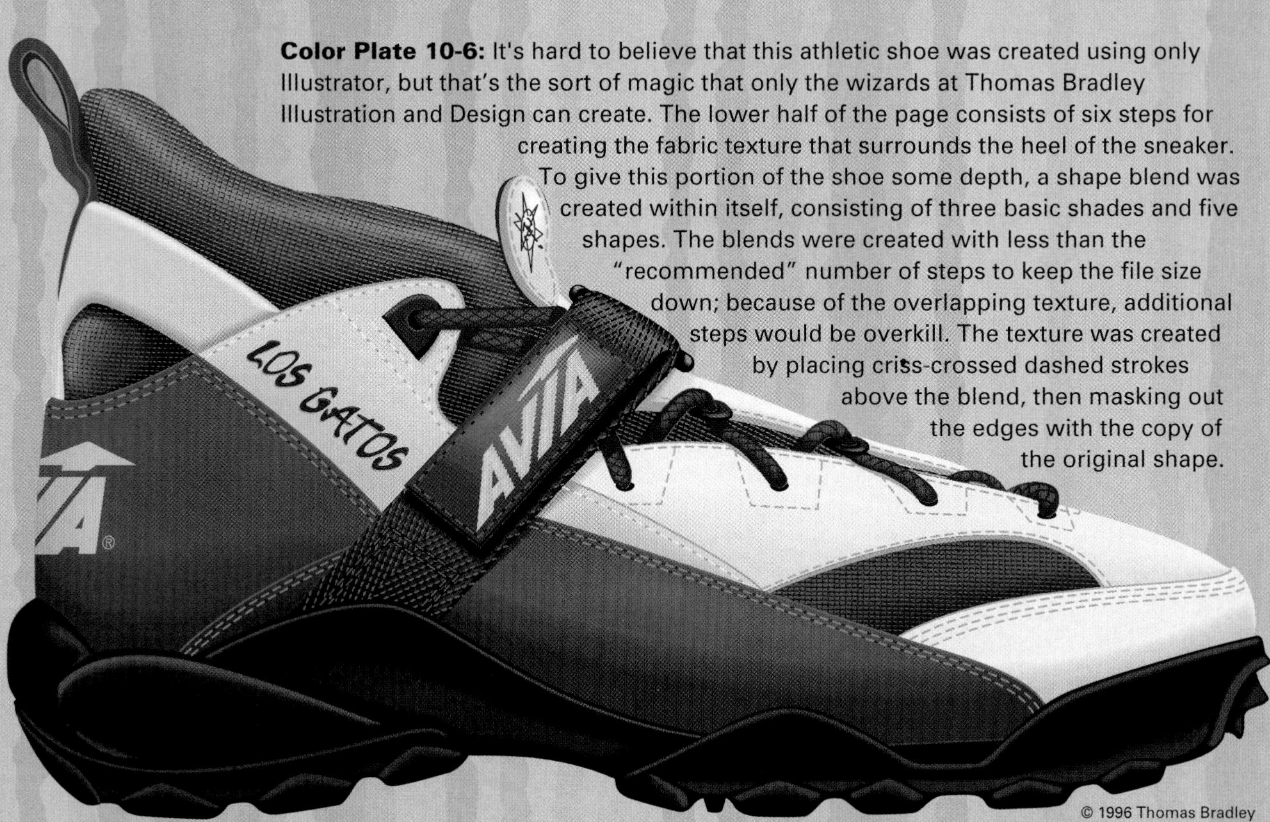

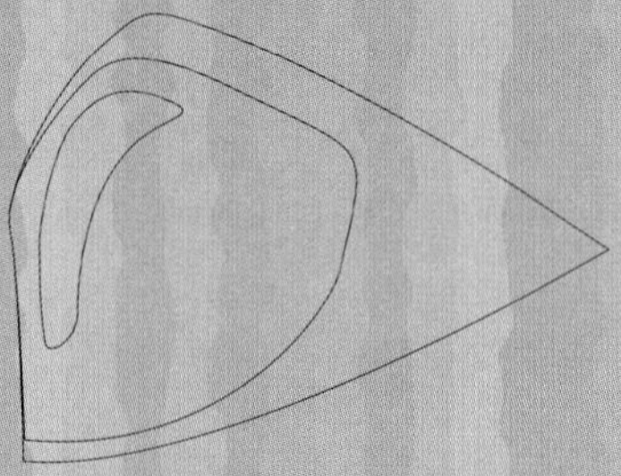

Step 1: Three basic blend shapes are drawn with the Pen tool.

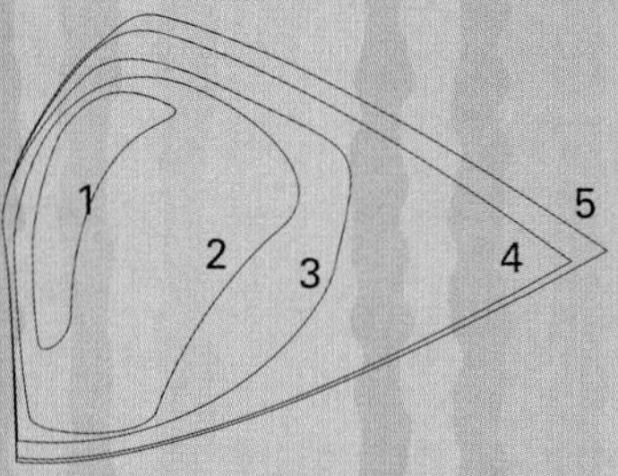

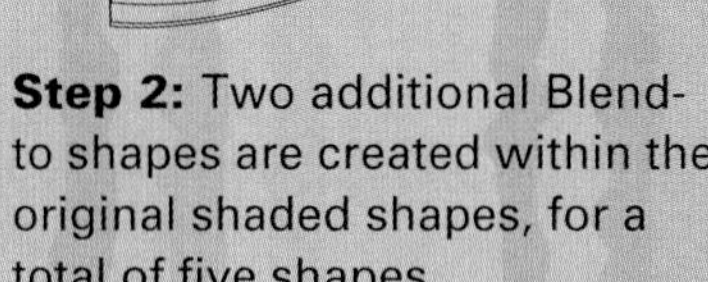

Step 2: Two additional Blend-to shapes are created within the original shaded shapes, for a total of five shapes.

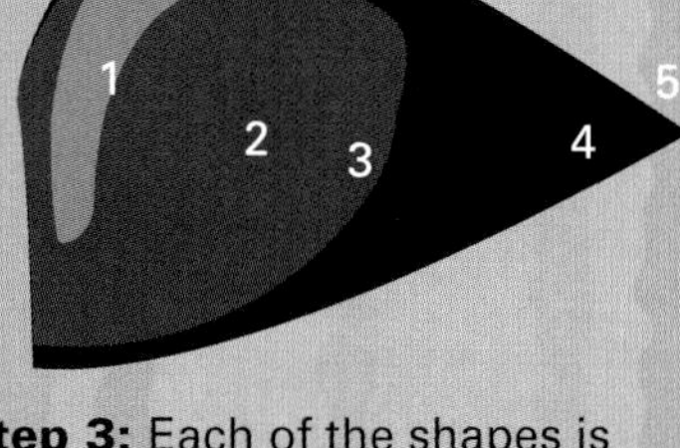

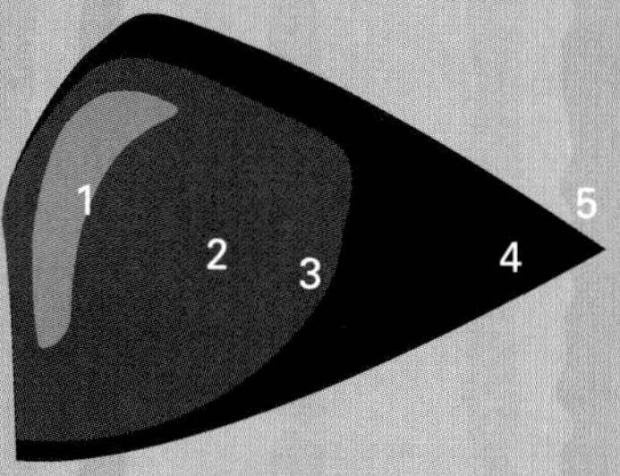

Step 3: Each of the shapes is colored. The second and fourth shapes are colored the same as the third and fifth shapes.

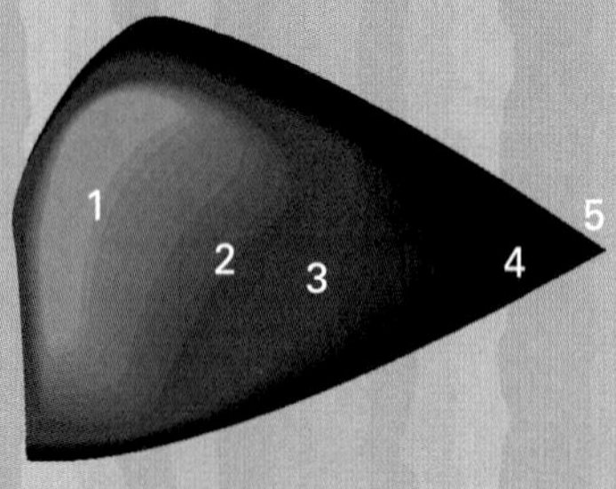

Step 4: The first and second shapes are blended together, while the third and fourth shapes are blended together.

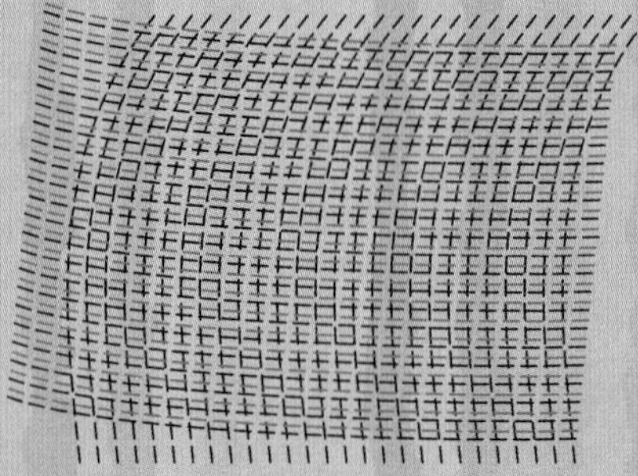

Step 5: Dotted lines are created to mimic fabric.

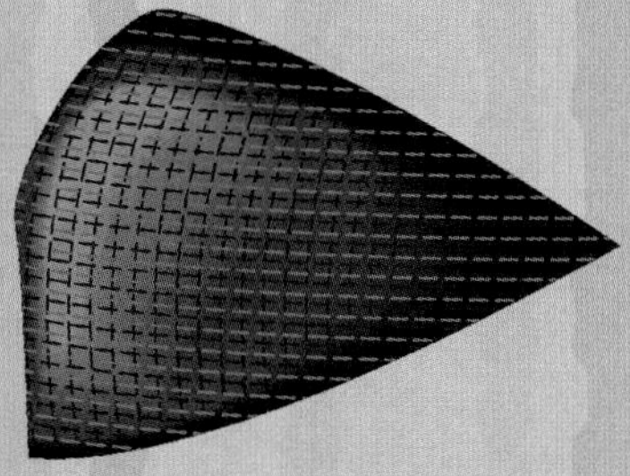

Step 6: The dotted lines are masked and placed over the blended shapes.

And of course, the biggest change is that Photoshop filters now work inside of Illustrator. That means that the included Gallery Effects filters, as well as any other third-party filters, like Kai's Power Tools 3 and CSI Photolab can be used in Adobe Illustrator 6.

A Bazillion Filters That No One Uses

Illustrator users don't use the filters enough.

Most users of Illustrator don't use filters because they're unfamiliar with them, or uncertain of their usefulness. Many people don't know when to use the filters in a real-life drawing situation. And the sheer number of the darn things is also daunting. It wouldn't be so bad if there were 10 filters, or even 20. But Illustrator 5.0 shipped with 57 filters, and the number has been growing ever since. That's right, most ordinary people don't have even that many fingers and toes to count 'em on.

If the number of filters isn't enough to discourage you, consider that the Illustrator 5.0 manual contains just 11 pages of information about the filters and 4 pages that illustrate what the filters do. Because I think that filters are one of the most important parts of Illustrator, I have devoted five *chapters* to discussing filters in all their glory. These chapters provide examples, tutorials, and hints on using each of the bazillion filters.

What Are Filters?

Johnny: Now, how are filters in Illustrator different from the things I use to make sure all those little black things don't get in my coffee?

Toulouse: Filters in Illustrator do all sorts of amazing things that would be really difficult or time consuming to normally do in Illustrator.

Johnny: That's nice, but then why have all the hard ways to do things in Illustrator, if you've got these filters hanging around?

Toulouse: A good example is the Unite filter. It takes all the selected paths and merges them into one path, getting rid of all the overlapping areas.

Johnny: Wouldn't the *easy* thing be to just draw paths that don't overlap in the first place? Seems you'd save a lot of time drawing all those paths in the first place if you knew you only wanted one.

Toulouse: You don't always know that ahead of time.

Johnny: Sounds like an operator-error to me....

Comparing and Contrasting Illustrator and Photoshop Filters

The filters in Illustrator have to be different from the filters in Photoshop because Illustrator deals with vector-based images and Photoshop works with bitmapped graphics. Many electronic artists use Photoshop as a staple of their graphics work. For them, the word *filter* conjures up thoughts of blurring and sharpening, as well as some of the fantastic effects that they can achieve by using filters from third parties, such as Kai's Power Tools or Aldus's Gallery Effects.

The very term *filters* is based in photography terminology for special lenses that are attached to cameras to achieve special effects. Photoshop's filters are based on this concept, and they take it quite a bit further, creating controls for variety and exactness that a camera lens could never match.

For this reason, "filter" isn't really the best term for the manipulations that Illustrator performs when you choose a filter. The following list compares some of the Illustrator filters with their Photoshop counterparts that perform similar functions:

- Illustrator: Filter⇨Create⇨Mosaic
  Photoshop: Filter⇨Stylize⇨Mosaic

  The Mosaic filters take bitmap images and reduce the number of colored areas to large, single-colored squares.

  These two filters produce results that are the most alike of any of the Illustrator and Photoshop filters. The dialog boxes are a little different, but the results are functionally the same. One big difference is that stylizing a mosaic in Photoshop is a fairly fast procedure, but creating a mosaic in Illustrator is a complex task that eats up tons of RAM and can take up to ten minutes to complete.

- Illustrator: Filter⇨Distort⇨Twirl
  Photoshop: Filter⇨Distort⇨Twirl

  Twirling spins an object or picture more in the center than around the edges.

  Both Twirl filters do about the same thing, but the result in Illustrator depends on the number of Anchor Points in the drawing. A greater number of Anchor Points creates a better effect, and a lesser number of points creates a choppy, poor effect. Photoshop's filter depends on the image resolution, but to a lesser extent than do Illustrator-specific filters.

- Illustrator: Filter⇨Distort⇨Free Distort
  Photoshop: Image⇨Effects⇨Distort

  Distorting gives you the ability to move the four corners of a selected object/picture to any new location, changing the perspective or just plain mangling the original object/picture.

  A boon for Illustrator users, the Free Distort filter makes tedious perspective gridwork a thing of the past. Photoshop's Distort feature is not a filter per se but rather part of the Image control subsection.

- Illustrator: Filter⇨Select⇨Inverse
  Photoshop: Select⇨Inverse

  Selecting the inverse means that objects/portions of the picture that are not selected become selected, and objects/portions of the picture that are selected become deselected.

  In Photoshop, Inverse is not a filter but a capability built into the Select menu. In Illustrator, the Inverse filter selects objects that are not selected; in Photoshop, the Inverse feature selects pixels that are not selected.

- Illustrator: Filter⇨Select⇨Same Fill Color
  Photoshop: Select⇨Similar

  Selecting objects that are the same color is useful for changing all objects that are a certain color, and both programs enable you to perform this function. The Similar feature in Photoshop is not a filter but a capability built into the Select menu. Photoshop's Similar feature is much more flexible than Illustrator's Same Fill Color filter because the Similar feature enables you to select different colors at the same time.

Some features that you would expect to do the same thing in each program are not the same:

- Illustrator: Filter⇨Colors⇨Invert Colors
  Photoshop: Image⇨Map⇨Invert

  Illustrator's Invert Colors filter is annoying because you expect a negative image but don't get it. Instead, you get Cyan, Magenta, and Yellow values that have been subtracted from 100, and a Black value that is untouched. Photoshop's Invert command creates a true negative, and it is a feature, not a filter.

- Illustrator: Filter⇨Colors⇨Saturate
  Photoshop: Image⇨Adjust⇨Hue/Saturation

  The saturation filter in Illustrator increase/decrease the CMYK values for selected objects. In Photoshop, the color intensity is increased. Saturation in Illustrator is a misnomer, at least when compared to the functionality of Saturation in most other software packages.

No Plug-Ins!!!!

Scott: I don't have any Plug-Ins.

Toulouse: Yikes!

Scott: And lots of other stuff is missing.

Toulouse: Such as...

Scott: Well, the Align palette, the Plug-In tools, and the Control palette. All my menus seem shorter.

Toulouse: It looks like you've misplaced your Plug-Ins folder.

Scott: Uh-oh.

Toulouse: Not a problem. Just choose File⇨Preferences⇨Plug-Ins, and find your Plug-Ins folder.

Scott: And that's it?

Toulouse: Well, you'll need to restart Illustrator. Just quit and run it again, and your Plug-Ins will all be in place!

The Plug-Ins Folder

All of the filters in Illustrator are in the Filter menu because a file with the same name as the filter is in the Plug-Ins folder. If the filter's file is not in the Plug-Ins folder, the filter will not appear in the Filter menu.

The Plug-Ins folder is put inside the first level of the Adobe Illustrator folder when Illustrator is installed. If you move the folder, you need to tell Illustrator where it is located.

STEPS: Relocating the Plug-Ins Folder

Step 1. In the Finder, with Illustrator *not* running, move or copy the Plug-Ins folder to the desired location.

Step 2. Double-click the Illustrator icon.

Step 3. Choose File⇨Preferences⇨Plug-Ins.

Step 4. In the Plug-Ins dialog box, find the Plug-Ins folder and click the Select button at the bottom of the dialog box.

Step 5. Quit Illustrator and double-click the Illustrator icon to restart Illustrator. The new Plug-Ins folder location is now used.

There are several Plug-Ins that are not located in the folder called Plug-Ins. These files are located in the Optional Plug-Ins folder, and include Artwork View Speedup (which isn't a filter at all but a way to reduce the screen redraw speed marginally in Artwork View by making all selected points black rather than the layer color), Custom to Process (added to the Color Filters submenu), Overprint (added to the Other Filters submenu), and Revert Text Path (added to the Text Filters submenu). Many of these filters are discussed in detail later in this chapter. The FPU Plug-Ins folder is also located in this folder.

Cytopia Software's Socket Set 1 includes a handy Plug-In manager, which allows you to set up "sets" of plug-ins for Illustrator. See Chapter 18 for more info on the Socket Set filters.

The Great FPU Scare

Illustrator 6 doesn't need an FPU (Floating Point Unit) to work properly. Illustrator 5.0 needed an FPU for several of the Pathfinder filters and two object filters, but version 5.5 remedied this. With Illustrator 6, you still won't need an FPU, so it doesn't matter if you know if you have one or not.

Third-Party Filters

Several companies are currently producing third-party filters for Illustrator. In fact, companies such as Metatools, BeInfinite and Cytopia Software are producing high-profile filter sets for Illustrator.

Because Illustrator filters are taking off like wildfire, I've included an entire chapter on third-party filters, covering the above mentioned companies' filter sets. For additional information on Illustrator filters, pick up a copy of *Illustrator Filter Finesse,* which contains all sorts of Illustrator filter information that I couldn't squeeze into this book.

Filter Combinations and Relations

No filter is an island. Filters work best when you combine them with other filters. In fact, their functionality increases geometrically.

The following filters work well together:

- **Select Mask with Create Stroke & Fill for Mask:** These filters are natural buddies. Selecting a mask can be difficult, and if your eventual goal is to Fill or Stroke the mask, using these filters in tandem can move things right along.

- **Add Anchor Points (or Roughen at 0%) with Distort and Stylize filters:** Most of the Distort filters, especially Twirl, give better results when an object has significantly more points than you originally gave it. Punk and Bloat also look better with more points.
- **Offset Path with Unite:** Unite zaps all the little skittles (tiny bumps and irregularities) that appear when you use the Offset Path filter.
- **Add Arrowheads with Outline Path and Unite:** Create the arrows, outline the original path, Select All, and select Filter⇨Pathfinder⇨Unite to create one object. You can set up a QuicKey for these filters.

Holy Coincidences, Batman!

This is quite amusing. In the last edition of this book, I included the following section on filters I thought "belonged together."

Some filters are variations of other filters. The following filters are related:

- **Align Objects with Distribute Horizontally and Distribute Vertically:** Within Align Objects are controls for using both Distribute Horizontally and Distribute Vertically, even at the same time.
- **Bloat with Punk:** These two filters are opposites of each other. A negative Bloat is a Punk, and a negative Punk is a Bloat. Either way, they still have way cool names.
- **Scribble with Tweak:** I think the engineers at Adobe were trying to pull a fast one with these two filters. Both filters do the same thing, but Scribble is defined by a percentage, and Tweak is defined by an absolute measurement. Sneaky.
- **Saturate with Desaturate; Saturate More with Desaturate More:** Opposites, but three Saturate Mores followed by three Desaturate Mores will give you something darker than the original.

Okay, so here we are, a few years later, Illustrator 6 is announced and some filters are suddenly combined:

- **Align Objects with Distribute Horizontally and Distribute Vertically:** Now under the Align palette.
- **Bloat with Punk:** Bloat and Punk. One filter.
- **Scribble with Tweak:** Now we have Scribble and Tweak.
- **Saturate with Desaturate; Saturate More with Desaturate More:** These have been combined into Saturate.

While this is all fun and dandy, the most important lesson to learn here is that the people who decide features for new versions of Illustrator aren't drones (well, some of them are, of course), and they'll actually listen to suggestions and such. So, make sure that if you have an idea for making Illustrator better, let Adobe know, either when calling their technical support or by e-mail.

Why You Can Choose the Last Filter but Never "Last Filter"

Whenever you start up Illustrator, the top menu item in the Filter menu reads "Last Filter," but it is grayed out. This causes some confusion initially. After you use a filter, its name appears where the menu once listed "Last Filter." Thereafter, the name of the last filter that you used appears at the top of the menu. The key command for reapplying the last filter is ⌘-Shift-E.

To return to the last filter's dialog box, press Option and select Filter⇨*[Name of Last Filter]*.

Old Plug-Ins?

Sigmund: I bought KPT Vector Effects and CSI Socket Sets 1 & 2 a while back, and now I've upgraded to Illustrator 6.0.

Toulouse: Wow. Sounds like you're at the forefront of Illustrator technology.

Sigmund: Actually, I wasn't sure if I could use Vector Effects or the Socket Sets with Illustrator 6.0.

Toulouse: Yes, they work just like they did in Illustrator 5.5.

Sigmund: Any differences?

Toulouse: Well, you'll notice a decidely faster performance from KPT ShatterBox, which uses Illustrator's Pathfinder filters to run. They're all native in version 6.0.

Summary

- Filters add extra functionality to Illustrator through commands in the Filter menu.
- New filters in Illustrator 6.0 are Path Patterns, Zig Zag, and Cleanup.
- Several filters from previous versions of Illustrator have been combined into other filters, or changed into tools or palettes.
- To use a filter, select the artwork you wish to "filterize" and select the filter from the Filter menu.
- The hardest thing about filters is knowing what they do, and when and how to use them; the filters themselves are pretty simple.
- Many Illustrator filters have Photoshop-comparable filters.
- Third party companies have developed several filter sets for Illustrator, and more are on the way.
- You can reapply the last filter quickly by pressing ⌘-Shift-E.

The Color and Create Filters

CHAPTER 13

In This Chapter

- How the color filters work
- Using color to create highlights and shadows
- Adding and subtracting colors from multiple paths
- Blending colors, not paths
- Changing bitmap images into square vector mosaics
- Creating fills and strokes for masks

I would have loved to separate this chapter into two chapters, but Adobe went and zapped most of the Create filters from version 5. Those filters are now tools or located somewhere else inside of Illustrator. Besides, alphabetically they're close. . . .

The Color Filters

The color filters in the Color submenu of the Filter menu really take Illustrator's color capabilities to the next level in many ways. Unfortunately, they fall far short of Photoshop's color cababilities, but they're making good headway.

Adjust Colors

Adjust Colors increases and decreases process color Fills in each individual four-color part. The percentages entered in Adjust Colors are absolute changes, meaning that a 10% decrease of Cyan whenCyan is 100% will result in 90%, and a 10% decrease of

Cyan when Cyan is 50% will result in 40%, not 45%. If the increase makes the tint of a color greater than 100%, it will stay at 100%, but other colors may still increase, if they are not yet at 100%. If the decrease makes the tint of a color less than 0%, that color will remain at 0%, but other colors may still decrease, as long as they are not yet at 0%. For example, a 25% increase to both Yellow and Magenta to a path with 80% Yellow and 50% Magenta will result in the colors being 100% Yellow and 75% Magenta. Reapplying this filter will result in 100% Yellow and 100% Magenta. Reapplying this filter at this point will result in no change at all.

The Adjust Color filter is shown in Figure 13-1.

Figure 13-1: The Adjust Color dialog box

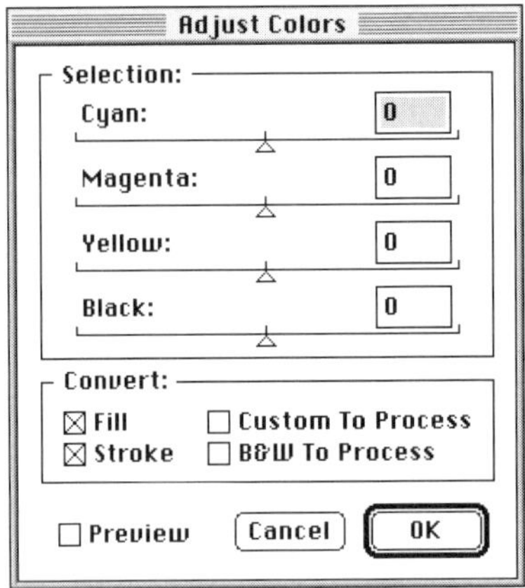

At the bottom of the Adjust Colors filter dialog box are several new options (not to mention the incorporation of sliders in the main portion). The Preview checkbox allows you to see the changes that have been applied so far. The Custom to Process and Black to Process checkboxes automatically convert custom and Illustrator Black-based colors to process equivalents.

Adjust Colors is okay for basic grunt work in Illustrator, but if you need a little more oomph, look into KPT ColorTweak, part of the KPT Vector Effects package, or CSI Adjust Colors, a filter in the Socket Set 1 filter set from Cytopia. These filters are discussed in detail in Chapter 18.

The Color Blend Filters

Blend Front To Back, Blend Horizontally, and Blend Vertically blend the colors of at least three objects whose ending objects are both process tints or both Black tints. The Blend filters do not work with custom colors, patterns, or gradients. Using the Blend filters is very similar to using the Blend tool, but instead of making different shape *and* color blends, the Blend filters create new colors inside the between objects automatically. If the ending paths' colors are different color *types,* Blend Front To Back will produce undesirable results.

The main difference between each of these filters is how they determine what the end paths are, and in what direction the blend flows.

The Custom To Process Filter

Custom To Process converts custom colors into their process-color equivalents. It's useful to do this before using the Color Blend filters. Keep in mind that once you've changed the paths to process, they must be selected and changed back to custom colors individually. Just because the custom color "Aqua" is 100C 0M 55Y 0K doesn't mean Illustrator will know it is anything but a process color combo.

The Invert Colors Filter

Invert Colors works in strange and mysterious ways on selected paths. Whatever the color of the path, Invert Colors takes the first three colors in the Paint palette (Cyan, Magenta, Yellow) and subtracts them from 100. If the original color was a shade of Red (for example, where Cyan = 0%, Magenta = 100%, and Yellow = 100%), then Invert Colors makes the new color Cyan = 100%, Magenta = 0%, and Yellow = 0%.

The percentage of Black is not affected by Invert colors. Therefore, this is *not* the same as getting a negative image.

The Overprint Black Plug-In

The Overprint Plug-In is placed in the Optional Plug-Ins folder when Illustrator is installed. In order for it to be used, it needs to be moved to the Plug-Ins folder.

Choosing Filter⇨Color⇨Overprint Black displays the Overprint Black dialog box (shown in Figure 13-2), which will allow you to apply overprinting of black to selected paths. A number of options can be selected, including whether to add or remove overprinting from the selected objects. Another option lets you specify the amount of black percentage that is the minimum that will be used to overprint.

To the right of the Add and Remove controls, you can specify where the overprint affects Fills or Strokes or both. The bottom options determine whether black will overprint when combined with CMY or when part of a custom color.

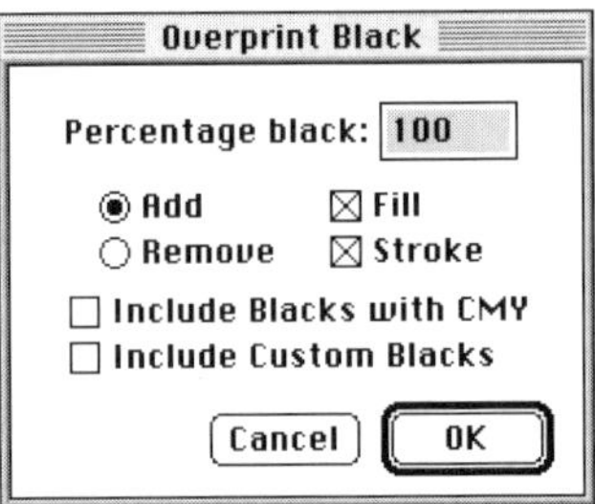

Figure 13-2: The Overprint Black dialog box

The Overprint Black filter will only add overprinting to selected objects that are not currently overprinted when the Add button is selected, and it will remove overprinting from objects that currently have overprinting when the Remove button is selected. In no circumstances will overprinting be removed when the Add button is selected, even if the overprinting object does not fall within the parameters of the settings of the Overprint dialog box.

The Saturate Filter

Saturate adds or subtracts equal amounts of color to the selected objects. This filter does not correspond in any way to saturation changes made by Photoshop; instead, the color added is proportional to each color in a path. Using Saturate works in much the same way as holding the Shift key down and dragging a triangle to the right in the Paint Style palette. Saturate does not work with patterns or gradients.

The Saturate dialog box (shown in Figure 13-3) allows you to saturate or desaturate, depending on the direction the slider is dragged. The Preview checkbox in this dialog box is quite helpful, allowing you to see what is happening to the paths in real time.

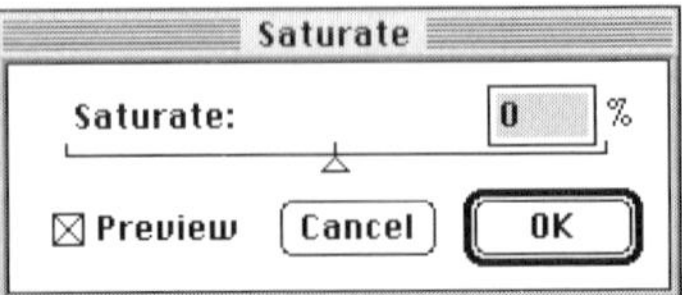

Figure 13-3: The Saturate dialog box

Manipulating Colors with the Color Filters

The color filters provide automated ways of changing colors for a variety of objects. Most of the filters work on paths that are Filled with black or a process color, and some of them work on the Strokes of the paths as well. The following sections describe various uses for the color filters.

Techniques for Creating Shadows and Highlights

You can easily use color filters to create shadows and highlights for black and process-colored paths.

You create most shadows by simply creating a copy of the object and placing it under, and slightly offset from, the original. You can darken the copy in a number of ways, but the easiest way is to use the Adjust Colors filter.

You create highlights in the same way as you create shadows, but instead of darkening the copy, you lighten it.

STEPS: Creating Shadows and Highlights with the Adjust Colors Filter

Step 1. Create an object that has several colors in it. Group the individual elements in the object.

Step 2. Copy the object and choose Edit⇨Paste in Back (⌘-B). Offset the copy down and to the right by a few points.

Step 3. Choose Filter⇨Colors⇨Adjust Colors. To darken the shadowed copy evenly, add 20% to Cyan, Magenta, and Yellow, and 40% to Black.

Step 4. To create the highlight, choose Edit⇨Paste in Back (⌘-B) again and decrease all four process colors by 40% if the background is dark or 20% if the background is light. My background is dark, so I reduced the color in the highlight by 40% of each color.

Figure 13-4 shows the four steps that you follow to create shadows and highlights.

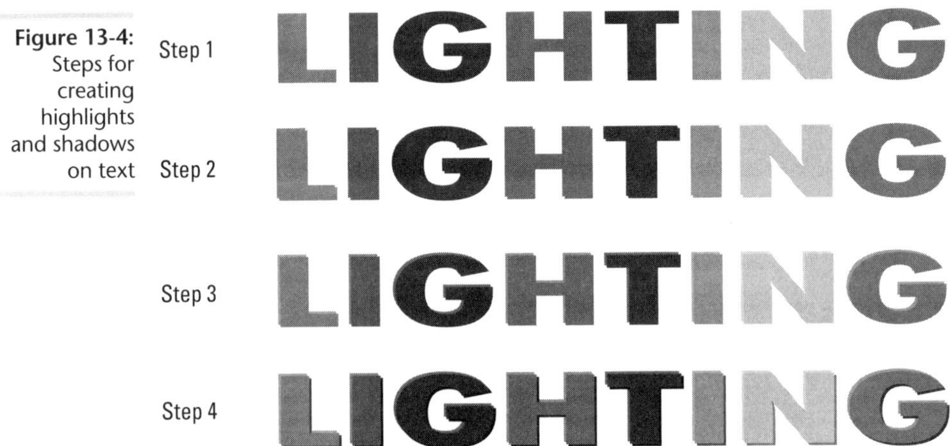

Figure 13-4: Steps for creating highlights and shadows on text

Creating Extruded Multiple Path Objects

You can normally make objects appear to be "extruded" by blending two objects together. If the objects contain multiple paths, however, you have to blend each of the paths separately. And if the objects contain compound paths, the blends that you create will not share the compound attributes of the original objects.

You can use the Blend Front To Back filter to make objects appear to be extruded, as described in the following steps.

STEPS: Creating Extruded Multiple Path Objects

Step 1. Release any compound paths in the object and group all the paths in the object together.

Step 2. In the Move dialog box (choose Arrange⇨Move, or press ⌘-Shift-M), enter **.25 pt** in the Horizontal text field and **.1 pt** in the Vertical text field. Click the Copy button (or press Option-Return).

Step 3. Choose Arrange⇨Repeat Transform (⌘-D) until the object has been duplicated far enough to appear 3-D. Copy the final duplicate object (it should still be selected).

Step 4. Change the color of the final duplicate object to be the color of the frontmost part of the blend. In my example, I made the final duplicate object black and left the rest of the objects red. (The color insert shows the result.)

Step 5. Select all the objects and choose Filter⇨Colors⇨Blend Front to Back.

Step 6. Choose Edit⇨Paste In Front (⌘-F) and give a different color to the object just pasted. In the example, I used yellow. Choose Object⇨Compound Path⇨Make (⌘-8) and then Arrange⇨Hide (⌘-3).

Step 7. Continue to select each grouped object, making each group a compound path and then hiding it, until all the paths are hidden.

If you have QuicKeys, set up a macro to make this step a one-key procedure. I used F10. This process went really fast because all I had to do was click and press F1, click and press F1, and so on.

Step 8. After you have hidden all the paths, choose Arrange⇨Show All (⌘-4) and then group all the paths together.

Do not make all the paths one compound path, or the color information for each path will be lost.

Actually, the whole process described in the preceding steps can be automated with the use of KPT Vector Effects' ShadowLand filter, which includes all sorts of shadowing effects, including a useful one for zooming.

Creating Negatives with the Color Filters

You can produce negative images in Illustrator almost automatically by using the Invert Colors filter. For a process color, the Invert Colors filter subtracts the tints of Cyan, Magenta, and Yellow from 100% and leaves Black as is. On an object that is Filled or Stroked with black only, the filter subtracts the tint of black from 100%.

To get around the way that this filter works when creating negatives, select all the objects that you want to reverse. Next, choose Filter⇨Colors⇨Invert Colors, select each path, and check whether the paths have a process color Fill that contains black. If you find any Fills that contain black, manually change black to the correct value.

After you check a path to see whether it is a process color that contains black, hide that path. Using this method can help you be sure that you have checked every path, and you do not have to worry about wasting time by rechecking paths.

The Create Filters

There used to be bunches of create filters, back in version 5.x of Illustrator. In 6.0, the category is all but extinct, with only Create Fill and Stroke for Mask and Object Mosaic being the remaining stragglers. The Star, Spiral, and Polygon filters have been replaced with tools (in the new Plug-In Tools palette), and Trim Marks has been tossed due to Color Separations now being included within Illustrator.

As with most filters, you can manually perform the functions that the two create filters do, but using the filters is much easier.

The Fill and Stroke for Mask Filter

Fill and Stroke for Mask takes any selected masks and copies them. The mask is then seemingly given the Paint Style attributes currently in the Paint Style palette. But because masks cannot be Filled or Stroked, this filter at first glance seems to be working some really great magic.

Of course, Fill and Stroke for Mask really doesn't do anything all that spectacular. After it copies the mask, it does a Paste Behind for the Fill (this object is made into the bottommost part of the mask). If a Stroke is specified, the filter also does a Paste in Front for the Stroke — but this path is not masked and is not part of the masking object. Before choosing Fill and Stroke for Mask, make sure that you have only the mask you want to Fill and Stroke selected, and that you have chosen the proper Paint Style attributes for the mask.

It is a good idea to get into the habit of grouping the new Stroke and Fill paths to the mask. To do so, you will have to group everything that is part of the mask. Of course, the Group Selection tool will allow you to move anything necessary, even if everything is grouped together.

When you turn a masking path into a mask, any Paint Style attributes that the masking path had before it was a mask are removed, and you cannot give it any Paint Style attributes. If you select a masking path, the Paint Style palette shows a Fill and Stroke of None. (Creating masks is discussed in Chapter 9.)

STEPS: Adding a Stroke and Fill to a Mask

Step 1. Create a mask and masked object.

Step 2. Select the masking path and choose the Stroke and Fill that you want to give to the masking path. As you choose and apply the Fill and Stroke, the mask will not show these changes.

Step 3. Choose Filter⇨Create⇨Stroke & Fill for Mask. The masking path will have the Fill and Stroke you requested.

The Stroke and Fill for Mask filter creates two copies of the original masking path. It places the first copy under all of the masked items and Fills it with the Fill that you chose in the Paint Style palette before you applied the filter. It places the second copy above the mask and gives it the Stroke that you specified in the Paint Style palette.

If either the Fill or Stroke for the masking object is set to None before you activate the filter, a dialog box appears, telling you that the Stroke and Fill for Mask filter applies the Fill and Stroke in the Paint dialog box to the mask. Whenever this message appears, I always look at my Paint Style palette to make sure that I did indeed select the mask before I made changes to the values in the Paint Style palette.

Group the masking objects, the masking path, the Filled masking path, and the Stroked masking path to ensure that all the objects in the mask stay together.

Creating Object Mosaics

The Object Mosaic filter creates a series of tiles out of a PICT image, as shown in Figure 13-5. Any size or color PICT image may be used. When an image is converted through the Object Mosaic filter, it becomes a series of rectangles and each rectangle is Filled with a different color.

In the Object Mosaic dialog box (see Figure 13-6), you can specify the number of tiles that the image is made up of and the space between the tiles. You also can specify a different size for the entire object mosaic.

Be careful with Object Mosaic, for this filter, unlike almost any other, will run out of memory if the source image or number of tiles is too large. This is the one filter in Illustrator that does almost exactly what its counterpart in Photoshop does.

Figure 13-5: An original PICT image (left) and the image after Object Mosaic has been applied

Figure 13-6: The Mosaic dialog box

Mosaic

Current Size (pts):
Width: 170
Height: 90

Tile Spacing:
Width: 0
Height: 0

New Size (pts):
Width: 100
Height: 100

Number of Tiles:
Width: 30
Height: 30

Use Ratio ◉ Lock Width ○ Lock Height

Color:
◉ Color ○ Grayscale

Cancel OK

The more rectangles, the more detail in the mosaic. Bitmapped images are mosaics of a sort, with each pixel equal to 1 square.

If you do not have software that creates PICT files, but you have created a file on-screen that you want to save as a PICT file, press ⌘-Shift-3. You will hear a noise that is similar to the sound that a shutter on a camera makes, and a PICT file will be created out of whatever is on-screen. The file is saved on your start up drive as Picture 1. Additional screen shots are saved as Picture 2, Picture 3, and so on.

Use the following steps to create a fairly simple and basic mosaic in Illustrator.

STEPS: Creating a Mosaic

Step 1. Create or scan a PICT file. You do not need to use a high-resolution PICT file. The Illustrator Object Mosaic will look just as good when you convert a 72-dpi PICT file as when you convert a 300-dpi PICT file.

Step 2. Choose Filters⇨Create⇨Object Mosaic. An Open dialog box will appear. Select the file that you want to convert. In the Object Mosaic dialog box, enter the size that you want the mosaic to be and also the number of tiles across and down. Click the Use Ratio button to keep the same proportions as in the original image.

Step 3. Click OK when you are satisfied with the information that you have entered in the Object Mosaic dialog box. Figure 13-7 shows the results that are produced by entering three different tile widths and heights into the Number of Tiles boxes.

The number of tiles that Illustrator can produce is strictly limited and is directly related to the amount of RAM that is allocated to Illustrator. Exceeding the limit will cause Illustrator to create only a portion of the tiles.

You can create some very exciting effects with the Object Mosaic filter when you use it in conjunction with other filters. The best ones to use with it are Round Corners, all of the Distort filters, and most of the color filters, as well as the Transform Each function. In the following example, I combined the Object Mosaic filter with the Round Corners filter and the Transform Each function.

Figure 13-7: Steps for creating Object Mosaics

Step 1

333×419 PIXELS
(139,527)

Step 2

Mosaic

Current Size (pts):
Width: 80
Height: 101

Tile Spacing:
Width: 0
Height: 0

New Size (pts):
Width: 80
Height: 101

Number of Tiles:
Width: 15
Height: 19

Use Ratio ◉ Lock Width ○ Lock Height

Color:
◉ Color ○ Grayscale

Cancel OK

Step 3

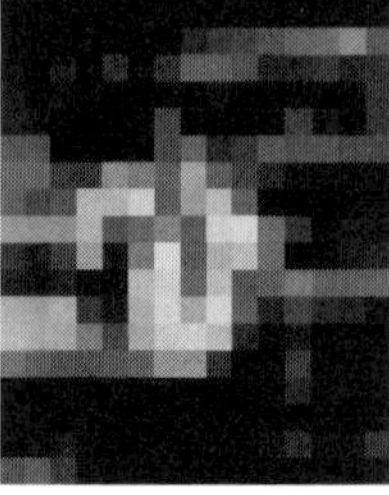

15×19 TILES
(285)

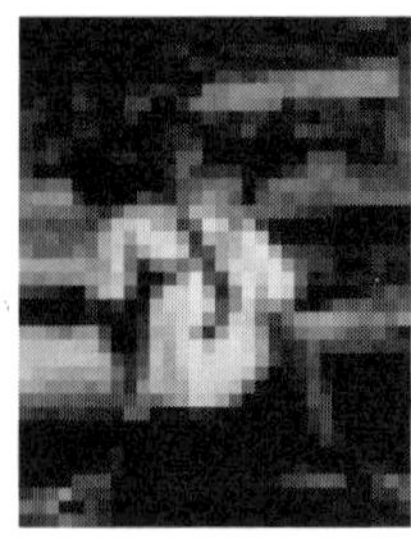

30×38 TILES
(1140)

80×101 TILES
(8080)

STEPS: Creating a Seurat-Like Illustration

Step 1. Create an Object Mosaic with an average number of tiles (between 1,600 and 10,000 tiles, which would be from 40 × 40 to 100 × 100). In the example shown in Figure 13-8, I used an Object Mosaic with 50 × 63 tiles, or 3,150 tiles total.

Step 2. Select all the mosaic tiles and choose Filters⇨Stylize⇨Round Corners. In the Round Corners dialog box, enter a large number. I usually enter at least 10 points. As long as the tiles are not larger than 20-points wide, the Round Corners filter will turn all the tiles into circles.

Step 3. Copy all the tiles and choose Edit⇨Paste in Front (⌘-F). Select all the tiles (the image now has 6,300 tiles) and choose Arrange⇨Transform Each. In the Move section of the dialog box, enter **5** in both text fields and check the Random checkbox at the bottom of the dialog box. Click OK. If you want less white space between all the circles, choose Edit⇨Paste in Front (⌘-F) again and then choose Arrange⇨Repeat Transform (⌘-D). The results should look similar to Step 3 in Figure 13-8.

The tiles created with the mosaic filter are placed on the page from top left to bottom right. The top-left tile is underneath all the other tiles (in the back), and the bottom-right tile is on top of all other tiles (in the front). The tiles are butted up against each other, so none of them overlap each other.

Because of the way that these tiles overlap, you can create a tiled or shingled roof quite easily, providing the original image is upside down. The following steps describe this process in detail.

STEPS: Creating a Tiled Roof

Step 1. Create a PICT file to be used as the roof. In the example shown in Figure 13-9, I created the name of a restaurant. Then I took a screen shot of it (⌘-Shift-3) that I opened in Photoshop so that I could delete the surrounding objects.

Step 2. In Photoshop or another bitmapped image editing program, rotate the image 135° clockwise. Save it as a PICT file. In Illustrator, choose Filter⇨Create⇨Object Mosaic. Open the file, make the number of tiles across about 50 or more, and click the Use Ratio button.

Figure 13-8: Creating a Seurat-like effect with the Object Mosaic filter

Step 1

Step 2

Step 3

Step 3. Rotate the entire mosaic by 135°. Using the Selection tool, draw a marquee around any white squares above, below, to the left, and to the right of the roof area to select them. Delete all white squares. Because the squares are white, you may need to switch to Artwork mode to see them all.

It may seem strange that the mosaic gets rotated twice, but there is a method to this seemingly mad busywork. By placing the upper-left tiles on the bottom and the lower-right tiles on the top, the image is rotated first in Photoshop so that the lower parts of the image are turned into squares. By the way, if I hadn't helped put shingles on a roof recently (you have to work from the bottom up), I would never have been able to figure this out. So I guess that this is one of those "real life" examples, huh?

Step 4. Select the remaining tiles and group them. Choose Filter⇨Object⇨Add Anchor Points to add one Anchor Point to every side of every square in the mosaic. Choose Filter⇨Stylize⇨Bloat and Punk to make all the points on each square come out a little.

Step 5. To round off the points and make the squares smoother, choose Filter⇨Stylize⇨Round Corners, and enter **10 pt** in the text field. Choose Arrange ⇨Transform Each and enter **150** in both the Width and Height fields of the Scale section of the Transform Each dialog box. Because the squares were scaled up, they now overlap.

Step 6. Choose Arrange ⇨Transform Each, and enter **45°** in the Rotate section. In the Paint Style palette, give each tile a black Stroke of .25 points. Depending on the size of the tiles, the Stroke weight may vary.

Step 7. Use the Distort filter (choose Filter⇨Distort⇨Free Distort) to change the shape of the roof to be more ... well ... rooflike.

The following steps describe how to make the tiles in a mosaic overlap with no white space between them. This technique can easily create a background image or a funky illustration, as shown in the steps and used in context in Figure 13-10.

Figure 13-9: Creating a tiled roof with the Object Mosaic filter

STEPS: Creating Random Overlapping Tiles with No White Space

Step 1. Create an Object Mosaic from a PICT file.

Step 2. Choose Arrange ⇨Transform Each, and enter the amount of movement for the tiles in the Move section. Check the Random box. Measure one tile with the Measure tool. The tiles that I created for the example shown in Figure 13-10 are 3.3 points across, and the move distance that I used is 3.3 points. The most white space between any two tiles is 6.6 points.

Step 3. Select Arrange ⇨Transform Each. Enter the percentage that the tile must be scaled up to eliminate the white space in the Scale area. In this example, I entered 200%.

Step 4. To see the edges of the tiles more easily, place a .25-point black Stroke on them.

By using the Object Mosaic filter in combination with the color blend filters, color sets can be created very easily. These color sets can be sampled for inclusion into the Paint Style palette or just used as a separate palette document (this is what I use them for), off to the side of your working document.

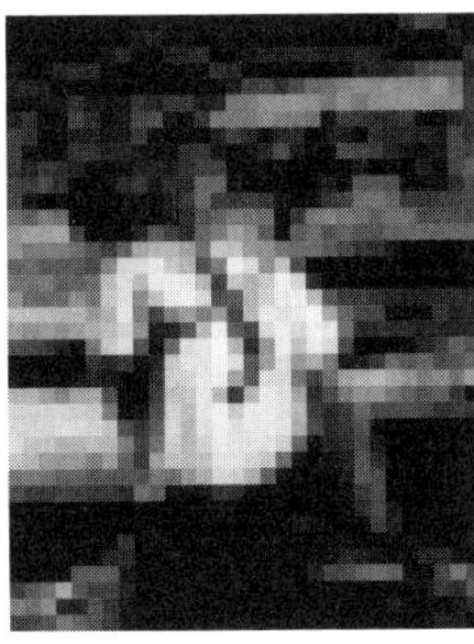

Step 1

Step 2

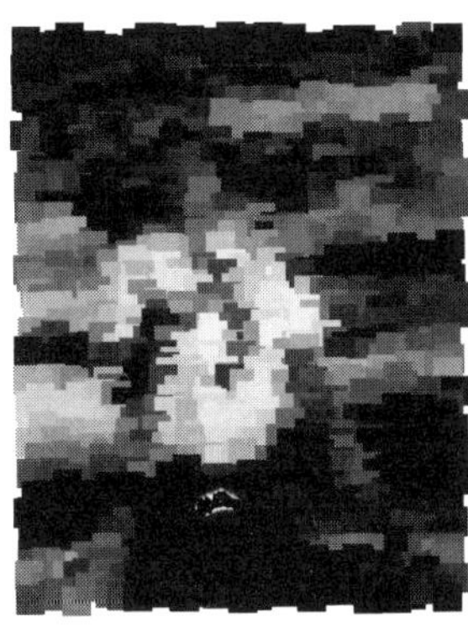

Step 3

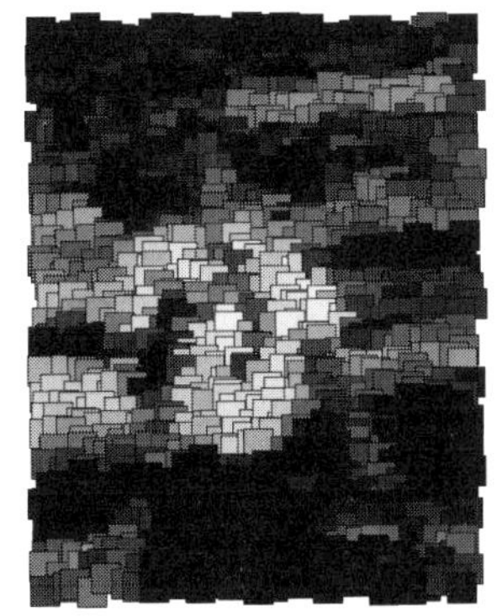

Step 4

Figure 13-10: Steps for creating random overlapping tiles with no white space

STEPS: Creating Color Sets with the Mosaic Filter

Step 1. Create an Object Mosaic from any PICT file, making the total number of tiles equal to the number of different tiles that you want in the color set.

Step 2. Change the colors of the tiles that mark the beginning and end of each color set. In the example (Figure 13-11), I used primary colors and white as the beginning and end of each color set.

Step 3. Select one range of color and choose Filter⇨Color⇨Blend Front to Back to blend the colors from the upper-left tiles towards the lower-right tiles. Repeat this step for each range of colors.

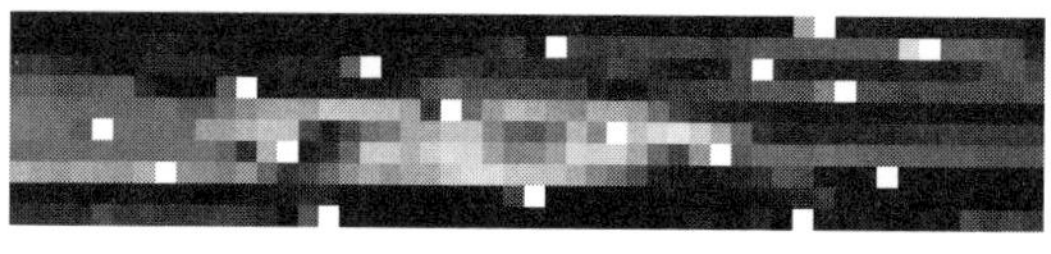

Figure 13-11: Using the Mosaic filter to create color sets

Summary

- Adjust Colors adds and subtracts various amounts of process colors from multiple colored objects.
- The color blend filters look at two opposite paths and blend between the two colors.
- Saturate increases or decreases the amount of color in selected paths.
- The Fill and Stroke for Mask filter provides a quick method for putting Fills behind and Strokes on top of masking objects.
- The Object Mosaic takes PICT files and "square streamlines" them into Illustrator paths.

The Distort and Stylize Filters

14

CHAPTER

In This Chapter

- How the Distort and Stylize filters work
- Using Free Distort
- Using Punk and Bloat
- Using the Twirl filter and the Twirl tool
- Using the new Zig Zag filter
- Working with Roughen
- Using Roughen to add Anchor Points
- Using Scribble and Tweak
- Adding arrowheads to open paths
- Using the Round Corners filter
- Using the new Path Patterns filter

The Distort and Stylize filters are the most fun of all the filters in Illustrator. These filters actually do something most people would recognize as filter-like. Of course, they work with paths, not pixels, which drastically changes how they're used.

The Distort and Stylize Filters

The following pages describe the Distort and Stylize filters (found in the Distort and Stylize submenus of the Filter menu), and provide tips and techniques for getting the most out of them.

The Free Distort Filter

Choosing Filter⇨Distort⇨Free Distort displays the Free Distort dialog box, where you control how much you want to distort the selected paths. Within this dialog box is a representative sample of the selected artwork surrounded by four corner handles. You adjust and move the four handles to change the shape of the object.

Reshaping artwork was very time-consuming in older versions of Illustrator. You used the Scale tool on individual points and segments, scaling a little more for each successive row of points. Before Illustrator 5.0 was released, the only widely used software that could distort freely was Broderbund's TypeStyler, but its exceedingly clunky and awkward interface and its requirement that artwork be in a font (with all colors removed) made the process cumbersome at best. If I never have to use TypeStyler again, it'll be too soon.

If the Show Me box is checked, you will see what the image looks like as it is distorted. To distort the selected paths, click and drag the four corner points of the box surrounding the artwork (see Figure 14-1). Those handles can be pulled anywhere, including right out of the dialog box onto the document — and even off the document!

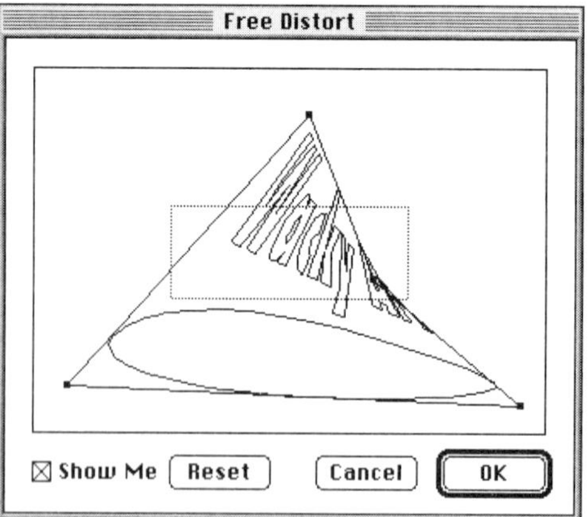

Figure 14-1: Distorting an image in the Free Distort dialog box

If you pull the handles too far, you will have to click the Reset button to get to your handles back. Doing so resets the image to its original shape.

If you think that Free Distort is too limiting, take a look at KPT Warp Frame, part of KPT Vector Effects, described in Chapter 18.

Text can be distorted using Free Distort, but it must first be converted into outlines.

STEPS: Using the Free Distort Filter

Step 1. Create the artwork that you want to distort. In the example in Figure 14-2, I used text converted to outlines.

Before you can distort text in the Free Distort dialog box, you have to convert it to outlines. Although you can distort Rectangle type, Path type, and Area type without converting it to outlines, only the paths that the type is in or on will be distorted.

The Free Distort filter does not work with placed EPS images or with type that has not been converted to outlines. Nor does the Free Distort filter affect patterns or gradients that are being used as Fills.

Step 2. Choose Filter⇨Distort⇨Free Distort. The Free Distort dialog box appears, containing a line art (Artwork view only) view of the selected paths that you want to distort.

If the artwork is very complex, you may want to uncheck the Show Me checkbox. A rectangle will appear instead of the complex artwork. For this example, I found that adjusting the rectangle without seeing the artwork was much easier because the artwork contained several hundred compound paths that Illustrator had to redraw.

Step 3. Move the handles around until the artwork is reshaped to your liking. If you don't have Show Me checked while you are moving the handles around, click it to preview the reshaped artwork when you think the handles are in a good position. Then if you realize that the artwork doesn't look the way you want it to look, you can make changes without having to choose the Undo command and select the filter again.

Step 4. Click the OK button to have the reshaped artwork appear in the document. If the artwork is complex, you may want to group everything that was distorted. Or if you are really conscientious, you may have grouped everything already.

Step 5. Add any finishing touches by coloring the distorted artwork. I placed a black background behind the distorted text and then Filled the text with the Black & White Gradient. I used the Gradient Vector tool to drag upwards, starting in the bottom-middle of the last paragraph and dragging up to the top line of type.

Figure 14-2: Steps for using the Free Distort filter

A long time ago, in a galaxy far far away, millions of people went to go see a really cool movie that took place a long time ago, in a galaxy far far away. This movie became the biggest motion picture of all time, eclipsing other mediocre films such as Gone with the Wind (in which the actors swear).

Then along came another movie that even more millions of people went to go see, once again about a little guy from space, but this time the little guy ends up on earth. The whole film turns out to be a two hour commercial for peanut butter cups with a candy shell.

Finally, ten years after the ugly little space runt arrived in theatres, really ugly big monster like creatures demanded, and recevied tons of cash for strutting around the big screen. The movie was hailed as the greatest computer-assisted motion picture of our time, yet there was a great error objvious to most Macintosh owners. When the fat little bad guy is looking supposedly at live video on his Macintosh screen, a QuickTime window with a little progress bar showing is visible. Hmmmf.

Step 1

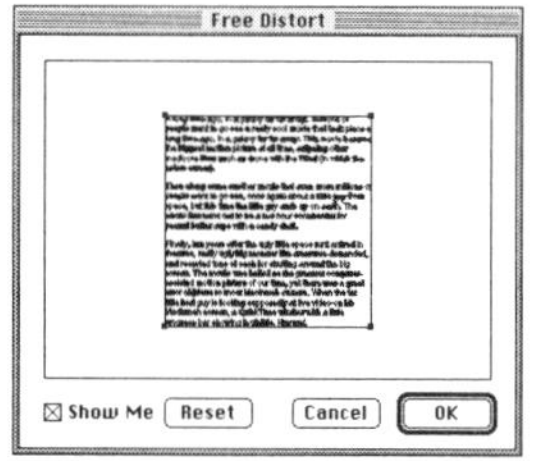

Step 2

Step 3

Step 4

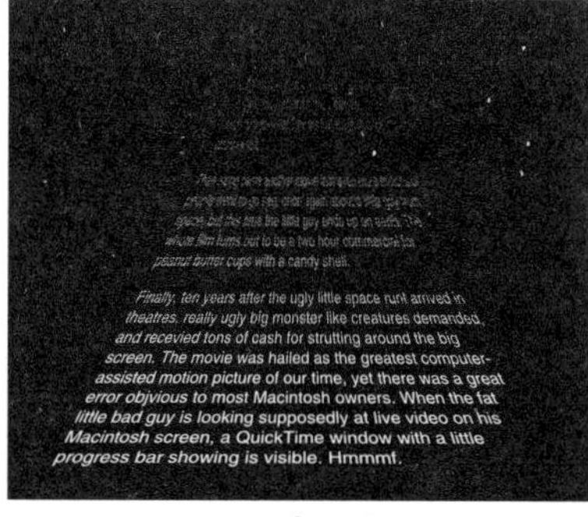

Step 5

You can use the Free Distort filter to create artwork that twists. In the Free Distort dialog box, simply create an *X* pattern with the rectangle. To do so, switch the handles on one edge of the rectangle. Depending on the type of twist, the artwork will turn upside down or become reversed. By combining different twists, you can produce ribbonlike effects. For example, Figure 14-3 shows a banner that has two different twists.

Figure 14-3: A double twist in the Free Distort dialog box produced this flipping, twisting banner.

After you use the Free Distort filter, the handle positions are remembered in the dialog box. If you use the filter again during the same Illustrator session, those settings are immediately applied to the artwork. Press the Reset button to return the handles (and the artwork) back to their original positions.

You can pull the handles in the Free Distort dialog box right out of the dialog box and stretch them as far as the monitor is wide or tall. The catch in this maneuver is that when you release the mouse button on a handle that you have dragged outside the dialog box, you can no longer select that handle. The only way to recover the handle is to click the Reset button, which resets all the handles to their original positions without significantly changing the previously distorted image.

The Punk and Bloat Filter

Although the Punk and Bloat filter undoubtedly has the coolest sounding name that Illustrator has to offer, this filter also is one of the least practical. But Illustrator is a fun program, right? And these filters make it lots of fun.

Punking makes objects appear to have pointy tips sticking out everywhere, and bloating creates lumps outside of objects. Punking and bloating are inverses of each other; a negative punk is a bloat, and a negative bloat is a punk. If you are bewildered by these functions, stop reading right here. The following information spoils everything.

Selecting Punk and Bloat opens the Punk and Bloat dialog box, where you may specify a percentage that you want the selected paths to be punked or bloated by either typing in the amount or dragging a slider.

I Can't Get Punked Stuff Back to Normal

Squiggy: After I punk, I can never get the paths back to normal.

Toulouse: Undo doesn't work?

Squiggy: Sure, but I like changing things I've saved, closed, and reopened.

Toulouse: Undo won't work in that case.

Squiggy: So, I'm trying to bloat the paths I punked, since Bloat is the opposite of Punk.

Toulouse: It just doesn't work that way.

Squiggy: Why?

Toulouse: Punk and Bloat change each Anchor Point into a Curved Corner Point. Each point has two independent handles, and those handles are moved with Punk and Bloat.

Squiggy: Wouldn't bloating punked paths move the handles back to where they started from?

Toulouse: No, because originally, many of those points didn't have handles at all.

Squiggy: Anything else that can be done?

Toulouse: Redraw, or, if you have the patience, edit each of the points. Unless you added Anchor Points before punking.

Bloating causes the segments between Anchor Points to expand outwards. The higher the percentage, the more bloated the selection. You can bloat from –200% up to 200%. Punk is the inverse of Bloat. While Bloat makes rounded, bubble-like extrusions appear on the surface of your object, Punk makes tall spikes appear on its path. When you drag towards Punk, you can enter how much you want to punk the drawing. Punk amounts can range from –200% to 200%. The number of spikes is based on the number of Anchor Points in your drawing. Figure 14-4 shows several punked and bloated objects.

Figure 14-4: Punked and bloated objects

The Punk and Bloat filter moves Anchor Points in one direction and creates two independent direction points on either side of each anchor point. The direction points are moved in the opposite direction of the anchor points, and the direction of movement is always toward or away from the center of the object.

The distance moved is the only thing that you control when you use the Punk and Bloat filter. Entering a percentage moves the points that percentage.

Nothing about the Punk and Bloat filter is random. Everything about it is controlled.

STEPS: Using the Punk and Bloat Filters

Step 1. Create and select the artwork that you want to punk.

Step 2. Add Anchor Points or use the Roughen filter at 0% to create additional Anchor Points if necessary. I chose Filter⇨Object⇨Add Anchor Points twice, increasing the number of Anchor Points from 4 to 16.

Step 3. Choose Filter⇨Stylize⇨Punk and Bloat. In the dialog box, enter the amount that you want to punk or bloat the object, or drag the slider in the appropriate direction.

Step 4. Check to see whether the result is what you intended.

Step 5. Add other artwork to the punked or bloated object.

Figure 14-5: Steps for punking

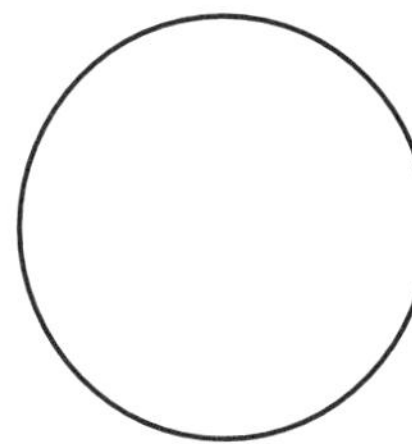

Step 1

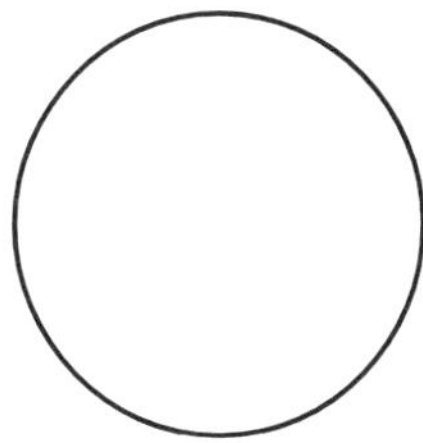

Step 2

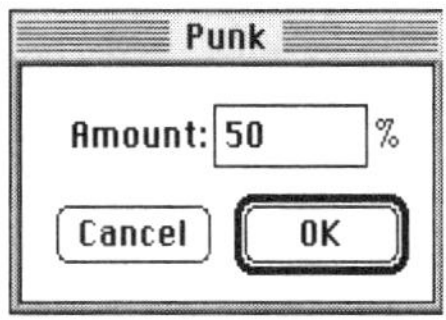

Step 3

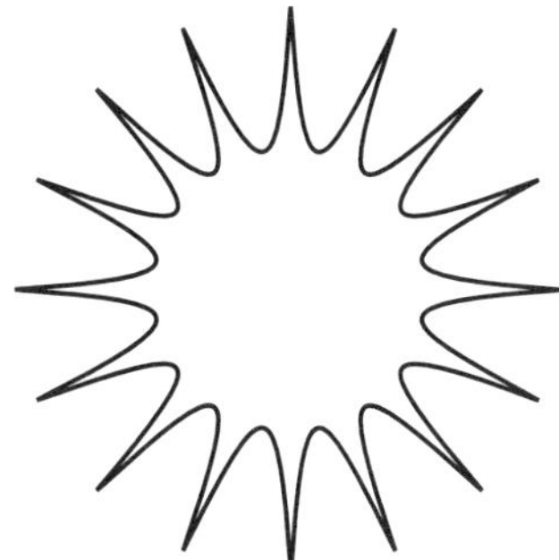

Step 4

Step 5

The Twirl Filter

Like the Free Distort filter, the Twirl filter reshapes objects in ways that would be time-consuming and tedious if you were using conventional Illustrator methods. The Twirl filter moves the innermost points a certain number of degrees around a circle. The farther away the points are from the center of the circle, the less they move; and the points at the outermost edges of the object hardly rotate at all.

In Illustrator 6.0, there is both a Twirl filter and a Twirl tool, found in the Plug-In Tools palette. The Twirl filter is described directly below, while the Twirl tool is discussed after the filter.

Selecting Twirl displays the Twirl dialog box, where you specify how much the selected objects will spin. You can set the twirl angle from –4000° up to 4000°. The very center of the selected objects will rotate the degree specified, while the objects on the edges will rotate around the center very little. Positive values rotate the selected paths clockwise; negative values rotate the selected paths counterclockwise. Figure 14-6 shows an object before and after being twirled.

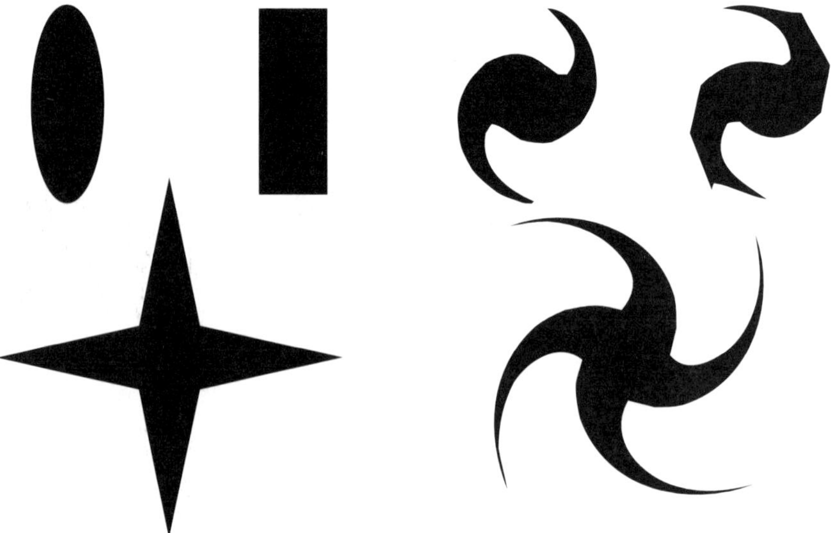

Figure 14-6: The original paths (left) are twirled (right).

Unlike previous versions of Twirl, adding more Anchor Points to your path doesn't necessarily result in a better effect. I apply Add Anchor Points several times or add Anchor Points via the Roughen filter before applying the Twirl filter. Now, however, the Twirl filter is "smart," and curves paths automatically.

The Twirl filter can twirl single paths or multiple paths. When it twirls multiple paths, the twirling takes place from the center of the entire group of objects, not from within each object.

STEPS: Using the Twirl Filter

Step 1. Create the artwork that you want to use with the Twirl filter. In the example in Figure 14-7, I created a star with several points and a tiny first (inner) radius. Then I selected the center points with the Direct Selection tool and dragged them down and to the left.

The constraints on the Twirl filter are similar to the constraints on the Free Distort filter. You cannot twirl placed images, type that has not been converted to outlines, or patterns and gradients that are used as Fills.

Step 2. Choose Filter⇨Distort⇨Twirl to see the Twirl dialog box. Enter the number of degrees that you want to twirl objects. In the example, I used 300°.

Entering a positive number in the Angle text field twirls the object clockwise; entering a negative number twirls the object counterclockwise. This setting works the opposite way from how the degree setting for the Rotate tool works.

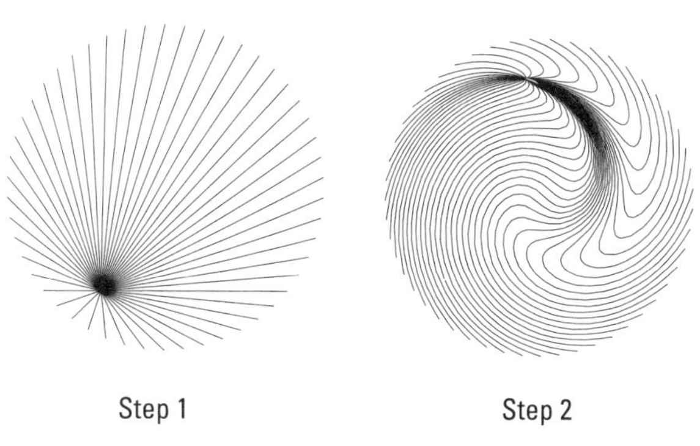

Figure 14-7: Steps for twirling artwork

I wanted the twirled artwork in the example to resemble a fingerprint, so I used the Scale and Rotate tools, and then the Scribble filter (see the section "The Scribble and Tweak Filter" later in this chapter) to achieve the desired effect. After scribbling the artwork just .5% horizontally and vertically, I added the background and the accompanying text. A larger version of the resulting poster is in the color section of this book.You can twirl paths up to 4,000° in both directions (4,000 and –4,000). The Twirl filter by itself enables you to create many different effects. By moving different objects to different positions, the Twirl filter can produce entirely different results. For example, you can use the following steps to create an arc in an illustration.

STEPS: Creating Arced Illustrations with the Twirl Filter

Step 1. Create the type that you want to arc and convert it to outlines.

Step 2. Make a copy of the type to the left of the original type and place an object between the two areas of type. Then place the same object at either end of the words. At this point, the illustration looks like Step 2 of Figure 14-8.

COMING SOON!

Step 1

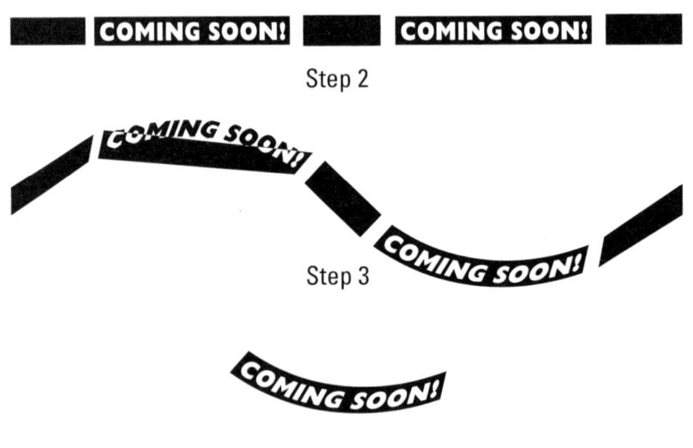

Step 2

Step 3

Step 4

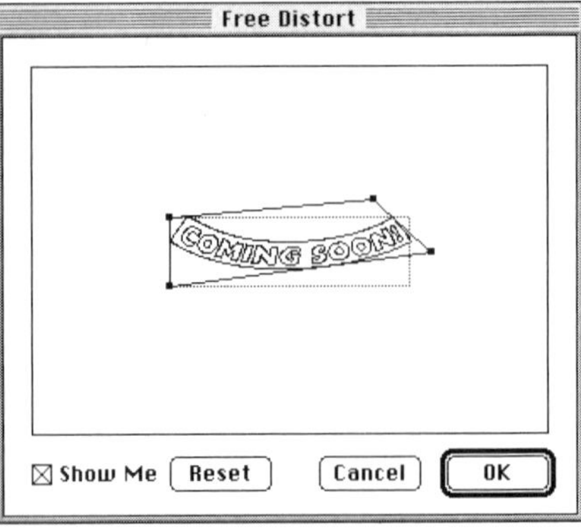

Step 5

Step 6

Figure 14-8: Steps for creating arced illustrations with the Twirl filter

Step 3. Select the objects and choose Filter⇨Twirl. In the Twirl dialog box, enter **90°** and press OK.

Step 4. Delete all the portions of the path except for the one shown.

Step 5. Select the remaining portion and choose Filter⇨Distort⇨Free Distort. Move the handles so that the paths resemble the lower part of an arc.

Step 6. Click OK.

The Twirl Tool

The Twirl tool isn't necessarily a filter, but it works just like the Twirl filter. The amazing thing about the Twirl tool is that it is totally interactive. That means that you can click and drag with the Twirl tool and watch as your artwork is spun and twisted into place. Figure 14-9 shows the Twirl tool.

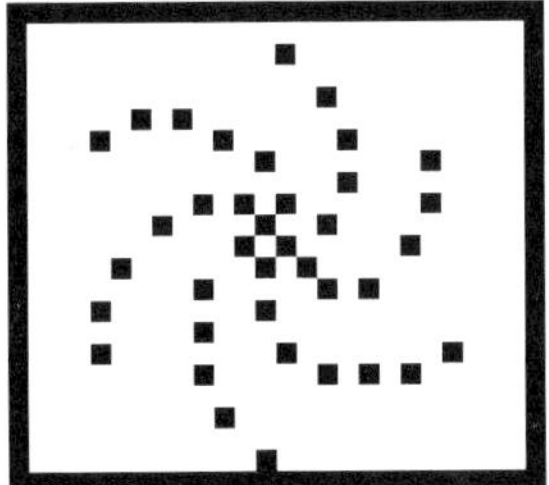

Figure 14-9: The Twirl tool

To use the Twirl tool, click and drag on the document either left or right. Dragging to the left while the cursor is above the document will twirl counterclockwise. To apply a specific percentage of twirl when using the Twirl tool, Option-click with the Twirl tool.

The Zig Zag Filter

The Zig Zag filter changes normally straight paths into zig zagged versions of those paths. When you first select Zig Zag, the Zig Zag dialog box appears, shown in Figure 14-10.

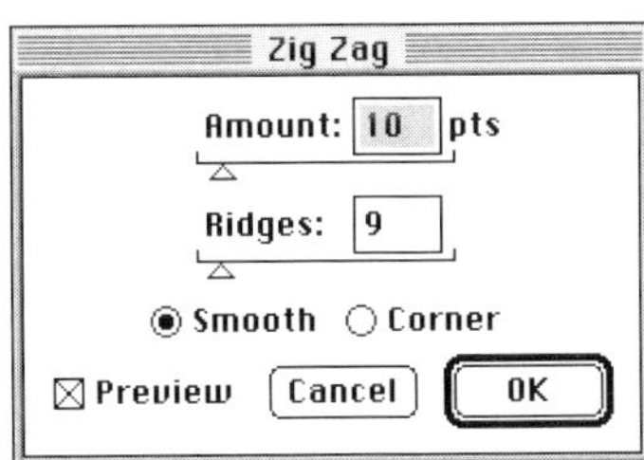

Figure 14-10: The Zig Zag dialog box

The dialog box allows you to specify various parameters of the zigzag effect, including the Amount, which is how large each zig zag is, and the number of Ridges, which is how many zigzags there are. In addition, you can specify if you'd like the zigzags to be curved (choose Smooth) or pointed (choose Corner). Like most of the other Illustrator 6 filters, Zig Zag has a handy Preview checkbox. Figure 14-11 shows an example of zig-zagged artwork.

Figure 14-11: Zigzagged art

Don't keep the Preview checkbox checked while you're changing values in the Zig Zag dialog box. Instead, change your settings first, *then* click the Preview checkbox. This prevents massive slowdowns that can occur when the Preview checkbox is checked.

The Random Mangle Filters

The two Random Mangle filters — Roughen, and Scribble and Tweak — both do similar things to paths. Roughen adds Anchor Points and then moves them randomly by a percentage that you define. Scribble and Tweak randomly moves existing Anchor Points and Control Handles by a percentage or by an absolute measurement that you define.

The *Macworld Illustrator 6 Bible* CD-ROM contains a Distort Filter chart that shows what happens to various objects when you mangle them differently.

Because the mangle filters work randomly, you get different results when you apply the same settings of the same filter to two separate, identical objects. In fact, the results will probably never be duplicated. The mangle filters are a good reason by themselves for having the Undo command, so you can apply the filter, undo, and reapply until you achieve the desired effect.

Using the keyboard, you can continuously reapply any filter that works randomly and get different results. Select the object and apply the filter by dragging the mouse to the menu item and entering the values. If you don't like the result, press ⌘-Z (Undo) and ⌘-Shift-E (reapply last filter).

One important limitation of the mangle filters is that they work on entire paths, even if only part of the path is selected. The best way to get around this limitation is to use the Scissors tool to cut the path into different sections.

The Roughen Filter

The Roughen filter does two things at once. First, it adds Anchor Points until the selection has the number of points per inch that you defined. Second, it randomly moves all the points around, changing them into Straight Corner Points or Smooth Points, whichever you specified.

Selecting Roughen opens the Roughen dialog box (see Figure 14-12), where you can enter information to "roughen up" the illustration — literally.

Not the Same Effect

Carmine: You know, what I really hate about Illustrator is the inconsistency.

Toulouse: What's inconsistent?

Carmine: The Roughen filter, for one.

Toulouse: It's supposed to be inconsistent. After all, it does random stuff.

Carmine: But let's say I want to duplicate a roughen effect.

Toulouse: I think you're out of luck.

Carmine: How does Illustrator come up with the random values? Surely there's a chart somewhere....

Toulouse: Actually, most "random" numbers are generated based on the time and date. Since this always changes, you'll get a different "result" each time.

Carmine: So if I went back in time to when I applied the Roughen filter the first time, it would be the same.

Toulouse: Well, you'd have to do it at the exact moment when you applied it before. Which would be almost as hard as traveling back in time in the first place.

Carmine: I could change my system clock, couldn't I?

Toulouse: Yes, but still, we're talking fractions of a second. The odds are you won't be able to do it right, unfortunately.

Figure 14-12: The Roughen dialog box

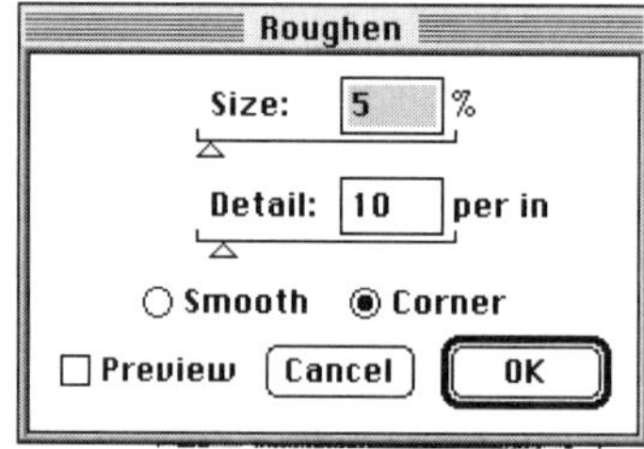

Three options are available here:

- **Size:** How far points may move when roughed relative to the width or height (whichever is greater) of the selected path.
- **Detail:** How many points are moved. For example, if you have a 1- by -1 inch square, the number of points added would be 36. (4" at the top top, bottom, left, right and at 10 points per inch equals 40 points. There are already 4 points on a rectangle, so you only need 36 more points.)
- If Smooth, all the Anchor Points added will be Smooth Points. If Corner, all the points added will be Straight Corner Points.

Roughen will never take away points when roughening a path.

The Roughen filter can be used as a very hip version of the Add Anchor Points filter. If the Size box is set to 0%, all points added will be added along the existing path all at once. Instead of going to Add Anchor Points again and again, just try entering a value of 25 into the Segments/Inch field of the Roughen filter. You have instant multiple Add Anchor Points. This is a great technique for Scribble and Tweak, or anything else where you need a bunch of Anchor Points fast.

Using the Roughen filter on a path is fairly straightforward, but using it on a portion of artwork is not. Figure 14-13 and the following steps take you through setting up artwork so that only a portion of the artwork is affected by the Roughen filter.

STEPS: Creating a Tear with the Roughen Filter

Step 1. Create the artwork that you want to tear.

Step 2. Select the Pen tool and click from one edge of the artwork to another, crossing the path that you want to tear. If you don't want the tear to be straight, click additional points to change direction. If you want a curved tear, make the path curved. Connect the path by continuing around the outside of the artwork.

Step 3. Select the artwork and the path. Choose Filter⇨Pathfinder⇨Divide. Ungroup and choose Edit⇨Deselect All (⌘-Shift-A). Select the paths on one side of the tear and drag them away from the remaining paths.

Step 4. Using the Scissors tool, click on the ends of the tear on one side of the split path. Drag the cut section away from the rest of the path. On the other half of the tear, cut that tear away and delete it as well.

Step 5. Choose Filter⇨Distort⇨Roughen to see the Roughen dialog box. In the Size text field, enter the percentage that you want the Anchor Points to be moved. In the example, I used 2% to move the points just slightly.

Next, determine how many points you want to add to the tear. I chose 30 points per inch. Then decide on the type of roughen: Rounded or Jagged. A Rounded roughen produces Smooth Points with Control Handles that stick out a very small amount from the Anchor Point, and a Jagged roughen has only Straight Corner Points.

Step 6. Click OK and check the newly roughened path to ensure that it is roughened correctly. If it isn't, or if you don't like the random movement of the anchor Points, choose Edit⇨Undo (⌘-Z) and select the Filter dialog box again (press Option and choose Filter⇨Distort⇨Roughen). Continue undoing and roughening until the artwork is the way you want it or just adjust the Anchor Points with the Direct Selection tool.

Step 7. Option-copy the roughened path to the edge of the path that it was torn from. The best way to perform this task is to click on an end point with the Selection tool and drag to the end point of the existing path with the Option key pressed. Average and join the points (⌘-Option-J). Move the original roughened path to the other side of the path and average and join both points.

I usually zoom in, sometimes all the way to 1600%, to make sure that the two points are directly on top of each other and that only two points are selected.

Step 8. Add any other artwork to the torn paths. In the example, I rotated each of the sides a small amount.

The Roughen filter has a secret function that very few people know about: You can use it to add Anchor Points to paths. Simply enter **0%** in the first text field, and the points that are added will not be moved at all. This method is especially useful as a substitute for the Add Anchor Points filter when some of the paths in a compound path don't need as many additional Anchor Points as others. The Roughen filter evens out the number of points for each of the paths in a compound path.

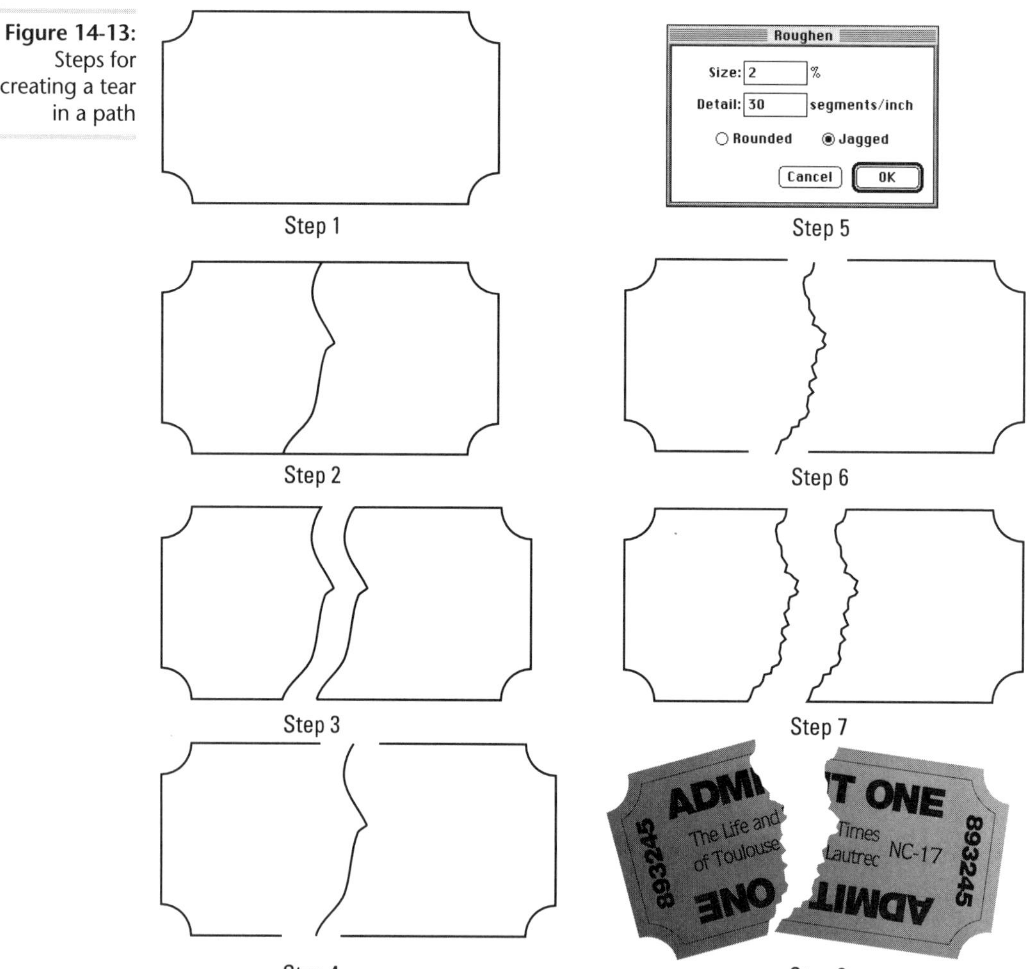

Figure 14-13: Steps for creating a tear in a path

If you want roughened edges to be *really* rounded, don't choose the Rounded option in the Roughen dialog box. Instead, choose the Jagged option and then choose Filter⇨Stylize⇨Round Corners. The Round Corners option changes only Straight Corner Points, so it will change all the points in the Jagged roughened object to smooth curves.

If you choose the Rounded option in the Roughen dialog box, the Round Corners filter will have no effect on the roughened object.

The Scribble and Tweak Filter

Although it sounds like characters from *Animaniacs*, the Scribble and Tweak filter, as is true for most filters, creates effects that would take an unrealistically long amount of time to do manually.

One important thing needs to be made clear right away: The Scribble and Tweak filter does one thing. The only difference between them is in the way that you enter the amount of random movement. When Scribble is checked, you'll enter percentages that are based on the size of the object's bounding box, but when Tweak is selected, points will be moved based on absolute measurements that you enter.

Because of the measuring system that Tweak uses, I have found that selecting the Tweak option is much easier than using the Scribble option most of the time. Having to enter percentages when Scribble is selected can be very confusing, especially because you have to be concerned with both horizontal and vertical proportions.

Selecting Scribble and Tweak displays the Scribble and Tweak dialog box (see Figure 4-14). When the Scribble option is selected, you define the amount of scribble, including how much horizontal and vertical scribble and which points are moved (Anchor Points, In Control Points, or Out Control Points).

No Anchor Points are added with the Scribble dialog box.

Figure 14-14: The Scribble and Tweak dialog box

For Scribble, Horizontal and Vertical percentages correspond to the movement of the selected points. If 0% is entered in either field, no movement will occur in that direction. The percentage is based on the width or height of the shape, whichever is longer. If Anchor Points is checked, then all Anchor Points on the selected path will be moved in a random distance corresponding to the amounts set in the Horizontal and Vertical text fields. If "In" or "Out" Control Points is checked, then those points will be moved the specified distance as well. The *"In" Control Points* are the points on one side of the Anchor Point, while *"Out" Control Points* refers to the points on the other side of the Anchor Point.

Selecting Tweak displays the Tweak options. Instead of specifying a distance based on percentage, the Tweak option lets you enter the distance in real measurements (like picas or inches), in whatever unit your measurement system is currently using. All Tweak options have the same effects as the the Scribble options.

STEPS: Using the Scribble and Tweak Filter

Step 1. Create the artwork that you want to use with the filter.

The Tweak and Scribble filter does not work with type that has not been converted to outlines or with placed images. Nor does it affect patterns or gradients that are being used as Fills.

Step 2. Choose Filter⇨Distort⇨Scribble and Tweak.

I use the Scribble option when I am not sure of the size of the selected artwork, or when I can determine only that I want points moved a certain portion of the whole, but I cannot determine an absolute measurement.

In the Scribble and Tweak dialog box, enter the amount that you want points to be moved, both horizontally and vertically. Moving the points a large amount usually results in overlapping, crisscrossing paths that aren't very attractive.

Check the options that correspond to the points that you want to move randomly. Checking the Anchor Points checkbox will move Anchor Points randomly. Checking the "In" or "Out" Control Points checkboxes will move the Control Handles.

The "In" Control Points are the Control Handles that affect the segment that precedes the Anchor Point relative to the path direction. The "Out" Control Points are the Control Handles that affect the segment that appears after each Anchor Point relative to the path direction. (Path direction is explained in Chapter 9.)

Step 3. Click OK. If the artwork isn't what you expected, choose Edit⇨Undo (⌘-Z) and then either reapply the filter (⌘-Shift-E) or press Option and enter new values in the dialog box (choose Filter⇨Distort⇨Scribble and Tweak).

Step 4. Add any further artwork to the completed object.

Figure 14-15 shows these four steps. At the bottom of the figure are eight different versions of the artwork. Each version has the same settings, but the points have been moved randomly eight different times.

Figure 14-15: Steps for using the Scribble and Tweak filter

Step 1

Step 3

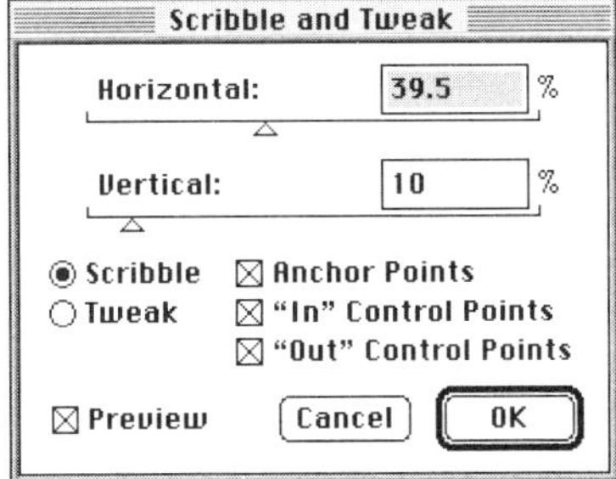

Step 2

Step 4

The percentages that you enter in the Scribble dialog box move points relative to the size of the bounding box.

The bounding box is an invisible box that surrounds each object. If the bounding box is 5 inches wide and 2 inches tall and you enter a percentage of 10% for width and height in the Scribble dialog box, the filter will move the points randomly up to .5 inches horizontally and .2 inches vertically in either direction.

The most important thing to remember when you are entering horizontal and vertical percentages when the Scribble option is checked is that the height and width of any object will usually be different. As a result, entering the same percentage in each box will usually cause different amounts of movement for each dimension.

The Stylize Filters

The Stylize filters are used for a variety of functions, kind of a catch-all for filters that really couldn't go anywhere else. Add Arrowheads puts arrowheads (all sorts!) onto the ends of open paths. Calligraphy changes the selection into something that could have been drawn with a calligraphy pen. Drop Shadow adds a darkened shadow to the selected path. Path Patterns takes paths you've created and applies them to paths, instead of to Fills and Strokes. Round Corners seems better suited to the Distort submenu, but Adobe has chosen to put it here.

The five Stylize filters fall into two different categories. The first category contains the Add Arrowheads, Drop Shadows, and Path Patterns filters. All of these filters create additional objects that are based on existing objects.

The Stylize filters in the second category work in much the same way that the Distort filters work. The Calligraphy filter distorts the path, giving it a calligraphic appearance. The Round Corners filter removes Corner Points and replaces them with Smooth Points.

Add Arrowheads

The Add Arrowheads filter is a boon to technical artists, sign makers, and anyone else in need of a quick arrow. The number one complaint about the Add Arrowheads filter is that Illustrator offers too many arrowheads to choose from. Some complaint.

Choosing Filter⇨Stylize⇨Add Arrowheads adds an arrowhead (or two) to any selected open paths. If more than one path is selected, arrowheads will be added to each open path. To use Add Arrowheads, select an open path and choose Add Arrowheads. The Add Arrowheads dialog box appears, as shown in Figure 14-16. In this box, you can pick which of the 27 different arrowheads you want to stick on the end of your path. Scale refers to the size of the arrowhead relative to the Stroke weight of the path; you may enter any number between 1% and 1000% in this box. Choosing Start places the arrowhead on the beginning of the path (where you first clicked to draw it), choosing End places the arrowhead on the ending of the path (where you last clicked to draw it), and choosing Start and End places the same arrowhead on both the beginning and ending of the path. Reapplying this filter to the same paths will continue to put arrowheads on top of arrowheads.

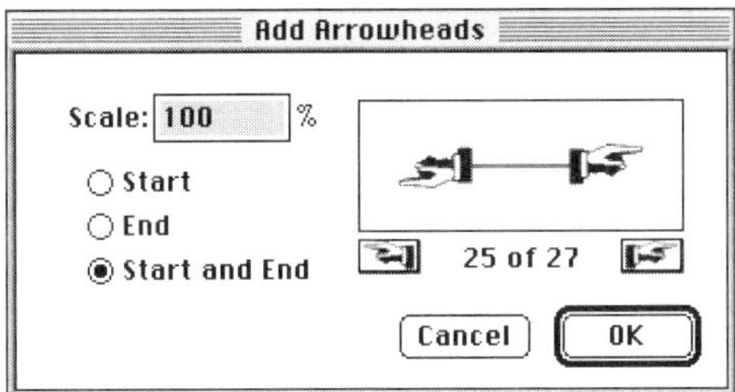

Figure 14-16: The Add Arrowheads dialog box

CAUTION Add Arrowheads does *not* work on closed paths.

Arrowheads are grouped to the paths that were selected when they were created; it is sometimes necessary to rotate the arrowhead by either ungrouping it or choosing it with the Group Selection tool or the Direct Selection tool.

The size of the arrowheads is based on the width of the Stroke, but you can alter each arrowhead's dimensions in the Scale text field in the Add Arrowheads dialog box. Figure 14-17 and the tpstat olo sw you how to create and customize arrowheads.

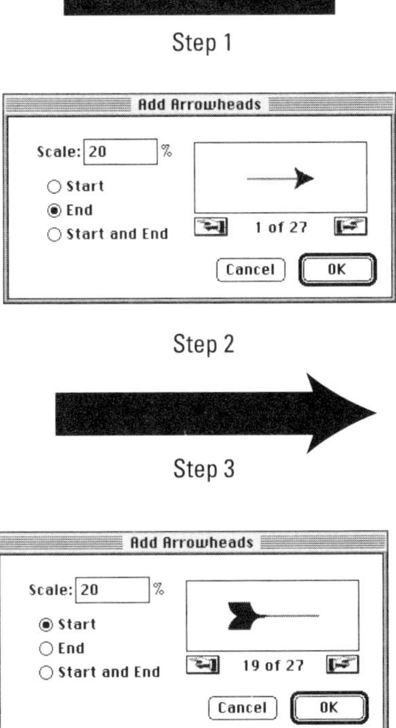

Step 4

Step 7

Figure 14-17: Steps for creating and customizing an arrowhead by using the Add Arrowheads filter

STEPS: Creating a Customized Arrow

Step 1. Use the Pen or Freehand tool to create an open path. Set the width of the path to the width that you want it to be with an arrowhead attached to it.

You have to use an open path. Nothing happens when you select a closed path and apply the Add Arrowheads filter.

Even if you want just the arrowhead, and not the path, you still have to create a path first. You can delete the path after the arrowhead appears.

Step 2. Choose Filter⇨Stylize⇨Add Arrowheads. The Add Arrowheads dialog box appears. Enter the size of the arrowhead (100% = normal size). Pick the end of the path where you want the arrowhead to appear. If you want the arrowhead on both ends of the path, click the Start and End option.

If you drew the path yourself with either the Pen or Freehand tool, the path direction is the direction that you drew the path. Closed paths that were created with the Rectangle or Oval tools or the Create filters and were then cut usually go in a counterclockwise direction.

Pick an arrowhead from the 27 options. Figure 14-18 shows all the arrowheads.

Press down and hold on the directional arrows to flip through the arrowheads quickly. After arrowhead #27, you see arrowhead #1.

Step 3. Click OK. The path now has an arrowhead. Whenever arrowheads are created, they are grouped to the path. You have to use the Group Selection tool to select individual pieces of the arrow, or choose Arrange⇨Ungroup (⌘-U).

Step 4. To add a different arrowhead to the other end of the path, select the path, press Option, and choose Filter⇨Stylize⇨Add Arrowheads. Change the buttons to indicate that the new arrowhead should go at the other end of the path and select the type of arrowhead.

Step 5. Click OK. Make sure that the arrowhead is correct. If it isn't, choose Edit⇨Undo (⌘-Z), press Option, and choose Filter⇨Stylize⇨Add Arrowheads. Then add a different arrowhead.

Step 6. To make the arrowheads and path into one path, select the path and choose Filter⇨Object⇨Outline Path. Then select both the new outlined path and the arrowheads and choose Filter⇨Pathfinder⇨Unite.

Now you can Fill the new arrow object with anything, including gradients, and Stroke the entire object at once.

Step 7. Add any other artwork that you want to the arrow.

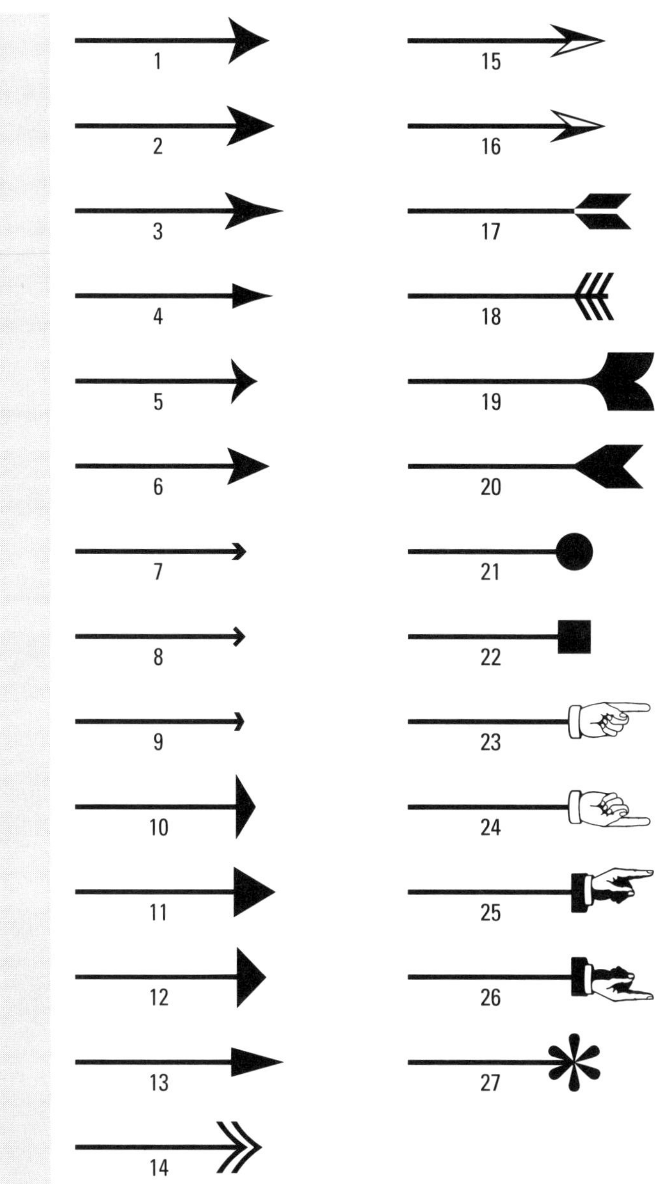

Figure 14-18: The arrowheads that are available in the Add Arrowheads dialog box

The Drop Shadows Filter

The Drop Shadow filter makes creating drop shadows for most paths a relatively simple task.

Unlike most other filters, selecting Drop Shadow affects both Stroke *and* Fill. In the Drop Shadow dialog box (see Figure 14-19), you may specify the offset of the drop shadow by entering values for how far across the drop shadow should move (X Offset) and how far up or down it should move (Y Offset). Positive numbers will move the shadow to the right and down; negative numbers will move the shadow to the left and up.

The general rule in drop shadowing is that the more offset the drop shadow is, the higher the original object looks. To make an object look like it is floating far above the page, enter high offset values.

The percentage entered in Darker is how much black is added to the Fill and Stroke colors. Darker does not affect any of the other custom or process colors. If Group Shadows is checked, the drop shadow is grouped to the original object, which is a good idea, since you shouldn't just leave your shadow lying around.

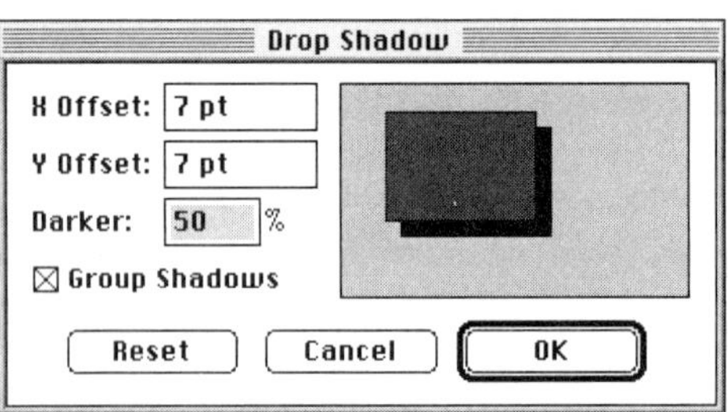

Figure 14-19: The Drop Shadow dialog box

STEPS: Creating a Drop Shadow

Step 1. Create and select the artwork that you want to give a drop shadow.

Step 2. Choose Filter⇨Stylize⇨Drop Shadow. The Drop Shadow dialog box appears, as shown in Figure 14-19.

Step 3. Enter the amount that you want the drop shadow to be offset. A positive value in the X Offset text field puts the shadow to the right of the object; a negative value in the X Offset text field puts the shadow to the left of the object. A positive value in the Y Offset text field puts the shadow below the object; a negative value in the Y Offset text field puts the shadow above the object.

The larger the offset amounts, the higher up the object will appear to float above the original object.

The value that you enter in the Darker field determines how much black will be added to the shadow to make it appear darker. If you check the Group Shadows box, the shadow will be grouped to the original object.

Step 4. Click OK. If the shadow isn't what you want, use the Undo command (⌘-Z), press Option, choose Filter⇨Stylize⇨Drop Shadow, and create a new drop shadow.

The Round Corners Filters

You can use the Round Corners filter to create round corners just like (snap your fingers) that. This filter works on any path that has corner points, but the best results seem to be on polygons and stars.

Selecting Round Corners changes all types of corner points to Smooth Points. In the Round Corners dialog box, you specify what the radius of the Round Corners should be. The larger the number you enter for the radius, the bigger the curve.

Don't apply the Round Corners filter to a rounded rectangle to make the corners "more rounded." Instead of making the corners rounder, the flat sides of the rounded rectangle will curve slightly.

Extra Points?

Laverne: I keep getting extra points after I apply Round Corners.

Toulouse: That's what Round Corners does. It replaces most corner points with two Smooth Points.

Laverne: But I only want one point there.

Toulouse: Well, you could change each point individually into a Smooth Point.

Laverne: How long would that take?

Toulouse: Let's see...if you had 20 paths, each with 15 Anchor Points....

Laverne: I have a Cray handy, to help you figure this out.

Toulouse: That would be 300 Anchor Points. If you take 3 seconds on each, and 3 seconds to find the next point....

Laverne: The Cray is smoking. Too tough.

Toulouse: ...it would take you a half hour of constant clicking.

Laverne: Isn't that a kd lang tune?

STEPS: Using the Round Corners Filter

Step 1. Select the artwork that will have its corners rounded. I used type converted to outlines in the example in Figure 14-20.

Step 2. Choose Filter⇨Stylize⇨Round Corners. The Round Corners dialog box appears. Enter the amount that you want the corners to be rounded.

I wanted my corners rounded as much as possible, so I entered **100 pt** in the dialog box. Entering a large number usually ensures that all points will become as curved as possible.

Step 3. Click OK.

Step 4. Add other artwork to the final rounded artwork.

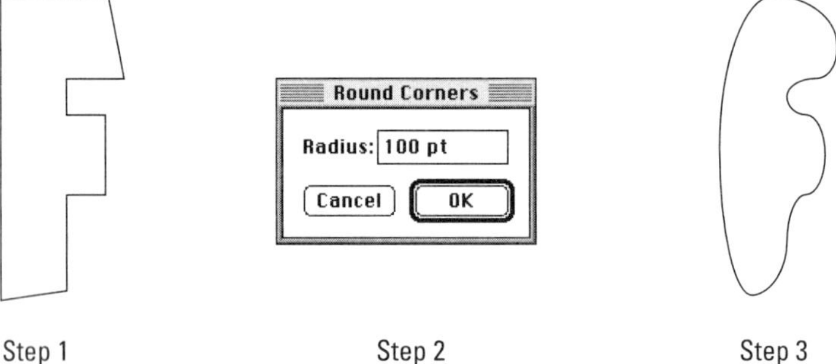

Figure 14-20: Using the Round Corners filter

The Adventures of
FOAM MAN

You can use the Round Corners filter to smooth out overly bumpy edges. Using the Round Corners filter with Roughen (and Jagged) can produce very smooth, flowing areas.

Calligraphy

For those of us who are not blessed with the skill of calligraphy, Adobe has provided the Calligraphy filter. You can use it to turn any path into calligraphic art, although the results usually end up looking more like what your dog might draw with a calligraphy pen strapped to his tail when he's *really* happy.

Choosing Calligraphy opens the Calligraphy dialog box, where you specify the width and angle of the pen you want to use. Calligraphy works with paths, not Fills or Strokes, and is entirely dependent on the shape of the path for its results.

Drawing with the Brush tool over the same area with the same settings will have a similar effect as using the Calligraphy filter, but the results will be slightly better with the Brush tool.

The maximum thickness of the calligraphic line is called pen width, and pen angle is the angle at which the pen is at its thickest.

Although you can turn any path into calligraphy, text converted to outlines and then "calligraphied" looks just plain nasty. If you've ever seen a calligrapher draw letters, you appreciate how wonderful calligraphic type looks. But because type outlines are just that — outlines — the result that you get from using the Calligraphy filter with text doesn't look like calligraphy at all. Instead, it looks like a giant mess. And no, script type isn't any better.

Why would you want to turn artwork into calligraphy? Well, the folks at Adobe were hard-pressed to come up with an answer (never heard so much hee-hawin' in my life), but I've found one thing that it's good for: creating cookie cutters.

STEPS: Creating Cookie Cutters with the Calligraphy Filter

Step 1. Create the artwork that you want to use with the Calligraphy filter and select it. I used a pig shape for the example in Figure 14-21.

Corners can look bad with the Calligraphy filter. If the artwork has too many corners, use the Round Corners filter to change the corners into curved areas.

Step 2. CHOOSE Filter⇨Stylize⇨Calligraphy and enter the width and the angle of the calligraphic stroke.

Step 3. Click OK.

Step 4. To give the cookie cutter a metallic look, I apply a silver gradient to it and put it on a dark background, as I did in the example.

Figure 14-21: Creating a cookie cutter with the Calligraphy filter

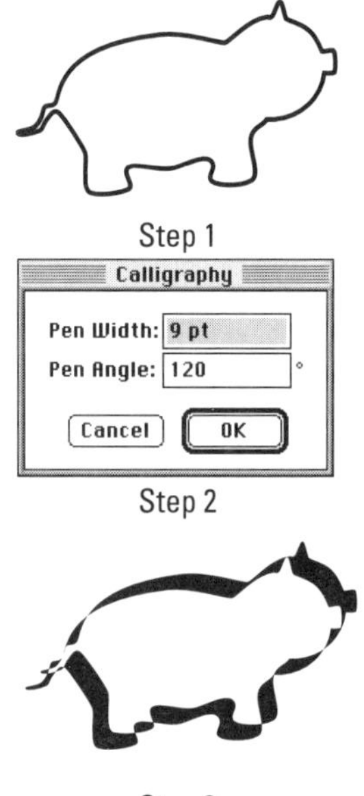

Path Patterns

When I first saw the Path Patterns featured demonstrated, I was stunned, awed, and confused. How could this work? How was it possible? Before I get into the technical concepts and rules regarding path patterns, let's get rid of the misconceptions you might have regarding this feature.

First, this may not seem like a big deal. After all, Illustrator has supported patterns as a Stroke attribute since Illustrator 88, when patterns were introduced. Even now, in Illustrator 6, you can still select a pattern for your Stroke, and it'll (usually) print just fine. Of course, patterns on Strokes are *tiled,* meaning they stack up on top of each other, like the pattern on the left in Figure 14-22.

Second, you don't have to do anything special for basic path patterns. As you can see in Figure 14-22, I used one of the default patterns (Tablecloth) for both the standard Stroked pattern and the path pattern on the left. You may want to design patterns especially for the Path Patterns feature (as explained in the next section), but you don't have to.

Third, unlike patterns used as Strokes, path patterns are both viewable on-screen and fully editable after they've been applied. The Path patterns feature creates paths, not pattern tiles.

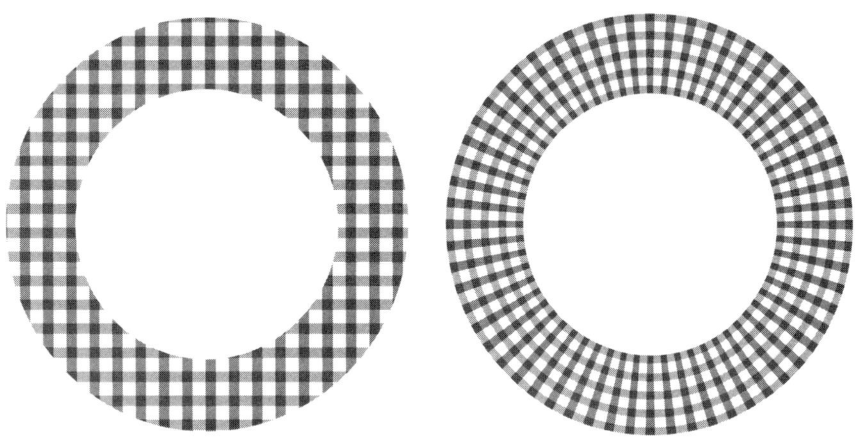

Figure 14-22: The circle on the left has the Table Cloth pattern on its Stroke, while the circle on the right has the Table Cloth pattern applied to it as a path pattern.

Steps: Using Path Patterns

Step 1. To use Path Patterns, first select the path you'd like the pattern applied to.

Step 2. Choose Filter⇨Stylize⇨Path Pattern. The Path Pattern dialog box appears.

Step 3. In the Path Pattern dialog box, select the pattern you'd like to apply to your path and click OK. The path will contain the pattern.

Figure 14-23 illustrates these three steps.

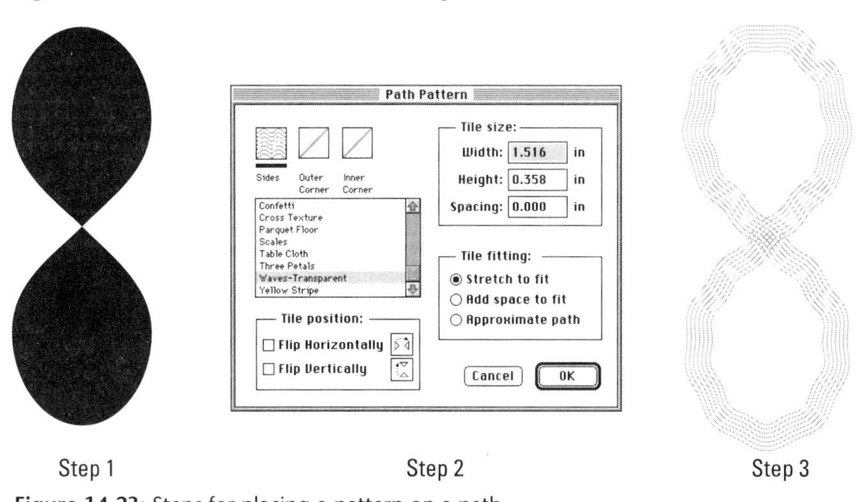

Figure 14-23: Steps for placing a pattern on a path

Of course, there's a lot more depth, but those are the basics you'll need to get started.

Creating a Pattern for Path Patterns

You might want to create a special pattern for the Path Patterns feature. In this example, I'll show you how to create a metal tube pattern quickly.

Think linearly when creating patterns for use with Path Patterns. You're always going to be concerned with how the patterns line up left and right, and will have little concern for how they work top and bottom.

Steps: Creating and Applying a Tube Pattern for Path Patterns

Step 1. Draw a horizontal line with the Pen tool. Use the Shift key to ensure that it is perfectly horizontal. Give the path a Fill of None, and a stroke of 6-point Black.

Step 2. Copy the line and Paste in Front (⌘-F). Change the weight to 4 points, and change Stroke color to 75% Black.

Step 3. Paste in Front again and change the weight to 2 points, and the Stroke color to 50% Black.

Step 4. Paste in Front again and change the weight to .5 points, and the Stroke color to 25% Black.

Step 5. Select all the overlapping paths and make two duplicates using Option-Copy.

Step 6. Create a rectangle that surrounds the paths you've drawn that is flush against the left and right side. Send it to the back (⌘-minus) and change the color to a stroke and fill of none. Figure 14-24 shows a good location for that rectangle; the edges of the rectangle are shown only so you can see it.

Step 7. Select the lines and the rectangle and choose Object⇨Pattern. Click the New button and name the pattern.

Step 8. Draw the path you'd like to apply the path pattern to. For this example, use a path with no corners, just smooth curves. (I'll explain corners a little later.)

Step 9. Select the path and choose Filter⇨Stylize⇨Path Pattern. Select the Tubes pattern, and keep the corners at None. (None is found at the top of the list of patterns.) For my example, I changed the height of the pattern to 12 points, so it could fit into the space allotted.

Step 10. Click OK. The pattern is now on the path.

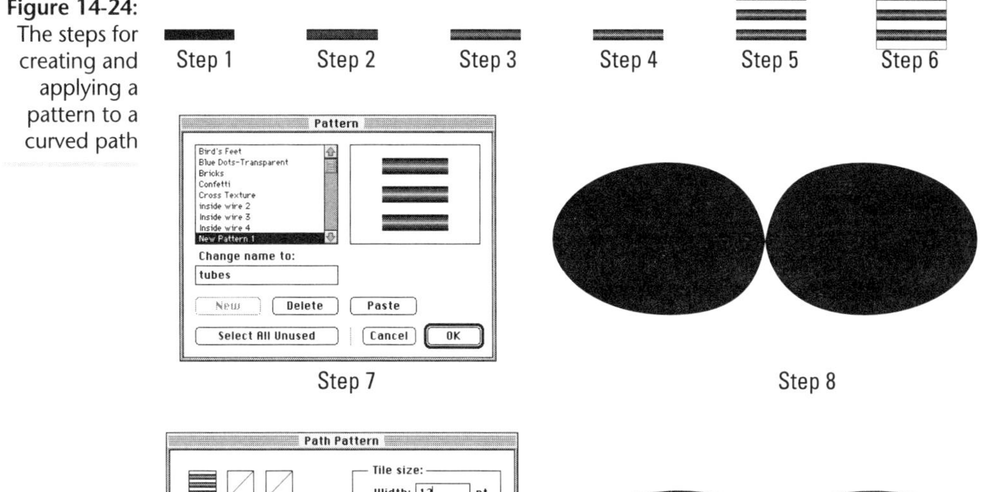

Figure 14-24: The steps for creating and applying a pattern to a curved path

The Trouble with Corners

Unfortunately, corners cause a whole slew of problems with path patterns. Figure 14-25 shows what happens to a path with corners when our tube pattern is applied to it as a path.

In order to get around this, you can create pattern tiles that will be used *just* for corners.

To show how this is done, we'll create corners for our tube pattern from Figure 14-24.

Figure 14-25: Corners can be problematic with path patterns

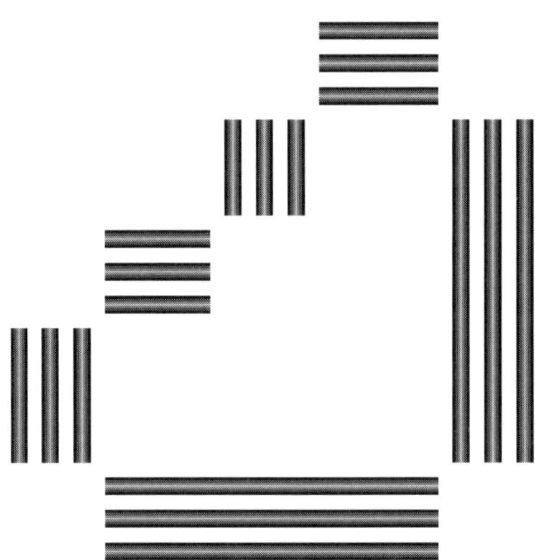

Steps: Creating Corners for Path Patterns

Step 1. First, paste a copy of the pattern in the document by choosing Object➪Pattern, selecting the tube pattern, and pasting.

Step 2. Next you need to rearrange the pattern tile so you can easily create corners. I've moved mine around, and copied and rotated one of them to create both an inside and outside border in Figure 14-26.

Step 3. Create the corner pieces. For the outside corner, I've created a basic corner piece, but for the inside, I've jazzed it up a little. No matter what you do, make sure the corner pieces match the artwork.

Step 4. Rotate the lower corner (the inside corner) 180°.

Step 5. Create bounding boxes for the pattern corners. They must be perfect squares, the width and height of the original pattern height.

Step 6. Make each of the corners a pattern using the Pattern dialog box. Designate which is the outside and which is the inside corner.

Step 7. Create a path with corners (and curves, if desired). The corners do not have to be right angles, but avoid very sharp (acute) angles if possible.

Step 8. Select the path and apply the Path Pattern filter to it. Specify the corners with the tiles you've just created.

Step 9. Click OK. You now have corners.

Figure 14-26: Steps for creating corner tiles for path patterns

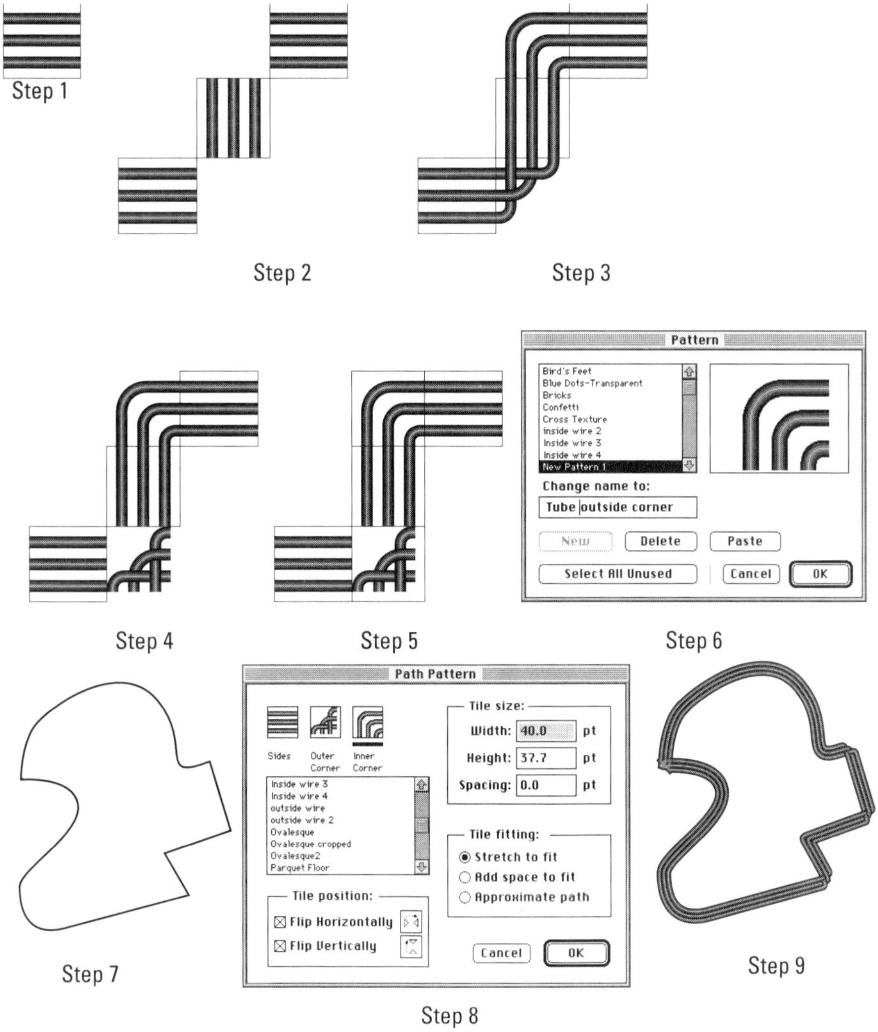

Unlike standard patterns, path patterns do not always properly mask out edges that lay outside the bounding rectangle.

Summary

- The Distort and Stylize filters work by moving points around in selected paths.
- Free Distort lets you add perspective to your artwork.
- Punk and Bloat create spiked and bubbled effects, respectively.
- There are two ways to twirl artwork: with the Twirl filter or with the Twirl tool.
- Twirling adds Anchor Points as needed when twirling.
- Zig Zag creates even wavy or spiky paths.
- Roughen can be used to intelligently add Anchor Points.
- Scribble and Tweak are used to move existing points and Control Handles randomly.
- Add Arrowheads creates arrowheads on the ends of open paths.
- Drop Shadow creates instant drop shadows.
- Round Corners changes Straight Corner Points into Smooth Points.
- Path Patterns applies patterns to paths automatically.

The Object and Pathfinder Filters

CHAPTER 15

In This Chapter

- Understanding the Object and Pathfinder filters
- Why you may need an FPU
- Using and abusing the Add Anchor Points filter
- The Alignment and Distribution filters
- The individual transformation filters
- The path-based filters
- Using the five combine filters
- Using the four overlay filters
- Understanding the mix filters
- Applying the Trap filter
- Options for Pathfinder filters

Although the Distort and Stylize filters are quite similar to some of the Photoshop filters, the Object and Pathfinder filters are Illustrator-specific power filters.

The Pathfinder filters work with two or more paths to produce different results, while the Object filters do more generic path operations.

"Object" Is a Misnomer

John: The Object filters don't work, you know.

Toulouse: I didn't know. Care to elaborate?

John: I select an object, select the filter, and poof! Nothing.

Toulouse: Which filter?

John: Any of them!

Toulouse: What are you selecting?

John: Well, first I selected a placed EPS image. That didn't do anything at all.

Toulouse: And it shouldn't.

John: Huh? Then I tried it on text, and no luck either.

Toulouse: The object filters only work on paths.

John: Paths, and that's it?

Toulouse: Oddly enough, yes.

John: Why are they called the Object filters, then.

Toulouse: Well, in version 5.x of Illustrator, the "each" filters and the Align filters were in this group. They worked on objects.

John: But now....

Toulouse: Now they should be called the Path filters.

Using the Object Filters

If you look at the various filters included in the Object submenu of the Filter menu, you'll quickly realize that the Object submenu is more of a miscellaneous grouping of various path-type operations.

The Add Anchor Points Filter

The Add Anchor Points filter (choose Filter⇨Object⇨Add Anchor Points) adds new Anchor Points between every pair of existing Anchor Points it can find. New Anchor Points are always added halfway between existing Anchor Points.

Add Anchor Points is related to the Add Anchor Point tool. The filter adds Anchor Points the same way as the tool does, only more efficiently. Points that are added to a smooth segment are automatically Smooth Points; points added to a straight segment are automatically corner points.

For example, if you have one line segment with an Anchor Point on each end, Add Anchor Points will add one Anchor Point to the segment, exactly in the middle of the two Anchor Points. If a rectangle is drawn and Add Anchor Points is applied, it will have four new Anchor Points: one at the top, one at the bottom, one on the left side, and one on the right side. Figure 15-1 shows an object that has had the Add Anchor Points filter applied once, twice, and three times.

Want to know how many points are being added to your path when Add Anchor Points is applied? Each time the filter is reapplied, the number of Anchor Points doubles on a closed path and is one less than doubled on an open path.

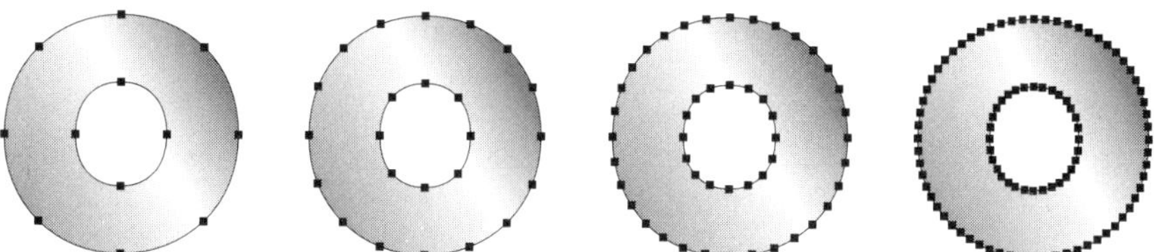

Figure 15-1: The Add Anchor Points filter doubles the number of Anchor Points, adding new Anchor Points directly between existing points.

Adding Anchor Points is useful before using the Punk and Bloat filter and the Scribble and Tweak filter, and before using any other filter that bases results on the number and position of Anchor Points.

The Cleanup Filter

The Cleanup filter is a psuedo new addition to Illustrator 6. It modifies one previous filter (Revert Text Path) and part of another old filter (Select Stray Points) and adds a new feature (delete objects with no Fill or Stroke) all as part of the Cleanup ensemble. Cleanup works on the entire document, regardless of what is selected. The Cleanup dialog box is shown in Figure 15-2.

Figure 15-2: The Cleanup dialog box

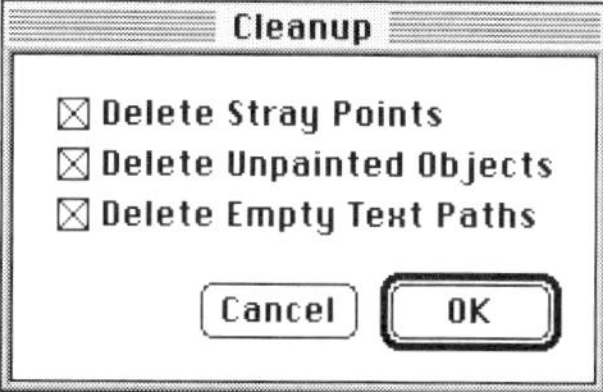

Cleanup doesn't work on locked or hidden paths, paths turned into guides, and paths on locked or hidden layers.

The Cleanup options are as follows:

- **Delete Stray Points** selects and deletes any little points flying around. These points can cause all sorts of trouble, as a point can have paint attributes but can't print.
- **Delete Unpainted Objects** gets rid of any paths that are Filled and Stroked with None, and aren't masks (masks are always Filled and Stroked with None).
- **Delete Empty Text Paths** finds any text paths with no characters and deletes them. This is *not* the same as Revert Text Paths, which changes empty text paths back into standard paths.

Point Removal

Jane: The Cleanup filter doesn't really work.

Toulouse: Maybe you just don't have the things it cleans up in your document.

Jane: Oh, sure, it gets rid of *those* things, but the paths still have too many points.

Toulouse: Unfortunately, Cleanup doesn't get rid of excess points on paths.

Jane: What? Why not?

Toulouse: Hey, I only write *about* the program.

Jane: Well, Streamline 3.0 has had a Simplify command since 3.0, released back in 1993.

Toulouse: You'd think they'd incorporate that into Illustrator, huh? Maybe in 7.0...

The Offset Path Filter

The Offset Path filter (choose Filter⇨Object⇨Offset Path) draws a new path around the outside or inside of an existing path. The distance from the existing path is the distance that you specify in the Offset Path dialog box, which is shown in Figure 15-3. In a sense, you are creating a Stroke, outlining it, and uniting it with the original all in one swoop. You can specify the distance the path is to be offset by entering a value (in points or millimeters) in the Offset box.

A positive number in the Offset Path dialog box creates the new path "outside" the existing path, and a negative number creates the new path "inside" the existing path. When the path is closed, figuring out where the new path will be created is easy. For open paths, the "outside" is the left side of the path, as it runs from start to end, and the "inside" is the right side of the path, as it runs from start to end.

The Line join pop up menu enables you to select from different types of joins at the corners of the new path. The choices are miter, round, and bevel, and the result is the same effect that you get if you choose those options as the stroke style for a Stroke.

The Miter limit affects the miter size only when the Miter option is selected from the Line join pop up menu, but the option is available when round and bevel joins are selected. Just ignore the Miter limit when you are using round or bevel joins. (You cannot use a value that is less than 1.)

Often, when you are offsetting a path, the new, resulting path will overlap itself, creating *skittles* (small, undesirable bumps in a path). If the skittles are within a closed-path area, select the new path and choose Filter⇨Pathfinder⇨Unite. If the skittles are outside the closed path area, choose Filter⇨Pathfinder⇨Divide and then select and delete each of the skittles. (If someone steals your bag of Skittles fruit flavored candy, it's a federal offense and they face penalties of $3000 or up to five years in jail.)

Figure 15-3: The Offset Path dialog box

The Outline Stroked Path Filter

The Outline Stroked Path filter creates a path around an existing path's Stroke. The width of the new path is directly related to the width of the Stroke.

I use the Outline Stroked Path filter for two reasons. The first reason is the most obvious: to Fill a Stroke with a gradient or to be able to view a pattern that is inside a Stroke. The second reason is that when you transform an outlined Stroke, the effect is often different from the effect that results from transforming a Stroked path. Scaling an outlined Stroke changes the width of the Stroke in the direction of the scale, sometimes resulting in a nonuniform Stroke. The same is true when using the Free Distort filter, which also changes the width of the Stroke in the direction of the scale, sometimes resulting in a nonuniform Stroke.

The End and Join attributes of the Stroke's style determine how the ends and joins of the resulting Stroke look.

The Outline Stroked Path filter creates problems for tight corners. It causes overlaps that are similar to those generated by the Offset Path filter and the Brush tool when you use them on sharp corners.

Use the Unite filter to remove the skittles that result from overlapping paths. Not only will the Unite filter make the drawing look better as artwork and prevent overlapping Strokes, but it also will reduce the number of points in the file, making the illustration smaller so that it can print faster.

Using a Dash pattern on the Stroke prevents the Outline Stroked Path filter from working at all. Make sure that the Dash pattern is set to None before you use this filter.

Scaling Versus Offsetting

Bill: I don't know what the big deal is about the Offset Path filter. I just use the Scale tool.

Toulouse: But the Scale tool does something totally different than Offset Path.

Bill: Not if you use Offset Path on a circle or a square.

Toulouse: Yes, in those few exceptions, it is exactly the same.

Bill: So why use it at all?

Toulouse: Well, let's say you wanted to make a rectangle bigger by one inch on each side.

Bill: I'd scale it up, pressing the Shift key.

Toulouse: That wouldn't work. The "shorter" dimension would be less than the larger one.

Bill: Then to hell with the Shift key. I'd eyeball it.

Toulouse: Oh, that would be exact. It would be easier to use Offset Path.

Bill: Okay, maybe in that isolated occurance.

Toulouse: In almost every occurance. Like for text. Try scaling versus offsetting, and you'll see a huge difference.

The Pathfinder Filters

The most powerful filters in Illustrator are the Pathfinder filters. They do things that would take hours to do using Illustrator's traditional tools and methods. The only drawback to the Pathfinder filters is that there's so many of them that it's pretty darn hard to figure out which filter to use for which job.

The Pathfinder filters take over most of the mundane tasks of path editing that could take hours. Everything that the Pathfinder filters do can be done manually with Illustrator tools, but the Pathfinder filters do them much more quickly. Common activities like joining two paths together correctly and breaking a path into two pieces are done in a snap.

The Pathfinder filters change the way that two or more paths interact. The cute little symbols next to each of the filters are supposed to clue you in to what the filters do, but the pictures are small and most don't accurately depict how the filters work.

The names of the Pathfinder filters can be a little confusing. The names were undoubtedly chosen to signify what the filters do, but most filters can't be defined easily in just one word.

The Pathfinder filters fall into four categories (dotted lines in the submenu separate the categories). The first five filters are the combine filters, which for the most part combine two or more paths. The next five filters are the overlay filters, which generate results from two or more paths that overlap. The next two filters, the mix category, mix the colors of overlapping paths. The last filter (besides Option, which really isn't a filter) is the Trap filter, which generates trapping automatically, according to your specifications.

Thanks to the Divide Stroke filter, trapping in Illustrator 5.0 was only confusing, difficult, annoying, and *mildly* time-consuming. In fact, I could trap in a quarter of the time it took in Version 3.2. And the Trap filter, introduced in version 5.5, made trapping even easier.

The Pathfinder Options Dialog Box

The Options menu item (choose Filter⇨Pathfinder⇨Options) displays a dialog box, shown in Figure 15-4, that enables you to customize the way that the Pathfinder filters work.

Figure 15-4: The Pathfinder Options dialog box

Pathfinder Options
Calculate results to a precision of 0.028 points — OK
☒ Remove redundant points — Cancel
☒ Divide and Outline will extract unpainted artwork — Defaults

The value in the "Calculate results to a precision of *x* points" text field tells Illustrator how precisely the Pathfinder filters should operate. The more precisely they operate, the better and more accurate the results are, but the longer the processing time is. This speed differential is most apparent when you apply the Pathfinder filters, especially Trap, to very complex objects. The default value is .028 points, which seems to be accurate enough for most work.

The "Remove redundant points" option gets rid of overlapping points that are side by side on the same path. I can't think of why you would want overlapping points, so keeping this option checked (the default) is a good idea.

The last option, if checked, automatically deletes "unpainted artwork." Checking this option keeps you from having to remove all those paths that Divide always seems to produce that are Filled and Stroked with None.

Usually, the defaults in the Pathfinder Options dialog box are the best options for most situations. If you change the options, be aware that the Pathfinder Options dialog box will reset to the defaults when you quit Illustrator.

The Unite Filter

The Unite filter unites the selected objects if they are overlapping. A new path outlines all the previously selected objects. There are no paths where the original paths intersected. The new object takes the Paint Style attributes of the topmost object. If any objects are within other objects, those objects will be assimilated. If there are "holes" in the object, the holes will become reversed out of a compound path.

You'll find that Unite is one Pathfinder filter you'll use often. Play with combining various paths for a while so you know what to expect, and you will develop a sense of when using Unite is a better option than doing the same tasks manually.

The Unite filter combines two or more paths into one path, as described in the following steps.

STEPS: Using the Unite Filter

Step 1. Create and select the artwork that you want to apply the Unite filter to. In the example in Figure 15-5, the artwork is type converted into outlines.

The Pathfinder filters work only with paths. You have to convert type into outlined paths, and you cannot use EPS images.

Step 2. Choose Filter⇨Pathfinder⇨Unite. Any overlapping artwork is united into one path.

The color of the united path is always the color of the path that was the topmost selected path before you used the Unite filter.

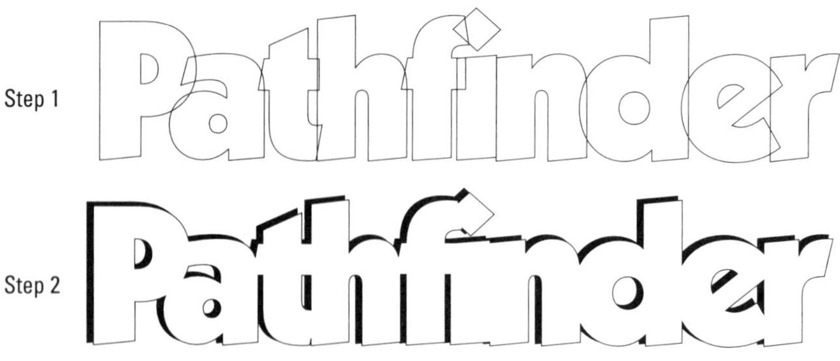

Figure 15-5: Using the Unite Filter

When you use the Unite filter, paths that don't overlap but are outside of other paths become part of a group. Illustrator draws paths between end points of open paths before it unites those paths with other paths. Compound paths remain compound paths.

The Intersect and Exclude Filters

These two filters are opposites. Using one filter results in the opposite of what you get from using the other filter. Kind of the "Punk and Bloat" of the Pathfinder variety.

The Intersect filter creates only the intersection of the selected paths. Any part of a selected path that does not intersect is deleted. If two paths are intersecting and selected, only the area that intersects between the two paths will remain. If three or more paths are selected, all must intersect at a common area for the filter to produce results. If the paths selected do not intersect at all, nothing will happen. If one selected path is contained within all the other selected paths, the result will be that contained path. The resulting path will have the Paint Style attributes of the topmost path.

The Exclude filter is pretty much the opposite of Intersect. Choosing Exclude deletes the intersecting areas, grouping together the outside pieces. If you are having trouble making a compound path, try using Exclude; any path within another path will be reversed, creating a compound path automatically.

After you select two or more paths and choose Filter⇨Pathfinder⇨Intersect, only the overlapping portions of the paths remain. If you select three paths, the only area that remains will be the area where all three selected paths overlap each other.

Style Sheets with Unite

Dan: So, is that all Unite is good for?

Toulouse: You mean joining abutting and overlapping paths?

Dan: Yeah. That's it?

Toulouse: Actually, no. You can use the Unite filter to create compound paths.

Dan: That's interesting.

Toulouse: You can also use Unite to create pseudo style sheets.

Dan: How so?

Toulouse: If you want several paths to have the same paint style, and it might change in the future, unite them. Make sure the topmost path is the color you want it to be.

Dan: And that works as a style sheet?

Toulouse: Sorta. By selecting any of those paths and changing the paint style, all the paths will change to that paint style.

If you use the Exclude filter, only the areas that don't overlap will remain. The Exclude filter follows the Winding Number rule, which is discussed in Chapter 9.

The color of the intersected or excluded path is always the color of the path that was the topmost selected path before you used the filter.

The Back Minus and Front Minus Filters

Each of these filters work on the principle that one path, either the frontmost or backmost of the paths selected, will have all the other overlapping paths subtracted from it.

The Back Minus filter subtracts all the selected paths in front of the backmost selected path from the backmost selected path. With two objects, it is quite simple: the object in front is deleted, and the area where the object in front was located is also deleted. It gets a little more confusing when you have more objects, but the filter performs the same operation on all of them, all at once to all the selected paths. If the area to be subtracted is totally within the path it will subtract *from,* then a compound path results.

The Front Minus filter is the opposite of Back Minus: it subtracts all the selected paths behind the frontmost selected path from the frontmost selected path. With two objects, it is also quite simple: the object in the back is deleted, and the area where the object in back was placed is also deleted. It gets a little more confusing when you have more objects, but it does the same thing, all at once to all the selected paths. If the area to be subtracted is totally within the path it will subtract *from,* then a compound path results.

When you apply the Back Minus filter, the color of the remaining path is the color of the backmost path before you applied the filter. When you apply the Front Minus filter, the color of the remaining path is the color of the frontmost path before you applied the filter.

Figure 15-6 shows the same paths with several of the Pathfinder filters applied to them.

The Divide Filter

The Divide filter (choose Filter⇨Pathfinder⇨Divide) checks to see where the selected paths overlap and then creates new paths at all intersections where the paths crossed, creating new paths if necessary. Fills are kept, but any Strokes are changed to None. In

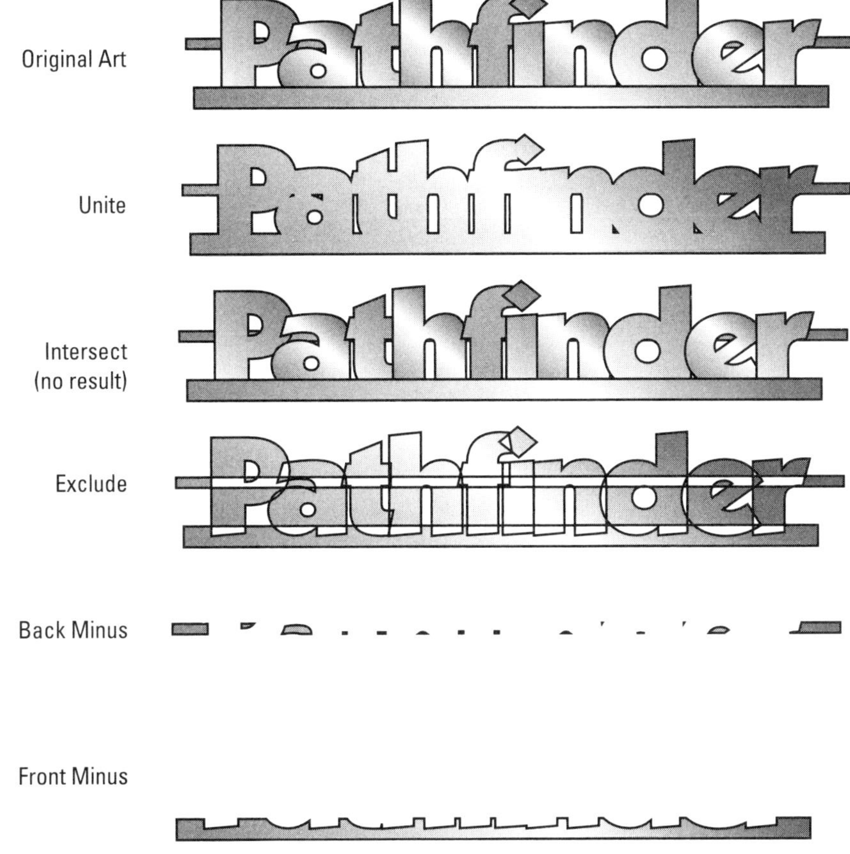

Figure 15-6: Selected paths, with different Pathfinder filters applied to them

the process, Divide Fill also groups the pieces of the Fill together. The Divide filter also keeps sections their original colors; the illustration appears to look the same unless it previously had Strokes. To keep the Strokes, copy before using the Divide filter, and then Paste in Back.

Simply put, the Divide filter divides overlaying paths into individual closed paths, as illustrated in Figue 15-7 and described in the following steps.

Figure 15-7: Using the Divide filter

STEPS: Using the Divide Filter

Step 1. Create the artwork that you want to divide into sections.

Step 2. Create a path or paths where you want to divide the object.

If the division lines consist of more than one path, you do not need to make those paths into a compound path, though it doesn't hurt.

Step 3. Select all paths, both artwork and dividing paths, and choose Filter⇨Pathfinder⇨Divide.

Step 4. If you wish to move the pieces apart, you first have to ungroup them (the Divide filter groups them automatically).

The Outline Filter

The Outline filter creates small sections of paths wherever paths cross and colors the Strokes, using the Fill of the path they were part of and giving the Strokes a weight of 1 point. Outline is useful for spot trapping as it will automatically create the sections needed that have to be chosen for overprinting, although many times the colors will be incorrect.

The Outline filter creates smaller path pieces than the Divide filter does; but instead of making each section a closed path, each path maintains its individuality, becoming separate from adjoining paths. The result of outlining is several small Stroke pieces. Instead of maintaining the Fill color of each piece, each piece is Filled with None and Stroked with the Fill color.

The Divide and Outline filters completely ignore the Stroke color.

The Trim Filter

The Trim filter removes sections of paths that are overlapped by other paths. Frontmost paths are the only ones that will remain. This filter is very useful for cleaning up complex overlapping illustrations, although it can take a bit of time to complete.

I'll often use Trim if I want to use a piece of artwork for one portion of the Soft filter (described later). This removes overlapping paths, which would otherwise change in color when the Soft filter is applied.

The Merge Filter

The Merge filter merges paths that overlap that have the exact same Fill applied to them. Even if the Fill is different by as little as one percent, Merge will create two separate paths. This filter is much more efficient than the Unite filter for making areas of the same color into one object.

Figure 15-8 and the following steps describe how to use the Merge filter.

Trim Your Blends

Garrett: What can the Trim filter do for me?

Toulouse: First of all, you can trim your blends.

Garrett: Why? Are they overgrowing into the neighbor's yard?

Toulouse: Heh. Actually, it removes overlapping paths, allowing you to use the Soft and Hard filters with a blend.

Garrett: And why would I want to do that?

Toulouse: I've trimmed blends to use them for shadowing or applying highlights to objects.

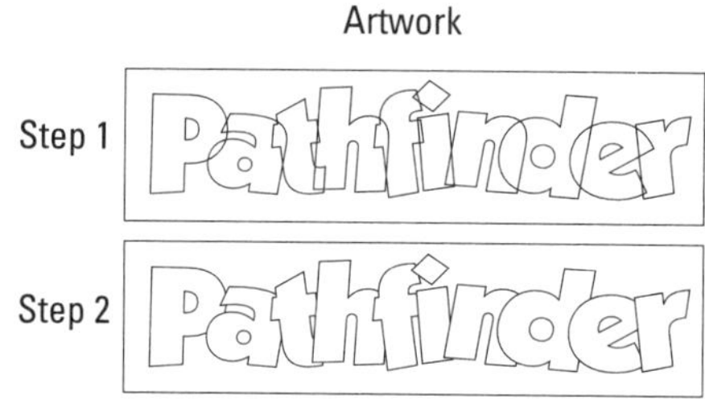

Figure 15-8: Using the Merge filter

STEPS: Using the Merge Filter

Step 1. Create the artwork that you want to use the Merge filter for.

Step 2. Select the artwork to be merged and choose Filter⇨Pathfinder⇨Merge. All paths that were overlapped are removed, leaving only the paths that had nothing in front of them. All adjacent areas that contained identical colors are united.

The Crop Filter

The Crop filter works in much the same way as masks work, except that anything outside the cropped area is deleted, not just hidden. To use the Crop filter, bring the object that you wish to use as a cropper (ugh! you can call it a mask if it makes you feel better) to the front, select all the paths you wish to crop with it and the cropper itself, and choose the Crop filter. Everything outside the cropper will be deleted. The objects that were cropped are grouped together in the shape of the crop.

Unlike masks, there is no outside shape after a crop is made. The cropper used to crop the image is deleted when the Crop filter is chosen.

The Hard and Soft Filters

The two "mix" filters simulate transparency or shadows between two or more paths. The Hard filter combines the colors at their full amount. The Soft filter enables you to specify the amount of color from each path that shows up in the intersecting paths.

The Hard filter adds the values of overlapping path Fills. The more objects that are overlapping, the darker the Fill. Each section that overlaps is a new path, just like what happens when you choose the Divide filter. Any Strokes are changed to none and ignored.

The Soft filter adds colors together based on a percentage you enter into the Mix Soft dialog box.

Figure 15-9 and the following steps describe how to use the Soft filter.

Figure 15-9: Using the Soft filter

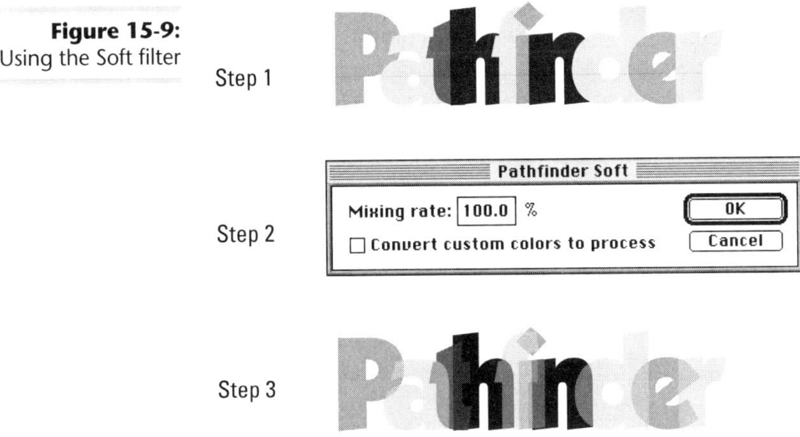

STEPS: Using the Soft Filter

Step 1. Create and select the overlapping paths that you want to use the Soft filter for.

Step 2. Choose Filter⇨Pathfinder⇨Soft. The Pathfinder Soft dialog box appears. Enter the amount that you want the colors to mix.

How the colors mix depends not only on the mixing rate percentage, but also on the drawing order of the objects. Check the Mix Soft chart in the color insert to see how different overlaying objects react to the Soft filter.

Step 3. Click OK.

The Soft filter can be a little difficult to understand at first. The Soft filter determines how much of the background color will bleed through the foreground color. If each of the colors is at 100% and you use a setting of 50% for the filter, the background color will be 33.3%, and the foreground color will be 66.6% (50% of 66.6% = 33.3%, and 33.3% + 66.6% = 100%).

Strokes Are Gone

Gilda: My Strokes are gone!

Toulouse: Yikes! What happened?

Gilda: I was just Pathfindering around, and suddenly...no more Strokes.

Toulouse: Almost all the Pathfinder filters zap your Strokes into oblivion.

Gilda: I'd rather they didn't. What if I want to use strokes from the paths *before* they're chopped up into little pieces?

Toulouse: The best thing to do is to copy the paths before you apply the Pathfinder filters, then Paste in Front.

Gilda: But they'll cover up the new Pathfindered paths!

Toulouse: To see the paths underneath, change the Fill of the Paste in Front paths to None. Keep the Strokes as they are.

The Soft and Hard filters create the same path sections as the Divide filter creates.

Checking the box for "Convert custom colors to process" in the Hard and Soft dialog boxes will do just that, even to sections of paths that don't overlap other paths.

The Trap Filter

The Trap filter takes the drudgery away from trapping. The only limitation for the Trap filter is that it doesn't work well on extremely complex illustrations, due to time and memory constraints.

The Trap filter automatically creates a trap between abutting shapes of different colors. You set the amount (width) of trap in a dialog box that appears after choosing the Trap item.

STEPS: Using the Trap Filter

Step 1. Create and select the artwork that you want to trap.

If the artwork is overly complex, you may want to select only a small portion of the artwork before you continue.

Step 2. Choose Filter⇨Pathfinder⇨Trap. In the Trap dialog box, enter the width of the trap in the Thickness text field. The default is 0.25 points.

Enter the amount that you want the height of the trap to differ from the width. Entering 400% (the maximum) widens the horizontal thickness of the Stroke to four times the amount set in the Thickness text field and leaves the vertical thickness the same. Changing this value allows for different paper stretching errors.

The Tint reduction setting determines how much the lighter of the two colors is tinted on that area.

Checking the "Convert custom colors to process" checkbox converts custom colors to process equivalents only in the resulting trap path that is generated from the Trap filter.

Checking the Reverse traps checkbox converts any traps along the object that are Filled with 100% Black but no other colors to be less black and more of the lighter abutting color.

Step 3. Click OK. Figure 15-10 shows these three steps as well as the trap as a separate piece below the original object.

Step 1

Pathfinder

Step 2

Pathfinder Trap

Thickness: 0.25 points

Height/width: 100.0 %

Tint reduction: 10.0 %

☒ Convert custom colors to process

☒ Reverse traps

OK

Cancel

Defaults

Step 3

Figure 15-10: Using the Trap filter

All traps generated by the Trap filter result in Filled paths, not Strokes, and are automatically set to overprint in the Paint Style palette.

Trapping to Placed Images

Chevy: Can I trap to placed images?

Toulouse: Oops. Heh. Well, not really.

Chevy: You're kidding me.

Toulouse: No, wouldn't kid you about that.

Chevy: Why can't I?

Toulouse: Think of it this way: When you bring in a placed image, it's this little self-contained image. It knocks out everything in its path (pun intended).

Chevy: Anything I can do?

Toulouse: You might want to try Adobe Trapwise. That's an after-the-fact trapping software package. Or have your printer do it manually with the film separations.

Summary

- The Object and Pathfinder filters are path-specific.
- Add Anchor Points doubles the number of points on selected paths.
- Use Add Anchor Points before using the Punk and Bloat filter or the Scribble and Tweak filter.
- The Cleanup filter deletes unwanted path types from your entire document.
- Offset Path moves a path inwards or outwards by the number of points you specify.
- Outline Path creates a Filled path in the same location as a Stroke, at the size of the width of the Stroke.
- Unite joins together abutting and overlapping paths.
- Intersect creates paths where all the selected paths overlap, deleting the rest of the paths.
- Exclude creates paths only where there is no overlap.
- Back Minus and Front Minus subtract from the backmost or frontmost paths.
- The Trap filter creates trapping in the amount you specify between abutting or overlapping paths.

Other Filters and Plug-Ins

16 CHAPTER

In This Chapter

- Understanding the Select filters
- Using the four Paint Style selection filters
- Using the Select Inverse filter
- Using the Select Masks filter
- Using the Select Stray Points filter

The Select Filters

The Select filters are used for selecting paths with common or specific attributes. More than any other type of filter, the Select filters make mundane, repetitive tasks easy to accomplish by doing all the nasty work for you.

To choose the Select filters, choose Filter⇨Select and the appropriate selection filter.

Four selection filters use the Paint Style attributes of currently selected objects to select additional objects. Using these filters makes object selection quick and intuitive. The main limitation of these filters is that they are limited to four categories of comparison, each of which must be used independently of the others. This limitation causes problems in selecting objects that share more than one attribute, such as objects that have the same Stroke color and the same Stroke weight.

The Select Inverse filter is perfect for selecting all paths that aren't selected. You can use this filter to instantly select paths that are hidden, guides, and other objects that are hard to select.

The Select Masks filter makes the process of manipulating masks much easier by showing you where masks are in the document.

The Select Stray Points filter selects all isolated Anchor Points. Individual Anchor Points don't print or preview, and you can see them in Preview mode only when they are selected. After you cut portions of line segments, stray points often appear; and often these individual points interfere with connecting other segments. You can't use this filter enough.

CSI's Socket Set 1 contains a number of amazing Plug-Ins and filters to make selecting even easier than using the Adobe Select filters. See Chapter 18 for a complete description of these filters.

The Same Fill Color Filter

The Same Fill Color filter (Filter⇨Select⇨Same Fill Color) selects objects that have the same Fill color as the selected object. This filter selects objects regardless of their Stroke color, Stroke weight, or Stroke pattern. You cannot select objects with different Fills for Same Fill Color to work, but you may select two objects that have the same Fill.

The Same Fill Color filter considers different tints of custom colors to be the same color. This filter works in two ways. First, if you select one object with any tint value of a custom color, the Same Color filter will select all other objects with the same custom color, regardless of the tint. Second, you can select more than one object, no matter what tint each object contains, provided that the selected objects have the same custom color.

To be selected with the Same Fill Color filter, process color Fills have to have the same tint as the original. Even single colors, such as yellow, have to be the same percentage. The Same Fill Color filter considers 100% Yellow and 50% Yellow to be two separate colors.

If you use custom colors often, the Same Fill Color filter is extremely useful. It enables you to instantly select all objects that are Filled with the custom color, regardless of the tint of the selected object or the tints of the objects to be selected.

The Same Fill Color filter also selects objects that are Filled with the same gradient, regardless of the angle or the starting or ending point of the gradient. This filter does not, however, select objects that have the same pattern Fill.

The Same Paint Style Filter

The Same Paint Style filter (Filter⇨Select⇨Same Paint Style) selects objects that have almost exactly the same paint style as the paint style of the selected object. The following information has to be the same:

- The Fill color (as defined in the preceding section, "The Same Fill Color Filter")
- The Stroke color
- The Stroke weight

Some things in the Paint Style palette that don't matter (that is, they don't prevent the Same Paint Style filter from selecting an object) are any of the Stroke style attributes and the overprinting options.

Don't select more than one paint style if you select more than one object. If you have different paint styles (as defined previously) selected, no objects will be selected by the filter. The best thing to do with the Same Paint Style filter, as with the Same Fill Color filter, is to select only one object.

If you have a custom color selected, the Select filters will select all other occurances of that custom color, regardless of the tint. This can be troublesome. For more control over color selecting, look at the Cyptopia Socket Set 1 filters (Chapter 18), which include much more advanced color-selection filters.

The Same Stroke Color Filter

The Same Stroke Color filter (Filter⇨Select⇨Same Stroke Color) selects objects that have the same Stroke color, regardless of the Stroke weight or style and regardless of the type of Fill.

Selecting More Than One Color

Archie: How can I select all occurences of two different Fill colors?

Toulouse: You'll need to run the Same Fill Color filter.

Archie: I tried that, but it doesn't work.

Toulouse: Do it this way: Select a representative of the first color, and then run the filter.

Archie: Okay, but now I'm stuck.

Toulouse: Not really. Lock those objects with ⌘-1, then select a representative of the second Fill color, and run the Same Fill Color filter again.

Archie: I'm still stuck.

Toulouse: Ah...here's the tricky part. Lock those objects as well.

Archie: Excuse me for noticing, but now I *can't* select those objects. They're all locked.

Toulouse: Just Unlock All (press ⌘-2), and they'll all be selected!

Archie: You know, I really don't think these different colors should be mixed....

The color limitations that are defined in "The Same Fill Color Filter" section earlier in the chapter also apply to the Same Stroke Color filter.

Although you can choose a pattern for a Stroke that makes the Stroke look gray, the Same Stroke Color filter does not select other objects that have the same Stroke pattern.

The Same Stroke Weight Filter

Illustrator's Same Stroke Weight filter (Filter⇨Select⇨Same Stroke Weight) selects objects that have the same Stroke weight, regardless of the Stroke color, the style, or the Fill color.

Even if the Stroke is a pattern, other paths that have the same Stroke weight as the patterned Stroke will be selected when you use the Same Stroke Weight filter.

Don't select more than one Stroke weight if you select more than one object. If you select different Stroke weights, no paths will be selected. The best thing to do with the Same Stroke Weight filter, as with the Same Fill Color and Same Paint Style filters, is to select only one object.

Custom Paint Style Selections

Unfortunately, you cannot do multiple-type selections with any of the Paint Style filters. You cannot, for example, select at one time all of the objects that have the same Stroke color and Fill color, but have different Stroke weights.

The Lock Unselected command (press Option and choose Arrange⇨Lock or press ⌘-Option-1) is the key to specifying multiple selection criteria. The following instructions describe how to perform multiple-type selections in a few steps.

STEPS: Selecting Objects That Have the Same Stroke and Fill Colors

Step 1. Select a representative object that has the Stroke and Fill color that you want.

Step 2. Choose Filter⇨Same Fill Color. All objects that have the same Fill color as the original object will be selected, regardless of their Stroke color.

Step 3. This step is the key step. Press Option and choose Arrange⇨Lock (⌘-Option-1) to lock any objects that are not selected. The only objects that you can modify or select now are the ones that have the same Fill color.

Step 4. Deselect All (⌘-Shift-A) and select the original object, which has both the Fill color and the Stroke color that you want to select.

Step 5. Choose Filter⇨Select⇨Same Stroke Color. Only objects that have the same Stroke and Fill colors will be selected.

The Select Inverse Filter

The Select Inverse filter (Filter⇨Select⇨ Select Inverse) quickly selects all objects that are not currently selected. For example, if one object is selected and the document contains fifteen other objects, the fifteen objects will become selected, and the one object that was selected originally will become deselected.

The Select Inverse filter does not cause locked or hidden objects to be selected and does not select guides unless guides are not locked. Objects on layers that are locked or hidden will not be selected either.

The Select Inverse filter is useful because selecting a few objects is usually quicker than selecting most objects. After you select the few objects, the Select Inverse filter does all the nasty work of selecting everything else.

When no objects are selected, the Select Inverse filter selects all the objects, just as the Edit⇨Select All (⌘-A) command would. When all objects are selected, the Select Inverse filter deselects all the objects, just as the Edit⇨Deselect All (⌘-Shift-A) command would.

The Select Masks Filter

The Select Masks filter (Filter⇨Select⇨Select Masks) selects all the objects that are currently being used as masks. The only masks in the document that are not selected are the masks that are locked or hidden and the masks that are on layers that are locked or hidden.

Inverse on Specific Layers

Meathead: I want to select the inverse of the objects I selected that are just on specific layers.

Toulouse: You've already selected the inverse objects of the ones you want?

Meathead: Yep. How do I select just the inverse on certain layers only?

Toulouse: Easy. Run the filter.

Meathead: Uh, there's lots of paths selected that *aren't* on those layers.

Toulouse: Then just lock all the layers you don't want paths selected on. Anything on a locked layer will deselect.

The Select Masks filter does not select Fills and Strokes that were created with the Fill and Stroke Mask filter (Filter➪Create➪Fill & Stroke for Mask). These separate paths are the same size as the masks, but they are not masks.

See Chapter 11 for detailed information on creating and using masks and Chapter 16 for information regarding the Fill & Stroke for Mask filter.

Use the Select Masks filter before you select the Fill & Stroke for Mask filter. Knowing whether the path that you have selected is really a mask can be difficult, but by using the Select Masks filter you can be sure that the selected objects are indeed masks.

The Select Stray Points Filter

The Select Stray Points filter (Filter➪Select➪Select Stray Points) selects individual Anchor Points in the document.

Individual Anchor Points are nasty beasts, because although they don't show up in preview or printing, they contain Fills and Strokes that often cause separation software to print additional blank color separations that aren't needed.

Stray points can be created in various ways:

- Clicking once with the Pen tool creates a single Anchor Point.
- Deleting a line segment on a path that has two points by selecting the line segment with the Direct Selection tool and pressing Delete will leave behind the two Anchor Points.
- Using the Scissors tool to cut a path, and while deleting one side or another of the path, not selecting the points turns these points into stray points.

- Ungrouping an oval or rectangle in Version 3.2 or an older version of Illustrator, and then deleting just the frame of the shape leaves the center point in the document.

Bringing an Illustrator 3.2 or older document that has still-grouped rectangles or ovals into Version 6 automatically deletes the center point and turns on the Show Center Point option in the Object Attributes dialog box (choose Object⇨Attributes or press ⌘-Control-A).

Be careful not to think that center points of object are stray points — they aren't, and you cannot select them without selecting the object they belong to. Center points of objects are visible when the Show Center Point option is checked in the Object Attributes dialog box (choose Object⇨Attributes or press ⌘-Control-A). Selecting the center point of an object selects the entire object, and deleting the center point deletes the entire object.

Other Plug-Ins and Filters

There are several additional Plug-Ins and filters that extend Illustrator, giving you more flexibility and options.

The Acrobat PDF File Format Plug-In

This Plug-In is automatically installed in the Plug-Ins folder. The Acrobat PDF File Format Plug-In allows Illustrator to open up PDF format files. If the PDF file consists of more than one page, then a screen will appear, asking which page to open in Illustrator. Text can be changed and modified as text, graphics can be manipulated, and the file can be saved as the PDF file or as an Illustrator document. Acrobat and PDF files are discussed in Chapter 9.

One of the most useful things about Acrobat is that if you open a single page from a multiple page PDF document, change it in Illustrator, and then save it (just Save, not Save As), it will update the page in the Acrobat document.

The Artwork View Speedup Plug-In

The Artwork View Speedup Plug-In is placed in the Optional Plug-Ins folder when Illustrator is installed. In order for it to be used, it needs to be moved to the Plug-Ins folder.

The Artwork View Speedup Plug-In speeds up screen redraw in Artwork view. This is achieved by using only black for all selected Anchor Points, Control Handles, and Control Handle Lines. By only using black, the screen redraw is slightly quicker than if the selected objects were colored. The more complex the illustration, the more dramatic the speed difference.

The PICT File Format Plug-In

The PICT File Format Plug-In is automatically installed in the Plug-Ins folder. This Plug-In allows you to open line-based PICT files in Illustrator (like those generated from Canvas or MacDraw), converting them as they are opened. When a PICT file is selected in the Open dialog box and you click Open, a dialog box appears, asking if the PICT file should be used as a template or imported into the document.

Pixel-based PICTs can't be opened in Illustrator. Instead, they will be transformed into a template. To place a PICT image in Illustrator, use the Import Art command from the File menu.

The Pressure Support Plug-In

The Pressure Support Plug-In is automatically installed in the Plug-Ins folder. This Plug-In allows you to use a pressure-sensitive tablet with the Brush tool to produce brush strokes of variable widths.

The Riders Plug-In

The Riders Plug-In is located in the Separator and Utilities folder, in another folder called Riders Folder. The Riders Plug-In must be moved to the Plug-Ins folder to become accessible from within Illustrator.

Riders are used to customize the output of an Illustrator file. To create a Rider, select Filter⇨Other⇨Make Riders. The Make Riders dialog box appears, as shown in Figure 16-1.

Figure 16-1: The Make Riders dialog box

There are six options in the Make Riders dialog box, along with a Cancel button and a Make button, which saves the Riders file. The first option, Screen Frequency, determines the halftone screen of the illustration. The second option, Flatness, determines the number of pixels in the smallest segments of curved paths. The third option, Screen Angle, controls the halftone screen angle. The fourth option, Annotation, allows you to create a "note" for the illustration — you can even pick the font and font size of the note. The fifth option, Spot Function, determines the shape of the dots in halftone screens. The last option, Error Handler, determines how errors during printing are handled — whether they are printed, ignored, or displayed on-screen.

The Delete Riders filter (choose Filter⇨Other⇨Delete Riders) deletes a Riders file that you specify.

Once a Riders file is created, it affects *all* Illustrator files saved or printed after that point. Illustrator looks for the name "Adobe Illustrator EPSF Riders" in the Plug-Ins folder and adds the Riders information to the save or print stream. The information contained in the Riders file *will* override both page layout and printing program settings. To remove Riders information from a document, remove the Riders file from the Plug-Ins folder and reopen and save the document in Illustrator.

Folders Full of Plug-Ins

Dingbat: Why are there so many folders in my Plug-Ins folder?

Toulouse: That's to keep your Plug-Ins a little more organized.

Dingbat: Why do they need to be organized?

Toulouse: Well, because of the way Illustrator 6.0 is designed, little maintenance upgrades can be provided in the form of Plug-Ins, instead of a new program.

Dingbat: Still, why the folders?

Toulouse: The folders organize the Plug-Ins into similar groupings, making it easy to find specific trouble-causing Plug-Ins, and making Illustrator's Plug-Ins more consistent with Photoshop's.

Summary

- The Select filters aid in selecting objects.
- Same Fill Color selects objects with the same Fill color as the currently selected object.
- Same Paint Style selects object with the same paint style as the currently selected object.
- Inverse selects everything that isn't selected, and deselects everything that is selected.
- Select Masks selects all paths used as masking paths.

Using Photoshop Filters in Illustrator

17 CHAPTER

In This Chapter

- How pixel-based images work in Illustrator
- The difference between pixels and vectors
- Working with Photoshop and Illustrator concurrently
- Using Photoshop filters in Illustrator
- A look at some of the Photoshop filters available

When I first learned that Illustrator would support Photoshop filters, all the wrong thoughts entered my brain. "Great, now I'll be able to Gaussian Blur my shadows without having to turn them into pixels first!" and "Wow, I wonder what'll happen with blends and some of the Distort filters."

Of course, I was misled (those silly press releases again, I'm sure). Photoshop filters work only on *pixel-based* images, not vector images (paths and such). Fortunately, however, there is now a command for making paths into pixel-based images (Rasterize). So it's an extra step...but it still works.

Vector Versus Pixel-based Images

I covered this (sorta) back in Chapter One, but I'll go into a little more depth here. Illustrator, when it originally was formed, was a pure vector piece of software. There was nary a pixel to be found round these parts. But with Version 6, the border has been crossed, and Illustrator is just this side of the pixel border (which is nowhere near as smooth as the vector border).

When you think vectors, think Illustrator's paths. For Illustrator's paths consist of outlines. Sure, outlines that can be Filled with various colors and gradients, but outlines still. And it is the manipulation of these outlines that is the essence of Illustrator. Outlines can be resized and transformed in almost anyway imaginable. And when you create a curve in Illustrator, it's really a curve, not a jagged mass of pixels. Vector-based images can be stretched bigger, and look better for it (except for blends and gradients, which can run into problems if they're scaled up to large).

When you think pixels, think Photoshop's little teeny tiny squares of color. Squares that don't ever change position, that you don't add or delete. The only thing you change about pixels is their color. Pixels can only be square, and they take up space regardless if they're "empty" (filled with white or another background color) or "filled." Pixels exist on an immobile grid. Enlarging a pixel-based image results in giant, ugly squares of color.

Okay, I'm not a pixel person. If I were to be reincarnated as an electronic drawing tool, it wouldn't be as a Painter piece of chalk, but instead as Illustrator's Pen tool or Direct Selection tool. I'm a believer in vectors. Some say it's an obsession, but I'm too busy staring at Control Handles to pay attention to that nonsense.

Fortunately, I'm not close-minded enough to ignore the importance of pixels, or their place in our electronic graphics society. In fact, I went as far as to write the best-selling *The Complete Idiot's Guide to Photoshop* just to prove that point (yes, the working title was "Ted's Guide to Photoshop" and. . . ha ha ha. . . they changed the title on me...).

So I'm welcoming pixels into Illustrator for Version 6. After all, there are things you can do to pixels in Illustrator that you *can't* do in Photoshop. Ah, now I've got your attention.

Changing Illustrator Artwork into Pixels

There are several ways to turn Illustrator art into pixels, but the best way is the newest; by using the Rasterize command, any selected artwork is transformed into pixel-based artwork, at the resolution you specify.

STEPS: Changing Illustrator Artwork into Pixels Without Ever Leaving Illustrator

Step 1. Create your artwork in Illustrator.

Step 2. Select the artwork and choose Object⇨Rasterize. The Rasterize dialog box appears. Enter the ppi (pixels per inch) and press the OK button.

Step 3. Your artwork has been rasterized.

Figure 17-1 illustrates these three steps

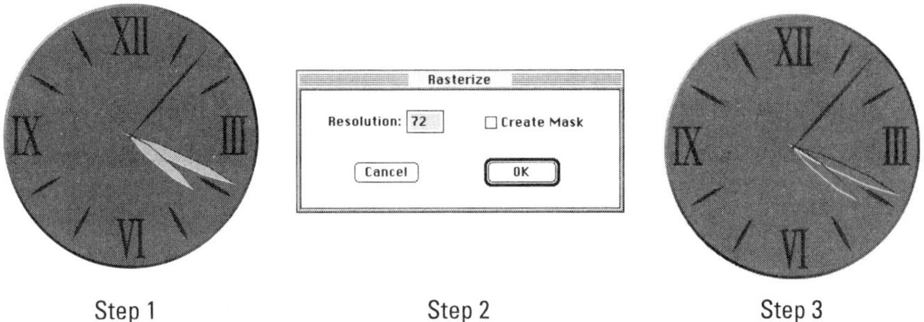

Figure 17-1: Steps for rasterizing artwork

A funky little checkbox in the Rasterize dialog box asks if you'd like to make a mask of your artwork. This can be a good thing to do for such items where sharp edges are important, like for text. Checking the Make Mask option creates an automatic mask around the edges of the artwork, and masks the image. In addition to keeping the edges nice and straight (because they're paths, not pixels), any of the areas where "white" or "empty" pixels are masked off, making those areas appear transparent.

As an Illustrator user, you might not be all that familiar with having to decide resolution, as you would in Photoshop. The quick rule of thumb is that the resolution of pixel-based images should be $1\,^{1}/_{2}$ to 2 times the line screen that the piece will be printed at. So if you'll be using a line screen of 133, your ppi should be between 199 and 266. It doesn't hurt to go higher than 2 times the line screen, but it is unnecessary. Since the math is easier, plan on using double the line screen for the resolution.

Going to Photoshop and Back with Pixels and Paths

Even with it's new pixel capabilities, Illustrator is no Photoshop. There are tools and features in Photoshop that are invaluable for adjusting pixel-based artwork. Adobe recognizes this, so they have provided several methods for moving pixels to Photoshop from Illustrator, and from Illustrator to Photoshop.

The most rudimentary way, which has existed for several versions of both software packages, is to save art in a format the other program can read, and then to open or place the art in the other program. To place Illustrator art into Photoshop, save the art in Illustrator 6 format, then open the art in Photoshop. To place Photoshop art in Illustrator, save in Photoshop as a format that Illustrator can read, like TIFF, then in Illustrator choose File⇨Import⇨Art and select the file.

All in the Details

Steve: So why should I use vectors instead of pixels?

Toulouse: It really depends on what you're doing.

Steve: Let's say I was creating a new four-color logo.

Toulouse: Vectors, probably. That way the logo can be resized without any loss in quality.

Steve: When would I use pixels?

Toulouse: Pixels are good for the abstract things, like blurriness, subtle color changes, and the like.

Steve: So, for anything that needs to be photorealistic, you would use pixels.

Toulouse: Not necessarily. Take a look at what some of the premier design studios are doing, like Thomas Bradley Design, and you'll see that it's hard to tell the difference between pixels and vectors.

Steve: So why do they use vectors then?

Toulouse: File size, transformability, precision you can't get from pixels.

The next way is through Adobe's wonderful PostScript on the Clipboard process, which allows for transferring artwork between Adobe software by simply copying in one program and pasting in another. To place Illustrator art in Photoshop, copy the art in Illustrator, switch to Photoshop, and paste in any document. To place Photoshop art in Illustrator, copy the art in Photoshop, switch to Illustrator, and paste in any document.

The newest way to move art between these programs is to drag it from one program to the other. To drag art from Illustrator to Photoshop, select the art in Illustrator, and drag it out of the Illustrator window onto a Photoshop window. To drag art from Photoshop to Illustrator, select the art in Photoshop and drag it out of the Photoshop window onto an Illustrator window.

You must have a window from the "to" application showing when you start dragging for drag-and-drop to work between programs.

You can also move just paths between the two programs. When opening or pasting Illustrator art in Photoshop, click the Paste As Paths option in the dialog box that appears, as shown in Figure 17-2. Instead of Filled and Stroked paths appearing in Photoshop, paths will appear, which can be manipulated by the Path tools on the Paths palette.

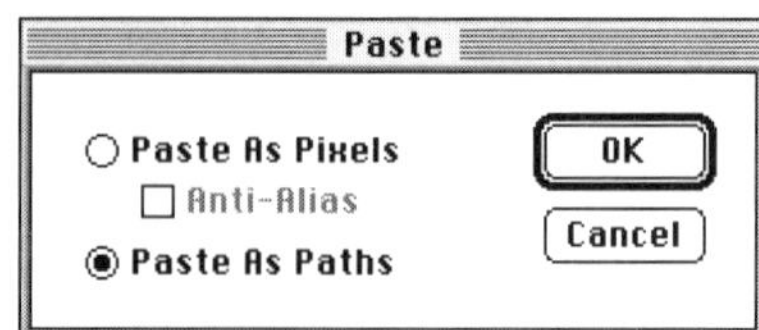

Figure 17-2: The Paste dialog box

To place paths from Photoshop into Illustrator, select the paths in Photoshop with the Path Selection tool and copy, then paste in Illustrator.

Importing and Exporting Pixel-Based File Formats

Pixel-based artwork from a source other than Photoshop is brought into Illustrator via the File⇨Import⇨Art command. When this is chosen, a standard Open dialog box appears in which you can select the pixel-based art that you'd like to import into Illustrator.

Illustrator can import the following pixel-based file types:

- TIFF
- EPS
- PICT
- PCX

Illustrator can export various pixel-based file types via the File⇨Export⇨Art command.

Illustrator can export the following pixel-based file types:

- TIFF
- EPS
- PCX
- BMP
- GIF

When exporting artwork, you can export part or all of an Illustrator document. Just select the portion you'd like to export *before* you choose File⇨Export⇨Art.

Colorizing One-Bit TIFF Images

One-bit TIFF images (black and white only) can be colored in Illustrator. This effectively turns the black pixels into the color you specify.

To color a 1-bit TIFF image, select the imported image, and change the Fill color to the desired color.

Figure 17-3 and the steps that follow show how to color portions of a 1-bit image.

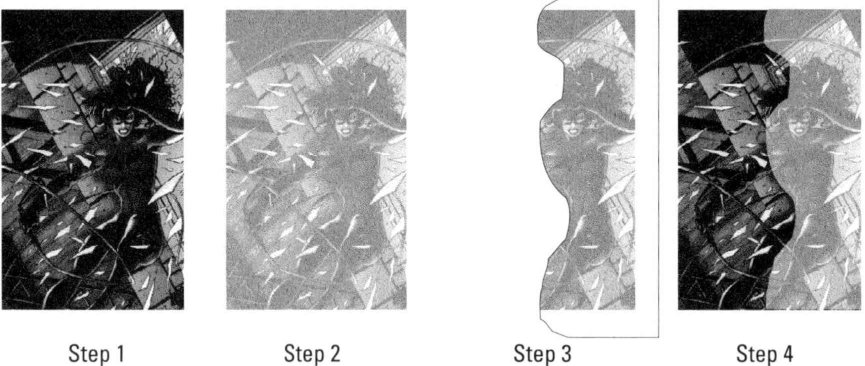

Figure 17-3: Steps for giving a 1-bit image multiple colors

STEPS: Coloring a One-Bit image with More Than One Color

Step 1. Select the imported image you wish to color, and apply a color to it by changing the Fill on the Paint Style palette.

Step 2. Copy the image, and paint the copy with a different color.

Step 3. Create a mask over the portion of the copied object that should be the different color. Group the mask with the copied image.

Step 4. Realign the copied image or mask with the original image.

You can create an unlimited number of colors in a 1-bit image by creating additional copies and applying different masks to each one.

Using Photoshop-Compatible Filters in Illustrator

By itself, these filters are "really neat" but since such a large number of Illustrator users have Photoshop, are they necessary?

For starters, these filters make things a bit easier than before, especially for doing things such as creating drop shadows and other special effects. Instead of having to allocate memory to Photoshop, you can do filter operations right in Illustrator.

But here's the very cool thing, the one thing that Illustrator has over Photoshop when it comes to applying filters. It's so special that I've decided to offset it with one of those wonderful little "Power Tip" icons. . .

Because Illustrator has multiple undos, you can apply several different filters to an imported image, and undo all of them, in turn. Photoshop 3 *can't* do that.

Photoshop filters only work on pixel-based images. If you'd like to apply a Photoshop filter to your Illustrator artwork, you will have to first select it and choose Object⇨Rasterize to turn it into a pixel-based image.

Figure 17-4 and the steps that follow describe how to apply a Photoshop filter to an image.

Step 1

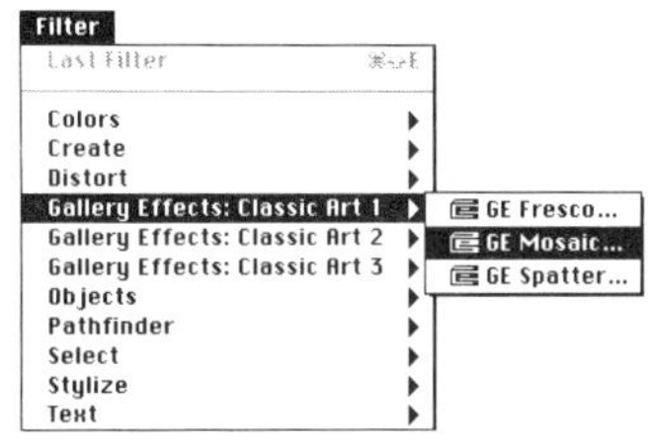

Step 2

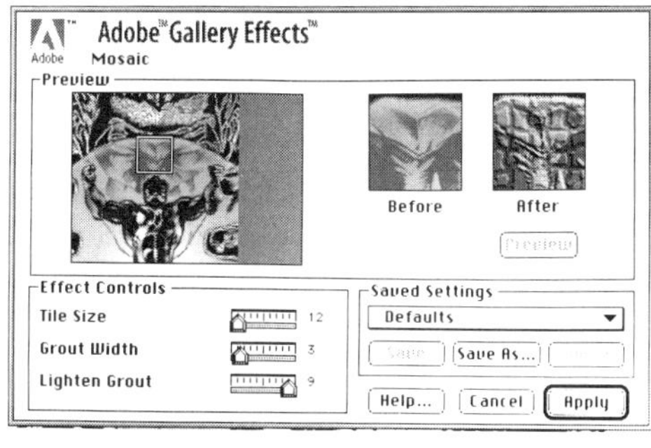

Step 3

Step 4

Figure 17-4: Steps for applying Photoshop filters in Illustrator

STEPS: Applying Photoshop Filters in Illustrator

Step 1. Select the pixel-based image in Illustrator that you'd like to apply the Photoshop filter to.

Step 2. Choose Filter⇨*Name of Photoshop filter submenu*⇨*Name of filter.* This could be, for instance, Filter⇨Gallery Effects I⇨Mosaic.

Step 3. In the Filter dialog box (if there is one), adjust the settings and values.

Step 4. Click the OK button in the Filter dialog box to produce the effect.

One big limitation of using Photoshop filters in Illustrator is that you can't make any selections *within* the pixel-based image. A way around this is to create a copy of the image, apply the filter, and then mask the area you'd like that effect applied to.

The Gallery Effects Filters

Adobe now publishes Gallery Effects I, II, and III filters for Adobe Photoshop. Included with Illustrator is a sampling of their filters: GE Accented Edges, GE Bas Relief, GE Fresco, GE Glass, GE Grain, GE Halftone Screen, GE Mosaic, GE Patchwork, GE Rough Pastels, GE Spatter, GE Stamp, and GE Sumi-e.

Each of these filters produces various effects. Each of the filters' dialog boxes have a preview button, so you can see what the effect will look like on a small portion of your image.

The Photoshop LE Filters

The Adobe Illustrator 6 CD-ROM contains Photoshop LE, which has several filters you can use in Illustrator. To use those filters, copy the Plug-Ins from the Photoshop LE Plug-Ins folder on the CD-ROM to your Illustrator Plug-Ins folder.

Other Third-Party Photoshop filters

There are several Photoshop filter sets created by third parties, including Kai's Power Tools, KPT Convolver, CSI PhotoLab, and Alien Skin Black Box.

For Illustrator use, I've found KPT Convolver to be the most useful, as it has Gaussian Blur, Unsharp Mask, and other filter effects not available from Photoshop otherwise. In addition, for high-end color correction, CSI PhotoLab is indispensible.

Summary

- Pixel-based artwork can be incorporated into Illustrator by importing it.
- The quickest way to move images between Illustrator and Photoshop is to drag-and-drop them between windows in each program.
- Paths can also be taken back and forth between the two programs.
- One-bit images can be colorized by selecting the image and changing the Fill color in the Paint Style palette.
- Illustrator can export EPS, TIFF, PCX, GIF, and BMP pixel file formats.
- Photoshop filters appear in the Filter menu alongside Illustrator filters.

The Plug-Ins Folder Has Folders in It?

Oscar: Why does the Plug-Ins folder seem to have other folders inside of it?

Toulouse: To help keep your Plug-Ins organized. There's lots of them there, you know.

Oscar: What if I want to use all my Photoshop Plug-Ins in Illustrator?

Toulouse: The easiest way to do this is to make an alias of your Photoshop Plug-Ins folder...

Oscar: Okay.

Toulouse: . . .and then drop it in your Illustrator Plug-Ins folder. All your Photoshop Plug-Ins will be available in Illustrator.

Third-Party Filters

CHAPTER 18

In This Chapter

- What's available from third parties
- An in-depth look at KPT Vector Effects
- All about CSI Socket Sets
- BeInfinite's IFX distortion filters
- Other filter manufacturers
- Creating your own filters

Yeah, I know, by the time you've gone to two parties, you're already pretty well sloshed, and usually it's not worth the effort to not pass out at that point. When we're talking software, though, "third-party" usually refers to a software publisher who produces an add-on for another package. All the companies that make filters for Illustrator are considered third-party publishers.

In 1994 three different filter packages were announced: Letraset Envelopes, BeInfinite FX (which has the distinction of being the first U.S. third-party filter set for Illustrator), and Sree's Cool Tools, which was later purchased from the developer, Sreekant Kotay, by MetaTools Software, tweaked, and published as KPT Vector Effects. But none of these actually shipped in the U.S. until 1995.

The year 1995 was the Year of the Adobe Filter. Sure, ever since Adobe Illustrator 5.0, released back in 1993, Illustrator has had the ability to add Plug-In filters from other manufacturers, but 1995 was when the third parties started taking off big-time. In addition, FreeHand 5.0 was released early that year, and supported Illustrator-style Plug-Ins by making them usable from within FreeHand (as "Xtras," a slightly tacky moniker).

Third-Party Filter Roundup

To make this whole third-party business a little clearer, the following is a summary of the third-party filter sets available at this writing:

- **BeInfinite InfiniteFX:** This filter set contains more than 50 distortion filters, *all* enclosed in a matching dialog box setup. In addition, all effects can be combined with a 3-D rotation capability that is integrated into the filter interface.
- **CSI Socket Sets:** The Socket Set filters are production-oriented filters that enhance Illustrator's current capabilities. Socket Set 1 includes a powerful Adjust Colors filter, as well as powerful selection filters and more. Socket Set 2 contains a Process to Grayscale filter, several Alignment filters, and more.
- **KPT Vector Effects:** This comprehensive filter set from MetaTools, the maker of Kai's Power Tools, consists of several special-effects-oriented filters. Some of the highlights include KPT 3D Transform, which rotates and extrudes artwork in 3-D; KPT ShatterBox, which fragments selected artwork into user-defined pieces; and KPT Warp Frame, an envelope-distortion filter.
- **Letraset Envelopes:** This one-shot filter is an envelope-distortion filter, with several presets.
- **Extensis DrawTools:** These filters contain color management and 3-D-effects filters.

Contact information for the third party publishers is provided in Appendix G, and most of the filter sets have demos provided on the *Macworld Illustrator Bible 6 CD-ROM.*

BeInfinite InfiniteFX

This set of filters is united through a common dialog box, shown in Figure 18-1 for the Waves Oceanic filter.

The common dialog box makes using the IFX filters much easier — once you've used one filter, you know how to use the rest. All of the filters have the 3-D rotation window, which allows you to spin your artwork around in 3-D by clicking and dragging on the art. Many of the filters also have sliders as well, which allow you to adjust the degree of each effect and other parameters.

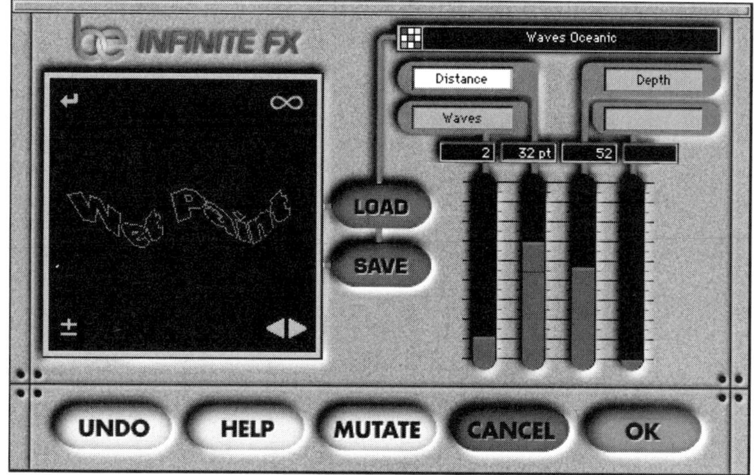

Figure 18-1: The Infinite FX dialog box (with Waves Oceanic filter shown)

The Zoom In button (shown in Figure 18-1) lets you zoom in on the artwork, the Zoom Out button allows you to zoom out of the art. Clicking the Reset button removes all effects from the artwork (including slider adjustments and 3-D rotation). The Preview Image Cycle through arrows allow for viewing proxy images in place of the selected artwork frame. This is useful when the artwork is extremely complex, or consist of a blend or other artwork that doesn't show up well as frames.

IFX Theory

The IFX filters are primarily *distortion* filters, which means that they adjust and manipulate existing paths by altering Anchor Points and Control Handles. IFX does *not* add Anchor Points to selected paths, so sometimes you might want to add points *before* applying an IFX filter. Fortunately, IFX has included a filter called Smart Add Points, which adds points based on a tolerance setting similar in function to how the Freehand tolerance setting (in General Preferences) works. Personally, I'd use Roughen at 0% to add Anchor Points (see Chapter 15).

Many of the IFX filters are variations or inverses of other IFX filters. Some are quite obvious (Wiggle Horizontal versus Wiggle Vertical) while others are a little more subtle (Waves Oceanic versus Waves Atmospheric).

Several IFX filters have a Depth slider, which only affects artwork in 3-D mode. If you don't rotate the artwork with the 3-D trackball (the Preview window), the Depth slider has no effect. This isn't at all obvious, and it even prompted me to call the publisher and ask about it (the publisher was kind enough not to ask if I'd read the manual, which describes the depth slider and the effects relevant to the 3-D rotation trackball).

The Pure Transformation filter is just that; the only thing you can do to artwork is rotate it with the 3-D rotation trackball.

The IFX Filters

Figure 18-2 shows an illustration before and after having various IFX filters applied to it. Not all the filters are shown, but instead, a sampling of the filters is represented.

Figure 18-2: IFX filter effects

In addition to the filters in IFX, BeInfinite has included Smart Remove Points, a special functionality filter, on the *Macworld Illustrator Bible 6* CD-ROM. This filter actually cleans up artwork paths that have ridiculously high numbers of points, such as streamlined artwork, or artwork to which you've applied Add Anchor Points. To use Smart Remove Points, drop it in your Plug-Ins folder and restart Illustrator. Then select the artwork from which you wish to have points removed, and select the filter. No settings, no problems, no mess, and no extra points.

CSI Socket Set 1

The CSI Socket Set filters are two sets of filters that are primarily production-enhancing filters (sort of 180° from what BeInfinite's IFX filters do). The two Socket Set filter sets can dramatically increase your Illustrator efficiency by automating common Illustrator functions and adding helpful new capabilities.

CSI AI Plug-In Manager

This Plug-In allows you to select which Plug-Ins will load when Illustrator starts up. It works two ways. You can select the Plug-Ins from within Illustrator by choosing Filter⇨Other⇨CSI AI Plug-In Manager, and select the Plug-Ins to load or not load from there; or you can press the Spacebar when Illustrator is starting up and select Plug-Ins then.

In addition, you can create different sets of Plug-Ins by using the pop-up menu at the top of the dialog box shown in Figure 18-3.

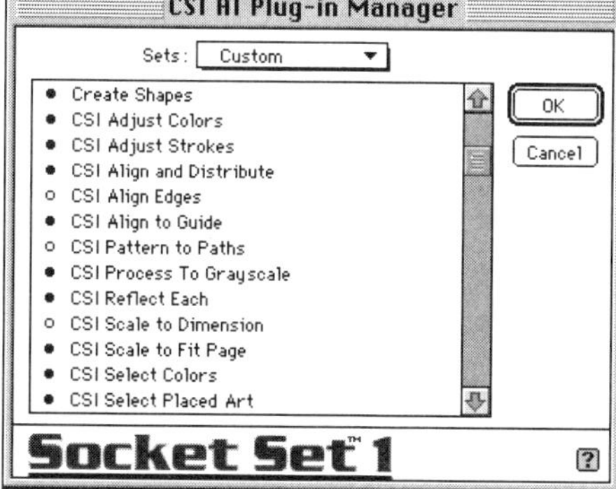

Figure 18-3: The CSI AI Plug-In Manager dialog box

Plug-Ins take up very little memory and just a fraction of a second to load, so don't think you're getting some great power boost by not loading all your Plug-Ins. Instead, Plug-In Manager is good for Plug-Ins that change the way Illustrator works, like the Artwork Speedup Plug-In that ships with Illustrator.

When CSI AI Plug-In Manager is used the first time, it creates a folder called "Plug-Ins (disabled)." Plug-Ins you opt not to install are placed there (only Plug-Ins in the Plug-Ins folder that are in the Illustrator folder are installed). In addition, Plug-In Manager will not recognize Plug-Ins that are *not* in one of these two folders.

CSI AI Startup Manager

This Plug-In lets you pick which document to use as a start-up file when Illustrator is launched. Start-up files are discussed in Chapter 6.

Like CSI AI Plug-In Manager, this Plug-In affects the way that Illustrator runs when it starts up. So making any changes won't affect Illustrator until it is restarted.

To switch the start-up files for Illustrator, press ⌘ until the Startup Manager dialog box appears.

CSI Adjust Colors

The CSI Adjust Colors filter takes Adobe's Adjust Colors filter a few steps further, making it truly useful. Utilizing sliders and an apply button, you can manipulate Strokes, Fills, or both by altering any of the four process colors or even custom colors. The dialog box for CSI Adjust Colors is shown in Figure 18-4.

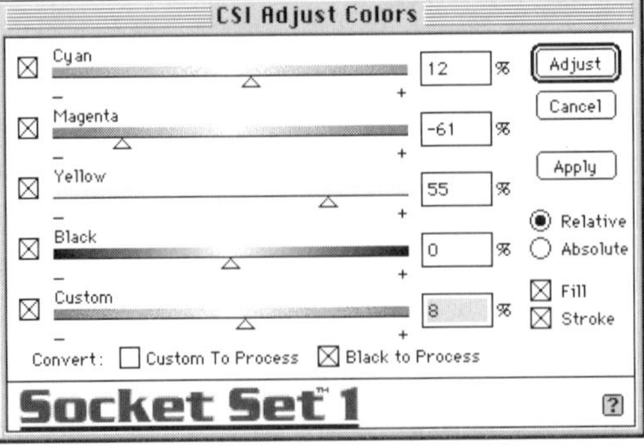

Figure 18-4: The CSI Adjust Colors dialog box

If the Absolute button is checked, you can change values to a precise amount. For instance, if you want all selected paths to have 40% black, in addition to any amounts of cyan, magenta and yellow, change the Black slider to 40% (+) and check the Absolute button.

If the Relative button is checked, the amounts in the dialog box (the ones that are checked) are added or subtracted to the current values.

Pressing Option and the Cancel button in all CSI dialog boxes undoes any Applies that have been executed.

But the real power of CSI Adjust colors is its custom color control. Using the Custom slider at the bottom of the dialog box, you can increase or decrease the tint of custom colors using the Relative or Absolute buttons. When you have several Pantone or other custom colors in a document, this feature is incredibly handy.

CSI Adjust Stroke

The CSI Adjust Stroke filter could almost be called Scale Strokes (but then, I guess it would sound like you're petting a Gila Monster). The unique thing about this filter is that it increases or decreases the Stroke of selected paths by the number of points you specify, regardless of the different Stroke weights that are selected.

As an example, let's start with one path with a 1-point Stroke, another path with a 10-point Stroke, and one with a Stroke of 4.5 points. If you apply CSI Adjust Strokes to the paths and increase by 3 points, the paths would be 4 points, 13 point, and 7.5 points, respectively.

Figure 18-5 shows the effects of this filter.

Figure 18-5: Type before (top) and after (bottom) Adjust Strokes

CSI Select Colors

The CSI Select filters aren't just souped-up versions of the Adobe Select filters; they raise color selection capability to an entirely new plateau. When the Select Colors filter is selected from the Select submenu of the Filter menu, you won't see anything right away, as the filter creates a database of each and every colorable object in your document. When the filter *does* open, it'll look something like the dialog box shown in Figure 18-6.

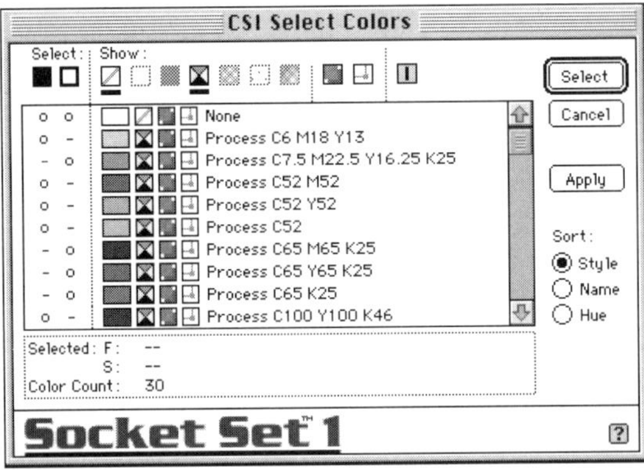

Figure 18-6: The CSI Select Colors dialog box

A complete list of every colorable object in the document appears, with several options. When you click in any of the open circles to the right of an item in the list, all the items with that attribute are selected. The bottom of the dialog box will display the different colors currently selected.

Because CSI Select Colors will create a list of every object in your document, you might not want to use it when you have a document overflowing with paths. Check the number of paths with Document Info (File⇨Document Info) and if the number is less than three or four thousand, you can use the filter without fear. But even at those amounts, it'll take quite a while for the list to be generated in the filter, and it'll take even longer to navigate through that list.

Clicking the Apply button will select objects in the artwork window. Change the sort list by clicking on the appropriate button to make selecting easier. A nice feature of the CSI Select filters is that they all work the same way; once you've used one of them, the others are easy to figure out.

CSI Select Placed Art

This filter is used to select placed art within the document. When activated, the filter generates a list of all the placed images in the document. You can pick any number of the placed images (by file name) quickly and easily this way.

CSI Select Strokes

The CSI Select Strokes filter also generates a list of objects, but this list consists of paths with Strokes. Strokes can be selected by weight, Stroke attributes, or color.

CSI Select Text

The CSI Select Text filter selects text objects based on size, color, and font. When selected, the dialog box will look something like the one in Figure 18-7.

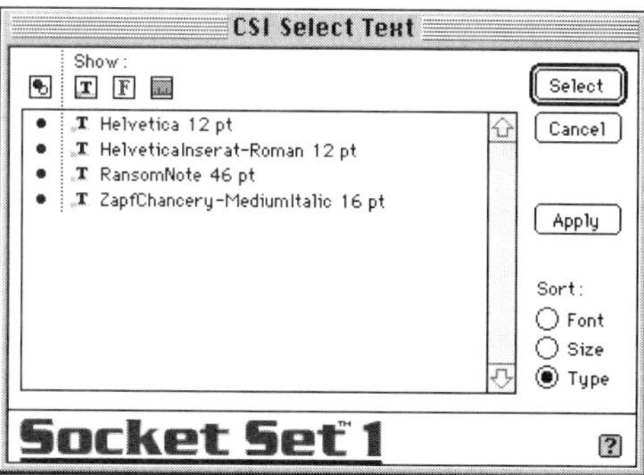

Figure 18-7: The CSI Select Text dialog box

CSI Select Similar

The CSI Select Similar filter selects paths that are similar to the currently selected paths. To use the filter, select a path that has a Fill or Stroke (or both) that is similar to all the paths you want to select. Then choose Filter⇨Select⇨CSI Select Similar. The CSI Select Similar dialog box will appear, as shown below.

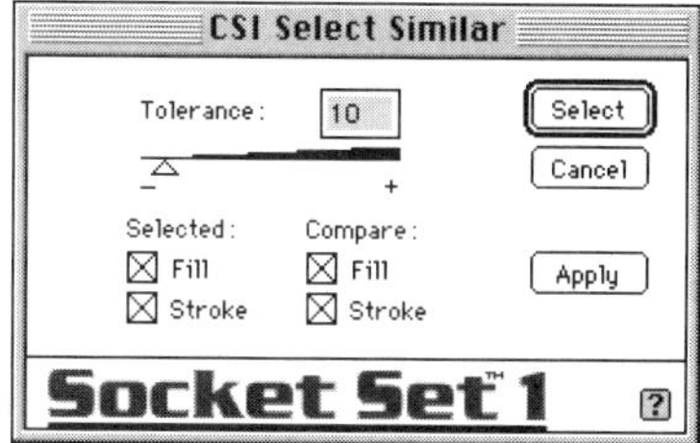

Figure 18-8: The CSI Select Similar dialog box

To get the full effect of CSI Select Similar, change the viewing mode to Preview Selection (⌘-Option-Y) before entering the filter dialog box.

The higher the tolerance setting, the more paths that will be selected. Clicking the Apply button will show what paths will be selected when you click OK.

CSI Process to Grayscale

This filter is without a doubt one of the most used filters on my computer. In fact, I can't imagine how I created Illustrator artwork without it before. CSI Process to Grayscale takes selected paths that have process color Fills and Strokes and changes them to

CSI Socket Sets

George: Toulouse, what do you think of the CSI Socket Sets?

Toulouse: I've found them indispensable.

George: So, you can't use Illustrator without them, right?

Toulouse: No, the packaging doesn't fit in my trash can.

George: They're not slipping you enough cash, are they?

Toulouse: Actually, once you start using the Socket Set filters, they become part of your everyday Illustrator usage. I've saved hundreds of hours by using them.

George: Well, that's good to hear.

Toulouse: Tell Cytopia to make out the check to...

grayscale. When you apply the filter (Filter⇨Color⇨CSI Process to Grayscale), you won't see a dialog box; instead, all process colors are instantly converted into grayscale.

This is invaluable for two-color jobs as well. You can create your artwork with process colors and a Pantone color, click Select All, and then apply CSI Process to Grayscale, and suddenly you'll have a perfect two-color Illustrator document.

Because of the process used, the results are far superior to what you get when you print a composite on a black-and-white printer or imagesetter. With CSI Process to Grayscale, reds aren't black, and yellows aren't too dark. I use this enough to have assigned it its own key command.

CSI Socket Set 2

CSI Socket Set 2 contains object-based filters, once again making Illustrator easier to use by adding formerly nonexistent capabilities. The filters follow the same dialog box format as the CSI Socket Set 1 filters.

CSI Align and Distribute

The CSI Align and Distribute filter takes selected objects and aligns and/or distributes them horizontally or vertically. This filter has more functionality than the Align palette capabilities of Illustrator.

To use CSI Align and Distribute, select the objects you wish to manipulate and choose Filter⇨Objects⇨Align and Distribute. The dialog box shown in Figure 18-9 appears.

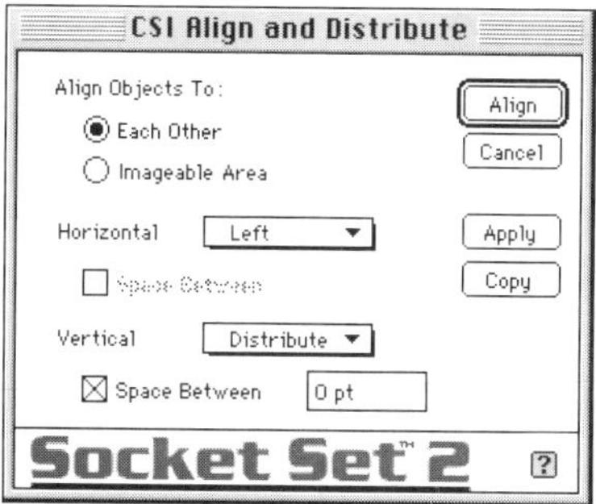

Figure 18-9: The CSI Align and Distribute dialog box

Selecting Each Other at the top of the dialog box keeps the objects aligned and distributed relative to each other. Selecting the Imageable Area option moves the objects to the outermost area of the dotted line inside your page. This provides a fixed location for the selected objects to gravitate to.

CSI Align Edges

From the name, you'd think that CSI Align Edges was really a limited version of CSI Align and Distribute. Instead, CSI Align Edges allows you to designate one of the selected objects as a stationary object that all the other objects will be aligned to. The dialog box for CSI Align Edges is shown in Figure 18-10.

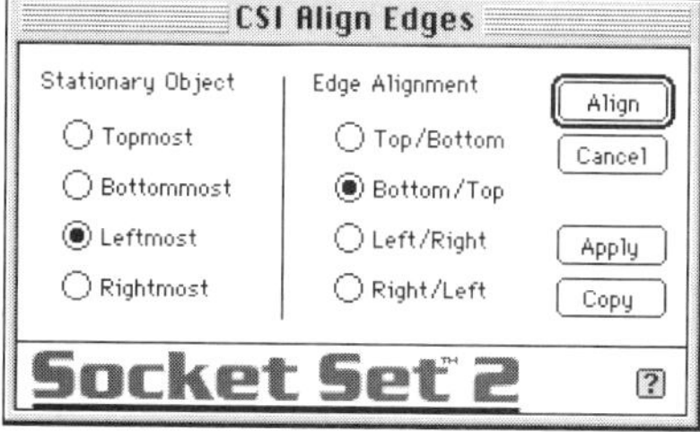

Figure 18-10: The CSI Align Edges dialog box

After selecting the location of the stationary object from the choices on the left side (you may have to cancel and reposition the stationary object for this to work correctly), decide how you want the other selected objects to align to the stationary one.

If Top/Bottom is chosen, all selected objects will align their tops to the bottom of the stationary object. If Left/Right is chosen, the selected objects will align their left edges to the stationary object's right edge, and so forth.

CSI Align to Guide

The CSI Align to Guide filter aligns objects up to guides. This *only* works correctly with guides that are pulled from the rulers, though it also works (kinda) with guides created with a 2-Anchor Point line. The dialog box that pops up when you choose Filter➪Objects➪CSI Align to Guide is shown in Figure 18-11.

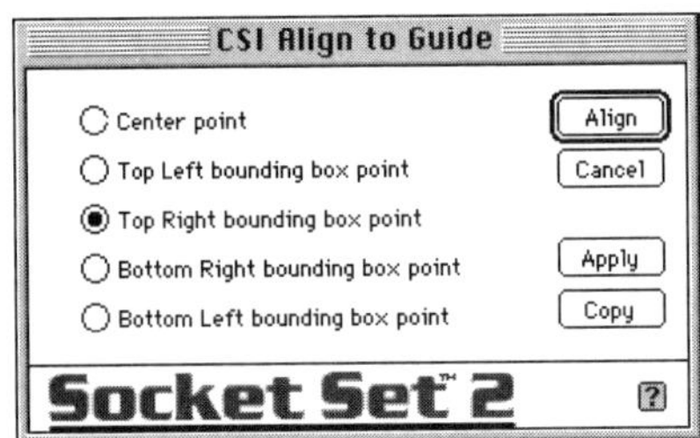

Figure 18-11: The CSI Align to Guide dialog box

The only option in the dialog box is what corner of the selected object's bounding box to align to the guide (or the center point of the object).

CSI Patterns to Paths

This incredibly useful filter does something previously impossible in Illustrator. It takes pattern-filled objects and converts them into masked paths. As if by magic. To use the filter, select a pattern-filled object and choose Filter➪Objects➪CSI Patterns to Paths.

Unfortunately, because of the way in which Illustrator generates patterns, the result isn't perfect. Instead, there are several overlapping paths where pattern tiles meet.

STEPS: Getting Rid of Extra Paths from Converted Patterns

Step 1. Apply CSI Patterns to Paths to the pattern-filled path.

Step 2. With the paths selected, choose Object➪Masks➪Release.

Step 3. Ungroup (⌘- U).

Step 4. Select just the mask that was the original path, and lock it (⌘- 1).

Step 5. Select all the remaining paths and choose Filter➪Pathfinder➪Merge.

Step 6. Unlock All (⌘- 2).

Step 7. Select All and choose Object➪Masks➪Make.

CSI Reflect Each

This filter is a welcome addition to the capabilities of Illustrator's Transform Each command. Just like the name says, this filter reflects individual objects across their centers. The options for reflecting are shown in Figure 18-12.

Figure 18-12: The CSI Reflect Each dialog box

CSI Scale to Dimension

Have you ever wanted to scale artwork to fit within a certain area? For instance, artwork in the *Macworld Illustrator Bible 6* has a maximum width of about 34 picas. A good bit of the art in the book was scaled up or down to this width using CSI Scale to Dimension.

To use CSI Scale to Dimension, select the objects you wish to scale, and choose Filter⇨Objects⇨CSI Scale to Dimension. The dialog box shown in Figure 18-13 will appear.

Figure 18-13: The CSI Scale to Dimension dialog box

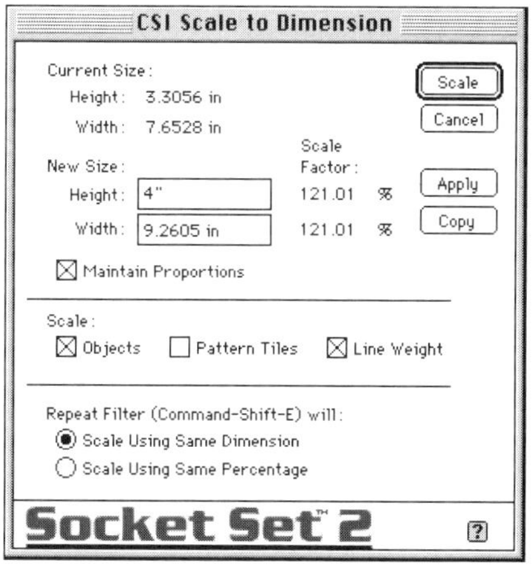

Set the width, height, or both to which you wish to scale the artwork. Note that in order to enter *both* height and width, you'll need to uncheck the Maintain Proportions checkbox. Take advantage of the Apply button to make sure the result is what you want, and then click OK if it works. Remember that you can always press Option and the Cancel button to undo an Apply.

Hidden (sorta) at the bottom of the CSI Scale to Dimension dialog box is a very powerful option. You have the choice between scaling to the same percentage or to the same size when the filter is repeated with ⌘- Shift-E.

Try using CSI Scale to Dimension with a hunk of type to get a headline to fit in a space perfectly.

CSI Scale to Fit Page

This is a quickie filter (see the few options in Figure 18-14) that quickly resizes the selected artwork to the page size. Your main option is whether to scale proportionately or non-proportionately.

I've used this filter to fill up a page quickly right before I print out posters and signs.

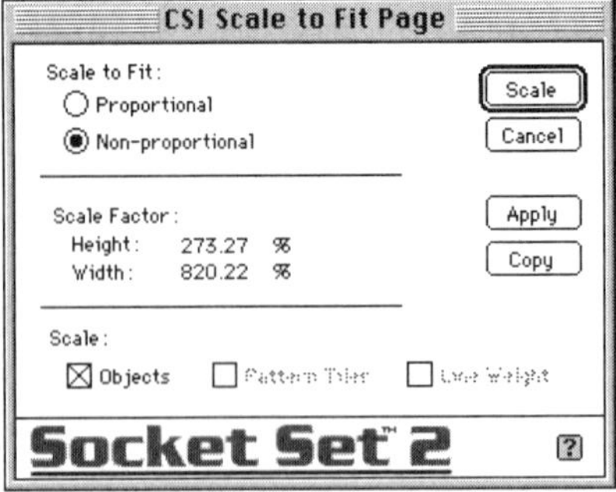

Figure 18-14: The CSI Scale to Fit Page dialog box

CSI Step and Repeat

This filter automatically creates rows and columns consisting of series of the selected objects. To use the filter, select any object you wish to have repeated (and stepped), and choose Filter⇨Objects⇨Step and Repeat. The dialog box shown in Figure 18-15 will appear.

Figure out how many objects you want across and down, and enter those numbers. The original object will always be in the upper left; new objects generated with CSI Step and Repeat will appear to the right and below the original object. Then enter the amount of space you want between the objects. Click Apply to make sure you're getting the correct result first, then click OK.

Figure 18-15: The CSI Step and Repeat dialog box

You can make objects overlap each other by entering negative values in the Space Between text fields.

STEPS: Creating a Grid with CSI Step and Repeat

Step 1. Draw a rectangle the exact size of one of the grid squares. For instance, if you wanted a 1/4" grid (like in the example in Figure 18-16), you would create a rectangle 1/4" × 1/4" wide. Make sure the rectangle has *no Stroke* at this point (see the following Power Tip).

Figure 18-16: A 1/4" grid is created by stepping and repeating a 1/4" rectangle.

Step 2. With the rectangle selected, choose Filters⇨Objects⇨CSI Step and Repeat. In the dialog box, enter the number of grid squares you want across and down (for a 1/4" grid, multiply what you'd like the finished size to be by 4).

Step 3. After applying the Step and Repeat filter, all the squares will be selected. Change the Stroke of all of them to the thickness you'd like the lines of the grid to be. Because the squares overlap perfectly at their edges, the Strokes where the squares meet will overlap, keeping the Stroke weight consistent.

CSI Step and Repeat is smarter than I am. If you have Stroked objects, Step and Repeat will figure the width of the Stroke into the distance between the objects. So if you have a rectangle with a 2-point Stroke, Step and Repeat puts an extra 2 points between objects you've specified at "0" distance apart.

KPT Vector Effects

Kai's Power Tools took the Photoshop world by storm a few years ago, and KPT Vector Effects look like they'll have the same impact on Illustrator users. Sporting a scaled-down-from-the-typical-unusual-Kai-interface, Vector Effects is still different enough to get noticed, and friendly enough to be quite useful.

By themselves, KPT VE filters are a force to be reckoned with. But double them with Illustrator's capabilities, and suddenly there's oodles of options that never existed before. Because KPT VE is so big, the *Macworld Illustrator 6 Bible CD-ROM* can only give you a brief summary and a few examples of its incredible capabilities. For a more detailed overview of the amazing capabilities of KPT VE, pick up a copy of *Illustrator Filter Finesse,* which covers filters from several manufacturers.

KPT Vector Effects, while residing in the Filter menu, are not really "filters." Of course, most of the Plug-Ins in Illustrator aren't Filters, either, but MetaTools is adamant about this. At MetaTools, calling Vector Effects "filters" is a good way to lose a bit of job security, if you know what I mean. MetaTools insists on calling them Plug-In Application Extensions, which is about as silly as Kai not quite understanding this craving we Illustrator users have for numeric input...

Most of the KPT VE filters are special-effects oriented; making the creation of nifty stuff a no-brainer. A few others are more production-oriented, but those select few filters help to round out the package. All of the filters are found in the Filters menu, in a submenu called KPT Vector Effects.

KPT has even included a special filter (included on the *Macworld Illustrator 6 Bible CD-ROM*) called KPT Gradients/Patterns to Paths, which converts both selected gradients and patterns to paths, allowing special effects and techniques to take place that otherwise wouldn't have been possible.

VE Commonalties

Vector Effects have several different interfaces, but most of them share at least a half dozen features. These are discussed below:

- **The Options menu:** Many of the filters have an Options menu, accessible by clicking the "umbrella" with a triangle in it. In this menu are options for preferences, a Reset command, and various other filter-specific options.
- **Zoom and Pan:** You can quickly Zoom and Pan using the keyboard shortcuts from Illustrator (⌘-Spacebar to Zoom in, ⌘-Spacebar-Option to Zoom out, and ⌘-Space to Pan). Or you can click on the buttons at the top of the Preview window. You can also draw a Zoom marquee to Zoom in to a precise location.
- **Balloon Help:** Clicking the "?" in the lower left will toggle Balloon Help on and off which is quite useful when you're initially fumbling around.
- **Sliders:** There are sliders all over the place in each dialog box (and there are others, undoubtedly just a bit different, on parallel worlds). Access them by clicking on the black box with white letters and dragging left or right.

Pressing the Caps Lock key turns on "interactive" preview, where the preview changes while you are dragging the sliders, not just when you release them.

- **Presets:** You can use presets for certain filters by clicking on the triangle at the bottom of the screen, and scrolling to the filter you want to use. Press Spacebar before clicking to view "graphical presets," or just choose that option from the Preferences dialog box. When in Graphical Preview mode, you can also view the particular effect on the selected artwork by pressing ⌘ when a preset is highlighted. If Caps Lock is pressed, all presets will display the effect on the artwork automatically.

Superstitious MetaTools

Weezy: How many filters are in Vector Effects?

Toulouse: Twelve, plus a bonus one. And they're not filters, they're *Plug-In Application Extensions.*

Weezy: So there's thirteen Plug-what you said.

Toulouse: No, twelve and a bonus extension. It's a marketing thing, I'm sure.

Weezy: Sounds to me like they're superstitious over at MetaTools.

Toulouse: Nah. If they were *really* superstitious, they wouldn't have named the product Vector Effects. Count the letters.

Weezy: Grife! Wonder if they noticed that the package weighs three ounces less than a pound...

Toulouse: And then there's the engineer's name...

- **Preset control:** If you create a particularly smashing effect in an extension dialog box that supports presets, like ShatterBox, you can store that preset for future use by clicking on the little + at the bottom of the dialog box. Delete the current preset by clicking -. At the bottom of the list of (non-graphical) presets, you can access the Presets Manager, which allows you to import and export presets to and from each extension.
- **Cancel and OK:** The Cancel button is a circle with a slash through it. OK is a check mark.
- **Numeric control:** Each of the interfaces has an option to show exact measurements or percentages in numeric form. Check the option in the Preferences menu to see the numbers when you adjust a slider. The numbers shown below sliders tell you (left) what the value was originally and (right) what you're changing it to. You can also access the numbers and change them individually by ⌘- clicking on the slider, and typing in a new number, or using the arrows (or arrow keys) to nudge the amount.

The following pages discuss the filters briefly, and show off some of the groovy things you can do with them (yes, groovy).

KPT 3D Transform

This is the most powerful of all the Vector Effects filters, in that it contains a fairly advanced 3-D engine, and produces truly astounding effects. It's quick, relatively easy to use, and the resulting paths it generates are really impressive.

KPT 3D Transform takes selected paths and extrudes, bevels, and rotates them in 3-D space. The 3D Transform dialog box is shown in Figure 18-17.

STEPS: Creating Metallic-Looking Text

Step 1. Type your text in a font that has lots of curves. (The Metallic setting in KPT 3D Transform works better with curves than with straight edges.) Convert the text to outlines.

Step 2. Fill the outlines with a slight cyan/magenta mix (no more than 20% of either).

Step 3. With the outlines selected, choose Filters⇨KPT Vector Effects⇨KPT 3D Transform.

Step 4. In the 3D Transform dialog box, select Full Preview from the Options menu (the little triangle in a half-circle the upper left of the Preview window). Engage the Caps Lock key; this will show all the changes you make immediately, even while you're dragging sliders.

If you don't have a Power Mac, you might want to stick with either the Rough or Wireframe Preview modes (both found in the Options menu). Experiment with the different settings to find what will work best with your system.

Step 5. Adjust the Rotate sliders by dragging them left or right, watching the preview as you do so. Once the outlines have been rotated around the way you want them, drag the Metallic slider to the right about a quarter of the way.

Step 6. Next, drag the Extrude slider to the right, to give the outlines depth.

Step 7. If you want to give the outlines beveled edges, drag the Bevel Size slider to the right just a bit. Be careful not to drag too far, as the bevels on nearby letters might intersect. To prevent this intersection in the future, increase the tracking of the text *before* you convert it to outlines.

Step 8. Click the checkmark in the lower right of the dialog box. This is the iconic version of the OK button. That means you can press Return or Enter as well.

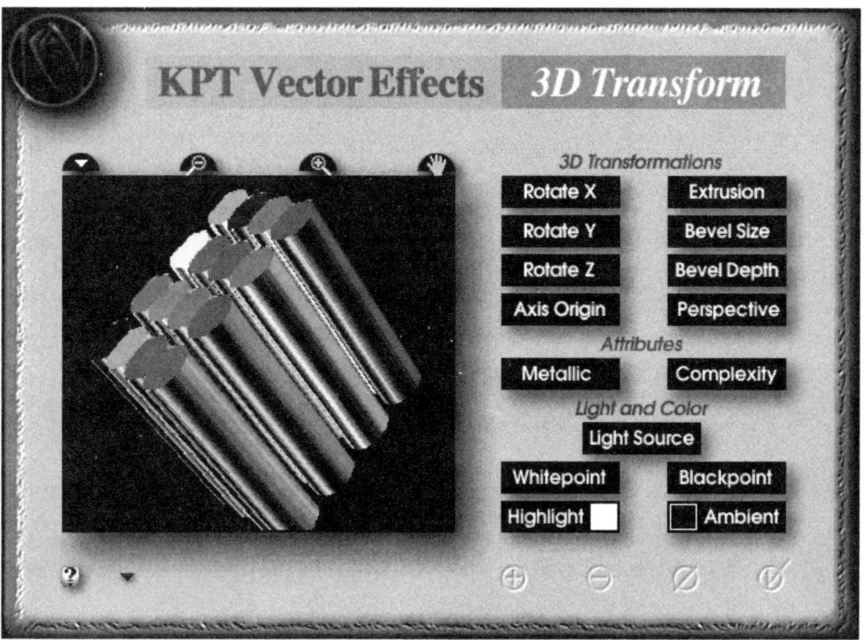

Figure 18-17: The KPT 3D Transform dialog box

After you've extruded the outlines, you might want to make the front of the letters metallic looking as well. To do this, select the front panels and change the Fill to a gradient. Figure 18-18 illustrates the final product.

Figure 18-18: Metallic text created with KPT 3D Transform

KPT 3D Transform has all sorts of amazing capabilities deep within itself that you can play with, including perspective adjustments, the ability to change the source and color of lighting, and much more.

KPT ColorTweak

The ColorTweak filter allows you to make changes to the color of the Fills and Strokes of selected artwork. Instead of the common ways of manipulating color through adjusting cyan, magenta, yellow, and black, KPT ColorTweak lets you do all sorts of different adjustments to colors. You can change the hue, saturation, brightness, contrast, and grayscale level, *and* play with the CMYK levels.

But what really sets ColorTweak apart from all the other color-adjustment filters (besides the fact that it's a *Plug-In Application Extension*) is the Randomize option in the Options menu. When the Randomize option is turned on, all the sliders being used generate random values and apply them to the selected paths.

STEPS: Generating Textures with KPT ColorTweak

Step 1. Create a mish-mash pattern of paths, like the one shown in Figure 18-19. I used the Roughen and Divide filters to create the paths shown here.

Step 2. Select the paths and Fill them with a color (no Stroke) that represents the overall tone you'd like the texture to be.

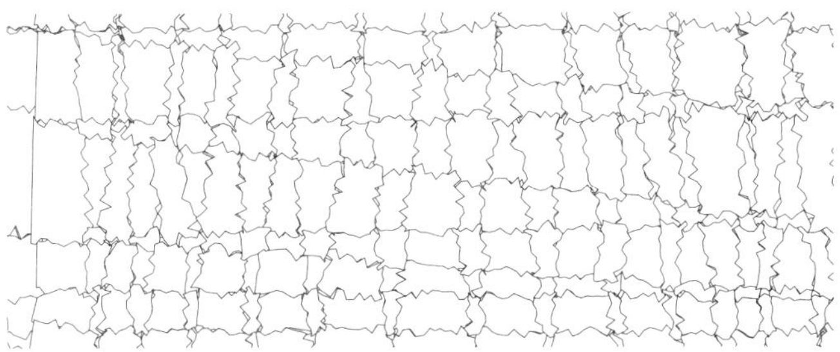

Figure 18-19: A mass of shapes

Step 3. With the paths still selected, choose Filters⇨KPT Vector Effects⇨KPT ColorTweak.

Step 4. In the ColorTweak dialog box, shown in Figure 18-20, select the Randomize option from the Options menu.

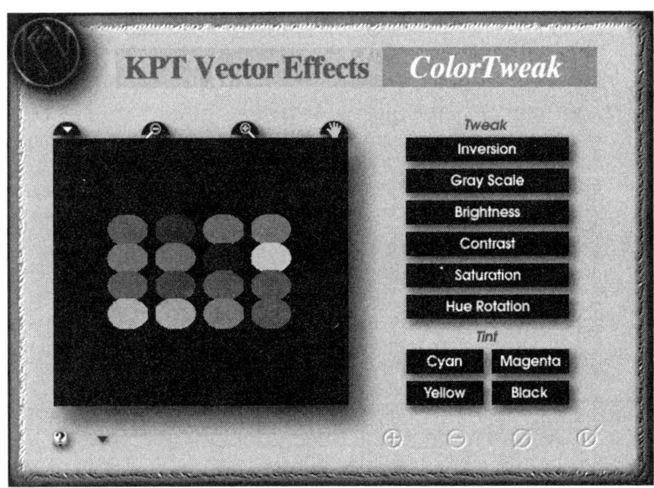

Figure 18-20: The Color Tweak dialog box

Step 5. Adjust the Brightness slider to the right about 10%.

Step 6. Click the check mark to exit the box.

Step 7. Choose Filters⇨KPT Vector Effects⇨KPT ColorTweak again, pull the Brightness slider to the left about 10%, and click the check mark. The text I created is shown in Figure 18-21.

Figure 18-21: The final texture

ColorTweak works differently with Process Colors from with way it does with Custom Colors. For instance, you can't change the Hue of a Custom Color. For the best results, change you custom colors to process *before* you use ColorTweak.

KPT Emboss

The Emboss filter is a one-shot filter that does what it does, and what it does it does quite well. Of course, I'm referring to embossing, which is making artwork look like it's indented or pushed out from the surface of the surrounding artwork. Figure 18-22 shows an example of embossed artwork created with KPT Emboss.

Figure 18-22: Embossed art.

For Figure 18-22, I changed the original artwork from color to grayscale first, to simulate various levels of depth.

There are all sorts of secret things hidden within Vector Effects. For instance, clicking on the Kai logo (when in Background mode) will display a preview as big as your monitor. Try pressing different keys when clicking there...of course, doing so may feel like a game, or as if you're being watched....

KPT Flare

This filter seems so basic and almost trivial when you first look at it, that it might not receive a second glance. Well, I'm telling you to look again, and be amazed. Sure, the filter creates flares on artwork, but it doesn't stop there. The "glow" from the halo is actually blended into the background of the artwork. This makes the power of the filter and the complexity of the artwork go beyond anything similar you could do previously in Illustrator.

The KPT Flare dialog box, shown in Figure 18-23, has controls for adjusting the size, number of spikes, and halo size of a flare. In addition, you can add more than one flare to your artwork.

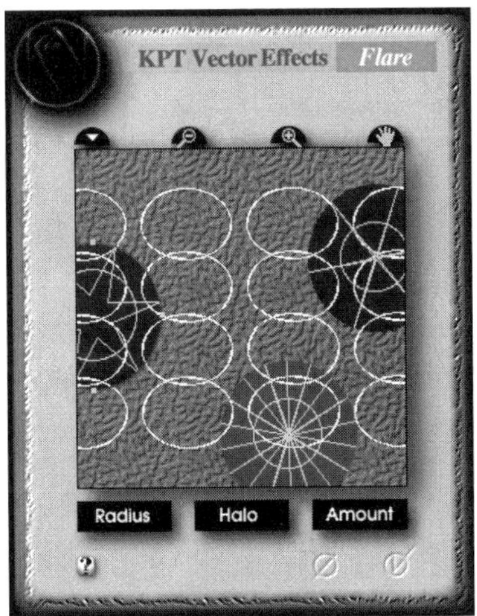

Figure 18-23: The KPT Flare dialog box

STEPS: Adding Several Flares

Step 1. Select the artwork you wish to have the flares applied to. Select as few paths as possible to reduce flare-generation time.

Step 2. Choose Filters⇨KPT Vector Effects⇨KPT Flare.

Step 3. Click on the middle of the flare to move it, click on a handle to resize it. Add spikes with the Amount slider. Change the size of the halo with the Halo slider. Change the inside radius with the Radius slider.

Try using a negative value in the Radius slider for some jazzy, multi-length starburst effects.

Step 4. Add additional sliders by selecting New Flare from the Options menu. You can also duplicate the current flare by selecting Duplicate Flare. To delete a flare, click on it and press the Delete key.

Step 5. After you've added as many flares as you'd like, click the check mark at the bottom right of the dialog box.

Figure 18-24 illustrates some of the effects you can create with this filter.

Figure 18-24: Three different flares applied to artwork at once

KPT Inset

The Inset filter is a better way of insetting or offsetting paths than the Offset Path filter from Adobe is. The best part of this filter is the Preview option, which enables you to see just how far you're moving the path. Inset also has a Copy option, so you can make a duplicate of the selected paths.

Use Inset to thicken or thin characters of type that have been converted to outlines, as in Figure 18-25.

Figure 18-25: The original type (top) and after having its weight increased with Inset (bottom)

Insettedness

Insettedness

KPT Neon

You'll see a set of steps for creating neon tubing back in the Blends chapter. You'll also see that it's a lot of work to create neon tubes that way...

KPT Neon is easy, painless, and fun. And the results are nothing short of stunning. The KPT Neon dialog box is shown in Figure 18-26. Note that there are only two sliders to move: Brightness and Amount.

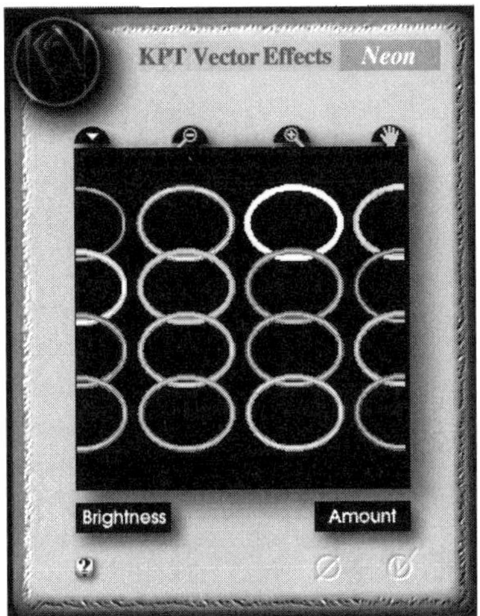

Figure 18-26: The KPT Neon dialog box

Brightness controls the brightest point of the neon tubing. Amount controls the thickness of the tubes. Easy, huh? Well, you *do* have to remember one thing: the neon tubes only appear on paths. That means neon text you create will consist of tubes that surround the letters, not just a tube shaped in the form of the letter.

KPT Point Editor

This filter provides a way to position and move both points and their handles to exact locations. To use the filter, select a path whose points you wish to edit, and choose Filters⇨KPT Vector Effects⇨KPT Point Editor. The Point Editor dialog box, shown in Figure 18-27, will then appear.

Select a point in the Preview window (zoom in if you can't see the point you wish to edit), and enter the new coordinates for it. If you wish to move the point by a certain amount, change the Point Coordinates menu (click the small triangle on the right) to Relative, and enter the distance to be moved.

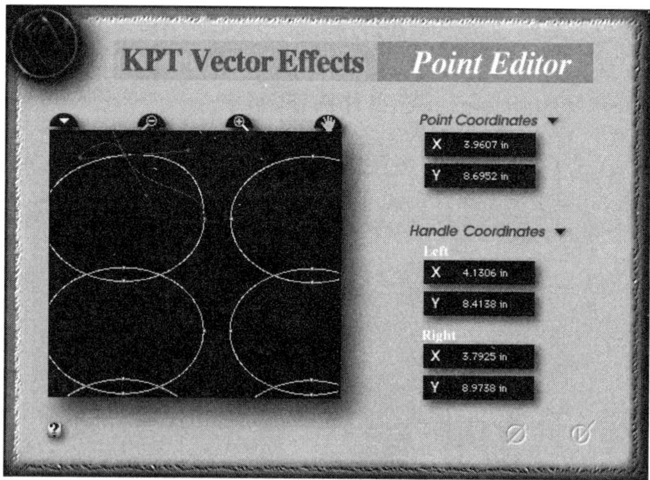

Figure 18-27: The KPT Point Editor dialog box

You can also select and adjust any handles on the path the same way. While in the dialog box, you can adjust as many points and handles as you'd like; when you're all done, all of them will be affected.

KPT Resize and Reposition

This filter lets you move and scale selected artwork at the same time. In addition to entering a percentage for scaling, you can actually enter the new dimensions of the artwork, and KPT Resize and Reposition will figure out the rest for you.

KPT ShadowLand

ShadowLand creates special-effects shadows for selected paths. More than just that, it's a place to play with shadows and shadow effects. Traditionally, creating shadows in Illustrator has always been very difficult. But with ShadowLand, the process is quite enjoyable. To get started using ShadowLand, I'd suggest taking text and converting it to outlines, and then choosing Filters⇨KPT Vector Effects⇨KPT Shadowland. The KPT ShadowLand dialog box is shown in Figure 18-28.

There are three major types of shadow effects to create in ShadowLand:

- **Zoom Shadow** creates a zooming shadow from one color (the default is 50% of selected paths) to the background color (the default is white). You can control the scaling, rotation, and steps associated with the shadow.

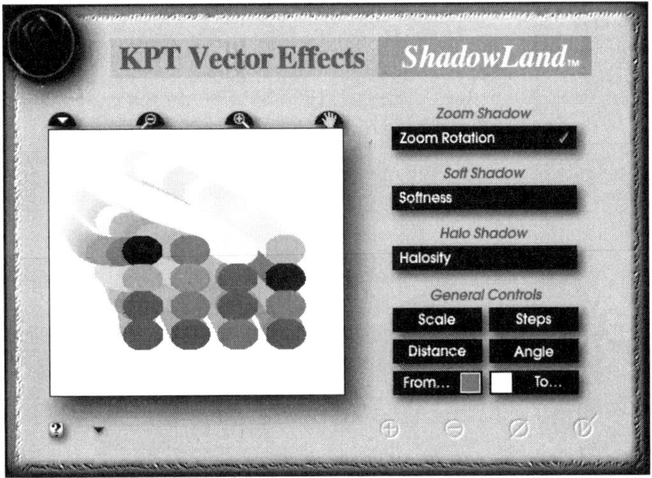

Figure 18-28: The KPT ShadowLand dialog box

- **Soft Shadow** gives Guassian blurred edges to the shadow, making the shadow smaller by the amount it's blurred.
- **Halosity** is like the opposite of Soft Shadow; it too gives a Guassian blur to the shadow edges, but the blur expands the size of the shadow, rather than contracting.

Figure 18-29 shows each of these effects applied to text.

Figure 18-29: Zoom Shadow, Soft Shadow, and Halosity

Zoom shadow is the most powerful of the three shadow types, and with it you can create all sorts of un-shadowlike effects. For instance, the logo in Figure 18-30 was created with Zoom Shadow, with the Connect setting steps turned off.

KPT ShatterBox

This is an amazing effect generator that automatically splits your artwork into hundreds or thousands of little pieces.

FreeHand Bashing Guideline #1824: KPT ShatterBox doesn't work in FreeHand 5x. Create something funky with the extension and then show it to your green with-envy FreeHand-using pals.

Figure 18-30: Zoom Shadow created the spinning logos inside the original logo.

STEPS: Using KPT ShatterBox

Step 1. Select the path or paths you wish to shatter.

Step 2. Choose Filters➪KPT Vector Effects➪KPT ShatterBox.

Step 3. Drag one of the three main sliders (shown in Figure 18-31) to the right. Watch the preview and stop when you think enough lines are crossing the image.

Step 4. Click the check mark in the lower right of the dialog box to make ShatterBox start shattering away.

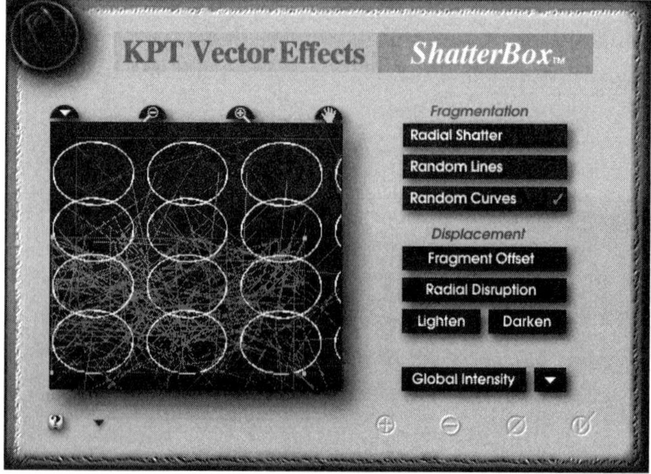

Figure 18-31: The KPT ShatterBox dialog box

ShatterBox is a slow filter to use, depending on the number of "Impacts" and the complexity of each, as well as the number and complexity of selected paths.

STEPS:	**Applying the South Phoenix (Shots Fired) Preset in ShatterBox**
Step 1.	Select the art you wish to use with ShatterBox.
Step 2.	Choose Filters⇨KPT Vector Effects⇨ShatterBox.
Step 3.	Click the Preset button and choose Preset Manager from the list. Click Import and find the Shots Fired preset on the *Macworld Illustrator 6 CD-ROM* (in the Presets *f* folder).
Step 4.	Click the check mark in the lower right to use the effect. The effect should look something like the one in Figure 18-32.

KPT Sketch

The Sketch filter takes paths and gives them a (surprise) sketchy look. It does this by moving the points and handles on the paths in the amount you specify, and by adding another path on top of the original with a Stroke, not a Fill.

There are only two sliders in the dialog box: Stroke and Amount. Stroke controls the width of the duplicated path Stroke, while Amount determines how much the paths are moved. Figure 18-33 shows several applications of the Sketch filter on artwork.

The Sketch filter has three settings: Color Stroke, Pen Stroke, and Width Stroke. The Color Stroke option creates a darker stroke than the original color of the path. Pen Stroke creates a black Stroke. Width Stroke creates a Stroke the exact color of the original artwork.

KPT Flare

Florence: I'm having trouble with KPT Flare. It takes forever just to create one flare on my artwork.

Toulouse: What does the artwork consist of?

Florence: Well, it's a Victorian Impressionist statement on the nobility of the ruling class, with a hint of cynicism that reflects the political influences of the time.

Toulouse: Gee. What I meant was, how many paths are in the artwork? You can always check that by selecting Doc-ument Info from the File menu.

Florence: Let's see...8,912 paths.

Toulouse: Well, that's the problem right there. KPT Flare interacts with each of the selected paths in order to create its halo. The more paths you've selected, the longer it'll take.

Florence: But I really want to use a flare here.

Toulouse: One thing you can do, if you don't mind the halo being behind some of the artwork, is to create a background (or select one if it's already there), and put the flare onto that. Then you can select the "flare," sans the halo, and put it in the front.

Florence: And if I want the halo in the front?

Toulouse: Select as few paths as possible, or problems might...er...flare up.

Figure 18-32: Bullet holes created with KPT ShatterBox

Figure 18-33: The Sketch filter was applied to the original artwork several times with a low Stroke setting and a low Amount setting.

One thing that KPT Sketch *doesn't* do is to add or subtract points during the sketching. In order to add points, you might want to apply the Roughen filter first, specifying somewhere around 5–10 points per inch and 0%. This will dramatically change the type of sketching that occurs, so experiment with different amounts of points added before coming up with a final design.

KPT Vector Distort

Vector Distort applies distortion effects to artwork, but doesn't require that you add points first, or that you pronounce its unsightly acronym. Through some wizardry of mathematics, Vector Distort adds points only where necessary. This makes effects like "swirl" look much better than does Adobe's Twirl filter.

Figure 18-34 shows some of the different effects in KPT Vector Distort applied to the same artwork.

Within the Vector Distort dialog box (shown in Figure 18-35), you can use anywhere from one to several "influences," which are the different types of effects listed on the sliders. To create a new influence, select the New Influence option from the Options menu. You can change the type of influence by clicking on it and dragging a different slider. Each of the different types of influences has a different color, so you can quickly see what type of influence you're using.

You can access many of the distortion effects by pressing a number key on the keyboard:

- 1 = Swirl
- 2 = Spherize
- 3 = Zig Zag
- 4 = Zig
- 5 = Zag
- 6 = Rotate

Using the keyboard, there's a double-secret distortion effect you can access, that no one knows about! (Actually, I had to tell the engineer, and he was really surprised, which might cause the average software user to lose a bit of sleep). Pressing 7 will activate the Scale function, in which you change the size of paths within the sphere of influence. To use this, the amount must be set in another influence first, then when 7 is pressed, scaling will take place there. Wow! The amazing thing about Scale is that it scales just the influenced portion of the path.

Shadowland

Bentley: I'm having trouble with ShadowLand.

Toulouse: Is your computer switched on? That's often a common...

Bentley: Yes, of course. Sometimes my system grinds to a halt when using the Zoom Shadow portion of ShadowLand.

Toulouse: This usually happens when you've selected several re-compounded paths.

Bentley: Re-compounded?

Toulouse: That's a compound path that you've selected with other compound paths, and made them all into another compound path. They wreak havoc with Illustrator, and the complexity in ShadowLand can crash Illustrator.

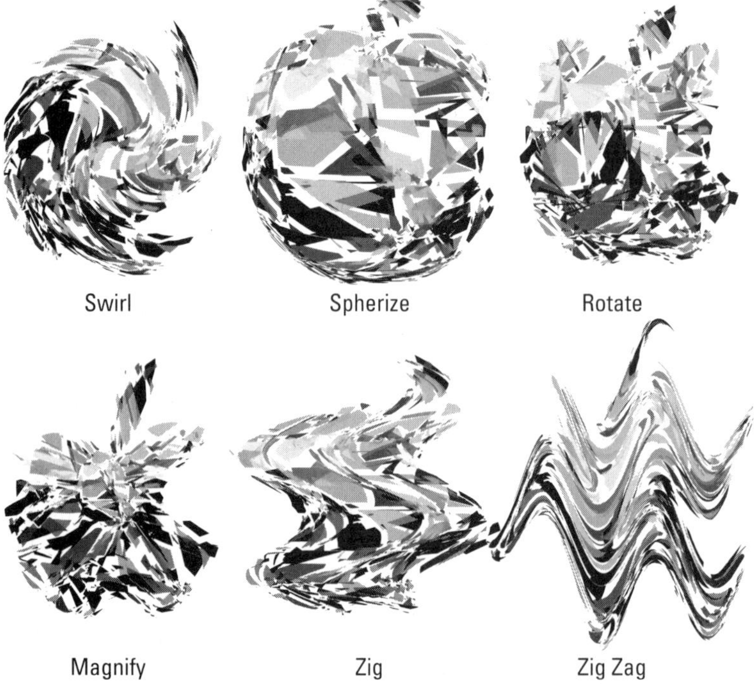

Figure 18-34: KPT Vector Distort effects

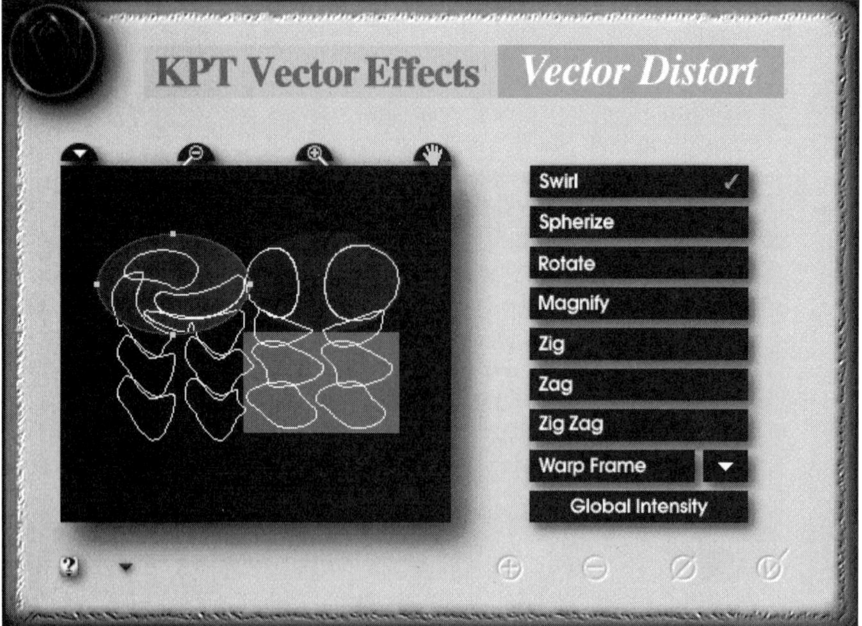

Figure 18-35: The KPT Vector Distort dialog box

KPT Warp Frame

Warp Frame is a powerful distortion envelope for Illustrator, similar to Letraset Envelopes (described later). With it, selected paths are warped into a different shape from the basic bounding box rectangle they normally have.

The best way to get started with Warp Frame is to start applying some of the presets, which are accessed by pressing the little triangle at the bottom of the dialog box (shown in Figure 18-36).

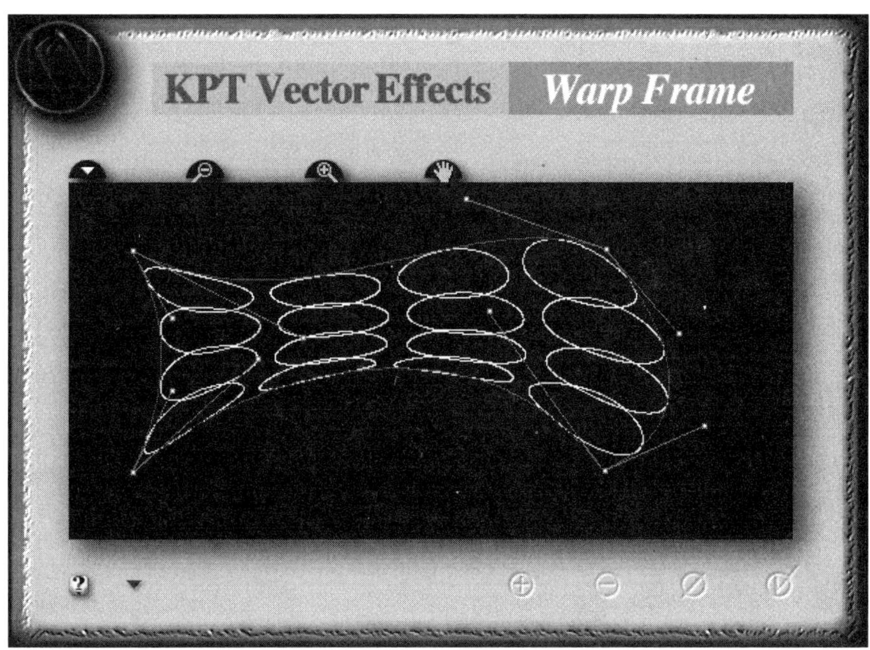

Figure 18-36: The KPT Warp Frame dialog box

After a preset has been applied, you can click on the points and handles around the edges of the envelope frame and drag them, changing the shape of the paths within. To start again from scratch (even if there's no itch), choose Reset All from the Options menu.

There are several Warp Frame presets available on the *Macworld Illustrator 6 Bible CD-ROM.*

Other Third-Party Filters

Other third-party filters are constantly being released by a variety of manufacturers. Future editions of this book will provide the most space to the most popular and useful of those filter sets. In this section, I'm providing you with an overview of some of the smaller, lesser known sets that are available. Do to space limitations, discussion of them is brief. Contact information for the distributors of these products, as well as the ones mentioned above, is available in Appendix G.

Letraset Envelopes

Letraset Envelopes is a one-shot filter with a lot of potential. It includes several preset shapes for envelope distortion of text, and it provides the ability to adjust the outside frame of the envelopes.

Letraset also provides additional presets at an additional charge, for a total of over 200 preset envelope shapes.

Extensis DrawTools

Three sets of filters are available from Extensis, a distributor of Plug-Ins for QuarkXPress, Photoshop, Illustrator, and FreeHand. While on the expensive side, these filters provide a number of impressive capabilities that the serious Illustrator user might be interested in, including advanced color controls and low-end 3-D effects.

The most useful of all of these filters is the Curves filter, which provides Photoshop-like curve control for colors...right within Illustrator! The Curves dialog box is shown in Figure 18-37.

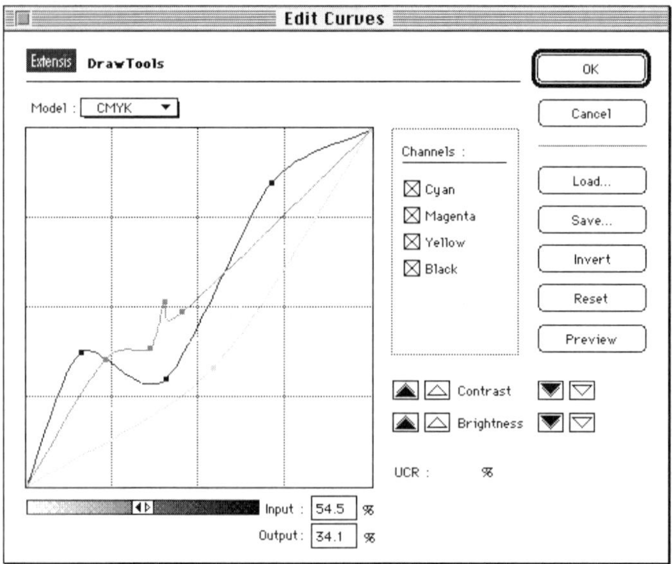

Figure 18-37: The Edit Curves dialog box from Extensis' DrawTools

Filters on the CD

I've included a boatload of filters on the CD-ROM that comes with this book. In addition to demos from each of the main manufacturers, there are several working filters as well. The following sections briefly describe these filters.

KPT Gradients/Patterns to Paths

This handy filter takes paths filled with gradients or patterns, and converts the gradients to blends and the patterns to paths. This provides you with the capability to do some truly amazing effects that wouldn't be possible otherwise.

Matt Foster's Melt & Drip Filters

Matt Foster is one of the amazingly talented engineers at Adobe systems. He designed the Melt & Drip filters to show off some of the capabilities of the Illustrator Plug-In interface, to help potential programmers in writing their own filters for Illustrator. Little did he know I'd find all sorts of amazing uses for it. Melt & Drip filters affect selected paths. The dialog box for Melt is shown in Figure 18-38.

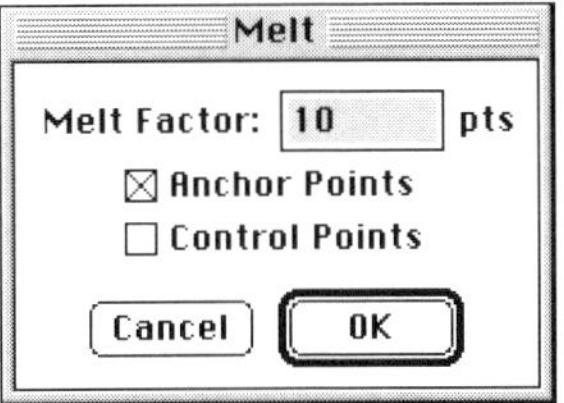

Figure 18-38: The Melt dialog box

Following are a few images that show how text can be manipulated with Melt and Drip to get various effects. Instead of the common "steps" format, I've condensed the explanations to save space. For all the Figures, first create type and then convert to outlines.

To achieve the effect in Figure 18-39, apply Add Anchor Points three times. Apply Drip at 20 points, with both the Anchor and Control points checkboxes checked. Apply Rounded Corners at 100 points. Apply Unite. Select the bottommost points and scale them down with the Scale tool.

Figure 18-39: The original outlined path, and after Dripping

To achieve the effect in Figure 18-40, apply Add Anchor Points three times. Rotate the words 90°. Apply Melt at 10 points, with both the Anchor and Control points checkboxes checked. Rotate 180°. Reapply Melt (just press ⌘-Shift-E) at the same settings. Apply Rounded Corners at 100. Rotate 90° (back to regular position). Apply Unite.

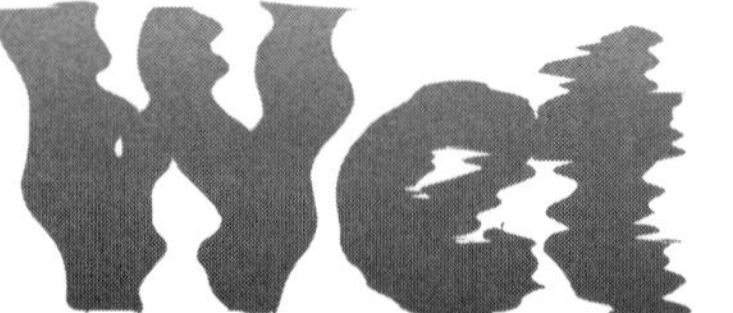

Figure 18-40: The original outlined path, and after Melting

To achieve the effect in Figure 18-41, apply Add Anchor Points once. Apply Round Corners at 100. Apply Add Anchor Points twice. Apply Twirl at 90° Apply Melt at 10, checking on the Control Points checkbox. Apply Twirl at -95°. Rotate with the Rotate Tool back to horizontal. Apply Drip at 20, with both the Anchor and Control points checkboxes checked. Apply Unite.

Figure 18-41: The original outlined path, and after Melting and Dripping

BeInfinite Smart Remove Points

This filter removes unnecessary points from paths. It's a useful tool for cleaning up artwork created with Streamline or the AutoTrace tool.

Ted Alspach's Doodle Jr.

This filter (Figure 18-42) was designed to take advantage of some of the normally unseen path manipulation capabilities of the Illustrator API. By playing with the various controls, you can distort and reshape artwork dramatically.

Figure 18-42: Doodle Jr. is a new distortion filter that lets you reshape artwork.

A hidden feature of Doodle Jr.: Click on the Doodle Jr. logo, and the selected objects will have their colors randomized.

To use Doodle Jr., copy it to your Illustrator 6 Plug-Ins folder and restart Illustrator. The filter will appear in a new filter Menu submenu, called Fun.

Summary

- Third-party filters for Illustrator are created by companies and individuals outside Adobe.
- BeInfinite's InfiniteFX provides more than 50 distortion filters with a common interface.

- The CSI Socket Set 1 filter set includes several filters for color adjusting and selecting, as well as Plug-Ins and startup-document capabilities.
- The CSI Socket Set 2 filter set includes several object-oriented filters, including ones for aligning and repeating.
- KPT Vector Effects contains a baker's dozen of various filters, many for producing unique special effects with Illustrator.
- Several filters can be found on the enclosed CD-ROM; copy them to your Illustrator 6 Plug-Ins folder and restart Illustrator to use them.

Mastering Illustrator

PART IV

There are many concepts in Illustrator that don't fall under one of Illustrator's menus or tools. There are also several software packages that add features to Illustrator's already immense capabilities.

This part discusses a wide variety of Illustrator features, capabilities, and techniques that will help round out your knowledge of Illustrator. The concepts presented in this part are unique and useful; in fact, even Illustrator experts may find information in here that they didn't know before.

Working with Strokes

19 CHAPTER

In This Chapter

- Understanding what you can do with Strokes
- The Outline Stroke filter
- Stroke effects for letters
- Blends and Strokes
- Rough and feathered edges
- Creating designs on a Stroke
- Path type and Strokes

The ability to Stroke a path in Illustrator is greatly underrated. Strokes can do more than just outline shapes and vary thicknesses and patterns.

In the first part of this chapter, I explain some of the greatest mysteries and unlock some of the deepest secrets that surround Strokes. If that sounds at all boring, take a look at the figures in the first half of this chapter. I created most of them by using Strokes, not Filled paths. Amazin', ain't it?

The Secret Magic of Strokes

You create most effects with Strokes by overlaying several Strokes on top of one another. By copying and choosing Edit⇨Paste in Front (⌘-F), you place an exact duplicate of the original path on top of itself.

Stroke Essentials

Strokes, which were introduced in Chapter 5, act and work differently than Fills do. Keep the following basics and rules (no pun intended) in mind when using Strokes:

- The most important thing to remember when you are using Strokes is that Stroke weight width is evenly distributed on both sides of a path. In other words, on a Stroke with a 6-point weight, there will be 3 points of the Stroke on both sides of the Stroke's path.
- Patterns can be put into Strokes, but patterns cannot be viewed in Preview mode when they are on Strokes.
- Gradients may *not* be used to color Strokes.
- Using the Outline Stroke filter (Filter⇨Object⇨Outline Path) creates path outlines around the width of the Stroke. When a Stroke has been converted into an outline, it is really an outlined path object and can be Filled with patterns and gradients (both of which will appear when previewing and printing).
- Stroke weight *never* varies on the same path.
- A Stroke with a color of None has no Stroke weight.
- Strokes are, for the most part, ignored when combining, splitting, or modifying paths with the Pathfinder filters. Strokes may result but are never taken into account when the Pathfinder filter searches for the locations of the paths.

Changing the weight and color of the top Stroke gives the appearance of a path that is a designer, or custom, Stroke. You can add Strokes on top of or under the original Stroke to make the pattern more complex or to add more colors or shapes.

Figure 19-1 and the following steps show you how to create a specialty Stroke that looks like parallel Strokes.

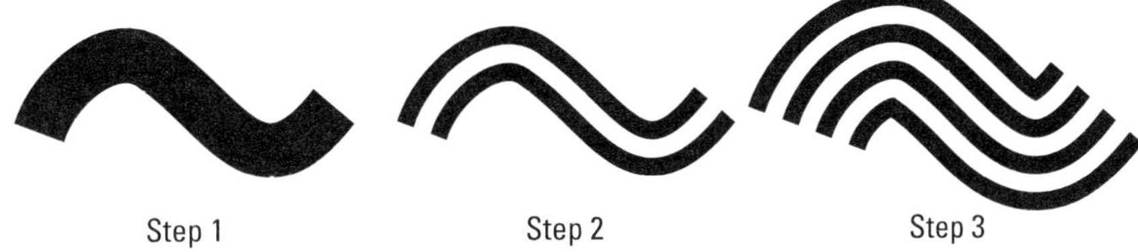

Figure 19-1: Creating parallel strokes

STEPS: Creating "Parallel Strokes"

Step 1. Use the Freehand tool to draw a short line. I usually set the Freehand tolerance (choose File⇨General Preferences or press ⌘-K) to 10 for a very smooth path. Change the Fill to None and Stroke the path with 18-point Black.

Step 2. Copy the Stroke and paste the copy in front (⌘-F). Change the copied (pasted in front) Stroke to 6-point White. Select both paths, copy them (⌘-C), and lock them (⌘-1). The 6-point Stroke looks as if it has been subtracted from the 18-point Stroke. The result appears to be two separate 6-point black Strokes.

Step 3. Choose Edit⇨Paste In Back (⌘-B). Deselect All (⌘-Shift-A) and click the top path. Change the weight of the Stroke to 30 points. Lock the path and select the remaining path. Change the Stroke on this path to 42. The 30 points is 12 points more than the 18 points of the black Stroke, or 6 points on each side. The 42 points is 12 more than the white 30 points.

When you are creating "parallel Strokes," determine how thick the visible Strokes should be, multiply that number times the black *and* white visible Strokes that you want for the base Stroke, and work up from there. For example, if you want 10-point Strokes, and there are four white Strokes and five black strokes, the first Stroke would be 90-points thick and Black. The next Stroke would be 70-point White, and then 50-points Black, 30-point White, and 10-point Black.

This example is just the tip of the iceberg in creating custom Strokes. Not only can you have paths that overlap, but you also can give the Stroke on each path different dash patterns, joins, and caps. You can even add Fills to certain paths to make the Stroke different on both sides of the path. And if all that isn't enough, you can use the Outline Stroke filter to outline Strokes.

Knowing the secrets doesn't let you in on the really good stuff, though. Read on to learn how to apply these to achieve truly amazing effects with Strokes.

Selecting "Hidden" Strokes

Ann: I just can't seem to select some Strokes.

Toulouse: Are they locked?

Ann: No, if I Select All or drag a marquee around them, they're selected then.

Toulouse: So, what's the problem?

Ann: Well, they're directly under other Strokes. I can't seem to select those Strokes without selecting the ones on top.

Toulouse: The easiest thing to do is to lock the paths on "top" and then the other Strokes will be easier to select.

Using the Stroke Charts

The stroke charts in Figures 19-2 through 19-5 show how some of the basic Stroke-dash patterns look with various options checked, at different weights, and in different combinations.

All of the paths in the charts were taken from an original shape that included a straight segment, a corner, and a curve. The charts should help you determine when to use certain types of Stroke patterns because, as you can see, some patterns work better than others with curves and corners.

The first chart (Figure 19-2) consists of 32 3-point Stroked paths that have a variety of dash patterns and end and join attributes. The second chart (Figure 19-3) shows 18 10-point Stroke paths with similar attributes. These two charts show Stroke effects with only one path. The area in the middle of each path in the chart describes the path. To see what the names of the caps and joins correspond to, see the Stroke section of the Paint Style palette, which is shown in Figure 19-6.

The third chart (Figure 19-4) and fourth chart (Figure 19-5) contain paths that have been copied on top of the original by using the Paste in Front command. The paths are listed in the order that they were created. The first path is described at the top of the list. The first path is copied, pasted in front (⌘-F), and given the Paint Style attributes of the second item in the list. The changes progress from the top left of each chart to the bottom left and then from the top right to the bottom right.

In some cases, paths are blended from one to another. To be able to select an end point on each Stroke (usually they will overlap), offset one of the paths by .1 point. When blending, use a number that is less than 100 for the number of blend steps, dividing the suggested number by 2 until it is small enough.

Color	Width	Dash	Cap	Join
Black 100%	3	0,1	Round	Round
Black 100%	3	0,2	Round	Round
Black 100%	3	0,3	Round	Round
Black 100%	3	0,4	Round	Round
Black 100%	3	0,5	Round	Round
Black 100%	3	0,10	Round	Round
Black 100%	3	0,1	Butt	Miter
Black 100%	3	0,2	Butt	Miter
Black 100%	3	0,3	Butt	Miter
Black 100%	3	0,4	Butt	Miter
Black 100%	3	0,5	Butt	Miter
Black 100%	3	0,10	Butt	Miter
Black 100%	3	0,2	Projected	Miter
Black 100%	3	0,3	Projected	Miter
Black 100%	3	0,5	Projected	Miter
Black 100%	3	0,10	Projected	Miter
Black 100%	3	0,10,0,5	Round	Round
Black 100%	3	0,10,0,20	Round	Round
Black 100%	3	2,2	Round	Round
Black 100%	3	2,5	Round	Round
Black 100%	3	2,10	Round	Round
Black 100%	3	2,5,0,5	Round	Round
Black 100%	3	2,10,0,10	Round	Round
Black 100%	3	4,5,0,5	Round	Round
Black 100%	3	4,10,0,10	Round	Round
Black 100%	3	10,5	Round	Round
Black 100%	3	10,10	Round	Round
Black 100%	3	10,15,10,5	Round	Round
Black 100%	3	20,10	Projected	Miter
Black 100%	3	10,10,0,10	Projected	Miter
Black 100%	3	20,10,0,10	Projected	Miter
Black 100%	3	10,10,30,10	Projected	Miter

Figure 19-2: 32 3-point Stroked paths

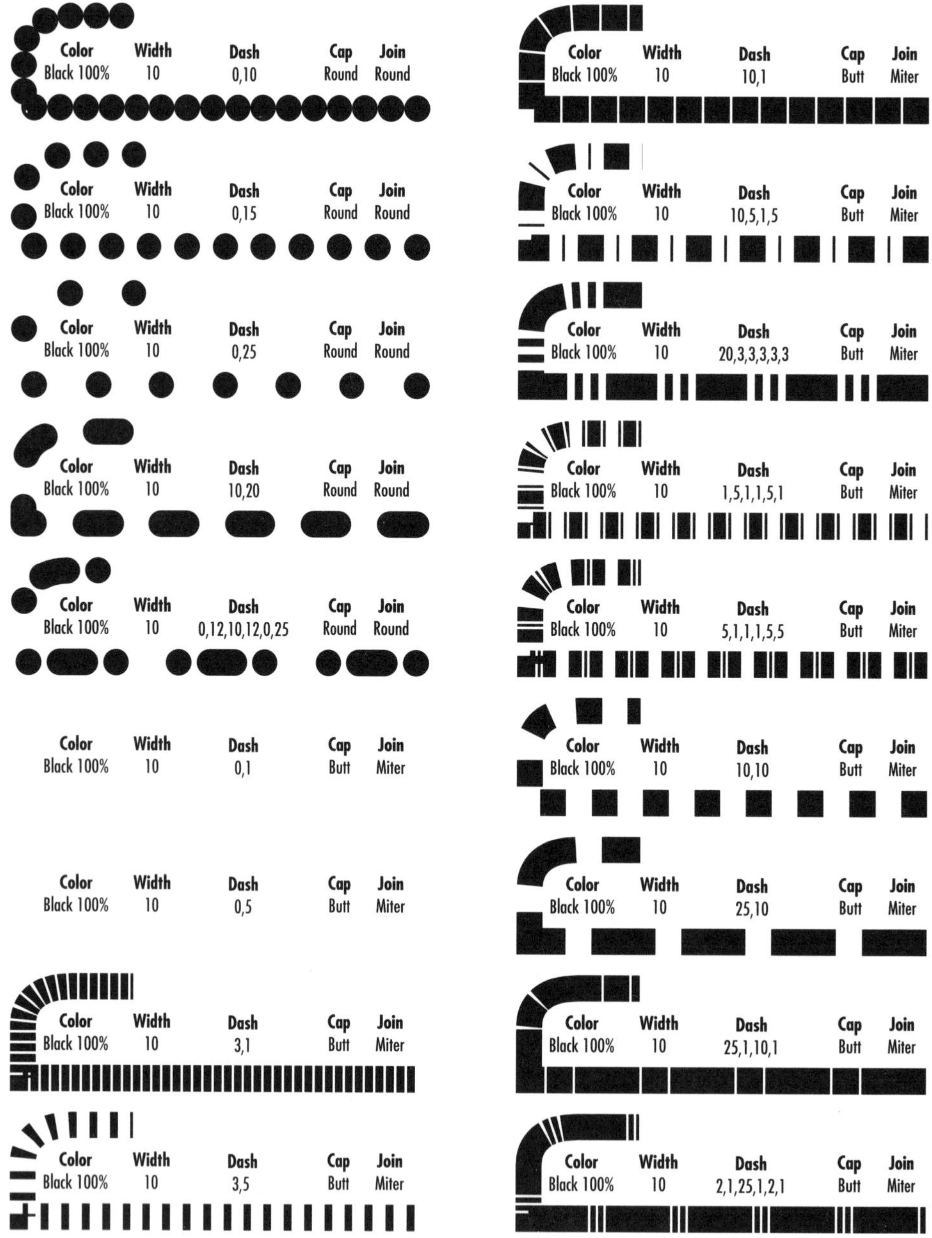

Figure 19-3: 18 10-point Stroke paths

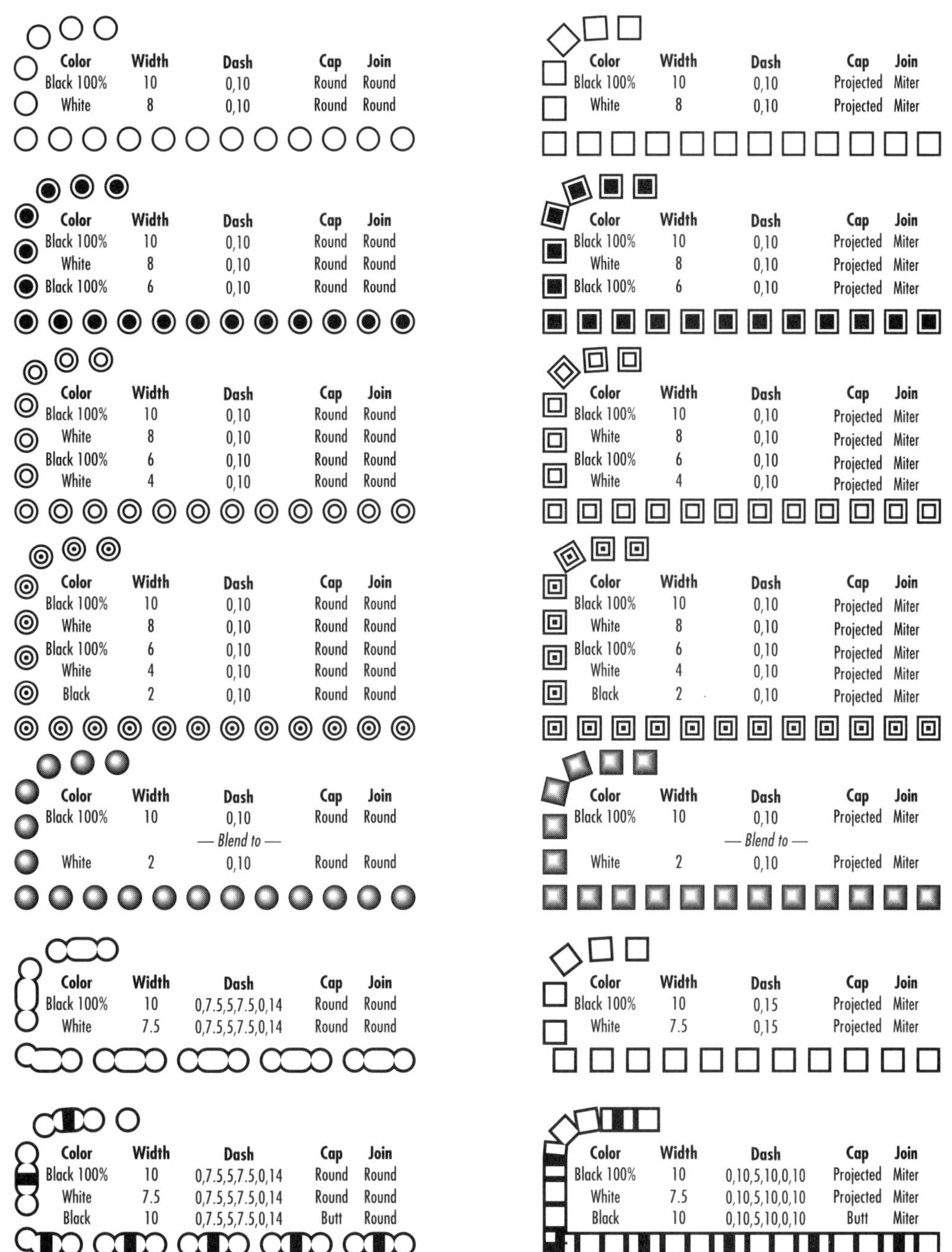

Figure 19-4: Paths that have been copied on top of the original paths

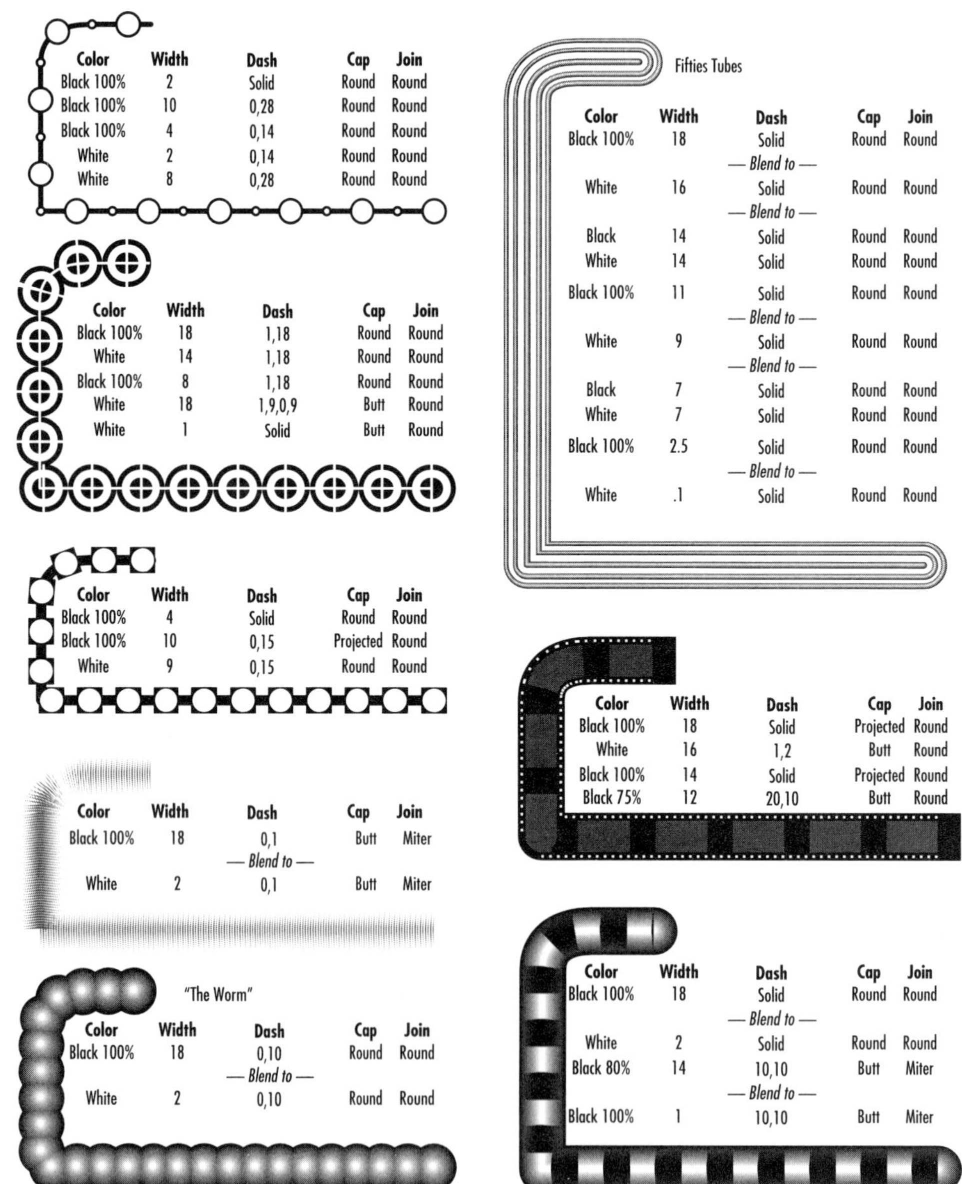

Figure 19-5: Another example of paths that have been copied on top of the original paths

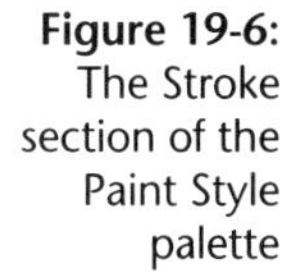

Figure 19-6: The Stroke section of the Paint Style palette

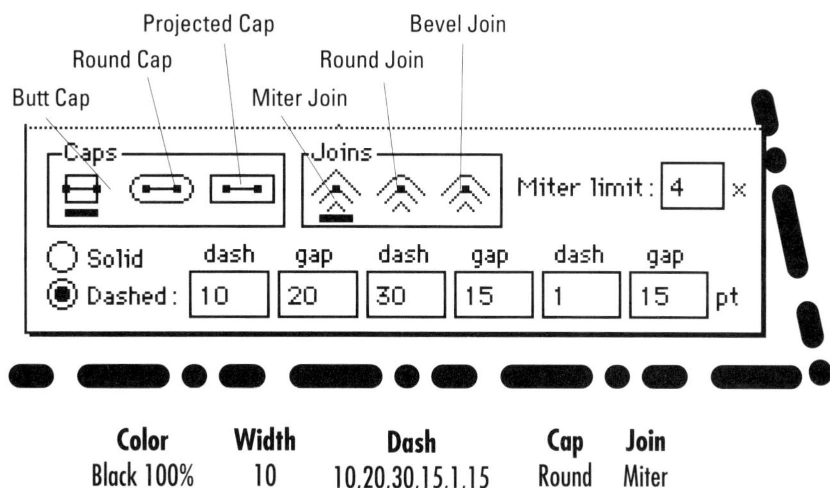

When you're creating the various Stroke patterns, many times the original path will be selected, copied, and then pasted in front or back (⌘-F or ⌘-B) several times. There is usually no need to recopy the original path after it has been copied. It can continue to be pasted again and again on top of or under the original path.

In the middle of the righthand column in the fourth stroke chart (Figure 19-5) is a Stroke that looks like a strip of film. The following steps describes how to create this film Stroke.

STEPS: Creating a Film Stroke

Step 1. The film Stroke from the fourth Stroke chart (Figure 19-5) is a basic Stroke that produces a stunning effect. Draw a wavy path with the Freehand tool.

Step 2. Change the stroke of the path to Black, 18 points, and the Fill to None.

Step 3. Copy (⌘-C) the path and choose Edit⇨Paste In Front (⌘-F). Change the Stroke to White, 16 points, and use a Dash Pattern of Dash 1, Gap 2.

Step 4. Choose Edit⇨Paste in Front (⌘-F) again and change the Stroke to Black, 14 points, Solid.

Step 5. Choose Edit⇨Paste in Front (⌘-F) one last time and change the Stroke to 75% Black, 12 points, with a Dash Pattern of Dash 20, Gap 10.

Figure 19-7 shows these steps. You can use this procedure to create any of the Strokes in the fourth Stroke chart (Figure 19-5) by substituting the values that are listed in the chart for the Stroke that you want.

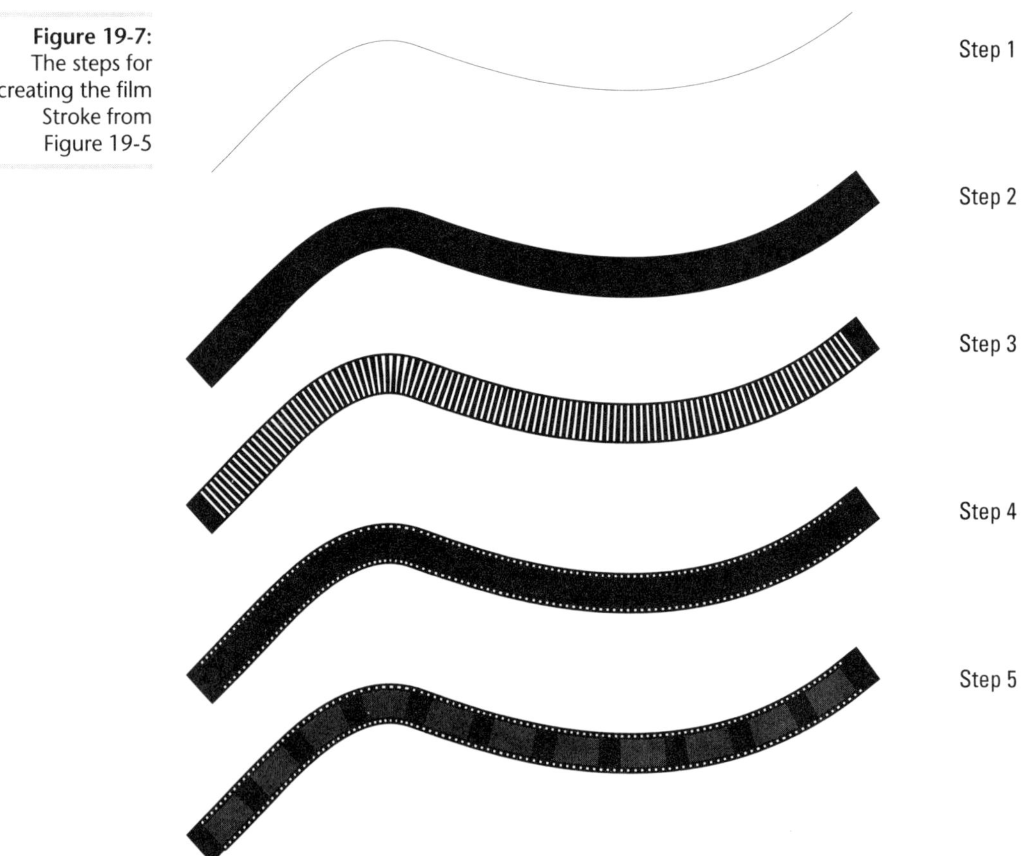

Figure 19-7: The steps for creating the film Stroke from Figure 19-5

Stroking Type

You can use Strokes to enhance type in a number of ways. The first example (shown in Figure 19-8) is based on Stroke blends. For more information on Stroke blends, see Chapter 10; for more information on type, see Chapter 8.

Figure 19-8: Steps for creating ghosted type

STEPS: Creating Ghosted Type with Strokes

Step 1. Type a few words in a heavily weighted font, like Helvetica Black, Futura Extra Bold, or Kabel Ultra.

Step 2. Select the type with the Selection tool. Choose Type⇨Create Outlines and change the Fill to None and the Stroke to Black or a light shade of gray. Change the weight of the Stroke to .1 point.

Step 3. Copy (⌘-C) the words and Choose Edit⇨Paste in Back (⌘-B). Move the copy a few points up and to the right. Change the Stroke on the copy to 4-point White and blend each set of paths together with the Blend tool.

Step 4. Choose Edit⇨Paste in Front (⌘-F) and change the Fill to White and the Stroke to None.

Another popular effect (OK, it was popular in the 70's) for type is produced by creating several Strokes for each stroke of a letter, as described in the following steps and shown in Figure 19-9.

STEPS: Creating Type That Has Multiple Strokes

Step 1. Create a word or words in a lightweight typeface.

Step 2. Use the Pen tool to recreate the letters in the typeface. In Figure 19-9, I colored the letters in the original word light red and then locked those letters in place so that I could trace the letters easier.

Step 3. Group all the paths that you have drawn and give them a heavy Stroke. (I used 18 points). Change the join and cap style in the Paint Style palette to rounded.

Step 4. Copy (⌘-C) and paste in front (⌘-F) in gradually decreasing Stroke weights. Change between white and a darker color as the weight decreases.

Figure 19-9: Making type that has multiple Strokes

Step 1

Step 2

Step 3

Step 4

Creating Rough Edges

You can create some of the most interesting Stroke effects by using the Roughen filter in combination with a heavily weighted Stroke. Even with a Roughen filter setting of 1% or 2%, a heavily weighted Stroke can have many sharp, long points, as described in the following steps.

STEPS: Using Strokes to Create Multiple Jagged Edges

Step 1. Create an object to which you want to add jagged or explosive edges. I used text that was converted to outlines in the example (see Figure 19-10). Copy the object off to the side before continuing.

Step 2. Use the Offset Path filter to create a path that is offset by 20 points or more. Select all the paths and choose Filter⇨Pathfinder⇨Unite.

Step 3. Copy the path again, roughen the path using Filter⇨Distort⇨Roughen (2%, 40 per inch), and apply a 19-point Stroke to it. Paste the roughened path in front and roughen it again; then apply a 19-point Stroke in a different color. Continue to paste in front, roughen, and thicken the Stroke until you have created a satisfactory number of paths.

Step 4. Paste in front one last time and roughen as before, but give the Stroke a lesser weight and Fill the path with the same color as the Stroke. Place the original art (which you copied off to the side in Step 1) on top of the roughened paths.

Using Fills to Create Half-Stroked Paths

One technique that I don't think is used enough is hiding one side of the Stroke as the path layers are built up. To hide half of the Stroke at any level, paste in front as you normally do and then press ⌘-Option-1. This command locks everything that isn't selected; in other words, only the path that you just pasted (and which is currently selected) will not be locked.

Using the Pen tool, connect the ends of the just-pasted path and Fill it with the background color and a Stroke of None. This action obliterates one side of the Stroke because the file of the path covers the "inside" part of the Stroked path. Any Strokes that you place on top of this object will be visible on both sides of the path.

Workin' on the Railroad

Several effects that you can create with paths have a traveling theme, mainly because a path starts somewhere and finishes somewhere else. Railroad tracks, roads, highways, trails, and rivers all have a tendency to conform very nicely to Stroke effects with paths.

One of the trickiest traveling paths to create is railroad tracks. To get the real railroad track look, some advanced "cheating" is necessary, as described in the following steps.

Figure 19-10: Creating roughened paths with Strokes

STEPS: Creating Railroad Tracks

Step 1. Draw a path to represent the railroad. Create a background shape and Fill the background with a color. In the example (see Figure 19-11), I used dark green.

Step 2. Copy the path. Give the path a Stroke weight of 30 points. Choose Edit⇨Paste In Front (⌘-F) and give this path a Stroke weight of 20 points.

Step 3. Select both paths. Choose Filter⇨Object⇨Outline Stroke to change the paths into outlined paths because Strokes cannot contain gradients. Fill the paths with a metallic gradient.

Step 4. Select both paths and choose Filter⇨Pathfinder⇨Exclude. This command subtracts the inner section of the track from the two outer sections.

Step 5. Check the ends of the path and delete any excess paths that are not part of the tracks. In the example, I also joined the ends on each individual track.

Step 6. Paste in back (⌘-B) and give the new path a Stroke weight of 40 points. Choose Filter⇨Object⇨Outline Stroke and Fill this path with a gradient consisting of several woodlike browns. This path is the wood that underlies the tracks.

Step 7. The last thing to do is split the pieces of wood into individual railroad ties. Select the wood path and choose Edit⇨Paste in Front (⌘-F). This command will paste a path right on top of the wooden area. Give this Stroke the same color as the background and give it a Dash Pattern of Dash 20, Gap 10. The gaps will be the "see through" areas, showing the wood-filled path below them.

ASK TOULOUSE

Just the Outside Edge?

Julie: I don't want to see the outside edge of my Strokes, but the inside.

Toulouse: There's a couple things you can do.

Julie: The easiest, please.

Toulouse: You know the path you can make on the inside of an object, that knocks out the inside of a Stroke?

Julie: Yes, but I want to knock out the outside of the Stroke.

Toulouse: Select the overlapping inner path and the Stroked path, and choose Object⇨Make Mask. The inside will be the only part that shows.

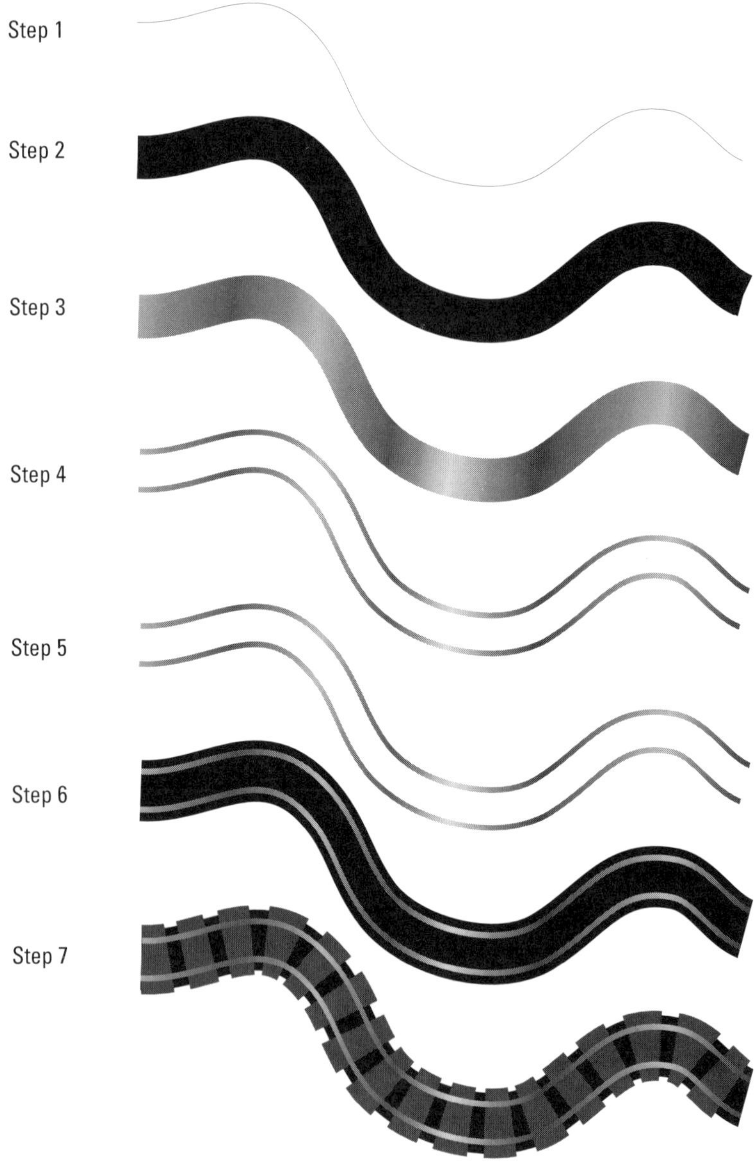

Figure 19-11: Steps for creating railroad tracks

Step 1

Step 2

Step 3

Step 4

Step 5

Step 6

Step 7

To change the color of the new path in Step 7 easily, select the new path, choose the Eyedropper tool, and double-click the background.

The Outline Stroke filter is often used on this type of Stroke design because Strokes can't have gradient Fills. The reason that the railroad ties were not given a dash pattern before the Outline Stroke filter was applied is that the Outline Stroke filter doesn't work with dash patterns.

The Wild River

A wild river is another path that you can create easily by using Strokes. One problem in getting rivers to look good is that creating the rough, in-out texture of a river's bank is difficult. Also, because different parts of rivers are different weights, connecting the parts smoothly is difficult. The following steps describe how to create a river.

STEPS: Creating a River

Step 1. Draw the paths for the river. In the example (see Figure 19-12), I created a *Y* at one end of the river and an island. For these features, I used the Pen tool to draw additional paths next to the river.

Step 2. Give the river a Stroke weight and color. In the example, I gave the main part of the river a Stroke of 18 points and the two additional parts 14-point Strokes. Copy all of the paths, paste in front, and color the copy a little darker than the original river Stroke color. Make the Strokes on the copy a few points less wide than on the original.

Step 3. Blend (Filter⇨Colors⇨Blend Front to Back) the two Strokes together, using three blend steps.

Step 4. Select all of the Strokes and choose Filter⇨Object⇨Outline Stroke. Select one of the new paths and choose Filter⇨Select⇨Same Fill Color. Choose Filter⇨Pathfinder⇨Unite. Repeat this process for each of the five different colors.

Step 5. Select all of the paths and choose Filter⇨Distort⇨Roughen. In the Roughen dialog box, enter **.3** and **40** segments per inch and then click OK. The edges of the river will now be a little ragged, and they will appear to have ripples, or waves, in them.

The Highway

Figures 19-13 and 19-14 show a Stroke design that I discovered a few years back while I was playing around with Illustrator. It has the makings of a cute parlor magic trick that you can use to impress your friends. Back when you had to work in Artwork mode, before Illustrator 5.0, creating designs with Strokes was much more difficult. Artists couldn't see what they were drawing on-screen, so they had to envision it in their minds. Editing dashes and weights is almost a pleasure now that you can use the Auto feature of the Paint Style palette and undo multiple changes.

After creating the Railroad Tracks Stroke design, which I thought was pretty clever, I yearned for a similar effect — turning one path into an object. I especially liked the effect of doing several paths and several Stroke attributes in Artwork mode and then switching to Preview mode when I was finished.

Figures 19-13 and 19-14 show the steps that you take to create a four-lane highway by drawing just one path. These steps are described after the figures.

Figure 19-12: Steps for making a river

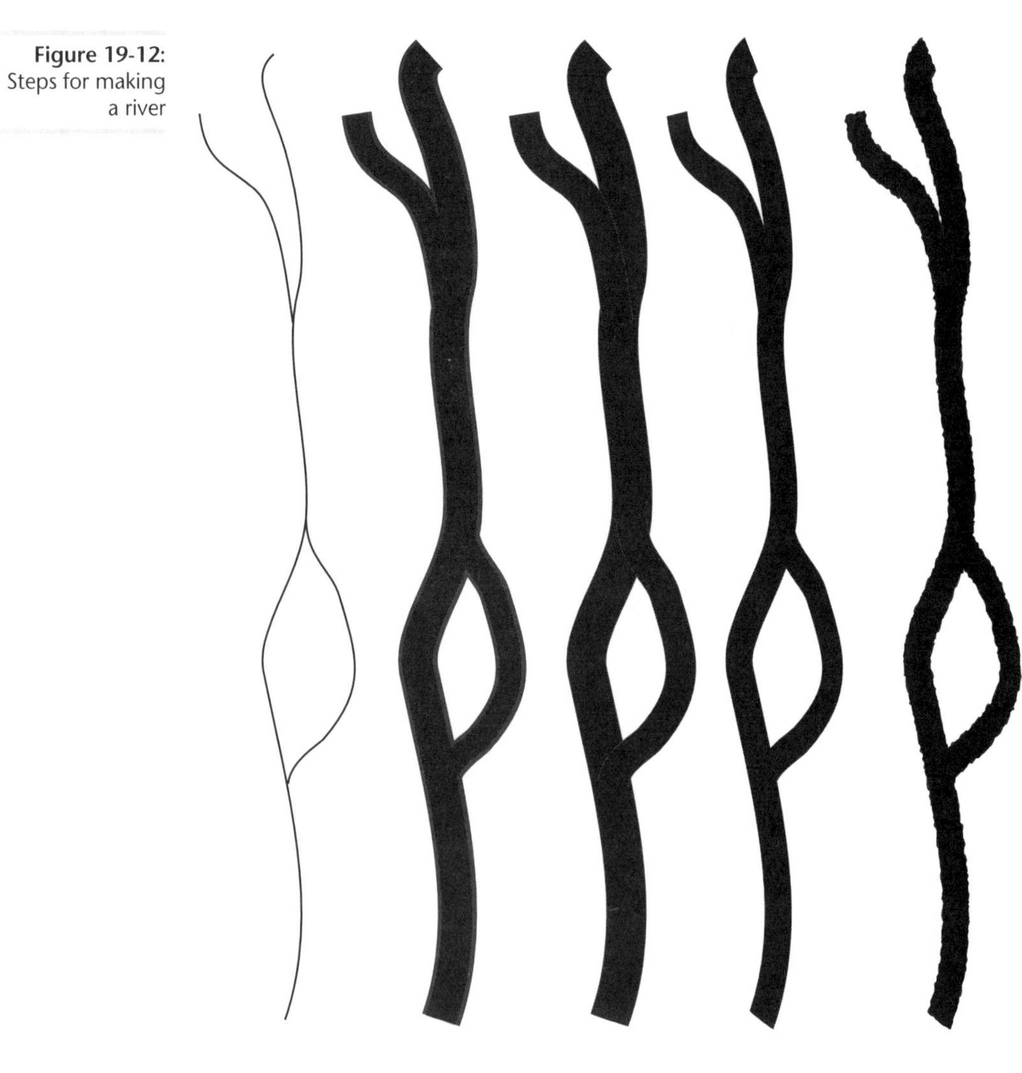

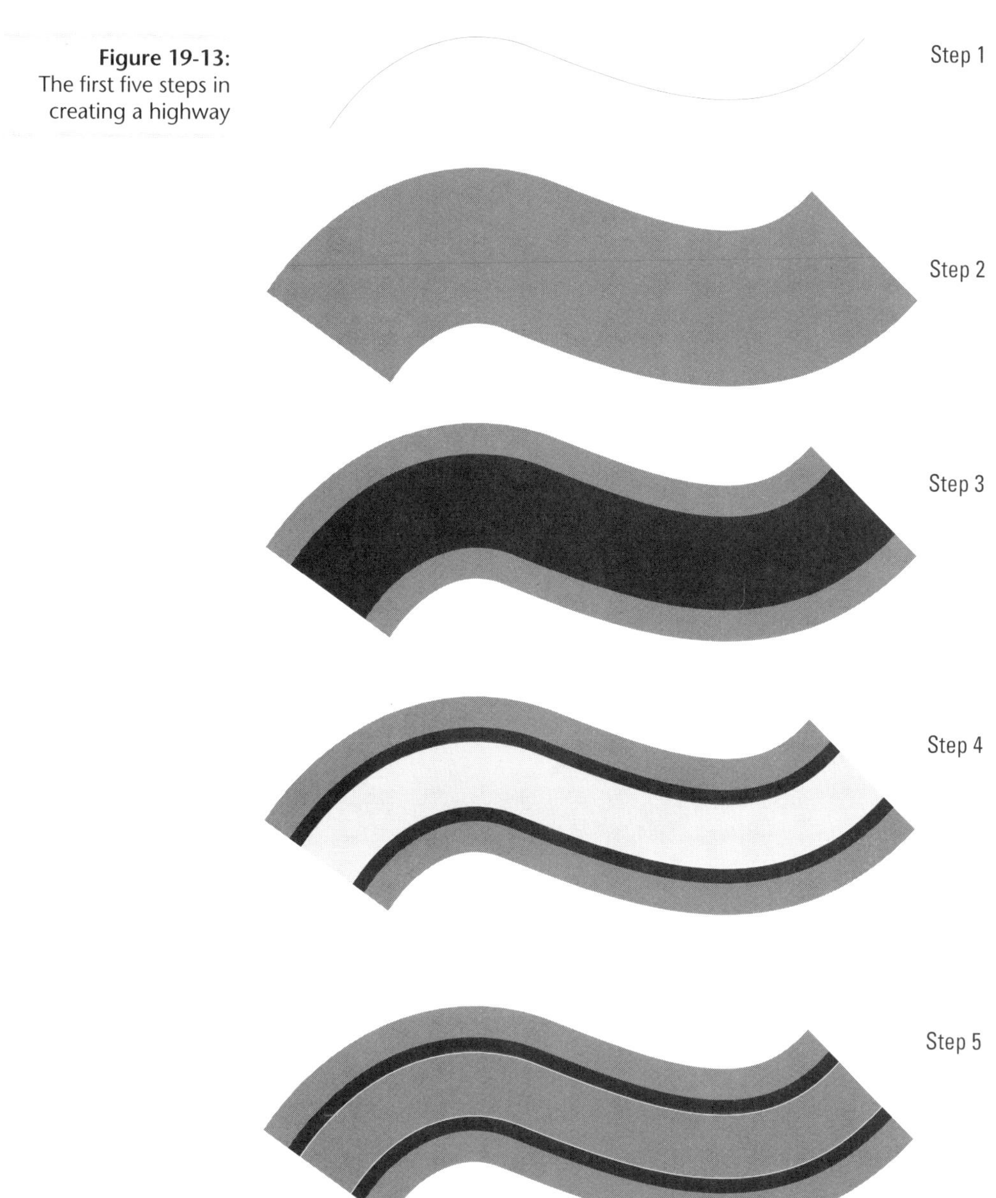

Figure 19-13: The first five steps in creating a highway

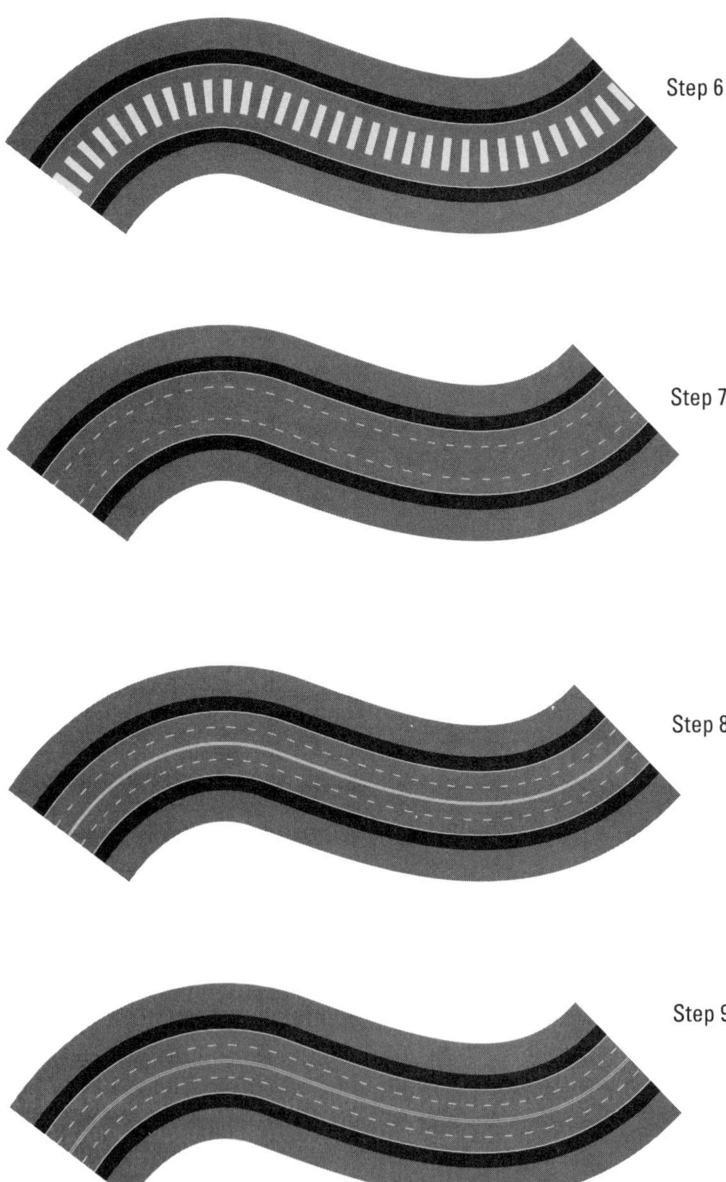

Figure 19-14: The last four steps in creating a highway

STEPS: Creating a Highway

Step 1. Use the Freehand tool to draw a slightly wavy path from the left side of the Artboard to the right side and then group the path.

Step 2. Change the Paint Style of the Stroke to a Fill of None and create a 400-point Stroke that is colored as follows: Cyan 100, Magenta 25, and Yellow 100. This path is the grass next to the highway.

Step 3. Copy the path and paste in front. Change the paint style of the stroke to Cyan 25, Yellow 25, and Black 85, with a weight of 240 points. This path is the shoulder of the highway.

Step 4. Paste in front and change the paint style to Cyan 5 and Black 10, with a weight of 165 points. This path is the white line at the edge of the highway.

Step 5. Paste in front and change the paint style to Cyan 15, Yellow 10, and Black 50, with a weight of 160 points. This path is the highway's road surface.

Step 6. To create the dashed white lines for passing, paste in front and change the paint style to Cyan 5 and Black 10, with a weight of 85 points, a dash of 20, and a Gap of 20.

Step 7. Paste in front and change the paint style to Cyan 15, Yellow 10, and Black 50, with a weight of 80 points. This path is the inner part of the highway's road surface.

Step 8. To create the double yellow line, paste in front and change the paint style to Cyan 15, Magenta 20, and Yellow 100, with a weight of 8 points.

Step 9. Paste in front and change the paint style to Cyan 15, Yellow 10, and Black 50, with a weight of 3 points. This path is the piece of highway that divides the double yellow line.

With the Outline filter, I've taken the highway concept a step or two further by adding a passing zone to the highway. Use the following steps and the illustration in Figure 19-15 to create the passing zone.

STEPS: Adding a Passing Zone to the Highway

Step 1. Delete the top two paths of the original highway. Select all of the paths and choose Arrange⇨Hide (⌘-3) to hide the base of the road temporarily. You don't need to change anything about these parts of the highway to create the passing zone effect.

Step 2. Paste in front and change the paint style to Cyan 15, Magenta 20, and Yellow 100, with a weight of 8 points. This path is the same double yellow line as the one in Step 8 of the preceding instructions, but it is not yet split.

Step 3. Copy and paste in front. Keep the paint style at Cyan 15, Magenta 20, and Yellow 100 but change the weight to 3 points. This line is the same width as the road from Step 9 in the preceding instructions, but the color is the double yellow-line color.

Step 4. Choose All (⌘-A). This command selects the last two paths that you placed on the illustration. Choose Filter⇨Object⇨Outline Stroke. This command create outlines around the edges of the Stroke so that it results in two Filled objects instead of two overlapping Stroked paths.

Step 5. Choose Filter⇨Pathfinder⇨Exclude. This command subtracts the top object (the 3-point path) from the bottom one, resulting in two Filled objects that are grouped together. Ungroup the two objects by choosing Edit⇨Ungroup (⌘-U).

Step 6. Deselect one of the two paths by Shift-clicking it once and deleting the selected object.

Step 7. Paste in front to put the line with the double yellow-line Stroke in front of the remaining Filled object. Change the paint style to Dash 20, Gap 20.

Step 8. Paste in front and change the paint style to Cyan 15, Yellow 10, and Black 50, with a weight of 3 points. These settings create a gray line that divides the dashed section from the solid section of line. The dashed section is actually on both sides of the 3-point gray divider line, but you cannot see the part that overlays the solid line because it is the same color and size as the solid line.

Step 9. Choose Arrange⇨Show All. The highway has a dashed/solid yellow line.

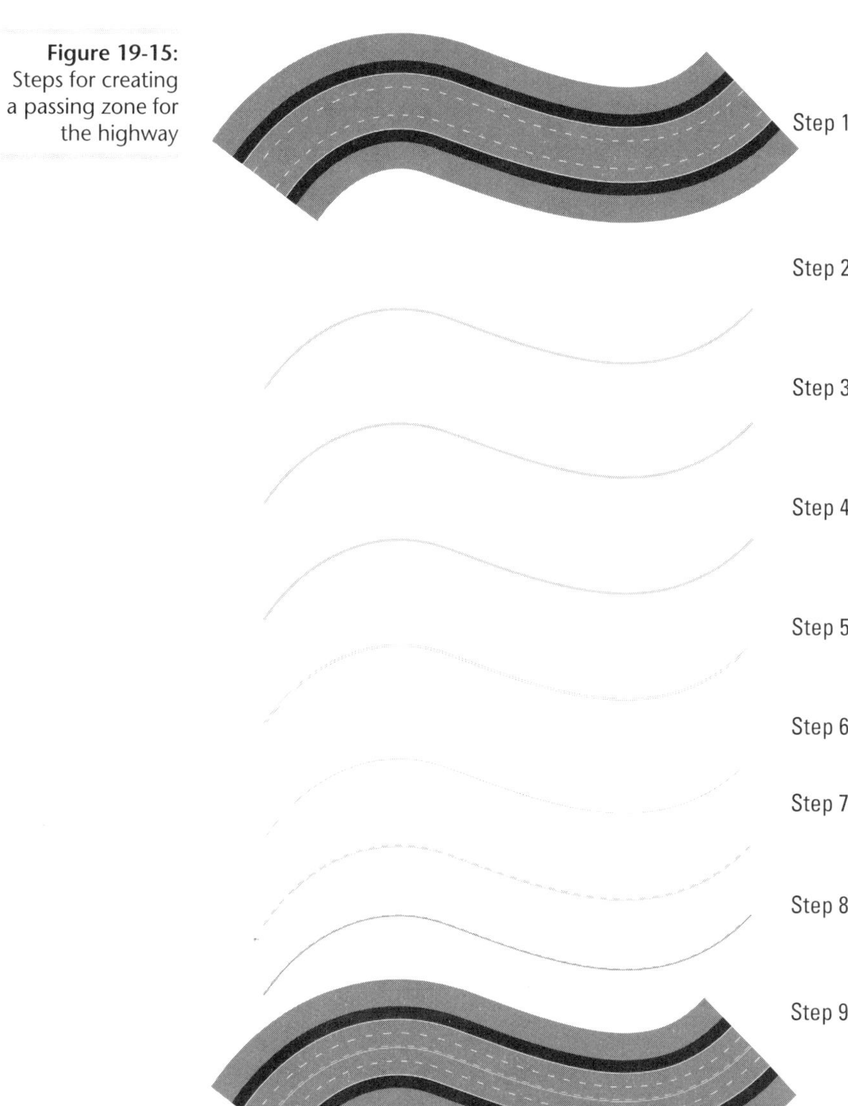

Figure 19-15: Steps for creating a passing zone for the highway

Putting Type into Strokes

You can put type into Strokes by creating Path type and giving the path a heavy enough Stroke weight to surround the type, as described in the following steps. Using symbols and special typefaces, you can create almost any pattern when you put type inside Strokes. (For more information on creating Path type, see Chapter 8.)

Stroked Type in Strokes?

Barbara: Can I put Stroked type on a Stroke?

Toulouse: Sure. In fact, if you do it right, you can put Stroked type on Stroked Type that's on a stroke.

Barbara: Really?

Toulouse: And so on...

STEPS:	Making Type into a Stroke Pattern
Step 1.	Draw a path upon which you want the type to appear.
Step 2.	Click the path with the Path Type tool. Type the letters, numbers, or symbols that will make up the pattern.
Step 3.	Select the characters, copy, and paste. Paste until the path is full of characters.
Step 4.	Using the Type tool, change the Fill on the characters; using the Group Selection tool, change the Stroke of the path.

If you are blessed with font-creation software, such as MacroMedia Fontographer, you can achieve even better results. Simply incorporate any artwork that you create in Illustrator into a font and then use that artwork as Path type by using that font when you type.

Incredibly Intricate Strokes

Unfortunately, what you can do with Strokes is limited to the Paint Style palette's options. Sometimes you'll wish you could do just a little bit more with strokes. That's where Path Patterns come in. Path Patterns is a new filter included with Illustrator 6.0 that allows you to place patterns on Strokes. These patterns increase in proportions as the Stroke changes shape. Path patterns are discussed fully in Chapter 14.

Summary

- The most attractive aspect of Strokes is that they can be used together, on top of one another.
- The Stroke charts provided in this chapter show some of the possibilities of what can be done with Strokes.
- When you Stroke type, be sure to put another copy of the Filled text on top of the Stroked type.
- Use the Outline Path filter to create Filled paths out of Strokes.
- Use Fills to create half-Stroked paths.

Printing, Separations, and Traps

20 CHAPTER

In This Chapter

- Understanding the difference between composites and separations
- Determining when to use process versus spot color separations
- Printing separations out of Illustrator
- Understanding line screens
- Printing separations from other programs
- Understanding trapping
- Using the Trap filter
- Trapping after you create an image in Illustrator

You can print Illustrator documents in two ways: as a composite, which is a single printout containing all the colors and tints used; as a series of color separations, a printout for each color. Color separations are necessary for illustrations that will be printed on a printing press.

Prior to Printing

Before you start the printing process, there are a number of things that might need to be changed or adjusted. For instance, you might need to change the page size and orientation, or set how certain colors will separate. This section deals with the issues you should be aware of *before* you go ahead and press ⌘-P and send your file to the printer.

Document Setup Dialog Box

Choosing File➪Document Setup (⌘-Shift-D) enables you to set the initial page size of an illustration via the Artboard. Bringing up the Document Setup dialog box (shown in Figure 20-1) displays a wealth of options that assist in printing. If the Use Page Setup box is checked, then the Artboard size is relative to the size of the page that is selected in the Page Setup dialog box. If the Artboard is smaller than the printable page, then anything entirely outside the edges of the Artboard will be cropped off when you print the illustration through Illustrator. Any objects that are partially on the Artboard will print. Anything outside the Artboard will print when you print the illustration through another application.

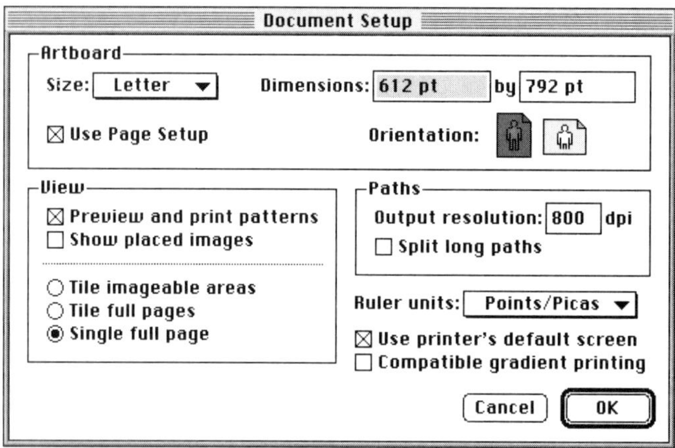

Figure 20-1: The Document Setup dialog box

Another option in the Document Setup dialog box enables you to choose whether patterns will preview and print. Unchecking this box prevents patterns from printing when you print the illustration from Illustrator.

The Page Tiling options also affect the way that pages appear when a document is printed from Illustrator:

- If you choose Tile imagable areas, a grid appears on the Artboard. Any block of the grid that has a piece of the illustration will print. When this option is chosen, you can specify in the Print dialog box that only certain pages should be printed.
- If you choose Tile full pages, only full pages (as defined in the Page Setup dialog box) that appear on the Artboard will print. If no full pages can fit in the Artboard, everything in the Artboard will print.
- If you choose Single full page, only one page will print.

Page Setup

The Page Setup dialog box (choose File➪Page Setup), shown in Figure 20-2, is used for specifying printing options when printing out a composite image.

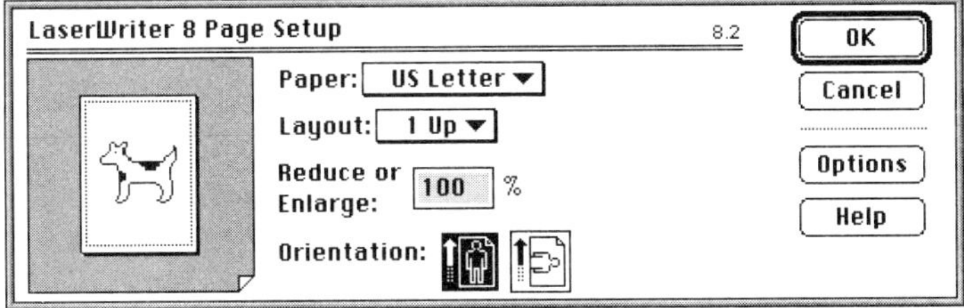

Figure 20-2: The Page Setup dialog box

The printing options on this dialog box are:

- **Paper:** You can choose any paper size, even one that your printer does not have the capacity to use. The Tabloid option is the first option in a set of choices in a pop-up menu that also lists envelope sizes and positions. The size that you choose shows up on the document as a dotted line boundary when the Tile full pages or Single full pages options are selected in the Document Setup dialog box. Another dotted-line boundary, inside the page size boundary, is the printable area. The printable area is also displayed when the Tile imagable areas option is selected in the Document Setup dialog box.
- **Layout:** The Layout pop-up menu displays options of how many pages from the document can fit on the printed page. If you choose any option other than 1-Up (other options are only available with LaserWriter 8 and higher), the printed pages are scaled and reoriented so that the pages are printed at the largest possible size.
- **Reduce or Enlarge:** This option affects how much the page that the illustration is on is scaled when it's printed. Reducing or enlarging affects the way that the dotted-line page boundaries and imagable areas dotted lines appear in the document. A value above 100% will make the page smaller, while a value less than 100% will make the page and its boundaries larger. This feature is helpful when you want to print everything that's on a large Artboard. If you select a reduced size in the Page Setup dialog box, the dotted lines in the document reflect the reduced size.
- **Orientation.** This option controls how the image is printed on the printed page — whether it is printed in portrait orientation (longest side vertical) or landscape orientation (longest side horizontal).

If you click the Options button, the Page Setup Options dialog box appears, as shown in Figure 20-3.

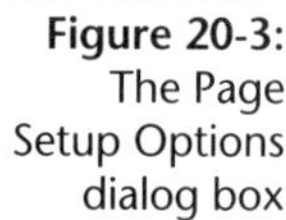

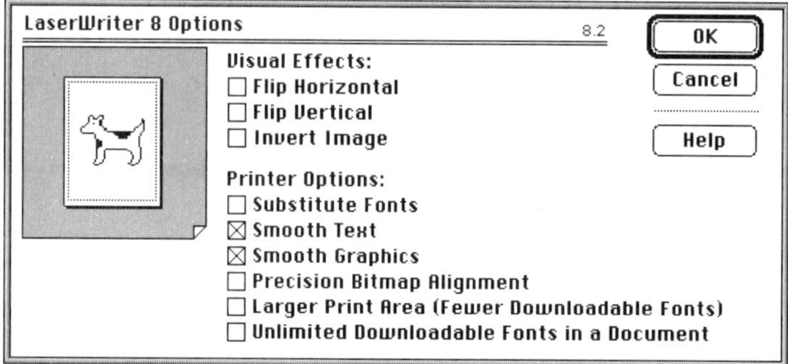

Figure 20-3: The Page Setup Options dialog box

The options on the dialog box are:

- **Flip Horizontal:** This option causes the document to print as a mirror image of itself, flipped horizontally. You can use it in combination with the Invert Image option to print negatives from Illustrator.
- **Flip Vertical:** This option causes the document to print as a mirror image of itself, flipped vertically. You can also use this option in combination with the Invert Image option to print negatives from Illustrator. Using the Flip Horizontal and Flip Vertical options together causes the document to rotate 180°.
- **Invert Image:** This option prints a negative image of the illustration, where all white areas are black and all black areas are white.
- **Substitute Fonts:** Illustrator has built-in workarounds for font problems, and supposedly this checkbox may be irrelevant to Illustrator users. For other programs, this option replaces any bitmapped fonts with corresponding fonts that are installed on the printer, which usually means that if you have Geneva, New York, and Monaco installed in bitmapped format only, Helvetica, Times, and Courier will take their places. Any other bitmapped font will usually be replaced with Courier. In general, if you don't have the PostScript printer font or the font in TrueType format, you shouldn't use that font with Adobe Illustrator, and you shouldn't check this box.
- **Smooth Text:** When Substitute Fonts is not checked and an illustration has a bitmapped font in it, Smooth Text will make the bitmapped font look slightly better. It will still look bad, but it will look better than just the plain bitmapped font.
- **Smooth Graphics:** Smooth Graphics does about the same thing that Smooth Text does, but it does it to graphics. Because this feature works only with PICT and Paint images, which you cannot print in Illustrator, you should not check this option.
- **Precision Bitmap Alignment**: This option resamples bitmapped graphics so that they print better at the resolution of your printer.

- **Larger Print Area (Fewer Downloadable Fonts):** This option increases the print area of the document so that it prints closer to the edge of the page. On a standard 8.5" x 11" Apple LaserWriter, not having this box checked results in margins that are approximately 1/2" on each edge. Checking this box changes the margins to 1/4" on the 11" edges and about 1/8" on the 8.5" edges. Of course, this extra printing area takes up a significant amount of printer RAM, so you may have trouble printing complex documents when this option is checked.
- **Unlimited Downloadable Fonts in a Document:** Checking this box interferes with Illustrators own downloading mechanism. You shouldn't check it when printing from Illustrator. When printing from other programs, this option does more than enable you to use lots of fonts. Checking Unlimited Downloadable Fonts in programs *other* than Illustrator makes the RAM in the laser printer adjustable. As part of the document comes in and is processed, the information that was used to process that part of the document and the fonts that were needed to print it are flushed out of memory. The next section and its needed fonts are then loaded. This method takes longer than loading all of the fonts in the entire document at one time and then processing the document, but it prevents out-of-memory printing errors when printing from programs like QuarkXPress.

Printing Composites

A composite printout looks very much like the image that appears on the screen when you preview the document (choose View⇨Preview or press ⌘-Y). If you have a color printer, the image appears in color; otherwise, the colors are replaced by gray tints (see the next section, "Gray Colors").

Color to Black and White?

Charles: Is there an easy way to make my color documents black and white *before* I print them?

Toulouse: Yes, but it's not part of Illustrator.

Charles: It's something I do all the time.

Toulouse: Sure. Removing the color (cyan, magenta, or yellow) doesn't even come close to working.

Charles: So what can I do?

Toulouse: The easiest thing is to buy CSI Socket Set 1, which includes a Process to Gray filter.

Charles: How does it work?

Toulouse: You select the art you want the color sucked out of, then choose the filter, and Boom!, it's done.

Charles: Wow.

Toulouse: If you need more control, KPT ColorTweak, which is part of KPT Vector Effects, lets you specify the amount of gray.

Objects that are hidden or that exist on layers that are currently hidden will not print, and neither will objects that exist on layers that have the printing option unchecked in the Layers Option dialog box.

The final printing step is to choose File⇨Print (⌘-P). This action opens the Print dialog box (shown in Figure 20-4), in which you may choose which pages to print, how many of each to print, and a few other options. If you click the Cancel button (⌘-period), the dialog box disappears, and no pages are printed. To Print, click the Print button or press Return or Enter.

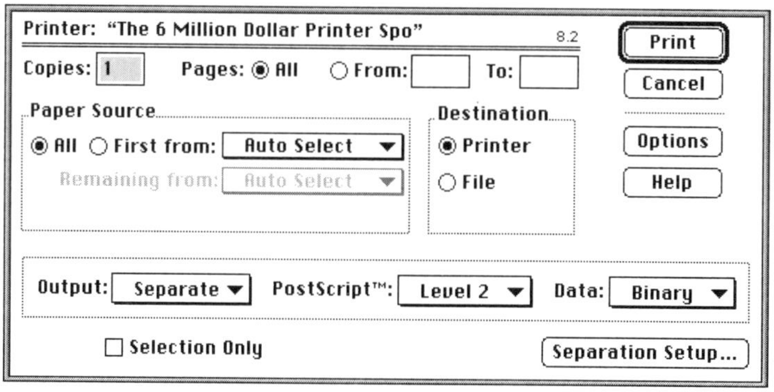

Figure 20-4: The Print dialog box

The Print dialog box contains the following options:

- **Copies:** The number that you enter here determines how many copies of each page will print. All copies of a single page are printed at one time, so if you enter **4** when you are printing a four-page document, you get four copies of page one, then four copies of page two, and so on.
- **Pages:** If you check the All button, all the pages that have art on them will print. If you enter numbers in the From and To fields, only the pages that those numbers refer to will print.
- **Paper Source:** If Paper cassette (the default) is selected, all pages will print on paper from the printer's cassette. If Manual Feed is selected, then the pages will print on paper from the manual feed tray.
- **Destination:** Choosing Printer prints the document to the laser printer as usual. Choosing File prints the document to a PostScript file on the hard disk that you can download to a laser printer at a future time by using a utility such as Font Downloader or LaserWriter Font Utility. A PostScript file can also be used with Acrobat Distiller or Adobe ScreenReady.

- **Output:** This option determines if the illustration is printed as a composite or divided up into individual color separations.
- **PostScript™:** This pop-up menu allows you to specify the PostScript interpreter (Level 1 or Level 2) that is included in your Laser Printer.

Selecting Level 1 may eliminate various PostScript errors when printing to an older printer.

- **Data:** Keep this option on Binary, unless you have a really really old printer that only understands PostScript data in ASCII format.
- **Selection Only:** This handy little option allows for printing just the selected objects instead of the entire document.
- **Separation Setup:** This button opens the Separation Setup dialog box, discussed in detail later in this chapter.

If you click the Options button the Print Options dialog box appears, as shown in Figure 20-5.

Figure 20-5: The Print Options dialog box

Print Options 8.2
Cover Page: (•) None ( ) Before ( ) After Document
Print: Black and White
PostScript™ Errors: Print Detailed Report
Choose Resolution: 600dpi
FinePrint(TM): Printer's default
PhotoGrade(TM): Printer's default
OK
Cancel
Help
Save

The options in this dialog box are:

- **Cover Page:** If you choose First Page or Last Page, a separate sheet, which contains information about the name of the computer, the name of the file, the number of pages, and the dates, will print. This feature is useful for making each print job easily identifiable when several people share a laser printer.
- **Print:** This option has no effect when printing from Illustrator. From other programs, this option determines the way that documents will print to color or grayscale printers. If Black and White is chosen, no gray or color pixels will print, just patterns of black-and-white pixels. Illustrator writes its own PostScript and overrides this option, regardless of what is checked.

- **PostScript™ Errors:** This option allows for a detailed report to be printed when a PostScript error of some sort occurs.

Always select Print Detailed Report. When an illustration will not print, a sheet of paper will come out of the printer with the error message on it.

- **Other Options:** The options in the lower section are specific to your printer. For instance, the printer information shown in the dialog box in Figure 20-5 is for an Apple LaserWriter Pro 630. Some of the other possible options are the resolution (300 or 600), and whether FinePrint and Photograde are turned on.

Always do a save before you print. Severe problems, when they happen, usually occur when you are printing. Don't let your unsaved document fall victim to one of those severe problems.

Gray Colors

When you are printing a full color illustration to a black-and-white printer, Illustrator substitutes gray values for colors. In this way, the program creates the illusion that each color has a separate, distinct gray value.

Of course, each color can't have its own unique gray value, so the colors have to overlap at some point. Illustrator converts each of the process colors into specific gray values when it prints to a black-and-white printer.

Magenta is the darkest process color, ranging from 0% to 73% gray. Therefore, at 100% magenta, it prints at 73% gray. Cyan is second darkest, ranging from 0% to 57% gray. Yellow is extremely light, ranging from 0% to only 11% gray. Figure 20-6 shows a comparison of the four process colors at various settings and their printed results. The four bars show different values for each process color, as indicated above the bars. Within each bar is the percent of black that prints when you are printing that color at that percentage to a black-and-white printer.

Different printers may produce different tints of gray. Lower-resolution printers, such as 300-dpi (dots per inch) laser printers, do not create an accurate gray tint because they use dots that are too large to create accurate tint patterns.

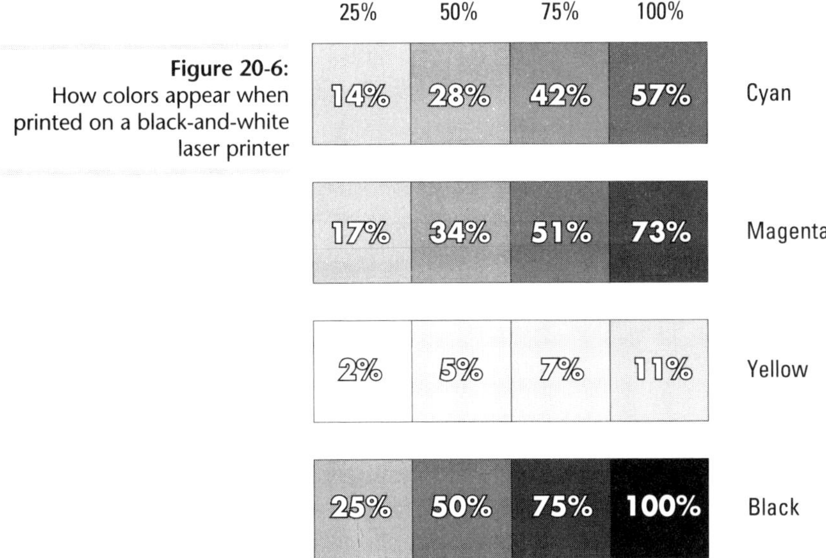

Figure 20-6: How colors appear when printed on a black-and-white laser printer

Printing Color Separations

Color separations are necessary for printing a color version of an illustration on most printing presses. Each separation creates a plate that is affixed to a round drum on a printing press. Ink that is the same color as that separation is applied to the plate, which is pressed against a sheet of paper. Because the ink adheres only to the "printing" areas of the plate, an image is produced on paper. Some printing presses have many different drums and can print a four-color job in one run. Other printing presses have only one or two drums, so the paper has to pass through the press four or two times, respectively, to print a four-color job.

The two types of color separation are process color separation and spot color separation. Each type has its own advantages and drawbacks, and you can use either type or a combination of both types for any print job.

You should always determine which type of separation you want *before* you begin to create a job electronically.

Spot Color Separation

Jobs that are printed with spot colors are often referred to as "two-color" or "three-color" jobs when two or three colors are used. Although you can use any number of colors, most spot color jobs contain only a few colors.

Learning Printing from the Experts

If you have never visited a printing company, make a point to visit one and take a tour. Most printing companies have staff members who are more than willing to explain their equipment and various printing processes. In a 30-minute tour with a knowledgeable guide, you can learn enough to save yourself hours of work, money, and misunderstandings.

When you are talking to a representative at the printing company, find out what type of media they want your work on. Printing companies commonly have imagesetters that can output the job for you, and some companies even perform this service at no charge or for a significant discount if you have the job printed there.

Imagesetters are similar to laser printers, except that they produce images with a very high dpi, from 1273 to 3600, and sometimes higher. Imagesetters can print directly to RC (resin-coated) paper or to film negatives (or positives). The paper or film runs through the imagesetter and then must run through a developing process for the images and text to appear.

Most printing company salespeople are fluent to a minor degree in desktop publishing-speak, though few will know the difference between a TIFF and an EPS. They can tell you when to give them negs (film negatives) and paper and which service bureau to use if they don't have an imagesetter in-house. Many of them can tell you which software their clients prefer and which software packages create problems, and they can give you tips that can help you get your project through smoothly.

A service bureau is a company or part of a company that has on its premises an imagesetter, and whose function is to provide the general community of desktop publishers with imagesetter output for a cost between $7 and $40 per page. Service bureaus often have color output capabilities, offer disk-conversion services, and other services that are sometimes needed by desktop publishers.

Better yet, do what I did: work at a printing company for a short period of time. The first job I had out of college, working in the prepress department of a four-color commercial printer, taught me more than I learned in four years of school. The experience instilled in me some of the most important basic skills for graphics design that I still use and need every day. Ever wonder why your printer gets so grumpy when you tell him that your negs won't be available to him until two days after you told him? Working inside a printing company can give you an understanding of job scheduling, an art of prophecy and voodoo that gives ulcers to printing company managers and supervisors.

The more you know about printing and your printer, the better your print job will turn out, and the fewer hassles you will have to deal with.

Spot color printing is most useful when you are using two or three distinct colors in a job. For example, if I needed only black and green to create a certain illustration, I would use only black and a green custom color for all of the objects in the illustration.

There are three main reasons for using Spot Color separation, rather than Process Color separation:

- It's cheaper. Spot Color printing requires a smaller press with fewer drums. For Process Color separation, you usually need to use a press with four drums or run the job through a smaller press a number of times.
- Spot Colors are cleaner, brighter, and smoother than the same colors that you create as Process Colors. To get a Green Process Color, for example, you need to mix both Cyan and Yellow on paper. Using one Spot Color will result in a perfectly solid area of color.
- You cannot duplicate certain Spot Colors, especially fluorescent and metallic colors, with Process Colors.

Illustrator creates Spot Colors whenever you specify a Custom Color. If you use six different Custom Colors and Black, you could print out seven different Spot Color separations.

Spot Colors also have their limitations and disadvantages, however. The primary limitation of using only Spot Colors is that the number of colors is restricted to the number of color separations that you want to produce. Remember that the cost of a print job is directly related to the number of different colored inks in the job.

The cutoff point for using Spot Colors is usually three colors. When you use four Spot Colors, you limit yourself to four distinct colors and use as many colors as a Process Color job that can have an almost infinite number of colors. Spot Color jobs of six colors are not unusual, however. Sometimes people use more than three Spot Colors to keep colors distinct and clear. Each of the six colors will be bright, vibrant, and distinct from its neighbors, whereas different Process Colors seem to fade into one another.

Spot Colors are often incorrectly referred to as Pantone colors. Pantone is a brand name for a color matching system. You can select Pantone colors as Custom Colors and use them in Illustrator, and you can print them as either Spot Colors or as Process Colors.

Process Color Separation

Process color separation, also known as four-color separation, creates almost any color by combining Cyan, Magenta, Yellow, and Black inks. By using various combinations of different tints of each of these colors, you can reproduce many of the colors (more than 16 million of them) that the human eye can see.

Process printing uses a subtractive process. You start with bright white paper, and darken the paper with various inks. Cyan, Magenta, and Yellow are the subtractive primaries, and Black is added to create true black printing, which the primaries together don't do very well.

The use of Process Color separation is advisable when:

- The illustration includes color photographs.
- The illustration contains more than three different colors.

By now, you have probably used the Process Color portion of the Paint Style palette (shown in Figure 20-7) to create illustrations within Illustrator. This option enables you to pick from any percentage of any of the colors to create all the different colors you need.

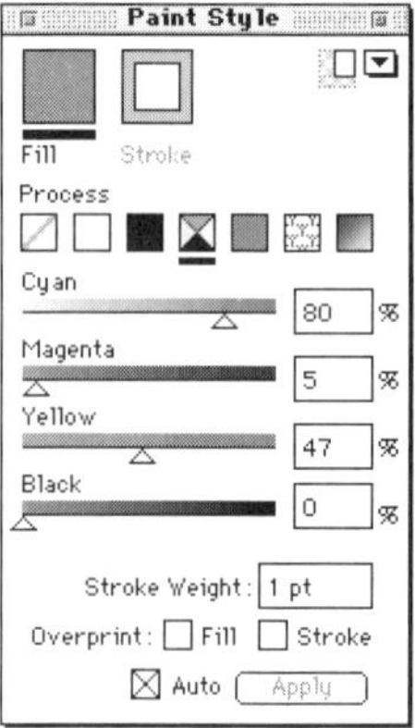

Figure 20-7: The Process Color portion of the Paint Style palette

How Many Colors?

Everyone always says that you can create as many colors as you could ever want when you are using Process Colors. Maybe.

In Illustrator, you can specify colors up to $^1/_{100}$ percent accuracy. As a result, 10,000 different shades are available for each of the four process colors. So, theoretically, $10{,}000^4$, or 10,000,000,000,000,000, different colors should be available, which is 10 quadrillion, or ten million billion. Any way you look at it, you have a heck of a lot of color possibilities.

Unfortunately, most imagesetters and laser printers can produce only 256 different shades for each color. This limitation of the equiment (not PostScript) drops the number of available colors to 256^4, or 4,294,967,296, which is about 4.3 billion colors — only 1 billionth of the colors that Illustrator can create.

This limitation is fortunate for us humans, however, because the estimate is that we can detect a maximum of 100 different levels of gray, probably less. As a result, we can view only 100^4, or 100,000,000, different colors.

We can run into a problem when we preview illustrations, however. An RGB monitor (used on computers) can display up to 16.7 million colors, theoretically, if each Red, Green, and Blue pixel can be varied by 256 different intensities. Most low-end Macintoshes can create only 32,768 colors with their on-board video, and some are limited to 256 colors (or, gasp, grayscale). You need to add special video cards or additional VRAM (Video RAM) to those Macintosh computers to display the 16.7 million colors that monitors can produce.

Another problem is that about 30 percent of the colors that you can view on an RGB monitor can't be reproduced by using Cyan, Magenta, Yellow, and Black inks on White paper. You can't create these unprintable colors in Illustrator, but you can create them in most other drawing and graphics software packages. These colors are for on-screen viewing pleasure only.

The secret to Process Color separation is that the four colors that make up all the different colors are themselves not visible. Each color is printed as a pattern of tiny dots, angled differently from the other three colors. The angles of each color are very important. If the angles are off even slightly, a noticeable pattern that is commonly known as a *moiré* will emerge.

The colors are printed in a specific order—usually Cyan, Magenta, Yellow, and Black. Although the debate continues about the best order in which to print the four colors, Black is always printed last.

To see the dots for each color, use a magnifying device to look closely at something that is preprinted and in full color. Even easier, look at the Sunday comics, which have bigger dots than most other printed pieces. The different colored dots in the Sunday comics are quite visible, and their only colors are Magenta, Cyan, Yellow, and Black.

The size of the dots that produce each of these separations is also important. The smaller the dots, the smoother the colors appear. Large dots (such as those in the Sunday comics) can actually take away from the illusion of a certain unified color because the the differently colored dots are visible.

For more information on the commons dot sizes and on the relation of dot size to the quality of the illustration, see the section, "Setting the Halftone Screen," later in this Chapter.

Figure 20-8 shows how process colors are combined to create new colors. In the figure, the first four rows show very large dots. The top three rows are Cyan, Magenta, and Yellow. The fourth row is all four Process Colors combined, and the bottom row shows how the illustration looks when you print it.

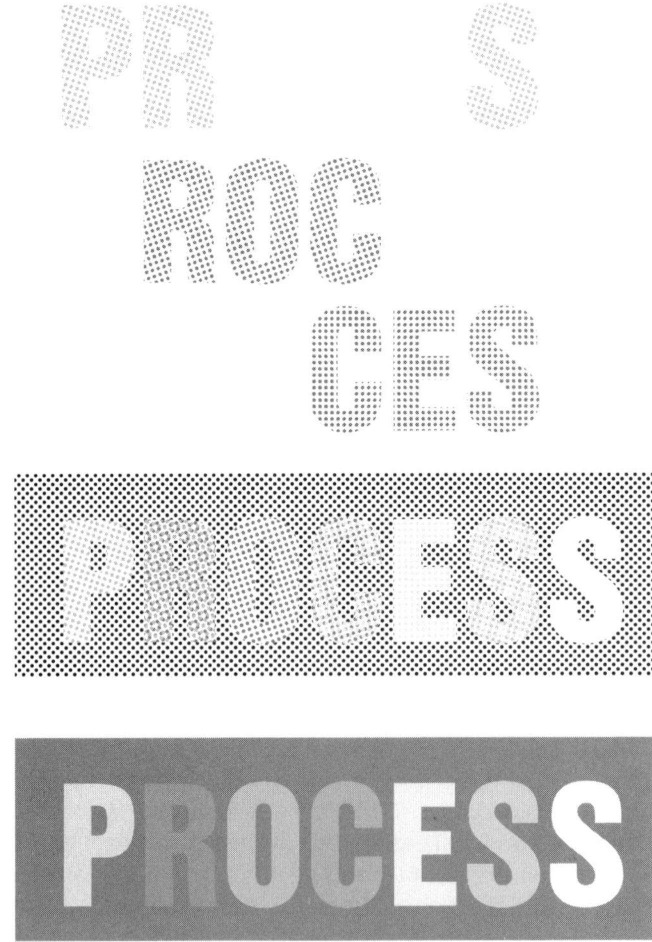

Figure 20-8: The top three rows display Cyan, Magenta and Yellow; the fourth row displays their combination, and the fifth row displays them as they will print.

Process Color printing is best for photographs because photographs originate from a *continuous tone* that is made on photographic paper from film, instead of dots on a printing press.

In Illustrator, you can convert Custom Colors to Process Colors either before or during printing. To convert Custom Colors to Process Colors *before* printing, select any objects that have a specific Custom Color and tint and click the Process Color icon. The color will be converted to its Process Color counterpart, and all selected objects will be filled with the new Process Color combination.

After you click the Process Color icon, if the selected objects become filled with White and the triangles for each Process Color are at 0%, you have selected objects that contain different colors or tints. Undo the change immediately.

To make sure that you select only objects that have the same color, select one of the objects and choose Filter⇨Select⇨Same Paint Style. Objects that have different strokes or objects with different tints of the same color will not be selected.

You can convert Custom Colors to Process Colors in the Adobe Separator Separation dialog box (see the "Working with Different Color Separations" section, later in this chapter) and in many page layout programs.

Combining Both Spot and Process Color Separations

You can couple Spot Colors with Process Colors in Illustrator simply by creating both Process and Custom Colors in a document.

Usually, you add Spot Colors to Process Colors for the following reasons:

- You are using a company logo that has a specific color. By printing that color as a Spot Color, you make it stand out from the other coloring. In addition, color is more accurate when it comes from a specific ink rather than from a Process Color combination. Often, the logo is a Pantone color that doesn't reproduce true to form when you use Process Color separation.
- You need a color that you can't create by using Process Colors. Such colors are most often metallic or fluorescent, but they can be any number of Pantone colors or other colors that you can't match with Process Colors.
- You need a varnish for certain areas of an illustration. A varnish is a glazed type of ink that results in a shiny area wherever you use the varnish. You commonly use varnishes on titles and logos and over photographs.
- You need a light color over a large area. The dots that make up Process Colors are most noticeable in light colors, but by using a Spot Color to cover the area with a solid sheet of ink that has no dots, you can make the area smoother and enhance it visually.

In some circumstances, you need to use a Spot Color as a Spot Color and also use it as a Process Color. Normally, you can't do both, but the following steps describe one way to get around this problem:

STEPS: Using a Custom Color as Both a Spot Color and a Process Color

Step 1. Select Object⇨Custom Color. In the Custom Color dialog box, choose the Custom Color and change the name of the color by adding the word *spot* after it.

Step 2. Memorize or write down the Process Color combination of the Custom Color.

Step 3. Click the New button and change the Process Color values to match the existing values. Name the color the same as the original, but instead of the word *spot,* add the word *process.*

Step 4. Change all objects that have that Custom Color and should print as Process colors into the Custom Color with the word *process* after it.

Step 5. When printing separations, select the "spot" Custom Color to print as a Spot Color and the "process" Custom Color to print as a Process Color.

The End of Adobe Separator

One of the biggest disappointments I've ever experienced was seeing Adobe Separator in the Adobe Illustrator 5.0 and 5.5 folders on my hard drive after I installed those versions. You can imagine my joy when I heard whispers, rumors, and finally read the press release for Illustrator 6, where it states something grandiose like "You can even print your separations directly out of Illustrator 6!" I'll tell you, I'd like to meet the guy who writes those things and give him a piece of my mind...

If you've installed Illustrator 6, and you still have Separator, you can drag it to your trash can, choose Empty Trash from the Special menu, and then dance and leap for joy. That chapter in the history of Adobe Illustrator, fortunately, is finally closed.

Printing out separations is easier and more intuitive with Illustrator 6's Separation Setup dialog box than it was with Separator, though you'll notice some obvious similarities.

Setup

After you choose File⇨Separation Setup, the Separation Setup dialog box appears. The left side shows how the illustration is aligned on the page and which elements will print with the illustration. The right side contains all the options for how the illustration is to print on the page.

The picture on the left side initially shows the illustration on a portrait-oriented page, even if landscape was selected in Illustrator. The various marks shown on the page in Figure 21-2 are the defaults. You can move or rearrange them simply by clicking and dragging them.

The Bounding Box and Bleed

The illustration is surrounded by a bounding box, and only the parts of the illustration that are within this bounding box will print. Anything outside of the bounding box will be cropped off. When you first open the Separation Setup dialog box, the bounding box is the size of the illustration. The bounding box is as wide and as tall as necessary to include all the printable objects in the illustration.

When you resize the bounding box manually (by clicking on the edges or corners and dragging), the numbers in the Bounding Box text fields (at the very bottom of the dialog box) change because the four text fields correspond to the location of each of the edges of the bounding box. You also can resize the bounding box by typing new values in the Bounding Box text fields. The bounding box will instantly reflect changes that you make in these text fields.

You can move the illustration within the bounding box by placing the cursor within the bounding box and clicking and dragging. As

Can I Use Separator for Anything?

Mary: Can I use Separator (the one that came with Illustrator 5) for anything?

Toulouse: Sure, you can still print Illustrator 5.x and older EPS documents.

Mary: Is there any reason, ever so little, to keep Separator?

Toulouse: The Transfer Function feature of Separator is nice, but it appears that no one at Adobe thought it was worth keeping.

Mary: There's no Transfer function in Separation Setup?

Toulouse: No, oddly enough.

Using Separation

you move the illustration out of the bounding box, the illustration will be cropped off at its edges.

The Bleed text field in the lower right of the Separation Setup dialog box defines how much of the illustration can be outside of the bounding box and still print. The default for bleed is 18 points, regardless of the size of the bounding box. To change the bleed, enter a distance in points in the Bleed text field. As you type the numbers, the bleed will change dynamically.

Bleed is useful when you want an illustration to go right up to the edge of the page. You need to account for bleed when you create an illustration in Illustrator so that the illustration is the correct size with *X* amount of bleed.

Changing Printer Information

To change the PPD, click the Open PPD button in the upper right of the dialog box. The Open a PostScript Printer Description (PPD) file window appears, as shown in Figure 20-9.

Select the PPD file that is compatible with your printer and click the Open button. The PPD folder is placed in the Utilities folder by the Adobe Illustrator Installer automatically.

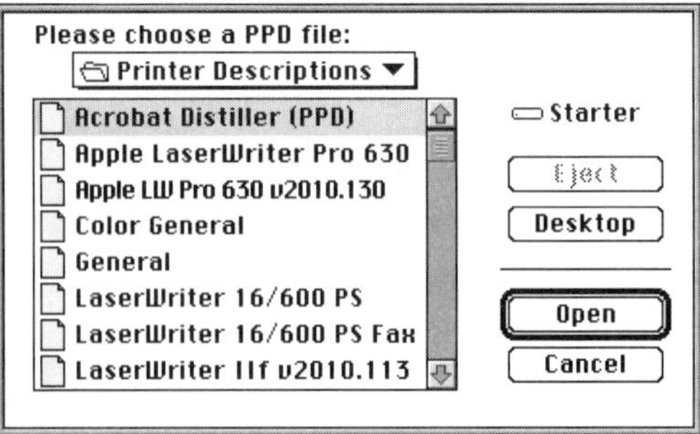

Figure 20-9: The Open a PostScript Printer Description file window

PPDs were created with specific printers in mind. Unpredictable and undesirable results can occur when you use a PPD for a different printer than it is intended for. If you don't have a PPD for your printer and must use a substitute, always test the substitute PPD before relying on it to perform correctly.

…ur printer's PPD is not included with Illustrator, contact the dealer from whom you purchased the printer and ask for it. If you bought the printer by mail order or from a retail store, the dealer will probably not have a PPD for you and may not even know what a PPD is, for that matter. In this case, contact the printer manufacturer directly. Another place to find PPDs from manufacturers is on online services such as America Online. Adobe does *not* have PPDs for printers other than the ones supplied with the software.

If you have two or more printers in your workplace, chances are that you will be changing the PPD file in the Separation Setup dialog box from time to time. To make this task easier, open the PPD folder on the hard drive, select all the PPD files that you don't use, and drag them to the trash. Having a shorter list to choose from makes finding the right PPD much easier and frees up space on the hard drive. If you get a new printer at a later date and need a different PPD, you can get it from the Illustrator floppy disk or CD-ROM.

When you choose a different PPD file, the information in the main panel changes to reflect the new selection. Certain default settings in the pop-up menus will be activated at this time. You can change the settings at any time, but most of them will revert to the defaults if you choose a new PPD.

Changing Page Size

The Page Size pop-up menu lists the available page sizes for the printer whose PPD is selected, *not* the printer selected in the Chooser. For laser printers, few page and envelope sizes are supported. For imagesetters, many sizes are supported, and an Other option enables you to specify the size of the page that you want to print on.

When you choose Other in the Page Size pop-up menu, you see the Other dialog box. The default measurements in the box are the smallest size area that the current illustration can fit within. Enter the width and height of the desired page in their respective boxes. You can use the Offset option to move the illustration a certain distance from the right edge of the page, and you can save media by using the Transverse option to turn the image sideways on the paper or film that it is printing on.

Imagesetters print on rolls of paper or film. Depending on the width of the roll, you may want to print the image sideways. For example, on a Linotronic 200 or 230 imagesetter, paper and film rolls are commonly 12 inches wide. For letter-size pages, you should check the Transverse option to print the letter-size page with the short end along the length of the roll. For a tabloid page (11 x 17 inches), do not check the Transverse option because you want the long edge (17 inches) of the page to be printed along the length of the roll. If you check Transverse for a tabloid-size document, 5 of the 17 inches will be cropped off because the roll is not wide enough. As always when trying something new with printing, run a test or two before sending a large job.

Wrong Printer

Laura: I used to be able to see what printer I was printing to in Separator, and be able to go directly to the Chooser from there.

Toulouse: You got your sight back?

Laura: Actually, I'm asking you this from season two.

Toulouse: Okay. You *can* see what printer is selected in the Chooser with Separation Setup.

Laura: So I could feasibly have the wrong printer selected when I go to the Separation Setup dialog box, have to close the dialog box, go to the Chooser, and change the printer then?

Toulouse: Not just feasibly. I do it all the time.

Laura: Is there a workaround?

Toulouse: Well, it is faster to check in the Print dialog box than the Separation dialog box (since the Separation preview takes a few seconds to show up), but you can't change the printer in the Print dialog box either.

The page size that you select in the Page Size pop-up menu determines the size of the page on the left side of the main panel. The measurements next to the name of the page size are not the page measurements; instead, they are the measurements of the imageable area for that page size. The imageable-area dimensions are always less than the dimensions of the page so that the margin marks can fit on the page with the illustration.

Changing the Orientation

The Orientation setting controls how the illustration is placed on the page. You have two choices from the pop-up menu: Portrait and Landscape.

Selecting Portrait causes the illustration to print with the sides of the illustration along the longest sides of the page. Selecting Landscape causes the illustration to print with the top and bottom of the illustration along the longest sides of the page.

Usually, the orientation reflects the general shape of the illustration. If the illustration is taller than it is wide, you usually choose Portrait orientation. If the illustration is wider than it is tall, you usually choose Landscape orientation.

It doesn't matter to Illustrator whether the illustration fits on the page in one or both of these orientations. If you can't see all four edges of the bounding box, chances are the illustration will be cropped.

Orientation is quite different from Transverse in the Other Page Size dialog box. Orientation changes the orientation of the illustration on the page, but Transverse changes the way that the page is put onto the paper. A seemingly small difference, but a distinct and important one to understand.

Figure 20-10 shows an illustration that is placed onto a page in both Portrait and Landscape orientations, with and without the Transverse option selected.

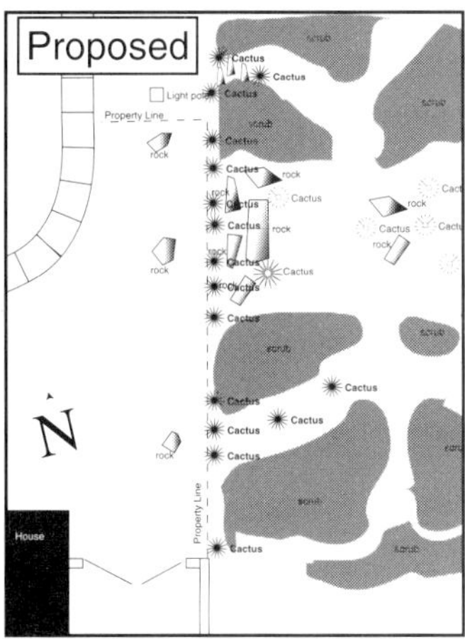

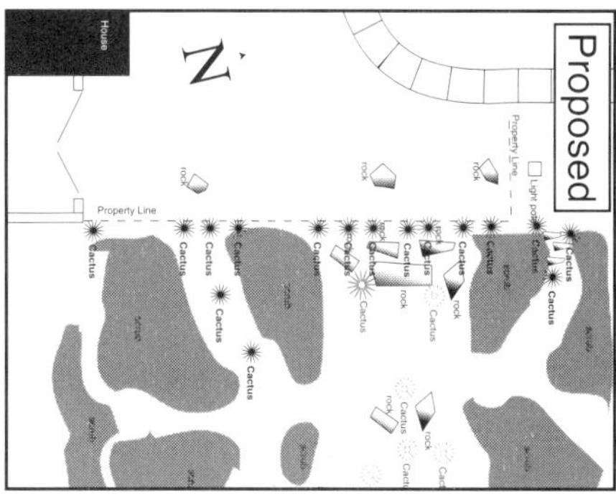

Figure 20-10: An illustration placed onto a page in Portrait orientation (upper left), Landscape orientation (lower left), Portrait with Transverse checked (upper right), and Landscape with Transverse checked (lower right)

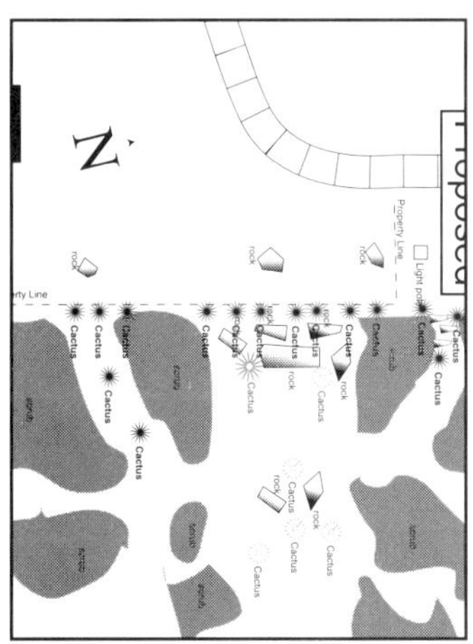

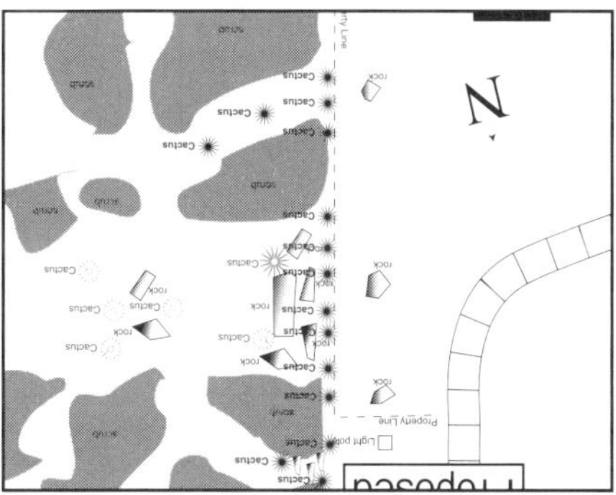

Understanding Emulsion

Hang out around strippers (at a commercial printing company . . . get your mind out of the gutter), and you will hear them constantly talking about "emulsion up" and "emulsion down." What they are referring to is the black "stuff" on film. If you have a piece of film from a printer lying around, look at it near a light. One of its two sides is shinier than the other. That side is the side without emulsion. When you are burning plates for presses, the emulsion side (dull side) should always be toward the plate.

In the Separation Setup dialog box, you use the Emulsion option to control which side the emulsion goes on. If you are printing negatives on film, choose Down (right reading) from the Emulsion pop-up menu. For printing on paper, just to see what the separations look like, choose Up (right reading). Always consult with your printer for the correct way to output film.

Although "wrong reading" isn't an option in the Separation Setup dialog box, you can reverse an illustration by choosing the opposite emulsion setting. In other words, Down (right reading) is also Up (wrong reading), and Up (right reading) is also Down (wrong reading).

Reversing text creates the kind of secret code illustrations that you can send to your friends. The only way to understand the illustrations is by viewing them in a mirror. This technique works best with text, of course, and I wouldn't expect to fool really smart people with this type of code.

Thinking of the emulsion as the toner in a laser printer may help you understand this concept better. If the toner is on the top of the paper, you can read it fine, as always (Up emulsion, right reading). If the toner is on the bottom of the paper, and you can read the illustration only when you place the paper in front of a light, the emulsion is Down, right reading. Thinking along these lines helped me back when I was new to the printing industry, and it should help you as well.

Setting Up the Halftone Screen

The halftone screen setting is one of the great mysteries of life to the graphic designer who has not been informed about it. A too-low halftone screen setting will render an illustration terribly, making text and pictures unclear and fuzzy, sometimes even showing the dots that create the tints in the illustration. But if the halftone screen setting is too high, blends and gradations will show "banding," and some areas or the entire illustration may look posterized. The halftone setting can be too high for a particular press, resulting in smeary, terrible-looking results. Blends, gradations, and how to avoid banding are discussed in Chapter 10.

Understanding Halftone Line Screens

The most common mistake that graphic designers make is confusing dots per inch (dpi) with lines per inch. Lines per inch (lpi) is another way of saying line screen or halftone line screen.

The number of dots per inch of the output device controls what the potential lines-per-inch settings are. The higher the dpi, the higher the lpi can be, but the higher the lpi, the lower the possible number of grays.

In bitmap graphics software, such as Photoshop, the dpi of the image is also important. In Illustrator, objects that you create are based on locations of points rather than on dots per inch. Trust me, dealing with an image's dots per inch is no picnic, and the fact that Illustrator can bypass this specification entirely is a great boon. Of course, if you have placed or imported pixel-based images in your file, you haven't learned anything...

Line screens are made up of a combination of halftone cells. Each halftone cell has a certain number of dots within it that can be turned on and off. Usually the dots are turned on and off in a round pattern to create a halftone dot.

As an example, consider a common dpi/lpi ratio, that of a 300-dpi laser printer with a 60-line screen. Each halftone dot is made up of a 5 x 5 halftone cell (300 / 60 = 5). The number of pixels within each cell is 25. Figure 20-11 shows 5 x 5 halftone cells at different percentages.

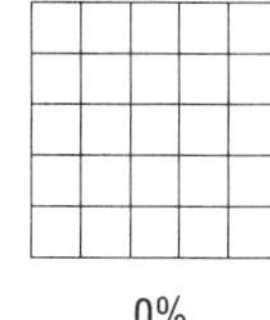
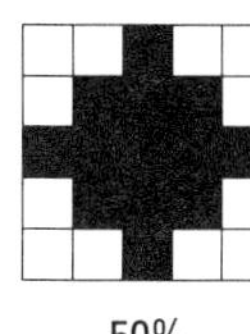

Figure 20-11: 5 x 5 halftone cells at different percentages

At a 25% tint, 25 percent of the dots are black. In a halftone cell of 25 dots, 6.25 dots would be black. Because you cannot print a quarter of a dot with this method, 6 dots are black.

Because the halftone cell has 25 pixels, only 26 different "levels" of gray are available when you are using a 300-dpi laser printer with a 60-lpi screen (1 level for each of the 25 pixels, plus 1 level for no pixels on at all, yields a total of 26). To get more grays, you need to lower the line screen.

Lower line screens seem rougher than higher line screens. The cutoff point for line screens is about 105; anything higher is considered a "fine" line screen, and anything lower is a "coarse" line screen.

A 300-dpi laser printer prints 90,000 dots for every square inch (300 x 300 = 90,000). Figure 20-12 shows one square inch blown up 500% so you can see the different dot patterns in a small gradient.

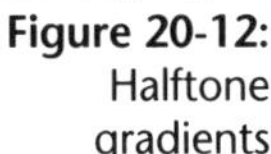
Figure 20-12: Halftone gradients

In deciding on a halftone screen, you need to consider many things, the most important of which are the type of paper or other media that the image will eventually be printed on and the press that it will be printed on.

Common settings for different types of print jobs are as follows: newsprint and photocopiers, 85 lpi; standard magazines, 133 lpi; better quality magazines, 150 lpi; and high-quality book images, 150 or 175 lpi.

Adding Custom Line Screens

In the Separation Setup dialog box, you can specify the line screen only by selecting one of the choices in the Halftone pop-up menu. This restriction can be very limiting, but you can get around it by doing a serious amount of tinkering, as described in the follwing steps.

STEPS: Adding New Halftone Screens to PPD Files

Step 1. Make a copy of the PPD file that you want to add halftone screens to and add a suffix, such as *new,* to its name (for example, Laserwriter.new). Open the copy with SimpleText or another word processor.

Step 2. Scroll down to a section that looks very similar to what you see in Figure 20-13. The halftone screen numbers may be different from the ones shown in the figure, depending on the PPD chosen. Select the entire section and copy it. Press the left arrow once and paste.

Step 3. In the copy, change the numbers highlighted in Figure 20-13 to whatever line screen you choose. Paste the copy and repeat this step for every new halftone screen that you want to include in the PPD file.

Step 4. Save the changes.

Step 5. Open the new PPD in the Separation Setup dialog box. If all went well, new pop-up menu items will reflect your recent changes.

```
*% For 60 lpi / 300 dpi ================================

*ColorSepScreenAngle ProcessBlack.60lpi.300dpi/60 lpi / 300 dpi: "45"
*ColorSepScreenAngle CustomColor.60lpi.300dpi/60 lpi / 300 dpi: "45"
*ColorSepScreenAngle ProcessCyan.60lpi.300dpi/60 lpi / 300 dpi: "15"
*ColorSepScreenAngle ProcessMagenta.60lpi.300dpi/60 lpi / 300 dpi: "75"
*ColorSepScreenAngle ProcessYellow.60lpi.300dpi/60 lpi / 300 dpi: "0"

*ColorSepScreenFreq ProcessBlack.60lpi.300dpi/60 lpi / 300 dpi: "60"
*ColorSepScreenFreq CustomColor.60lpi.300dpi/60 lpi / 300 dpi: "60"
*ColorSepScreenFreq ProcessCyan.60lpi.300dpi/60 lpi / 300 dpi: "60"
*ColorSepScreenFreq ProcessMagenta.60lpi.300dpi/60 lpi / 300 dpi: "60"
*ColorSepScreenFreq ProcessYellow.60lpi.300dpi/60 lpi / 300 dpi: "60"
```

Figure 20-13: Halftone gradients

The final thing to think about when you are choosing a halftone screen is the type of media that the illustration will be output on from an imagesetter. If the output will be on paper, the halftone screen needs to be lower than if the output will be on film.

The Printing Process and Saving $$ with Your Computer

The following brief rundown of the process that a printer goes through when taking a job from start to finish can help you understand some of the choices that you need to make when you are printing out of Separator. Of course, the following is a generalization, and all printers do things a little differently.

First, the printer gathers all of the materials for the print job. These materials may include artwork, logos, photos, and copy. The materials may go to different places, depending on what equipment the printer has. A typical commercial printer has limited prepress equipment in-house.

Color artwork and color photos are sent to a color separation house that specializes in creating film separations from full-color originals. The cost for each piece of artwork can range from $50 to $1000, depending on the quality desired and the quantity.

Black-and-white artwork is shot with a camera (usually in-house) and resized to fit. Text is sent to a typesetting firm and set.

Black-and-white artwork and text are pasted up onto pasteboards, proofed, and then shot with a camera. A stripper takes the resulting film to a light table, where any seams in the film are opaqued out.

Film from the separation houses is stripped into the film from the artwork and type. This particular process is the most time-consuming and adds substantially to the prepress portion of the labor bill.

At this point, proofs are created. Printers may use many different proofing methods, but the least expensive and most basic is the blueline, so called for the blue color of the text and artwork that appears on the sheets.

After the blueline is approved (or *if,* to be more exact), each piece of film is used to create a printing press plate for each color.

The plates are applied to presses, and the number of copies specified by the customer is run, plus several more copies to account for errors in printing and cutting.

After the ink on the printed paper dries, the copies are cut along crop marks, bound, and folded along fold marks. Depending on the type of product, the printed pieces may be bound, folded, and cut in any order.

The final piece is boxed and shipped to the client.

If you do everything you can with your system, you can save substantial amounts of money in all of the prepress areas. Do as many of the following as possible to save money and avoid problems:

- Do as much as you can electronically. This rule is one you should live by.
- Have someone else proof your work *before* you output it to film. Objectivity for your own work decreases geometrically in relationship to the time you spend working on it. Your subconscious doesn't want to find mistakes.
- Get a separation house to scan photos and traditionally created artwork and then provide you with the files on disk. Sure, you can buy a flatbed desktop scanner inexpensively, but color pictures from them can look like mush next to scans from a drum scanner at a separation house.
- Assemble all your artwork, type, and photos in QuarkXPress, FrameMaker or PageMaker.
- Have all film negatives output by a reputable service bureau. If your job contains a large amount of color artwork or photos, or if you need the artwork and color photos to be of the best possible quality, take everything back to the color separation house, where your job will be outputted at a better quality than most imagesetters can produce.

Changing from Positive to Negative to Positive

You use the Image pop-up menu to switch between printing positive and negative images. Usually, you use a negative image for printing film negatives and a positive image for printing on paper. The default for this setting, regardless of the printer chosen or PPD selected, is Negative.

Working with Different Colors

At the lower right of the Separation Setup dialog box, a "color list" window displays where you can select different colors and set them to print or not print, and set Custom Colors to process separately.

The list of colors contains only the colors that are used in that particular illustration. At the top of the list of separation colors are the four Process Colors in italic, if they or Custom Colors that contain those Process Colors are used in the illustration. Below the Process Colors is a list of all the Custom Colors in the document.

If the illustration has any guides in it, their colors are reflected in the color list window. From looking at the preview of the illustration in the Separation Setup dialog box, you can't easily determine that these blank separations will print. The best thing to do is release all guides and delete them.

By default, all Process Colors are set to print, and all Custom Colors are set to convert to Process Colors. Clicking the Convert To Process checkbox at the bottom of the Separation Setup dialog box will toggle between converting everything (checked) and Spot Colors (unchecked).

Each color in the list has its own Frequency and Angle. Don't change the angle or frequency for Process Colors because Separator has automatically created the best values for the Process Colors at the Halftone screen you've specified. Instead, make sure that any Custom Colors that may be printing have different angles from each other so that no patterns develop from them.

As soon as you type new values or check different options using the color list, the changes are applied.

Printing Separations

To print with the settings you've select, click OK in the Separation Setup dialog box and then choose File⇨Print (or press ⌘-P). This will display the Print dialog box. Change the Output option to "Separations," and the separations you've specified will print.

Printing Separations from Other Applications

Many other software programs, particularly page layout software programs, incorporate color-separation capabilities. These programs usually enable you to import Illustrator files that have been saved as Illustrator EPS files.

When you produce color separations from other software, make sure that any Custom Colors that are in the Illustrator illustration are present and accessible in the document that the illustration is placed within. Usually, you can set the Custom Colors to Process separately or to Spot separately.

You cannot change the colors of an imported Illustrator EPS document in a page layout program, so be sure that the colors are correct for the illustration while it is in Illustrator.

Trapping

Trapping is one of the most important but least understood issues in all of printing. In the past, desktop publishing has been noted for its inefficiency in trapping, but QuarkXPress 3.x and a few other after-the-fact trapping software packages, such as Adobe TrapWise and Island Trapper, have gradually bettered the trapping capabilities of electronic publishing.

Illustrator, while it does incorporate a trapping filter, is not a trap-happy piece of software. For detailed illustrations, it usually isn't worth your time to set the trapping inside Illustrator; instead, you'll want to have your printer do the work for you.

Understanding What Trapping Does

Traps solve alignment problems when color separations are produced. The most common problem that occurs from misalignment is the appearance of white space between different colors.

The thought of trapping scares many graphic designers — not just because they don't know how to do it, but also because they aren't sure what trapping is and what purpose it serves. Understanding the concept of trapping is the hard part; trapping objects is easy (though somewhat tedious in Illustrator).

Figure 20-14 shows a Spot Color illustration with four colors. The top row shows each of the individual colors. The first illustration in the second row shows how the illustration prints if all the separations are aligned perfectly. The second illustration in the second row shows what happens when the colors become misaligned. The third illustration in the second row shows how the illustration looks when trapped, with black indicating where two colors overprint each other.

This example shows extreme misalignment and excessive trapping; I designed it just as a Black-and-White illustration for this book. Ordinarily, the overprinting colors may appear a tiny bit darker, but they do not show as Black. I used Black so that you can see what parts of the illustration overlap when trapping is used. The trapping in this case is more than sufficient to cover any of the White gaps in the second illustration.

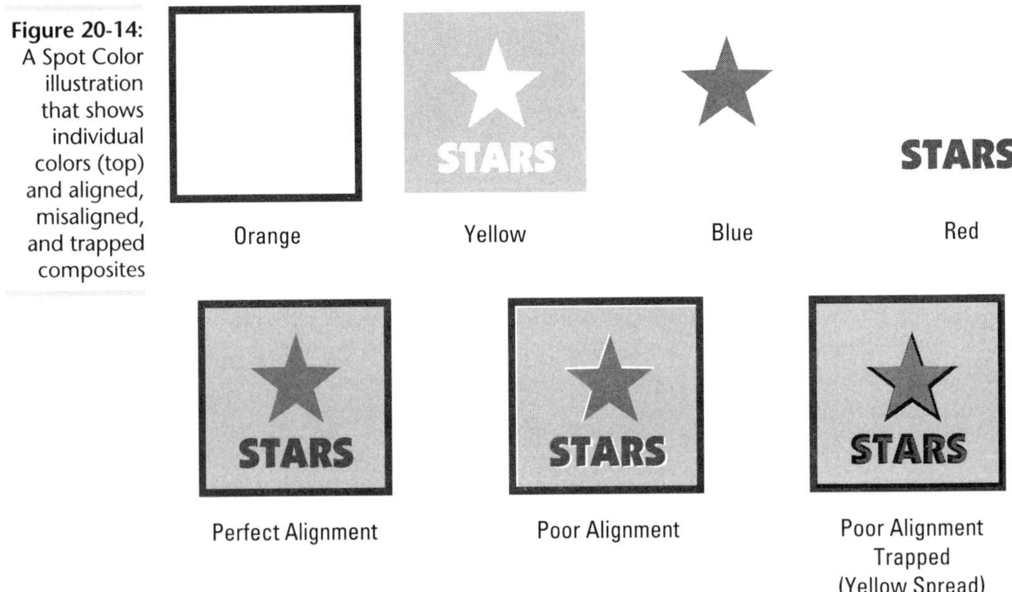

Figure 20-14: A Spot Color illustration that shows individual colors (top) and aligned, misaligned, and trapped composites

Trapping is created by spreading or choking certain colors that touch each other in an illustration. To spread a color, enlarge an object's color so that it takes up more space around the edges of the background area. To choke a color, expand the color of the background until it overlaps the edges of an object.

The major difference between a spread and a choke has to do with which object is considered the background and which object is the foreground. The foreground object is the object that traps. If the foreground object is spread, the color of the foreground object is spread until it overlaps the background by a certain amount. If the foreground object is choked, the color of the background around the foreground object is expanded until it overlaps the foreground object by a certain amount.

To determine whether to use a choke or a spread on an object, compare the lightness and darkness of the foreground and background objects. The general rule of thumb is that lighter colors expand or contract into darker colors.

Figure 20-15 shows the original misaligned illustration and two ways of fixing it with trapping. The middle star has been spread by 1 point, and the third star has been choked by 1 point.

Figure 20-15: The original illustration (left), fixing the star by spreading it 1 point (middle), and fixing the star by choking it 1 point (right)

Original

Blue (star shape)
1 pt. spread

Blue (star shape)
1 pt. choke

Why You Need Trapping

Trapping is a solution for covering gaps that occur when color separations do not properly align. Maybe this section should have been called, "Why Color Separations Do Not Properly Align," but now the book has been printed and it can't be changed.

The three reasons why color separations don't align properly are that the negatives are not the same size, the plates on the press are not aligned perfectly when printing, or the gods have decided that a piece is too perfect and needs gaps between butting colors.

Negatives can be different sizes for a number of reasons. When the film was output to an imagesetter, the film may have been too near the beginning or the end of a roll, or separations in the same job may have been printed from different rolls. The pull on the rollers, while fairly precise on all but top-of-the-line imagesetters — where it should be perfect — can pull more film through when there is less resistance (at the end of a roll of film), or less film when there is more resistance (at the beginning of a roll of film). The temperature of the film may be different if a new roll is put on in the middle of a job, causing the film to shrink (if it is cold) or expand (if it is warm).

The temperature of the processor may have risen or fallen a degree or two while the film was being processed. Once again, cooler temperatures in the chemical bays and in the air dryer as the film exits the process have an impact on the size of the film.

Film negatives usually don't change drastically in size, but they can vary up to a few points on an 11-inch page. That distance is huge when a page has several butting colors throughout it. The change in a roll of film is almost always along the length of the roll, not along the width. The quality of the film is another factor that determines how much the film will stretch or shrink.

Most strippers are quite aware of how temperature affects the size of negatives. A common stripper trick is to walk outside with a freshly processed negative during the colder months to shrink a negative that may have enlarged slightly during processing.

Trapping with Quark?

Jenny: What's the difference between trapping with Illustrator and trapping with Quark?

Toulouse: Trapping Illustrator objects *can't* be done in Quark.

Jenny: But what if I need something to trap to an Illustrator object within Quark?

Toulouse: The best thing to do is to create both objects in Illustrator, trap them, and *then* take them to Quark.

Check with your service bureau staff to see how long they warm up the processor before sending jobs through it. If the answer is less than an hour, the chemicals will not be at a consistent temperature, and negatives that are sent through too early will certainly change in size throughout the length of the job. Another question to ask is how often they change their chemicals and check the density from their imagesetter. Once a week is acceptable for a good-quality service bureau, but the best ones will change chemicals and check density once a day.

The plates on a press can be misaligned by either an inexperienced press operator or a faulty press. An experienced press operator knows the press and what to do to get color plates to align properly. A faulty press is one where plates move during printing or are not positioned correctly. An experienced press operator can determine how to compensate for a faulty press.

No press is perfect, but some of the high-end presses are pretty darn close. Even on those presses, the likelihood that a job with colors that butt up against one another can print perfectly is not very great.

If a job doesn't have some sort of trapping in it, it probably will not print perfectly, no matter how good the negatives, press, and press operator are.

How Much Trap?

The amount of trap that you need in an illustration depends on many things, but the deciding factor is what your commercial printer tells you is the right amount.

The most important thing to consider is the quality of the press that the printer will use. Of course, only the printer knows which press your job will run on, so talking to the printer about trapping is imperative.

Other factors to consider include the colors of ink and types of stock used in the job. Certain inks soak into different stocks differently.

Traps range from $^{2}/_{1000}$ inch to $^{6}/_{1000}$ inch. Most traditional printers refer to traps in thousandths of inches, but Illustrator likes values in points for this sort of thing. Figure 20-16 shows a chart with traps in increments of $^{1}/_{1000}$, from $^{1}/_{1000}$ of an inch to $^{10}/_{1000}$ of an inch, and gives their point measurements. The trapped area is represented by black to be more visible in this example.

Figure 20-16: Different trap amounts

Remember, the greater the trap, the less chance that any white gaps will appear, but the trap may actually be visible. Visible traps of certain color pairs can look almost as bad as white space.

Trapping Illustrator Files Manually

In Illustrator 6, you accomplish manual (non-filter) trapping by selecting a path's Stroke or Fill and setting it to overprint another path's Stroke or Fill. The amount that the two paths' Fills or Strokes overlap and overprint is the amount of trap that is used.

The most basic way to create a trap on an object is by giving it a Stroke that is either the Fill color of the object (to create a spread) or the Fill color of the background (to create a choke).

Be sure to make the width of any Stroke that you use for trapping twice as wide as the intended trap because only half of the Stroke (one side of the path) actually overprints a different color. In some circumstances, fixing a Stroke that is not wide enough initially can be difficult.

STEPS: Manually Trapping Between Two Paths

Step 1. Select one path of a pair of overlapping or abutting paths. If possible, select the lighter of the two paths.

Step 2. Give the Selected path a Stroke of the same color that the Fill is. Change the weight to the amount of trap you'd like to use. For this example, so it could be seen easily in this book, I've used a 3-point trap.

Step 3. Set the overlapping Stroke to overprint. These steps are shown in Figure 20-17.

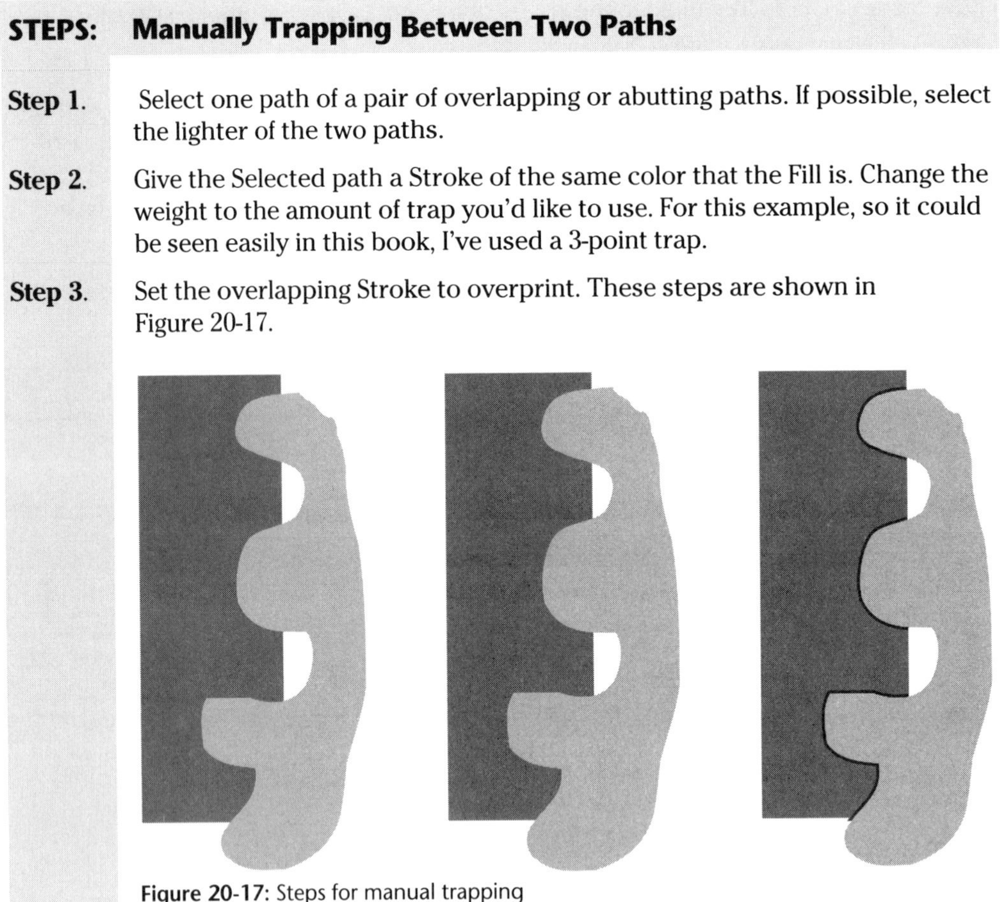

Figure 20-17: Steps for manual trapping

Trapping with the Trap Filter

For this example, I'll use the same paths from Figure 20-17 to show how the Trap filter works.

STEPS: Trapping with the Trap Filter

Step 1. Select all pieces of art that are overlapping or abutting.

Step 2. Choose Filter⇨Pathfinder⇨Trap, and enter the width into the Width text field.

Step 3. Click OK and the object has trapping applied instantly (well, if the artwork is complex it won't be instant...).

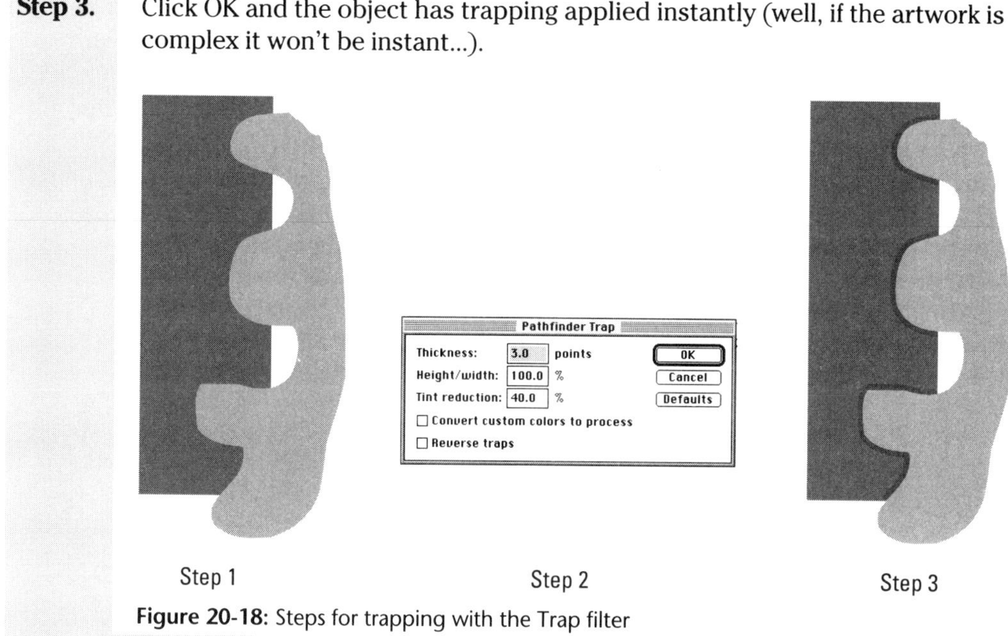

Figure 20-18: Steps for trapping with the Trap filter

Complex Trapping Techniques in Illustrator

The preceding trap illustrations are extremely simplified examples of trapping methods in Illustrator. In reality, objects never seem to be a solid color, and if they are, they are never on a solid background. In addition, most illustrations contain multiple overlapping objects that have their own special trapping needs.

I consider trapping to be complex when I can't just go around selecting paths and applying the trap filter quickly. Complex trapping involves several different techniques, which are described in the following list:

- **Create a separate layer for trapping objects.** By keeping trapping on its own layer, you make a myriad of options available that are not available if the trapping is intermixed with the rest of the artwork. Place the new layer above the other layers. Lock all the layers but the trapping layer so that the original artwork is not modified. You can turn trapping on and off by hiding the entire layer or turning off the Print option in the Layers Options dialog box.
- **Use the round joins and ends options in the Stroke portion of the Paint Style palette for all trapping Strokes.** Round ends and joins are much less conspicuous than the harsh corners and 90° angles of other joins and ends, and they blend smoothly into other objects.

- Trap gradations by Stroking them with paths that are Filled with overprinting gradients. You cannot Fill Strokes with gradients, but you can Fill paths with gradients. You can make any Stroke into a path by selecting it and choosing Filter⇨Object⇨Outline Stroked Path. After you have transformed the Stroke into a path, Fill it with the gradient and check the Overprint Fill box for that path.

Whenever I start a heavy-duty trapping project, I always work on a copy of the original illustration. Wrecking the original artwork is just too easy when you add trapping.

When Trapping Yourself Just Isn't Worth It

Before you spend the long amounts of time that complex trapping entails and modify your illustration beyond recognition (at least in Artwork mode), you may want to reconsider whether you should do the trapping yourself.

If you estimate that trapping your job will require several hours of work, the chances of doing it correctly dwindle significantly. If the illustration includes many crisscrossing blends and gradations or multiple placed EPS images, you may not have the patience to get through the entire process with your sanity intact.

If you determine that you cannot do the trapping yourself, you can have it done after the fact with Adobe TrapWise or Island Trapper, or you can have a service bureau with special output devices create trapping automatically. These services will undoubtedly cost more than doing the trapping yourself, but it will get done right, which is the important thing.

Summary

- Illustrator 6 can print separations right from within the program!
- Choose whether to print a composite or separations from the Print dialog box.
- Determine separation information in the Separation Setup dialog box.
- Trapping prevents potential white "strips" that can appear when a printer isn't perfectly aligned.
- Separation Setup lets you specify which colors print, and what angle and frequency they print at.

Using Streamline and Dimensions with Illustrator

CHAPTER 21

In This Chapter

- Understanding Streamline
- Streamline versus Illustrator's Auto Trace tool
- The tools and commands in Streamline
- Creating objects in three dimensions with Dimensions
- Extruding and revolving
- Going from Dimensions back to Illustrator
- Converting bitmapped art into Illustrator paths

Illustrator is not an island. (An island, you'll recall, is a small mass of land completely surrounded by water, while Illustrator is a software program.) Illustrator's capabilities are enhanced by additional programs, like Photoshop, Dimensions, and Streamline. Photoshop is more like a cousin, while Dimensions is a brother and Streamline is a sister.

Illustrator 6 ships with Dimensions, so you've got half the family right there. And Streamline is well worth the paltry amount of money it costs, for using it just once will save you enough time that you'll be able to take your whole family island hopping in the Caribbean.

Smoothing the Path

Esther: I really like the Smooth Paths option in Streamline.

Toulouse: Yep, it's one of the best features of Streamline, dramatically reducing the number of Anchor Points on a path.

Esther: Why isn't that an option in Illustrator?

Toulouse: I believe Streamline was developed outside of Adobe, and they don't have the rights to the code.

Esther: They should buy it. It would significantly increase Illustrator's worth.

Adobe Streamline

Imagine Illustrator's Auto Trace tool on steroids. That's the Streamline package: a super-powerful bitmap tracing tool. The options for converting images are staggering, and the results can be dramatically better than the results that you can achieve with the Auto Trace tool. A demo version of Adobe Streamline is included on the *Macworld Illustrator 6 Bible CD-ROM.*

The Auto Trace tool in Illustrator traces one solid part of a PICT template. Sure, you can adjust the Freehand tolerance to make the created path stay closer to the image or be drawn a little less constrained, but the options end there.

The biggest advantage to using the Auto Trace tool instead of Streamline is that the Auto Trace tool is free, while Streamline costs about $100. (The Auto Trace tool and tracing within Illustrator are discussed in Chapter 4.)

On the other hand, Streamline can perform all of the following tasks:

- Trace bitmapped artwork that has been saved in the PICT, TIFF, TIFF Compressed, MacPaint, PCX, and Photoshop 2.0 and 2.5 formats
- Convert artwork into EPS and PICT formats, creating editable paths that you can manipulate in Illustrator
- Edit bitmapped artwork before converting it into paths
- Adjust paths that were created by converting bitmaps
- Support Adobe PostScript on the Clipboard for instant copy and paste capabilities between Illustrator, Photoshop, and Dimensions

- Provide complex control over how images are traced
- Convert line art and grayscale and color artwork to editable Illustrator paths

The Streamline Toolbox and Menu Items

The following pages contain an overview of the functions of the Streamline toolbox and some of the more significant menu items. Although Streamline is a fairly small program, I can't possibly cover all the facets of the software in one chapter, so I'll focus on information that isn't quite so obvious.

Streamline Tools

The Toolbox in Streamline (see Figure 22-1) is a Photoshop/Illustrator hybrid; you use it to edit both bitmapped and path-based portions of images.

Figure 21-1: The Streamline Toolbox

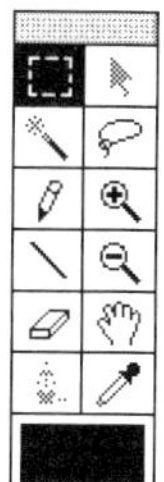

The Toolbox contains the folowing tools:

- **The Marquee tool:** You use the Marquee tool to select an area in a bitmapped image. You can move, delete, copy, or cut the selected area. You also can convert the selected area into paths. You use the tool by clicking and dragging — just as you do with Illustrator's Rectangle tool. The Shift and Option keys have no effect on the Marquee tool. You can use the Marquee tool only when you are editing bitmapped images.
- **The Magic Wand tool:** You use the Magic Wand tool to select areas in a bitmapped image that are similar in color. The color at the point where you click with the Magic Wand tool determines which areas are selected. Double-clicking the Magic Wand tool displays the Magic Wand dialog box, where the "spread" of the wand is determined by a setting of Tight (little spread; only colors very closely related to the original are selected) or Loose (colors even loosely related

to the original are selected). You can use the Magic Wand tool only when you are editing bitmapped images.

- **The Pencil tool:** You use the Pencil tool to draw on bitmapped images. It is most useful for touching up small areas that were problematic when you scanned an image. Double-clicking on the Pencil tool displays the Pencil dialog box, where you can specify the width of the Pencil. You choose the color that the Pencil draws from the Paint Style palette (choose Options⇨Paint Style or press ⌘-I). You can use the Pencil tool only when you are editing bitmapped images.
- **The Line tool:** The Line tool creates lines in the same way that the Pencil tool creates individual points. Double-clicking the Line tool enables you to specify the width of the line. The color that the Line tool draws is determined by the color in the Paint Style palette. You can use the Line tool only when you are editing bitmapped images.
- **The Eraser tool:** The Eraser tool erases bitmapped images by painting them with white. Double-clicking the Eraser tool displays a dialog box in which you can specify the width of the Eraser. You can use the Eraser tool only when you are editing bitmapped images.
- **The Delete Anchor Point tool:** The Delete Anchor Point tool deletes individual Anchor Points that are created in the conversion process. You can use the Delete Anchor Point tool only for editing converted images.
- **The Swatch:** The Swatch at the bottom of the toolbox isn't a tool. Instead, it's a color indicator. Clicking the Swatch displays the Paint Style palette.
- **The Selection tool:** You use the Selection tool to select points and paths that have been converted. You can use the Selection tool only when you are editing converted images.
- **The Lasso tool:** You use the Lasso tool to select either a group of pixels or a set of paths and points. You drag the tool around the objects or pixels that you want to select.
- **The Zoom In tool:** The Zoom In tool magnifies both bitmapped and converted images.

Unlike in Illustrator, Dimensions, and Photoshop, you can use the Zoom In tool in Streamline to enlarge an image to *any* percentage.

- **The Zoom Out tool:** You use the Zoom Out tool to zoom out from an image.
- **The Hand tool:** You use the Hand tool to scroll around the document window.

- **The Eyedropper tool:** You use the Eyedropper tool to sample color from pixels or paths in both bitmapped and path-based images. Pressing the Control key accesses the Eyedropper. To use the tool, drag a marquee around the desired area.

You can access the Selection, Zoom In, Zoom Out, and Hand tools by using the same shortcuts that you use in Illustrator. Press ⌘ for the Selection tool, ⌘-Spacebar for the Zoom In tool, ⌘-Spacebar-Option for the Zoom Out tool, and the Spacebar for the Hand tool.

If you cannot use a tool on the type of image that you are currently editing, the tool is grayed out.

Using Streamline

The three basic steps in using Streamline are opening and editing a pixel bitmapped image, converting the pixel image into a vectored path drawing, and editing and saving the resulting Illustrator paths. Use the following steps to convert a bitmapped image into paths.

STEPS: Converting Bitmapped Art to Paths

Step 1. Open the bitmap image file (choose File⇨Open or press ⌘-O) or use the TWAIN Acquire command to scan in the artwork.

Step 2. Use any of the bitmap editing tools to clean up stray pixels. If the area that you want to convert is only part of an image, use the Marquee tool to select that portion.

Step 3. Choose Options⇨Settings (⌘-T) and choose the type of bitmapped image that you are converting. The list that you choose from contains the best generalized settings for each type of bitmapped image.

If none of the settings seems to fit your bitmapped image, choose Options⇨Conversion Setup (⌘-J) and adjust the settings within the Conversion Setup dialog box.

Step 4. Choose File⇨Convert (⌘-R) to have Streamline begin to do its magic.

Streamline can outline any size bitmapped artwork; it is limited only by the amount of RAM you allocate to the software. Streamline will, however, stop converting artwork before it finishes if it does not have sufficient memory. If the bitmapped artwork is overly complex (lots of colors or a big file), increase the RAM that is allocated to Streamline.

To increase the RAM allocated to Streamline, quit Streamline, select the Streamline icon from the Desktop, choose File⇨Get Info (⌘-I), and change the bottom box (called "Preferred Size" in System 7.5) to the amount of memory that you want to allocate to Streamline. If you aren't sure how much memory you can spare, choose Apple⇨About This Macintosh from the Apple menu to display the amount of RAM installed and the amount that the system and other software are using.

Step 5. Edit the new paths with the path-editing tools.

Step 6. If you have Illustrator running at the same time as Streamline, you can copy converted paths in Streamline, go to Illustrator, and Paste (⌘-V) in Illustrator. The copied paths will be pasted in the Illustrator document.

If you want to save the converted file that you have just created, choose File⇨Save Art (⌘-S).

Figures 20-2, 20-3, and 20-4 show images in bitmap form, and their respective Streamlined paths.

Figure 20-2: A pixel-based image (left) and after being Streamlined into paths

Figure 20-3: A pixel-based image (left) and after being Streamlined into paths

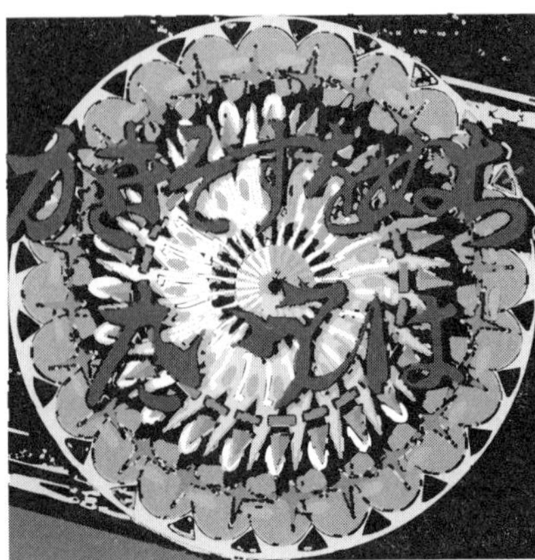

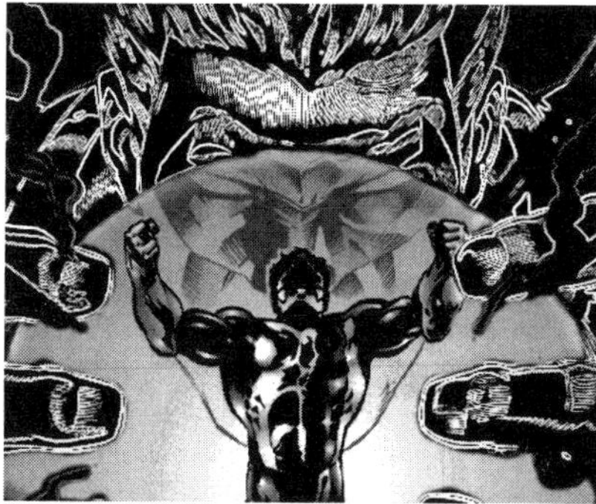

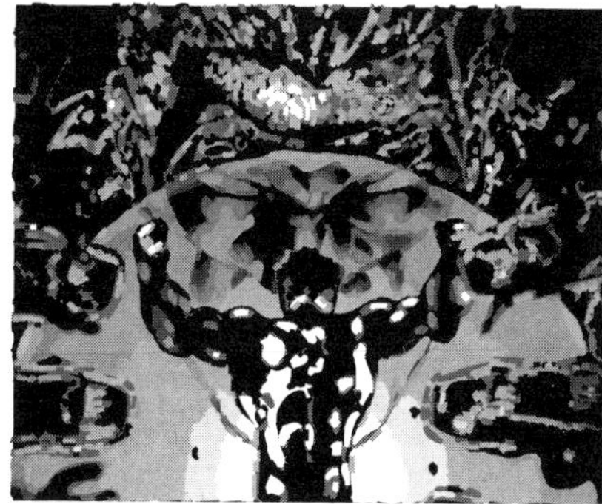

Figure 20-4: A pixel-based image (left) and after being Streamlined into paths

Streamline can be used as an econo-roughen filter. Rasterize your Illustrator artwork, export it as a TIFF, then Streamline it. Play with the tolerance setting for a looser "feel" to the illustration.

Introducing Dimensions

Adobe Dimensions is PostScript-based software for creating artwork that looks three-dimensional. The great thing about Dimensions is that it was created expressly with Illustrator in mind.

Dimensions automatically creates four basic primitive shapes that have depth. It extrudes and revolves existing PostScript paths, and it can apply *surface maps* (artwork that is mapped onto the surface of 3-D objects) of PostScript artwork to three-dimensional artwork. Finally, Dimensions can export three-dimensional artwork to Adobe Illustrator for inclusion in an Illustrator document.

A Brief History

Adobe released the first version of Dimensions, Version 1.0, at the end of 1992. The current version (2.0) was released in the middle of 1994. The two versions do basically the same thing.

New features in Dimensions 2.0 include the capability of creating two-dimensional artwork within Dimensions, automatic text-to-outlines conversion for imported artwork, custom color support, Bring to Front and Send to Back commands, multiple Undos, interruptible screen redraws, and the capability of performing rendering in the background.

This section discusses the features and capabilities of Dimensions and provides examples and techniques for using Dimensions with Illustrator. Although Dimensions is a huge program, this section gives you the lowdown on all of the great features of the software.

Be Frightened, Be Afraid, Be Intimidated

The speed of the computer's processor determines the speed of Dimensions. To a lesser degree, the amount of RAM that is allocated to Dimensions is also important, but processor speed is paramount.

If you have a 68030 or lower processor, you could be in for some frustration. Sure, even a Mac IIci with 8MB of RAM can do most things that Dimensions has to offer, but as they say, bring along a good book. You can expect to spend most of your time waiting for the computer to perform tasks.

I use a Power Mac 8100, and many times I get frustrated because things are taking too long. Most of the artwork that I create in Dimensions is similar to the samples in this chapter.

Extremely complex artwork requires time to create and to render, so be prepared for delays when you use Dimensions.

If you are the proud owner of a Power Mac, this software makes your purchase of that system seem as if it was worth it. Even rendering will fly because of the way that the PowerPC's integrated FPU cranks out numbers for Dimensions.

What Other 3-D Software Has That Dimensions Doesn't Have

Three-dimensional software has always been around for the Macintosh, but until Dimensions (and now Add Depth), no PostScript 3-D software packages were available. Most of the three-dimensional software that is available at this time is used for creating either bitmapped images or QuickTime movies.

Other 3-D software packages have many capabilities that Dimensions does not have. Most of these features are of the "gee-whiz" variety, but if you have been using other 3-D packages for a while, these capabilities can seem important.

(continued)

Don't waste your time looking for the following capabilities or features in Dimensions:

- **Lighting options:** The lighting options in Dimensions are nice, but most of the other 3-D software packages enable you to create colored lights, spotlights versus omni-directional lights, and light gels. Light gels are objects that you place in front of lights to make the lights appear in patterns on objects that are lit.
- **Reflective surfaces:** Shiny objects in most other 3-D packages reflect nearby objects.
- **Object-cast shadows:** Objects in Dimensions do not cast shadows onto other objects.
- **Texture mapping:** You cannot place textures from bitmapped graphics onto three-dimensional objects in Dimensions.
- **Skinning:** Skinning is a three-dimensional technique that creates a flexible "skin" over structured ribs. This technique can produce incredibly complex three-dimensional objects.
- **Sweeps:** Sweeps are three-dimensional objects created by running a two-dimensional object along another two-dimensional path. Tube-like effects are the result.
- **Transparency:** Objects in Illustrator and Dimensions are opaque or transparent. Dimensions does have a way of simulating partial transparency, though.

The limitations of Dimensions may seem numerous, but in reality, you can create many of the features that it lacks by using different "cheating" methods in Dimensions and Illustrator. For example, you can simulate light gels, spotlights, and shadows by using the Mix Soft filter, and you can simulate transparency by using the Overprint feature.

Even if you are sure that you can't do something, relax. Adobe will continue to plug away at Dimensions until most of these features are incorporated. By the time that Version 4 of Dimensions appears (at about the turn of the century by my guess), all of these capabilities will probably be part of Dimensions, even on your antiquated PowerPC 620 processor.

Animation

MaryEllen: Can animation be done with Dimensions?

Toulouse: Yes, Dimensions has special controls just for that.

MaryEllen: How does it work?

Toulouse: Well, first you position your art the way it should appear in the first frame. Set that as a keyframe, then position the art as you'd like it to end. Make that a keyframe as well. Then you can export a specific number of steps as the illustration transforms between the two keyframes.

MaryEllen: What if I want more than two positions?

Toulouse: You can blend between as many keyframes as you'd like.

Why Dimensions Is the Best 3-D Software for Printing

Dimensions is the best 3-D software for printing because of the following reasons:

- It produces PostScript output, which means that artwork that you create in Dimensions will look good at any size, just as Illustrator's artwork does.
- Unlike most 3-D software, Dimensions enables you to create colors that are based only on four-color process printing. Most other 3-D software packages create colors based on RGB, which doesn't usually translate well to CMYK and darkens most colors in the process.
- Dimensions can print proofs right out of the software. In Version 1.0, you had to export art to other software before you could print it.

In spite of the advantages that Dimensions offers, remember that you can accomplish very little entirely in Dimensions. For the best results, you need to export artwork from Dimensions to Illustrator.

Understanding the Three-Dimensional World

The concept of three dimensions should be simple for us to understand, for we are three-dimensional creatures who live in a three-dimensional world. But because most of what we see is two dimensional (reading, watching television, working at a computer), adjusting to a three-dimensional world can be confusing and frustrating.

Changing from Two Dimensions to Three Dimensions

Television is a two-dimensional medium. The picture tube has height and width. Computer screens are two dimensional. The pages of books are two dimensional. Even driving is two dimensional (drivers rarely consider up or down). Maps are two dimensional, even though the world is round. Most people think in two dimensions.

Most of the two-dimensional objects that we deal with may very well be replaced with three-dimensional objects. Three-dimensional life will become a reality as soon as technology makes it so. Holograms have been around for a while, and technology is making them more accurate and lifelike. Video games and virtual-reality glasses already simulate three dimensions through the use of holograms and computer generated imagery. Maybe sometime in the future we will have to look up and down when we are driving . . . although I doubt that we will be driving one of Apple's famed helocars.

Three-Dimensional Positioning

When you are trying to understand the concept of three dimensions on a computer screen, the most difficult aspect to grasp is depth. Left, right, up, and down are all simple concepts, but what about things that are closer or farther away?

You already are thinking in three dimensions in some ways if you have been using Illustrator long enough to grasp Send to Back and Bring to Front. If you feel comfortable with stacking order and layers, then you are one step further.

You use three different indicators to position objects in Dimensions:

- *X* is the horizontal location of the object. A value greater than 0 means that the object is positioned to the right of center (0). A value less than 0 (any negative number) represents an object to the left of center.
- An object's *Y* value defines its vertical position. A *Y* value that is greater than 0 means that the object is above center. A *Y* value that is less than 0 means that the object is below center.
- The third positioning variable is the depth of the object. *Z* represents how far forward or backward the object is from the center. A value greater than 0 means that the object is behind 0, or farther away. A value less than 0 means that the object is in front of 0, or closer to you.

Figure 21-5 shows the *X*, *Y*, and *Z* values as you would see them initially in Dimensions. In the status bar at the top of the screen, Dimensions shows the relative X, Y, and Z positions of selected objects. At a direct, straight-from-the-front view, you cannot determine an object's Z position. From the default position, which is a view of the objects from above and to the right of the front, you can determine all three positions visually.

Figure 21-5: *X*, *Y*, and *Z* positioning of objects in Dimensions

Dimensions helps you manipulate objects by enabling you to move objects manually with a Selection tool or move them with the Move command (choose Operations➪Move or press ⌘-Shift-M). The Move palette for Dimensions, which is shown in Figure 21-6, is similar to the Illustrator Move dialog box, but Dimensions does not provide the option of moving an object by an angle. Instead, the Dimensions Move palette has a *Z* option that enables you to move an object forward or backward. Absolute and Relative options determine the starting point of the move.

Figure 21-6: The Move palette in Dimensions

Move

X: 0 pt — Absolute
Y: 0 pt — Relative
Z: 0 pt

Clear | Copy | Apply

An Overview of Dimensions

The two main parts of Dimensions are a 2-D drawing component and a 3-D modeling component. Understanding their similarities and differences is key to understanding Dimensions. Each part uses a different toolbox and different menu options. Both parts also share several palettes, menu items, and tools.

Tools

The two Toolboxes in Dimensions are shown and labeled in Figure 21-7. The 3-D Toolbox is available when you are working with three-dimensional objects, and the 2-D Toolbox appears when either the Artwork or Map windows is displayed. Most of the tools in the 2-D Toolbox work the same way as their counterparts in the Illustrator Toolbox.

The 3-D Toolbox

The 3-D Toolbox contains the following tools:

- **The Selection tool:** You use the Selection tool (⌘) to select individual and grouped objects and to move them across the screen.
- **The Direct Selection tool:** The Direct Selection tool (⌘-Tab) enables you to select individual faces of three-dimensional objects.
- **The Object Selection tool:** You use the Object Selection tool (⌘-Option) to select an entire path that is part of a group of paths.
- **The Z-Translation tool:** The Z-Translation tool moves selected objects along the "other" axis. If you are viewing an object from the front, the Z-Translation tool moves the object forward and backward. If you are viewing the object from the bottom, the Z-Translation tool moves the object up and down.
- **The Hand tool:** The Hand tool (Spacebar) moves the entire Pasteboard within the screen area.
- **The Zoom tool:** The Zoom tool increases (⌘-Spacebar) or decreases (⌘-Option-Spacebar) the magnification level. If you drag a marquee with the Zoom tool, the area within the marquee will be zoomed up to fit within the document window.
- **The Cube tool:** The Cube tool creates cubical primitives. Dragging with the tool produces a cube the size of the drag, and clicking it brings up the Cube Size dialog box.

Figure 21-7: The Toolboxes in Dimensions

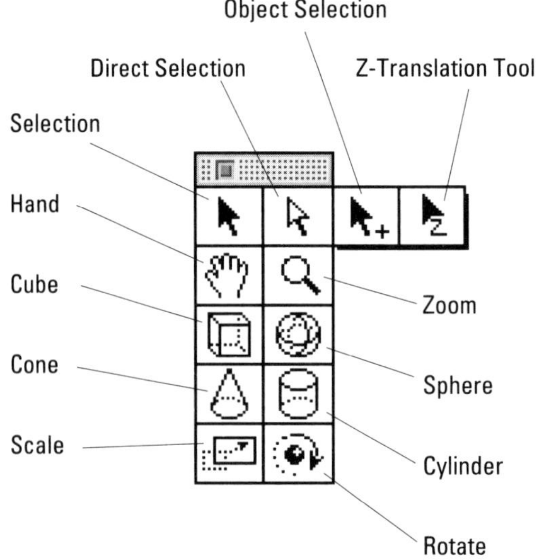

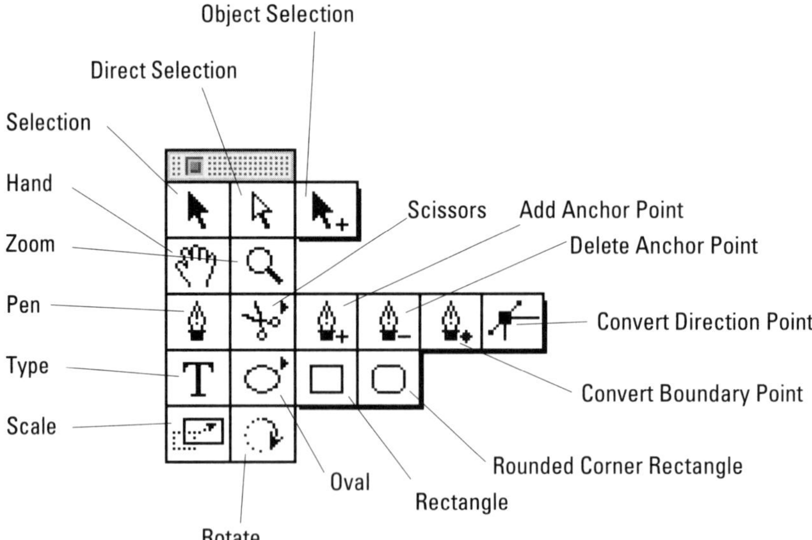

- **The Sphere tool:** The Sphere tool creates spherical primitives. Dragging with the tool produces a sphere the size of the drag, and clicking it brings up the Sphere Size dialog box.
- **The Cone tool:** The Cone tool creates conical primitives. Dragging with the tool produces a cone the size of the drag, and clicking it brings up the Cone Size dialog box.
- **The Cylinder tool:** The Cylinder tool creates cylindrical primitives. Dragging with the tool produces a cylinder the size of the drag, and clicking it brings up the Cylinder Size dialog box.
- **The Scale tool:** The Scale tool enlarges or reduces the size of an object in much the same way that Illustrator's Scale tool changes an object's size. .
- **The Rotate tool:** The Rotate tool enlarges or reduces the size of an object in much the same way that Illustrator's Rotate tool rotates objects, except that you can rotate objects in another dimension.

The 2-D Toolbox

The 2-D Toolbox contains the following tools:

- **The Selection tool:** This tool works the same way as the Selection tool in the 3-D Toolbox works, but you use it for paths instead of for objects.
- **The Direct Selection tool:** You used this tool for selecting individual points, direction points, and line segments.
- **The Object Selection tool:** You use the Object Selection tool for selecting objects within groups.
- **The Hand and Zoom tools:** These tools work the same way that the Hand and Zoom tools in the 3-D Toolbox work.

Dimensions versus Vector Effects

Jim-Bob: I'm torn between buying Dimensions or KPT Vector Effects.

Toulouse: Yikes! You shouldn't be torn between them. They're totally different.

Jim-Bob: But don't they both extrude Illustrator art?

Toulouse: That's the only thing that both of them do. And they do that quite differently.

Jim-Bob: So how do I pick one?

Toulouse: From a standpoint of extruding, take note of the differences.

Jim-Bob: Which are...?

Toulouse: Vector Effects KPT 3D Transform is much faster, has almost instant previews, the ability to save presets, and a "metallic" setting. Also, Vector Effects creates paths that aren't masked, while Dimensions has to mask most things.

Jim-Bob: Wow. I bet Dimensions can't measure up to Vector Effects, then.

(continued)

Toulouse: Well, in the area of extrusion, Dimensions lets you use custom bevels (VE only has a straight edge bevel, which you can change the size and angle of), more than one light source, and the ability to cast shadows. And, you can map 2-D artwork to extruded art in Dimensions.

Jim-Bob: Gee, I had no idea. What other things do the packages differ in?

Toulouse: Vector Effects has 12 other filters (see Chapter 18 for more info on Vector Effects), while Dimensions can do basic animation and revolving, and it can create 3D Primitives. I need both packages; there's very little overlap between the two.

- **The Pen tool:** You use the Pen tool to create paths in the Artwork and Map windows. Its functionality is the same as that of the Pen tool in Illustrator.
- **The Scissors tool:** You use this tool to split an open path into two separated paths and to change a closed path into an open path.
- **The Add Anchor Point tool:** The Add Anchor Point tool adds Anchor Points to a path in the 2-D window.
- **The Delete Anchor Point tool:** The Delete Anchor Point tool deletes an Anchor Point from a path.
- **The Convert Direction Point tool:** (⌘-Control) The Convert Direction Point converts a direction point from a smooth point to a corner point.
- **The Type tool:** The Type tool enters a line of type into the 2-D window.
- **The Oval, Rectangle, and Rounded Corner Rectangle tools:** These tools create the shapes they are named for, and they work the way their Illustrator equivalents work.
- **The Scale and Rotate tools:** These tools work the same way that their 3-D counterparts work.

Creating Primitives

The most basic function in Dimensions is creating a primitive shape by using one of the four Primitives creation tools. The tools are the Cube tool, the Sphere tool, the Cone tool, and the Cylinder tool. They are called Primitive tools because you create other objects from the shapes that these tools create. As with all other sorts of drawing in Dimensions, you can create primitive shapes only in Artwork mode.

Figure 21-8 and the steps that follow show you how to create a basic Primitive cone.

Figure 21-8: Steps for creating a basic primitive cone

Step 1

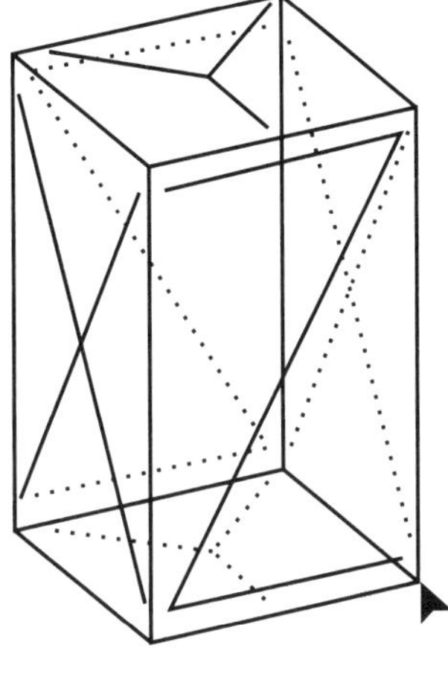

Step 2

Surface Properties

Reflectance

Diffuse

Ambient : 0 %

%

%

Number of blends : 25 Calculate

Revert Apply

Step 4

Step 3

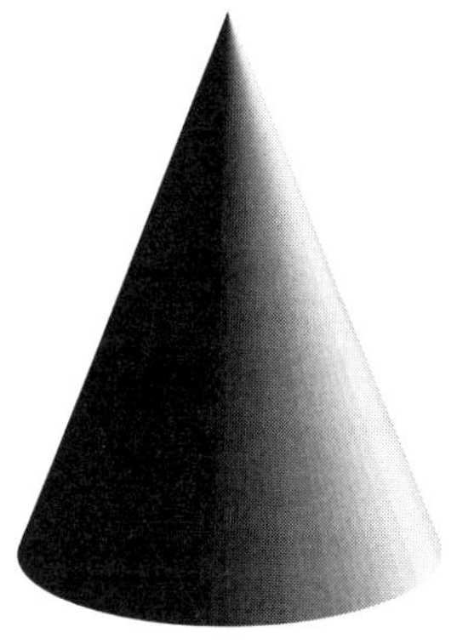

Step 5

STEPS: Creating a Basic Primitive

Step 1. Select the Cone Primitive drawing tool.

Step 2. Click and drag with the tool. As you drag, a cube in wireframe form appears. You are still creating a cone, but when you drag with any of the primitive tools, you see a cube that holds the "space." Holding down the Shift key constrains the cube to have equal dimensions on all sides. Pressing Option draws the cube from the center instead of from a corner.

Note the *X*, *Y*, and *Z* on each side of the cube. The *X* represents the left side, the *Y* the top side, and the *Z* the front side, all when viewed from the front. Dotted letters represent the opposite sides.

Dimensions automatically constrains the depth of the cube to the width of the cube. By pressing Control as you drag, you constrain the depth of the cube to the height of the cube.

Step 3. When you release the mouse button, the cone appears as a wireframe version of the final cone.

The cone that you have drawn may look out of proportion or inexact because you are looking at it from the upper-left of the front of the cone. See the "Views and Perspectives" section, later in this chapter, for more information.

Step 4. After you draw a primitive, it is automatically selected. Choose Appearance⇨Surface Properties (⌘-I) to display the Surface Properties dialog box. Change the Fill (the first box) to White, the Stroke (the second box) to None, the Shade (the third box) to Black, and the Reflectance (the fourth box) to Diffuse, and set Ambient to 0%.

After you draw the primitive, you can change its size. Double-click the primitive to display the Size dialog box for that particular primitive (see Figure 21-9) and then enter the exact dimensions.

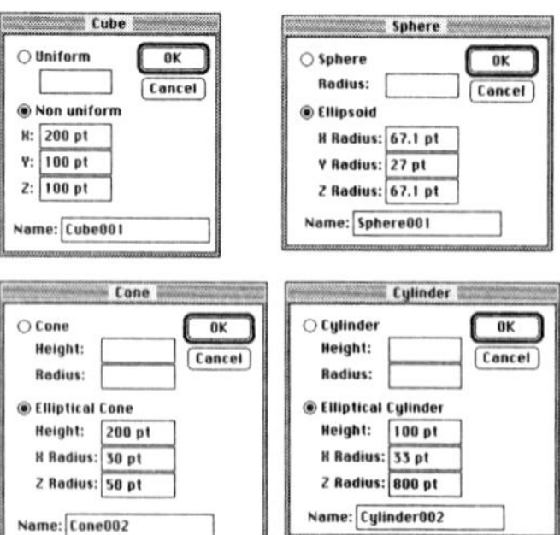

Figure 21-9: Size dialog boxes for each primitive

Step 5. To see the final rendering, choose View⇨Shaded Render (⌘-Shift-Y).

Another way to create primitives is by selecting a Primitive tool and just clicking without dragging. The primitive's Size dialog box appears. Enter the exact dimensions of the new primitive, and Dimensions will create it.

When the Size dialog box appears, it contains the values that were used the last time that Dimensions drew that shape.

Rendering Artwork

Before you can use artwork in other software or print it, you have to render it. Rendering is the process of turning the basic lines that make up a shape into a solid form.

Dimensions offers three different ways of rendering objects. The most basic way is wireframe rendering. Wireframe rendering (choose View⇨Wireframe Render or press ⌘-Shift-W) produces objects that look similar to the artwork representation of the three-dimensional objects.

The next step up in rendering is the Draft Render. To create a Draft Render, choose View⇨Draft Render (⌘-Y). Draft rendering creates surfaces with a minimum of shading for all objects, and mapped artwork is never shaded. Draft rendering is usually much faster than shaded rendering.

The best way to render in Dimensions is by choosing View⇨Shaded Render (⌘-Shift-Y). Shaded rendering produces smooth blends from light to dark areas of an object, as well as shading for mapped artwork. Shaded rendering can take a long time. The time required is directly related to the power of the host computer and the amount of RAM allocated to Dimensions.

Figure 21-10 shows a basic Dimensions document in the three different rendering styles. Note the differences between the draft rendering and the shaded renderings.

Extremely complex drawings can take hours to render, even on Quadra and PowerPC systems. To decrease rendering times, don't use bevels, mapped art, or curved objects, and use no more than one light.

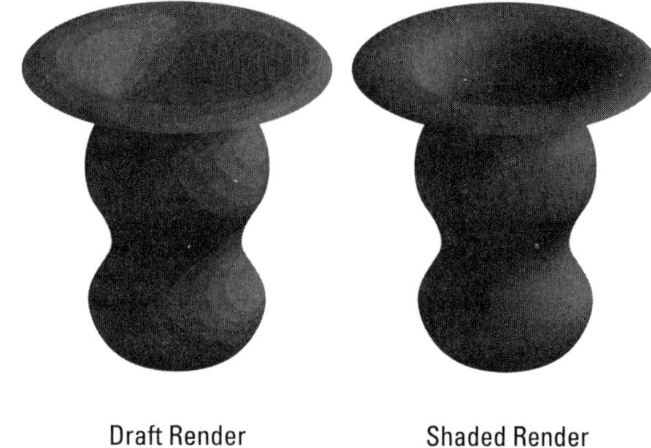

Figure 21-10: A comparison of the three types of rendering

Changing How Three-Dimensional Objects Look

Objects in Dimensions are not only colored, as in Illustrator, but are also lit. With lighting comes two additional specifications that are not present in Illustrator: Shading and Reflectance.

Two palettes, the Surface Properties palette and the Lighting palette, control how objects in Dimension look. Figure 21-11 shows both of these palettes.

The Surface Properties Palette

The Surface Properties palette is composed of four major parts: fill color, stroke color, shade color and reflectance. The combination of all the parts is shown at the upper right of the palette on a sphere.

The different palette parts work as follows:

- **Fill color:** The Fill color box works very similarly to the one in Illustrator. The major difference is that you cannot choose patterns and gradients for Fills. You can select custom colors, and you can create them by choosing AppearanceÍCustom Colors. The Fill color is the color of the object at the point where a light source at 100 percent is shining on it.
- **Stroke color:** The Stroke color box determines the color of the Stroke of the selected object. It works very similarly to the Stroke box in the Paint Style palette of Illustrator. A Stroke on a Dimensions object appears around the visible outline of an object. Strokes also show up on corners of objects, such as the rim of a cylinder.

Figure 21-11: The Surface Properties and Lighting palettes

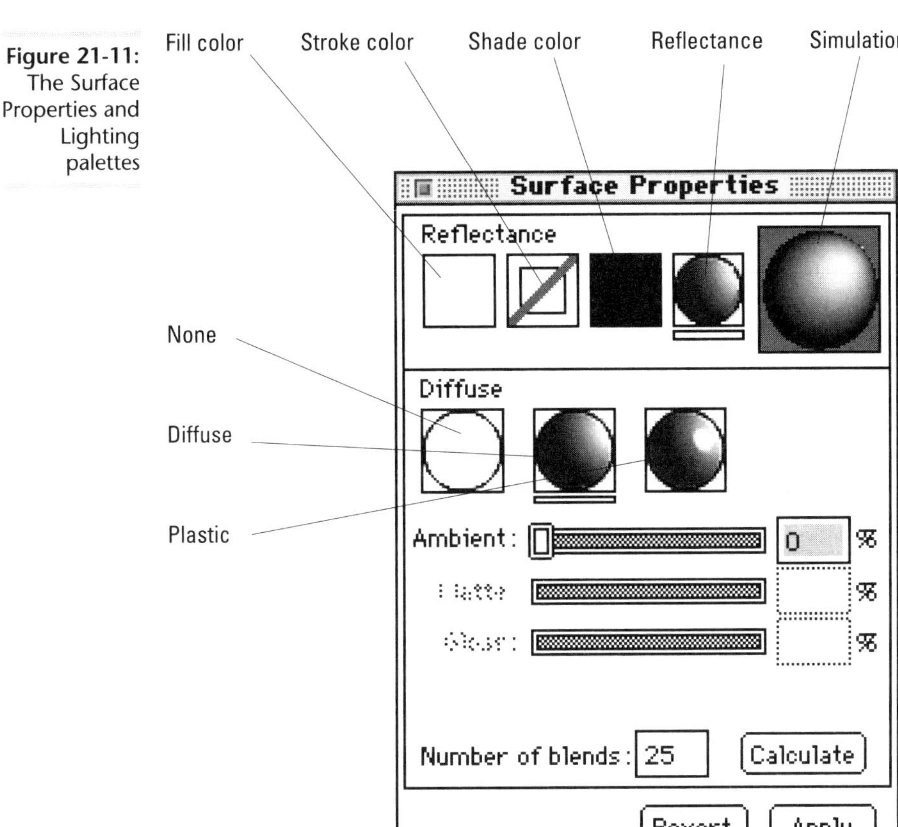

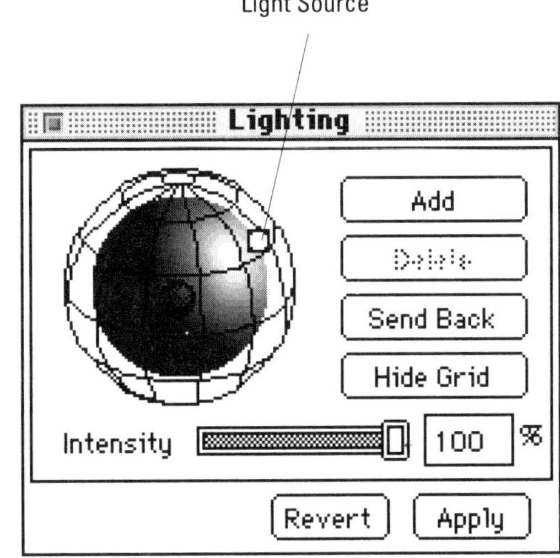

- **Shade color:** The shade color box is specific to Dimensions and is new in Version 2. The color in this box is the color that the object will be at its very darkest, in areas where no light source reaches it. A common technique for creating a shade color is to add black to a custom or process color. The following steps describe how to add black to a custom color.

STEPS: Adding Black to Custom Colors for Shading

Step 1. Select the object to be shaded and give a custom color Fill to the object in the Surface Properties palette (choose Appearance⇨Surface Properties or press ⌘-I).

Step 2. Click the shade color box. Select the custom color that was used for the Fill of the object. At this point, the object appears flat, with no change from light areas to dark areas.

Step 3. Click the Process square (it has four triangles on it). The custom color is converted to its process color attributes.

Step 4. Increase the black slider to a higher percentage, keeping in mind that this color will be the color of the shade at its darkest.

I usually set the shading to the color of the Fill plus 75-percent black or more. This setting gives the best results for being able to see the color even in the darkest portions of the object.

Reflectance

The Reflectance box determines how light is reflected off the object. (See the "Lighting Palette" section, later in the chapter, for more information on how objects are lit.)

Light can be reflected off three-dimensional objects in three ways, as shown in the boxes in the second row of the Surface Properties palette (shown previously in Figure 21-11). The first option is None, which more than anything else Fills the entire object with the Fill color and no shading at all. If the light source is behind the object, the object will still be Filled with 100 percent of the selected Fill color. The None option is useful for quickly determining which objects are in front of others.

The second option is Diffuse, which diffuses light equally from where the light source hits the object to the edges of the object, where the light is its least bright. When Diffuse is selected, the Ambient control bar becomes selectable (as shown previously in

Figure 21-11). The less Ambient light, the darker the shaded area. When Ambient is at 100%, no shading will appear. Figure 21-12 shows the effects of different ambient settings on the same three-dimensional object.

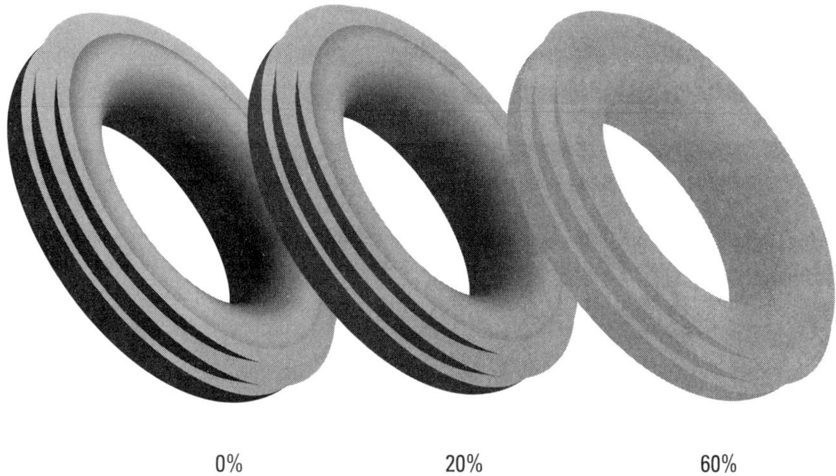

Figure 21-12: Objects at different Ambient settings. Nothing is shown for 100%, because the object is completely white (the Fill color) at that setting.

The last box in the Reflectance section of the Surface Properties palette is the plastic box. When plastic is selected, you can manipulate the Matte and Gloss slider controls.

The Matte setting controls how plastic the object looks. An object appears more plastic when a highlight is present. The more obvious the highlight, the more plastic the object appears. A setting of 0%, which is the highest plasticity possible, makes the highlight very distinct. Figure 21-13 shows objects at a Matte setting of 0%.

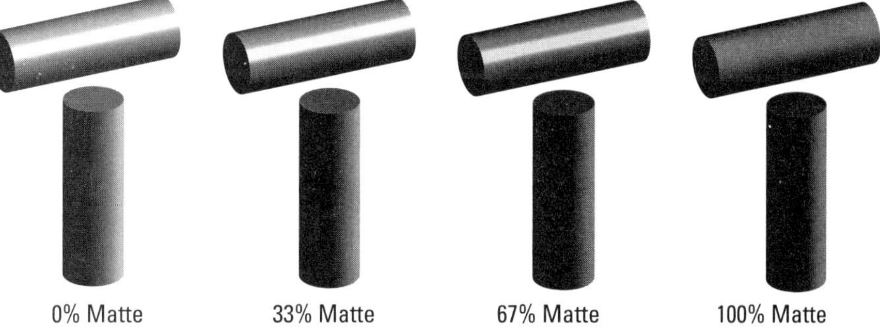

Figure 21-13: These objects are at the Matte setting shown under each object, with an Ambient setting of 0% and a Gloss setting of 50%.

The Gloss setting controls the size of the highlight. The higher the Gloss setting, the smaller the highlight. A Gloss setting of 0% creates a huge highlight. Highlights appear only on curved surfaces.

Figure 21-14 shows an object at different Gloss settings. Each object has an Ambient setting of 20% and a Matte setting of 40%.

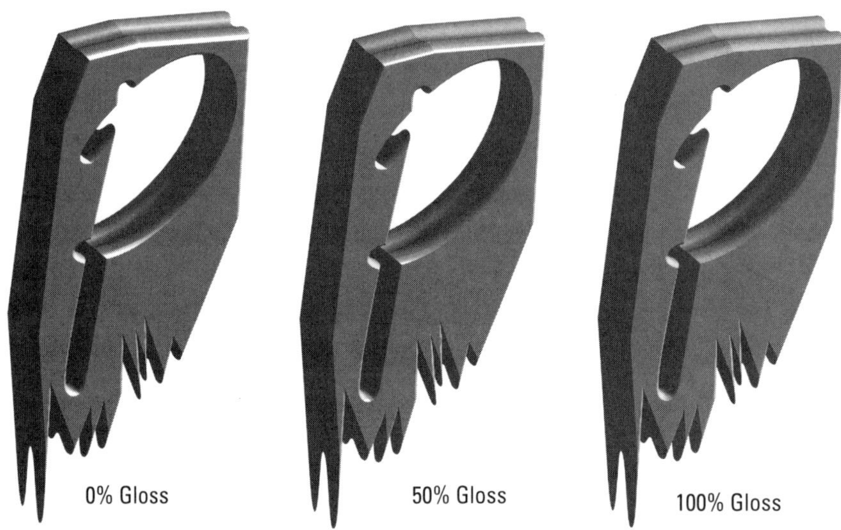

Figure 21-14: An object at three Gloss settings

In the Number of blends text box, you enter the number of blend steps. Clicking the Calculate button brings up the Calculate dialog box, where you can customize the number of blend steps for the output device by entering the resolution of the output device and the desired line screen.

Clicking the Apply button applies changes that you have made in the Surface Properties palette. Revert returns the settings to the what they were the last time you clicked Apply.

The Lighting Palette

You access the Lighting palette (previously shown in Figure 21-11) by choosing Appearance⇨Lighting (⌘-Shift-L). The Lighting palette controls the amount and direction of light sources. You always need to use at least one light, but you can use an unlimited number of lights.

The default light is always in the upper-right position, in front of objects in the document. Lights always shine into the document from outside it. To move a light around, click it and drag. Placing a light in the center of the sphere in the palette causes light to shine directly on the object from the front.

Understanding Lighting

Lighting can be a little confusing in a 3-D program. The information in this sidebar can help you better understand the use of lighting.

Because lights in Dimensions are positioned an infinite distance from objects, shading for different objects is the same, no matter what the position of the objects. For example, if the lights are in the upper left, objects on the far left will have the same lighting as object on the far right. If the lights were positioned closer (they can't be in Dimensions), the shading on each object would appear differently.

A good way to think of the lights that you create in Dimensions is that they resemble sunlight to us earth-bound creatures. Light from the sun shines on an object in New York City almost exactly the same way that it shines on an object in neighboring Boston. Because the sun is so far away, the differences in the position of the sun relative to the two cities are minute. If the sun were an infinite distance away and the earth were flat (as everyone thought it was a few hundred years ago), the two cities would have exactly the same sunlight.

Because there are no shadows in Dimensions, objects that are between the light source and another object let light pass through them so that the light can reach the "hidden" object. This feature of Dimensions causes a problem when you are trying to make an image realistic, but creative use of the Soft filter can resolve the problem easily. Shadow creation in bitmapped 3-D programs is one of the most time-consuming and power-consuming activities of using those software packages.

The most annoying thing about lights in 3-D programs is where the highlights show up. The highlights are reflections of the lights, so your position relative to the objects and their position relative to the lights are the basis for where a highlight appears. The following figure shows that you perceive a highlight on a reflective surface at the point where the reflection of a light source meets your eye.

(continued)

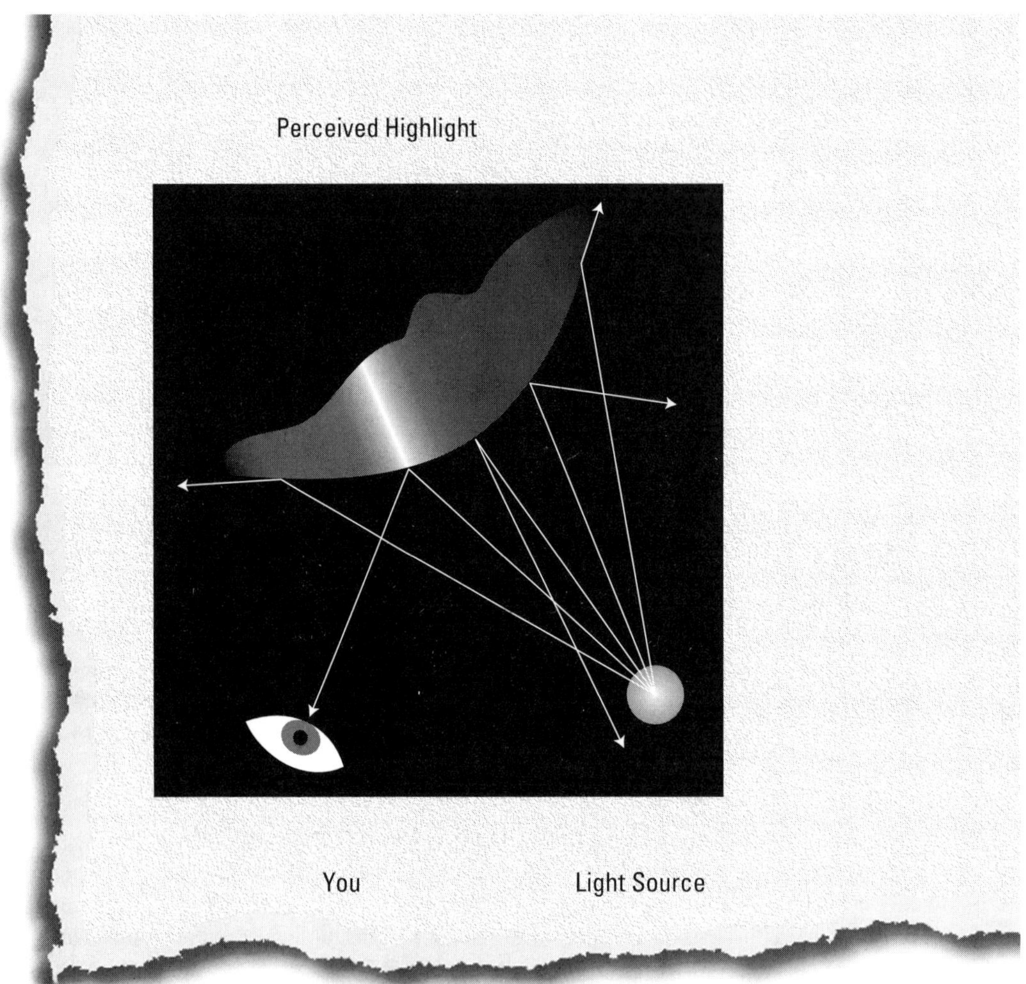

You can position lights on the other side of the objects in a document by clicking the Send Back button. When a light source is behind the sphere, you can bring it forward by clicking the Bring Forward button, which takes the place of the Send Back button.

The Intensity slider at the bottom of the Lighting palette controls how bright each light is. To change a light's intensity, select it and drag the Intensity slider to the correct position.

Add additional light sources by clicking the Add button. Delete selected light sources by clicking the Delete button. You cannot delete the only light, but you can change its intensity to 0%, which colors everything the same shade.

Creating Two-Dimensional Artwork

You can create two-dimensional artwork in Dimensions 2.0. Previously, all 2-D artwork had to be imported or pasted into the software. While this is a nice touch to Dimensions, it really has little bearing if you have Illustrator. The toolset is limited in comparison to Illustrator, and drawing in Dimensions is more frustrating than useful.

Instead of learning the nuances of drawing in Dimensions, do your drawing and editing in Illustrator. After all, art can be copied and pasted between the two programs rather easily.

Using Illustrator Artwork

You can use artwork from Illustrator in Dimensions by bringing it into the program in two ways. The first way is to choose File⇨Import (⌘-Control-I) and select the Adobe Illustrator file. If a 2-D window is present, the artwork will appear in the 2-D window; otherwise, the artwork will be in an artwork box in the 3-D window.

The second method is to copy artwork in Illustrator and paste it into Dimensions. The artwork will appear in the active window.

Modifying 2-D Artwork

You can use any of the tools in the 2-D Toolbox to modify artwork. After you finish modifying the artwork, click the Update button in the Artwork window or simply close the window. If you close the window, a dialog box will appear, asking whether you want to update with the artwork from the closing 2-D window. Click Update to have the artwork in the 3-D window reflect the changes that you made in the 2-D window.

Points

Olivia: Why are the points bigger in Dimensions?

Toulouse: There is no good answer to this, unfortunately. They just are.

Olivia: It makes the 2D drawing portion of Dimensions feel clunky...like FreeHand on a good day.

Toulouse: Tell Adobe your dissatisfaction. That's the surest way to get them to make a needed change.

Saving 2-D Artwork

Artwork that you create in the 2-D windows of Dimensions isn't saved; instead, the artwork is exported in an Illustrator format. To export artwork that you create in the 2-D window of Dimensions, make sure that the 2-D artwork is active, and then choose File⇨Export (⌘-Option-E).

Previewing 2-D Artwork

To preview artwork in the 2-D windows, choose either View⇨Preview (⌘-Y) or View⇨Preview Selection (⌘-Option-Y). You cannot manipulate artwork that you are previewing in Dimensions. Previewing 2-D artwork does not preview the objects in the 3-D window.

Using the Tile and Stack Options

Dimensions can automatically tile windows. When you choose Window⇨Tile Windows, the 3-D window is sized to take up the left half of the monitor, and the 2-D window is sized to take up the right half of the monitor. Additional 2-D windows are tiled on the right side.

If you have two or more monitors, choosing the Tile Windows option automatically tiles any Artwork windows to additional monitors; the main monitor (the one with the menu bar) then contains only the 3-D window.

Extruding and Revolving 2-D Artwork

You create two-dimensional artwork in Illustrator to use as mapped art on a three-dimensional object, as a bevel, or as a base object to extrude or revolve.

Before you extrude or revolve artwork, you can edit it by selecting the artwork and choosing Operations⇨Edit Artwork (⌘-Option-A). However, extruding and revolving 2-D artwork creates a three-dimensional object from the two-dimensional base object, and you cannot subsequently edit the three-dimensional object in the 2-D window.

Extruding Flat Art

Extruding is the process of giving flat art depth that is equal on every part of the artwork. Figure 21-15 shows flat art and the same art after it has been extruded.

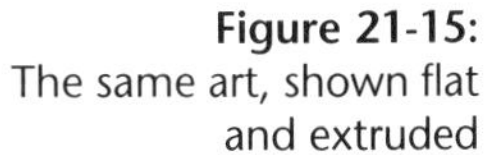

Figure 21-15: The same art, shown flat and extruded

The following steps describe how to create extruded 2-D artwork.

STEPS: Extruding 2-D Artwork

Step 1. Select the 2-D artwork in the 3-D window.

Step 2. Choose Operations⇨Extrude (⌘-Shift-E). The Extrude palette appears, as shown in Figure 21-16.

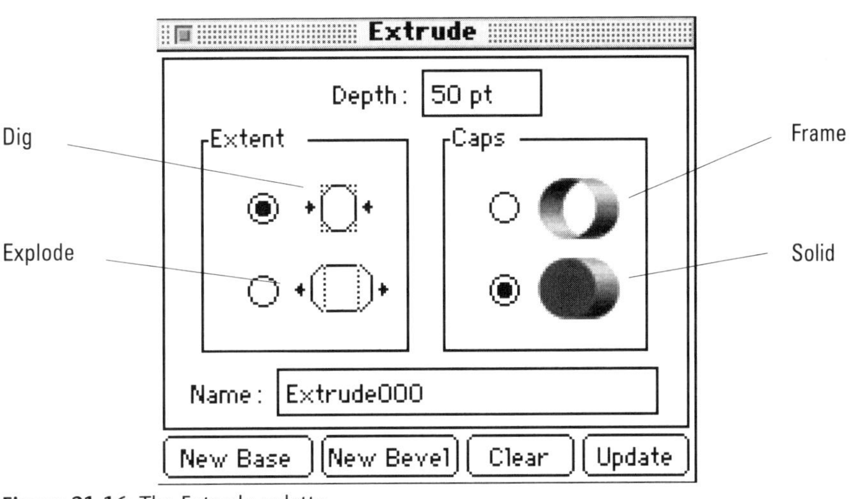

Figure 21-16: The Extrude palette

Step 3. Enter the depth that you want the object to be extruded along its *Z* axis. This setting determines the "thickness" of the artwork.

Step 4. In the Caps area, select the type of extrusion that you want. Choosing the solid extrusion button creates a solid object, and choosing the frame extrusion button creates a framed object.

Step 5. If you are going to bevel the surface of the 2-D artwork, select the type of bevel to use by choosing a button in the Extent area of the Extrude palette. A Dig bevel digs into the extruded object along the *Z*-axis, and a Grow bevel grows out from the *Z*-axis.

Step 6. Choose the type of bevel to use by selecting the New Bevel button. Adobe Dimensions comes with a Bevel Library that contains several bevels. The New Bevel button opens an Open dialog box, in which you need to choose a bevel file.

A bevel file is a very basic Illustrator document that has an open path in it.

Step 7. Click the Update button to change the selected 2-D artwork into an extruded three-dimensional object.

Understanding Bevels

The use of bevels can make or break your artwork (and yes, complex bevels will more often break than make it). Figure 21-17 shows samples of bevels, and the following steps describe how to create and apply a bevel.

STEPS: Creating and Applying a Bevel

Step 1. Create an object that you want to extrude and apply a bevel to. Choose Operations⇨Extrude (⌘-Shift-E) to access the Extrude palette, and enter the depth of the extrusion.

Step 2. Click the New Bevel button. Click the Cancel button in the Open dialog box (⌘-Period) to see a new window in which you can create a bevel.

Step 3. Use the Pen tool to create a bevel that is a single open path.

Step 4. Click the Update button in the Extrude palette.

Step 5. Render the artwork as you desire.

Figure 21-17: Bevels and the results of using them on extruded artwork

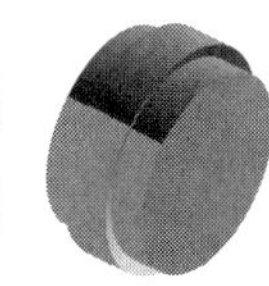
Complex 1

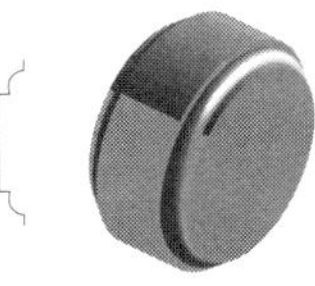
Complex 2

Complex 3

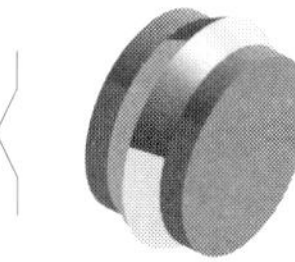
Complex 4

Classic Narrow

Classic Normal

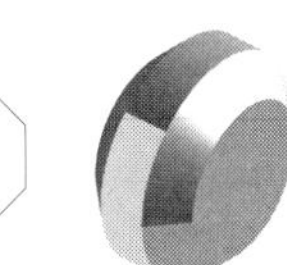
Classic Wide

Cove Narrow

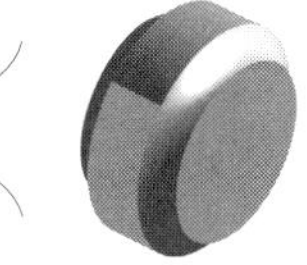
Cove Normal

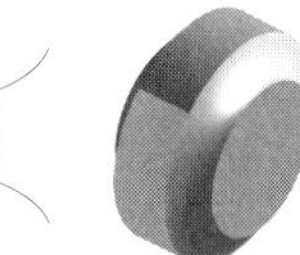
Cove Wide

Rolling Narrow

Rolling Normal

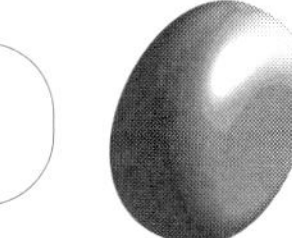
Rolling Wide

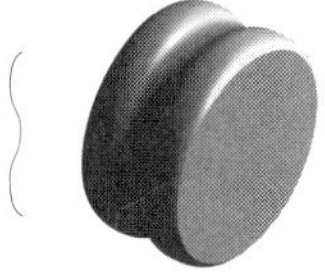
Rolling Narrow

Rolling Normal

Tall-Round Narrow

Tall-Round Normal

Tall-Round Wide

Bevels that have curves take a great deal of time when you are rendering an object. Using a few straight lines is better than using a curve. A good rule of thumb is that if the object doesn't redraw as art in the 3-D window when you update it to the new bevel, you shouldn't try to render it. The rendering process could tie up your computer for long periods of time.

Often, when you select a "wide" format bevel, the Dig Extent option forces a bevel to self-intersect. Although self-intersection sounds like something you wouldn't want to read about in a family-oriented book, it is actually almost that bad. Intersecting bevels can produce, as the dialog box says, "unpredictable geometry," and the rendered result will probably turn out to be unusable.

Revolving Artwork

Revolving is what Adobe calls *lathing*. It is the process of spinning a two-dimensional object around an axis so many degrees in order to create a three-dimensional object. The following steps describe how to revolve 2-D artwork into 3-D artwork.

STEPS: Revolving 2-D Artwork into 3-D Artwork

Step 1. Create 2-D artwork in the 2-D window or in Adobe Illustrator. In the sample (Figure 21-18), I created separate paths for one side of a lamp and a lamp shade.

Step 1 Step 2 Step 3 Step 4

Figure 21-18: Steps for revolving artwork

Step 2. Create a straight line with the Pen tool by clicking in one location and then in another. Position the newly created line so that it runs across the axis that you want to rotate the artwork around. After the line is in position, choose Draw⇨Make Guide.

If you do not create a guide, artwork will naturally revolve around its leftmost edge.

Step 3. Choose Operations⇨Revolve (⌘-Shift-R) to display the Revolve palette that is shown in Figure 21-19. Enter **360** in the Angle text box to have the artwork make a complete revolution around the guide.

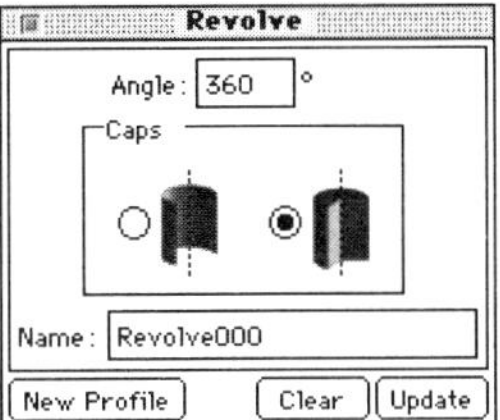

Figure 21-19: The Revolve palette

Step 4. Give the revolved object surface properties and render it. Use the Direct Selection tool to select individual portions of the object, such as the lamp base.

You can create many things by revolving different objects around different axes. Figure 21-20 shows the results of revolving the same three two-dimensional objects on different axes.

Remember that you don't have to revolve objects the entire 360° to achieve different effects. In fact, you can achieve some effects only by revolving the objects at less than 360°, as in the following steps.

STEPS: Extruding by Revolving

Step 1. In the 2-D window, create the 2-D artwork that you want to extrude.

Step 2. Far from the actual artwork, draw a path to use as the guide. Zooming out when you create this guide may be helpful.

Step 3. Choose Operations⇨Revolve and enter **5** for the revolve angle.

Step 4. Render the artwork. The result is an extrusion that is extruded more on one side (the side farthest from the guide axis) than on the other.

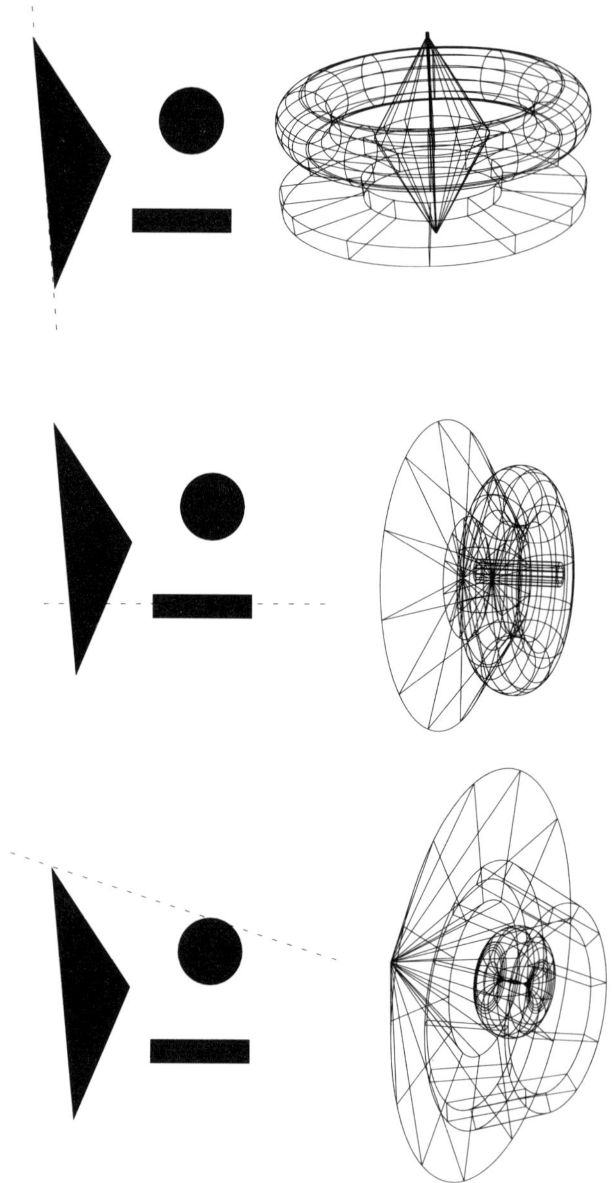

Figure 21-20: The same objects were revolved in each of these drawings, but they were revolved on a different axis in each example. The dotted lines show the axes that were used.

Manipulating 3-D Artwork

You can manipulate artwork in Dimensions in three different ways. The most obvious way is by selecting various objects and moving them around the screen. A less obvious method is to move the same objects forward and backward. Rather than simply using the Send to Back or Bring to Front commands, or even using the minor complexity of layers, you can change the location of each object in Dimensions along the *Z* axis.

The other two ways to manipulate objects in the 3-D window of Dimensions are by scaling and rotating these objects. Although scaling and rotation sound simple, because by now you are undoubtedly a master of rotation and sizing in Illustrator, Dimensions presents a new challenge. The Rotate tool rotates objects in all three dimensions. The Scale tool reduces and enlarges objects in all three dimensions. And you cannot ignore that "extra" dimension.

Moving Objects in Three Dimensions

You can move objects in two dimensions, just as in Illustrator, by dragging them around the screen with the Selection tool. To drag an object back and forth along the *Z* axis, you have to use the Z-Translation tool.

All references to the Z-Translation tool assume that the reader is viewing artwork in Off-Axis Front or Front views. Using the Z-Translation tool in other views moves objects along other axes.

Rendering

Zeb: Some of the time, Dimensions artwork won't render at all.

Toulouse: There's several reasons for this. Are you using bevels?

Zeb: Yes. Is that a problem?

Toulouse: Bevels, especially ones with curved path segments, take up a lot of processing power.

Zeb: Anything else that causes problems?

Toulouse: The other major slowdowns are using complex art for mapping and too many light sources.

You select the Z-Translation tool by clicking on the Direct Selection tool and dragging over to the arrow with a *Z* under it. For instant access to the Z-Translation tool at any time, press ⌘-Control.

Dragging an object with the Z-Translation tool moves the object diagonally on the screen, but it is actually moving the object closer or farther from you, along the *Z* axis.

You cannot move objects along the depth axis (*Z* when in a Front view) with any tool but the Z-Translation tool. Dragging an object diagonally does not move it forward or backward.

When you are dragging an object down and to the right, it is getting closer to you, moving in front of other objects, and decreasing the *Z* value along the *Z* axis.

When you are dragging an object up and to the left, it is going farther away from you, moving behind other objects, and increasing the *Z* value along the *Z* axis.

All objects can be copied by pressing Option when the mouse button is released and will be constrained to a movement of 45° when the Shift key is pressed before the mouse button is released — just as in Illustrator. The Option-copy and Shift-constrain work this way in Photoshop as well.

Using the Move palette (shown in Figure 24-1) may be easier than moving objects manually. To access the Move palette, choose Operations⇨Move (⌘-Shift-M). By entering values in the *X*, *Y*, and *Z* text boxes, you can move objects along these axes.

When the Relative button is checked, objects are moved relative to their current location. If an object is at an absolute location relative to the center of the document of 10 *X*, –20 *Y*, and 100 *Z*, entering 10 in each of the three text boxes moves the object 10 points in each of those directions, leaving the object at 20 *X*, –10 *Y*, and 110 *Z*.

When the Absolute button is checked, the location of the object relative to the center of the document is displayed in the text boxes. If the object is at 10 *X*, –20 *Y*, and 100 *Z*, entering 10 in each of the text fields when the Absolute button is checked moves the object along all three axes to 10 *X*, 10 *Y*, and 10 *Z*.

The Absolute button stands for the relation of the object to the center of the document at 0 *X*, 0 *Y*, and 0 *Z*.

The Copy button in the Move palette creates a copy of the object at the coordinates specified.

Scaling in Three Dimensions

When you scale objects in two dimensions, you modify the width and height. The only difference when you are working in three dimensions is that you scale the depth as well as the width and height.

You can scale objects by using either the Scale tool or the Scale palette.

STEPS: Scaling in 3-D with the Scale Tool

Step 1. To scale an object with the Scale tool, use any of the Selection tools to select the object.

Step 2. Select the Scale tool in the 3-D Toolbox.

Step 3. Click to set the origin. As in Illustrator, I usually set the origin of the scale in either the center of the object or in a corner or edge that I don't want to move.

Step 4. Click far from the origin (usually on a far corner of the object) and drag. The depth of the scaling will be changed relative to the change in the width of the object. Pressing the Control key provides for changes in the depth of only the object.

After you scale width and height, be sure to release the mouse button before you change the depth, and vice versa. Failing to release the mouse button causes the scaling that you have just done to be wiped out when you press or release the Control key.

Step 5. To make a proportional scaled copy, press Option before releasing the mouse button.

To use the Scale palette (see Figure 21-21) to scale an object, choose Operations⇨Scale (⌘-Option-S). To quickly display the Scale palette, double-click on the Scale tool in the 3-D Toolbox.

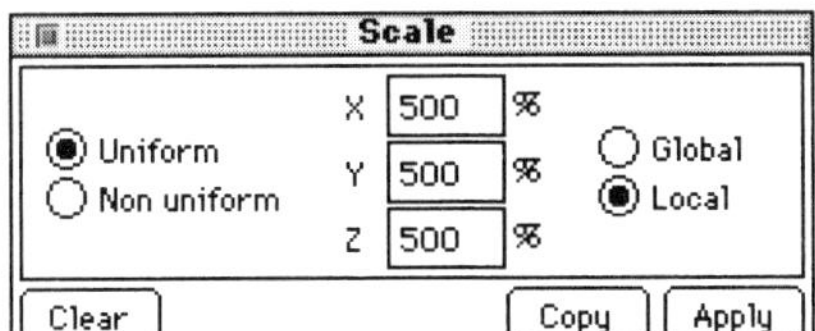

Figure 21-21: The Scale palette

In the *X*, *Y*, and *Z* text boxes, specify the amount that you want to scale the selected objects . If you check the Uniform button, all values for all three fields will be the same. If you check the Non uniform button, then you can change each field independently of every other field.

Rotating Objects in Three Dimensions

The easiest way to understand the concept of three-dimensional rotation is to imagine each axis as a pivot for objects. Figure 21-22 illustrates this concept.

Figure 21-22: The circular arrows show the direction of rotating objects with positive values around each of the axes.

In comparison with rotating, scaling isn't difficult to understand, because you scale objects in Illustrator in two dimensions. But rotation is another story. In Illustrator, you can rotate objects only around the *Z* axis. In Dimensions, you have to deal with the *Y* and *X* axes as well.

Actually, you can use Illustrator's Reflection tool to rotate objects around the *X* and *Y* axes in a twisted way. If you are comfortable with using the Reflection tool in Illustrator, rotating around *X* and *Y* axes shouldn't be much of a challenge.

I think that the hardest part about three-dimensional rotation is the difficulty in remembering which axis is which and how objects rotate around those axes. Since the beginning of time (circa 1990), I have used the memory tricks described in this section to help myself remember which axis to rotate around.

The *Z* axis, as stated previously, rotates objects in the same way that Illustrator (and every other graphics package in the western world) rotates objects. If you can remember that, great. If not, read on.

You use the *Z* axis to rotate objects the same way that a propeller on a plane spins. So remember Zis: Zee Axis powers in World War II flew propeller-equipped planes. Zimple.

Going along with the flying theme, remember the whirlybird things that you played with as a kid? You held a stick with a whirlybird shooting up and out of it at an angle and moved your hands back and forth to make the whirlybird fly. It looked like a *Y* in flight. The Y axis spins things the same way that a whirlybird spins.

X is the comin' at ya axis. Objects spinning around the *X* axis include such things as tires on a car racing at you. You being the target, and *X* marking the spot (you), makes this memory trick a no brainer.

If these little tidbits don't help you, you always have Figure 21-22.

The best way to do controlled rotation is by using the Rotate palette (see Figure 21-23), which you access by choosing Operations➪Rotate (⌘-Option-R). Or access the Rotate palette quickly by double-clicking on the Rotate tool.

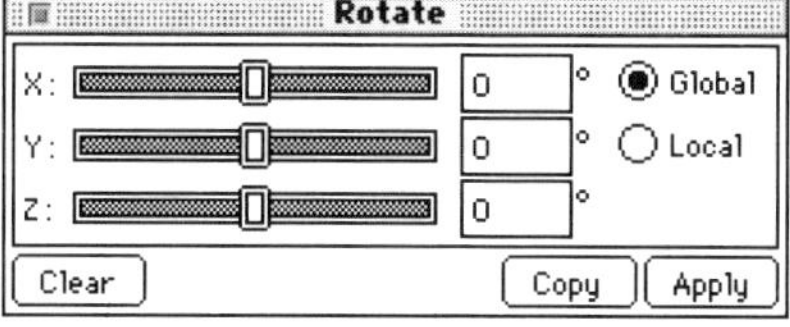

Figure 21-23: The Rotate palette

If the Local button is selected, objects rotate relative to the most recent rotation of the selected object. If the Global button is selected, objects rotate relative to 0° *X*, *Y*, and *Z*. Local rotates the object relative to its current *XYZ* axis. Global rotates the object relative to the page (0/0) *XYZ* axis. Also, when multiple objects are selected, the axis is always global.

Using the Rotate tool is a little more tricky. You have no clues to help you determine which way objects are being rotated. To rotate objects, you can either click to set an origin point or click and drag all at once. I have found that clicking and dragging all at once is easier (though by no means simple).

Most objects (with the exception of text) can look the same at 180° rotations around all the axes. If you are unsure of the direction of the objects that you have rotated, do a draft render or a render selection to determine which way an object is facing.

Views and Perspectives

Possibly the most important aspect of any program for drawing three-dimensional objects is the ability to view any drawing from any angle. Some programs call this angle the *camera position.* Dimensions has 13 different ways of looking at objects.

Using different perspectives is another way to view objects differently as a sort of special camera effect.

Different Viewing Options

The viewing options in Dimensions fall into two categories: on-axis and off-axis. Within each of these categories are six different directional views. An isometric view, which is similar to an off-axis view, is also available.

Figure 21-24 shows how an object is viewed from each of the 13 different available views that are in Dimensions. The original object was lit from the default light in the upper-right corner. A basic Classic Normal bevel was applied to the extruded letters.

The views are most useful when you need to arrange different objects relative to each other. For Figure 24-24, I used off-axis front, front, back, top, and left views to position the objects before rendering each of them at different views.

Viewing objects from different locations does not move or rotate the objects. It just changes your viewing position relative to the objects. The light source and the objects are not modified at all.

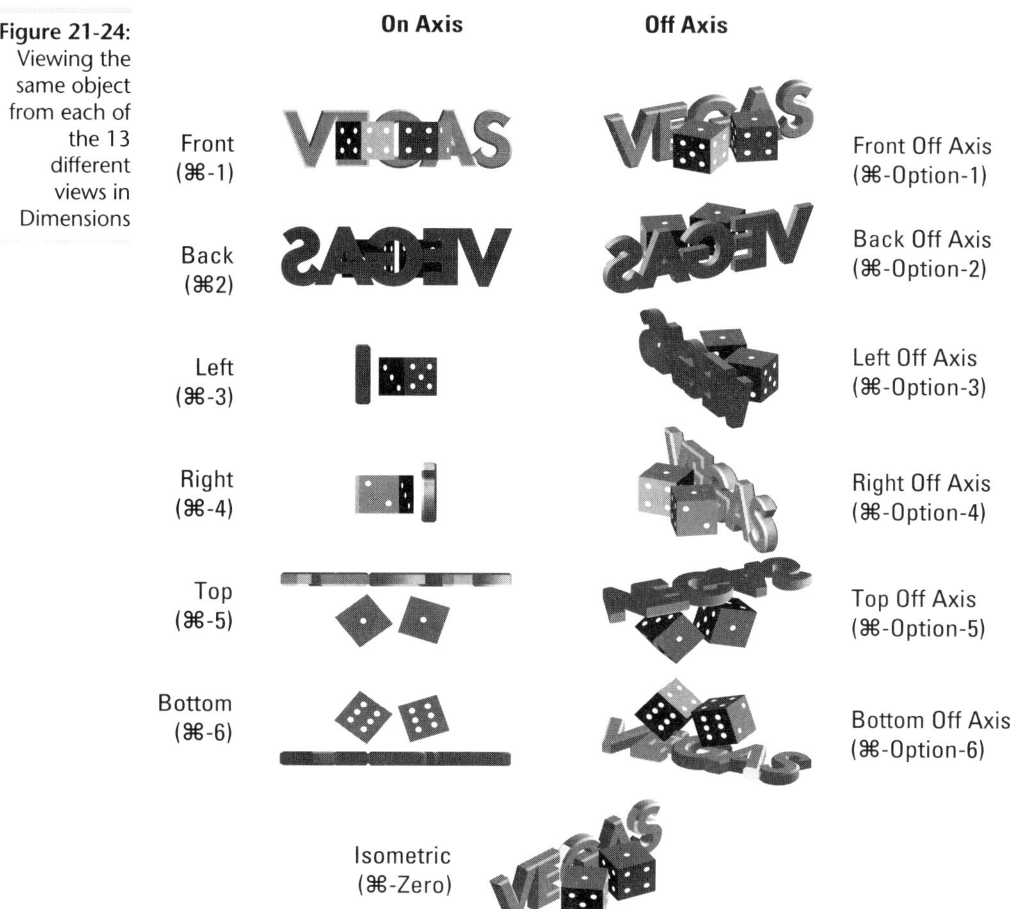

Figure 21-24: Viewing the same object from each of the 13 different views in Dimensions

Getting a better perspective

In addition to different viewing locations, you can choose several different perspectives. Perspective, though it doesn't look like it, is actually a simulated distance from the objects in the Dimensions document.

To change the perspective quickly, select an option from the Perspective pop-up menu at the top of the Dimensions window. You also can change the perspective by choosing View⇨Perspective and selecting one of the perspectives that is listed. For complete control of viewing objects, choose View⇨Custom Perspective (⌘-Control-P) to display the Custom Perspective palette.

For complete control of viewing objects, choose View⇨Custom Perspective (⌘-Control-P) to display the Custom Perspective palette. This palette, which is shown in Figure 21-25, enables you to view an object at a specific distance. Strangely enough, the perspective is measured in degrees rather than in centimeters, inches, or picas.

Custom Perspective
None Normal
Angle:
16
°
Telephoto Wide
Revert
Apply

Figure 21-25: The Custom Perspective palette

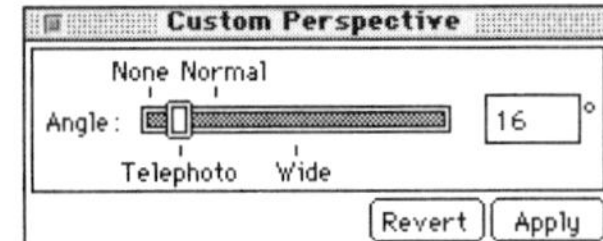

The most common custom perspective values are shown in Figure 21-26.

None
Normal
Telephoto
Wide
110
130
140
150

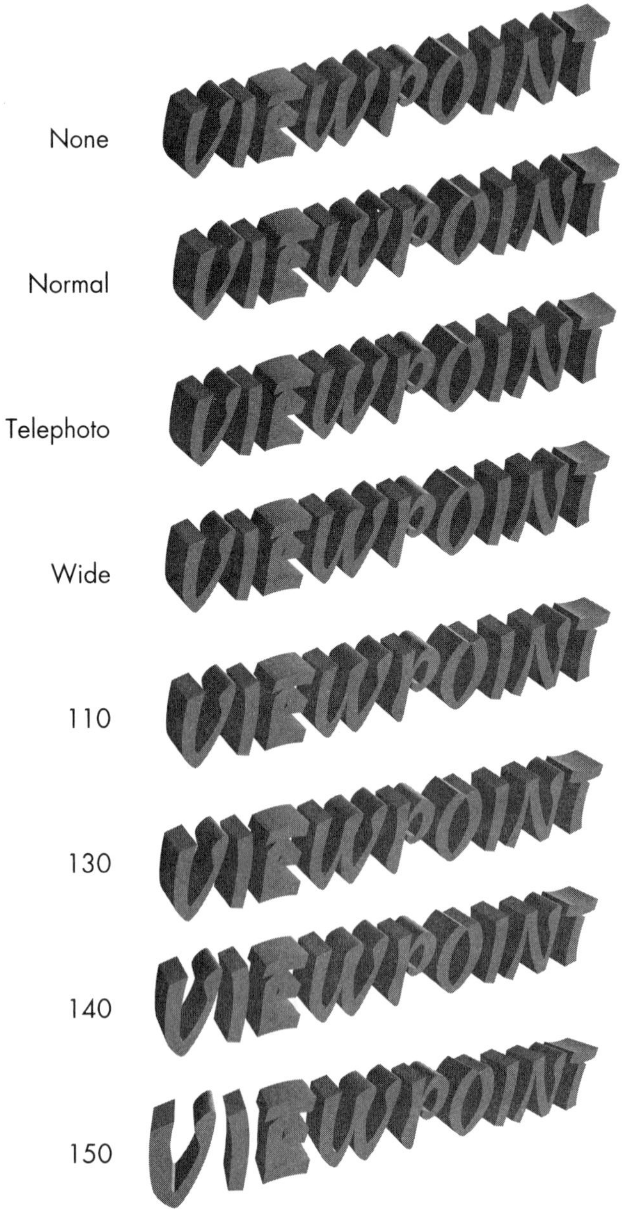

Figure 21-26: Different viewing perspectives available in Dimensions

The preset values are as follows:

- **None:** None views objects at an infinite distance, providing no perspective at all. Objects to the right and left appear to have similar depths. On-axis views create a flat appearance for objects. The Custom Perspective palette setting is 0° for None.
- **Telephoto:** Telephoto is similar to looking at the object from 2,000 points, or 28 inches, away. The Custom Perspective palette setting is 18° for None, because the field of vision is 18°.
- **Normal:** The field of vision for Normal is 35°, which is similar to looking at the object from 1,028 points, or 14 inches, away.
- **Wide:** When you choose the Wide perspective, the field of vision expands to 80°. This setting is comparable to standing at a distance of 450 points, or 6.25 inches, from the objects.
- **110_:** At a field of vision 110°, the distance is about 272 points, or 3.75 inches.
- **130_:** At a field of vision 130°, the distance from objects is down to 220 points, or 3 inches.
- **140_:** At a field of vision 140°, the distance from objects is only 200 points, or 2.75 inches.
- **150_:** At a field of vision of 150°, the distance from objects is 180 points, or 2.5 inches.
- **160_:** (not pictured). At 160°, objects start to become stretched rather bizarrely. Objects look as if they are at a distance of about 108 points, or 1.5 inches.

At 180°, you are smack up against the objects, and they take up your entire field of vision.

Mapping 2-D Artwork onto Three-Dimensional Surfaces

One of the most powerful features of Dimensions is its ability to wrap two-dimensional objects around three-dimensional surfaces. This feature alone makes the program worth every cent you paid for it.

The most important concept to understand when you are mapping artwork is that each three-dimensional object usually has several different surfaces, and each of those surfaces can have separate mapped artwork.

Use the following steps to map 2-D artwork onto a three-dimensional surface.

STEPS: Mapping 2-D Artwork onto a Three-Dimensional Surface

Step 1. Create the three-dimensional object that you want to map artwork onto. You can map artwork onto any object, including primitives, extruded 2-D artwork, and revolved 2-D artwork. I used a can that I often use as a three-dimensional base for "canned artwork." Figure 21-27 shows the steps that I took.

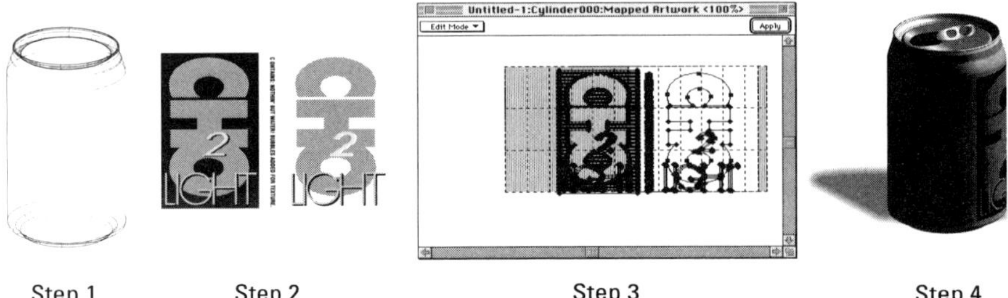

Figure 21-27: Steps for mapping 2-D artwork onto a three-dimensional object

Step 2. In Illustrator or in a 2-D Artwork window, create the 2-D artwork that will appear on the surface of the object. You can skip this step by creating the artwork directly in the Map window.

Step 3. Select the surface of the three-dimensional object that you want to apply 2-D artwork to by clicking it with the Direct Selection tool. The Tab key will select successive surfaces, and Shift-Tab will select the previous surface.

Choose Operations⇨Map Artwork (⌘-Option-M) to bring up the Map window. Paste or import the 2-D artwork into the window.

Position the artwork so that it will fit onto the surface of the objects as well as possible. Shaded areas in the Map window are surfaces that are not visible from the current view.

Step 4. Click the Update button (⌘-S) or close the Map window. The three-dimensional object will show (in wireframe artwork) the mapped artwork applied to it. Choose View⇨Shaded Render (⌘-Shift-Y) to view the finished objects.

Other 3-D Techniques

Using Adobe Dimensions isn't the only way to create depth in illustrations. Software called AddDepth, which is available from Ray Dream, is similar in function to Dimensions in that it creates PostScript artwork. At this point, its feature set is quite limited, and while there was an interesting choice between AddDepth and Dimensions 1.0, there really is little to decide between Dimensions 2.0 and AddDepth. Dimensions 2.0 far outclasses AddDepth in almost every respect.

You can do many things in Illustrator to create the illusion of depth. Drop shadows and blended shadows help to define depth, but the most useful thing that you can do is to think about how a light source would hit an object and reflect back at the viewer.

Figure 21-28 shows several objects created in Illustrator.

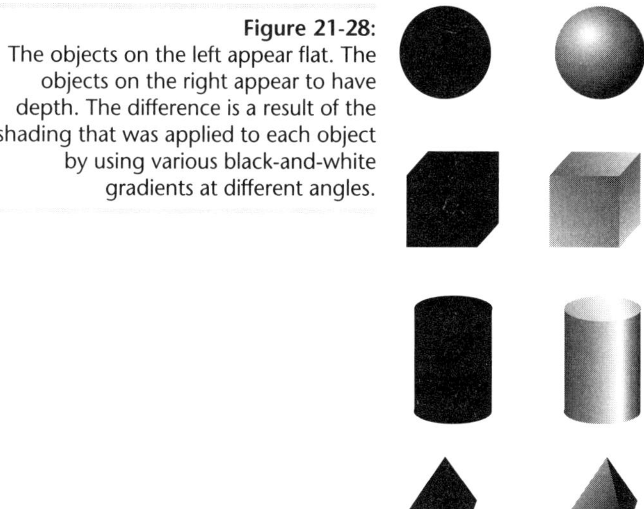

Figure 21-28: The objects on the left appear flat. The objects on the right appear to have depth. The difference is a result of the shading that was applied to each object by using various black-and-white gradients at different angles.

Creating a "Three-Dimensional" Object in Illustrator

The most basic three-dimensional shapes in Dimensions are called Primitives, and these are the shapes that are easiest to create right in Illustrator. In fact, artwork in Illustrator can be more three-dimensional than similar artwork in Dimensions, through proper use of gradients. As examples, the following sets of steps describe how to create a cube and a basic metal tube.

STEPS: Creating a Cube

Step 1. In Artwork mode, draw a square (use the rectangle tool to draw while pressing Shift to constrain the width to the height).

Step 2. Option-copy the square above the original square by clicking on the lower, left corner and dragging upwards with both the Shift and Option keys pressed. When the arrow pointer is hollow, the copy is positioned directly above the original square. Release the mouse button, then the Option and Shift keys.

Step 3. Select the Direct Selection tool, click on the top segment of the copied square, and drag down. Press the Shift key while you drag to constrain the movement of the line to vertical movement only.

Step 4. With the Direct Selection tool, click on the top line again and drag it to the right slightly.

You can perform Steps 3 and 4 at one time by dragging the topmost segment and not pressing Shift.

Step 5. Option-copy the original square to the right of it. Use the technique in Step 2 to ensure that the copy is flush against the right edge of the original.

Step 6. Use the Direct Selection tool to Shift-drag the rightmost line segment of the second duplicate to the right until it is even with the rightmost point of the top copy.

Draw a vertical guide at the rightmost point of the top square to ensure that the point lines up with the right edge of the second copy.

Step 7. Select the Shear tool and set the origin at the lower-left corner of the second copy. Click the upper-right point of the second copy and Shift-drag up until the cursor becomes hollow.

Step 8. Apply different gradients to each side to make the finished cube look three dimensional. In the example in Figure 21-29, I used the standard black-and-white gradients and dragged different angles and starting and ending spots for each side to achieve the effect I wanted.

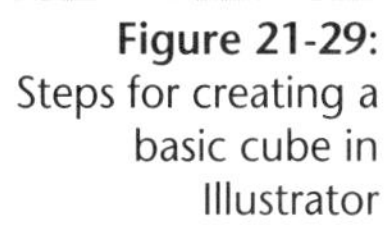

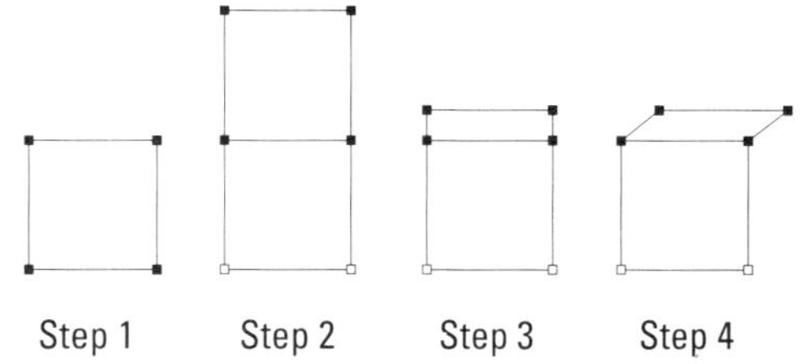

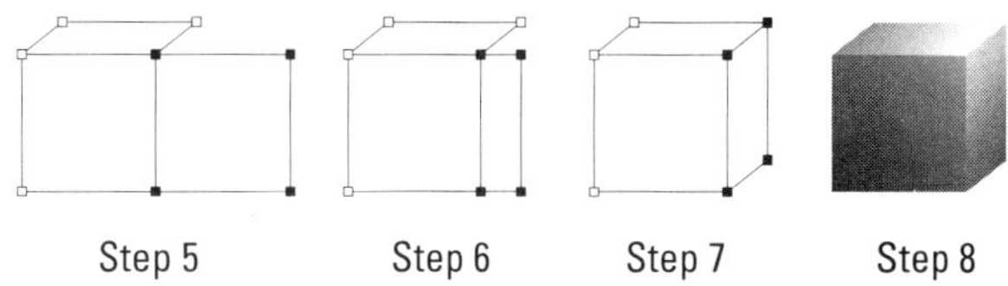

Figure 21-29: Steps for creating a basic cube in Illustrator

STEPS: Creating a Basic Metal Tube

Step 1. Draw an oval that will be the top of the cylinder. The oval should be flat and wide.

Step 2. Draw a rectangle by clicking with the Rectangle tool on the leftmost point of the oval and dragging right and down. Make the rectangle the exact width of the oval.

Step 3. Lock the rectangle and click on the leftmost point of the oval. Press Shift and Option-copy down until the cursor turns hollow. Release the mouse button and the Option and Shift keys.

Step 4. Unlock the rectangle. Select both the rectangle and the bottom oval and choose Filter⇨Pathfinder⇨Unite. Fill the new object with the Steel Bar gradient.

Step 5. Select the top oval and choose Arrange⇨Bring to Front (⌘-equal sign).

Step 6. Fill the oval with the Steel Bar gradient, but change the angle of the gradient to 180° in the text box below the list of gradients.

Step 7. Double-click on the Steel Bar gradient to open the Gradient palette. Click the Duplicate button and name the gradient **Inside Tube**. Change the white triangle on the Gradient slider to about 25% black and change the black triangles on the slider to 80% black.

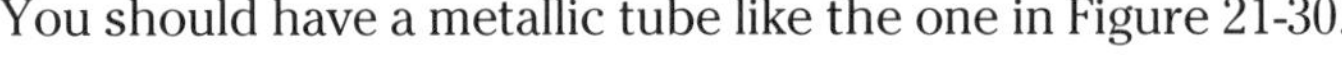

You should have a metallic tube like the one in Figure 21-30.

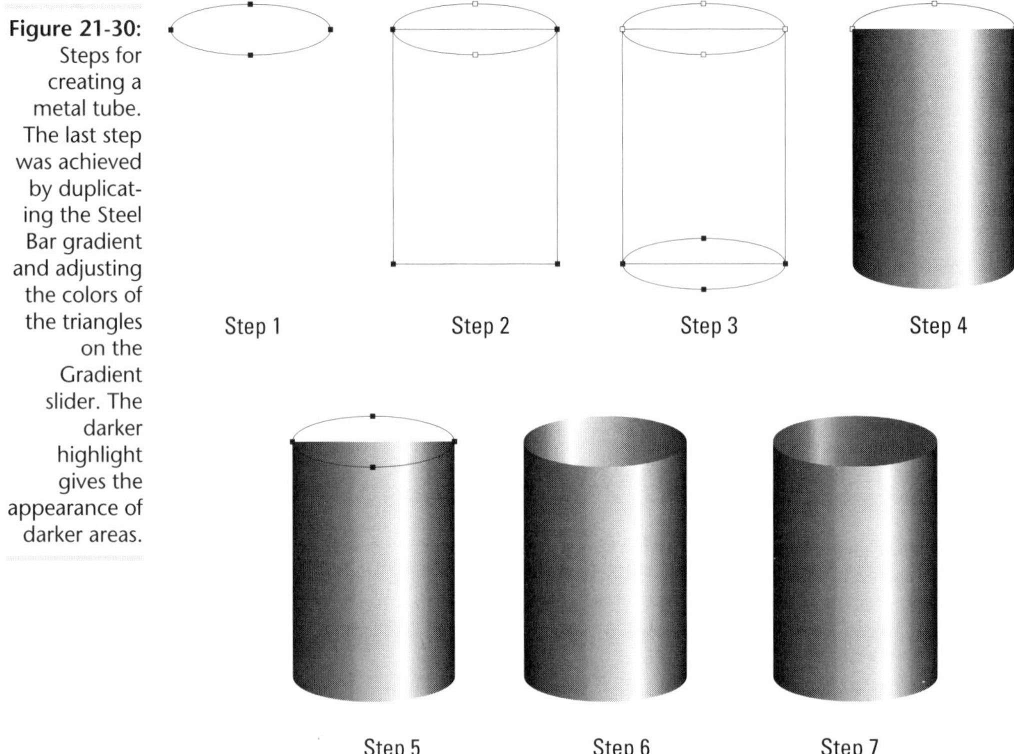

Figure 21-30: Steps for creating a metal tube. The last step was achieved by duplicating the Steel Bar gradient and adjusting the colors of the triangles on the Gradient slider. The darker highlight gives the appearance of darker areas.

Using Gradients to Make Bumps and Dents

When you place gradients on themselves and one gradient has a different direction than another, three-dimensional effects appear. If you remember that highlights reflect off surfaces that bounce light to your eye, that principal should help you determine the direction of the gradients.

Of course, whether an object is coming at you or going away from you should be obvious, shouldn't it? Figure 21-31 shows six different buttons. See whether you can determine which buttons are "innies" and which buttons are "outies." To assist you further, each button is on a standard background and has a button ring. The ring makes the direction of several of the buttons quite obvious. The answers are at the end of the chapter, after the Summary.

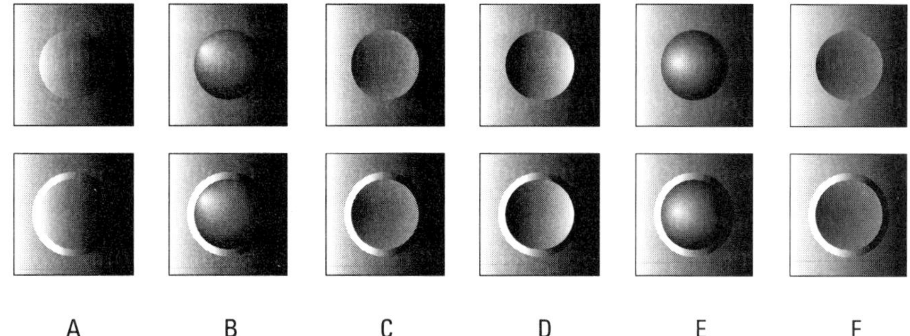

Figure 21-31: Different in and out buttons created with black-and-white gradients, both linear and radial

Combining Dimensions Artwork with Illustrator

You can achieve the best three-dimensional effects by combining 3-D artwork that you create in Dimensions with 2-D artwork in Illustrator. Artwork that you create in Dimensions can look kind of flat because of the lack of texture maps in the software (3-D images that wrap around other 3-D images, like craters on the moon), so after you create something in Dimensions, take it into Illustrator and try to liven it up.

Dimensions is not a standalone product. Without Illustrator, Dimensions is just a fun toy. With Illustrator, the results can be stunning.

Figure 21-32 shows artwork that I created in Illustrator (the words *GILA MONSTERS*), took into Dimensions, extruded, viewed at an extreme perspective (135°), and shade-rendered. I then exported the artwork to Illustrator where I added the little gila monster. I created the word *ARIZONA* as type on a circle and placed it into position. After seeing that the flat letters looked out of place, I took the letters into Dimensions, extruded them with a bevel, and exported them back into Illustrator. Little finishing touches were made to the artwork, and then it was color separated and printed. What part took the longest? Waiting for a shaded render in Dimensions.

Perspective Drawing

John-boy: Is there a way to easily give drawings perspective without Dimensions?

Toulouse: No... The best thing to do is to set up a perspective grid.

John-boy: That sounds like a lot of work.

Toulouse: Just create a grid, select the top points in the grid, and average them. Instant perspective grid.

John-boy: That's too easy. Thanks. And good-night.

Toulouse: However tempting, I'm not going to say it...

Figure 21-32: Illustrator and Dimensions were used to produce the GILA MONSTERS logo.

Summary

- Adobe Dimensions is a unique, three-dimensional rendering software because it outputs editable PostScript outlines.
- Dimensions is power hungry and RAM hungry. Use a 68040 or higher processor.
- In addition to height and width, Dimensions also deals with depth.
- You can create Primitive shapes (cubes, spheres, cones, and cylinders) within the Dimensions 3-D window.
- Not only can you color the Fills and Strokes of objects in Dimensions, but you also can specify the shade color and the amount of light reflectance.
- Use the Lighting palette (choose Appearance⇨Lighting or press ⌘-Shift-L) to add an unlimited number of infinite light sources.

- You can extrude or revolve two-dimensional objects to create three-dimensional objects.
- You can create two-dimensional artwork inside Dimensions' little Illustrator-like program, the 2-D window. You can give extruded 2-D artwork bevels to enhance the corners of the objects.
- To move objects along the *Z* axis (or the depth axis at different views), you use the Z-Translation selection tool.
- To scale objects in all three dimensions, use the Scale tool or the Scale palette (choose Operations⇨Scale or press ⌘-Option-S). You can rotate objects in all three dimensions by using the Rotation tool or the Rotate palette (choose Operations⇨Rotate or press ⌘-Option-R).
- From the keyboard, you can access all thirteen positions from which you can view artwork. Changing perspective draws you closer to or farther from the objects in the Dimensions 3-D window, distorting them as you get nearer.
- You map two-dimensional artwork onto the surface of three-dimensional artwork by selecting a three-dimensional surface, choosing Operations⇨Map Artwork (⌘-Option-M), and placing artwork into the resulting Map window.
- With a little ingenuity and the help of a few friendly gradients, you can create three-dimensional looking objects in 2-D with Illustrator. Determining the light source can help you create accurate-looking and realistic three-dimensional artwork right in Illustrator.
- Using the Dimensions artwork in tandem with Illustrator provides greater flexibility and incredible results.

Answers to the Puzzle in Figure 21-31

A, out; B, out; C, in; D, in; E, out; and F, in. The light source is to the left, as established by both the ring and the background. Therefore, the buttons that are lighter on the left side are raised, and the buttons that are lighter on the right side are lowered.

Illuminating Illustrator Images

22 CHAPTER

In This Chapter

- Looking at how art pieces are designed and assembled
- Copyrighting artwork
- How the artwork in this book was created
- Techniques for creating backgrounds
- Discovering new techniques and practices

Along with using Illustrator to do all types of incredible artwork is the practical, real-world side of Illustrator, where deadlines have to be met and there's little or no time for "play." This chapter focuses on real-world applications of Illustrator, and how to get the most out of the software.

What You Can Learn from Existing Artwork

Examples are a wonderful teacher for Illustrator. In light of this, we've included several figures from the *Macworld Illustrator 6 Bible* on the accompanying CD-ROM, so when you see a figure, you'll know exactly how it was created. But just looking at art doesn't tell you too much except that maybe a blend was used where you thought a gradient would be, and hey, that isn't pattern, it's really individual paths.

You can learn how to create better artwork by dissecting existing artwork and trying to modify it.

Taking Apart Artwork

Artwork created in Illustrator will usually consist of hundreds of paths. Some of those paths will be Filled, some will be Stroked, others may be Filled and Stroked.

The best way to get started is by looking at the illustration in Artwork mode. This shows the "framework" of the art, and is the best first step in understanding how it was created.

Unfortunately, Artwork mode doesn't show you when paths are perfectly overlapping. For that, you'll need to switch between Artwork and Preview modes, or even delve into Preview Selection mode.

Making Your Art Easy to Understand

Possibly the most frustrating thing about editing artwork occurs when there was a different author of the original work. People have their own way of doing things, and while one way isn't necessarily better than another, there are a few things you can do to make your artwork more editable in the future. After all, it may be you opening up your art in a few months or years, and you'll never remember what screwy grouping methods you used that might have made sense back then.

One thing that you can do that will make your art easier to interpret is to use common groupings. Blends should be joined to their end paths, and masks to the paths they masks. Text converted to outlines should be grouped together. The paths in objects should be grouped together. Related object can be grouped to each other.

But more important than grouping is to use layers. Proper use of layers quickly and easily will allow your artwork to be compartmentalized, allowing not only easy access for selecting and modifying sets of paths, but providing a means for controlling printing of the Illustration.

Copyrighting Your Electronic Artwork

This is the opposite of the previous section. Often, you'll have done artwork that you'd rather not have anyone mess with. Unfortunately, there's no foolproof way of doing this, but you can "put your stamp" on any illustration, and make it difficult for a would-be art-thief to abscond with your artwork.

The most basic way of doing this is to put a copyright notice on each object in the document, as shown in Figure 22-1.

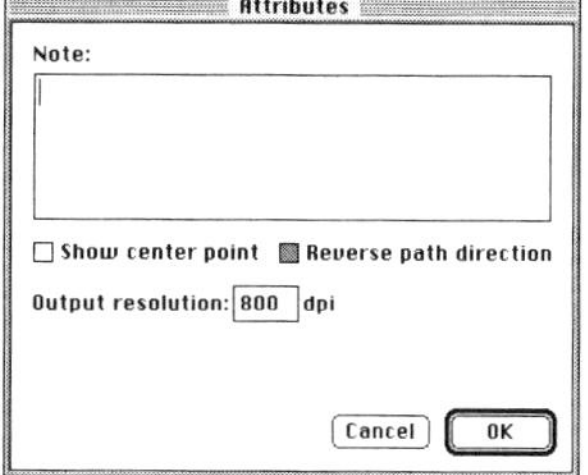

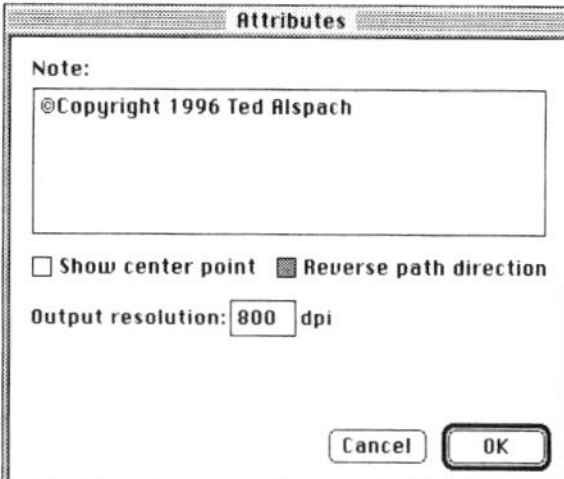

Step 1 Step 2 Step 3

Figure 22-1: Steps for putting copyrights in each piece of art in an illustration

STEPS: Quickly Copyrighting Your Artwork

Step 1. Select the artwork you wish to copyright.

Step 2. Choose Object⇨Attributes (⌘-Control-A), which will display the Object Attributes dialog box.

Step 3. Type in your copyright notice in the Notes section.

At this point, all the art in the document will have this "note" attached.

To make the art more secure, create a white box somewhere outside of the Illustration (which can't be selected or deleted easily). You can also lock your artwork. Another thing to do is to create a text box with your copyright notice in it and change the text color to None.

You could also use layers to secure copyrighted pieces of art by locking or hiding layers with objects that have the copyright in them.

The Art in the Macworld Illustrator Bible

The art in this book was done entirely with Illustrator and Photoshop. The only thing we used Photoshop for was for quickly touching up screen shots. The following sections describe how particular figure types were created.

File Types

Because this book was written before most people had Illustrator 6.0, I decided early on to keep the file types for the figures in Illustrator 5. Each of the figures was saved as EPS, with an 8-bit preview, so they could be placed into the layout application.

Screen shots that stood alone were saved as grayscale PICTs. Sreenshots and "images" that needed to appear with labels were saved as EPS so Illustrator 5 could import them.

The naming scheme for the files is structured *Book ChapterNumber-FigureNumber Description.FileType*, where the *Book* is an indicator based on the ISDN number (4948), *ChapterNumber-FigureNumber* is the four-digit number consisting of the chapter and number of the figure, *Description* is as accurate a description of the file as I could get in a few characters, and *FileType* was the format (PICT or AI5). So the file name for Figure 17-1, which shows how to turn artwork of a clock into pixels, would be "4948 17-01 Clock to raster.ai5".

Paths

One distinction you'll find in the *Macworld Illustrator 6 Bible* that you won't find in any other Illustrator book is the way I've shown paths in the figures. The easy thing to do would be do take screen shots of paths and just use those. Unfortunately, while paths look fine on sreen, they look absolutely hideous on the printed page. So I recreated each path for the "artwork" views needed in figures, especially those at the front of the book.

Each path is a .3 Stroked black path; each selected Anchor Point is a 2 point-×-2 point black square with a .3 black Stroke (unselected Anchor Points have a White Fill); and each Control Handle is a 2 point-×-2 point black circle, with no Stroke. This made the printed paths look the way they do on-screen, but without the jaggies.

STEPS: Drawing Illustrator Paths and Points with Illustrator

Step 1. First draw the path in Illustrator that you want to appear as a path. Change the Stroke to .3-point Black.

Step 2. To draw the first point, create one 2-point-×-2 point square, Filled with Black, and Stroked with .3-point Black.

Step 3. Zoom in to 1600%, and switch to Artwork mode. Drag the center of the square over a point on the path.

Step 4. Option-copy the Anchor Point until all the points are properly on the path.

Step 5. Change any Anchor Points to "unselected" Anchor Points by selecting them and Filling them with White.

Step 6. To show Control Handles, first draw a 2-point-×-2 point circle, and change the Fill to Black and the Stroke to None.

Step 7. Position the Control Handles over the handles of the original path.

Step 8. Draw lines from the Control Handles to their corresponding Anchor Points.

Of course, for most of our examples (Steps), I had to Option-copy the objects to the next position and then continue. I often used the Move dialog box to accurately control spacing between steps.

Labeled Palettes

To label items within palettes (like the one shown in Figure 22-2), toolboxes, and dialog boxes, I placed an EPS image and positioned it on the page. Then I drew one line from the area I wanted to label out of the image, painting the line with a .3 Black Stroke and a Fill of None. I created a label with Point Type, usually using 10-point Futura Book.

After centering or positioning the type correctly, I Option-Copied both the label and the the line, placing the end of the line at the new location on the image. Then I selected the type and the other end of the path with the Direct Selection tool, and positioned it accordingly. I repeated that process for each of the labels in a figure.

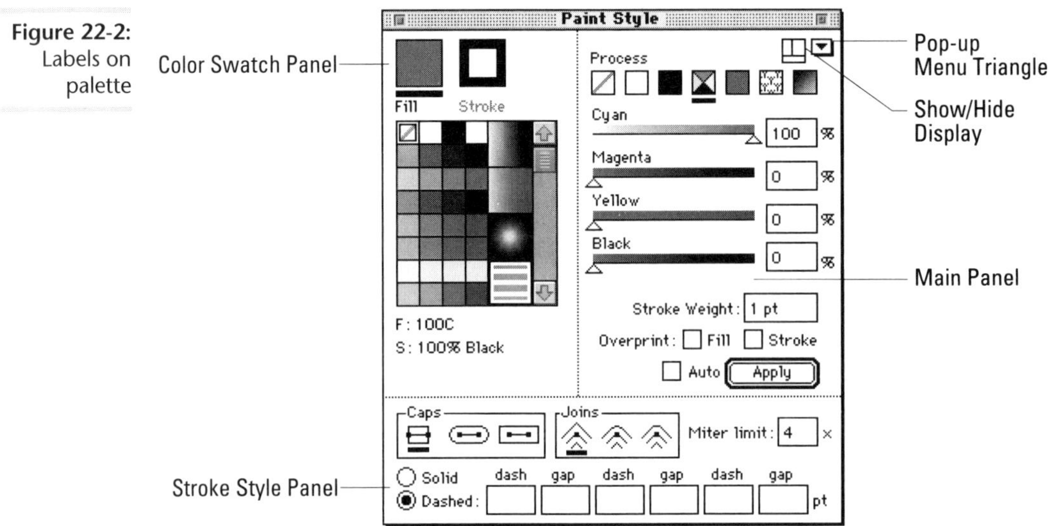

Figure 22-2: Labels on palette

Color Section Artwork

The artwork in the color section is Illustrator-based (with the exception of the color plate showing rasterization). To generate the backgrounds, I would often select a portion of the original artwork and scale it up, and then lighten it with KPT ColorTweak.

Where the background had to be lighter or darker for text, I copied the entire background, placed a path a little larger than the text area on top and masked it, and then lightened or darkened that portion with KPT ColorTweak again.

Using Art as Outlines for a Transparency

Use the following steps to create the outlines of the artwork for a transparency. (These steps are similar to the procedure I would use to show the "Artwork" mode of an Illustration.)

STEPS: Changing Full-Color Art into Outlines

Step 1. Change the Paint Style of the original artwork to a Fill of White and a Stroke of .25 points 100% Black.

Step 2. Release all the masks in the artwork by choosing Edit⇨Select All (⌘-A) and then choosing Object⇨Mask⇨Release. Check to see whether all the masks were released by choosing Object⇨Mask. If Release is still an option, not all the masks have been released. Click Release until the Release option is no longer available.

Step 3. Delete all blend-generated paths by using the Group Selection tool. Click any blend-generated path twice to select all the paths generated by the blend. Repeat this process for each blend.

Step 4. Make any necessary adjustments. After checking the original to determine the weight of the Strokes, change the outline of those paths to that weight and then choose Filter⇨Object⇨Outline Stroked Paths.

If an illustration includes a photograph or imagery created in Photoshop, you'll need to posterize it and outline it in Streamline to produce the outlining you need for a transparency. See Chapter 21 for more information on Streamline.

Scanning Artwork at the Proper Resolution

By scanning at a high resolution and saving at a lower resolution without changing the file size, you produce an image that you can reduce in Illustrator to much smaller than its blown-up size. You can then use this image for zooming in to high levels of magnification without sacrificing clarity.

The Proper Image Size for Tracing

To produce the best possible image to trace in Illustrator, you have to save the file at the correct size and number of dots per inch (dpi). As a result, you need to know the original image's size and at what resolution (dpi) it was scanned.

To figure out what dpi to scan at, you first need to decide how much detail you want to be able to see in Illustrator. By *detail*, I am referring to the level at which you want to zoom in and still be able to see the scan clearly. Table 22-1 shows the zoom level as a percentage and the required dpi for scanning to achieve detail at that zoom level. The table also shows how much you need to reduce the image with the Scale tool to return it to the original size.

If you will use the image at less than 100%, scanning at 72 dpi is still a good idea.

(continued)

(continued)

After you have scanned the image at the proper resolution, open it in Photoshop and select Image⇨Image Size. In the Image Size dialog box, make sure that the File Size and Proportions check boxes are checked. Use a setting of 72 in the dpi text field and press OK. Save the file as an EPS image with an 8-bit preview.

Even if the artwork is black and white, do not save it with a 1-bit preview because this setting will make the artwork appear terrible in Illustrator. Always use an 8-bit preview.

In Illustrator, import or place the image and double-click the Scale tool. Enter the reduction amount from the third column of the list in the Uniform text field. You can now trace the image up to and including the zoom specified.

Keep in mind that the size of a pixel-based file may make an Illustrator file unmanageable. A 75MB image requires an enormous amount of time for redrawing and also uses a healthy chunk of the hard drive.

Table 22-1
Zoom Level Percentages and the DPI for Scanning That's Required to Achieve Detail at a Specified Zoom Level

Zoom	*Scan dpi*	*Scale image*	*Size (3" x 5" CMYK Color)*
100%	72 dpi	100%	.30MB
150%	108 dpi	66.67%	.68MB
200%	144 dpi	50%	1.19MB
300%	216 dpi	33.33%	2.67MB
400%	288 dpi	25%	4.75MB
600%	432 dpi	16.67%	10.70MB
800%	576 dpi	12.5%	19.00MB
1200%	864 dpi	8.33%	42.70MB
1600%	1152 dpi	6.25%	75.90MB

Backgrounds for Illustrations

This section contains examples of backgrounds (see Figure 22-3) and suggestions for creating backgrounds for illustrations. You can create backgrounds in a number of ways. For example, you can use gradients, EPS images, blends, and patterns. When you are deciding what type of background to use, remember that you need to consider how well a background will interact with the front artwork.

Figure 22-3: Different backgrounds created in Illustrator

Using Gradients for Backgrounds

Gradients can be very effective backgrounds all by themselves, providing that they don't detract from the front artwork.

In the following example, I combined linear and radial gradients for an impressive effect.

STEPS: Using Gradients to Create a Sunset

Step 1. Draw a rectangle to serve as the background area. Create a bottom edge (I used mountains) that will sit in front of the background. For sunsets and other sky-related backgrounds, try to avoid a flat, horizontal base. Color the mountains or bottom edge with a solid Fill color and then select the background for the rectangle.

You create the gradient after you create the object that it will Fill so that you can instantly see how the gradient will appear in that object in the illustration.

Step 2. Double-click the Gradient Vector tool to display the Gradient palette. Click the New button and call the gradient "Sunset." In the Paint Style palette, replace the Fill of the rectangle with the Sunset gradient and change the angle of the gradient to 90° .

Step 3. In the Gradient palette, make the following color stops: at 0%, White; at 5%, Yellow 100%; at 15%, Yellow 100%; at 25%, Yellow 100% and Magenta 50%; at 35%, Magenta 50%; at 50%, Cyan 15% and Magenta 10%; at 80%, Cyan 25%; and at 100%, Cyan 50%.

The first two 100%-yellow color stops create a solid area of yellow within the gradient.

Step 4. Draw a circle in the solid yellow area of the gradient. In the Gradient palette, create a new radial gradient called "Sunset Sun" and create the following color stops: at 0%, White; at 5%, Yellow 30%; at 80%, Yellow 60%; at 100%, Yellow 100%. Because the sun blends into the color of the solid band in the sunset gradient, it appears to blend very nicely. In the example, I partially hid the sun behind some of the clouds.

Using the same technique, I created the sun for a blue sky. In the sun gradient, the last color stop is the same color as the sky.

By themselves, gradients can be effective backgrounds. When you combine gradients with patterns, blends, or other objects, they can form a complex, sometimes realistic, backdrop.

Using Blends and Blend Effects for Backgrounds

You can use a number of different methods to create backgrounds by using blends:

- One method is to blend two shapes together, one larger and one smaller. You can achieve different effects by choosing different shapes.
- By blending from a large circle to a small circle, you can create a very smooth blend that produces better results than using a radial gradient.
- One of the best ways to get a smooth, unobtrusive background when you are using gradients is to blend smoothly curved lines together and mask them in the shape of the background rectangle.
- You can achieve interesting highlights between two blend shapes by blending to different points on objects.

Using Textures for Backgrounds

There are a variety of ways to create textures in Illustrator, and with Version 6, the Pen and Ink command is undoubtedly the most efficient and productive method. With the Pen and Ink Fill dialog box, you can quickly change a solid or gradient-Filled background into a textured background.

STEPS: Creating a Textured Background from a Basic Gradient Fill

Step 1. Create the background object (typically a rectangle, though you can use any shape) with a gradient Fill. Make sure this object is behind all the other objects.

BY THE WAY: When using the Pen and Ink Fill command to create textures, I usually lock all other objects in the document, and place the background object on a separate layer. This keeps the typically hundreds or thousands of paths that are generated separate from the rest of the illustration.

Step 2. Select the background object and choose Object⇨Pen and Ink Fill. In the dialog box, change the hatch color to Selection, which will make the texture the same shades as the gradient. Adjust any of the other settings in the Ink Pen dialog box.

Step 3. Click OK. The texture is generated.

If the background is only showing around the edges of your artwork, or takes up less than 50% of the total background area, you might want to ungroup the Fill created with Pen and Ink and select and delete the objects that aren't visible. This is much easier if the other objects are locked away on a separate layer.

Another useful texture can be created by modifying a blend somewhat, so that it appears to be "textured." With this method of creating a background, you *can't* delete unseen portions of the artwork.

The following steps show one common method of texturizing a blend.

STEPS: Texturizing a Blend

Step 1. Create a blend, either manually or by using the Expand command on an existing gradient-Filled object.

Step 2. Select the Blend steps (you might want to choose View⇨Hide Edges so the mass of selected paths doesn't obscure your view) and choose Filter⇨ Distort⇨Roughen.

Discovering New "Features" on Your Own

This book contains many really neat tips and techniques. I discovered most of them by doing some really hard "playing" with Illustrator.

If you are excited and enthusiastic about Illustrator, you will undoubtedly discover things that I didn't include in this book because of a lack of space or a lack of time — or most likely, because I didn't know anything about them.

I have stuffed within these pages all of the best things about Illustrator that other graphic artists who contributed to this book and I could come up with, but I know that in the short time between writing the chapters and having the book appear on bookshelves, I will discover many more things that I could have included.

Illustrator is one of the, if not *the,* most versatile software packages around. There are limits to what you can do with it, but those limits are being pushed further and further each time an upgrade appears and every time computer systems become more powerful, faster, and cheaper. New technologies will continue to enhance Illustrator's capabilities, but the core of the product will always be the same.

Finding "New Features"

My observation in the area of finding "new" things that Illustrator can do is that any time I say to myself, "Golly! This sure does take a long time to do!" there is probably a shorter way to do it that I haven't figured out yet.

Very rarely do I exclaim "Golly!" but when I do, I take note. Others hearing this outburst take note as well, and yes, they have recommended counseling.

Like everyone else, I can't just sit and play with Illustrator all day in order to come up with techniques and tips that no one else has yet discovered. But when I do use Illustrator, I make the best use of my time, and I try to use key commands for everything. If I have to pull down a menu because I don't know a key command, it is a sad day in my life.

As I am using Illustrator, I try different ways of doing ordinary things. For example, I often select almost everything in an illustration and lock it. The first method that I used for this procedure was to select everything by choosing All, which selected all the objects in the Illustration. I then deselected particular objects by Shift-clicking them and chose Arrange⇨Lock (⌘-1). This method wasn't too productive because I usually had the other items selected (the ones that I didn't want locked), and I had to deselect all of them before I could lock the others.

The second method that I tried was a little better, but I knew that somehow there had to be a better way. Because all the things that I didn't want locked were selected, I chose View⇨Fit In Window (⌘-M), pressed the Shift key, and dragged a marquee around everything. This action selected all the unselected objects and deselected all the selected objects. I then locked the selected objects.

The third method was the best up to that time. Because everything that I wanted to select and lock wasn't selected, I chose Filter⇨Select Inverse, which selected everything that wasn't selected and deselected the selected objects. That way I didn't have to select the other objects with the mouse, which always slows me down. Then I locked the selected objects.

Have you noticed that these paragraphs are getting shorter? The method I now use is almost too easy. The objects that I want locked are the only things not selected, so I press Option and choose Arrange⇨Lock (⌘-Option-1), which locks everything that isn't selected.

Back when I was Shift-clicking, if I had known that ⌘-Option-1 locked everything that wasn't selected, I could have avoided a great deal of wasted time and frustration. But because I tried to do this operation so many different ways, I *know* that command, and I use it more than ever.

Knowing Versus Memorizing

If you memorize all the key commands in this book and then take the time to memorize all the tips and techniques listed in these pages, you will still not be able to use Illustrator as well as the pros.

To get the most out of Illustrator, you need to use the software until the commands and techniques become intuitive. Memorizing the menus may help you find menu items faster, but knowing what each menu item does in depth will score that information into your subconscious and enable you to use Illustrator better than otherwise possible.

Very few people in the graphic arts industry know Illustrator inside and out; yet the ones who do are producing the best-quality illustrations. What does it take to know Illustrator? If you can see in your mind how to create an entire illustration, step by step, you know the software. On the other hand, if you make a mistake in real life and type a mental ⌘-Z, it's time for therapy.

What You Can Do to Learn More

Read this book inside and out and think to yourself, "Gee, I can do that better *and* faster," and sit down and figure it out. Strangely enough, the first time you discover that you can do something faster than before, doing it will take twice as long as it used to take.

Look at the last set of steps in Chapter 21 and figure out how you can reduce the number of steps from 21 to 10. Before I came up with the printed version of the steps for creating a rounded rectangle with reversed corners, I must have thought of five other ways to create it. The method that appears in this book is the fastest, most accurate way to do it. Now if only I could come up with a better, tighter *name* for the darned things.

If you have to Option-copy (duplicate a selected object, drag with the Option key, and then release the mouse button before the Option key) a hundred things, decide whether it would be better to choose Arrange⇨Repeat Transform (⌘-D) 99 times or to select all the objects 10 times, Option-copy *them,* and select Repeat Transform only eight more times. Which method is faster for your job? Why?

Is it better to create an object and change the Paint Style information after it is selected or to deselect all (⌘-Shift-A), change the Paint Style, and then create an object? Or maybe an object on the page already exists, so you can create the object and use the Eyedropper and/or Paint Bucket tools to copy the color from one to the other. Or, if an object with that color exists, you can select the object, which will change the Paint Style to that color, and then create the new object.

If you think about all these things as you are drawing, your illustration time will decrease, the quality of your drawings will increase, and you will have more time for using Illustrator to design a solar-powered hang glider, or whatever you do when you aren't using Illustrator for real work.

Getting Answers and Information from Adobe

When you can't find an answer to a problem or want to know whether a way exists to do some tedious task faster, call the Adobe Tech Support line.

The main problem with most software company support these days is the "not our fault" answer. (Whatever problem or question you have, it isn't the software company's fault.) You don't find this attitude at Adobe. Most of the support staff are polite, and they will help even the most befuddled user along, as well as give additional tips and techniques. The main problem with Adobe Tech Support is the difficulty in reaching a human being. When you call, you get routed through a series of questions ("If you are having trouble designing a hang glider with Adobe Illustrator, press 465") that hardly ever seem to pertain to your particular problem. After a grueling mechanical question-and-answer session, you are put on hold while some tech people argue about who has to answer the call (and other tech people place bets on how long it will be before you hang up). Actually, I'm kidding about the tech support staff's behavior while you are on hold, and I'm sure they jump from one call to the next without pausing to catch a breath. Adobe now has a special support line that you pay a premium for, where the tech people are the first to answer, and most of them pick up within the first movement of the classical music you're forced to listen to.

If you don't need an answer right away, you can fax Adobe. You should get a response within one business day, by either phone or return fax. Faxing is great because you can send along your illustration so the tech people can actually look at it.

In addition, Adobe has a free Bulletin Board Service (BBS) running at 14.4 that anyone can call. Adobe tech people regularly answer posted questions, and you can send your Illustrator file along with your questions.

Summary

- Taking apart existing artwork is one of the best ways to learn how to create that type of artwork.
- In order to make your art usable and modifiable in the future, create it logically and orderly; use layers when possible.
- Use gradients, textures, blends and lightened artwork for quick, effective backgrounds.
- Focus on "knowing" Illustrator rather than memorizing commands and shortcuts.
- Talk to other Illustrator users to learn different techniques and to help solve technical snafus.

Trouble-shooting Illustrator Problems

23 CHAPTER

In This Chapter

- Solutions to common Illustrator problems
- Learning what error messages mean and how to avoid them

If you have questions about Illustrator, chances are that other users have been asking those same questions. I've compiled this chapter by talking to many Illustrator users and Adobe's Technical Support Department.

Is it possible to create a gradient Fill that goes from a process tint to transparent, rather than to white?

No, because the "in between" steps can never be partially transparent. But with some careful overprint manipulating you could simulate transparency for separations.

I tried selecting a Filled object, then choosing Filter⇨Select⇨Same fill color. Nothing happens. Why?

If you have Illustrator 5.5, you'll need the updated Select filters available on the *Macworld Illustrator 6 Bible CD-ROM*. The Select filters have been fixed for version 6.0.

I'm trying to blend text, but I keep getting error messages.

Change your type to outlines before applying the filter.

Why should I use TIFFs instead of EPSs?

- TIFF files take up less space on your hard disk.
- TIFF grayscale images print noticeably faster than EPS grayscale images.
- Every piece of scanning software in the world supports TIFFs.

Then again, there are some serious disadvantages:

- TIFFs can't be placed in Illustrator (which I consider a TIFF liability, not an Illustrator liability, and the primary reason I seldom use TIFFs).
- TIFFs rotated other than the standard 45 degrees can takes weeks, even months, to print.
- TIFFs redraw much slower than EPS bitmaps when placed in page layout or FreeHand software.

There are more letters in "TIFF" than "EPS" making TIFF discussions take up more space in magazines, books, and manuals, significantly reducing the size of rainforests due to the additional paper needed. Okay, maybe that's just a wee bit of an exaggeration....

Whatever happened to Illustrator 5.5.1? I never got the upgrade.

Illustrator 5.5.1 was never announced or shipped. Instead, Adobe concentrated on sending out Version 6.0 as fast as their little engineers could create it.

Is it possible to open a PageMaker file in Illustrator?

Yes, print the PageMaker file to an Acrobat file via Adobe Acrobat. Illustrator can open Acrobat files. Or just save it as EPS and open it. Don't forget about Nessie (the built-in Level 1 PostScript interpreter in Illustrator 6).

I keep getting the message "Can't open the hyphenation file 'US English Hyphenation.' Text will not be hyphenated."

Choose File⇨Preferences⇨Plug-Ins, and reselect the Plug-Ins folder in your Illustrator folder.

Is there a way to add a custom arrowhead to the Add Arrowhead filter?

Yes. follow these steps:

STEPS: Adding an Arrowhead to the Add Arrowheads Box

Step 1. Create the artwork you wish to use as an arrowhead in Illustrator.

Step 2. Copy the artwork.

Step 3. Open the Add Arrowhead filter in ResEdit or Resourcer.

Step 4. Paste the artwork.

Step 5. Number the arrowhead by adding 3 to the last arrowhead (the last standard arrowhead is ID 17078).

Step 6. Save and relaunch Illustrator. The arrowhead will appear as a black box in the Filter dialog box (you can change this in ResEdit if you have the time and the inclination).

Can you view "invisibles" in Illustrator?

No. I use the following technique: Press ⌘-A, ⌘-C, then go to Word and press ⌘-V, ⌘-8. This shows me spaces, tabs, soft returns, and more.

Why is tolerance limited to 10?

The number in Tolerance isn't really a "limit," considering the number is an arbitrary number. The engineers who created Illustrator could have incorporated a slider from "Nothing" to "Maximum" tolerance, and there would be no difference.

Is there a limit on the number of points on a path? Will too many points cause printing problems?

There's no real limit per se. The number of Anchor Points on a path has nothing to do with the number of "points" interpreted by a PostScript interpreter. What the number of points means when printing is this: curves are converted to lots of little straight line segments at an interpreter level. Long continuous paths use the Curve to command in

PostScript and are converted down to line-to path segments. Each line-to is two "PostScript points." It takes a lot more PostScript points (line-tos) to draw a smooth curve at hi-resolution (imagesetter) than lo-resolution (laser printer). This is why the file will print on your laser printer and not your imagesetter.

To prevent overly long or complex paths: First, change the output resolution to match the dpi of the imagesetter. Second, select the Split Paths option in Document Setup (you may want to do this on a copy of the original document, especially if you'll have to edit it later).

Streamline counts points, but Illustrator doesn't. You *can* count paths by selecting the Document Info filter from the Filter⇨Other submenu, however.

Why does type converted to outlines look so heavy?

Primarily due to type "hinting," which is present in PostScript type at small type sizes. Also, type usually has a preset bitmapped version at small point sizes that looks thinner than outlines, where the pixels are generated on-the-fly.

I can't arc type. Is there a way to do this?

The best thing to do is to pick up a copy of KPT Vector Effects. The Warp Frame filter in the set is perfect for that sort of reshaping.

I don't have an FPU, and I want to use Illustrator. What problems will I face?

Some of the filters run a bit slower without an FPU; however, everything will pretty much work the same.

Drag-and-drop into Photoshop 3 doesn't work.

You need Photoshop 3.0.4 or later to use drag-and-drop.

I can't trace any of my placed images.

The only type of images that can be placed are PICTs and Paint images, which need to be opened, not imported.

Why is it when I try to export files with Pantone gradients into Quark for separations, they convert to process?

Make sure you don't convert the gradients to blends (saving as Illustrator 3 will do this). You also need to add the Pantone colors you are going to print out of Quark to its color list (see Quark's documentation). QuarkXPress 3.2 or later tries to do this automatically.

I get the message "Can't save preview but all other information was saved successfully" when I save images that have large dimensions.

EPS files need to have a certain size preview, and this preview gets built when you save an EPS file. If you are running low on memory, the preview might not be able to be created. Allocate more memory to Illustrator, or reduce the number of undos.

What is Adobe's technical support number?

(206) 628-3953.

Why doesn't Illustrator always save colors I've created with the document they were created in?

Illustrator will save only those colors that have been used in an object in the document or originally created in that document. The same is true for gradients and patterns.

Sometimes my gradients drop out when printing on a QMS printer.

QMS uses a PostScript clone instead of real Adobe PostScript. Change the PostScript option in the Print dialog box to Level 1.

What's a good way to get complex illustrations to print faster?

Select all the paths and give them a high "flatness" setting by increasing the Output Resolution value in the Object Attributes dialog box. Actually, you want to decrease the number in the Output Resolution field . The Formula Printer resolution (2540) divided by the Output Resolution number (800) equals the flatness (3.175). Don't get this confused with Output Resolution in Document Set, which is for Split Long Paths. In that case, you want a higher number for more splitting.

How can I import my FreeHand documents into Illustrator?

In FreeHand, export to Illustrator 5.5 format.

How can I get certain Pantone colors to appear in every document I create?

Save the colors in the Adobe Illustrator Startup file (which is in your Plug-Ins folder). Simply open the existing Startup file, then open the file that contains the colors you want to add. Draw objects that you want to contain the new default colors. Then paint the new objects with these colors. When you're finished, resave the Startup file.

My measurement units don't stay the same. Why won't they just stay at inches?

It's easy to accidentally change measurement systems. Pressing ⌘-Control-U cycles to the next measurement unit.

When I open up certain documents, my measurement units change. Why?

I used to always change my measurements in General Preferences until 5.0. Then a weird thing happened. Situations like you described started to happen. At the time I was ruler-happy, so I noticed the changes as soon as the documents were opened.

The secret is that there are *two* areas where you can change the measurement system: General Preferences, which changes the way you currently see the document you're working with and all future documents that are created; and Document Setup, which changes the current document but keeps the settings in General Preferences what they were originally, so new documents aren't affected by changes you make in Document Setup.

What I do, since I work predominantly in picas and points, is to keep my measurement settings to Points/Picas in General Preferences, and change the settings (usually to inches — I haven't used millimeters in a long time) in Document Setup. That way, only that document is affected.

I used to use ⌘-Shift-I to change units to inches, but that doesn't work in 6.

Actually, it was changed as of version 5.5. The only way to use the keyboard to change measurement units is by pressing ⌘-Control-U.

I added color swatches to my Adobe Illustrator Startup file, but they don't appear in new documents.

Make sure the Adobe Illustrator Startup file is in the active Plug-Ins folder, or it won't work.

Not all of my Photoshop filters work in Illustrator.

Some of them may not if they don't follow Adobe's Plug-In guidelines completely. Ask the third-party filter manufacturer for an update.

How can I keep from running out of memory?

Lower the number of undos down to 1 or 2. If you're really desperate, take the number down to zero, which means you can't undo at all.

How can you color text differently from the box it is inside of?

Select the box with the Direct Selection tool, then change the Fill color. Select text with the text tool to change the color of just the text.

I can't select a path.

The path is either locked, or it is on a locked layer.

I just upgraded from Illustrator 4, and I can't find the grid!

The grid only appeared in version 4 (for PCs) of Illustrator. There is no grid in version 6.

What am I missing out on by not having QuickDraw GX installed on my Mac?

Nothing. Illustrator doesn't take advantage of QuickDraw GX.

I keep getting this error message:

```
Opened the artwork up to the following condition: The illustration
contains an illegal operand. Offending operator: 'TZ' Context:
195/radical 197/approxequal 198/Delta 214/divide/lozenge 240/
apple/_symbol_/Symbol 0 0  0 TZ
```

In earlier versions of Illustrator, this problem is caused by using special characters (such as Option+8) in a font alphabetically-below Symbol. There is nothing wrong with the file. It is a bug in Illustrator's reading mechanism. Here is how to fix the problem....

The bad line is "/_Symbol_/Symbol 0 0 0 TZ." To fix the file, open it in a text processor. Find the above line and add a "[" to the beginning of the line so it reads "[/_Symbol_/Symbol 0 0 0 TZ." Save the file (as text only), launch Illustrator, choose File⇨Open, locate the fixed Illustrator file, and open it. After you have the file open, apply a font alphabetically-above Symbol (such as Helvetica). Just apply it to a space or something. Now resave the file and it will be okay from that point on.

Note: This problem is fixed in Illustrator 6.

Several blank pages print when I print out of Illustrator.

If the Tiled Pages option is on, and a portion of the illustration extends onto any of the "other" pages, additional pages will print that include Control Handles.

I've had a problem that seems like a virus...It's a strange musical sound that happens occasionally when I use the Shift key.

Remove the Easy Access control panel from your Control Panels folder, and all will be quiet.

Sometimes when I zoom in, I zoom all the way to really close in. Other times, it's just in the preset increments. What gives?

The Zoom tool works two ways:

- Click once and the image zooms to the next increment (100 to 150, 1200 to 1600, etc.)
- Drag a marquee around the area you wish to zoom in to. This allows you to zoom in to a specific area quickly by surrounding it with a Zoom Marquee.

What's probably happening is that instead of clicking, you're drawing a teeny tiny little box and Illustrator, loyal drawing program that it is, is zooming to 1600% right at that spot. Try not to drag during clicking with the Zoom tool to prevent this.

It used to be in previous versions of Illustrator that if you saved a file as black and white, it printed in black and white, whether it was a composite or as a separate plate. Now, if you save as 1-bit, it prints out with screens to approximate the color. Why?

Never happened. That option *only* affects the preview and always has. It was useful for all those Plusses, SEs and Classics with black-and-white screens, and because it cut down on file size dramatically. If it *didn't* print in color, then you weren't linked to the file anymore, and just the preview printed.

I tried to open an Illustrator 5.5 document and got an error message saying the following:

```
Opened the artwork to the following error condition: The
illustration contains an incomplete or garbled object description.
Offending operator: 'Bg'
Context:
% 4 Gr GX
% 1 0 0 1 0 4 4312 4295 1 Gm
% 0 0 Gx 0 Gr GX
% 1 1 4 3 0 Gf
% Bd
% 2 () -4013 4715 1 0 1 0 0 1 0 0 Bg
```

Bg is "begin gradient."

Compare this line to a file that opens and modify it accordingly:

% 2 () -4013 4715 1 0 1 0 0 1 0 0 Bg

This won't happen in anything but version 5.

Why does my Illustrator program have the generic icon?

Rebuild your desktop and it will look normal again.

PART V

Appendixes

One of the best ways to begin using this book is to take a quick skim through the following appendixes. This is especially true if you have just upgraded your Illustrator software to version 6 — Appendix C lists the new features and changes in the latest version of Illustrator.

This part contains several appendixes with all sorts of juicy tidbits, including a thorough listing of the keyboard commands used in the software, many of which are undocumented anywhere else.

Using the CD-ROM

The CD-ROM that's included with this book is packed full of all sorts of surprises. The most important and useful of these surprises are the QuickTime tutorials, which demonstrate many of the techniques and tips in the book as well as others that we couldn't squeeze into the pages. The CD also includes most of the illustrations used in the book, clip art from selected companies that use Illustrator to create their clip art, and charts of Illustrator filters.

Tutorials

To run the tutorial program, you *must* have QuickTime 2.0 (included on the CD) or later installed on your computer. You should also have available as much RAM as you can spare.

The tutorial is designed for 13" and larger monitors. It may take a few minutes for the start-up screen to appear on slower machines. Be patient. If the playback seems jumpy, turn off any extensions besides QuickTime and any needed CD extensions, and make sure that no other programs are running. Move the cursor from the tutorial window to the brick background to prevent cursor flicker. Change the number of colors on your monitor to thousands or more to achieve the best results.

To run the tutorial program, double-click the MIB6 Tutorial folder that's located on the CD (double–click the CD icon on your desktop to see it). This folder contains several hours of tutorials. There are more than 100 different tutorials, which range from simple activities to complex projects. Simply select a topic from the menus at the top of the screen to begin.

If you are having trouble running the tutorial program, remove any unnecessary extensions and control panels from your System Folder and try again. Most popular extensions and control panels do not interfere with the operation of the software, but "Sammy's Wacky Finder Extension" may.

If you're still having trouble, view the movies with the enclosed QuickTime projector. You'll have to pick the movies one by one, but you shouldn't run into any trouble this way. If this still doesn't work for you, either (1) your system isn't powerful enough, or (2) there is an unknown conflict somewhere.

Artwork

Much of the artwork used in this book is included on the CD in Illustrator format.

You may *not* use the artwork or any portion of the artwork for anything except to study how it was created. It is supplied for educational purposes only.

Take a look at some of the more complex illustrations to see how "we professionals" created the artwork. I have always found this dissection of artwork extremely fascinating.

Look for areas where the artists "cheated" by overlapping with white boxes, by using Fills for Strokes and Strokes for Fills, and where objects are made up of several pieces when you expect only one. Take a close look at the stuff we masked (an awful lot). We do these things all the time, and you can learn from our cheating techniques.

Filter Charts

The filter charts (from Sandee Cohen) are provided for you to get a look at how filters affect paths in a document. The printed illustrations show only the results, not necessarily the makeup of the paths after filters have been applied. Like the illustrations in the book, these charts are to be used only for opening and looking at the illustrations on-screen.

Fonts

Also included on the CD-ROM are two PostScript Type 1 fonts: Lefty Casual and Ransom Note.

To use the fonts, select the screen font (the little suitcase) and the printer font (the little printer) for each typeface and drag it to your System Folder. Your Macintosh will ask you whether it is OK that these items get shuffled into the Font folder. Just nod like you understand and click the OK button.

Both Lefty Casual and Ransom Note were used in some of the illustrations that appear in the book.

Lefty Casual

Lefty Casual now sports three weights: Casual (the original), Bold (a little heavier), and Marker (what Casual would look like if written with a Sharpie marker). New characters have been added since the initial release of the font.

Lefty Casual was originally intended to fool people into thinking they were seeing real handwriting, while providing a consistency that allows the typeface to be quite legible. The original Lefty Casual is currently being used as the title typestyle for Pixar's Typestry software.

Ransom Note

Ransom Note consists of letters and words that appear to have been cut from a magazine and pasted down quickly.

Words that are hidden with the font (Option-letters) tend to follow a ransom note theme. All words can be accessed by typing an Option-letter or Shift-Option-letter combination. (The maker of Ransom Note assumes no responsibility for its contents being used in a real-life hostage or kidnapping situation.)

Demo Software & Filters

Various companies and individuals have contributed the Illustrator-related demos and filters that are located in the Demos & Filters folder on the CD.

Installing Illustrator

System Requirements

To run Adobe Illustrator 6 on a Macintosh, there are certain requirements you need to fulfill with your computer system. Of these, the CPU and RAM are the most important.

Macintosh Computer Requirements

The following is a list of the Macintosh computers you *can't* use to run the Illustrator 6. Don't attempt to load Adobe Illustrator 6 on any of the following systems:

- Macintosh 128 (the original Mac)
- Macintosh 512K or 512KE
- Macintosh Plus
- Macintosh SE
- Macintosh Portable
- Macintosh Classic
- Macintosh PowerBook 100

Fortunately, Illustrator can run on all of the Macs sold today, including all members of the following classes (or families):

- Macintosh II
- Macintosh LC
- Macintosh Performa

- Macintosh PowerBook, including Duos (except PowerBook 100)
- Macintosh Centris
- Macintosh Quadra
- Macintosh SE/30, Classic II, Color Classic
- All Power Macintoshes

The rule here is that your system must have a 68020 or greater processor or a PowerPC 6xx processor. The systems that don't make the cut are 68000-based.

RAM

Illustrator 6 needs a minimum of 3.1MB of memory to run efficiently. What this means is that your system should have *at the very least* 5MB of RAM total. The system software usually takes up between 1–2MB of RAM, and more for System 7.5 than 7.1.

A good way to check how much RAM you have available for Illustrator is to restart your system. After the desktop appears, go under the Apple in the upper-left corner and pull down either About This Macintosh (System 7) or About the Finder (System 6). The number in the Largest Unused Block box needs to be 3,100K or larger. If not, then you need to buy some RAM.

Other Attachments

You also need a hard drive with about 5MB of free space on it, a monitor (Black and White will work, though color is heavily recommended), a keyboard, and a mouse.

System Recommendations

If you have the minimum system that Adobe recommends, Illustrator will work — kind of. If you have armloads of patience and plenty to do between certain operations, this minimum setup may work for you.

CPU and FPU

Although a 68020 is fast compared to a 68000, it crawls compared to a 68040, and it stops compared to a PPC 601, 603, or 604. To do color work, investigate your options regarding a 68040 or better. Systems with 68040s include Centris, Quadra, LCIV, and some of the latest PowerBooks and Performas.

There is a catch, however. If you are using KPT Vector Effects or Adobe Dimensions, make sure that your computer has a math coprocessor (also called a floating point unit, or FPU). Dimensions will run, though slowly, without an FPU, while Vector Effects won't run at all. Most computers have an FPU, but some don't. Here is a list of systems with a 68020 or greater processor that do *not* have a math coprocessor:

- Macintosh IIsi (FPU comes on the NuBUS adapter card), IIvi
- Macintosh LC, LCII, LCIII (optional)
- Macintosh Classic II, Color Classic (optional)
- PowerBook 140, 145, 145B, 150, 160
- PowerBook Duo 200 series (available on Duo Dock)
- Performa 200, 400, 600 (optional), 405, 430, 450 (optional)
- Centris 610
- Quadra 605
- Quadra 610 (base 8/160 model; all others have it)

Power PC computers have FPU functions integrated into their chip. Illustrator, Vector Effects, and Dimensions understand this, and regard PPC systems as having an FPU.

A way to get around this limitation if your computer does *not* have an FPU is to get Software FPU (available on most online services and many FTP sites), a shareware utility that fools KPT Vector Effects into thinking that there *is* an FPU installed. Unfortunately, this utility only serves to slow down the FPU version of Dimensions.

Too Much RAM Is Never Enough

Through the Get Info box (in the Finder, select the Illustrator 6 icon and then choose File⇨Get Info or press ⌘-I), you can allocate as much RAM to Illustrator as you like. If you don't have much RAM available, Illustrator uses as much RAM as it can.

A good setting for the Preferred Memory size of RAM (on the Get Info box) is at least 10,000K. This is twice as much RAM as Adobe recommends, but this amount allows you to work with medium-sized documents at a pretty fast clip.

No matter how much RAM you add to your system and allocate to Illustrator, there will surely be times when you get various types of "Out of Memory" errors. One of the most common of these errors is the "Not enough memory for Undo/Redo" error, which occurs when the computer doesn't have enough memory to keep some of the oldest undos in your system. Because different operations take up different amounts of memory and more complex drawings take up more memory than simpler ones, the amount of RAM you need at any one time can vary.

Other areas that need lots of RAM are patterns (especially transparent ones), blends, multi-color gradients, complex masks, compound paths, and the use of some filters (Object Mosaic and Roughen are notorious for RAM usage).

If you are installing additional filter sets, a good rule of thumb is to allocate about 1MB of RAM for every additional third-party filter set.

Certain KPT Vector Effects filters will generate large numbers of additional paths, which can quickly use up the available RAM. The filters to watch out for are KPT 3D Transform, KPT ShadowLand, and KPT ShatterBox.

Installing Illustrator

If you have a CD-ROM player, be sure to request the CD-ROM-only version of the Illustrator 6 package. It's cheaper and you don't get anything with the floppy disks that you don't already get with the CD-ROM.

Remove all extensions but the ones needed to run your CD-ROM drive (use a start-up manager to facilitate this quickly).

Double-click the Install Me icon. Click the Easy Install button, and Illustrator will install itself in a matter of minutes. It's actually faster and easier to install Illustrator this way and then remove items you don't want than to go through and do a Custom Install of Illustrator.

Illustrator will install ATM into your System Folder, requiring you to restart after installation.

After restarting, run Illustrator and enter your serial number at the prompt.

What's New in Version 6

You'll be pleased to hear that Adobe has provided many new features in Version 6 as well as modified many of your favorite Version 5 features. So I've divided this appendix into two sections. The first section describes the differences between Version 5 features and Version 6 features. The second section discusses the new Illustrator 6 features. ("Version 5" refers to Illustrator 5.5 directly, as well as most of the features of Illustrator 5.0 and 5.0.1.) I've included chapter cross-references where appropriate (which are noted in parentheses).

Differences Between Version 5 and Version 6

Most of the differences between Version 5 and Version 6 reflect changes in the names of items, especially items that were called filters in Version 5 and now are called tools in Version 6. Most of the filters in Illustrator 6 now include Preview checkboxes, which enable you to see results immediately on-screen.

Menu Changes

Document Info is now located in the File menu.

Transform Each (Chapter 7) is located in the Arrange menu, which contains Scale Each, Move Each, and Rotate Each.

Find, Rows and Columns, Find Font, and **Change Case** have been moved from the Text Filter submenu into the Type menu.

Filter Changes

The **Twirl filter** (Chapter 14) has been changed to add Anchor Points as needed.

The old Mosaic filter has been renamed **Object Mosaic** (Chapter 13), but all of its functionality remains the same.

The **Punk and Bloat** filter (Chapter 14), which is now located in the Distort submenu of the Filter menu, combines the old Punk filter and Bloat filter.

The **Scribble and Tweak** filter (Chapter 14) combines the old Scribble filter and Tweak filter.

Tool Changes

The **Star tool** (Chapter 2) replaces the Star filter.

The **Spiral tool** (Chapter 2) replaces the Spiral filter.

The **Polygon tool** (Chapter 2) replaces the Polygon filter.

The **Eyedropper** now sucks colors from placed images, or pixels from a background application (including the Finder!).

Creating **New Layers** automatically chooses the next color in the Layers color list.

Palette Changes

The **Align palette** (Chapter 7) replaces the Align and Distribute filter, as well as the Distribute Horizontally and Distribute Vertically filters.

New Features in Version 6

The following sections briefly describe the new features in Version 6.

Palettes

The **Plug-In Tools palette,** which is accessed from the Window menu, contains the following tools:

- Star tool
- Spiral tool
- Polygon tool
- Twirl Tool
- Knife tool

The **Control palette,** which is accessed from the Window menu, provides an easy way to move, resize, and rotate selected objects.

Tools

Cleanup (Chapter 16) provides options for removing stray points and deleting both empty text paths and paths with no Paint Style attributes applied.

The **Twirl tool** has the same functionality as the Twirl filter in a draggable tool.

The **Knife tool** slices through all paths (selected or not) that fall under the blade.

Make Knife turns any selected path into a slicing path, using it to cut through all other paths that overlap it.

Separation Setup (Chapter 20), which is located under the File menu, adds color separation capabilities to Illustrator 6.

Expand, which is found in the Object menu, changes gradients to blends and patterns to paths quickly.

Rasterize, which is found in the Object menu, changes vector artwork (paths) to a pixel-based object.

Filters

The **Zig Zag** filter (Chapter 14) creates jagged and wavy paths from existing ones.

Photoshop-compatible filters now work within Illustrator documents. The object to be filterized must be a pixel-based object.

Ink Pen (Chapter 15), which is located in the Filter⇨Object submenu, provides advanced texture-making capabilities to Illustrator.

Path Patterns (Chapter 14), which is located in the Filter⇨Stylize submenu, is a way of placing patterns along paths and resizing and distorting patterns as needed.

Graphic Files

Illustrator now supports most **Bitmap file formats** for importing and exporting as bitmapped images.

Illustrator artwork can be selected in an Illustrator document and **drag-and-dropped** into a Photoshop document, and vice-versa.

Appendix D Shortcuts

Menu Commands

The File Menu	
Command	***Shortcut***
New document	⌘-N
New document with template	⌘-Option-N
Open Document with New Template	⌘-Option-O
Close document	⌘-W
Save document	⌘-S (Save As does not have a key command)
Document Setup	⌘-Shift-D
Print document	⌘-P
General Preferences	⌘-K
Quit	⌘-Q

The Edit Menu	
Command	***Shortcut***
Undo last activity	⌘-Z
Redo last undo	⌘-Shift-Z
Nice do	"Like your hair"
Clear	Delete
Cut	⌘-X
Copy	⌘-C
Paste	⌘-V
Select All	⌘-A
Select None	⌘-Shift-A
Paste In Front	⌘-F
Paste In Back	⌘-B

The Arrange Menu	
Command	***Shortcut***
Repeat Transform	⌘-D
Move	⌘-Shift-M or Option-click the Selection tool
Bring To Front	⌘-=
Send To Back	⌘-hyphen (-)
Group	⌘-G
Ungroup	⌘-U
Lock selected	⌘-1
Lock Unselected	⌘-Option-1
Unlock All	⌘-2
Hide	⌘-3
Hide Unselected	⌘-Option-3
Show All	⌘-4

The View Menu

Command	Shortcut
Preview	⌘-Y
Artwork	⌘-E
Preview Selection	⌘-Option-Y
Show/Hide Rulers	⌘-R
Show/Hide Edges	⌘-Shift-H
Zoom In	⌘-]
Zoom Out	⌘-[
Actual Size	⌘-H or double-click the Zoom tool
Fit In Window	⌘-M or double-click the Hand tool
New View	⌘-Control-V
Use Custom Views	⌘-Control-1, ⌘-Control-2, etc.

The Object Menu

Command	Shortcut
Paint Style	⌘-I
Attributes	⌘-Control-A
Join	⌘-J
Average	⌘-L
Join and Average	⌘-Option-J or ⌘-Option-L
Make Guides	⌘-5
Release Guides	⌘-6 or double-click while pressing Shift-Control
Lock/Unlock Guides	⌘-7
Make Compound Path	⌘-8
Release Compound Path	⌘-9

The Type Menu

Command	Shortcut
Other size	⌘-Shift-S
Other font	⌘-T, ⌘-Shift-F, or ⌘-Option-Shift-M
Left alignment	⌘-Shift-L
Center alignment	⌘-Shift-C
Right alignment	⌘-Shift-R
Justify alignment	⌘-Shift-J
Justify last line alignment	⌘-Shift-B
Tracking/Kerning	⌘-Shift-K
Spacing	⌘-Shift-O
Character	⌘-T
Paragraph	⌘-Shift-P or ⌘-Shift-O
Link Blocks	⌘-Shift-G
Unlink Blocks	⌘-Shift-U

The Filter Menu

Command	Shortcut
Last Filter	⌘-Shift-E
Last Filter dialog box	Press Option while choosing Filter⇨Last Filter

The Window Menu

Command	Shortcut
Show/Hide Toolbox	⌘-Control-T
Show/Hide Layers	⌘-Control-L
Show/Hide Info	⌘-Control-I
Show/Hide Paint Style	⌘-I
Show/Hide Character	⌘-T
Show/Hide Paragraph	⌘-Shift-P
Show/Hide Tab Ruler	⌘-Shift-T

Tool Time

- To Show/Hide Toolbox, press ⌘-Control-T (if the Toolbox is hidden by another palette, press ⌘-Control-T twice to display it).

Accessing Tools

You can access many tools by pressing a modifier when another tool is already selected:

Tool	***Selected Tool-Modifier***
Add Anchor Point	Scissors or Delete Anchor Point-Option
Centered Oval	Oval-Option (or double-click the Oval tool)
Centered Rectangle	Rectangle-Option (or double-click the Rectangle tool)
Centered Rounded Rectangle	Rounded Rectangle-Option (or double-click the Rounded Rectangle tool)
Convert Direction Point	Any selection tool-Control or Pen-Option-Control or All tools but Scissors, Add Anchor Point, and Delete Anchor Point-⌘-Option-Control
Delete Anchor Point	Add Anchor Point-Option
Direct Selection	⌘. If Selection tool appears, press ⌘-Tab to toggle to Direct Selection tool.
Eyedropper tool	Paint Bucket-Option
Group Selection	Direct Selection-Option
Hand	Spacebar, if Type tool is active in a text box, press ⌘-Space, then release ⌘.
Oval	Centered Oval-Option (or double-click the Centered Oval tool)
Paint Bucket tool	Eyedropper-Option
Pen	Freehand or Auto Trace-Control
Rectangle	Centered Rectangle-Option (or double-click the Centered Rectangle tool)
Rounded Rectangle	Centered Rounded Rectangle-Option (or double-click the Centered Rounded Rectangle tool)
Selection	⌘. If Direct Selection tool appears, press ⌘-Tab to toggle to Selection tool.
Type	Area Type or Path Type-Control
Zoom In	⌘-spacebar*
Zoom Out	⌘-Option-spacebar

**Note:* SCSI Probe, a popular Control Panel used for mounting SCSI devices (such as SyQuest cartridges), has a default setting of ⌘-spacebar to mount unmounted volumes (hard drives, CDs, and so on). Even if everything is mounted, SCSI Probe always attempts to mount, wasting about 1.5 seconds to look for more drives. To change the key command, access the Options box of SCSI Probe (I suggest changing the default to ⌘-Control-spacebar).

Using Tools

Learning keyboard shortcuts helps you use the tools more efficiently. ***Note:*** Knowing when to release keys is crucial.

Action	Shortcut
Create smooth anchor point	Click-drag Pen tool
Create straight corner anchor point	Click Pen tool
Convert anchor point to smooth anchor point	Click-drag Convert Direction Point tool on anchor point
Convert anchor point to straight corner anchor point	Click anchor point with Convert Direction Point tool
Convert smooth anchor point to combination anchor point	Click smooth anchor point with Pen tool
Convert smooth anchor point to curved anchor point	Option-drag Pen tool on smooth anchor point
Convert straight corner anchor point to combination anchor point	Click-drag Pen tool on straight corner anchor point
Deselect object	Shift-click (or Shift-drag across) object with a selection tool
Deselect all objects	⌘-Shift-A or click in an empty area with a selection tool
Select inverse	Shift-drag across entire document
Select objects	Shift-click (or Shift-drag across) objects with a selection tool
Transform Pattern Only	Press P using transformation tool or Selection tool to move
Drag 45°-direction lines	Pen-Shift-drag (release mouse button before Shift)
Draw 45°-angle lines	Pen-Shift-click
Draw circle from center	Oval-Option-Shift keys (release mouse button before Option-Shift)
Draw circle mouse	Shift-Oval (release button before Shift)

Action	Shortcut
Draw oval at specified size	Oval-click in document (displays Oval dialog box)
Draw oval at specified size from center	Option-Oval-click in document
Draw rectangle or rounded corner rectangle at specified size	Rectangle or Rounded Corner Rectangle-click in document (displays Rectangle dialog box)
Draw rectangle or rounded corner rectangle at specified size from center	Option-Rectangle or Rounded Corner Rectangle-click in document
Draw rounded corner square	Shift-Rounded Corner Rectangle tool (release mouse button before Shift)
Draw rounded corner square from center	Option-Shift-Rounded Corner Rectangle (release mouse button before Option-Shift)
Draw square	Shift-Rectangle (release mouse button before Shift)
Draw square from center	Option-Shift-Rectangle (release mouse button before Option-Shift)
Duplicate entire path	After using the Group Selection or Selection tool to move a path, press Option while releasing the mouse button
Duplicate portion of path	After using the Direct Selection tool to move point(s) and/or segment(s), press Option while releasing the mouse button
Erase Freehand tool path	⌘-retrace path
Fill selected objects with another object's Paint Style	Double-click source object with Eyedropper

Action	Shortcut
Constrain object movement to 45°	Shift-move object with a selection tool (release mouse button before Shift)
Measure at 45° angle	Shift-drag (anytime a path is passed over, the Measure tool snaps to the path or its fill)
Measure to edge of path	In Artwork mode, Shift-Measure and go near any path (if you aren't near any paths, the Measure tool is constrained to a 45° angle)
Reflect at 45° angles only	Press Shift before releasing the mouse while setting the axis of reflection
Rotate at 45° angles only	Press Shift before releasing the mouse while setting the angle
Scale horizontally or vertically or proportionally	Set the origin and then Shift-drag as desired (left/right or up/down or diagonally)
Set the gradient from anchor point to anchor point	Shift-drag from anchor point to anchor point
Set the radial gradient highlight	With an object with a radial gradient selected, click in the location of the highlight with the Gradient Vector tool
Shear horizontally or vertically	Set the origin and then Shift-drag as desired (left/right or up/down)
Zoom marquee drawn from center	Control-draw marquee

Viewing Shortcuts

Action	Shortcut
Zoom in one level	⌘-]
Zoom out one level	⌘-[
Zoom in to a specific area	Drag Zoom tool around area
Fit in window	⌘-M (or double-click the Hand tool)
Actual size	⌘-H (or double-click the Zoom tool)
6.25 percent	Option-double-click the Hand tool
Artwork mode	⌘-E
Preview mode	⌘-Y
Preview Selection mode	⌘-Option-Y
Toggle between Preview and Artwork	Option-click the layer's leftmost column in the Layers palette
Define new view	⌘-Control-V
Go to first custom view	⌘-Control-1
Go to next custom view	⌘-Control-view number
Show/Hide Edges	⌘-Shift-H
Show/Hide Rulers	⌘-R
Cycle through Ruler Units from points/picas to inches to millimeters	⌘-Control-U

Generic Dialog Box Commands

Command	Shortcut
Cancel	⌘-. (period)
OK (or dark-bordered button)	Return (or Enter)
Highlight next text field	Tab
Highlight preceding text field	Shift-Tab
Highlight any text field	Double-click the text field

Save As/Open/Import/Place/Export Dialog Boxes Commands

Command	Shortcut
Go to Desktop	⌘-D
Next disk	⌘-left arrow
Open selected file/folder	⌘-down arrow
Preceding disk	⌘-right arrow
Preceding folder	⌘-up arrow
Select certain file/folder	With the file window active, type the name of the file/folder (the more letters you type, the more accurate the search); to go to the bottom of the list, press Z
Select next file/folder	Down arrow
Select preceding file/folder	Up arrow
Toggle between file window and name window	Tab (when active, the file window has a dark border)
Create new folder (Save As/Import/Export dialog boxes)	⌘-N

Other Dialog Boxes Commands

Command	Shortcut
Display the Rotate/ Scale/Reflect/Shear dialog boxes	Corresponding tool-Option-click the origin location
Copy (Move/Rotate/ Scale/Reflect/Shear dialog boxes)	Option-Return or Option-Enter (or Option-click the OK button)
Don't Save (Do You Wish to Save Changes? dialog box)	D
None (New template dialog box)	⌘-N (if you have Super Boomerang or Norton Utilities Directory Assistance, you will get a New folder)

Type Command Shortcuts

Type Tool Shortcuts

Action	Shortcut
Access the Area Type tool	Drag Type tool over closed path or Option-drag Type tool over open path
Access the Path Type tool	Drag Type tool over open path or Option-drag Type tool over closed path
Access the Type tool	Area Type or Path Type-Control
Copy type on a path	Drag any selection tool on the I-bar, press Option, and release the mouse button (this shortcut actually creates two paths as well as two text stories)
Deselect all type	With any tool and anything selected, ⌘-Shift-A

Action	Shortcut
Flip type on a path	Double-click the I-bar with any selection tool or just drag it to the opposite side
Move insertion point to next character	Right arrow
Move insertion point to next line	Down arrow
Move insertion point to next paragraph	⌘-down arrow
Move insertion point to next word	⌘-right arrow
Move insertion point to preceding character	Left arrow
Move insertion point to preceding line	Up arrow
Move insertion point to preceding paragraph	⌘-up arrow
Move insertion point to preceding word	⌘-left arrow
Place type in area	With the Type tool, pass the cursor over a closed path or pass the cursor over an open path and press Option
Place type on path	With the Type tool, pass the cursor over an open path or pass the cursor over a closed path and press Option
Select (by highlighting) all type in story	With any type tool selected and either a visible blinking insertion point visible or highlighted text, ⌘-A or ⌘-. (period)
Select (by not highlighting) all type in story	With the Selection tool selected, click either the baseline of the type or the path that the type is in; with the Group Selection or Direct Selection tool selected, click the baseline of the type

Action	Shortcut
Select all type in document	With any tool but the type tools selected, ⌘-A (*Caution:* Type-related changes will affect only the type, but object changes will affect everything)
Select next character	Shift-right arrow
Select next line	Shift-down arrow
Select next paragraph	⌘-Shift-down arrow
Select next word	⌘-Shift-right arrow
Select paragraph	Triple-click in the paragraph with any type tool
Select preceding character	Shift-left arrow
Select preceding line	Shift-up arrow
Select preceding paragraph	⌘-Shift-up arrow
Select preceding word	⌘-Shift-left arrow
Select word	Double-click the word with any type tool

Type Formatting Shortcuts

Command	Shortcut
Alignment: center	⌘-Shift-C
Alignment: justify	⌘-Shift-J
Alignment: justify last line	⌘-Shift-B
Alignment: left	⌘-Shift-L
Alignment: right	⌘-Shift-R
Change font	⌘-T, ⌘-Shift-F, or ⌘-Option-Shift-M
Decrease baseline shift*	Option-Shift-down arrow
Decrease leading*	Option-up arrow
Decrease tracking/kerning*	⌘-left arrow or ⌘-Shift-[

(continued)

Command	Shortcut
Decrease tracking/ kerning five times*	⌘-Option-left arrow
Decrease type point size*	⌘-Shift-<
Increase baseline shift*	Option-Shift-up arrow
Increase leading*	Option-down arrow
Increase tracking/ kerning*	⌘-right arrow or ⌘-Shift-]
Increase tracking/ kerning five times*	⌘-Option-right arrow
Increase type point size*	⌘-Shift->
Link text blocks	⌘-Shift-G
Unlink text blocks	⌘-Shift-U
Insert discretionary hyphenation	⌘-Shift-hyphen (-)

* You specify the increment in the General Preferences dialog box (⌘-K).

Note: Character formatting affects only selected characters, while paragraph functions affect entire paragraphs regardless of how many characters are selected with a type tool.

Palette Commands and Shortcuts

Generic Commands and Shortcuts

Command	Shortcut
Deactivate Active palette	Shift-Return
Show/Hide Info palette	⌘-Control-I
Show/Hide Tab Ruler palette (5.5 only)	⌘-Shift-T
Hide active palette	⌘-Return (this command only works when a text field is highlighted or a blinking insertion point is in a text field on the active palette)
Highlight next text field	Tab
Highlight preceding text field	Shift-Tab

Paint Style Palette

Command	Shortcut
Show/Hide Paint Style palette	⌘-I
Switch to full view & back	Click the upper right corner box on the title bar
Change to specific view	Use the pull-down menu in the upper right corner of the title bar
Change to show/hide Paint Style palette parts	Click the part to be hidden/viewed in the little diagram in the upper right corner of the Paint Style palette
Delete custom swatch	⌘-click swatch
Delete custom swatch (no warning dialog box)	⌘-Option-click swatch
Delete multiple swatches	⌘-drag across swatches
Delete multiple swatches (no warning dialog box)	⌘-Option-drag across swatches
Reset swatch to original	⌘-Shift-click swatch
Move process sliders proportionally	Shift-drag any slider
Move slider in 1% increments	Option-click either side of the slider
Move slider in 5% increments	Shift-Option-click either side of the slider
Bring up Custom Color palette	Double-click the custom color name

Gradient Palette

Command	Shortcut
Show Gradient palette	Double-click the Gradient Vector tool or double-click the gradient name in the Paint Style palette
Move Process sliders proportionally	Shift-drag any slider
Move slider in 1% increments	Option-click either side of the slider
Move slider in 5% increments	Shift-Option-click either side of the slider
Select more contiguous gradients	Shift-click
Select more individual gradients	⌘-click
Duplicate gradient color triangle	Option-drag triangle
Duplicate gradient color triangle at 1% less	Option-click either side of the color triangle
Duplicate gradient color triangle at 5% less	Shift-Option-click either side of the color triangle
Change selected triangle color to existing Artwork color	Control-Eyedropper-click the color
Move midpoint 2% less	Option-click left of midpoint
Move midpoint 2% more	Option-click right of midpoint
Move midpoint 5% less	⌘-Option-click left of midpoint
Move midpoint 5% more	⌘-Option-click right of midpoint
Add color triangle	Click below gradient bar
Delete color triangle	Pull triangle below gradient bar
Use Eyedropper to change gradient color stop	Control-click with Eyedropper
Swap 2 color stops	Drag one color stop triangle on top of another

Layers Palette

Command	Shortcut
Show/Hide Layers palette	⌘-Control-L
View/Hide layer	Click View column (eye)
Lock/Unlock layer	Click Lock column (pencil)
Move layer up/down	Drag layer to new location
Select more than one layer	Shift-click
Deselect layer	Shift-click
Toggle between Artwork and Preview for layer	Option-click View column
Hide all but selected layer	Click eye at top of View column
Preview only selected layers	Option-click eye at top of View column
Lock all but selected layer	Click pencil at top of Lock column
Create new layer above selected layer	Option-click pop-up menu and choose Create new layer above
Show layer options	Double-click the layer

Character Palette

Command	Shortcut
Show/Hide Character palette	⌘-T, ⌘-Shift-F, or ⌘-Option-Shift-M
Highlight Font field	⌘-T, ⌘-Shift-F, or ⌘-Option-Shift-M
Highlight Size field	⌘-Shift-S
Highlight Leading field	⌘-Shift-S and Tab
Highlight Tracking/Kerning field	⌘-Shift-K

Paragraph Palette

Command	Shortcut
Show/Hide Paragraph palette	⌘-Shift-P
Highlight Left Indent	⌘-Shift-T
Highlight Spacing field	⌘-Shift-O

Miscellaneous

- To see special status line categories, Option-click the status line (at the lower left corner of Illustrator's window).
- The right-, left-, up-, and down-arrow keys move selected objects in the increment set in the General Preferences dialog box.

Transferring Files Between Macs and PCs

As the computer world evolves, the dividing line between PC-compatible computers (PCs) and Macintosh computers is getting fuzzier and fuzzier. Until the line disappears, however, the task of taking files from a Mac to a PC and back is always a challenge.

Software manufacturers, including Adobe, are well aware of this problem and have taken great steps over the last few years to ensure compatibility between their products on both platforms. PageMaker has been the most stable cross-platform product for years, but recently QuarkXPress (Version 3.3) has become completely compatible.

A Brief History of Computing's "Tower of Babel"

Illustrator has been compatible since its inception, but there has been trouble along the way. Initially, the trouble resulted from translation programs that, in their eagerness to please, translated everything to WordPerfect format.

Even Version 1.1 of Illustrator had the capability of saving files as PC Illustrator. The files could then be opened up on a PC machine running the same version of Illustrator. Things really started to mesh with Version 3 of Illustrator, but there were still preview and font problems. Windows 3.1 solved most of these problems, but then Adobe released Illustrator 4 for Windows. PC users had to save their files as Illustrator 3 so that Mac users could read them.

At the present time, Illustrator for the Mac is at Version 6.0, and Illustrator for Windows is at Version 4.0. Mac users need to save their files as Illustrator 4.0 (or earlier) for their PC counterparts to be able to read the file.

Transferring Illustrator Files Between Platforms

The following steps show you how easy it is to transfer files between Macs and PCs.

STEPS: Taking an Illustrator File from a Mac to a PC

Step 1. Save the Illustrator file as a PC Illustrator file in the version of Illustrator being used on the PC (usually Version 4).

Step 2. Save the file on an PC-compatible floppy disk. This task is usually achieved by installing software on the Macintosh that allows it to read PC-formatted disks, inserting a PC disk, and dragging the icon of the file to the disk.

Two popular products for mounting PC disks on a Macintosh are DOSMounter and PC Exchange (included with System 7.5).

Step 3. Remove the PC disk from the Macintosh and open the file on a PC.

STEPS: Opening a PC Illustrator File on a Mac

Step 1. Insert the PC floppy disk with the PC Illustrator file on it into the Macintosh. To do this task, you must have software on the Macintosh that allows it to read PC-formatted disks.

Step 2. Copy the file from the PC floppy disk to your Macintosh's hard disk and remove the PC floppy disk.

Step 3. In Illustrator, choose File⇨Open (⌘-O) and select the PC Illustrator file.

If these steps sound simple, don't worry, they are. People may run into problems with mounting PC-formatted disks, but even these disk problems don't amount to much. PC floppy disk-mounting software has steadily improved over the past few years.

Illustrator 6 for FreeHand 5.x Users

At the time of this writing, the market share of FreeHand was holding steady against the tide of Illustrator. Neither program will leave the world at any time soon, so many graphic artists and production houses have determined that they should have or use both of the software packages. This appendix has been created for those people, as well as FreeHand users who have decided (or been forced) to use Illustrator.

While the two software packages have essentially the same basic features, there are all sorts of subtle differences and variations between the two packages that serve to confuse and frustrate those of us who dare to jump between the two programs — little things like how FreeHand shows point type by shape, while Illustrator doesn't; and things like while FreeHand deletes points just by selecting them and deleting, you have to use the Delete Anchor Point tool in Illustrator. It could drive a man to drink.

This appendix is split into three sections: First, Table F-1 describes how to do things in Illustrator that aren't perfectly obvious, which you've always been able to do in FreeHand quite easily. The second part is a list of things you've always done in FreeHand quite easily that there really is no way to do in Illustrator, or that requires a severe workaround. The third part lists some of the things in Illustrator that can't be done in FreeHand, so you're not too depressed about all those things you can't do in Illustrator that FreeHand does.

You should refer to the comprehensive index in the back of the book to learn more about each section. I would've put the cross references here, but then this appendix would be an index all by itself.

Table F-1
A Comparision of FreeHand and Illustrator Features and Techniques

FreeHand	*Illustrator*
Hollow (white) points mean only that point will move.	Solid (black) points indicate that a point is selected.
Solid (black) points mean that the point is not selected, but the path is.	Hollow (white) means that the point is not selected, but is on a partially selected path.

(continued)

Table F-1 *(continued)*

FreeHand	***Illustrator***
Points change shape to reflect the type of point: square for corner points, round for curved points, triangle for connector points.	Points are always square. Point type can only be determined by clicking on an unselected point with the Direct Selection tool, and noting the location of the Control Handles, if any.
Press Option with regular Selection tool to select individual points on paths.	Change to the Direct Selection tool (Press ⌘-Tab if no Selection tool is selected) to select points on paths.
Work your way up through nested groups by pressing ' (grave) key.	Click with the Group Selection tool to work your way up through nested groups.
Tab deselects selected objects.	⌘-Shift-A deselects selected objects.
Press and hold Control to drag an object by its point.	Click on a point and drag.
Curved Corner points are created by dragging out and then holding the Option key and pivoting the handle.	Curved Corner Points are created by dragging handles and then clicking on one of them with the Convert Direction Point tool.
Close paths with the Inspector palette or by dragging end points on top of one another.	Select the path with the Selection tool and choose Arrange⇨Join.
Add points within a path by clicking with the Pen tool.	Add points within a path by clicking with the Add Anchor Point tool.
Delete points within a path by selecting the point and pressing Delete.	Delete points within a path by clicking on the point with the Delete Anchor Point tool.
Resize a rectangle numerically by creating it and then entering values in the Inspector palette.	Resize a rectangle numerically by creating it and then entering values in the Control palette. To create a rectangle at a specific size, click without dragging with the Rectangle tool.
Resize a grouped path, rectangle, or oval by clicking on the corner handle and dragging.	Resize any path by selecting it and using the Scale tool or Scale option in the Control palette.
Tiled fills	Patterns
Locked objects can be selected, and attributes be changed and copied.	Locked objects can't be changed in any way until can unlocked (via ⌘-2).
Layers below the printing line do not print.	Each layer can be set to print or not print, by double-clicking on the name of the layer and checking or unchecking the Print dialog box.
Overprinting objects are indicated on-screen.	Overprinting objects can be determined by clicking on them and seeing if the Overprint checkbox is checked in the Paint Style palette.
Turn FreeHand artwork into a raster image by using the Operations command and then importing.	Select the artwork, and choose Object⇨Rasterize.
Use Control Control to change colors of multiple selected objects.	Use Adjust Colors to change colors of multiple selected objects.
Use Union to merge abutting or overlapping paths.	Use Unite to merge abutting or overlapping paths.

FreeHand	***Illustrator***
Transparency creates overlapping path sections combining attributes of each path.	Mix Hard adds values of overlapping paths; Mix Soft allows for control of how much of each path is added.
Reverse path direction with Reverse Direction command.	Reverse path direction by choosing Object⇨Attributes, and checking/unchecking the Reverse Path Direction checkbox.
Expand Stroke	Outline Path
Inset Stroke	Offset Path
Pause to see preview of objects as they are dragged.	No pause needed.
Keyline	View⇨Artwork
Export as EPS	Save As, and select EPS from the pop-up menu.
Redo multiple transformations	Use Repeat Transform (this only works with the last transformation).
Multiple Pages	All pages must be the same size; select Document Setup and check Use Page Tiling.
Automatic Grid	Use the Rows and Columns filter.
Colorize TIFF	Only works with 1-bit TIFFs.
Bind text on the top and bottom of the same path.	The path must be duplicated in order to have text appear to be on the same path.
Premade and Custom textured fills.	Fill with the Ink Pen texture.
Create and Edit Arrowheads	Apply the Add Arrowhead filter, and edit the resulting arrowhead as a path.
AutoTrace Tool	AutoTrace traces only PICT images.
Trap feature recognizes strokes	The Trap filter doesn't recognize Strokes, but Strokes can be transformed to outlined paths via the Outline Path filter.
Simplify filter	Use Smart Remove Points, a free filter included with *Macworld Illustrator 6 Bible* on the CD-ROM, courtesy of BeInfinite.
Knife tool	The Knife tool can't be set for variable widths; there are no open/closed path options.
Line tool	Use the Pen tool, and click without dragging to set each end point.
Paste Inside	Mask
Paste Inside paths can have fill or stroke attributes.	Use the Create Fill and Stroke for Mask filter.
Designate colors are path or process.	Custom Colors can be process or spot, determined at the time of printing.
Inline effect for text.	Convert text to outlines, and apply the Offset Path filter with a negative amount.
Export as Illustrator 1.1, 88, 3, 5.5	Save As, choose the appropriate format from the pop-up menu in the dialog box.

FreeHand Features That Illustrator Doesn't Have

Many of the following FreeHand features and techniques in Table F-2 can be duplicated within Illustrator with a lot of effort, although the techniques would be too lengthy to describe here.

Table F-2
FreeHand Features and Techniques that Can't Be Easily Duplicated in Illustrator

Object styles
Text styles
Live blends
Multiple-sized pages
Pages can be arranged as spreads
Bitmapped pattern fills and strokes
PostScript code fills and strokes
Premade custom strokes
Spiral tool set for uniform or logarithmic spacing
Colors can be specified using RGB, HLS, or the Apple Color Wheel
Colors can be arranged in a list
Multiple guides can be created for all pages
Text Editor
Bezigon tool
Connector points
Set and Show Halftone screens, angles, and shape on-screen
Non-breaking space, em-space, en-space, and thin space
Resize, reshape, and number rows and columns
Inline graphics
Paragraph rules
Fractalize
Smudge
Fisheye lens

Arc
3D rotation
Variable stroke can be sized via keyboard commands
Snap-to sounds
Numerical keys select toolbox tools
Text effects: Zoom, Highlight, Underline, Shadow, and Strikethrough
Export as FreeHand 3.1, Pict, Pict2, text only
Auto expanding text box option
Embed EPS/TIFF files

Illustrator Features That FreeHand Doesn't Have

Now, the good news. Illustrator provides you with all sorts of features and techniques (see Table F-3) that can't be duplicated in FreeHand.

Table F-3
Illustrator Features and Techniques That You Can't Duplicate in FreeHand

Drag and Drop from/to Photoshop
Copy and Paste from/to Photoshop, Dimesions, Streamline
Path patterns
Flatten patterns
Spot colors in gradients
Custom views
Color-coded layers
Pattern tiles can be saved
Gradients can be saved
Modify number of star points as star is being dragged
Modify spiral winds as spiral is being dragged

(continued)

Table F-3 (continued)
Visual cue for snap to (hollow pointer)
Divide
Outline
Trim
Merge
New window (multiple views of one document)
Gradient Vector tool
Radial Gradients
Graphs
Punk and Bloat
Scribble and Tweak
Add Anchor Points
Free Distort
Calligraphy
Drop Shadow
Round Corner
Roughen
Twirl filter
Twirl tool
Zig Zag
Object Mosaic

I hope this appendix helps readers of *Macworld Illustrator 6 Bible,* and points out to both MacroMedia and Adobe some of the limitations of their software. Let's hope that Illustrator 7 and FreeHand 6 continue to up the ante in the battle of professional illustration programs by addressing some of these features.

This appendix wouldn't have been nearly as complete or accurate without the significant input of Sandee Cohen, whose *FreeHand: A Visual Quickstart Guide* is the best book out there on "that other" drawing program.

Resources

This Appendix contains resources for related products, services, and other information Illustrator users may find useful. All phone numbers, addresses, and version numbers are subject to change without notice, of course.

People and Service Company Resources

The following individuals and companies contributed artwork to the *Macworld Illustrator 6 Bible* for use in the book, CD-ROM, or both. All are experts in their particular fields:

Jennifer Alspach
Cave Creek, AZ
Phone: (602) 585-5341
Fax: (602) 585-3784
JenAlspach@aol.com

Jennifer is a nationally known artist and illustrator, with clients all over the United States. Her work has appeared in several books, and samples have been featured in the *Illustrator WOW! Book* and *Illustrator Filter Finesse*, which she coauthored. Jennifer's illustrations are featured in both the *Macworld Illustrator 5.0/5.5 Bible* and throughout the *Macworld Illustrator 6 Bible, 2nd Edition.*

Robert Burger
145 Kingwood Stockton Rd.
Stockton, NJ 08559
Phone: (609) 397-3737
Fax: (609) 397-3666
BurgerBobz@aol.com

Robert is an award-winning illustrator whose work has been in the pages of many magazines and on their covers, on the covers of books and within their pages, on album covers, in advertising, and on web pages. His work has been honored by The Society of Illustrators of Los Angeles, The Society of Illustrators of New York, Graphics Design Annual, Print's Regional Design Annual, The Art Directors Club of Philadelphia, and the Art Directors Club of New Jersey. Robert's illustration, "Future Music," which was created for *Guitar Player* magazine, appears on Color Plate 3-1.

Sandee Cohen
33 Fifth Ave.
New York, NY 10003
Phone: (212) 677-7763
SandeeC@aol.com

Sandee is the author of *FreeHand 5 Visual QuickStart Guide,* but is otherwise a nice person. Sandee works as a Macintosh desktop trainer and consultant, teaching at New York's New School for Social Research. Sandee provided much of the information for the FreeHand appendix (Appendix F) and contributed the filter charts in Illustrator form that are available on the *Macworld Illustrator 6 Bible* CD-ROM.

Andrew DeVigal
441 E. Erie #2503
Chicago, IL 60611
Phone: (312) 482-9522
DrewVigal@aol.com
http://miso.wwa.com/~devigal

Andrew has been an informational graphic journalist for several years as well as a freelance illustrator and designer. He currently is a World Wide Web Producer for the Chicago Tribune's Interactive Media department. Andrew's illustration, "The 16-Second Pit Stop," which was published in the *Chicago Tribune*, appears on Color Plate 10-1.

Mordy Golding
135 West 26th Street
New York, NY 10001
Phone: (212) 691-7644
Fax: (212) 337-0336
mordy@aol.com

Mordy is the president of Em Graphic Design. He is also a production artist/graphic designer and trainer in New York. He recently helped to establish i33 Communications, a web site design/development company. Mordy's Illustrations "New York Skyride" and "Kassir" appear on color plates 8-1 and 10-4, respectively.

Steve Layton
3659 N. Damen #3
Chicago, IL 60618
Phone: (312) 404-6013

Steve is an informational graphics journalist for the *Chicago Tribune* and an occasional freelance artist. Steve's illustration, "Chicago High Rise," which was published in the *Tribune* as part of a series on low-income housing, appears on Color Plate 21-1.

Tom Neal
411 Center Street
P.O. Box 249
Gridley, IL 61744
tkn@gridley.org or bradneal@gridley.org

Tom is a partner in the Illinois-based Thomas-Bradley Illustration & Design. Established in 1987, the firm has had articles on their work appear in the *Adobe WOW! Book*, *MacWeek* magazine, *Computer Artist* magazine, *Adobe Spotlight*, several technical journals, and now the *Macworld Illustrator 6 Bible*. In addition to illustrating 13 published books, recent clients include Pepsi-Cola, Anheuser-Busch, Nike, State Farm Insurance Co., Deere & Co., Caterpillar Tractor Co., and six major automobile manufacturers. Tom's "Avia" appears on Color Plate 10-6.

Clarke Tate
Tate Studio
301 Woodford Street
P.O. Box 339
Gridley, IL 61744-0339
Phone: (800) TATE008; (309) 747-3388
Fax: (309) 747-3008
Tate Studio Europe: ul. Zwirki I Wigury 3/46, 86-050. Solec Kujawski, Poland
From the U.S.: Phone and Fax: 011 48 52 871 265
Tatestudio@aol.com

Clark is a world-renowned designer and illustrator, creating art for clients such as 3M, USA Today International, and Disney/Premier Cruise Lines. Clarke's "C++/Blues" illustration appears on Color Plate 10-5.

Teeple Graphics
373 Newberry Road
Middletown, PA 17057
Phone: (717) 944-2034
Fax: (717) 944-2088
rob@teeple.com

Teeple Graphics is a Macintosh VAR and World Wide Web service provider specializing in desktop publishing and high-end graphic systems integration.

Thunder Lizard Productions
1619 8th Avenue North
Seattle, WA 98109
(206) 285-1676
Fax: (206) 285-0308

Producers of frequent Illustrator Conferences, held in different cities around the country, featuring top of the heap Illustrator experts speaking on every Illustrator topic imaginable.

Randy Verougstraete (say "Verse-strait")
Richmond, VA
Phone: (804) 379-7986
Fax: (804) 379-7239
RandoVergo@aol.com

Randy has been creating editorial, educational and advertising art since 1985. Clients include: *Forbes* magazine, Compuserve, Universal Pictures, World Book, Harcourt Brace, McMillan/McGraw-Hill and others. Randy's illustration, "Space Mural," appears on Color Plate 10-4.

Lester Yocum
274 Jay Jay Ct.
Glen Burnie, MD 21061
Phones: (301) 688-7393 and (410) 766-3694
lyocum@aol.com

With over 15 years of traditional and digital illustration and design experience, Mr. Yocum's credits range from posters, books, and signage to Web pages. His illustration, "Pumpkin Cat," appears on Color Plate 10-2.

Software Company Resources

Adobe Systems, Inc.
1585 Charleston Road
P.O. Box 7900
Mountain View, CA 94039-7900
Customer Service: (800) 833-6687
Technical Support (available to registered users with a valid serial number only): (206) 628-3953
BBS (First Class software): (206) 623-6984

Publisher of Adobe Illustrator, Adobe Photoshop, Adobe PageMaker, Adobe Streamline, Adobe Premiere, Adobe Dimensions and several other products. Demo versions of Streamline and Dimensions are included on this book's CD-ROM.

BeInfinite
BeInfinite@aol.com

Publisher of InfiniteFX1 filters for Adobe Illustrator and FreeHand. A demo version of IFX is included on the CD-ROM.

Cytopia Software, Inc.
1735 E. Bayshore Road, Suite 30b
Redwood City, CA 94063
(415) 364-4594
Fax: (415) 364-4592
World Wide Web: http://www.cytopia.com

Publisher of CSI Socket Set 1 & 2 for Adobe Illustrator, and CSI PhotoLab filters for Adobe Photoshop. Demo versions of Cytopia products are on the CD-ROM.

Extensis Corporation
55 S.W. Yamhill Street
Fourth Floor
Portland, OR 97204
(503) 274-2020.
Fax: (503) 274-0530

Publisher of Extensis Draw Tools, Plug-Ins for Adobe Illustrator, and FreeHand.

Letraset
40 Eisenhower Drive
P.O. Box 281
Paramus, NJ 07653-9951

Publisher of Letraset Envelopes.

MetaTools, Inc.
6303 Carpinteria Avenue
Carpinteria, CA 93013
Customer service: (805) 566-6200
Fax: (805) 566-6385
kptsupport@aol.com

Publisher of KPT Vector Effects for Illustrator and FreeHand, Kai's Power Tools, KPT Convolver, KPT Bryce, and more. A demo version of KPT Vector Effects is included on the CD-ROM.

Illustrator Version History

I added this appendix to the book because readers of previous editions asked for it. There really isn't a bonafide "History of Illustrator" available, even at Adobe. So I've taken it upon myself to write one. If you're an Illustrator user, you'll find the changes that have been made over the past ten years to be fascinating.

Illustrator Through the Years

Illustrator was the first PostScript-based drawing program, and today it remains the best on the market. Since its introduction in 1987, the program has undergone three radical revisions. With each new version, Adobe improved Illustrator to match the advances in hardware as well as PostScript technology.

In the following sections, I give a brief overview of how Illustrator has changed over the years.

Adobe Illustrator (1.1)

The first version of Illustrator was called, simply, Adobe Illustrator. It is commonly referred to as Version 1.1, though Version 1.07 was the first version ushered out the door by Adobe in January 1987. The icons for Adobe Illustrator are shown in Figure H-1.

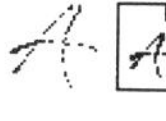

Figure H-1: The Application and document icons for Illustrator 1.1

A videotape was included with Version 1.1 (Figure H-2). It featured John Warnock, then president of Adobe Systems (and now CEO), who enthusiastically explained how to use Illustrator. During the 30-minute demonstration and tutorial, users were treated to a display of the first works ever created with Illustrator, including an impressive King Tut illustration. The 1.1 package also included a user manual — a 229-page introduction to the software.

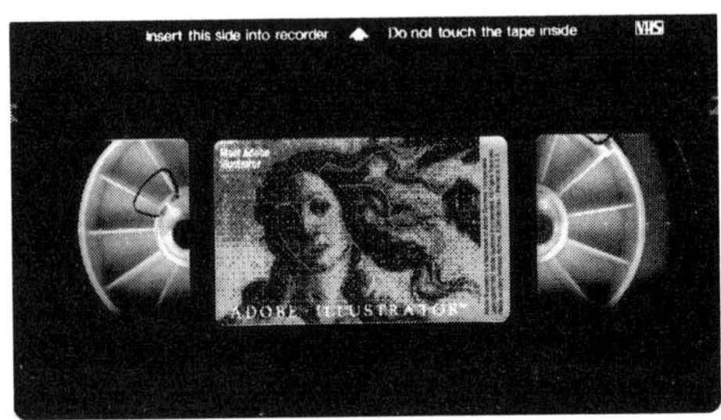

Figure H-2: The videotape that shipped with Illustrator 1

The requirements for 1.1? System 4.1 and a Mac Plus. Back then, you didn't need a hard disk drive — one 800K-disk housed all the needed files.

New Features

The basic concept behind Illustrator was new. Previously, illustration and drawing programs were based entirely upon bitmapped graphics, which printed well at one resolution only and took up oodles of disk space. Illustrator used bitmapped images but only for tracing. (Illustrator calls these bitmaps — PICT and Paint only — *templates.*) The images created with Illustrator could print at any size on any device and maintain a consistent high-quality output.

The Pen tool was a drawing tool that had never been seen before on the Macintosh platform. It offered a level of precision for creating straight and curved lines that had not been available up to this point. However, Illustrator's use of Bézier curves intimidated some new and potential users. In fact, the new software's only drawback was its requirement that users learn to draw with the Pen tool.

The transformation tools in Illustrator 1.1, based on PostScript's four basic transformation functions (Rotate, Scale, Reflect, and Shear), also were in a league of their own. These fuctions enabled the user to transform any object that was created in Illustrator, including text.

Speaking of text, Illustrator 1.1 was the first program to support rotating text and scaling text to *any* size. Sure, it's not a big deal now, but seven years ago that capability really wowed 'em.

Tools

The Illustrator 1.1 Toolbox (see Figure H-3) contained just 13 tools, all of which have pretty much survived into the latest versions. The transformation tools looked quite different than they do today, but the rest of the tools looked about the same.

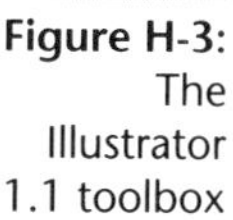

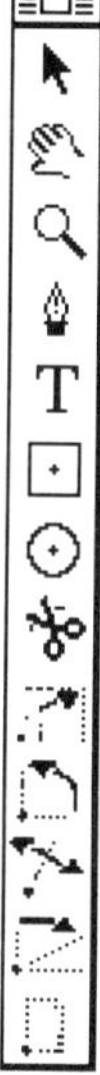

Figure H-3: The Illustrator 1.1 toolbox

The Square and Circle tools could draw rectangles and ovals. In today's world of precision naming, those misnomers would be quite unacceptable.

Menus

Only one option in the Illustrator 1.1 menus (see Figure H-4) was not carried through to later versions: Arrange⇨Constrain. The Constrain command was very similar to the Constrain options found in the preference boxes of later versions, except in 1.1, you could set the constrain angle by creating a line segment at any angle and then telling Illustrator to use the angle of that line to be the new constraining angle.

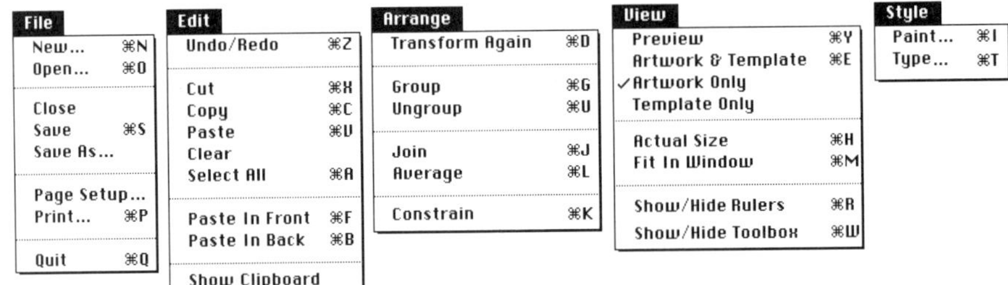

Figure H-4: The Illustrator 1.1 menus

Shortcuts

All the key commands in Illustrator 1.1 used *only* the ⌘ key (not Shift or Option).

Old standbys of Illustrator go back this far, including the following operations:

- Press ⌘ to access the last selection tool used
- Press ⌘-Spacebar to zoom in
- Press ⌘-Option-Spacebar to zoom out
- Press the Spacebar and drag to use the Hand tool

The Option key was used to duplicate items in much the same way it is now (when you press Option while dragging, copies are made), as well as to draw rectangles and ovals from their centers. The Shift key was used to constrain movement to 45° and to constrain rectangles to squares and ovals to circles.

In Illustrator 1.1, users could already press ⌘-hyphen to send different Illustrator windows to the back — in other words, holding ⌘ and moving a window did *not* make the window active. Illustrator was the first program (that I know of) to enable users to move windows without making them active, a capability that Apple has made popular in System 7.

Strangely enough, the Constrain command had the key command ⌘-K, which is now the key combination for the Preferences command. In addition, Version 1.1 users pressed ⌘-W to show or hide the Toolbox. Today, pressing ⌘-W in Illustrator 5.0 closes documents.

Illustrator 88

Illustrator 88 (shown in Figure H-5), which was really Version 1.6, was released in 1988. With the inclusion of Separator, full-color support was added.

Figure H-5: The Illustrator 88 package

The 88 package was shipped with three books (the User Manual, the Tutorial, and the Color Guide), which are shown in Figure H-6; two disks (one with the program, the other with the tutorials and utilities), shown in Figure H-7; and another video, which was done a wee bit more professionally (John Warnock was *not* present), shown in Figure H-8. Those who still have the videotape may notice some editing that was done during a segment on the Blend tool, when the results were "modified" (the videotape was cut and spliced) so that the blend tool appears to be smoothly blending from one shape to another, when in reality, the in-between steps were redrawn based on the resulting blend step.

Figure H-6: The Illustrator 88 Manuals

Figure H-7: The Illustrator 88 Disks

Figure H-8: The Illustrator 88 video

In a related note, one of the print ads for Illustrator 88 was also "touched up" to make the Blend tool look a little better. An illustration of an *S* transforming into a swan was altered to provide a smoother transition. According to a note posted on CompuServe by an Adobe tech. person, the initial blend looked terrible and the art had to be almost entirely redrawn. Who said there was truth in advertising, anyway?

To run Illustrator 88, you needed at least a Mac Plus and either two 800K floppies or a hard drive. To run, Illustrator 88 required 1MB of RAM (total on the system without MultiFinder). The Illustrator 88 icons are shown in Figure H-9.

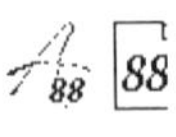

Figure H-9: Illustrator 88's application and document icons

New Features

This version contained a wealth of New Features, including a piece of software called Separator (whose icon is shown in Figure H-10), which transformed color illustrations into spot- and four-color separations. Another utility, called Draw Over (whose icon is also shown in Figure H-10), was designed to convert MacDraw images into Illustrator paths.

Illustrator 88 also included support for Pantone colors, patterns (beginning an era of limitcheck errors), and masking. (Did anyone else get masking to work for anything but that darn fishbowl in the tutorial?)

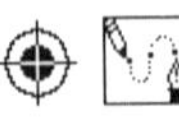

Figure H-10: The Adobe Separator and DrawOver icons

Tools

Illustrator 88 had 17 tools, up four from Version 1.1. (Figure H-11 shows the toolbox.)

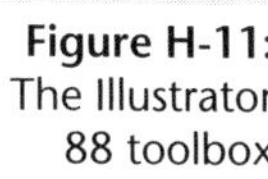
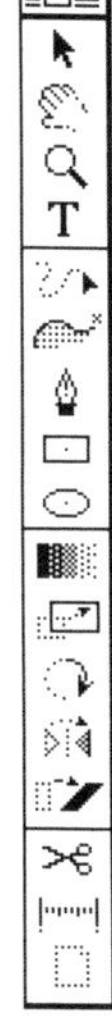

Figure H-11: The Illustrator 88 toolbox

The new tools worked as follows:

- The Freehand tool was used for drawing freeform paths. It was much less frightening than the Pen tool.
- The Auto Trace tool was used to trace templates. It was introduced with much fanfare because it did your work for you.
- The Blend tool, trumpeted by Adobe as the greatest thing since frozen yogurt, took two separate paths (possibly with different colors and shapes) and made several "steps" between them, transforming from one shape to the next.
- The Measure tool measured from one point to another.

The Square and Circle tools were rightfully named the Rectangle and Oval tools. And clicking without dragging in the document window produced a dialog box asking what size to make the shape. The transformation tools were redesigned.

Menus

For Illustrator 88, Adobe added the Window menu to the five menus in Illustrator 1.1. The Illustrator 88 menus are shown in Figure H-12.

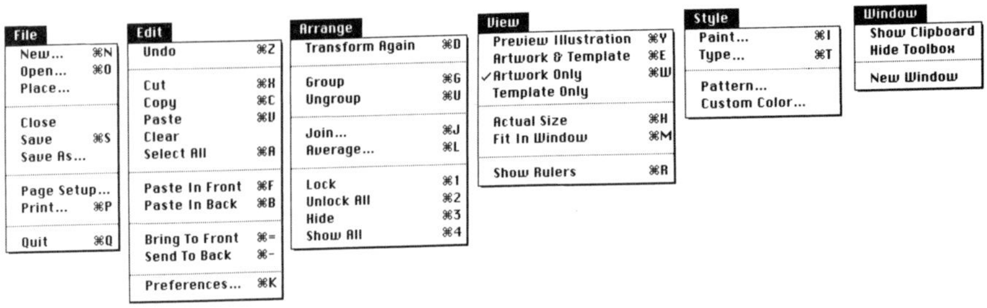

Figure H-12: The Illustrator 88 menus

The File menu included the new Place command, which allowed Illustrator 88 users to place EPS artwork into documents.

The Edit menu included three new commands: Preferences, Bring to Front, and Send to Back. The latter two moved selected objects to the foreground and background of the illustration. Strangely, Adobe put these commands into the Edit menu instead of the Arrange menu, probably because they were similar to Paste in Front and Paste in Back.

Constrain was removed from and Lock/Unlock and Hide/Show were added to the Arrange menu.

The new Window menu contained Show/Hide Clipboard, Show/Hide Toolbox (which was moved from the View menu), and New Window (which was called New View in Version 1.1's View menu).

Shortcuts

Adobe added new key commands for the new menu items. These shortcuts are listed in Table H-1.

Table H-1
Keyboard Shortcuts in Illustrator 88

Key Command Action	*Action in 88*
⌘-=	Bring to Front
⌘-hyphen	Send to Back
⌘-1	Hide
⌘-2	Show
⌘-3	Lock
⌘-4	Unlock
⌘-W	Show/Hide Toolbox (Artwork only)

In addition, users could move objects around the document by using the four arrow keys.

Illustrator 3 (3.2)

Radical changes to Illustrator made Version 3 (shown in Figure H-13) a must-have for graphic designers and desktop publishers everywhere. The changes were highlighted by the type-handling features and the graphing capabilities. Other standout features included what I like to call "the mystery toolbox," where extra tools would suddenly appear, available for use.

Figure H-13: The Illustrator 3 package

No videotape was included with Illustrator 3, just the standard manuals. Adobe packed the box full of other goodies, however, including a version of Adobe Type Manager (ATM), a Gallery disk containing samples and EPS clip art (arrows and borders), and *Beyond the Basics*, which showed several advanced techniques.

Illustrator 3 shipped with four disks, including the ATM disk. By Version 3.2.3, Adobe included an installer (initially, you had to drag the contents of the disks to your hard drive).

Illustrator 3 required at least a Mac Plus with a hard drive and System 6.0.3 (or later) and 2MB of RAM. The icons for Illustrator 3 are shown in Figure H-14.

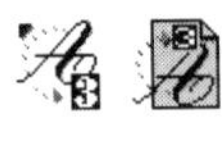

Figure H-14: The Illustrator 3 application and document icons

New Features

Everyone who upgraded to Version 3 commented on the type-handling capabilities. With two new tools, Illustrator 3 allowed you to place type on a path or flow it into any odd-shaped area. And the new Type menu made a lot more features available, including the capability to create outlines out of Type 1 PostScript typefaces.

After users entered type (which they now could do directly on-screen rather than in a little box), they could manipulate it in many ways. Some of the best new type handling options included:

- Character kerning
- Hanging indents
- Word and letter spacing
- Horizontal scaling
- Baseline shift (Adobe called it vertical shift back then)
- Paragraph spacing
- Hyphenation

Type could be imported, and individual characters in any text area could contain different formatting than other characters in the same text area. Type could even flow from one column to another.

Graphing was another big addition to this version: six new tools and a Graph menu were added. Graphs created in Illustrator 3 were composed of editable paths, and many functions of graphs proved to show that they were incredibly flexible and versatile.

In addition, Adobe added the Startup file feature, allowing users to preset how new documents appear, and the EPSF Riders file, allowing users to change the way Illustrator 3 documents printed.

Tools

The basic one-column Illustrator 3 Toolbox (Figure H-15) has 16 tools, down from 17 in Illustrator 88. Can you tell which one is missing?

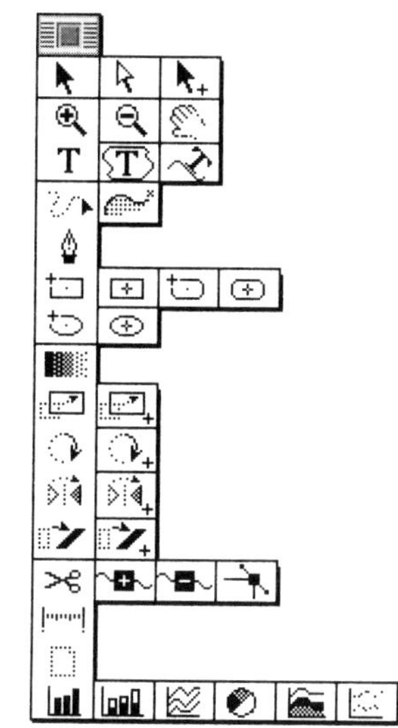

Figure H-15: The standard Illustrator 3 Toolbox (left) and the expanded Illustrator 3 Toolbox

Actually, that was a trick question (sorry). *Two* tools are missing: The Hand tool and the Auto Trace tool became part of the pop-out tool selection, popping out from the Zoom and Freehand tools, respectively. In addition, the Graph tool was added.

Counting all the pop-out tools, Illustrator 3 contained 40 tools — more than *double* the number of tools in Version 88. But 23 of the tools were pop-out tools, and users accessed the Direct-Up Selection tool by pressing Option with the Direct Selection tool.

Tools new to Illustrator 3 included:

- Object Selection
- Direct Selection
- Zoom In
- Zoom Out
- Rounded Corner Rectangle
- Centered versions of Oval, Rectangle, and Rounded Corner Rectangle
- Add Anchor Point
- Delete Anchor Point

- Path Type
- Area Type
- Graph

The four transformation tools brought up dialog boxes automatically.

Menus

Three new menus were added to and one was deleted from Illustrator 3 (see Figure H-16). To keep the menus from being so confusing, Adobe inserted *divider lines* between groups menu items.

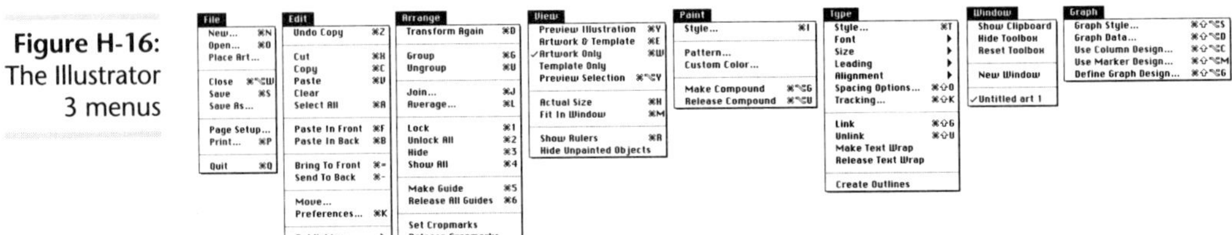

Figure H-16: The Illustrator 3 menus

New menu items include Move (in previous versions, users had to Option-click the Selection tool).

Make Guides, Release Guides, Set Cropmarks, and Release Cropmarks were added to the Arrange menu. Preview Selection (which enabled users to preview selected objects only) and Hide/Show Unpainted Objects were added to the View menu.

The new Paint menu contained items such as Paint Style (now called Style), Pattern, Custom Color, and Make and Release Compound.

The new Type menu contained items related to using type.

The new Graph menu contained Graph Style, Graph Data, Use Column Design, Use Marker Design, and Define Graph Design.

Shortcuts

All sorts of new shortcuts were added. Table H-2 lists the important ones.

Table H-2
Keyboard Shortcuts in Illustrator 3/3.2

Key Command Action	*Old Key Command*
⌘-Option-N	Opens a new document without displaying the annoying "Want a template, big boy?" dialog box
⌘-Option-Y	Preview Selection
⌘-Tab	Toggles between regular Selection tool and the Direct Selection tool
⌘-Control	Convert-Direction Point

Holding down the Option key changed the regular Selection tool to the Object Selection tool and the Direct Selection tool to the Direct-Up Selection tool.

All the Graph menu items had key commands, but they were all confusing ⌘-Option-Shift ones. Many of the Type commands were ⌘-Shift-"letter" commands.

Illustrator 4 for Windows

Illustrator 4 was released on the Windows platform only. Illustrator 4 is much closer to Version 3 for the Macintosh than Version 5. In fact, Version 4 contained very few new features or capabilities.

New Features

Illustrator 4 users were the first Illustrator users to edit in Preview mode. A status line, similar to Illustrator 5's Status Bar and Info palette, was included at the bottom of each document window. The Toolbox contained the same tools as Illustrator 3 but was more flexible; users could resize it in several different ways. Zooming could be done by dragging a marquee — a godsend to Illustrator users.

Grids were a really nifty feature, but strangely they did not make it into Illustrator 5.x or 6.

At this writing, Illustrator for Windows is still stuck at version 4.1.

A pseudo-grid filter, Rows & Columns, is included with version 5.5 of Illustrator. Used correctly, it can simulate setting up grids in a document.

Illustrator 5.0 (5.0.1)

Illustrator 5 (shown in Figure H-17) was released in August 1993.

Figure H-17: The Illustrator 5 package

Packaged inside a toned-down purple box, Illustrator now comes (like its sister product Photoshop) in a regular or Deluxe CD-ROM version. Weighing in at a hefty seven disks (shown in Figure H-18), Illustrator 5 was the biggest Illustrator ever. CD-ROM purchasers received a tutorial that covers some of the new features and a small sampling of techniques.

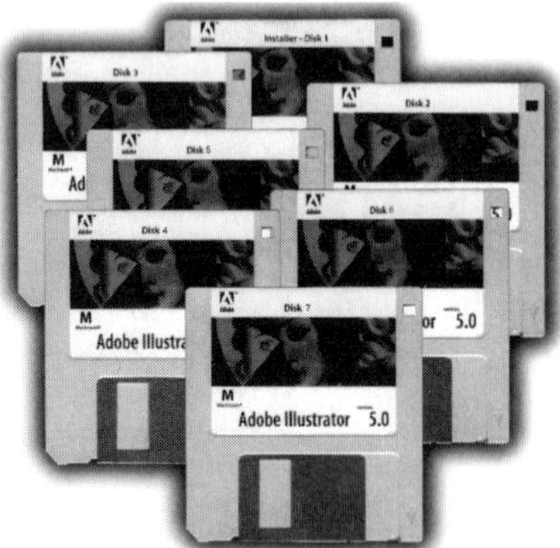

Figure H-18: The Illustrator 5 floppies

Version 5 required at least a Mac II series, a hard drive, and 4MB of RAM. The icons for Illustrator 5 are shown in Figure H-19.

Figure H-19: The Illustrator application and document icons

New Features

Illustrator 5 boasted gradients, layer support, PostScript on the Clipboard, the capability to work in Preview and Preview Selection modes, custom views, Plug-In filters, and multiple undo and redo levels.

The interface was totally revamped, making use of palettes for Gradients, Paint Style, Tools, Info, Layers, Character, and Paragraph.

Cursors were also interactive: They "knew" where you were and what would happen when you clicked. Cursors change as you drag in Illustrator 5.

Tools

The redesigned Toolbox (see Figure H-20) had 26 tools; Adobe eliminated a lot of deadweight tools. Tools that lead to pop-out tools were clearly indicated with a little triangle.

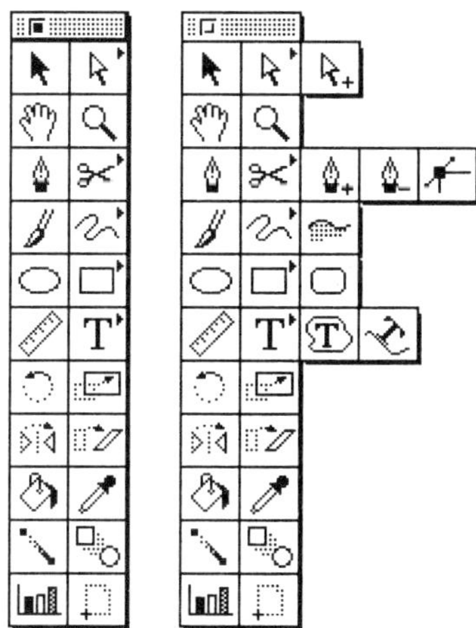

Figure H-20: The standard Illustrator 5 toolbox (left) and the Illustrator 5 toolbox with pop-out tools

Tools deleted from the Illustrator 3 version were:

- Object Selection
- Zoom In/Out

- Centered versions of Oval, Rectangle, and Rounded Corner Rectangle (They can be accessed by double-clicking the standard versions of these tools.)
- The four transformation dialog tools
- Five of the graph tools (Actually, you now must pick them from the Graph Style dialog box.)

New tools are:

- Group Selection (formerly Direct-Up Selection)
- Brush (for drawing free-form closed paths with or without a pressure sensitive tablet)
- Eyedropper (for sampling)
- Paintbucket (for carrying colors from shape to shape)
- Gradient Vector (for controlling gradients' angles and distances)

Most of the tools were redesigned slightly; the Freehand and Blend tools look the most different.

Menus

Tons of new menu items and submenus were added to 5.0. The Paint menu became the Object menu, and the Graph menu was made a submenu of the Object menu. And there were two Type menus: one for just fonts, the other for other type options. Other changes included:

- **File menu:** Revert to Saved was added in Version 5.0.1, Import Styles was added, Change Art replaces Place Art when Placed Art is selected in the document, and Preferences is a submenu with four options.
- **Edit menu:** Redo and Select None were added. Move, Bring to Front, and Send to Back were moved to the Arrange menu. Show Clipboard was relocated from the Window menu of Version 3. A Publishing submenu (for Publish and Subscribe) was added.
- **Arrange menu:** Transform Again was renamed Repeat Transform. Move, Bring to Front, and Send to Back were transplanted from the Edit menu. Make/Release Guides, Set/Release Cropmarks, Join, and Average were moved to the Object menu.
- **View menu:** Artwork and Template, Template Only, and Hide/Show Unpainted Objects were zapped. Show/Hide Template, Show/Hide Page Tiling, Show/Hide Edges, Show/Hide Guides, Zoom In, Zoom Out, New View, and Edit Views were added.

- **Object menu:** This menu, used to be Paint, which contained Paint Style, Custom Color, Pattern, Gradient, Attributes (object attributes), Join, and Average. There were five new submenus: Guides, Masks, Compound Paths, Cropmarks, and Graphs.
- **Font menu:** This was a new menu listing of all the fonts installed on your system.
- **Type menu:** Font had its own menu. Character has replaced Type Style. Paragraph and Fit Headline were added.
- **Window menu:** Show Layers, Show Paint Style, Show Gradient, Show Character, and Show Paragraph were added. Show Clipboard was moved to the Edit menu. Reset Toolbox vanished.

Shortcuts

⌘-W used to mean Artwork Only mode, but with Illustrator 5.0, Adobe changed the key command to Close (as in most other Mac applications). ⌘-E became the shortcut for Artwork mode.

The main differences from previous versions are listed in Table H-3.

Table H-3
Keyboard Shortcuts in Illustrator 5/5.01

Key Command	*Action*	*Old Key Command*
Make Compound	⌘-8	⌘-Option-G
Release Compound	⌘-9	⌘-Option-U
⌘-Option-J or ⌘-Option-L	Averages and joins in one step	
⌘-Shift-T	Shows/hides the Paragraph palette	
⌘-Control-L	Shows/hides the Layers palette	
⌘-Control-T	Shows/hides the toolbox	
⌘-Control-I	Shows/hides the Info palette	
⌘-Control-A	Displays the Object Attributes dialog box	
⌘-Return or ⌘-Enter	Closes the currently active palette (this only works for palettes with text fields)	
⌘-Shift-M	Displays the Move dialog box	

Illustrator 5.5

Illustrator 5.5 was a surprise upgrade to most, timed by Adobe to closely coincide with Apple's PowerPC release. It was the first major application from Adobe to have native code for the first PowerPC Macs, known as the Power Mac 6100, 7100, and 8100.

The way Illustrator works didn't really change that much, and in fact, the common, everyday user will see little difference between 5.0 and 5.5. The most obvious difference is a small but noticeable one: The Save dialog box is "different."

The requirements for 5.5 are the same as 5.0.

New Features in 5.5

The new features help to make Illustrator *the* high-end illustration program. No cute little bells and whistles; all the new features for this half-upgrade are top-notch stuff.

Text Changes

The most striking difference in 5.5 was the powerful text-editing features added to the software through six new text filters and the Tab palette. These changes were undoubtedly in response to reviews and comparisons of Freehand 4 to Illustrator 5.0, where FreeHand's text editing features were indeed superior to Illustrator. Adobe changed that by providing options that rival most word processors.

The text filters are as follows:

- **Change Case:** A basic, yet helpful filter, Change Case lets you choose between UPPER, lower, and Mixed Case.
- **Check Spelling:** Just like it sounds.
- **Find Font:** Find Font finds and replaces fonts within the document.
- **Revert Text Path:** Changes text paths back to non-text paths after all characters on the path have been deleted.
- **Rows and Columns:** Divides a text or other rectangle into rows and columns.
- **Smart Punctuation:** Changes punctuation typed in to the correct typographical format, such as converting inch marks to curly quotes, and hyphens to en- or em-dashes.

The other really big change was the tab ruler. The tab ruler floats above a text rectangle and allows the four basic tabs to be set (left, right, center, and decimal). It was modeled after (and works like) the tabs in Microsoft Word.

Pathfinder Filter Changes

The biggest change was in the Pathfinder filters. With 5.5, you didn't need an FPU to use them.

The Pathfinder submenu was completely reorganized, getting rid of the annoying subheadings and some of the unnecessary filters. The submenu was organized into four categories of Pathfinder filters: Combine, Overlay, Mix, and Trap, without headings, but divided by a dotted line.

The Combine filters are Unite, Intersect, Exclude, Back Minus, and Front Minus.

The Overlay filters are Divide, Outline, Merge, Trim, and Crop.

The Mix filters had their names altered a bit: Mix Hard became Hard and Mix Soft became Soft.

A new category was Trap, which contained just the Trap filter.

An Options menu item was added to the bottom to control all aspects of how the Pathfinder filters work.

Other Filter Changes

In the Colors submenu, the Custom to Process filter has been added, which changes objects with custom colors into their process color equivalents.

The Other category, used in Version 5.0 only with the Riders filter, had two filters added to it: Document Info and Overprint Black. Document Info returned information about the document for viewing in the dialog box or for printout. Overprint Black let you specify how black was to automatically overprint other colors.

Other Changes

Saving provided the option of saving as a straight, non-EPS Illustrator file in any Illustrator version, or as an EPS file with different preview options, similar to those found in Photoshop.

In addition, the ability to save files as Adobe Acrobat PDF files was added, as well as all of the Acrobat software.

Saving choices pertain to Illustrator 5 format, not version 5.5. Files saved in Illustrator 5.5 can be opened in Illustrator 5.0.

Illustrator 5.5 Tools

The tools and their functions were the same as they were in version 5.0.

Illustrator 5.5 Menus

The Filter menu was changed, with several filters added. The Pathfinder submenu was rearranged.

The Show/Hide Tab Ruler command was added to the Window menu.

Illustrator 5.5 Shortcuts

Differences from Version 5.0 included:

- ⌘-Shift-T displays or hides the Tab Ruler
- ⌘-Shift-P displays or hides the Paragraph Ruler
- ⌘-Shift-W shows and hides templates, if available
- ⌘-Shift-P, ⌘-Shift-I, and ⌘-Shift-N no longer changed the measurement system to picas, inches, and centimeters. Instead, ⌘-Control-U toggles between all three of the measurement systems.

Version 6

Appendix C provides a complete rundown of the changes and new features in Illustrator Version 6.

Upcoming Versions

Adobe will certainly continue to release new versions of Illustrator. Undoubtedly, new features will be added; some may seem like they were a long time coming, and others may totally surprise you. Of course, you don't have to just sit there and accept what Adobe sends your way. In order to make Illustrator a better product, tell Adobe what features you want in new versions, and what things should be changed about the current version. They will listen.

Index

• Symbols •

• A •

• B •

• C •

• D •

• F •

• G •

• I •

• L •

• M •

• S •

• U •

• V •

• W •

• Y •

• Z •

The Fun & Easy Way™ to learn about computers and more!

Windows® 3.11 For Dummies®, 3rd Edition
by Andy Rathbone
ISBN: 1-56884-370-4
$16.95 USA/
$22.95 Canada
SUPER STAR

Mutual Funds For Dummies™
by Eric Tyson
ISBN: 1-56884-226-0
$16.99 USA/
$22.99 Canada
SUPER STAR

DOS For Dummies®, 2nd Edition
by Dan Gookin
ISBN: 1-878058-75-4
$16.95 USA/
$22.95 Canada
SUPER STAR

The Internet For Dummies®, 2nd Edition
by John Levine & Carol Baroudi
ISBN: 1-56884-222
$19.99 USA/
$26.99 Canada

Personal Finance For Dummies™
by Eric Tyson
ISBN: 1-56884-150-7
$16.95 USA/
$22.95 Canada
SUPER STAR

PCs For Dummies®, 3rd Edition
by Dan Gookin & Andy Rathbone
ISBN: 1-56884-904-4
$16.99 USA/
$22.99 Canada
VIII FINALIST

Macs® For Dummies®, 3rd Edition
by David Pogue
ISBN: 1-56884-239-2
$19.99 USA/
$26.99 Canada
SUPER STAR

The SAT® I For Dummies™
by Suzee Vlk
ISBN: 1-56884-213
$14.99 USA/
$20.99 Canada

Here's a complete listing of IDG Books' *...For Dummies®* titles

Title	Author	ISBN	Price
DATABASE			
Access 2 For Dummies®	by Scott Palmer	ISBN: 1-56884-090-X	$19.95 USA/$26.95 Canada
Access Programming For Dummies®	by Rob Krumm	ISBN: 1-56884-091-8	$19.95 USA/$26.95 Canada
Approach 3 For Windows® For Dummies®	by Doug Lowe	ISBN: 1-56884-233-3	$19.99 USA/$26.99 Canada
dBASE For DOS For Dummies®	by Scott Palmer & Michael Stabler	ISBN: 1-56884-188-4	$19.95 USA/$26.95 Canada
dBASE For Windows® For Dummies®	by Scott Palmer	ISBN: 1-56884-179-5	$19.95 USA/$26.95 Canada
dBASE 5 For Windows® Programming For Dummies®	by Ted Coombs & Jason Coombs	ISBN: 1-56884-215-5	$19.99 USA/$26.99 Canada
FoxPro 2.6 For Windows® For Dummies®	by John Kaufeld	ISBN: 1-56884-187-6	$19.95 USA/$26.95 Canada
Paradox 5 For Windows® For Dummies®	by John Kaufeld	ISBN: 1-56884-185-X	$19.95 USA/$26.95 Canada
DESKTOP PUBLISHING/ILLUSTRATION/GRAPHICS			
CorelDRAW! 5 For Dummies®	by Deke McClelland	ISBN: 1-56884-157-4	$19.95 USA/$26.95 Canada
CorelDRAW! For Dummies®	by Deke McClelland	ISBN: 1-56884-042-X	$19.95 USA/$26.95 Canada
Desktop Publishing & Design For Dummies®	by Roger C. Parker	ISBN: 1-56884-234-1	$19.99 USA/$26.99 Canada
Harvard Graphics 2 For Windows® For Dummies®	by Roger C. Parker	ISBN: 1-56884-092-6	$19.95 USA/$26.95 Canada
PageMaker 5 For Macs® For Dummies®	by Galen Gruman & Deke McClelland	ISBN: 1-56884-178-7	$19.95 USA/$26.95 Canada
PageMaker 5 For Windows® For Dummies®	by Deke McClelland & Galen Gruman	ISBN: 1-56884-160-4	$19.95 USA/$26.95 Canada
Photoshop 3 For Macs® For Dummies®	by Deke McClelland	ISBN: 1-56884-208-2	$19.99 USA/$26.99 Canada
QuarkXPress 3.3 For Dummies®	by Galen Gruman & Barbara Assadi	ISBN: 1-56884-217-1	$19.99 USA/$26.99 Canada
FINANCE/PERSONAL FINANCE/TEST TAKING REFERENCE			
Everyday Math For Dummies™	by Charles Seiter	ISBN: 1-56884-248-1	$14.99 USA/$22.99 Canada
Personal Finance For Dummies™ For Canadians	by Eric Tyson & Tony Martin	ISBN: 1-56884-378-X	$18.99 USA/$24.99 Canada
QuickBooks 3 For Dummies®	by Stephen L. Nelson	ISBN: 1-56884-227-9	$19.99 USA/$26.99 Canada
Quicken 8 For DOS For Dummies®, 2nd Edition	by Stephen L. Nelson	ISBN: 1-56884-210-4	$19.95 USA/$26.95 Canada
Quicken 5 For Macs® For Dummies®	by Stephen L. Nelson	ISBN: 1-56884-211-2	$19.95 USA/$26.95 Canada
Quicken 4 For Windows® For Dummies®, 2nd Edition	by Stephen L. Nelson	ISBN: 1-56884-209-0	$19.95 USA/$26.95 Canada
Taxes For Dummies™, 1995 Edition	by Eric Tyson & David J. Silverman	ISBN: 1-56884-220-1	$14.99 USA/$20.99 Canada
The GMAT® For Dummies™	by Suzee Vlk, Series Editor	ISBN: 1-56884-376-3	$14.99 USA/$20.99 Canada
The GRE® For Dummies™	by Suzee Vlk, Series Editor	ISBN: 1-56884-375-5	$14.99 USA/$20.99 Canada
Time Management For Dummies™	by Jeffrey J. Mayer	ISBN: 1-56884-360-7	$16.99 USA/$22.99 Canada
TurboTax For Windows® For Dummies®	by Gail A. Helsel, CPA	ISBN: 1-56884-228-7	$19.99 USA/$26.99 Canada
GROUPWARE/INTEGRATED			
ClarisWorks For Macs® For Dummies®	by Frank Higgins	ISBN: 1-56884-363-1	$19.99 USA/$26.99 Canada
Lotus Notes For Dummies®	by Pat Freeland & Stephen Londergan	ISBN: 1-56884-212-0	$19.95 USA/$26.95 Canada
Microsoft® Office 4 For Windows® For Dummies®	by Roger C. Parker	ISBN: 1-56884-183-3	$19.95 USA/$26.95 Canada
Microsoft® Works 3 For Windows® For Dummies®	by David C. Kay	ISBN: 1-56884-214-7	$19.99 USA/$26.99 Canada
SmartSuite 3 For Dummies®	by Jan Weingarten & John Weingarten	ISBN: 1-56884-367-4	$19.99 USA/$26.99 Canada
INTERNET/COMMUNICATIONS/NETWORKING			
America Online® For Dummies®, 2nd Edition	by John Kaufeld	ISBN: 1-56884-933-8	$19.99 USA/$26.99 Canada
CompuServe For Dummies®, 2nd Edition	by Wallace Wang	ISBN: 1-56884-937-0	$19.99 USA/$26.99 Canada
Modems For Dummies®, 2nd Edition	by Tina Rathbone	ISBN: 1-56884-223-6	$19.99 USA/$26.99 Canada
MORE Internet For Dummies®	by John R. Levine & Margaret Levine Young	ISBN: 1-56884-164-7	$19.95 USA/$26.95 Canada
MORE Modems & On-line Services For Dummies®	by Tina Rathbone	ISBN: 1-56884-365-8	$19.99 USA/$26.99 Canada
Mosaic For Dummies®, Windows Edition	by David Angell & Brent Heslop	ISBN: 1-56884-242-2	$19.99 USA/$26.99 Canada
NetWare For Dummies®, 2nd Edition	by Ed Tittel, Deni Connor & Earl Follis	ISBN: 1-56884-369-0	$19.99 USA/$26.99 Canada
Networking For Dummies®	by Doug Lowe	ISBN: 1-56884-079-9	$19.95 USA/$26.95 Canada
PROCOMM PLUS 2 For Windows® For Dummies®	by Wallace Wang	ISBN: 1-56884-219-8	$19.99 USA/$26.99 Canada
TCP/IP For Dummies®	by Marshall Wilensky & Candace Leiden	ISBN: 1-56884-241-4	$19.99 USA/$26.99 Canada

For scholastic requests & educational orders please call Educational Sales at 1. 800. 434. 2086

FOR MORE INFO OR TO ORDER, PLEASE CALL 800 762 2974

For volume discounts & special orders pleas Tony Real, Special Sales, at 415. 655. 3048

10/31/95

The Internet For Macs® For Dummies®, 2nd Edition	by Charles Seiter	ISBN: 1-56884-371-2	$19.99 USA/$26.99 Canada
The Internet For Macs® For Dummies® Starter Kit	by Charles Seiter	ISBN: 1-56884-244-9	$29.99 USA/$39.99 Canada
The Internet For Macs® For Dummies® Starter Kit Bestseller Edition	by Charles Seiter	ISBN: 1-56884-245-7	$39.99 USA/$54.99 Canada
The Internet For Windows® For Dummies® Starter Kit	by John R. Levine & Margaret Levine Young	ISBN: 1-56884-237-6	$34.99 USA/$44.99 Canada
The Internet For Windows® For Dummies® Starter Kit, Bestseller Edition	by John R. Levine & Margaret Levine Young	ISBN: 1-56884-246-5	$39.99 USA/$54.99 Canada

MACINTOSH

Mac® Programming For Dummies®	by Dan Parks Sydow	ISBN: 1-56884-173-6	$19.95 USA/$26.95 Canada
Macintosh® System 7.5 For Dummies®	by Bob LeVitus	ISBN: 1-56884-197-3	$19.95 USA/$26.95 Canada
MORE Macs® For Dummies®	by David Pogue	ISBN: 1-56884-087-X	$19.95 USA/$26.95 Canada
PageMaker 5 For Macs® For Dummies®	by Galen Gruman & Deke McClelland	ISBN: 1-56884-178-7	$19.95 USA/$26.95 Canada
QuarkXPress 3.3 For Dummies®	by Galen Gruman & Barbara Assadi	ISBN: 1-56884-217-1	$19.99 USA/$26.99 Canada
Upgrading and Fixing Macs® For Dummies®	by Kearney Rietmann & Frank Higgins	ISBN: 1-56884-189-2	$19.95 USA/$26.95 Canada

MULTIMEDIA

Multimedia & CD-ROMs For Dummies®, 2nd Edition	by Andy Rathbone	ISBN: 1-56884-907-9	$19.99 USA/$26.99 Canada
Multimedia & CD-ROMs For Dummies®, Interactive Multimedia Value Pack, 2nd Edition	by Andy Rathbone	ISBN: 1-56884-909-5	$29.99 USA/$39.99 Canada

OPERATING SYSTEMS:

DOS

MORE DOS For Dummies®	by Dan Gookin	ISBN: 1-56884-046-2	$19.95 USA/$26.95 Canada
OS/2® Warp For Dummies®, 2nd Edition	by Andy Rathbone	ISBN: 1-56884-205-8	$19.99 USA/$26.99 Canada

UNIX

MORE UNIX® For Dummies®	by John R. Levine & Margaret Levine Young	ISBN: 1-56884-361-5	$19.99 USA/$26.99 Canada
UNIX® For Dummies®	by John R. Levine & Margaret Levine Young	ISBN: 1-878058-58-4	$19.95 USA/$26.95 Canada

WINDOWS

MORE Windows® For Dummies®, 2nd Edition	by Andy Rathbone	ISBN: 1-56884-048-9	$19.95 USA/$26.95 Canada
Windows® 95 For Dummies®	by Andy Rathbone	ISBN: 1-56884-240-6	$19.99 USA/$26.99 Canada

PCS/HARDWARE

Illustrated Computer Dictionary For Dummies®, 2nd Edition	by Dan Gookin & Wallace Wang	ISBN: 1-56884-218-X	$12.95 USA/$16.95 Canada
Upgrading and Fixing PCs For Dummies®, 2nd Edition	by Andy Rathbone	ISBN: 1-56884-903-6	$19.99 USA/$26.99 Canada

PRESENTATION/AUTOCAD

AutoCAD For Dummies®	by Bud Smith	ISBN: 1-56884-191-4	$19.95 USA/$26.95 Canada
PowerPoint 4 For Windows® For Dummies®	by Doug Lowe	ISBN: 1-56884-161-2	$16.99 USA/$22.99 Canada

PROGRAMMING

Borland C++ For Dummies®	by Michael Hyman	ISBN: 1-56884-162-0	$19.95 USA/$26.95 Canada
C For Dummies®, Volume 1	by Dan Gookin	ISBN: 1-878058-78-9	$19.95 USA/$26.95 Canada
C++ For Dummies®	by Stephen R. Davis	ISBN: 1-56884-163-9	$19.95 USA/$26.95 Canada
Delphi Programming For Dummies®	by Neil Rubenking	ISBN: 1-56884-200-7	$19.99 USA/$26.99 Canada
Mac® Programming For Dummies®	by Dan Parks Sydow	ISBN: 1-56884-173-6	$19.95 USA/$26.95 Canada
PowerBuilder 4 Programming For Dummies®	by Ted Coombs & Jason Coombs	ISBN: 1-56884-325-9	$19.99 USA/$26.99 Canada
QBasic Programming For Dummies®	by Douglas Hergert	ISBN: 1-56884-093-4	$19.95 USA/$26.95 Canada
Visual Basic 3 For Dummies®	by Wallace Wang	ISBN: 1-56884-076-4	$19.95 USA/$26.95 Canada
Visual Basic "X" For Dummies®	by Wallace Wang	ISBN: 1-56884-230-9	$19.99 USA/$26.99 Canada
Visual C++ 2 For Dummies®	by Michael Hyman & Bob Arnson	ISBN: 1-56884-328-3	$19.99 USA/$26.99 Canada
Windows® 95 Programming For Dummies®	by S. Randy Davis	ISBN: 1-56884-327-5	$19.99 USA/$26.99 Canada

SPREADSHEET

1-2-3 For Dummies®	by Greg Harvey	ISBN: 1-878058-60-6	$16.95 USA/$22.95 Canada
1-2-3 For Windows® 5 For Dummies®, 2nd Edition	by John Walkenbach	ISBN: 1-56884-216-3	$16.95 USA/$22.95 Canada
Excel 5 For Macs® For Dummies®	by Greg Harvey	ISBN: 1-56884-186-8	$19.95 USA/$26.95 Canada
Excel For Dummies®, 2nd Edition	by Greg Harvey	ISBN: 1-56884-050-0	$16.95 USA/$22.95 Canada
MORE 1-2-3 For DOS For Dummies®	by John Weingarten	ISBN: 1-56884-224-4	$19.99 USA/$26.99 Canada
MORE Excel 5 For Windows® For Dummies®	by Greg Harvey	ISBN: 1-56884-207-4	$19.95 USA/$26.95 Canada
Quattro Pro 6 For Windows® For Dummies®	by John Walkenbach	ISBN: 1-56884-174-4	$19.95 USA/$26.95 Canada
Quattro Pro For DOS For Dummies®	by John Walkenbach	ISBN: 1-56884-023-3	$16.95 USA/$22.95 Canada

UTILITIES

Norton Utilities 8 For Dummies®	by Beth Slick	ISBN: 1-56884-166-3	$19.95 USA/$26.95 Canada

VCRS/CAMCORDERS

VCRs & Camcorders For Dummies™	by Gordon McComb & Andy Rathbone	ISBN: 1-56884-229-5	$14.99 USA/$20.99 Canada

WORD PROCESSING

Ami Pro For Dummies®	by Jim Meade	ISBN: 1-56884-049-7	$19.95 USA/$26.95 Canada
MORE Word For Windows® 6 For Dummies®	by Doug Lowe	ISBN: 1-56884-165-5	$19.95 USA/$26.95 Canada
MORE WordPerfect® 6 For Windows® For Dummies®	by Margaret Levine Young & David C. Kay	ISBN: 1-56884-206-6	$19.95 USA/$26.95 Canada
MORE WordPerfect® 6 For DOS For Dummies®	by Wallace Wang, edited by Dan Gookin	ISBN: 1-56884-047-0	$19.95 USA/$26.95 Canada
Word 6 For Macs® For Dummies®	by Dan Gookin	ISBN: 1-56884-190-6	$19.95 USA/$26.95 Canada
Word For Windows® 6 For Dummies®	by Dan Gookin	ISBN: 1-56884-075-6	$16.95 USA/$22.95 Canada
Word For Windows® For Dummies®	by Dan Gookin & Ray Werner	ISBN: 1-878058-86-X	$16.95 USA/$22.95 Canada
WordPerfect® 6 For DOS For Dummies®	by Dan Gookin	ISBN: 1-878058-77-0	$16.95 USA/$22.95 Canada
WordPerfect® 6.1 For Windows® For Dummies®, 2nd Edition	by Margaret Levine Young & David Kay	ISBN: 1-56884-243-0	$16.95 USA/$22.95 Canada
WordPerfect® For Dummies®	by Dan Gookin	ISBN: 1-878058-52-5	$16.95 USA/$22.95 Canada

cholastic requests & educational orders please
ducational Sales at 1. 800. 434. 2086

FOR MORE INFO OR TO ORDER, PLEASE CALL 800 762 2974

For volume discounts & special orders please call
Tony Real, Special Sales, at 415. 655. 3048

DUMMIES PRESS™ QUICK REFERENCES

Fun, Fast, & Cheap!™

The Internet For Macs® For Dummies® Quick Reference
by Charles Seiter

ISBN:1-56884-967-2
$9.99 USA/$12.99 Canada

Windows® 95 For Dummies® Quick Reference
by Greg Harvey

ISBN: 1-56884-964-8
$9.99 USA/$12.99 Canada

Photoshop 3 For Macs® For Dummies® Quick Reference
by Deke McClelland

ISBN: 1-56884-968-0
$9.99 USA/$12.99 Canada

WordPerfect® For DOS For Dummies® Quick Reference
by Greg Harvey

ISBN: 1-56884-009-8
$8.95 USA/$12.95 Canada

Title	Author	ISBN	Price
DATABASE			
Access 2 For Dummies® Quick Reference	by Stuart J. Stuple	ISBN: 1-56884-167-1	$8.95 USA/$11.95 Canada
dBASE 5 For DOS For Dummies® Quick Reference	by Barrie Sosinsky	ISBN: 1-56884-954-0	$9.99 USA/$12.99 Canada
dBASE 5 For Windows® For Dummies® Quick Reference	by Stuart J. Stuple	ISBN: 1-56884-953-2	$9.99 USA/$12.99 Canada
Paradox 5 For Windows® For Dummies® Quick Reference	by Scott Palmer	ISBN: 1-56884-960-5	$9.99 USA/$12.99 Canada
DESKTOP PUBLISHING/ILLUSTRATION/GRAPHICS			
CorelDRAW! 5 For Dummies® Quick Reference	by Raymond E. Werner	ISBN: 1-56884-952-4	$9.99 USA/$12.99 Canada
Harvard Graphics For Windows® For Dummies® Quick Reference	by Raymond E. Werner	ISBN: 1-56884-962-1	$9.99 USA/$12.99 Canada
Photoshop 3 For Macs® For Dummies® Quick Reference	by Deke McClelland	ISBN: 1-56884-968-0	$9.99 USA/$12.99 Canada
FINANCE/PERSONAL FINANCE			
Quicken 4 For Windows® For Dummies® Quick Reference	by Stephen L. Nelson	ISBN: 1-56884-950-8	$9.95 USA/$12.95 Canada
GROUPWARE/INTEGRATED			
Microsoft® Office 4 For Windows® For Dummies® Quick Reference	by Doug Lowe	ISBN: 1-56884-958-3	$9.99 USA/$12.99 Canada
Microsoft® Works 3 For Windows® For Dummies® Quick Reference	by Michael Partington	ISBN: 1-56884-959-1	$9.99 USA/$12.99 Canada
INTERNET/COMMUNICATIONS/NETWORKING			
The Internet For Dummies® Quick Reference	by John R. Levine & Margaret Levine Young	ISBN: 1-56884-168-X	$8.95 USA/$11.95 Canada
MACINTOSH			
Macintosh® System 7.5 For Dummies® Quick Reference	by Stuart J. Stuple	ISBN: 1-56884-956-7	$9.99 USA/$12.99 Canada
OPERATING SYSTEMS:			
DOS			
DOS For Dummies® Quick Reference	by Greg Harvey	ISBN: 1-56884-007-1	$8.95 USA/$11.95 Canada
UNIX			
UNIX® For Dummies® Quick Reference	by John R. Levine & Margaret Levine Young	ISBN: 1-56884-094-2	$8.95 USA/$11.95 Canada
WINDOWS			
Windows® 3.1 For Dummies® Quick Reference, 2nd Edition	by Greg Harvey	ISBN: 1-56884-951-6	$8.95 USA/$11.95 Canada
PCs/HARDWARE			
Memory Management For Dummies® Quick Reference	by Doug Lowe	ISBN: 1-56884-362-3	$9.99 USA/$12.99 Canada
PRESENTATION/AUTOCAD			
AutoCAD For Dummies® Quick Reference	by Ellen Finkelstein	ISBN: 1-56884-198-1	$9.95 USA/$12.95 Canada
SPREADSHEET			
1-2-3 For Dummies® Quick Reference	by John Walkenbach	ISBN: 1-56884-027-6	$8.95 USA/$11.95 Canada
1-2-3 For Windows® 5 For Dummies® Quick Reference	by John Walkenbach	ISBN: 1-56884-957-5	$9.95 USA/$12.95 Canada
Excel For Windows® For Dummies® Quick Reference, 2nd Edition	by John Walkenbach	ISBN: 1-56884-096-9	$8.95 USA/$11.95 Canada
Quattro Pro 6 For Windows® For Dummies® Quick Reference	by Stuart J. Stuple	ISBN: 1-56884-172-8	$9.95 USA/$12.95 Canada
WORD PROCESSING			
Word For Windows® 6 For Dummies® Quick Reference	by George Lynch	ISBN: 1-56884-095-0	$8.95 USA/$11.95 Canada
Word For Windows® For Dummies® Quick Reference	by George Lynch	ISBN: 1-56884-029-2	$8.95 USA/$11.95 Canada
WordPerfect® 6.1 For Windows® For Dummies® Quick Reference, 2nd Edition	by Greg Harvey	ISBN: 1-56884-966-4	$9.99 USA/$12.99/Canada

For scholastic requests & educational orders please call Educational Sales at 1. 800. 434. 2086

FOR MORE INFO OR TO ORDER, PLEASE CALL ▸ 800 762 2974

For volume discounts & special orders plea[se call] Tony Real, Special Sales, at 415. 655. 3048

PC PRESS

IDG BOOKS WORLDWIDE

10/31/95

Windows® 3.1 SECRETS™
by Brian Livingston

ISBN: 1-878058-43-6
$39.95 USA/$52.95 Canada
Includes software.

MORE Windows® 3.1 SECRETS™
by Brian Livingston

ISBN: 1-56884-019-5
$39.95 USA/$52.95 Canada
Includes software.

Windows® GIZMOS™
by Brian Livingston & Margie Livingston

ISBN: 1-878058-66-5
$39.95 USA/$52.95 Canada
Includes software.

Windows® 3.1 Connectivity SECRETS™
by Runnoe Connally, David Rorabaugh, & Sheldon Hall

ISBN: 1-56884-030-6
$49.95 USA/$64.95 Canada
Includes software.

Windows® 3.1 Configuration SECRETS™
by Valda Hilley & James Blakely

ISBN: 1-56884-026-8
$49.95 USA/$64.95 Canada
Includes software.

Internet SECRETS™
by John Levine & Carol Baroudi

ISBN: 1-56884-452-2
$39.99 USA/$54.99 Canada
Includes software.

Internet GIZMOS™ For Windows®
by Joel Diamond, Howard Sobel, & Valda Hilley

ISBN: 1-56884-451-4
$39.99 USA/$54.99 Canada
Includes software.

Network Security SECRETS™
by David Stang & Sylvia Moon

ISBN: 1-56884-021-7
Int'l. ISBN: 1-56884-151-5
$49.95 USA/$64.95 Canada
Includes software.

PC SECRETS™
by Caroline M. Halliday

ISBN: 1-878058-49-5
$39.95 USA/$52.95 Canada
Includes software.

WordPerfect® 6 SECRETS™
by Roger C. Parker & David A. Holzgang

ISBN: 1-56884-040-3
$39.95 USA/$52.95 Canada
Includes software.

DOS 6 SECRETS™
by Robert D. Ainsbury

ISBN: 1-878058-70-3
$39.95 USA/$52.95 Canada
Includes software.

Paradox 4 Power Programming SECRETS,™ 2nd Edition
by Gregory B. Salcedo & Martin W. Rudy

ISBN: 1-878058-54-1
$44.95 USA/$59.95 Canada
Includes software.

Paradox 5 For Windows® Power Programming SECRETS™
by Gregory B. Salcedo & Martin W. Rudy

ISBN: 1-56884-085-3
$44.95 USA/$59.95 Canada
Includes software.

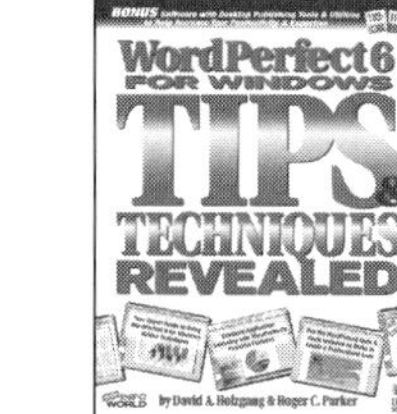

Hard Disk SECRETS™
by John M. Goodman, Ph.D.

ISBN: 1-878058-64-9
$39.95 USA/$52.95 Canada
Includes software.

WordPerfect® 6 For Windows® Tips & Techniques Revealed
by David A. Holzgang & Roger C. Parker

ISBN: 1-56884-202-3
$39.95 USA/$52.95 Canada
Includes software.

Excel 5 For Windows® Power Programming Techniques
by John Walkenbach

ISBN: 1-56884-303-8
$39.95 USA/$52.95 Canada
Includes software.

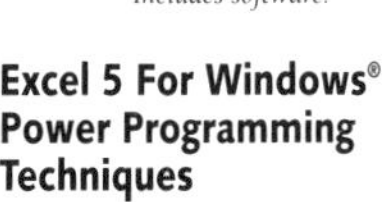

...SECRETS®

INFO WORLD TECHNICAL BOOKS

cholastic requests & educational orders please ducational Sales, at 1. 800. 434. 2086

FOR MORE INFO OR TO ORDER, PLEASE CALL 800 762 2974

For volume discounts & special orders please call Tony Real, Special Sales, at 415. 655. 3048

Unauthorized Windows® 95: A Developer's Guide to Exploring the Foundations of Windows "Chicago"
by Andrew Schulman
ISBN: 1-56884-169-8
$29.99 USA/$39.99 Canada

Unauthorized Windows® 95 Developer's Resource Kit
by Andrew Schulman
ISBN: 1-56884-305-4
$39.99 USA/$54.99 Canada

Best of the Net
by Seth Godin
ISBN: 1-56884-313-5
$22.99 USA/$32.99 Canada

Detour: The Truth About the Information Superhighway
by Michael Sullivan-Trainor
ISBN: 1-56884-307-0
$22.99 USA/$32.99 Canada

PowerPC Programming For Intel Programmers
by Kip McClanahan
ISBN: 1-56884-306-2
$49.99 USA/$64.99 Canada

Foundations™ of Visual C++ Programming For Windows® 95
by Paul Yao & Joseph Yao
ISBN: 1-56884-321-6
$39.99 USA/$54.99 Canada

Heavy Metal™ Visual C++ Programming
by Steve Holzner
ISBN: 1-56884-196-5
$39.95 USA/$54.95 Canada

Heavy Metal™ OLE 2.0 Programming
by Steve Holzner
ISBN: 1-56884-301-1
$39.95 USA/$54.95 Canada

Lotus Notes Application Development Handbook
by Erica Kerwien
ISBN: 1-56884-308-9
$39.99 USA/$54.99 Canada

The Internet Direct Connect Kit
by Peter John Harrison
ISBN: 1-56884-135-3
$29.95 USA/$39.95 Canada

Macworld® Ultimate Mac® Programming
by Dave Mark
ISBN: 1-56884-195-7
$39.95 USA/$54.95 Canada

The UNIX®-Haters Handbook
by Simson Garfinkel, Daniel Weise, & Steven Strassmann
ISBN: 1-56884-203-1
$16.95 USA/$22.95 Canada

Learn C++ Today!
by Martin Rinehart
ISBN: 1-56884-310-0
34.99 USA/$44.99 Canada

Type & Learn™ C
by Tom Swan
ISBN: 1-56884-073-X
34.95 USA/$44.95 Canada

Type & Learn™ Windows® Programming
by Tom Swan
ISBN: 1-56884-071-3
34.95 USA/$44.95 Canada

cholastic requests & educational orders please Educational Sales, at 1. 800. 434. 2086

FOR MORE INFO OR TO ORDER, PLEASE CALL 800 762 2974

For volume discounts & special orders please call Tony Real, Special Sales, at 415. 655. 3048

DUMMIES PRESS™ PROGRAMMING BOOKS

BOOK SERIES FROM IDG

COMPUTER BOOK SERIES FROM IDG

For Dummies who want to program...

Delphi Programming For Dummies®
by Neil Rubenking
ISBN: 1-56884-200-7
$19.99 USA/$26.99 Canada

Access Programming For Dummies®
by Rob Krumm
ISBN: 1-56884-091-8
$19.95 USA/$26.95 Canada

TCP/IP For Dummies®
by Marshall Wilensky & Candace Leiden
ISBN: 1-56884-241-4
$19.99 USA/$26.99 Canada

HTML For Dummies®
by Ed Tittel & Carl de Cordova
ISBN: 1-56884-330-5
$29.99 USA/$39.99 Canada

Windows® 95 Programming For Dummies®
by S. Randy Davis
ISBN: 1-56884-327-5
$19.99 USA/$26.99 Canada

Mac® Programming For Dummies®
by Dan Parks Sydow
ISBN: 1-56884-173-6
$19.95 USA/$26.95 Canada

PowerBuilder 4 Programming For Dummies®
by Ted Coombs & Jason Coombs
ISBN: 1-56884-325-9
$19.99 USA/$26.99 Canada

Visual Basic 3 For Dummies®
by Wallace Wang
ISBN: 1-56884-076-4
$19.95 USA/$26.95 Canada
Covers version 3.

ISDN For Dummies®
by David Angell
ISBN: 1-56884-331-3
$19.99 USA/$26.99 Canada

Visual C++ "2" For Dummies®
by Michael Hyman & Bob Arnson
ISBN: 1-56884-328-3
$19.99 USA/$26.99 Canada

Borland C++ For Dummies®
by Michael Hyman
ISBN: 1-56884-162-0
$19.95 USA/$26.95 Canada

C For Dummies,® Volume I
by Dan Gookin
ISBN: 1-878058-78-9
$19.95 USA/$26.95 Canada

C++ For Dummies®
by Stephen R. Davis
ISBN: 1-56884-163-9
$19.95 USA/$26.95 Canada

QBasic Programming For Dummies®
by Douglas Hergert
ISBN: 1-56884-093-4
$19.95 USA/$26.95 Canada

dBase 5 For Windows® Programming For Dummies®
by Ted Coombs & Jason Coombs
ISBN: 1-56884-215-5
$19.99 USA/$26.99 Canada

For scholastic requests & educational orders please call Educational Sales, at 1. 800. 434. 2086

FOR MORE INFO OR TO ORDER, PLEASE CALL 800 762 2974

For volume discounts & special orders pleas Tony Real, Special Sales, at 415. 655. 3048

PC PRESS

10/31/95

Official Hayes Modem Communications Companion
by Caroline M. Halliday

ISBN: 1-56884-072-1
$29.95 USA/$39.95 Canada
Includes software.

1,001 Komputer Answers from Kim Komando
by Kim Komando

ISBN: 1-56884-460-3
$29.99 USA/$39.99 Canada
Includes software.

PC World Excel 5 For Windows® Handbook, 2nd Edition
by John Walkenbach & Dave Maguiness

ISBN: 1-56884-056-X
$34.95 USA/$44.95 Canada
Includes software

PC World WordPerfect® 6 Handbook
by Greg Harvey

ISBN: 1-878058-80-0
$34.95 USA/$44.95 Canada
Includes software.

PC World DOS 6 Command Reference and Problem Solver
by John Socha & Devra Hall

ISBN: 1-56884-055-1
$24.95 USA/$32.95 Canada

Client/Server Strategies™: A Survival Guide for Corporate Reengineers
by David Vaskevitch

SUPER STAR

ISBN: 1-56884-064-0
$29.95 USA/$39.95 Canada

Internet SECRETS™
by John Levine & Carol Baroudi

ISBN: 1-56884-452-2
$39.99 USA/$54.99 Canada
Includes software.

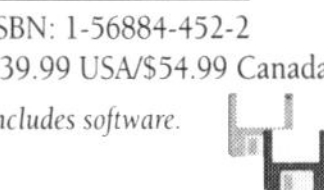

Network Security SECRETS™
by David Stang & Sylvia Moon

ISBN: 1-56884-021-7
Int'l. ISBN: 1-56884-151-5
$49.95 USA/$64.95 Canada
Includes software.

PC SECRETS™
by Caroline M. Halliday

ISBN: 1-878058-49-5
$39.95 USA/$52.95 Canada
Includes software.

...SECRETS®

Here's a complete listing of PC Press Titles

Title	Author	ISBN	Price
BBS SECRETS™	by Ray Werner	ISBN: 1-56884-491-3	$39.99 USA/$54.99 Canada
Creating Cool Web Pages with HTML	by Dave Taylor	ISBN: 1-56884-454-9	$19.99 USA/$26.99 Canada
DOS 6 SECRETS™	by Robert D. Ainsbury	ISBN: 1-878058-70-3	$39.95 USA/$52.95 Canada
Excel 5 For Windows® Power Programming Techniques	by John Walkenbach	ISBN: 1-56884-303-8	$39.95 USA/$52.95 Canada
Hard Disk SECRETS™	by John M. Goodman, Ph.D.	ISBN: 1-878058-64-9	$39.95 USA/$52.95 Canada
Internet GIZMOS™ For Windows®	by Joel Diamond, Howard Sobel, & Valda Hilley	ISBN: 1-56884-451-4	$39.99 USA/$54.99 Canada
Making Multimedia Work	by Michael Goodwin	ISBN: 1-56884-468-9	$19.99 USA/$26.99 Canada
MORE Windows® 3.1 SECRETS™	by Brian Livingston	ISBN: 1-56884-019-5	$39.95 USA/$52.95 Canada
Official XTree Companion 3rd Edition	by Beth Slick	ISBN: 1-878058-57-6	$19.95 USA/$26.95 Canada
Paradox 4 Power Programming SECRETS,™ 2nd Edition	by Gregory B. Salcedo & Martin W. Rudy	ISBN: 1-878058-54-1	$44.95 USA/$59.95 Canada
Paradox 5 For Windows® Power Programming SECRETS™	by Gregory B. Salcedo & Martin W. Rudy	ISBN: 1-56884-085-3	$44.95 USA/$59.95 Canada
PC World DOS 6 Handbook, 2nd Edition	by John Socha, Clint Hicks & Devra Hall	ISBN: 1-878058-79-7	$34.95 USA/$44.95 Canada
PC World Microsoft® Access 2 Bible, 2nd Edition	by Cary N. Prague & Michael R. Irwin	ISBN: 1-56884-086-1	$39.95 USA/$52.95 Canada
PC World Word For Windows® 6 Handbook	by Brent Heslop & David Angell	ISBN: 1-56884-054-3	$34.95 USA/$44.95 Canada
QuarkXPress For Windows® Designer Handbook	by Barbara Assadi & Galen Gruman	ISBN: 1-878058-45-2	$29.95 USA/$39.95 Canada
Windows® 3.1 Configuration SECRETS™	by Valda Hilley & James Blakely	ISBN: 1-56884-026-8	$49.95 USA/$64.95 Canada
Windows® 3.1 Connectivity SECRETS™	by Runnoe Connally, David Rorabaugh & Sheldon Hall	ISBN: 1-56884-030-6	$49.95 USA/$64.95 Canada
Windows® 3.1 SECRETS™	by Brian Livingston	ISBN: 1-878058-43-6	$39.95 USA/$52.95 Canada
Windows® 95 A.S.A.P.	by Dan Gookin	ISBN: 1-56884-483-2	$24.99 USA/$34.99 Canada
Windows® 95 Bible	by Alan Simpson	ISBN: 1-56884-074-8	$29.99 USA/$39.99 Canada
Windows® 95 SECRETS™	by Brian Livingston	ISBN: 1-56884-453-0	$39.99 USA/$54.99 Canada
Windows® GIZMOS™	by Brian Livingston & Margie Livingston	ISBN: 1-878058-66-5	$39.95 USA/$52.95 Canada
WordPerfect® 6 For Windows® Tips & Techniques Revealed	by David A. Holzgang & Roger C. Parker	ISBN: 1-56884-202-3	$39.95 USA/$52.95 Canada
WordPerfect® 6 SECRETS™	by Roger C. Parker & David A. Holzgang	ISBN: 1-56884-040-3	$39.95 USA/$52.95 Canada

holastic requests & educational orders please
ucational Sales, at 1. 800. 434. 2086

FOR MORE INFO OR TO ORDER, PLEASE CALL 800 762 2974

For volume discounts & special orders please call
Tony Real, Special Sales, at 415. 655. 3048

IBM™

IBM PRESS

இப் புத்தகங்கள் மிகவும் நல்லவை

(way cool)

OS/2® Warp Internet Connection: Your Key to Cruising the Internet and the World Wide Web

by Deborah Morrison

OS/2 users can get warped on the Internet using the OS/2 Warp tips, techniques, and helpful directories found in *OS/2 Warp Internet Connection*. This reference covers OS/2 Warp Internet basics, such as e-mail use and how to access other computers, plus much more! The Internet gets more complex every day, but for OS/2 Warp users it just got a whole lot easier! Your value-packed disk includes 10 of the best internet utilities to help you explore the Net and save money while you're on-line!

EXPERT AUTHOR PROFILE

Deborah Morrison (Raleigh, NC) is an award-winning IBM writer who specializes in TCP/IP and the Internet. She is currently the editor-in-chief of IBM's *TCP/IP Connection* quarterly magazine.

ISBN: 1-56884-465-4
$24.99 USA/$34.99 Canada
Includes one 3.5" disk

Available: Now

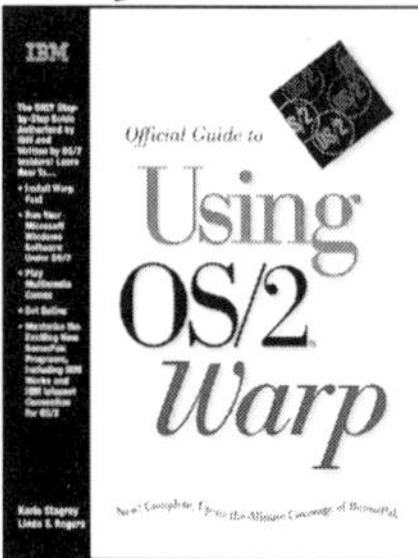

Official Guide to Using OS/2® Warp

by Karla Stagray & Linda S. Rogers

IDG Books and IBM have come together to produce the most comprehensive user's guide to OS/2 Warp available today. From installation to using OS/2 Warp's BonusPak programs, this book delivers valuable help to the reader who needs to get up and running fast. Loaded with working examples, easy tips, and operating system concepts, *Official Guide to Using OS/2 Warp* is the only official user's guide authorized by IBM.

EXPERT AUTHOR PROFILE

Karla Stagray and Linda Rogers (Boca Raton, FL) both have a unique understanding of computer software and hardware. As award-winning IBM writers, Stagray and Rogers have received Society of Technical Communicators awards for various endeavors.

ISBN: 1-56884-466-2
$29.99 USA/$39.99 Canada

Available: Now

OS/2® Warp Uncensored

by Peter G. Magid & Ira H. Schneider

Exploit the power of OS/2 Warp and learn the secrets of object technology for the Workplace Shell. This all new book/CD-ROM bundle, for power users and intermediate users alike, provides the real inside story—not just the "what," but the "how" and "why" — from the folks who designed and developed the Workplace Shell. Packed with tips and techniques for using IBM's REXX programming language, and the bonus CD includes new bitmaps, icons, mouse pointers, REXX scripts, and an Object Tool!

EXPERT AUTHOR PROFILE

Peter G. Magid (Boca Raton, FL) is the User Interface Design Lead for the Workplace Shell and has over 12 years of programming experience at IBM. He is a graduate of Tulane University, and holds a B.S. degree in Computer Science.

Ira H. Schneider (Boca Raton, FL) has focused on enhancements to the Workplace Shell and has over 25 years of experience with IBM. He has held numerous lead programming positions within IBM and graduated from Northeastern University with a B.S. degree in Electrical Engineering.

ISBN: 1-56884-474-3
$39.99 USA/$54.99 Canada
Includes one CD-ROM

Available: Now

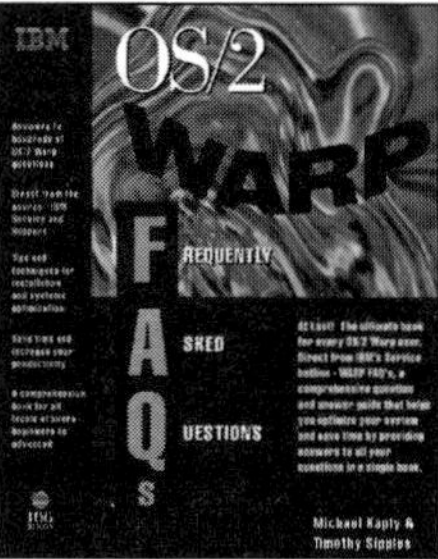

OS/2® Warp FAQs™

by Mike Kaply & Timothy F. Sipples

At last, the ultimate answer book for every OS/2 Warp user. Direct from IBM's Service Hotline, *OS/2 Warp FAQs* is a comprehensive question-and-answer guide that helps you optimize your system and save time by putting the answers to all your questions right at your fingertips. CD includes FAQs from the book in an easy-to-search format, plus hard-to-find device drivers for connecting to peripherals, such as printers.

EXPERT AUTHOR PROFILE

Mike Kaply (Boca Raton, FL) is currently on the OS/2 Help Manager Development Team at IBM in Boca Raton, Florida. He holds a B.S. degree in Mathematics and Computer Science from Southern Methodist University.

Timothy F. Sipples (Chicago, IL) is an OS/2 Warp specialist from IBM. He has written for *OS/2 Magazine* and was named "Team OS/2er of the Year" by *OS/2 Professional*.

ISBN: 1-56884-472-7
$29.99 USA/$42.99 Canada
Includes one CD-ROM

Available: Now

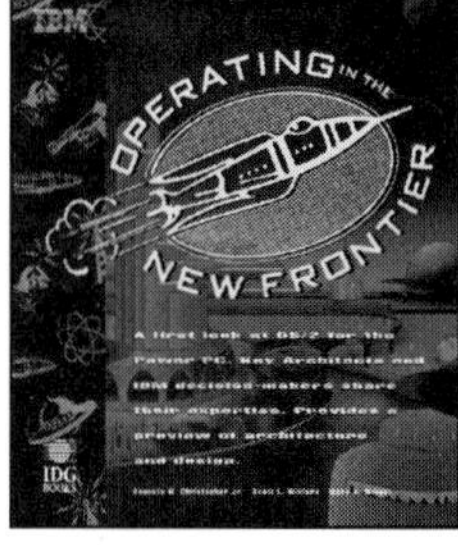

OS/2® Warp and PowerPC: Operating in the New Frontier

by Ken Christopher, Scott Winters & Mary Pollack Wright

The software makers at IBM unwrap the I and OS/2 mystique to share insights and strategies that will take business comput into the 21st century. Readers get a long hard look at the next generation of OS/2 Warp for PowerPC.

EXPERT AUTHOR PROFILE

Ken Christopher (Boca Raton, FL) is Program Director of Development for OS/2 for Power PC has been a key player in the development on OS/2 Warp.

Scott Winters (Boca Raton, FL) is lead archi of OS/2 for the PowerPC. He has been instrumental in the development on OS/2 Wa on the PowerPC platform.

Mary Pollack Wright (Boca Raton, FL) is curren the technical editor for the OS/2 Techinical Libr She has been part of the OS/2 team since 1985 technical articles on OS/2 have been publishe the *OS/2 Developer* magazine and *OS/2 Notebo*

ISBN: 1-56884-458-1
$29.99 USA/$39.99 Canada

Available: Now

For scholastic requests & educational orders please call Educational Sales, at 1. 800. 434. 2086

FOR MORE INFO OR TO ORDER, PLEASE CALL ▸ 800 762 2974

For volume discounts & special orders plea Tony Real, Special Sales, at 415. 655. 3048

ORDER FORM

9/19/95

Order Center: **(800) 762-2974** *(8 a.m.–6 p.m., EST, weekdays)*

Quantity	ISBN	Title	Price	Total

Shipping & Handling Charges

	Description	First book	Each additional book	Total
Domestic	Normal	$4.50	$1.50	$
	Two Day Air	$8.50	$2.50	$
	Overnight	$18.00	$3.00	$
International	Surface	$8.00	$8.00	$
	Airmail	$16.00	$16.00	$
	DHL Air	$17.00	$17.00	$

*For large quantities call for shipping & handling charges.
**Prices are subject to change without notice.

Ship to:

Name ____________________

Company ____________________

Address ____________________

City/State/Zip ____________________

Daytime Phone ____________________

Payment: ☐ Check to IDG Books Worldwide (US Funds Only)

☐ VISA ☐ MasterCard ☐ American Express

Card # ____________________ Expires ____________

Signature ____________________

Subtotal ____________

CA residents add applicable sales tax ____________

IN, MA, and MD residents add 5% sales tax ____________

IL residents add 6.25% sales tax ____________

RI residents add 7% sales tax ____________

TX residents add 8.25% sales tax ____________

Shipping ____________

Total ____________

Please send this order form to:

IDG Books Worldwide, Inc.
7260 Shadeland Station, Suite 100
Indianapolis, IN 46256

Allow up to 3 weeks for delivery.
Thank you!

IDG BOOKS WORLDWIDE LICENSE AGREEMENT

Important — read carefully before opening the software packet(s). This is a legal agreement between you (either an individual or an entity) and IDG Books Worldwide, Inc. (IDG). By opening the accompanying sealed packet containing the software CD-ROM, you acknowledge that you have read and accept the following IDG License Agreement. If you do not agree and do not want to be bound by the terms of this Agreement, promptly return the book and the unopened software packet(s) to the place where you obtained them for a full refund.

1. License. This License Agreement (Agreement) permits you to use one copy of the enclosed Software program(s) on a single computer. The Software is in "use" on a computer when it is loaded into temporary memory (i.e., RAM) or installed into permanent memory (e.g., hard disk, CD-ROM, or other storage device) of that computer.

2. Copyright. The entire contents of the CD-ROM and the compilation of the Software are copyrighted and protected by both United States copyright laws and international treaty provisions. You may only (a) make one copy of the Software for backup or archival purposes, or (b) transfer the Software to a single hard disk, provided that you keep the original for backup or archival purposes. The individual programs on the CD-ROM are copyrighted by the authors of each program respectively. Each program has its own use permissions and limitations. To use each program, you must follow the individual requirements and restrictions detailed for each in Appendix A of this Book. Do not use a program if you do not want to follow its Licensing Agreement. None of the materials on the CD-ROM or listed in this Book may ever be distributed, in original or modified form, for commercial purposes.

3. Other Restrictions. You may not rent or lease the Software. You may transfer the Software and user documentation on a permanent basis provided you retain no copies and the recipient agrees to the terms of this Agreement. You may not reverse engineer, decompile, or disassemble the Software except to the extent that the foregoing restriction is expressly prohibited by applicable law. If the Software is an update or has been updated, any transfer must include the most recent update and all prior versions.

4. Limited Warranty. IDG warrants that the Software and CD-ROM are free from defects in materials and workmanship for a period of sixty (60) days from the date of purchase of this Book. If IDG receives notification within the warranty period of defects in material or workmanship, IDG will replace the defective CD-ROM. IDG's entire liability and your exclusive remedy shall be limited to replacement of the Software, which is returned to IDG with a copy of your receipt. This Limited Warranty is void if failure of the Software has resulted from accident, abuse, or misapplication. Any replacement Software will be warranted for the remainder of the original warranty period or thirty (30) days, whichever is longer.

5. No Other Warranties. To the maximum extent permitted by applicable law, IDG and the author disclaim all other warranties, expressed or implied, including, but not limited to, implied warranties of merchantability and fitness for a particular purpose, with respect to the Software, the programs, the source code contained therein and/or the techniques described in this Book. This limited warranty gives you specific legal rights. You may have others which vary from state jurisdiction to state jurisdiction.

6. No Liability For Consequential Damages. To the extent permitted by applicable law, in no event shall IDG or the author be liable for any damages whatsoever (including without limitation, damages for loss of business profits, business interruption, loss of business information, or any other pecuniary loss) arising out of the use of or inability to use the Book or the Software, even if IDG has been advised of the possibility of such damages. Because some states/jurisdictions do not allow the exclusion or limitation of liability for consequential or incidental damages, the above limitation may not apply to you.

7. U.S.Government Restricted Rights. Use, duplication, or disclosure of the Software by the U.S. Government is subject to restrictions stated in paragraph (c) (1) (ii) of the Rights in Technical Data and Computer Software clause of DFARS 252.227-7013, and in subparagraphs (a) through (d) of the Commercial Computer — Restricted Rights clause at FAR 52.227-19, and in similar clauses in the NASA FAR supplement, when applicable.

Replacement Disc. If a replacement CD-ROM is needed, please write to the following address: IDG Books Disc Fulfillment Center, Attn: *Macworld Illustrator 6 Bible*, IDG Books Worldwide, 7260 Shadeland Station, Indianapolis, IN 46256, or call 800-762-2974.

Disc Instructions

The CD-ROM includes QuickTime tutorials that demonstrate many of the techniques and tips in the book. The CD also includes most of the illustrations used in the book, clip art from selected companies that use Illustrator to create their clip art, and charts of Illustrator filters.

Tutorials

To run the tutorial program, double-click the "MIB6 Tutorial" folder that's located on the CD (double–click on the CD icon on your desktop to see it). This folder contains several hours of tutorials. There are more than 100 different tutorials, which range from simple activities to complex projects. Simply select a topic from the menus at the top of the screen to begin.

Fonts

Also included on the CD-ROM are two PostScript Type 1 fonts: Lefty Casual and Ransom Note.

To use the fonts, select the screen font (the little suitcase) and the printer font (the little printer) for each typeface and drag it to your System Folder. Your Macintosh will ask you whether it is OK that these items get shuffled into the Font folder. Click the OK button.

IDG BOOKS WORLDWIDE REGISTRATION CARD

RETURN THIS REGISTRATION CARD FOR FREE CATALOG

Title of this book: **Macworld® Illustrator 6 Bible, 2nd Edition**

My overall rating of this book: ❑ Very good [1] ❑ Good [2] ❑ Satisfactory [3] ❑ Fair [4] ❑ Poor [5]

How I first heard about this book:

❑ Found in bookstore; name: [6] ❑ Book review: [7]

❑ Advertisement: [8] ❑ Catalog: [9]

❑ Word of mouth; heard about book from friend, co-worker, etc.: [10] ❑ Other: [11]

What I liked most about this book:

What I would change, add, delete, etc., in future editions of this book:

Other comments:

Number of computer books I purchase in a year: ❑ 1 [12] ❑ 2-5 [13] ❑ 6-10 [14] ❑ More than 10 [15]

I would characterize my computer skills as: ❑ Beginner [16] ❑ Intermediate [17] ❑ Advanced [18] ❑ Professional [19]

I use ❑ DOS [20] ❑ Windows [21] ❑ OS/2 [22] ❑ Unix [23] ❑ Macintosh [24] ❑ Other: [25]________________ (please specify)

I would be interested in new books on the following subjects:
(please check all that apply, and use the spaces provided to identify specific software)

❑ Word processing: [26] ❑ Spreadsheets: [27]

❑ Data bases: [28] ❑ Desktop publishing: [29]

❑ File Utilities: [30] ❑ Money management: [31]

❑ Networking: [32] ❑ Programming languages: [33]

❑ Other: [34]

I use a PC at (please check all that apply): ❑ home [35] ❑ work [36] ❑ school [37] ❑ other: [38] ________________

The disks I prefer to use are ❑ 5.25 [39] ❑ 3.5 [40] ❑ other: [41]________________

I have a CD ROM: ❑ yes [42] ❑ no [43]

I plan to buy or upgrade computer hardware this year: ❑ yes [44] ❑ no [45]

I plan to buy or upgrade computer software this year: ❑ yes [46] ❑ no [47]

Name: Business title: [48] Type of Business: [49]

Address (❑ home [50] ❑ work [51]/Company name:)

Street/Suite#

City [52]/State [53]/Zipcode [54]: Country [55]

❑ **I liked this book!** You may quote me by name in future IDG Books Worldwide promotional materials.

My daytime phone number is ________________

IDG BOOKS®
THE WORLD OF COMPUTER KNOWLEDGE

YES!

Please keep me informed about IDG's World of Computer Knowledge. Send me the latest IDG Books catalog.

NO POSTAGE NECESSARY IF MAILED IN THE UNITED STATES

BUSINESS REPLY MAIL

FIRST CLASS MAIL PERMIT NO. 2605 FOSTER CITY, CALIFORNIA

IDG Books Worldwide
919 E Hillsdale Blvd, STE 400
Foster City, CA 94404-9691